CONTINENTAL RECKONING

CONTINENTAL

History of the American West

SERIES EDITOR | Richard W. Etulain, *University of New Mexico*

RECKONING

➤ The American West in the Age of Expansion

ELLIOTT WEST

University of Nebraska Press | Lincoln

Publication of this volume was assisted by

a contribution from the University of Arkansas Alumni Association,

a grant from the Friends of the University of Nebraska Press, and

a gift from the Virginia Faulkner Fund, established in memory of Virginia Faulkner, editor in chief of the University of Nebraska Press.

The University of Nebraska Press is part of a land-grant institution with campuses and programs on the past, present, and future homelands of the Pawnee, Ponca, Otoe-Missouria, Omaha, Dakota, Lakota, Kaw, Cheyenne, and Arapaho Peoples, as well as those of the relocated Ho-Chunk, Sac and Fox, and Iowa Peoples.

Library of Congress Cataloging-in-Publication Data
Names: West, Elliott, 1945–, author.
Title: Continental reckoning: the American West in the age of expansion / Elliott West.
Other titles: The American West in the age of expansion
Description: Lincoln: University of Nebraska Press, [2023] | Series: History of the American West | Includes bibliographical references and index.
Identifiers: LCCN 2022013275
ISBN 9781496233585 (hardback)
ISBN 9781496234445 (epub)
ISBN 9781496234452 (pdf)
Subjects: LCSH: West (U.S.)—History—1860–1890. | West (U.S.)—History—1858–1860. | Land use—West (U.S.)—History. | West (U.S.)—Economic conditions—19th century. | West (U.S.)—Environmental conditions—History. | United States—Territorial expansion. | BISAC: HISTORY / United States / State & Local / West (AK, CA, CO, HI, ID, MT, NV, UT, WY) | HISTORY / United States / 19th Century
Classification: LCC F594 .W27 2023 | DDC 978/.02—dc23/eng/20220328
LC record available at https://lccn.loc.gov/2022013275

Set in Minion Pro.

For Suzanne,
again,
my ultimate companion

Contents

PART 3. WORKED INTO BEING

Illustrations

Maps

RICHARD ETULAIN

Series Editor's Introduction

Historical writing about the American West has undergone dramatic changes in the past half century and more. Specifically, historians have moved away from the frontier thesis of Frederick Jackson Turner and turned in new directions: earlier authors such as Henry Nash Smith and Earl Pomeroy helped us understand how the mythic West and western imitations of European and eastern American traditions shaped the history of the region. Other recent western histories highlight the roles of racial and ethnic groups, women and families, and urbanization in the development of the West. And widely recognized from the late 1980s onward is a new western history that has brought forth the darker, more complex sides of the region's past.

These historiographical shifts compel us to ask new questions about the history of the American West and to reexamine the past in light of our experiences in the late twentieth and early twenty-first centuries. Fresh sociological, demographic, and environmental topics are being addressed; for many specialists in the field, the regional West has supplanted the frontier West, with *place* being emphasized more than *process*.

It's time for a new comprehensive history of the American West, one that reflects new scholarship without overlooking past perspectives. Volumes in the History of the West series do just that. A history of the region in six volumes, the series builds on these recent historiographical treatments of gender, ethnicity, and the environment. The volumes reflect current thoughts about the West as a region, provide a judicious blend of old and new subject matter, and offer narratives that appeal to specialists and general readers.

In this book, Elliott West meets—and exceeds—the large goals of these series volumes. His wide-reaching overview of the American West from the 1840s to the 1880s overflows with storytelling achievements, superb research, and a new framework for viewing this near-half century. This volume illustrates why Elliott West ranks at the top of historians writing about the American West.

West knows how to tell interest-whetting stories. He employs numerous biographical vignettes and illuminative moments to give exceptional narrative power to his story. Pen portraits of individuals and notable events also enlarge the draw of his account.

In addition, West also displays his thorough, diligent research. He moves beyond the usual stories and adds new information, for example, about the California gold rush, the building of the transcontinental railroads, and frontier mining and agricultural endeavors. He shows, too, the ongoing, shaping influences of the East on the West. These cross-continental connections are invaluable for understanding this period of western history.

Readers will be drawn to West's superb use of statistics. West utilizes census and other statistical sources to substantiate and enlarge his overarching interpretations of the West—and often gives these interpretations with inviting bits of humor. This skillful use of numbers allows West to lard his history with dozens of valuable comparisons.

West also delivers a broad-based story. He displays manifold interests in topics such as race and ethnicity, gender, and the environment. Moving beyond earlier historians linked to the frontier interpretations of Frederick Jackson Turner, West delivers a narrative similar to that of the New Western historians but surpasses them in his balance and storytelling power.

The most important contribution of West's extensive and invaluable study is its illustration of his Greater Reconstruction thesis, the most notable historiographical idea advanced about the American West in the twenty-first century. West's Greater Reconstruction thesis urges historians to build a two-pronged story of this era of western history by bringing together simultaneous emphases on the coming of, the duration of, and the aftereffects of the Civil War alongside the major happenings of the westward movement stretching from the 1840s to the 1880s. Seen and considered together, these two major plot strains are at the center of West's Greater Reconstruction idea and of this book.

Altogether, then, this is an extraordinary Western history, full of provocative insights, fresh information, and storytelling power. It will capture readers and win major prizes.

MAP 1. (*pages xv–xviii*) The United States in 1844 and 1884. In 1844 the country west of the Missouri River was a mosaic of dozens of cultures and authorities overlain by vague claims by three outside powers. Forty years later that country was the West, a distinctive region yet bound well politically, economically, and culturally into a national whole. 1844 and 1884 detail: Map produced by Eugene Duflot de Mofras, 1844, Newberry Library; 1884: *Dollar Atlas of the United States and Canada*, Rand McNally, 1884, Newberry Library.

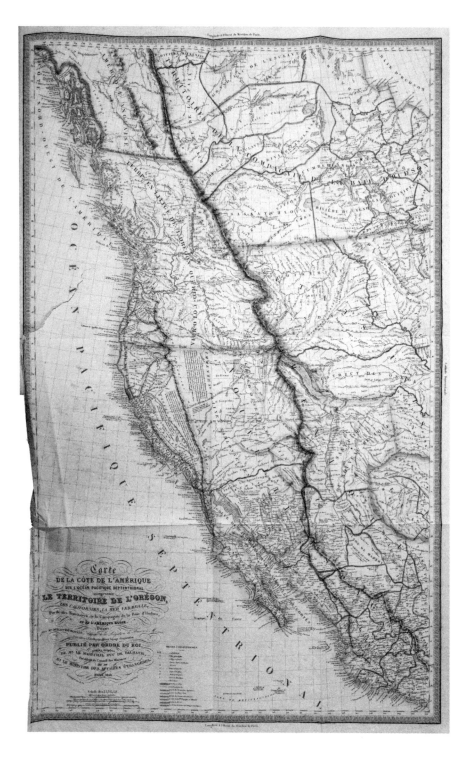

Carte
DE LA CÔTE DE L'AMÉRIQUE
SUR L'OCÉAN PACIFIQUE SEPTENTRIONAL
comprenant
LE TERRITOIRE DE L'ORÉGON,
LES CALIFORNIES, LA MER VERMEILLE,
Partie des Territoires de la Compagnie de la Baie d'Hudson,
et de L'AMÉRIQUE RUSSE,

PUBLIÉ PAR ORDRE DU ROI,
par les soins
DE M.r LE MARÉCHAL DUC DE DALMATIE,
ET LE MINISTRE DES AFFAIRES ÉTRANGÈRES,
PARIS, 1844

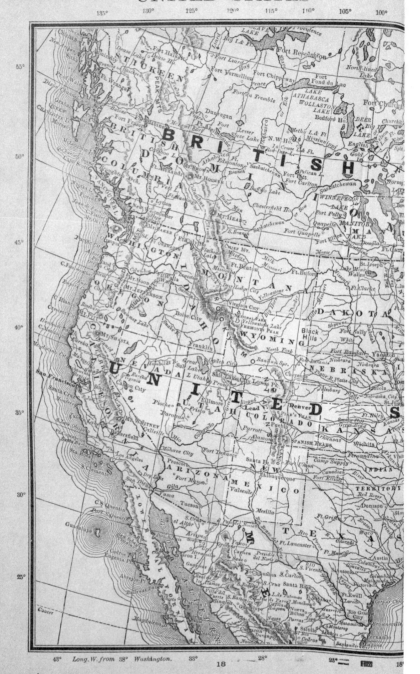

90° 85° 80° 75° 70° 65° 60° Long. W. 55° from Greenwich.

55°
50°
45°
40°
35°
30°
25°

HUDSON BAY

C. Southampton

Churchill
Port Nelson
York
Fort Severn

Cape Lookout

POSSESSIONS

JAMES BAY
RUPERT L.
Fort George
East Main Ft.

WOTCHISH MTS

LABRADOR

MINGAN MTS

Hopedale

LAKE NIPIGON

OF

LAKE SUPERIOR
Superior
Duluth

ONTARIO

CANADA

Quebec
Three Rivers
Ottawa

NEW BRUNSWICK
NOVA SCOTIA
Halifax

MICHIGAN

WISCONSIN

LAKE MICHIGAN
Milwaukee
Madison
Chicago
Detroit
Toledo

Montreal
VT.
N.H.
MASS. Boston
NEW YORK
CONN.

ILLINOIS
INDIANA
Springfield
St. Louis

OHIO
Cincinnati
Columbus

PENNSYLVANIA
Harrisburg
Philadelphia
Baltimore
Washington
MD.
DEL.

STATES

KENTUCKY
Louisville
Frankfort

VIRGINIA
Richmond

TENNESSEE
Nashville

N. CAROLINA
Raleigh

ARKANSAS
Little Rock

MISSISSIPPI
Jackson

ALABAMA
Montgomery

GEORGIA
Atlanta

S. CAROLINA
Columbia
Charleston

Savannah

FLORIDA

New Orleans
DELTA OF THE MISSISSIPPI

Galveston

GULF OF MEXICO

WEST INDIA
LUCAYAS
OR
ISLANDS
BAHAMA

13° 8° 3° 2° 7°

19

Prelude ➤ *773,510,680 Acres*

Between February 19, 1846, and July 4, 1848, the United States acquired more than 1.2 million square miles of land.[1] It was far and away the greatest expansion in the nation's history, more than half again what had been added in the Louisiana Purchase more than four decades earlier. Should the nation add that much today, expanding not to the west but to the south, our borders would embrace all of Mexico, Guatemala, Honduras, Nicaragua, Belize, El Salvador, Costa Rica, Panama, and more than half of Colombia. If you prefer to think more globally, imagine that during the twenty-eight months and fifteen days after you read this sentence, the United States will add to itself land just short of that in modern India.

The consequences over the next three or so decades were considerable. My goal has been to explore them in a couple of ways. I have tried to tell the birth of the West as a region—to see it take form as a political entity, as an arrangement of power, as part of a global community, and as imagined space. And I have tried to situate its birth in the broader narrative of American history.

For the first goal the problem was not finding things to write about but choosing among them and fitting them into something approaching a sensible whole. All history is about movement and change, but the pace and scope here was of a rare order. Events come quickly, stumbling over each other, crackling with energy, shifting and interlacing: a collective bewilderment. Trying to write their history can feel like being told to imitate a mockingbird or to cook authentic chili. Many episodes are well sited in popular memory—wagon trains rolling westward, horseback herdsmen, Indian wars, gold and silver strikes, homesteading mothers, Hispanic farmers with their acequias. I have tried to honor that popular interest while seeing those events freshly in light of new research, of wider perspectives, and of common sense. I have tried also to introduce much that has an equal claim to consequence and yet is too rarely seen in the traditional script—revolutionizing technologies, scientists reshaping basic human understandings, environmental upheavals and human atrocities, global bonds of commerce and capital.

As the second goal I have tried to suggest how those events and developments should encourage us to look anew at, to literally re-vise, what is by scholarly acclamation one of the most pivotal periods of American history. During the middle of the nineteenth century the trajectory of the United States shifted fundamentally onto a course that would carry it into what we would come to recognize as modern America. Among the changes were the steep acceleration of the nation's economic power and the rearrangement of that power, an increasing mastery of new technologies, the reordering of the nation's racial relations and its redefinition of citizenship, its growing engagement in global revolutions of knowledge, a profound transformation in its nonhuman environments, the expanding role of the federal government in its public life, and a wider, invigorated engagement with the larger world, one embracing both of the oceans that now formed its border.

To explain this new trajectory, historians usually have focused on the Civil War and the events that touched most immediately on its causes and consequences. We would do well, however, to avoid what Joel Silbey more than fifty years ago called the "Civil War Synthesis," which begins with the fact of the war, then views events around it only in relation to that fact.[2] In particular, we should broaden our view in both space and time. We should pull back spatially to a perspective from coast to coast that allows a far more prominent role for the emergence of the West and the changes it brought. That in turn requires us to pull back temporally, to view the shift in trajectory as beginning in the mid-1840s and coming into sharpening focus at the traditional end of the "Civil War era," around 1880. The Civil War and the birth of the West, that is, should be given something like equal billing in this crucial transition in national life. Each event has its own story and deserves its own narrative, but each was often in conversation with the other, and when each is properly considered in its broadest context, neither can be understood without the other.

Elsewhere I have suggested that the resulting picture is of a Greater Reconstruction—one that included not only rejoining the Southeast and Northeast after 1865 but also the remaking the nation at large during the thirty-plus years after expansion to the Pacific. The story is of events, East and West, that together preserved the republic while expanding it, reaffirming it, and binding its parts into a new America that was continental in scope and recast in its composition and purposes.

The birth of the West also offers a collective testimony—compelling, inspirational, horrifying, funny, bizarre—of what it was like to live through one of the more telling chapters of our common past. Such testimony should be considered part of an American literature, oral in this case, that deserves a place in a broader view of the contours of our past. When I could, I have tried to let the speakers have their say. The hope is to give at least parts of the story a somebodyness: to provide the big picture, with voices.

If the argument is that expansion between 1845 and 1848 began a fundamental restructuring of the nation, its prelude should start, briefly, with that expansion and the forces behind it. It came in three interrelated episodes.[3] The first was the annexation of Texas. In 1836 it had won its independence from Mexico, though Mexico continued formally to consider it a state in rebellion. Although opinion in Texas strongly favored joining the United States, a growing sentiment in the Northeast against expansion of African American slavery scuttled the possibility. For ten years Texas would remain its own nation. By then factions in the Democratic party strongly favored inviting the Lone Star Republic, and when the favorite for the 1844 nomination, Martin Van Buren of New York, opposed it, the party turned instead to James Knox Polk of Tennessee, who campaigned for annexing both Texas and the Oregon Country of the Pacific Northwest, territory strongly desired by voters in the anti-Texas Northeast. Polk's strategy, that is, was to offset opposition to some expansion, not by hedging his support for it, but by promising to expand still more. When he narrowly defeated the Whig stalwart Henry Clay of Kentucky, his victory was widely assumed to be popular approval of a vigorous and general expansion.

The current president John Tyler, an expansionist who had been read out of the Whig party for his views, meanwhile had negotiated a treaty of annexation, but the Senate rejected it after the new secretary of state, John Calhoun, publicly linked it to the preservation of Black slavery. Tyler, arguing that in the election voters had made their wishes clear, called for inviting the republic through a constitutionally dubious joint congressional resolution that needed only simple majorities in both houses. That passed by a whisker. On the eve of his departure, Tyler extended the offer to Texas, which approved annexation in a summer convention and by popular vote in the fall. Polk signed legislation admitting Texas two days before the end of 1845, and on February 19, 1846, Texas formally relinquished its sovereignty to the United States. The first gulp of new land was done.

The second was entwined with it. Polk had courted northeastern support by calling for acquiring the "Oregon Country," territory from the northern boundary of present California to the fifty-fourth parallel, forty minutes, today's southern boundary of Alaska. East to west it went from the continental divide to the Pacific Ocean. Spain and Russia had abandoned claims to the area, and the United States and England had agreed to allow each other's citizens to work and settle there and to forswear any military presence. The only land truly disputed was south of the forty-ninth parallel (our current boundary with Canada) and enclosed within the long curve of the Columbia River. England's Hudson's Bay had profited hugely from this beaver-rich country, and fur trade hopefuls in the United States looked on it covetously. Meanwhile, Methodist and Presbyterian missionaries were boosting the country below the Columbia as an agrarian wonderland, and by 1844 hopeful farm families were settling the fertile Willamette River valley.

It was to such interests that Polk appealed in 1844, and once in office he secretly proposed a division of the Oregon Country along the forty-ninth parallel. Through a slightly comic series of miscommunications, England seemed to refuse. Polk's response was to break negotiations, demand everything up to Russian America, and ask Congress to serve notice of ending joint occupation. The implication was that he was ready to fight. The English government in fact had been amenable to Polk's initial offer, the Hudson's Bay Company having moved its main post to the southern tip of Vancouver Island. A new government under Prime Minister Robert Peel and his secretary for foreign affairs, Lord Aberdeen, proposed dividing along the line long considered, the forty-ninth parallel, but bending around Vancouver Island to keep it in English hands. Polk accepted. For all the bluster, the confrontation was, writes historian Frederick Merk, one of a "kernel of reality and an enormous husk," with both sides agreeing to what was likely the outcome from the start.[4] The signing of the Oregon Treaty on June 15, 1846, gave the United States the present states of Washington, Oregon, Idaho, and a bit of Montana. The second gulp was accomplished.

The third, both bloodier and more complicated, brought the acquisition of California and the Southwest. Polk was committed to Texas's claim, based on virtually nothing, that its western boundary extended to the Rio Grande in its entirety, which would include Santa Fe, the mercantile and political center increasingly bound by trade to the Missouri Valley. Like the three presidents before him, he had further ambitions beyond Texas. California's Central Valley had a ripening reputation of an agrarian paradise and had already drawn small but growing numbers of farmers. There were, besides, California's ports, above all the bay at San Francisco, increasingly regarded as one of the world's finest, and which was nicely situated as a base for trade of whatever sort around the Pacific.

This left Polk playing a double, and contradictory, diplomatic game. He would press Mexico to recognize Texas annexation—to accept, that is, what Mexico considered an invasion—while also trying to persuade it to sell California and the Southwest in pursuit of his own political goals. It did not go well. In December of 1845 he sent John Slidell of Louisiana to offer up to $25 million to settle disputes and acquire New Mexico and California, but Polk sent Slidell as minister plenipotentiary, which in diplomatic language meant that meeting with him would imply that relations were reestablished, which in turn would imply that Mexico had accepted of the loss of Texas. A rebuffed Slidell wrote home that "a war would probably be the best mode" of getting what was desired.[5]

General Zachary Taylor and four thousand troops were already on the Nueces River, the actual extent of the Texans' occupation, and Polk now sent them down to the Rio Grande, clearly looking for a confrontation. None came. Polk was about to ask for a declaration of war based on Mexico's delinquency in paying a $2 million debt when word arrived that Mexican cavalry command had engaged American dragoons north of the Rio Grande and killed eleven. Polk hastily rewrote his address to charge that Mexico had invaded the nation and that "American blood [had been shed] upon the American soil." With some Whig opposition, Congress assented.

Many in Washington predicted a short and successful war. They were disappointed. Mexico put up far greater resistance than expected, and once its defeat was obvious, it was reluctant to concede. Taylor took Matamoros and Monterrey, and in February 1847 his outnumbered men defeated an untrained and exhausted command under Mexican president Antonio López de Santa Anna at the village of Buena Vista, near Saltillo. Texas was secure. New Mexico had been taken six months earlier. As Brig. Gen. Stephen Watts Kearny led the newly created Army of the West from Fort Leavenworth toward Santa Fe, a group of influential Anglos argued persuasively to Gov. Manuel Armijo that his position was untenable. Armijo negotiated a bloodless surrender and took off for Chihuahua. Local resentment, in particular among the clergy and Pueblo Indians, erupted in a rebellion in Taos, north of Santa Fe, that killed the new governor, Charles Bent, and a few other officials, but troops from Santa Fe commanded by Col. Sterling Price suppressed the revolt after a bit more than two weeks.

Six days before the rebellion, a treaty had secured California, at least on paper. In the summer of 1845 Col. John C. Frémont had led a well-armed expedition there, supposedly to explore but clearly meant to support, if not incite, a Texas-style rebellion. In mid-June 1846, a gaggle of Americans took the town of Sonoma in northern California, tapped Frémont to lead them, and declared their independence, two days before Cmdre. John Sloat arrived from Hawaii—he had been told a year earlier to take San Francisco should war begin—and announced (without authority) California's annexation. The conquest appeared complete, but in September Californios (Hispanic locals) struck back and took full control of much of Southern California. Even after Stephen Kearny arrived from New Mexico with a few hundred dragoons, he and Cmdre. Robert Stockton, who had replaced Sloat, had their hands full until Frémont joined them from up north. On January 13, 1847, a treaty with the Californios ended the resistance.

By late February 1847 American forces had taken control over everything that Polk had wanted, but with Mexican popular opinion virulently against the gringos, Santa Anna's government showed no sign of capitulating. The decision was made to force the point by moving on the national capital. After directing the first large-scale amphibious landing in his nation's history, Maj. Gen. Winfield Scott besieged and took the seemingly impregnable port city of Veracruz, bested Santa Anna's numerically superior force at the Battle of Cerro Gordo, and took the extraordinary risk of cutting loose from his support on the coast to lead more than eight thousand troops overland to Mexico City. He moved in stages over four months, allowing chances for his opponents to discuss terms, and arrived at the capital in August. Advancing unexpectedly from the south, Scott's force took the protective height of Chapultepec on September 13. The next day Santa Anna withdrew his troops and the city surrendered. Except for some guerilla assaults, the war was over.

The peace, however, was more than four months away. The path to it was worried by the popular loathing of the norteamericanos in Mexico, by its roulette of political affairs, and by the shifting of positions and opinions in Washington. Polk's negotiator, Nicholas Trist, first offered to pay almost what had been offered for areas originally sought, plus Baja California and rights to a canal across Mexican lands. Santa Anna (once again president) declined. Polk, reminiscent of his upping his demands on the Oregon Country, added demands for a sizable part of northern Mexico and ordered Trist to come home. Then Santa Anna was ousted again. When his replacement seemed more amenable, Trist, fearing with good reason that the situation might dissolve into chaos, chose to buck the president's order and press for a resolution. After protracted discussions and some amendments, an agreement was struck. An enraged Polk had Trist brought home in custody, but facing growing political turmoil, he followed Trist's reasoning and submitted the treaty. The Senate approved it on March 10, 1848, and the Mexican legislature on May 19.

The Treaty of Guadalupe Hidalgo, signed on February 2, 1848, acknowledged Texas's annexation and passed over to the United States all of today's California, Nevada, and Utah, as well as most of Arizona, western portions of Colorado and New Mexico, and a tad of Wyoming. In return the United States paid Mexico $15 million and assumed its debt to American citizens, now grown to a bit more than $3 million. Full citizenship was promised to all Mexican citizens who chose to relinquish their former allegiance. Washington agreed to control the Indian peoples on its side of the new border and to pay for damages that any inflicted in raids to the south—a commitment that proved full of problems and exceptionally expensive. Costs of any war, in human and financial terms, are ultimately incalculable, but the official tally for the United States was more than thirteen thousand dead, most by far from disease, and close to $150 million in expenses in the field, in payments from the treaty, and in veterans' benefits over the years.[6]

With that the land-gorging of 1845 to 1848 was complete, and with the after-dinner mint of the Gadsden Purchase in 1853, the boundaries of the contiguous United States were set. It was quite a growth spurt. In only a little more time than that between a child's birth and its speaking its first simple sentences, the United States expanded by 773,510,680 acres and change.[7]

Looking back on these events, it is easy enough to see them as serendipity (and, for Mexico, its opposite). There were so many turns of chance that, if they had turned differently, would have likely derailed the course of expansion. So striking are the chains of chance that it is easy to miss a critical underlying point. While each moment was a proximate step in expansion, all were at some remove responses to pressures and interests that had been building for the previous few decades. Four in particular go a long way toward explaining not only expansion but also the events that followed it.

Begin with population. The number of Americans more than tripled between 1800 and 1840, from 5.3 million to 17 million, and even with the size of the nation doubling with the Louisiana Purchase, the density of population per square mile grew by 60 percent. While the economy was shifting toward early industrialization, most families engaged in agriculture or closely related enterprises, and with a high birth rate each generation multiplied considerably the number of families hoping to start a farm. On the eve of expansion, the nation was increasingly crowded, at least by standards of the time, and basic math pushed the demand for land inexorably upward. Southern states could look beyond Louisiana and Arkansas to Texas, which by 1845 had a white population edging toward a hundred thousand, plus about thirty thousand enslaved Africans. Families in the Ohio Valley and around the Great Lakes could look to Michigan, Wisconsin, and Iowa, but the considerable land west of there was effectively off the agrarian table. This was "Indian Country." It had no political organization, had no effective connections to the East, and, it was thought, received too little rain for families to farm in accustomed ways. Plenty of land was still available in the Ohio Valley, but the rapid growth of population still prompted the impression that agricultural expansion might stall, as if running in place, which encouraged what was felt in the South, a scanning for places farther on that were friendly to farmers and their futures.

Thus Polk's twin appeal in 1844 in pledging to annex Texas and acquire Oregon. Reports from Oregon gushed over its agricultural potential, especially of the valley of the Willamette River, where the early booster Thomas Farnham described an arable corridor, 150 miles long by 60 miles wide, of rich vegetable mold 3 feet deep.[8] In 1838 the era's great storyteller, Washington Irving, published a popular account of the party sent by John Jacob Astor to establish a post in 1811–12. He reported a "serene and delightful" climate in coastal Oregon. One could "sleep in the open air with perfect impunity" and stand in the shade in high summer without breaking a sweat.[9] As eastern farmlands filled, Oregon beckoned, and by 1844 a couple of thousand Americans had settled there with more on the way, drawn by the prospect, in the phrase of the day, that if you planted a nail it would come up a spike.

A second demand was for commercial access to the Pacific world. Once Oregon was ours, John Frémont predicted in 1844, it would become "a thoroughfare for the East India and China trade" that Senator John Calhoun was sure would funnel goods and wealth from half the people on the planet straight to the Mississippi Valley and beyond.[10] The vision included California. Twenty-five years before the United States acquired Oregon and California, a New England congressman assured his colleagues that once the "swelling tide" of Americans had reached the Pacific, "the commercial wealth of the world is ours, and imagination can hardly conceive the greatness, the grandeur, and the power that awaits us."[11] In the years ahead a trade in sea otter furs and California cattle hides and a vigorous increase in whaling turned the interests of New Englanders increasingly to the Pacific coast and trade beyond it. Geography, however, posed a problem. Much of the Pacific coast consists of cliffs and heights, so interest came to focus on a handful of usable ports. In Oregon the Fuca Strait and Puget Sound had several good harbors, but to the south were only Monterey, San Diego, and the gem at San Francisco. "The glory of the western world," Farnham called its long, deep, wide, and placid bay. Even its bordering capes were "verdant and refreshing to the eye."[12]

A third force was a quarter century of exploration of land to the west, the tracing of routes of transit, and the development of new means of moving across and around it. The first overland emigrants in 1841 took paths used over the previous twenty years by fur trappers.[13] Over the following five years Lt. John Charles Frémont of the Corps of Topographical Engineers led a series of ambitious expeditions that clarified the road to Oregon, established a route across the Sierra Nevada, described parts of the Great Basin and central California, and reported on a trading route across the Southwest. His hugely popular official reports, written by his brilliant wife, Jessie, were essentially enticements that left readers feeling, as historian William Goetzmann suggests, that James Polk's push westward was not just acceptable but, to many, inevitable.[14]

The marking of ways into the West coincided with a time when the nation and the world were, in practical terms, shrinking. New Englanders were especially interested in Pacific ports in part because new ship designs had shortened the effective distance between Boston and San Francisco and between San Francisco and Hawaii and Hong Kong. By the 1840s the canals that had redirected movement in the East were showing up in westering dreams. President Polk sought the rights to build one across the Isthmus of Tehuantepec; Texas expansionists proposed one to link Galveston and the Gulf of California. Two new technologies especially pushed along this revolution in movement. In May 1844, as Frémont was on his second expedition, Samuel Morse and Alfred Vail officially tested the telegraph system that would soon girdle the globe. A month earlier the New York merchant Asa Whitney had arrived in San Francisco from more than a year in China. He was soon America's most impassioned advocate of the second technology, the railroad, as a link between the East, Pacific ports, and an Asian trade. Seven months after the Senate approved the Treaty of Guadalupe Hidalgo, Frémont set out with thirty-five men to find a usable Pacific rail route across the Rocky Mountains. Washington sent Howard Stansbury to do the same up the Platte road and through the Wasatch Mountains to the Great Salt Lake.[15]

By then the fourth development had given the vision of moving westward, quite literally, a distinctive coloration. There was a widely held conviction that expansion was both ordained and demanded by the nation's cultural and racial superiority. The world's peoples were arranged in a racial order, with Caucasians at the top and Anglo-Saxons at the top of them.[16] The true homes of these superiors were northern Europe, Germany, and especially England, and the United States—places where, unsurprisingly, these theories began and flourished most. Descriptions of the western land's beauty and promise were joined to others of peoples stunted in development and incapable of making of the country what God intended. In a small masterpiece of circular reasoning, Farnham described the elite *Californios* as men of "not a very seemly" bronze, then called them naturally indolent, offering as proof their "lazy color."[17]

All of these impulses drew on and reinforced each other. Anglo-Saxon farmers needed western land that, by happy chance, was properly theirs because retrograde Mexicans and Indians could never bring it to bloom. The railroads that promised to expand the nation's commerce and power were proof of its intellectual superiority and higher civilization. That in turn left Americans obligated to reach farther, into the Pacific. To Whitney, his rail line to the coast not only would benefit American farmers and merchants but in time would also feed starving Chinese and bless "the heathen, the barbarian, and the savage . . . [with] civilization and Christianity."[18]

Expansion of 1845–48 was both a child of chance and the product of forces that had been building for a quarter century. By 1845 those forces had come together under a gloss of confidence, summed up in the term "manifest destiny," that the United States was bound to dominate the lands between its current border and the Pacific. When the nation did in fact expand with such stunning speed, as sparks running through the stubble, it was natural to assume that what had brought the expansion would just as surely confirm America's command of the new country and its promised rise to new greatness.

Every force behind expansion was, in fact, unloosed into the new America, and in time expansion would indeed play vitally in the nation's steep rise in affluence and power. At the outset, however, that was anything but obvious. The events of 1845 to 1848 came close to destroying the republic. Their first fruits were turbulence, uncertainty, and the most contentious and violent time in American history.

The chapters that follow begin with that turbulent uncertainty. Part 1, "Unsettling America," covers the first seventeen years of the emergence of the West and its role in reconstructing the nation. The years were ones of growth and disordering, stunning revelations and unprecedented violence, continental fragmentation and disunion averted. Part 1 ends as the events of 1861–65 that preserved the Union in the East began also to establish genuine command over the West, including the defeat, dispossession, and confinement of Indian peoples.

The next fifteen or so years saw the new nation consolidated as the Northeast and Southeast were tentatively rejoined and the West was brought fully into the nation. Part 2, "Things Come Together," traces how spreading infrastructure and invigorated explorations were binding the West within itself and to the world beyond. It traces, too, how the West's role as a great laboratory in older and newer fields of science was expanding an understanding of the workings of the world while justifying Native dispossession and the fashioning of a national racial order.

Part 3, "Worked into Being," follows the story of how exploiting the West's prodigious resources continued to shape its contours of culture and power, even as it fed the needs and helped remake the nation's evolving economy. It is arranged by three familiar areas—ranching, agriculture, and mining—not only because each was critical to western development but also because all were prime examples of the misconceptions that have clouded our appreciation of what was happening. Their romanticized images of crooning cowboys, sturdy homesteaders, and crusty sourdoughs picture the West as a place apart. In fact ranching, farming, and mining all illustrated and often pioneered the new means of production, finance, and organization that after 1865 were increasingly evident elsewhere in the reconstructed nation. Each, too, was a prime case of how the working West was remaking America physically through environmental changes, ones as sweeping and often convulsive as any on earth at the time, and was continuing as well to expand the grasp of global science.

Two other threads run through the chapters. Every step of change affected Indian peoples, in virtually all cases for the worse. It began with California genocide and proceeded through the progressive loss of lands and independence, via treaty-making and warfare, but above all through the repurposing of the land by the overwhelming numbers of new occupiers. Parallel to that unseating were efforts to determine just where Native peoples fit within the human family and national household, a political concern that interlocked with African Americans in the East and Hispanos and Chinese in the West. Consigning the Native story to its own chapter felt like creating a kind of textual reservation. Instead it runs throughout, and it bears stressing in turn that the creation of the West, and certainly its moral meanings, cannot possibly be understood without it.

The story of Indian peoples is wound together with the other thread. Apart from what actually happened, as best as we can recover it, the West's role in reconstructing America was, for want of a better term, mythic. All regions are montages of collective impressions, but those of the West, more than with those of, say, the South or New England, have been projections of the fantasies, aspirations, and anxieties of others. As the new country was unsettling the nation, the West was the projecting ground of the East's increasingly stark and violent divisions, which nearly destroyed the continental Union. Once the crisis was resolved, the West's meanings reversed. Now its images and storylines, from belligerent Indians and insidious Chinese to railroads and stagecoaches, national parks, and heroic geologists, spoke of a nation unified and redirected toward a common greatness and national character.

In the final chapter I have hoped to bring into some coherence the resistant sprawl of events from 1848 to the 1880s. It is meant to sum up the two themes mentioned at the start—the birth of a distinctive part of the nation and how that birth was inherent to the nation's remaking and its shift onto a fundamentally new path. The trick is keeping the two in a rough balance. Wallace Stegner was one of the most insightful and influential observers of the West. His admirers are especially fond of quoting his thought that the West has been "America—only more so." Rarely if ever do they add what he wrote next: "Actually it is and it isn't."[19] Stegner understood that the West should be seen as an enlargement of the nation, its people, and its character, yet it also has its own nature and its own story that deserves its own telling. When we recognize both and work to see how they fit together, we will be closer to understanding ourselves and how we have come to be.

Acknowledgments

I have spent well more than twenty years, off and on, researching and writing this book. That translates into an army of friends and professionals to whom I owe my thanks. Doing history paradoxically is a solitary effort that cannot possibly be done without others helping you. In my case, their name is legion and their support is immeasurable.

I begin with thanks to Dick Etulain, editor of this series, for his extraordinary patience. From the first the "bald Basque" has given encouragement and invaluable advice. I am grateful for both and for a friendship that by my count goes back close to fifty years.

Fulbright College of the University of Arkansas and its several deans, most recently Todd Shields, have given me unwavering support of many sorts, as has the college's department of history. After forty-two years gladly serving in both, I retired coincident with this book going to press, an accident of timing that reminds me of how much I owe to friends and colleagues for their help in this and so many other areas. Exceptional thanks are due to the Huntington Library, which hosted me for two long-term fellowships as well as several shorter visits over many years. Besides its incomparable holdings in western history, the place I call Nirvana on the Pacific has a staff whose competence is surpassed only by their generosity of spirit. In particular I thank Roy Ritchie (and Roy and Louise for their hospitality), Peter Blodgett, Jennifer Watts, Steve Hindle, and the late, lamented Martin Ridge. Chicago's Newberry Library also hosted me for a year's fellowship in the early stages of this project. I benefited hugely from the collections of Yale's Beinecke Library, and in particular from the help of George Miles and encouragement of Howard Lamar, and from my study at the Bancroft Library, the Western History Collection at the Denver Public Library, the archives of the Harold B. Lee Library of Brigham Young University, and the state historical societies of Colorado, Montana, Arizona, Nebraska, Idaho, and Oklahoma. I thank as well the National Endowment for the Humanities, which funded one fellowship at the Huntington, and the faculty and staff of the Rothermere Institute of American History and Queen's

College at the University of Oxford, where I spent the most rewarding year of my professional life as Harmsworth Visiting Professor of American History.

As to individuals to whom I owe further thanks, where to begin? I suppose with those who read the entire manuscript. Besides Dick Etulain, Richard White and Andy Graybill did so and both provided invaluable criticism and advice. Anne Hyde and Megan Kate Nelson also read the whole shebang; I thank them for their generous words. Others read parts and helped greatly, pointing me in profitable directions and catching forehead-slapping errors: Virginia Scharff, Johnny Faragher, Ari Kelman, Jeannie Wayne, David Wishart, Fred Hoxie, Stephen Maizlish, Ben Madley, Michael Holt, Rachel St. John, Pekka Hämäläinen, and seminar students at the Rothermere Institute. Special thanks to Patty Limerick and dozens of teachers in her annual Gilder-Lehrman seminar, who read several chapters and graced me with their perceptive critiques. I had a lengthy exchange with two fine young(er) historians, Kevin Waite and Stacey Smith, hashing through our differing opinions on a key question, and for that I thank them heartily. Particular thanks also to the editorial staff at the University of Nebraska, especially Bridget Barry and Ann Baker, for their good work and patience with my digital befuddlements.

What follows is a portion of the large cast, several clustered at the Huntington, whose advice, suggestions, taunts, encouragement, eye-rolls, jokes, and general good spirits have kept me moving along over the years: Sherry Smith and Bob Righter, Carl and Jane Smith, Keven Leonard, Bill Deverell, George Sanchez, Nick Rogers, Dan Howe, David Igler, David Wrobel, Peter Mancall, Steve Hackel, Jenny Price, Louis Warren, Phil Deloria, and Mac Rohrbough. I thank particularly departmental colleagues Jeannie Whayne, Patrick Williams, Lynda Coon, Jim Gigantino, Calvin White, Randall Woods, and Dan Sutherland, as well as a platoon of research assistants. Special appreciation to Gary Anderson, for passing along material he gathered at the National Archives. My fine student Justin Gage shared his research, which helped me understand far better the Native experience described in the closing sections of the book. And a bittersweet expression of gratitude for the help and decades of friendship from the late, great David Weber.

More personally, I thank the Three Amigos for helping me through some rough stretches with their friendship and concern and by making me laugh as hard as anyone should dare to. And there is my family, whom I love more than air: the late Betsy and Dick West, Bob and Marcie Stoner, Jacqueline Floreen, nephews George, William, John, and Charles, brothers Richard and George, and their partners in life, Dena and Lynn, son Richard, son Garth, son Bill, and my most excellent daughter-in-law, Laura, daughter, Anne, and her partner, Danny, grandchildren Noah, Will, Christin, Jodie, and London, who daily graces our household. In the final stages of my writing this book we lost our daughter Elizabeth. I will use this occasion to salute her extraordinary character, humor, and courage, and thank her husband, Randy, for his loving and unwavering care for her.

I dedicate this book to my wife, Suzanne Stoner, who has the most generous heart, most infectious laugh, and loudest sneeze of anyone I have ever known. I could try to express how grateful I am for her integrity and moral courage, her grace, sense of humor, intelligence, and love, but I would fail, so I will just say that she is the greatest blessing of my life.

CONTINENTAL RECKONING

PART 1 ➤ Unsettling America

Expansion brought with it a long list of questions to answer and challenges to meet. The challenges began with the land itself. "The eastern half of America offers no suggestion of its western half," a New England journalist wrote of the new country.[1] Its mountains, deserts, savannas, and woodlands somehow had to be not only crossed and catalogued but brought under some degree of physical command. That would have to begin with simply coming to know the place. Past a point quickly reached, the leaders of the nation had only the vaguest understanding of what they had just gotten—how the land lay, what was on and within it, and how it could and could not be put to the uses they wanted.

That last question was especially pressing. Expansion's enthusiasts had crowed plenty about its economic promise, but what, in even the most general terms, did that mean? Most of the nation's working folk were farmers, but virtually nothing was known about where most of the new America could be farmed, what it could grow, and what methods had the slightest chances of success. Nor could anyone say what the West might offer for the nation's recent industrial stirrings or what surprises, good and ill, it held in the pursuit of global markets, especially beyond the new border on the Pacific. What technologies would be needed to wring benefits from the land, starting with the means to connect its various parts and its workplaces (themselves yet unknown) and to stitch them into a national whole?

The land was already well lived upon, and largely commanded, by many tens of thousands of Indian people divided among scores of different cultures, yet the nation's leaders had only the most glancing knowledge of who they were and where and how they lived, and the little information they had was comically—and, it turned out, tragically—distorted and naive. Precisely the same could be said about Native peoples' view of the newcomers who were claiming their land. How each would deal with the other—that is, the basic course of relations among scores of centers of power across a third of the nation—was wholly uncharted. There was, besides, a putative theocracy claiming control of a majority of the land taken from Mexico outside Northern California and New Mexico, and besides that, there were others who looked at the expanded America and wondered, "Why stop now?" In 1855 the secretary of war would complain that he had to deploy two-thirds of the army's "whole available force" to prevent filibusters from launching into Mexico from California, New Mexico, and Texas.[2]

The faith that the United States had been ordained by God or history or the fates or whatever to expand to the Pacific, caught up in the phrase "manifest destiny," supposedly held true for what would come next, the sure fulfillment of the land's promise as the nation perfected its command from coast to coast. As a predictor, however, that faith could not have been farther off the mark. In 1848 the future of what would become the West was more fluid and unsettled than it ever had been or would be. There was nothing destined about it. It was manifestly up for grabs.

Still more treacherous questions were afoot. Even before the land had been formally acquired, expansion had begun to pry apart the Northeast and Southeast over a particularly dangerous issue from the past—whether southeastern slaveowners would be allowed to take their human chattel westward into lands under federal control. A political bargain in 1820–21 had settled the issue for all lands inside the national boundaries in 1845. Then the three years of explosive growth undid that bargain and began to stress the nation's political order, eventually beyond its snapping point.

The remaking of the nation began when expansion unsettled it more profoundly than ever in its history. America at midcentury faced as many uncertainties, and ones as fundamental to its future, as at in any point in its history, and the attempts to cope with them set loose changes, East and West, as transformative as any that had come before or would come afterward. This continental unsettling culminated in 1861 in a continental crisis. The four years that followed, firmly seated in our memory as ones that preserved the older republic, kept the new West as well within the nation. They also began to consolidate the new country and truly to bring it, along with its Native peoples, fully into a national embrace.

Expansion alone, however, cannot fully explain the transformations that followed. At almost the exact moment when the nation's three-part leap to the Pacific was formally finished, another sequence of events began that would quicken every question. Together the paired episodes, the acquisitions to the Pacific and that other chain of changes, would create the West and would play a leading role in remaking the nation. The two came together one morning in early 1848 when a New Jersey carpenter looked down at his boots.

1 ➤ The Great Coincidence

When the first forty-niners arrived in what was now the far edge of their expanded nation, the world was shifting under their feet. The shifting was not of historical forces, although that shift was real enough. It was not metaphorical but literal. Like every place on earth, California rides like a raft on top of an ocean of molten rock. That raft, the North American plate, moves westward at about an inch a year, and as it does it runs against the Pacific plate, which comes at it at an angle. As the Pacific plate began to slide under California more than 150 million years ago, the friction caused by the grinding melted part of its crust, which flowed upward as plumes of magma. Part erupted as a string of volcanoes, but most remained deep in the earth and cooled into a batholith, a gigantic body of granite. Then water and wind eroded away the volcanic mountains and the land around them, and as they did, the granite batholith gradually came into the light. This became the mountain range later named the Sierra Nevada. At first it was no higher than today's Appalachians, but about twenty million years ago the area to its east began to stretch east to west. As it did, the eastern edge of the Sierra rose sharply, some of it to fourteen thousand feet above the sea, while the land to its east dropped down. The result was what exhausted overland immigrants would find as they approached their journey's end—a steep mountain face they would have to labor up before cresting it and descending gradually into California's Central Valley.

As the Sierra Nevada emerged, it brought with it a good bit of what humans for millennia have considered the very definition of wealth and beauty. Every ounce of gold on earth has arrived as a space traveler. Gold is made from dying stars. It is born in a supernova, the explosion of an especially massive star, or the collision of two unimaginably dense neutron stars. It is flung into the void as space dust, some of which coalesces with other elements to become planets and other celestial objects. By far most of the earth's gold is in its molten core, hopelessly inaccessible, but some arrived about two hundred million years after the planet's birth with the bombardment of some twenty billion billion tons of debris from meteors and asteroids. It was scattered and mixed unevenly into the earth's crust as part of those floating rafts. Some was in considerable concentrations. A stretch of faulted rock in the Sierra Nevada 150 miles long and 1 to 4 miles wide held veins of gold-bearing quartz up to 50 feet wide and more than 1,000 feet long.

A lot of gold remained in those veins, but a lot was freed as the land's endless erosion ate away at the Sierra. Gold is very inert—it combines with only a few other elements—and so it remained pure as it moved downhill in streams and eventually settled into the gravels of riverbeds. The streams came and went. Much of the eroded gold rested in the deep dry gravels of long-gone rivers. Some, however, was in the living watercourses that would be known by the first humans arriving at least thirteen thousand years ago, by the first Europeans coming in the sixteenth century, and three centuries later by Americans claiming the land as their destiny. Star-born, traveling billions of miles, churned deep into the earth and brought up with its mountains, then set loose to flow down toward the sea, this gold, what Egyptians called "the breath of God," lay beneath the water among rocks and pebbles, glittering, waiting to be seen.

"What Is That?"

At the end of the U.S.-Mexico War, Lt. William Tecumseh Sherman was in Monterey, California, an aide to Col. Richard B. Mason, the military governor. One morning in the spring of 1848, two men walked into his office and asked to speak privately to Mason. A few minutes later the governor called in Sherman and pointed to some glittering specks and pebbles the men had laid on a table. "What is that?" Mason asked. Sherman had seen gold mined in northwestern Georgia, and now he tried a couple of simple tests, noting the "metallic lustre" of the flakes and bending them with his teeth to check their malleability. They were the real item, he said. The men left. Weeks passed. In July Sherman accompanied Mason to the area along the American River where the gold had been found, and what he saw left him "quite bewildered." About four thousand men were laboring uncomplaining under a brutal sun and knee-deep in frigid water, buying overpriced supplies in brush-hut stores and sleeping on the ground under layers of pine needles. Mason was just as wide-eyed in the formal report he sent to the War Department a month later: men were finding gold in eighty-dollar chunks and two had cleared ten thousand dollars in a week. All the area's rivers—the Yuba, Feather, Bear, and others—he believed to be equally promising.[1]

The following December President James Polk told Congress that "officers in the public service" (that would be Mason and Sherman) had confirmed by "facts . . . on the spot" the tantalizing rumor heard over the past months: gold was abundant across a wide swath of the country just acquired from Mexico.

Things were happening fast, he reported. San Francisco's manhood—storekeepers and stevedores, liverymen, clerks, lawyers and layabouts, lots of soldiers and nearly all its sailors—had lit out for the mines. Goods and labor commanded preposterous prices. By the time Sherman left California in 1850, he could see that the discovery he had helped confirm had set loose a folk movement that would repeople the far edge of the continent.[2] So it happened that the man who, as much as any other, would determine the outcome of the Civil War also had a hand in the event that, as much as any other, would create the West and shift the nation's history.

The upheaval began at a millsite. James W. Marshall, a carpenter and builder, had drifted westward from New Jersey, first to Oregon and then to California, where he served under John Charles Frémont and then worked for John Sutter, grantee of nearly fifty thousand acres bordering the American River east of San Francisco.[3] As 1848 opened he was overseeing construction of a sawmill in partnership with Sutter. The millrace needed deepening. To gouge it out with minimal labor Marshall had ordered a temporary dam built and then opened several times to flush through the millsite. On the morning of January 24 he was inspecting the results. He looked down into the exposed gravel and noticed a sparkle. He stooped into the shallows and gathered a few flecks. First on his own and then with Sutter, Marshall did a simple assay, hammering his find with rocks, boiling it with lye, and applying nitric acid. Convinced it was gold, Sutter sent a sample to Governor Mason to secure title to the strike—the visit Sherman witnessed—but Mason demurred. The land was in legal limbo, he said, conquered but without civil authority. Sutter then tried to suppress the news, but workers at the mill tossed their shovels and saws and with just about everyone else in the vicinity were soon looking for gold up and down the river and in nearby streams. Word soon leaked to San Francisco, with the consequent jumbling of tents and brush huts Sherman and Mason found on their visit.[4]

For anybody at that time claiming that the fates were favoring the United States, Marshall's discovery of gold might have been exhibit A. Just nine days after he noticed the glitter at his feet, the treaty was signed that made the millsite, and around it the region soon called the Mother Lode, part of the nation. Within two hundred hours of its becoming part of the republic, that is, California began to be revealed as the most valuable real estate on the continent. The first flake Marshall picked up was worth about half a dollar.[5] When Mason visited the American River the following July, he estimated miners were clearing between thirty and fifty thousand dollars a day.

Strike followed strike. By 1854 the nation's gold production had increased seventy-three times over. California's output, plus that of Australia, which had its own strike in 1851, exceeded that of everywhere on earth during the previous 356 years, since the Columbian landfall. California's production of $65 million in its banner year of 1852 was greater than that of all the world's gold mines during the entire eighteenth century. By 1900 its output since Marshall's half dollar was estimated at $1.4 billion.[6] (A sardonic Marshall understandably had his own take on the figures. "Of the profits derived from the enterprise, it stands thus," he wrote in 1857: "Yankeedom $600,000,000. . . . Myself individually $000,000,000.")[7] Anyone needing a more kinesthetic image to appreciate those numbers might consider this: In 1856 the San Francisco mint was processing so much gold that considerable amounts were blown out its smokestack. Investigators found gilded rooftops a hundred yards distant.[8]

The effects rippled outward, ever farther. Markets boomed up and down the Pacific coast and around its rim as countries from Chile to Australia poured goods into California, and as word reached the Atlantic, manufacturers and shippers as far away as Norway began to eye it as a potential market. The impact of gold itself was seismic. Global prices surged, manufacturing capital doubled, and the exploding supply of money found its way into enterprises from French wheat farms to railroads and the Sardinian telegraph.[9] In the year of the discovery an amateur economist had published some thoughts on the relationship of labor and capital. Ten years later the impact of California and Australian gold had so shaken society that he felt compelled to reexamine his ideas in light of this "new stage of development." In 1867 Karl Marx published *Das Kapital*.[10]

Gold's initial jolt, however, had a far tighter radius. Someone sailing from New York in 1848 could get to India faster than to San Francisco, while the trip from California to Tasmania was weeks shorter than to Washington DC. Consequently it was eleven months before the President Polk officially confirmed the stunning news and another seven or eight before the first goldseekers from the Atlantic coast arrived in California. When they got there they found that thousands of others had been pulling money from the earth for months. Before the forty-niners, there were forty-eighters.

Everyone around him "seemed to have gone insane . . . apparently living in a dream," John Sutter's gardener wrote of the mobs that suddenly crowded the banks of the American River and its tributaries.[11] Colonel Mason figured that more than half of the four thousand men he saw were Indians from local tribes, working the streams with tightly woven willow baskets. Most at first were probably conscripted by Sutter and others or working as drudge laborers paid with food, crude shelter, and "gee-gaws of trifling value," but once they learned what gold would bring in the local stores, many turned independent and soon were sporting the results: pants and vests, scarves, gaudy shawls. "Heretofore so poor and degraded," Mason wrote, they "have suddenly become consumers of the luxuries of life." Some turned to prospecting and discovered several of the most valuable early deposits.[12]

Word seeped out to San Francisco in late April, and although editors tried to stem the flow, calling the rumors "a sham . . . got up to guzzle the gullible," the stampede was on. Rowboats that had cost fifty dollars now went for five hundred, dollar shovels for ten. In late May word reached Monterey, reportedly preceded by omens: a white raven playing with a child, owls ringing church bells. Prospectors heading north stripped the city of "every bowl, tray, warming pan, and piggin . . . everything, in short, that has a scoop in it that will hold sand and water."[13] Oregon heard the news in early August. Harvest was only weeks away, but, as a local versified:

> The farmer left his plough and steers,
> The merchant left his measure;
> The tailor dropped his goods and shears,
> And went to gather treasure.

By various reports two-thirds of Oregon's adult males left for California, leaving only five elderly men in Salem and in Oregon City nothing but women, children, and Indians.[14]

By then a wider immigration was underway. Late in the previous century Hawaiian Natives, called Kanakas, had begun working as trappers in the Northwest, and when a ship brought news of gold to Honolulu, five months to the day after Marshall's find, as many as three thousand were sailors on ships around the Pacific. Within weeks hundreds more, virtually all foreign-born men, had left the islands for California. The evaporating labor pool drove wages to new heights.[15] Considerably more goldseekers came via well-worn routes from Sonora and other Mexican border states; the French consul at Monterrey wrote in May of 1848 that ten thousand had passed by.[16] Chile and Peru received the word in late summer, and over the winter virtually every available vessel, including whalers, were shuttling to San Francisco passengers and cargoes of picks, shovels, boots, mirrors, shaving brushes, and whatever might sell. An estimated five thousand Chileans were in the hills by June.[17] Australia was in a depression when news arrived just before Christmas, and the exodus of goldseekers sent the price of houses tumbling even more. Tasmanians gathered around street placards: "GOLD! GOLD!" and "WHO'S FOR CALIFORNIA?" After their first crews deserted to the gold fields, captains from down under began hiring New Zealand Maoris, figuring they were more likely to stay aboard for the voyage home.[18]

The forty-eighters laid down the early basics of California mining.[19] Hispano locals and especially Mexicans and South Americans could draw on generations of mining experience. They tutored others in locating and extracting the most available dust. To process it they used mercury from nearby cinnabar deposits that, by another stroke of remarkable luck, had been discovered in the 1820s. Influences from outside California soon became part of the texture of daily life. The brightly colored Mexican banners and flags displayed in one camp reminded an early visitor of Asian bazaars. Hawaiians strolled about in colorful shirts and silk sashes, Chileans in distinctive wide belts and black ponchos, Indians in military coats but no pants. Already gambling was pervasive, and most popular was monte, the Mexicans' "great national game" that one man claimed they would play "in bed, on horseback, on their dinner plate or their father's corpse."[20] Eventually it would spread throughout the West. Women in street stalls sold Mexican-style meat rolled in tortillas, which was popular with the more acclimated but later avoided by easterners for its lower-class connotation and especially for its dramatic seasoning.[21] A visitor in the 1870s added a red pepper "the size of a minnow" to her salad, took a bite, and "Shades of vulcan! . . . Tears would not have flowed more freely if I had taken a coal of fire into my mouth. . . . The principle sources of heat are said to be the sun, the fixed stars, chemical action and electricity . . . [but] I am the first person who has ever discovered a latent hell in a red pepper. . . . I would warn all persons to beware of the pepper family entire."[22] Later arrivals picked up and adapted Mexican songs. A catchy musical phrase in "Donde vas, bueno caballero?" ("Where are you going, good sir?") became the chorus of "My Darling Clementine."[23] A western cultural artifact was born.

Forty-eighters established one of the West's prime characteristics. From that point on, the region would be the most culturally and ethnically mixed part of the nation. From Oregon to Arizona to the Dakotas, that human variety would enliven western society and quicken its development by bringing ideas and customs from virtually every part of the planet. It would also add immeasurably to the stresses that would soon make the emerging West one of the most violent places in the nation's history. The sheer pace of changes, plus the lustrous possibilities they unveiled in California and elsewhere in the region, naturally twisted ever tighter the usual tensions among disparate people thrown together. They would rupture within months, when the next wave of goldseekers, the forty-niners, washed into the country from the East.

That wave began to build only in the final months of 1848, but once it did, it swelled extravagantly. In yet another anticipation of a western theme, distance and sheer ignorance about the new country seemed to inflate hopes and fantasies. An early best-selling pamphlet, claiming firsthand experience but made from scant reports and lies, described a land of fertile soil, warm perfumed breezes, welcoming people, and terrain so friendly one could go by carriage from San Francisco to the mines as if riding down Broadway in Manhattan. Gold was everywhere. Approaching Sutter's land, the author's party stopped to dip a drink from stream, "and lo! at the bottom of the cup we found sparkling grains of gold."[24] The day after Christmas of 1848, James Gordon Bennett's *New York Herald*, the nation's most widely circulated newspaper, published the first of four special editions of the *California Herald*. They included maps, information on routes, and plenty about the glorious promise of the diggings. Philadelphia's *Christian Observer* assured readers that gold "lies on the open plain, in the shadows of the deep ravines, and glows on the summits of the mountains."[25]

Newspapers across the country and especially in the Midwest picked up the refrain during the first months of 1849. *Hunt's Merchants' Magazine and Commercial Review* gave instructions on gold-panning, adding offhandedly that men were regularly returning from the mines bent down by a hundred pounds of gold dust apiece.[26] Advertisements included a detector of the precious metal, "Signor D'Alvear's Goldometer," and "California Gold Grease," to be smeared over the body before rolling down hills to pick up the glittering powder that lay all across the landscape.[27] As for getting out to El Dorado, some proposals were an equal stretch of credibility. An editor of the *Scientific American*, Rufus Porter, suggested an "Aerial Locomotive," an eight-hundred-foot steam-powered dirigible that would carry two hundred passengers and their baggage on a smooth three-day flight from New York to California. Grizzly bears would gape in wonder far below, Porter predicted, as observers in Europe marveled at America's "soaring enterprise."[28]

Earthbound goldseekers had to stick to traditional options. Ships began leaving eastern ports for California early in 1849, and by late winter towns along the Missouri River were filling with crowds intent on an early start for an overland journey to the Pacific. With dreams of their own mercantile gold rush, Independence, Westport, and Saint Joseph in Missouri and Kanesville, Iowa, vied to become the preferred jumping-off place. Each boasted superior access to the trail west, the best and cheapest draft animals, and the most reliable liveries, farriers, dry goods merchants, flour mills, wagonmakers, wheelwrights, and saddle and harness makers.[29] Leaving before May was chancy, given the plains' unpredictable spring weather and the need for the grass to be up and hearty enough to feed their oxen, and impatient overlanders waited out the calendar in crowded tent cities. The buildup made a bottleneck of the first step of the trip, crossing the Missouri. On May 3 a man wrote his sister from

Saint Joseph of three to four hundred wagons in line to be ferried, a wait of three days, maybe four.[30] Once over the river the immigrant gathering looked westward across more than two thousand miles of what they knew only by rumor and leaps of fancy.

What followed was a microcosm of how the West would be shaped over the decades ahead. It anticipated the longer transformations to the land and its peoples, including devastations and assaults on tens of thousands who were bound to the place by centuries of intimacy. The more immediate picture was of outlanders coming into the country, older lives brought into new worlds, bearing the past yet startled and changed by what they found.

A Shout Westward

It was as if everyone living in Michigan and Arkansas in 1840 together picked up and walked west. Between then and 1860 more than three hundred thousand persons would trek overland to California, Oregon, and Utah, most of them to the gold country. More than a quarter million more would travel from the East Coast to San Francisco by sea between 1849 and 1860, crossing via Panama and Nicaragua, while thousands more would take the longer route around Cape Horn. Joining them were tens of thousands of persons from Europe. Just how many flocked to the Pacific coast is a speculation, but the mass migration was certainly one of the largest and most diverse in modern history. It was also an anticipation. Like so much in the next thirty years, the overlander experience both reflected American life at large and displayed the utter strangeness of the new world it was moving into.

Immigration by sea was by two routes. Nearly sixteen thousand persons sailed around Cape Horn, a voyage of six to eight months. The speed and quality of experience varied considerably. One voyager languished miserably in an "old fashioned tub of a vessel" that was "slower than justice."[31] The second way, via Panama, soon proved more popular.[32] The first arrivals from the East came by that route. Only twenty-nine passengers were on the steamship *Falcon* as it left New York City for Panama on December 1, 1848, four days before Polk's gold-confirming message. By the time the ship stopped at New Orleans the word had arrived by telegraph, and nearly 200 men clamored aboard and refused to leave. Passengers crossed from Chagras on Panama's east coast to Panama City on the other side. The steamship *California* carried the first of them to San Francisco—365 passengers, 100 above its supposed capacity and more than all persons taken to Panama the previous year. By year's end between 5,000 and 6,000 men had followed the firstcomers.[33] Twice as many took the Panama route the next year.

Chagras was a primitive town of bamboo huts along muddy streets full of naked children and lank dogs. Its few accommodations were strained impossibly by the "irruption of Americanos." Antsy for the goldfields, they took an ancient trail across the isthmus. The trip began in canoes, called bungoes, paddled by locals to the villages of Cruces and Gorgona near the peak of the Atlantic watershed. After resting and dining on "mule steaks, dead pork, and iguana pie," travelers went the rest of the way in the saddle, sloshing through swamps down a trail lined by dead and putrefying mules.[34]

Panama City was a traditional Spanish town with a decaying fort and white-washed houses with roofs of red tile. It was only 9 degrees north of the equator, 21 degrees closer than Boston and 16 closer than even New Orleans, and the searing sun alternating with curtains of rain left the unacclimated feeling as if they were living in a dog's mouth. "The climate of the Isthmus proved very trying," one wrote, a little daintily: "The air failed to satisfy the lungs."[35] Diseases, especially cholera, malaria, and yellow fever, flourished in the deplorable sanitation and tropical climate. Some waited weeks for a spot on a northbound ship. The priciest ticket bought a bed in a stateroom and meals of beef, duck, lamb, cheese, and fruit, but the great majority crowded together in steerage, "seething, swaying, quarreling, and cursing," sleeping on shelves and eating salt pork and black bread served out of tubs on deck.[36] A voyage of twenty to thirty days brought them to San Francisco.

For all its discomforts, the Panama route was far and away the fastest, and what had been scarcely a trickle of traffic before 1849, mostly officials and missionaries, swelled to more than twenty-six thousand by 1855. It jumped still more the next year when completion of a railroad (truly the first transcontinental) eased the crossing toward the gold fields and elsewhere around the Pacific.[37]

The overland route was far slower, but it was by far the cheapest way to go. Before 1849 about 19,000 had made the crossing. About 60 percent went to Oregon, drawn by accounts of land aplenty and of astonishing fertility, and about 25 percent had come with the early Mormon exodus to the Great Salt Lake in 1847 and 1848. The rest, only about one in six, went to California, most to John Sutter's grant. Marshall's gold changed that. In 1849 and 1850 nearly 80,000 persons journeyed overland, more than four times the total of the previous eight years, with nearly nine in ten landing in California, and nearly 65,000 followed during the next two years. The flow then slackened, only to jump again on the eve of the Civil War with discoveries of silver in what would be Virginia City, Nevada.[38]

In 1849 about five thousand persons followed the Gila River route to Santa Fe and then across the southwestern deserts to Southern California, but most crossed by the Platte River route.[39] From various towns along the Missouri River they converged on the Platte in what is now east central Nebraska and moved along the south bank before ascending the river's north fork to the continental divide at South Pass, a broad saddle between the northern and middle Rocky Mountains. Some would then branch off to the northwest to Oregon, while the California-bound would take a southwesterly route across the Great Basin, following the Humboldt River until it sank into the earth and then crossing forty miles of desert before ascending the Truckee and Carson Rivers to the Sierra Nevada. Unlike the Rockies, the Sierra had no easy gateway. In the journey's final and most difficult stage immigrants urged their spent oxen over Donner or Roller Pass before laboring down the western side.

From start to finish the trip was quite a physical test. Anyone crossing, warned a veteran, would "endure heat like a Salamander, mud and water like a muskrat, dust like a toad, and labor like a jackass." Another swore that he "would swim around Cape Horn on a log" before making the overland trip again.[40] Simply as a human experience, the overland migration was one of the most distinctive episodes of American history and a fitting prelude to the creation of the West. The travelers' responses to the land and to each other anticipated those across the region for the rest of the century, as did the appalling consequences for the land and its Native peoples.

The two-thousand-mile trip from the Missouri River to California or Oregon at first took four to six months, though over time improvements shortened the time. One man made it to California in an astounding seventy-six days.[41] A typical day's travel of ten to fifteen miles began before dawn with camp broken and breakfast cooked; in the middle came two or three hours of "nooning" for a meal and to rest the animals; travel ended close to dusk, with a new camp yet to be made, animals pastured, and dinner prepared. Most walked most of the way, and by the end their clothes showed the costs. "My skirts were worn off in rags above my ankles," a woman recalled: "My sleeves hung in tatters above my elbows . . . ; around my neck was tied a cotton square, torn from a discarded dress."[42] The grueling pace, repeated week upon week, was exhausting, although at day's end some found the experience inspiring. "Love is hotter her[e] than anywhere that I have seen," one traveler wrote: "When they love here they love with all thare mite & sometimes a little harder."[43]

Within a couple of hundred miles, emigrants found themselves an in increasingly alien world. Addison Crane marveled at the "wildest and most magnificent" scenes but then he gave up: "Any one who should seriously attempt its description would only make a fool of himself."[44] The West's openness and its yawning skyscape could leave outlanders feeling swallowed by space. The impression of sameness, of "an ocean of land the same day in and day out," could be unnerving. When a young man asked his toddler sister why she was crying, she answered that "we will never get to Oregon if we come back and camp in the same place every night."[45] Travelers were stunned at erratic swings of weather, like going to sleep in Nebraska and awakening in Siberia, one wrote, and at the ferocity of storms with "sheets of fire . . . pouring rain and the bellowing thunder" and hail "as if a field of ice had been put through a crusher, and then rained down upon us." In high summer they marveled at mirages as heat and refracted light showed them lakes that weren't there and lifted distant wagons into the shimmering air so they dipped and swayed like sloops at sea.

The western menagerie drew plenty of interest. Antelopes (more properly pronghorns) "glide[d] over the Prairie at a bird's wing pace."[46] Bison drew the closest attention. One woman called a bull a "prairie god" with enough hair on its chin for a dozen French emperors.[47] Travelers approached the trip with fears of lurking predators, but the anxieties were baseless. Stretches of the trail fairly writhed with rattlesnakes—one party killed fourteen under their wheels as they fled a camp—but bites were extremely rare, and the record has no cases of attacks by bears, wolves, and other creatures of eastern nightmares.[48]

Native residents often were lumped with other exotic fauna: "We have seen no wild animals except Indians, lizards, and black-tailed hares," wrote a diarist in Nevada.[49] As with animals, families often set out fearing that ruthless savages were waiting along the trails, as patient as spiders, ready to pounce. One mother cropped her daughter's hair to discourage scalping; another carried pellets of cyanide in a locket to take if facing rape. The closest study, however, shows only three overlanders out of every two thousand killed by Indians, and considerably more Indians killed by whites than vice versa (426 to 362 between 1840 and 1860).[50] Indians typically approached with overtures, not arrows. When about sixty Lakota hunters met David DeWolf's party along the North Platte in 1849, the lead horseman came forward with a flag crudely inscribed with the stars and stripes. "They were very friendly and understood begging," he wrote, but like other Native visitors, these were likely asking for a courtesy or for compensation for the loss of vital resources. There were occasional thefts of supplies or horses, but most meetings were of mutual curiosity and of exchanges of everything from moccasins and hats to feathers and hoop skirts. A delegation of Cheyennes was bored by a fiddle and watch—they had seen plenty—but quite taken with a jewsharp and ambrotypes of distant family.[51]

The true threats were ones of the overlanders' own making. In peak years campgrounds could be nearly as crowded as urban slums. As hundreds of parties stopped in the same places night after night, the garbage, offal, and human and animal waste quickly mounted, so by season's end the route was as much a gutter as a trail. An obvious result was, with accidents, one of the two most common causes of death—disease.[52] "Contact" diseases, passed person-to-person, flourished on the first five hundred miles or so before burning themselves out. Chronic ailments, dysentery the most common, persisted all the way. Their monotonous diet starved travelers of essential vitamins and left them vulnerable to scurvy once they arrived in California.[53] Some disorders, notably "mountain fever," transmitted via ticks, were picked up en route.

Cholera was the greatest killer. A bacterial intestinal infection passed usually by fouled water, it produces high fever, stomach cramps, and effulgent diarrhea that wrings the body of its fluids. Death can come within a day of the first symptoms, sometimes less. Cholera had last visited North America in 1832, but by grim luck it arrived in New York and New Orleans in December 1848, just as Polk was formally recognizing California's goldfields, and it swept up the Mississippi just in time for forty-niners to pick it up and carry it onto the trail. It struck again in 1852, the year of heaviest migration to California.[54] Physicians did the best they could—one treated more than seven hundred patients—but the losses could be horrific. One immigrant wrote of a train of eleven wagons, all driven by women; every man had died.[55] An Arkansan wrote in 1852:

> Huffmaster and wife and Manerad are dead. Uncle Enos is dead. James Hanen and wife and child are dead. Craig and wife and child are dead. James Crawfords babe is dead. David's child is dead, and Samuel Hanen has been at the point of death but was on the mend. . . . Nancy Graham and William Ingram's children are both dead. Elvy Hanen is delirious and is an object to look at. Jacob Rushes widow and little girl are dead.[56]

The other prime threat was accidents. Especially before toll bridges and ferries, emigrants drowned crossing the Platte and Green Rivers and floating down the Columbia. About as common were deaths by accidental gunshots from rifles and pistols kept primed and sometimes cocked, at the ready for dangers that weren't there. Children, spending their energies clamoring into and out of wagons, were especially prone to falling and being crushed under the wheels. Injuries normally non-fatal, such as a cut or broken bone, stood a fair chance of worsening by infection, sometimes to the point of death, under the physical exhaustion and dietary limits of the trip.[57]

Too often the dead were so hastily and shallowly buried that wolves and coyotes pulled them out and ate them, leaving bones scattered along the trail sides, which one traveler called a vast "city of the dead." While only informed guesses are possible, the total losses between 1840 and 1860 were between four-teen and twenty thousand, which has the mortality rate between 4 and 6 per-cent, higher than that for the general population back home and considerably higher than a sampling of young adults.[58] It was quite a toll, especially when imagined as an average of seven to ten graves per mile.[59]

The overland trails anticipated the emerging West in another way, their environmental impact—rapid, intense, wrenching, and catastrophic for native human and faunal populations. The popular image is of swaying wagons pass-ing single file across a great empty space. In fact in the busiest years the traffic could resemble that in central Boston or Philadelphia. Wagons sometimes traveled twelve abreast. Tens of thousands of iron-rimmed wheels and mil-lions of animal hooves tore at the soil and left a rutted road that in places was hundreds of yards across. The steady wind whipped the pulverized earth into choking clouds. Eyes stung; clothing itched; all food crunched. There were occasional advantages. When a young girl fell under her wagon and its wheel passed over her head, the dust was so deep she was simply pressed down into it. She jumped up, asking, "Am I killed?"[60] Oxen overgrazed what had been rich swards of grasses until by the summer's end the only pasture was a mile or more off the trail. The Platte valley had hosted great stands of timber, but by the mid-1850s virtually all were gone except some cedars well up feeder canyons. By then the overlanders' entry to the West was a metaphor for much of the land's later story: a mess of their own making.

The experience was in other ways a continuity, a carrying forward of lives left behind, starting with a sense of community. Many came as companies reflect-ing their origins: the Wolverine Rangers, Buckeye Rovers, Newark Overland Company, and Boston-Newton Company. Migrants from all sections of the country were coming together where sectional tensions were tightest in the 1850s, eastern Kansas, yet there is no record of serious conflict in the bivouacs. Once underway companies helped each other find stray stock, repair wagons, feed the foodless, nurse the sick, and bury the dead. A young girl caring for an infant whose mother had died en route would seek out a wet nurse at each night's campground over the final five hundred miles. She was never refused. There were predictable fractures among the rolling communities. A diarist wrote of a pair in his group who had started out together: "Dugan and Duhner not being able to agree made a division, sawing their wagon in two and making each a cart."[61] But in light of the stresses endured over the miles and months, the general mood was remarkably positive. "Never have I seen so much hos-pitality & good feeling," wrote one overlander, who had enjoyed coffee, warm biscuits, and butter in a neighboring camp the previous evening.[62] Travelers quickly grasped a lesson of much of western settlement ahead, even at its most competitive. Cooperation paid.

People brought other cultural fundamentals with their oxen and butter churns. Nothing showed this more clearly than families and how they operated. Their very absence highlighted their importance. More than 90 percent of those crossing in 1849 were men, with the portion even higher among the California-bound. Forced suddenly into women's work, many floundered pathetically. A diary of a later overland traveler to Colorado's gold fields shows a culinary nightmare of raw, fat meat, dried beef, and crackers. By the trip's end he was "never half so hungry in my life. . . . Oh, flesh potts of Edgept [sic], how I sigh for ye."[63] The double load of work was grueling. They had to "repair all breaks, wash and mend their own clothes, bake their own cakes, cook their own meat, brown and boil their own coffee," a months' long tutorial in a home economy most had taken for granted.[64] By 1853 the numbers were righting themselves. The portion of male overlanders dropped to 66 percent, and one out of five on the trail was a child.[65] Migration became more like what it had been before 1849, a family affair, and wives, husbands, children, and others stayed grooved in customary behaviors. Most women wore long, full skirts, perhaps for modesty in bodily functions along the crowded, treeless trails.[66] They hauled out furniture at the end of the day and set it up in a "home-like way" and went calling from wagon to wagon for what one called "feminine . . . diversions."[67] Children, called by one authority "respecters, even venerators of customs," carried their own traditions, a body of games, lore, rhymes, and language that in some cases dated back centuries. Along the Truckee and Platte Rivers they played "how many miles to Miley Bright," a rhyming game born of medieval English pilgrimages.[68] Rituals persisted. The most hurried funerals observed a few fundamentals and offered a hymn or two, and the rare marriage might be followed by a "shivaree," with a crowd shooting guns and banging pans, enough to "awaken the Seven Sleepers," outside the wagon of bedded newlyweds.

Lines of authority held firm. As the men in her company plotted the day's travel, Sarah Royce wrote, the women "were busy . . . cooking, washing, mending up clothes, etc."[69] The exception came on the Sabbath, as impatient men wanted to keep rolling and women, keepers of the family's moral life, wanted to stop.[70] They had a more mundane reason for observing the Sabbath. They needed the rest. Everybody on the trail worked hard, but they did not work hard at the same things. Men's traditional work in fields and shops was suspended on the trail, but much of women's labors in seeing to a family's needs continued, and under especially trying circumstances. Some had worked for weeks before leaving, drying fruit and preparing what they could in advance, and once under way they made more as well to cover the extra calories burned in the long trudge. In effect there were four or five meals a day. The mountain man and guide James Clyman watched a woman stand in a driving rain for two hours, holding an umbrella as she fried bread. Women mended clothes and did laundry in muddy rivers. Mothers fed, nursed, and bathed children—a typical family traveled with three or four—while caring for them in the baking heat of crowded, jolting wagons.[71]

While some children were lost along the way to accidents and disease, some were added. Remarkably, the birth rate on the trails apparently was a bit above the national average, with roughly one woman out of eight bearing a child during the trip.[72] These couples obviously knew that a child was on the way and that at some point on the journey, under primitive conditions and almost surely far from a doctor and likely without another woman experienced at midwifery, the wife would enter into the most dangerous thing a woman in those years could do—give birth. Perhaps this measures an allure of the new country strong enough to overbalance the most compelling reasons not to go, or at least to wait. Perhaps it reflects the family as patriarchy, with husbands overruling pregnant wives' objections to setting off, or perhaps childbirth was considered such a natural, recurring turn in the familial cycle that it should be taken, literally in this case, in stride. Whatever the explanation, two points are clear. Fundamental patterns of life in the East persisted, and as that life was borne westward by the hundreds of thousands crossing the continent, the patterns wore more heavily on women than on men.

There were plenty of lighter moments, also reflecting the cultural transfer. "Went swimming . . . , read four chapters of Proverbs, part of 'As You Like It,' shot at a mark five times . . . , ate supper and went to bed," a man wrote, and a woman did "not know when I have enjoyed anything so thoroughly" after she and a friend read aloud the poem "Locksley Hall." Frank Langworthy read his way westward by drawing on the plains "library," books others had tossed by the road. Along the Arkansas a man heard from a nearby camp airs by Mozart, "strangely out of place in the wild waste," and a woman was awakened by soldiers singing a chorus from "The Barber of Seville." There were impromptu dances and contests. At one stop a company made ice cream.

Mozart and dessert, half-devoured corpses and country beyond description: the journey was a rough metaphor for a larger experience. Taking control of the country would always be a process of cultural sift, and it started with the act of walking into it. As the miles unrolled and the oxen tired, and as the immigrants gradually grasped what they were in for, there began a recalculation of needs, hopes, and sentiments. Within a few weeks a sloughing began, and past the Rockies, as true exhaustion set in, the trail was littered with clothing, cook stoves, plows, anvils, furniture, firearms, and at least one iron safe and a diving bell. And just so in the years ahead. Those settling into the new country would toss aside other cargo—thoughts of the possible, identities, oughts and shoulds—while holding tenaciously to other presumptions and imposing them onto the new lives they were making.

One thing set the journey to the far West apart. It was one of two midcentury episodes, the other being the Civil War, in which hundreds of thousands of Americans were suddenly and wrenchingly tossed into experiences utterly alien to their lives until then. Unlike heading for the battlefield, however, the trip to the Pacific included persons of both sexes and all ages. Never in the nation's history has there been such a mass collective gawk. There were vast mounded communities of critters that looked like squirrels but yipped like dogs and scavenged human skulls at trailside, some still with hair and ribbons. There were hammering storms that upended whole wagons as electricity crackled around their iron wheel rims. Travelers drank water so thick with silt that "we could almost pick it up with our fingers" and met "bright, sprightly" Indian children, some bedecked in white buckskin and other "in puris naturalibus." Those crossing Panama and Nicaragua had their own memories. They told of trees draped in snakes, cigar-smoking children, freshwater sharks, and lizards the size of small dogs. A New Yorker attended a wake for a one-year-old boy whose corpse stood at the center of the room, dressed in a spangled robe and crowned with a flowered wreath. Only the mother appeared to grieve. Beside her sat a blind fiddler, his eyes rolling side to side as he sawed away. A gay crowd drank rum and danced around the dead child, whose open eyes were cast slightly down, as if he were deep in thought.[73]

2 ▷ Division and Multiplication

The westward flocking was a display of broader realities in national life. It reflected and amplified long-simmering tensions between Northeast and Southeast. It also spawned other, offsetting forces that quickly began to bind the emerging West into the evolving nation. The two themes—the West as divider, the West as unifier—would play out through the next three decades. So would another development begun by the great coincidence. By the end of the 1850s California's economy showed a maturity rivaling that of many eastern states. Its vitality would quicken the nation's turn into the Pacific world and would help propel a far wider economic growth that, in time, would help pull a diverse America into one and set it on a new course.

A Nation Divided and Connected

Northeast and Southeast had contested visions of what the West should be in its economic and cultural basics, and each tried vigorously to cultivate its particular views. In that contest the Southeast might seem to have had a definite edge. Only thirty-three years after the Louisiana Purchase of 1803, southern expansion had birthed a new nation, the Republic of Texas, and carried tens of thousands of persons beyond the nation's southwestern border. The push out of the Northeast meanwhile had been less than feeble. There was vigorous settlement in Minnesota, Wisconsin, and Iowa, but beyond that was Indian country, and farther on, past the northwestern boundary, what would become the states of Washington, Oregon, Idaho, and Montana contained at most a few dozen American citizens.

Texas's independence kicked southern expansionism into a more vigorous stage. Texas claimed, based on virtually nothing, that its western boundary was the Rio Grande, which would have given it Santa Fe, and in 1841 it sent an expedition to take command. It failed miserably, but Texan visions only expanded. By one scheme a link by rail, steamboat, and canal would allow a ten day passage from New Orleans through Texas to Guaymas on the Gulf of California. From there Texans could "converse with the people of China through a speaking trumpet."[1] Legislators further resolved that the republic now included the Mexican states of Chihuahua, Sonora, and Upper and Lower California, plus parts of four others—all together half of the neighboring nation.[2] Denial of their preposterous claim was an insufferable affront. "Jesus could be composed under insult," wrote a prominent attorney, "but the people of Texas are of a different breed."[3]

That south-to-west thrust persisted into the 1850s, and in the earliest stages of the gold rush, the Southeast was strongly represented. The considerable numbers of its people might seem to feed the hope that California would become a slave-based economy and culture, from its mines to the fields that would feed the miners.[4] Looking strictly at the previous decades, that might seem a natural outcome.

But the dynamic of America's westward tilt was fast changing.[5] The shift was most obvious in the Old Northwest. Illinois and Iowa quadrupled in population between 1840 and 1860; Indiana and Michigan tripled. Wisconsin residents increased twenty-five times over (30,945 to 775,881). The previous southern thrust of expansion was shifting sharply to the north, and the pressure to expand yet farther west was shifting with it.

A series of interlocking developments fueled that change. One was a tightening economic connection between the Ohio Valley and states to its east and north. In the past foodstuffs of the lower valley had gone mostly down the Mississippi River to southeastern states and to foreign markets through New Orleans. After 1840 the flow of goods was increasingly to the east to feed the expanding population in the industrializing region from Pennsylvania northward. Initially the main routes were through the Great Lakes—rates were cheap—and via the Erie Canal and Hudson River to New York City. Eastward traffic over the Erie Canal grew fourfold between 1841 and 1851, then nearly doubled again by 1860.[6] New canals from the lakes to the Ohio and Illinois Rivers brought ever more of the hinterland into commercial reach. That tendency was confirmed and amplified by the explosive growth of railroads starting in the early 1840s. Rail construction took place everywhere east of the Mississippi, including in the Southeast, but if it is imagined as a race among regions, the Old Northwest simply ran away from everybody else. Just under half of the new trackage was there, and when the mid-Atlantic and New England states were added, the figure rose to nearly two-thirds. That, with the accelerating ship traffic through the Great Lakes, firmed up the consolidation of the Northeast–Old Northwest link.

That link was further encouraged by the overland migration that began in the early 1840s. The new midwestern rail and water connections were a natural conduit to the overlanders' embarkation points along the Missouri River, and Marshall's find gave the tendency a forceful shove. The superintendent of the 1860 census wrote that California gold had been a prime cause behind the nation's recent spurt of rail construction. The effects in the Ohio Valley and Great Lakes were especially electric. People there, already "thoroughly aroused" to the railroads' effect on dropping transportation costs and quickening trade with the East, now saw them also as the easiest and fastest ways to jumping-off places from the Missouri Valley to the golden lands beyond.[7]

The census showed the effects. While a hefty portion of native-born immigrants to California in the first few years had come from the Southeast, the numbers quickly shifted. By 1860, 42 percent had been born in five states bound by the new bonds of economy and movement—New York, Pennsylvania, Ohio, Illinois, and Indiana. Add in New England and the portion rises to nearly two in three. The respective numbers for all thirteen slaveholding states were 28 percent, 9 percent for the deep Southeast, and when Virginia is held out, barely 5 percent. Nearly twice as many in California had originated in New York alone than in all the deep Southeast.[8]

These figures were a barometer of sectional power. As the populations of the Old Northwest and states to its east rose sharply, and as both areas pursued avidly the new systems of movement, their interests increasingly fused. The very notion of sections was evolving. Picture the new networks of commerce and movement as systems of chains binding New England and the mid-Atlantic states ever more tightly to the Ohio Valley and Great Lakes. By the latter 1850s they had fostered such a close economic and political kinship that it was sensible to speak of them together as a single region: the Northeast. Meanwhile, railroads to the south almost without exception were connecting the ports of the slave states to one another rather than running northward. Northeast and Southeast even used different gauges for their tracks.[9] The new sectional alignment was firming up just as the nation acquired the West and as Marshall made his discovery, and within a few years a growing majority of those heading into the new country came out of the Northeast, moving along the new routes to the Missouri Valley and beyond, in particular to the gold fields and San Francisco. After dominating the westward push for nearly half a century, the Southeast found itself outflanked and, as its share of the nation's population shrank, increasingly isolated.[10]

Southern expansionism, however, was anything but dead, and in fact the shifts of regional power gave it a kind of desperate energy, especially after news of gold arrived. Southeasterners had their own railroad dreams that would be central to their hopes to parlay political power into a clearer path to the Pacific for themselves and their institutions, in particular African slavery.

As some developments were straining relations between Northeast and Southeast, others were building the first links from the East to the Pacific. The two most consequential involved the federal government and business enterprises. They worked sometimes independently, often in partnership, and occasionally in opposition. Partnerships were most obvious at military posts on the overland trails, in particular Forts Kearny and Laramie along the Platte River and in eastern Wyoming. Up to four hundred travelers a day mobbed Fort Laramie, peppering soldiers with questions "on the simplest and best known points," an officer wrote: they "scarcely know where they are going."[11] Commanders at both posts handed out food gratis to the most desperate cases; blacksmiths repaired wagons; post doctors cared for injuries and more dire cases of illness.[12] Businesses from woodcutters to brothels sprang up around the forts and many more sprouted along the trails—ferries as a reprieve from treacherous crossings and slapped-together smithies for busted wheels and shoeless oxen. The first whiskey holes and crude "road ranches" gave way to well-stocked outfitters. Freighters to Salt Lake City and, after 1859, to Denver dropped off goods to stock the shelves—flour, smoked meat, coffee, sugar, clothes, wine and brandy, books, hardware, barrels, blankets, cutlery, window glass, and more.[13] One account book entry read: "Cocane, 1.00."[14] Itinerate merchants stuffed wagons with goods and marketed their way westward. Counting on the distant call of nicotine, a Missourian in 1850 bought a great supply of chewing tobacco at twenty cents a pound, sold it along the trail at five times as much, and unloaded what remained in Salt Lake City at five times that, a 2,500 percent markup. Another traveler arrived in California, sold everything he had, bought a load of essentials, then doubled back and set up shop on the trail at bloated prices. "All those traders we met out here skinned us emigrants for all we were worth," he explained, "and now I have come back here to skin all the balance."[15]

By 1860 long stretches of the overland road had stores and other businesses every ten miles or less, a sturdy thread of enterprise that after the war would feed other development all along its way. Culturally, it carried across the new country the entrepreneurial impulse that was so much a part of national life.

One federal function, the mail, played an especially vital role in binding East and West. From the republic's birth the postal service had been one of the federal government's few unquestioned responsibilities, one that settlement on the Pacific strained as never before. Besides the needs of government and the most basic business coordination across the continent, the mail nurtured the intimate bonds to a national diaspora. It is hard to exaggerate the gnaw of separation felt by many on the far coast, and hard as well to overstress the value of the post. Some men wrote letters home almost daily. There was something about writing on and touching paper that would be touched by distant loved ones that bridged the separation. One man went farther, leaving drops from a nosebleed: "I leave my mark here, with a little *sprinkling*." Often men waited despairingly for weeks without an answer. Then, with luck, elation. "There is a charm, a witchcraft in a letter from Home," William Perkins wrote: "a man is transported at once in spirit to the scenes he has left behind." Henry Page was "almost crazy for news from you," he wrote his wife, and so "let your motto be like . . . mine, write, write, write."[16]

Even before California was acquired, Congress contracted with two firms to meet the need, the United States Mail Steamship Company from New York to Chagres on Panama's east coast and the Pacific Mail Steamship Company from the other side to California and Oregon. In yet another of expansion's helpful coincidences, their first runs, in late 1848 and early 1849 by the steamships *Falcon* and *California*, provided the first maritime passage to the diggings, and in the years ahead goldseekers crowded the decks and berths of every postal ship. The maritime postal contracts were in effect a federal immigration subsidy. Contracted companies milked it to the maximum.

The first mail moving overland, government dispatches carried by Christopher "Kit" Carson, took three months to go from Monterey to Saint Louis.[17] By 1851 there was monthly service from Independence, Missouri, to Sacramento, but the huge demand and spotty service eventually demanded more. By then this fundamental service was caught up in rivalries between Southeast and Northeast. In 1857 Postmaster General Aaron V. Brown, formerly governor of Tennessee, contracted with John Butterfield's Overland Mail Company to carry the post by a long, looping route, called the "oxbow," from Saint Louis and the Gulf coast across southwestern deserts and then up California to San Francisco. The huge operation—more than 800 persons, 1,500 horses and mules, and 250 coaches, and 141 stations—crossed the 2,800 miles in the required time of twenty-five days or less in each direction.

Critics of the oxbow route called for a far shorter connection, roughly along the overland road (and favoring states to the north). They won a modest contract, but when its subsidy was slashed in 1859, it appeared doomed. The famed pony express was a last-ditch effort to save the Northeast's mail link to California— and with it one of the West's most prominent businesses.[18] The freighting firm of Russell, Majors and Waddell serviced army posts with thousands of tons of goods annually, but in 1860 the grand schemes of William Russell had left it teetering on collapse.[19] Their only chance, the owners decided, was to grab the plush government subsidy from Butterfield and to make the case for the central route they promised to deliver the mail in well less than half the time of the Overland Mail. On April 3, 1860, two riders set off from Saint Louis and Sacramento to begin relays between a hundred stations across the plains, Rockies, and Sierra Nevada. At five days riders exchanged bags and in five more they galloped into their respective destinations. The image of young men racing cross-country (the company called for "young, skinny, wirey fellows") enthralled the public, as it has ever since, but behind the show were larger lessons, with business powerhouses wrestling for millions in government funds, and behind them sectional politicians squaring off over control of the new country and the fate of the old.

The gamble failed. Even charging five dollars per every half ounce carried, Russell, Majors and Waddell lost money, and in October 1861 a transcontinental telegraphic connection made "the pony" irrelevant. The whole point of the effort, a government contract, did not materialize. The firm's debts spiraled up and its credit down until it went under in 1862. William Russell, the quixotic champion of a central route (and of his own baronial ambitions), rode ever stranger schemes into scandal and disgrace. At his death in 1872 he was selling patent medicines.

Even as events in the East slid toward disaster, however, the mail carried on. In 1859 the overland postal service bore twenty tons a month, and steamers delivered more than two million letters and nearly twice as many newspapers. The government eased the way. It charged a bulk rate for newspapers and dropped postage for letters from $0.40 to $0.06 in 1851, then raised it to $0.10 in 1855. Expenses were eight times receipts. The postmaster general figured his office was spending $4.14 per person west of the Rockies compared to the national average of $0.41. Service to the Pacific was "wholly impractical," he concluded.[20] But of course it continued. Sustaining a federal presence on the Pacific was a matter of connections, with letters of credit and letters from home equally vital, and so the government went deep into the red subsidizing the economic and emotional life in its new, far-flung outposts.

The role of business was even more emphatic on the westward route by sea. Out of it came an early case how the gold rush could rebound eastward in making financial barons of the age. Cornelius Vanderbilt, already commander of a system of steam transport centered in New York, hoped to challenge the United States Mail Steamship Company and the Pacific Mail Steamship Company with a second isthmian route, this one across Nicaragua. From Greytown on the Caribbean coast steamboats chugged up the San Juan river and across Lake Nicaragua before travelers finished with a short, steep descent to the Pacific by carriages, mules, and porters. As many as thirteen thousand persons chose the new route over the next five years. To carry goldseekers to Nicaragua Vanderbilt built several oceangoing steamships that became the basis for transatlantic business. He turned profits from that toward that other realm of steam power—railroads. On his death in 1877 Vanderbilt's estimated wealth equaled a full percent of the nation's gross domestic product.[21] Western gold, plus the technological revolution that was creating the West, propelled the career of one of the East's towering capitalists. There would be others.

Meanwhile in Panama, an even more ambitious project was under way. The tortuous, fever-ridden trudge across the isthmus quickly brought calls for a railroad, and William Aspinwall, president of the Pacific Mail Steamship Company, took the lead, organizing the Panama Railroad Company and raising a million dollars—a fifth of what was needed, as it turned out. The challenge was colossal. Tens of millions of cubic yards of gravel were poured into miles of swamp to build a roadbed. The rainy season of several months left workers slaving in water waist-deep. Yellow fever, malaria, and cholera forced the company constantly to shuttle out sickened workers and shuttle in new ones, sometimes fully flushing their workforce every two weeks. Still the project crept ahead, financed by travelers using the completed stretches on either side as they pinched toward the middle. Finally finished in 1855, the Panama Railroad ran 47 miles, crossing 170 bridges and rising as much as 60 feet in a mile. This first transcontinental link reduced travel from ocean to ocean from days to three hours. It had cost about 6,000 lives.[22]

Both isthmian options were pricey, about a thousand dollars for the full trip, but traffic increased as facilities improved. The 120,000 persons between 1855 and 1860 more than doubled the number of overlanders.[23] For all the popular fascination with the trek by wagon across plains, deserts, and mountains, by 1860 the majority of Americans who had traveled to the Pacific coast had come by sea, borne by a system made from a marriage of big business and government support. The partnered enterprises were a prelude to others in the West after the Civil War.

By 1860 the distance from east to west, measured not in miles but by the difficulty and time needed to cross it, had shrunk significantly. The making of those connections, from the repatterning of traffic in the East to the rivalries over mail routes in the West, initially fed the worsening sectional contest that nearly tore the nation apart, even as the connections themselves implanted unifying institutions into the new country: families, common customs, and powerful economic interests and more, bonds that would build vigorously after the Civil War.

In all this there was a certain irony. The earliest arrivals from the East called out desperately for more efforts to bridge what they felt was the terrible isolation of the far West. Developments of the 1850s—the mail coaches and steamships, military posts, ferries, businesses, and the isthmian railroad—answered the demand. And yet initially, and paradoxically, being so cut off from the world was a trigger of success. Separation, it turned out, could breed a dynamism that in turn would shape profoundly an emerging West.

Multiplication

California's early development was unique among American frontiers. Three overlapping circumstances explain why. The gold fields quickly generated enormous amounts of raw wealth. As scores of thousands crowded in to what was suddenly one of the most desirable destinations on earth, they created a voracious demand for a wide range of goods and services. Finally, there was California's isolation. It was thousands of miles, in many cases tens of thousands, from those who wanted to go there and from the obvious sources of what it needed. In practical terms California was what it appeared to be on the earliest maps—an island.[24] Each of the three circumstances is obvious by itself. It is together that they shed their brightest light. The combination—prodigious wealth, hungry demand, and isolation—created a unique dynamic.

Economists speak of the "multiplier effect." When money is spent, it not only brings something to the spender. Money also gives whoever gets it the chance to spend it again, and when they do, somebody else gets another chance. At each step, as money changes hands, it stimulates demand for whatever is bought, clothes or a meal or a spin of a roulette wheel, and that eventually has physical effects: new dry goods stores, restaurants, and gambling halls. Those businesses in turn take in money and hire workers, who spend their wages in other stores down the street. Thus a hundred dollars, as long as whoever gets it turns around and spends it, pays for economic activity many times its face value. Its effects multiply. That certainly happened in California. While much of its gold migrated elsewhere, much was spent where it was mined, and millions of dollars more poured in as investments. Strictly in economic terms, the rippling effects were impressive.

The multiplier metaphor can be pushed further. With so much to be done, and done so far from sources of support, much of the new society had to be built essentially from scratch. Rather like money's multiplying consequences, with each dollar bouncing and prodding activities in the same vicinity, each new development both met some new need and stimulated a need for some other, a demand that often had to be satisfied locally. It was development in ricochet. Precisely because much of that development began from a dead stop, unimpeded by any previous arrangements, those in command, if they could find a way on this far rim of the nation, could begin with advanced technologies and forms of organization. A good part of California's frontier economy was born modern.

Quickly the effects accumulated. Inside of a decade there was a collection of institutions and facilities far more elaborate and sophisticated than on earlier American frontiers. Those frontiers had been far closer to their motherlands and could rely on them more for their basic needs. California was both farther away and in far greater need. In effect it had to become its own motherland, especially in the crucial early years before the Panama Railroad quickened the flow of goods from the East. It produced everything from glassware and milled flour to boilers and workpants. It developed as well its own infrastructure of roads, coaches, steamboats, and, soon enough, rails to circulate within itself and to connect to the outside. Born from gold and the rush to get it, it was a historical multiplier that birthed a startlingly mature economy poised to reach into the interior and play a role for much of the West that the distant East had not played for it.

Agriculture was a good example. At the onset of the rush California was a growling stomach. Hunters soon exhausted most accessible game, and most foodstuffs had to come from Oregon, Mexico, Chile, Hawaii, and Australia. The sea turtle population on the Galapagos Islands crashed as hundreds were caught and shipped to California. Soon, however, local production boomed. The number of California farms grew from 872 to 18,716 between 1850 and 1860, improved land from a bit more than thirty thousand acres to nearly two and a half million. The value of farms in 1860 was a dozen times that of a decade before.[25] Garden produce that seemed to a local editor a "spontaneous production of the soil" brought stunning profits—$40,000 from sixteen acres of potatoes near Sacramento.[26] Especially impressive was the expansion in what Californians had grown for generations, starting with grapes for wine and brandy to slake the miners' prodigious thirst. The million bearing vines recorded in 1855 grew to eight million five years later and twenty-eight million in 1870. Forty counties reported orchards in 1860, the start of an industry that would boom spectacularly later.

The boom in wheat was even more dramatic. The long, hot, and dry summers in the San Joaquin and Sacramento River Valleys could produce huge harvests of grain that held up well when transported long distances. Great tracts of land, effectively a land monopoly, were turned to farming on a grand scale, and production soon was mechanized with gang plows, headers, and other machinery imported or made in San Francisco. A deep labor pool of Indians, Mexicans, and disappointed miners was on hand for planting and harvesting. Wheat production, virtually nil in 1852, consequently exploded to nearly six million bushels in 1860. By the mid-1850s markets in the mining camps and San Francisco were saturated. Producers looked abroad, not only around the Pacific to Australia, Chile, Peru, Hawaii, and China, but also, of all places, to England. Half of the state's wheat exports in 1860 went to Liverpool and London.[27]

So, too, with ranching. For decades ranchos in Southern California had raised large herds to export their hides and the tallow from their hooves and horns. With gold the price of meat spiked spectacularly. Tens of thousands of animals were driven north to be slaughtered at the diggings and tens of thousands more were driven in from the Midwest and border Southeast.[28] Within a dozen years of the gold discovery, the already considerable cattle population had increased tenfold, and California ranches were supplying markets in Oregon and Nevada.[29] Sheep increased during the same period from seventeen thousand to more than a million, and butter production from about seven hundred to more than three million pounds.[30] As in wheat production, ranching as a business rapidly matured. In the mid-1850s two German immigrant butchers, Henry Miller and Charles Lux, began raising cattle close to San Francisco to supply their shops there.[31] By the Civil War they were well on their way to fashioning an enterprise strikingly modern in structure, legal strategies, and manipulation of resources.

All these enterprises showed another of California's advantages. Its immigrant stewpot brought together traditions and innovations that made it an especially fertile ground for new enterprises. Agricultural developers came from careers in quarrying, meat packing, milling, and the China trade. Former trapper William Wolfskill settled in Los Angeles in the 1840s, married into the influential Lugo family, and began a winery that by 1859 produced fifty thousand gallons, 15 percent of the state's total. Another key figure in the expanding wine industry, the Hungarian Agoston Haraszthy, had founded a Wisconsin town, written a travel account of America, and operated a Mississippi steamboat.[32] The pattern, over and over, was of varied backgrounds and fertile ideas set to work where there were great needs but little precedent on how to meet them.

By the 1860s descriptions of agrarian California were as boosterish as those of the early mines. Winter was not winter at all, wrote the *Overland Monthly*, but "one long-subdued spring" before hot summers brought abundant yields.[33] Claims grew ever more extravagant. During a brief enthusiasm for silk, a promoter estimated that its foreign sales could retire the entire national debt.[34] Sprawling compendia appeared. One claimed California fields had produced a 210-pound squash, a 10-pound carrot, a beet 5 feet long, and a tomato 2 feet around.[35] The word was spreading. Haraszthy reported that Europeans were universally surprised that a state "so young and so isolated" had so quickly advanced in agricultural production and technique.[36] In fact it was exactly California's isolation and youth, plus lots of money and demand and a flood of new ideas, that brought about the impressive results. By the Civil War, California was not only mostly feeding itself. It was ready to send what it grew into a market with a radius worthy of the circumference of its tomatoes.

Manufacturing showed the same pattern, with a wrinkle. Scarcity of coal and iron held back heavier production, while high wages and interest rates and tastier opportunities in mining and land diverted investment elsewhere. Still, the demand of immediate needs brought a remarkable industrial burst, especially when raw materials and markets were close together, as with lumber and flour. During the 1850s lumber and flour mills increased respectively from 10 to 279 and from 2 to 91. There were other examples. California produced consumer goods ranging from beer, furniture, crackers, ground coffee and mustard, sugar, and coffins to woolens, sails, glassware, matches, boots and shoes, brooms, soap, pianos, and billiard tables.[37] The need for machines to turn out such goods inspired the start of heavier production. By 1870 one out of eight California steam engines was in a flour mill, most of them made in-state.[38] To provide for the diggings, factories south of San Franisco's Market Street produced hoses and nozzles for California hydraulic mining and later pumps, stamps, amalgamating pans, and retorts for the silver boom across the Sierra Nevada. In manufacturing San Francisco had a base it would build on after the war; in commerce it was soon serving a market second in size only to Chicago's.[39]

In the 1850s, well before Levi Strauss began making what would become the most popular style of trousers in history, California birthed other international consumer dynasties. In 1850 William Bovee established the Pioneer Steam Coffee and Spice Mills to offer coffee ready to use instead of the green beans miners had to grind and roast. To help build the shop and market the coffee he hired an ambitious New England teenager who saved his pay and bought into the business. At thirty-five he became a full partner in the firm, and seven years later James A. Folger bought out the others and gave his own name to what would become the leading coffee producer in the United States. John M. Studebaker took eight thousand dollars he had made building wheelbarrows in the market town of Placerville and invested it in his brothers' Indiana business making phaetons, sulkies, and other horse-drawn vehicles. Early in the next century, with "Wheelbarrow Johnny" as president, the firm began its first production of automobiles.[40]

The rapid, muscular development just as quickly began to offset one of the very conditions that had helped produce it—California's isolation. It had never been total, of course, and its sparse outside trade in 1848 spiked with the first word of gold. Almost all of it came by sea, and in fact it would for decades, even after completion of a rail connection to the East. San Francisco quickly became one of the busiest ports in the hemisphere. Nearly six hundred million pounds of goods arrived during the ten months after April 1849, and during the summer as many as five hundred ships stood at anchor.[41]

Those connections in turn fed what would be one of the gold rush's most consequential legacies. For more than half a century Americans and Europeans had shown a growing interest the vast Pacific Ocean.[42] Several expeditions, culminating with the remarkable United States Exploring Expedition (1838–42), toured the Pacific with an eye not only to filling in the map but also to feeling out commercial possibilities. Atlantic merchants sent hundreds of ships to traffic in the pelts of otters (sea and land), fur seals, and beavers and later the hides of the California cattle that would provide the first beefsteaks in the diggings.[43] As the fur trade declined another was rising sharply. An enormous fleet of American whalers, seven hundred of them in 1850, harvested tens of thousands of gray, right, sperm, and bowhead whales to supply illuminating and lubricating oil. Honolulu was an ideal pivot point for the quickening traffic. Between 1824 and 1848 nearly a thousand commercial ships docked there with cargoes ranging from cigars, bear skins, and "German stuff for trousers" to Italian brandy and, from one ship, fifty-one French accordions.[44] As 1848 opened, hundreds of ships sailed with growing confidence and familiarity along the sea lanes connecting Canton, Melbourne, and Hong Kong with Callao, Monterey, and Lima.

And then California gold. Goods began to pour into San Francisco as farmers in Oregon, Chile, and Peru sent shiploads of wheat, fruit, and beef on the hoof. Australia sent dray horses, bricks, tents, potatoes, and blankets of kangaroo hide. Hawaiian merchants shipped the food they had supplied to whalers as well as sugar, koa wood, salt, whale oil, and coffee. Soon the flow reversed as the telescoped economic development produced a surplus of some goods. On his visit to Taiwan in 1854 the California timber entrepreneur Nathaniel Crosby opened the first foreign trade there in two centuries. Traffic surged around the Pacific system. Between 1848 and 1864 the tonnage of freight arriving in Hong Kong grew tenfold; in 1856 nearly one ship in six arriving in San Francisco (42 of 246) was from China.[45] As eastern politicians crowed over the nation's blessed future in the gold fields, boosters along the coast had their own foretelling. "That we shall have the boundless Pacific for a market is manifest destiny," wrote an Oregon editor: "We are bound to command it."[46] The trade, and the bloviation, would only grow in the years ahead.

California's internal connections were developing as well. Goods landed at the Golden Gate were sent up the Sacramento River and its tributaries. In 1852, 165,000 tons of cargo arrived in the inland port of Sacramento, near the junction of its river namesake and the American River, and was carried from there to the mines.[47] The earliest traffic in skiffs and whaleboats shifted to steamboats by the summer of 1849, with at least fifty chugging along the Sacramento the next year. After vicious competition sank a ticket price from thirty dollars to one, rivals united into the California Steam and Navigation Company and carried people at ten dollars a head and freight at eight dollars a ton.[48]

Traffic along the first crude roads was by mule trains. Along a single route out of Marysville nearly four hundred Mexican *arrieros* (muleteers) worked 2,500 animals carrying foodstuffs, furniture, lumber, millstones, and at least one iron safe of 352 pounds (the mule carrying the safe died on arrival). As roads were improved wagons appeared and, in 1849, the first stagecoaches. Travel on them at first was what one woman called "the most excruciating . . . that it was ever my lot to be victimized in," but with few options companies proliferated.[49] By 1853 Sacramento alone hosted a dozen lines capitalized at a third of a million dollars. As conditions gradually improved, dozens, and eventually hundreds, of Concord coaches came by ship. In 1853 several firms combined into the California Stage Company, which bought and bullied its way into near-total control. Its routes ran nearly two thousand miles inside the state by 1858, the year it opened a line to Oregon.[50] The first means over the Sierra Nevada was "a little track like a footpath," but by 1858 sixty-four toll roads were operating. The discovery of silver that year in what would be the Comstock Lode upped the need for connection. Four years later a single toll road out of Placerville brought in $3 million a year by accommodating 50,000 persons and 30,000 tons of freight.[51]

By then each California town of significant size was well bound to every other. That in turn birthed other fusions of private and state enterprise. A prime example was the mail. After going to huge expense and effort to get the post to California, Washington failed miserably in getting it to addressees. San Francisco's single facility became in effect a general delivery office for tens of thousands of persons scattered over tens of thousands of square miles. A single shipment in November 1849 held forty-five thousand letters that took three days to sort. Alerted to a mail ship's arrival by a large black ball hoisted atop Telegraph Hill, crowds waited in long queues worked by coffee and food vendors. In the end many were turned away with a shake of the head.

The result was a new business, the express.[52] The first expressmen were smalltime entrepreneurs—William Ballou financed his business selling beans bought from a Chilean ship—who quickly became something like saviors with saddlebags.[53] The founder of one express company thought that anyone back home might have laughed at men greeting the mail: "such hoorahing, jumping, yelling & screaming."[54] The demand soon drew eastern firms, first Adams and Company (1850) and then Wells, Fargo and Company (1852), that offered the most direct, and by far the fastest, connections from coast to coast and then delivery to the camps. A parcel or letter sent between San Francisco and New York arrived in barely a month, well ahead of the government post. Driving it all was what drove everything else—gold. Expressmen first carried it in oyster cans and butter kegs, later in well-guarded strongboxes. The delivery fee was sweetened by juggling how gold changed in value as it traveled. William Brown, who started an early express after deciding he might mine for years "& not get my *whack*," carried coins with his letters, bought dust in the diggings for $16 an ounce, and sold it for $17 in San Francisco, a tidy 6.25 percent profit. Wells Fargo did the same continentally, buying California gold for $16–$17 an ounce and selling it to the Philadelphia mint for $18. Much of the gold it sent was from customers needing to transfer its worth across the country. A miner sending money home, or a merchant ordering goods, would provide dust to an agent for a fee and receive a letter of credit, which he would post (probably via Wells Fargo) somewhere back east, where the recipient would redeem it at a Wells Fargo office, again for a fee. Wells Fargo would carry the dust itself and would profit still more as its value appreciated between San Francisco and Philadelphia.

Every clerk was now a financial agent positioned to deal with both material things and with the movement of numbers. From there it was a small, predictable step into basic forms of banking. Wells Fargo and Adams and Co. soon offered loans based on the dust that sat in its safes, some of it waiting for redemption, some for safekeeping and drawing interest lower than what was charged for loans. Banking quickly became central to their operations. Adams and Company dominated until early 1855, when a financial panic forced all California banks to close their doors. Only Wells Fargo had kept adequate assets on hand, and it soon reopened and eclipsed the competition. Over about 120 hours, it emerged as master of two of California's leading enterprises, banking and the express.

The company's real product was something rarer than gold—predictability. A man paid Wells Fargo twenty cents to send a letter home, rather than a dime to the government, because he had more confidence that his letter would get there, and would get there faster. He used a Wells Fargo letter of credit to send his gold's value to his family because he believed that the credit was good, and he put his dust in a company safe because he believed it would be there when he asked for it. By marketing trust, the firm expanded in reach and operations. When the Civil War ended the southern oxbow route, Washington would contract with Wells Fargo to carry the overland mail via the central route. By its China Route it connected California's Chinese with the motherland. Its distinctive green letter boxes and its express offices, 126 of them on the eve of the Civil War, were scattered throughout the new country. Wells Fargo "went everywhere, did almost anything for anybody, and was the nearest thing to a universal service company ever invented," one historian writes. "Next to the whiskey counter and gambling table, Wells Fargo's office was the first thing established in every new camp."[55]

The company was responding to the new society's three defining traits—isolation, wealth, and the demands of an instantly prodigious population. It answered isolation by helping create an infrastructure that pulled the far West together and reached out to the world beyond. It turned the land's raw wealth into ciphered abstractions and connected them among uncountable contracting parties, some across the counter and others around the world. As for demands, the things it carried along its thousands of miles of routes met needs as primal as hunger, as everyday as wanting a fashionable hat, as existential as loneliness. In fewer than a hundred months, Wells Fargo parlayed the gold rush's unique conditions into an enterprise remarkably sophisticated in function and expansive in reach.

Something similar could be said about California's economy. Only a dozen years after the discovery of gold, it was remarkably mature. In its value of manufacturing output outside mining, it stood eighteenth among thirty-three states. It was twentieth in its amount of farmland and twelfth in wheat production. Its growth was financed through sophisticated arrangements and distributed through integrated systems of movement over land and sea. In 1848 San Francisco (Yerba Buena) was a coastal village of a few hundred persons. In 1860 it was the fifteenth-largest city in the nation. The consequences over time for the West and the nation were considerable—and one easily overlooked amid other events of the day. As pro- and anti-slavers grappled in Kansas, farmers were turning the Central Valley into a wheat bonanza that would soon feed Australians and Liverpudlians. When Roger Taney handed down the *Dred Scott* decision, San Franciscans were manufacturing boilers and bars of chocolate and Tasmanians were shopping in stores built of Pacific coastal redwood. Word of Lincoln's election came as Nevadans were fitting their silver mines with

California-made pumps and flywheels. Many of them doubtless went to bed that night wondering what the news would mean for the nation. When they did, some lay under blankets of kangaroo hide and set their heads on pillows stuffed with Hawaiian pulu fiber.

On the impact of gold on California's economy and growth, Carey McWilliams wrote that "the lights went on all at once, in a blaze, and they have never been dimmed."[56] He was wrong. The state's fortunes would dim and flicker and reblaze in different patterns over the decades ahead, but McWilliams did catch the underappreciated significance of prewar California. The great coincidence had produced a great multiplier, and by 1860 its telescoped development had positioned California to usher in transformations where, scarcely a decade before, the United States had been barely a whispered presence. It had expedited as well what would be one of the most momentous shifts of the coming century, the projection of national interests toward Asia. The potential for the changes in the course of the nation's history was more than considerable.

So, too, were its challenges, troubles, and costs. Besides deepening old sectional tensions in the East, expansion and gold brought convulsions in the new country that took a toll of human suffering rarely seen outside of battlefields. The costs were most evident where changes were the fastest and most sweeping, in California and environs, but the bloodshed and losses were from the Great Plains westward, a tragic counterpoint to what, then and later, was hailed as a time of soaring national accomplishment.

3 ➤ Letting Blood

The 1850s was the bloodiest decade in American history without a declared war. The point is easy to miss, given the carnage that followed from 1861 to 1865, but it is crucial to understanding how the expansion of the 1840s unsettled the nation from coast to coast. Even as it raised issues that would help pry Southeast from Northeast, expansion triggered unprecedented violence in what was now nearly two-thirds of the republic, lands west of the Missouri River. It began with bitter contention to control the raw wealth in what was now one of the richest places on earth—conflict that grew into genocidal assaults on Native peoples with losses far greater than in any other in the nation's history of Indian-white relations. The bloodletting in what was now the most culturally mixed part of the republic began more than a half century of a racial and ethnic reordering from California to the Dakotas to Mississippi and Georgia.

California Reconquered

The great coincidence had a troubling corollary. James Marshall's discovery might have given the nation an unexpected and immeasurably valuable gift, but controlling and exploiting the gift—that was another matter entirely. California's isolation in the long run proved a great advantage. Partnered with the colossal wealth being produced, it triggered the rapid growth and telescoped maturity of California society and economy. In the short run, however, isolation and wealth posed nettlesome difficulties and fed anxieties among eastern officials who contemplated that in crow-flying miles Washington was as far from the Mother Lode as it was from Iceland, while in travel time a passenger could reach Moscow more quickly than San Francisco. The same uneasiness took a more direct form in California. There the gap between legal possession and true control primed some of the ugliest violence of the stormy 1850s.

In June of 1848 Thomas O. Larkin, U.S. consul, wrote with typical effusion that a mere hundred square miles of the gold fields would yield enough money every year to match what the nation had paid for all land acquired in the Mexican War. At present, however, others were harvesting the wealth. Of the roughly two thousand miners on the scene, he wrote, "nine-tenths . . . [are]

foreigners."[1] The Indians and Californios Larkin saw had a far stronger claim as Natives than anyone from Virginia or Indiana, but to him, and to most Americans soon to arrive, anyone not from the eastern states was "foreign," and by those terms the place was peopled almost wholly by aliens. The first forty-niners from the East found the diggings occupied by thousands of forty-eighters—Kanakas (Hawaiians), Chileans, Tasmanians, Peruvians, Sonorans, and Maidu and Pomo Indians, a splay of peoples whose dress and tongues and food and habits were nothing like what they had known or thought should rightfully be there. All were busily pulling from the earth the riches presumed to be God's gift to the republic and its citizens. What followed, beginning in the summer of 1849, was essentially a second conquest of California.

Some miners simply served notice on "foreigners" and forced out any who resisted. In October 1849 a large party, waving an American flag and armed with pistols, rifles, and old shotguns, expelled all they considered inappropriate along a thirty-mile stretch of the Middle Yuba River. Some formalized the process with mining districts with exclusionist rules. A meeting late in 1849 declared that those who were "strangers alike to [the nation's] laws, its language, and its institutions" had no right to its soil and its riches. The documents often shimmered with high-blown rhetoric. Place real Americans anywhere away from home, "among mountains or in deserts," one stated, and they will quickly feel it their duty "to form a code of just laws" and to "ever acquit themselves honorably" in living by them. The "just laws" in this case included one limiting claims to "*bona fide* citizens of the United States," with any question decided by jury—one of men of impeccable citizenship, of course. The chair of the meeting was blunter: "the foreigners, and especially the d--d copper hides, every s--n of a b--h of 'em, should be driven from our diggings. They've got no business here in the first place."[2] These efforts seemed to have official sanction when Gen. Persifor Smith, en route via Panama to command the army, published an open letter proclaiming that noncitizens digging for gold were violating national law. "Nothing can be more unjust," he wrote, and he promised to put a stop to it as soon as he arrived.[3]

Smith was wrong. Noncitizens had just as much a legal right to work the diggings as anyone from the states—or, more exactly, they had no more right, since until 1866 the federal government reserved all mineral rights, making every claim technically void. In April 1850, however, the new state legislature tried to exclude foreigners by imposing a prohibitive tax of twenty dollars a month. In the mines around the Stanislaus and Tuolumne Rivers, hosting large concentrations of foreign-born, the response was almost instantaneous.[4] As many as five thousand Mexicans, Chileans, and Frenchmen marched into the town of Sonora to hear stemwinding "liberty or death" speeches denouncing the tax. Hundreds of armed Americans countermarched. By one account they arrived, led by a fife and drum, to find their opponents marching about waving banners and foreign flags, led by a paint-bedaubed naked Indian and singing "La Marseillaise."[5] The confrontation was loud but bloodless, as were others fueled by rumors and liquor.[6] The most effective opposition to the tax came not from its targets but from merchants who cared less about who their customers were than about the money and the dust that "falls into the . . . the capacious pockets of the Americans." Four months after it was passed, the tax was drastically reduced. The next spring it was repealed.[7]

"La Marseillaise": its chorus heard in anti-tax rallies sang of an especially large and contentious group of Europeans. Word of California gold arrived in France hard on the heels of its bloody revolution of 1848, and many were more than ready to leave for better prospects. By one estimate as many as thirty thousand had headed for the gold fields by 1853. Companies with names like La Fortune and L'Eldorado sold shares and financed emigration; twice a month the publication *La Californie* served up grand reports of fabulous wealth. The French government encouraged it all. In 1850 it urged the departure of the Garde Mobile, a paramilitary force used against street rioters during the upheaval, and sponsored the Lottery of the Golden Ingots, meant to send five thousand citizens to California at government expense. Arriving destitute and with no mining skills, many French goldseekers did not fare well, and their numbers and clannishness, plus suspicions that they represented the vanguard of a French takeover, soon drew the ire of Americans. French miners in turn could look down their Gallic noses at Americans, "the most famous boors that I have seen," according to one. In a confrontation over an especially rich hill a few hundred Frenchmen were driven from a hasty fortress, their tents burned and clothes distributed to local Indians.[8]

Franco-lashing to the contrary, most Europeans met little resistance. The flag-bearing mob expelling "foreigners" from the Middle Yuba River, for instance, included natives of Ireland and Germany; their targets were mainly Kanakas (Hawaiians). The foreign miner's tax apparently was rarely enforced against Germans, English, and other continentals besides Frenchmen. Legal and collective action was, rather, directed toward making what has recently been termed a *pigmentocracy*—a social and economic order ranked by ethnicity as defined by skin tone.[9] Hostility toward all darker peoples was sharp and, often enough, bloody.

That slant was inspired by two linked attitudes. One was simple racism. The common prejudices around the Mexican War portrayed Hispanos generally as degraded and far down the cultural scale, mongrel spawn of Spanish and Indians, nearly as low as African Americans.[10] The notions carried over into the gold rush. An Englishwoman heard forty-niners often dismiss all who spoke Spanish as "half-civilized black men," and Vicente Pérez Rosales saw a countryman nearly lynched as a "Chilean son-of-a-n--r."[11] That such persons should share the bounty that had fallen into the American lap was to many beyond the ken, as for a group tossing some Mexicans off their claim because "California had been ceded to the United States, and that white men had superior rights to the mines."[12]

The second reason was that currently heating politics back East to the fracturing point—free labor, the demand that independent workers be protected from competition from labor bound by force or contract and deployed as gangs under bosses. East and West, ideals of free labor were inextricable from issues of race.[13] In the East the focus was on opposition to African American slavery. Out West, the worry extended from slaves and free Blacks to other "colored" workers thought naturally submissive, lacking initiative, and inherently prone to drone work that threatened free white labor. Chinese were typically presumed to be docile "coolies" bound under bosses; Mexicans and Chileans were considered *péons* laboring for *patrónes*. A delegate to California's constitutional convention classed them with all darker peoples who were "as bad as any of the free negroes of the North, or the worst slaves of the South."[14] William Shaw and some fellow Englishmen saw this color code at work. They faced no resistance when they took up a claim until local Americans noticed their party included two "blacks," a Chinese, and a Malaysian. There was no place there for "coloured men," they were told. "Capitalists" were bent on massing them all under a "monopoly" and "gang system . . . obnoxious to Californians." Fired by paired racial and economic fears, Shaw reported, whites sent thousands of darker miners fleeing into the hills. The place was on the verge of "a war of race against race."[15]

And in fact the tension could take an especially nasty turn. Americans, wrote a Frenchman, are "terrible men. . . . They chase foreigners to death; they pillage them, they hunt them down, they kill them to remain masters of the country."[16] The first waves of forty-niners expelled Mexicans, Chileans, and Peruvians from the northern mines in the Sacramento River watershed, indirectly inspiring a riot against homeward-bound Chileans.[17] Displaced miners who remained shifted to the friendlier southern mines along the Mokelumne, Calaveras, Stanislaus, and Tuolumne Rivers, but when thousands of whites followed from the overcrowded north, expulsion decrees soon were issued against péons. In the Chili War in December 1849, a messy give-and-take left a couple of white Americans and perhaps a few Chileans dead. A few other Chileans were lashed and two had their ears cropped off.[18]

By 1851 most Chileans, Peruvians, and Frenchmen were vacating their claims, many of them returning home. Not until the next year did Chinese begin to come in numbers, so their story would have a different contour. That left two groups to bear the brunt of California's reconquest: Hispanos and Indians. The first included Californios, Spanish-speaking locals who until 1848 had been Mexican citizens, as well as thousands of goldseekers from the Mexican state of Sonora just over the new international boundary. The latter were among the first outsiders to hear the grand news, and they streamed northward along well-established routes and congregated in the southern mines. The area's main town took its name from the movement: Sonora. By one count as many as six thousand persons had journeyed north before the first forty-niners showed up, and thousands more came during the next couple of years.[19]

Forty-niners arrived with the rhetoric of conquest hanging in the air. "They are no men," a correspondent wrote of Mexicans that others shrugged off as "imbecile" and "pusillanimous" and, above all, "indolent" and "destitute of industry."[20] Yet there they were, laboring hard and profitably in El Dorado and, especially galling, teaching forty-niners with "cheerful alacrity" the basics of pulling gold—*their* gold—from the ground. As soon as the newcomers caught on, a British miner wrote, "with peculiar bad taste and ungenerous feeling," they organized to expel their instructors.[21] Whatever the roots—prejudice, lurid racial theories, or humiliation at relying on supposed inferiors—the antipathy could be extreme. Philosopher Josiah Royce remembered from his youth how his neighbors regarded a Californio: they "hated his whole degenerate, thieving, landowning, lazy, and discontented race."[22] "I was in the Mexican War," wrote a correspondent to the *Stockton Times* in the spring of 1850: "The men are made to be shot at, and the women are made for our purposes." The legislator sponsoring the foreign miners' tax wrote that he could "maintain a better stomach at the killing of a Mexican than at the crushing of a body louse."[23]

The ejections set loose a pernicious dynamic. Mexicans pushed to the fringes were impoverished and angry; some responded with theft and violence; whites reacted with told-you-so demands that Mexicans be systematically dispelled. A surge in crime in the summer of 1850 led to spasms of reprisals and a large gathering in Sonora that demanded all foreign miners turn in their weapons and disperse or forfeit all property. A local poetized about this "Great Greaser Extermination Meeting":

In Sonora one hot and sultry day,
Many people had gathered together,
They were bound to drive the Greasers away,
And they cared not a fig for the weather.
For folks had been robbed and folks had been killed,
And none but the Greasers would do it,
And the hearts of the people with vengeance were filled,
And they swore that the Greasers would rue it.[24]

The economics of reconquest also tipped against Hispanos. Mining of surface placers soon gave way to hydraulic mining, the elaborate use of water blasted from cannons onto great banks of ancient gravels, and then the tapping of underground lodes. Mining was industrializing, precisely the direction feared by champions of free labor, and one result was precisely what they had predicted. Darker-skinned Californians were organized into gangs for grunt wage labor apart from mining, not because it was their natural inclination, as critics had warned, but because, as a mass meeting in Sonora resolved in 1851, only a "native or naturalized American citizen" could claim and work an underground vein. Foreigners, they added, were free to work for wages, which at least gave Hispanos a place, but that place, as one correspondent put it, was of "hewers of wood and drawers of water to American capital and enterprise."[25]

As the pressure mounted, many Sonorans headed south, but enough stayed to fuel the dynamic of harassment and reprisal and counter-reprisal. Matters peaked in 1853. Early in the year mobs burned Sonorans' houses and began a systematic expulsion. "If an American meets a Mexican," the *San Joaquin Republican* reported, "he takes his horse, his arms, and bids him leave." An assembly resolved that "it is the duty of every American citizen . . . to exterminate the Mexican race from the county."[26] By year's end Hispanos not at work at wage labor were gone from all but isolated, poorly paying placers.

The expulsions took place against a backdrop of collective and interpersonal violence of rare extent and viciousness. At least 163 Mexicans were lynched in California between 1848 and 1860, most of them around the southern mines.[27] Mob violence had its counterpart in murders. Los Angeles was the urban center nearest the southern mines. There Sonorans and Native Hispanos congregated, and racial hostility followed them there from the diggings. Lethal hostility toward them helped account for the young city's extraordinary homicide rate during these years of racial reordering. More than 100 murders took place between 1850 and 1854. The 27 in 1854 amounted to 448 per 100,000 persons, or fifty-six times that year's rate in New York City.[28]

The killings say a lot about stresses of the place and time, but the lessons around them are wider than that. During the eighty years after expansion, the United States experienced the greatest racial and ethnic reordering in its history. The violence around that continental reordering began in the West, most bloodily in California with the discovery of gold and its consequent upheavals. Until recently historians have given most attention to the East, in particular to the years from around 1880 to 1930 as whites of the former Confederacy reasserted their control and forced recently freed African Americans back into subordinate roles and economic semi-bondage.[29] That time is often pictured as one of unprecedented violence. It was not. For one thing, racial violence in the Southeast during the quarter century before 1880 was more common than previously thought. More to the point here, when the view pulls back to one from coast to coast, events in the East after 1880 were a reprise of those in California and elsewhere in the West after the U.S.-Mexico War.

Anyone comparing racial and ethnic violence in East and West should tread carefully.[30] Students have given anti-Black violence in the Southeast far greater attention for far longer, and the numbers of victims there were far greater. The bloody patterning could differ considerably in particulars, which raises questions of what violence applied, and what didn't, in any effort to compare the different experiences. Still, the relative numbers suggest the western story may have been as grim as the other. During the dark years of 1880 to 1930, Mississippi's rate of lynching was the highest in the Southeast: 52.8 per every 100,000 persons. A study of lynching among Hispanos in California and the Southwest during the previous thirty years (1848–79) found a rate nine times greater: 473 per 100,000.[31] The Red River Valley of Louisiana was among the most blood-soaked parts of the Southeast after the Civil War. Its homicide rate from 1866 to 1880 was a stunning 196.3 murders per 100,000 persons. Although the area had only 13 percent of the state's population, it was the site of 59 percent of the murders of Blacks by whites.[32] In Los Angeles during the previous fifteen years (1850–64), a close study shows the homicide rate was roughly the same, between 179 and 209 per 100,000 persons.[33]

America's violent racial reckoning in the nineteenth and early twentieth centuries was both longer in time and wider in scope than in the usual telling. It began with expansion, and some of its more violent chapters were the earliest, with the reconquest of California after 1848.[34] What happened there was in one sense the reverse of the later events. In the former Confederacy whites would set out to reestablish command over a newly jumbled society. Whites coming to California began by jumbling the society they found, then they proceeded to force upon it their own control, including its ethnic pecking order. That command was essentially established by around 1880, just as another chapter in the continental story was building to the East.

But if patterns were different, the story was the same—establishing a white-topped racial and ethnic order in response to a profound social unsettling that began in the West in the late 1840s. That beginning went far beyond assaults on Californios, Sonorans, Chileans, and Kanakas. However great, their losses paled beside those of others, those with the deepest roots in the nation's newest country.

Swept Away

In early 1853 Pennsylvanian John Eagle was working a mining claim near Auburn, California. Every day, he wrote his wife, he and his fellows washed through their sluices "lizards, toads, frogs, bugs, worms, and all manner of creeping things, of almost every shape and size." Sometimes there was more. The week before, they had unearthed hundreds of human bones, "very much decayed. . . . These bones and skulls are all washed through, together with every thing else that is loathsome and filthy, to find the precious metal, *gold*."[35] Eagle's claim, like every square yard of the American West, was land with a deep human past, and all of it in some way was still being used by Indian peoples. Like Eagle, the outsiders who came there began immediately to live on the land by radically different visions and to use it in radically different ways. Directly and obliquely, they threatened to uproot and dispatch the older world, as Eagle's shoveling and sluicing were sweeping away the human remains from beneath his boots. As in so much else, California anticipated the story, this one catastrophic, soon to unfold across the West. If its reconquest was traumatic for Hispanos, for Indian peoples it was a nightmare.[36]

The Mother Lode, the watersheds of the Sacramento and San Joaquin Rivers, held one of the nation's densest Native populations. They were of several groups, among them the Miwoks, Yanas, Yukis, Pomos, Maidus, and Washoes, who lived in small villages, called *rancherias*, and supported themselves by hunting, fishing, and gathering. Indians and miners at first seemed to have looked on each other with a mix of curiosity, scorn, and bemusement. Luther Schafer was panning for gold next to several Maidu women gathering roots and wild onions when he and they suddenly burst into belly laughs, mutually struck by the silliness of the other's work.[37] In the first year or so some Indians did work the gravels, some as independents. To Samuel Ward, brother of the author of "The Battle Hymn of the Republic," a couple of hundred of them feverishly working a new strike were "a *fusion* of the worships of the Baptist and the dancing Dervish of India."[38] Most Indians, however, worked for others, hired or coerced into laboring in gangs as they had under the Spanish-Mexican system. By one report they made up half the workers in the gold fields in 1848; another said two-thirds.[39]

The thousands of forty-niners eliminated the early need for Native labor, but they did more than simply put Indians out of mining work. They regarded them with the same sentiments they had toward Mexicans and Kanakas—these were lesser beings prone to gang work that offended the ideals of free labor—but Indians were there in far greater numbers and living well rooted on far more of the land the newcomers saw as theirs. The responses against them were correspondingly far worse.

Native peoples were by no means helpless. Some in the Sacramento and San Joaquin Valleys were experienced raiders, and John Sutter employed an Indian army of two hundred infantrymen and cavalry in green and blue uniforms he acquired from Russians.[40] During the first few years after the discovery, there were some efforts to oust the goldseekers especially among Yokuts of the Central Valley around the southern mines. Ultimately, however, resistance was fruitless. Organized violence against Indians began in 1848, intensified in 1849, and by the time the rush entered its third year, Native peoples in every mining region were facing threats that would push some groups to the edge of annihilation. Some tipped over the edge and vanished.

It began with profound changes to the land itself that would be repeated again and again across the interior West. The reasons start with geography and geometry. Nearly every gold and silver strike came in remote western high country, much of it subject to extreme weather and often home to a small Native population. When a strike hit in some such mountain recess, the consequences spread outward in waves. The transformative burst had effects especially great because they grew by squared multiples. Imagine two frontiers, two lines of advancing settlement. The first is a section of land—one square mile, 640 acres—that has one side pushed outward by half a mile, as with a farming frontier entering new territory. Its area and influence grows by half, from 640 to 960 acres. The second shape is a circle, also of 640 acres, and its advancing frontier is its perimeter, as when the effects of a mining rush spread outward from its center point. As the circle's circumference grows all around, with the radius increased by half a mile, its impact grows, not by half, but by more than nine and a half times, from 640 to 2,276 acres.

As a geometry of conquest, the pattern of burst-and-ripple has it all over an advancing straight line. As California's rush was followed by another and another and another, the expanding circles in some of the West's remotest parts hammered at indigenous peoples who might otherwise have been largely ignored for years. The impact of the changes was worsened by the nature of Indian cultures. In nearly all the country where gold and silver would be found, Indians lived much as they did in California, by variations of a hunting-gathering-fishing economy. They hunted a rich range of large and small game. They fished from an abundance in mountain streams, sometimes damming them and tossing in pounded bodies of certain species to stupefy others. They gathered a wild bounty of seeds, plants, bulbs, berries, greens, and insects. Pacific coastal peoples gathered and stored enormous amounts of nutritious acorns; by one study a single family could collect seventeen tons in two weeks. The same environment provided medicines and the makings of clothes, housing, weapons, and tools.[41] It was a good life, but it laid down two rigid demands. Even a small population had to have access to a large territory, which left people scattered into groups of not much more than a hundred, often much less. And each group had to move by a precise annual choreography to cobble together what was needed. The Pomo people gave their thirteen lunar months names like "It will be difficult to go out (deep winter)," "You can get clover (late spring)," "We will still be gathering acorns (autumn)," and "There will be nothing to do (early winter)."[42] Paradoxically, such economies were both safe and vulnerable—safe because of the diversity of resources, vulnerable to disruptions of the intricate, rhythmic pursuit of them.

A gold or silver strike brought changes that were less a disruption than a derangement. A mining camp was the germ of an urban, industrial life that set loose an environmental assault, massive and sustained, on the native economy. Hunters quickly depleted everything four-legged and edible within a long radius. On one spree Franklin Buck and friends feasted on "venison stewed with pigeons and broiled quails, fricasseed squirrel, roast ribs, venison steaks, etc." Just two weeks later he wrote with pity of the "poor Indians . . . driven to actual starvation."[43] Fish populations crashed as work in the placers and erosion from cutting down trees quickly fouled the streams. Simply by being there, prospecting and moving from place to place, miners confounded the Indians' closely timed dance of survival. Then, as stockmen and farmers followed, cattle devoured the best grasses, plowing destroyed entire microhabitats, and fences blocked animal migrations. Soon the area around every strike was as one miner described his: "as sterile as a sandbar," with only reptiles, small game, and Indians.[44]

The environmental disordering brought on the same cycle that led to assaults on Hispanos being pushed to the margins. As wild game vanished and livestock appeared, Native men took to harvesting what was at hand. A white settler remembered that Indians "seemed to think they had the Same wright to the white man's stock, that they did to the deer," a presumption that must have rankled, as when a group of Miwoks took some mules and, gaining a hilltop, turned with "insulting gestures . . . [and] slapping their arses."[45] White responses escalated. As Indians would "sally out into the vallies to steal, + drive off Cattle, + mules, as an only alternative for starvation," an agent wrote, there would follow "the cry of Indian depredations, Invasion, murders + the absolute necessity for Exterminating the whole race!"[46] Reprisals like one reported by San Francisco's *Alta California* in 1853 were increasingly common. After losing several thousand dollars in livestock, ranchers hired two men "like other beasts of prey" to hunt and kill local Indians for eight dollars a month. A killing team might locate camps at night and rush in at first light, killing most and taking the rest as captives.[47]

By 1853 raids were systematic and increasingly formalized, part of what historian Benjamin Madley calls an emerging "killing machine." In 1848 and 1849 most raids were essentially vigilante operations or killings by individuals, but in 1850 a California law allowed for the creation of volunteer militia units that could call on the government for supplies, weaponry, ammunition, and pay. For most of the thirty-five thousand Californians in more than three hundred units, the militias were occasions for male socializing, like Masons with rifles, but a minority of militias, usually called "rangers," were state military enterprises that took a rising toll. By the opening of the Civil War, two dozen ranger expeditions had killed more than 1,300 Indians.[48] In early 1851 the legislature expanded its support by voting $500,000 to fund militia operations against Indians, and a bit more than a year later it added another $600,000.[49] Further legislation imposed a tax that provided another $410,000 for Indian-hunting operations. Legislators also outlawed giving or selling firearms to Indians, a ban that further tilted the odds against them and reduced still more their ability to feed themselves.[50]

The federal government also stepped up. President Millard Fillmore authorized supplying militias with weapons and in 1856 Congress provided nearly $1 million toward California's "war debt" of funds for militia campaigns. It provided another $400,000 four years later to both equip and pay state militiamen. Secretary of War Charles Conrad skeptically answered that such encouragement would likely produce results "revolting to humanity," but he still provided weapons for militias and would send more in the future.[51]

Much more damaging in the long run was Washington's refusal to apply the emerging system of reservations to California. During 1851 federal agents negotiated 18 treaties with 119 tribes that would set aside about 7.5 percent of the state for Indians to live on. Opposition quickly arose, and the Senate, at the urging of their two new colleagues from the Golden State, met in secret and unanimously rejected the treaties. In 1853 Congress authorized instead five "military reservations" with one-sixtieth as much land and with no federal support promised for those on it. The terms were so vague that the commander of the Department of the Pacific found no power to stop whites from moving onto the reserves or even "taking . . . Indians, squaws and children."[52] The practical effect was to leave Indians to the untender mercies of citizens of the state that was underwriting dozens of lethal raids against them. Several thousand Indians were confined on reserves where, by one estimate, rations had one-fourth the caloric value of an average American's. Two years later it had dropped to one-ninth (two or three ears of corn per person a day).[53] "I have seen this; and seeing all this I cannot help them," California's Indian superintendent, Edward Beale, wrote of starving Indians, who "perish by the hundreds." Nonetheless, Congress in 1859 reduced its funding for the reserves by nearly 70 percent.[54]

Washington's most direct participation was through military assaults. Some officers tried to shield those under their protection, but troops also took part in dozens of attacks, typically under the name of punishing Native wrongdoing or restoring order. One of the earliest and costliest in lives came in the spring of 1850, after a small group of Pomo Indians killed two ranchers, Charles Stone and Andrew Kelsey, notorious for their extraordinary, and sometimes lethal, abuse.[55] After vigilantes and dragoons killed some three dozen in retaliation, Gen. Persifor Smith, commanding the Pacific Division, decided that all Indians living nearby at Clear Lake were implicated and that a harsh lesson was needed: "Lenity now would be the extreme of cruelty" to all involved. On May 15 Brev. Capt. Nathaniel Lyon and a command of troops, wagons, a pair of whaleboats, and two howitzers attacked a large number of Pomos on an island in Clear Lake and pursued them into neighboring tule marshes, killing as they went. Many survivors drowned trying to swim to shore. Estimates of the dead range from sixty to eight hundred. Lyon's command suffered no deaths or injuries.[56] No future military engagements in the state would match the number of slain in Lyon's campaign, but a careful cataloguing shows that between 1846 and 1873 about 120 incidents involving federal troops and their auxiliaries claimed at least between 1,688 and 3,741 Native lives.[57]

Outright killing was only one reason for the desperate sag in population. By an 1850 law, ironically titled "for the Government and Protection of Indians," Indians "loitering or strolling about" could be arrested and contracted to work for the highest bidder. The law also outlawed the traditional practice of burning prairies and turned over those convicted to any white posting bond.[58] Men seized and put to work tending herds and fields lived for long stretches with only other men, housed in barracks while the women lived as domestics in white homes. In effect Native households were dismantled. A sampling in Butte County in 1860 found not a single Indian family living by a traditional arrangement. The birth rate naturally (or rather, unnaturally) collapsed.[59] Families were pulled apart more directly. The 1850 law and an amended version a decade later allowed the seizing and selling of Indian children under the guise of protecting them. The purchase prices of prime youngsters rose to $150 a head, and, a man testified in 1862, it was "a d--n poor [child] that's not worth $50." An early resident of Ukiah recalled a notorious character named Woodson who would kill the least marketable children and peddle the rest. He called them "cubs" and "quail," and indeed they lived "like caged birds," isolated and scattered through the area.[60] By one estimate ten thousand California Indians were kidnapped or enslaved between 1850 and 1863, twenty thousand if children are included.[61]

In some places the situation spiraled into a firestorm. Relations in Round Valley, in the Coastal Range northeast of Mendocino, were bloody from the start, in 1854, when the first whites to enter it "had a fight with the Indians, killing about forty of them."[62] The dead were Yukis, whose dozens of rancherias made Round Valley what one scholar believes was the densest Native population in California.[63] They fished the Eel River, gathered grass seed, acorns, and clover and hunted deer, small game, and hibernating bears. In 1856, when the government established a reserve for groups removed from the Sacramento Valley and ranchers began pasturing their cattle, horses, and pigs, the Yukis protested. "We were forced to kill many of them, which stopped their proceedings," an agent wrote. Ranchers launched their own attacks, "so many . . . I cannot recollect the number," one recalled.[64] The grisly climax came in 1859, when Gov. John B. Weller authorized a militia, the Eel River Rangers, to pacify the valley. A leading newspaper reported more than four hundred killed in seventy days.[65] By 1860 most surviving Yukis had been confined to the reserve, but local whites continued their killing as well as sending in their animals to devour the scanty crops. In 1862 the military was sent in and martial law declared.[66]

Still the regional horrors continued. In 1863 federal authorities stepped in to remove more than four hundred Konkow Maidu Indians to the already overcrowded Round Valley reservation. Without food or water or other supplies the refugees, some suffering from malaria, were soon in a desperate condition, and about 150 were left on the road, unable to go farther. When the reservation supervisor returned for them, he found them strung out over fifty miles, fevered and starving. Two or three were dying daily, "and the wild hogs were eating them up either before or after they were dead."[67]

Indians were not all passive in face of disaster. The Konkow episode was triggered by the deaths of a few whites in what seems to have been a guerilla campaign by groups withdrawn into the hills of Butte County. In 1851 the so-called Mariposa War, a five-month conflict involving organized roundups of Indians, began when Native workers killed three of their overseers. That same year a Cupeño chief, Antonio Garra, tried to unify several tribes to rid Southern California of all whites. Garra and eight others were captured, tried, and executed after a military campaign killed seventeen or more.[68] In most cases Indians killed one to three whites in isolated incidents. As always, the numbers are shadowy, but a meticulous search of sources finds that between 920 and 1,377 whites died at the hands of Indians between 1847 and 1873. The minimum estimates of Indians killed by whites is roughly ten times that.[69]

Raids and butcheries did not go unremarked by California whites. A young Bret Harte, later one of California's most celebrated writers, witnessed the results of one raid in 1860: corpses of elderly women "weltering in blood" and "infants scarcely a span long" with "faces cloven with hatchets and their bodies ghastly with wounds." A committee of the state legislature found "sickening atrocities and wholesale slaughters of great numbers of defenseless Indians" at Round Valley and estimated that more had been killed over four months than during the whole period of Spanish and Mexican rule. In a report to Congress, J. Ross Browne wrote of Indians starved and driven off military reserves "and then followed into their remote hiding places, where they sought to die in peace, and cruelly slaughtered."[70]

Nonetheless the assaults continued, even as the bleak consequences of the great coincidence reached much farther. Because most gold and silver strikes occurred well away from major white settlements, California's farthest of all, each demanded links to sources of supply, and as each expanding concentric circle reached outward for support, the West was soon crisscrossed by thousands of miles of roads and trails. Dozens of tribes saw their homelands become passways for tens of thousands of freight wagons, hundreds of thousands of persons, and millions of draft animals and livestock devouring resources along streams essential in Indians' annual cycle. By the end of one travel season an officer described the Upper Platte River: "The earth has a no more lifeless, treeless, grassless desert."[71] Farther on, through the Great Basin, thousands of rotting bodies of oxen, worn to death on the journey, only added to the desolation.

The new trails were highly efficient injectors of diseases into the country they crossed, and perhaps because of environmental and social disruptions, the toll on Indians from measles, influenza, and especially cholera was far greater than on immigrants.[72] Southern Cheyennes named 1849 the year "When the Big

Cramps Take Place," claiming that cholera took nearly half of their people. The Kiowas marked the year with a picture of a man with knees drawn to his chest and screaming in agony. Whole families and by some accounts entire camps died in what they would recall as "the most terrible experience in their history."[73] Contact diseases burned themselves out by the time immigrants crossed the continental divide, but endemic ailments such as tuberculosis and other lung diseases remained. Finlay McDiarmid, a doctor, found many in a Paiute camp along the Humboldt River in present-day Nevada dying of "congestive fever." In exchange for some horses he handed out pills to whomever he thought had a chance of living. The Paiutes took the medicine with "astonishing eagerness."[74]

McDiarmid was on his way to California, where the troubles of the Paiutes were amplified many times over. There were those who were appalled, but the most outraged typically agreed that the new country and its wealth would, and should, pass from Indian to white control. By the argument of what might be called confessional conquest, they admitted the massacres, gross mismanagement, and the tragedy of dispossession, but they agreed that the loss of land and lifeways was both inevitable and proper.[75] The cultural conversion of Indians needed only to be done more humanely, as on reservations being laid out for others across the West. Besides, that was also more economical: "*It will cost more to kill [Indians] than to let them live*," wrote an agent on the Fresno River (italics in original). For this, he said, the philanthropist, Christian, and political economist might all rejoice.[76] Senator John B. Weller, who as governor would later authorize the Eel River Rangers, was darker and blunter. All Indians were doomed, he told his colleagues in 1852. The best Washington could do was provide some palliative support as, by God's providence, they were ground down by advancing civilization. It was a melancholy fact, but a fact nonetheless: "Humanity may forbid, but the *interest* of the white man demands their extinction" (italics in original).[77]

California's Indians survived, but as environmental, economic, social, political, and demographic forces converged and ulcerated into something truly horrific, the Native population dropped from around 150,000 in 1845 to about a third of that six years later, and to as few as 16,000 in 1880, a plunge of 90 percent.[78] There, at least, the story devolved into genocide, an open and concerted effort at ethnic annihilation. The scale and numbers dwarf those elsewhere across the West.[79] Most popular and scholarly attention to the defeat and losses of Indian peoples has been after the Civil War in the Great Plains and Southwest, but if California's numbers had been replicated there, every Indian living in what would be Kansas, Colorado, Nebraska, Wyoming, Montana, the Dakotas, Arizona, and New Mexico would have vanished.

The disaster's scope makes it all the odder that, outside California, so little notice was taken at the time, and odder still that until recently so little has been taken since then. An obvious reason is timing. The California genocide occurred as the nation in the East was moving through its own crisis toward its own unprecedented bloodletting. Because stories of the massacres, child-stealing, and starvation among Yukis, Miwoks, Washoes, and others had no real influence on those events, they have lost their place in the narrative to stories that do. A prime example is Bleeding Kansas. The fight over whether Kansas would be slave or free soil undid the eastern political establishment and fanned the lit fuse that led to the Civil War. Its story began in 1854, the same year whites first stumbled into Round Valley, and it ended when the killing there finally ebbed around 1861. In Kansas an estimated fifty-six persons were killed over political issues.[80] More Yuki people than that might die in one raid, out of several in a single month, over seven years of slaughter. Sixteen people died in Virginia over two days when John Brown brought the Kansas violence eastward to Harpers Ferry on October 16, 1859. Scores of California Indians would be killed that autumn, twenty alone at Round Valley a few days before Brown's raid.[81] Surely there is no clearer case of how the Civil War has cast a deep shadow over western events than the relative attention given to Bleeding Kansas and Bloodier California.

Events in California, while especially tragic, were predictive of what would happen across the West during the thirty years after the discovery at Sutter's Mill. The tremors, in fact, could be felt within months as the news from the Pacific quickly began to bind the new country into the nation. A moment on the overland trail made the point. When a company of army engineers paused for a day along the North Platte, Howard Stansbury decided to visit five Indian lodges across the river. He approached with a flag of truce but met no one. Inside the first tipis he entered were bodies of Lakota men dead from cholera. In a lodge slightly apart was the body of a teenaged girl wrapped in two fine bison robes and richly dressed in scarlet leggings and in moccasins embroidered in porcupine quills. Stansbury returned to his own camp, where his fellows were celebrating. It was July 4, 1849, the year that would become synonymous with national promise and the seventy-third anniversary of the expanding republic's revolutionary birth.[82]

4 ➤ The Horse and the Hammer

The California upheavals occurred during what was already an exceptionally turbulent time in the interior West. There was a grappling among Indian peoples inspired by revolutionary changes begun with the arrival of Europeans and their reintroduction of horses—warfare that, ironically, aided the United States in its speedy conquest of the region. That conquest in turn began three decades of warfare between the United States and many Indian groups across more than two million square miles. Its first flashes were in the interior, where two continental powers, the United States and the Lakota Sioux, began a violent dance that would continue for a quarter century. There was violence as well against the land, environmental assaults that fell most harshly on the most vulnerable victims of the other calamities.

No clean tally is possible of deaths in the West directly and indirectly accountable to expansion during these years, but when those in the interior are added to the California carnage, they would surely number in the many thousands. If *civil war* is defined as substantial and sustained fatal conflict among groups of persons within the same national boundaries, America's began in the West in the 1850s, then spread eastward in 1861 into more terrible dimensions.

The Grass Revolution, I

Next to the men's corpses that Howard Stansbury found along the North Platte were spears and saddles, proud accoutrements of a life scarcely a few generations old. That life had carried Indians in the midcontinent to unprecedented power and wealth, even as Native peoples in California were suffering their unprecedented catastrophe. The heady rise to affluence and mastery was the result of an American revolution as consequential in its way as the one Stansbury and his comrades were celebrating along the North Platte. It began late in the seventeenth century, as Great Britain and France were beginning to grapple seriously for control of eastern North America, and it culminated around 1780, as the American colonies were securing their independence. Like the one in the East, this revolution had profound political, social, economic, and diplomatic consequences, and out of it, too, new identities emerged. This western revolution, however, was less political than environmental and biological. At its heart it had to do with animals and plants, in particular horses and grass. Like the other revolution it was accomplished through violence, and by its nature it spawned still more—wars and bloody rivalries that added greatly to the mayhem in the West of the 1850s.

The modern horse, *Equus ferus caballus*, evolved out of the southern Great Plains over fifty million years. Its long, powerful legs fit it for the rolling open spaces of the American savannah. Its large, high-crowned teeth could graze the land's tough grasses. Its elongated head with elevated eyes alerted it to its many predators. By a bit less than a million years ago early horses had migrated across the bridge of land that periodically connected modern Alaska with Siberia (passing early bison migrating the other way). They flourished in the Old World from England to Japan and mutated into such new forms as zebras and asses.[1] As historian Dan Flores has put it, all of the earth's varieties of *Equidae* "are more or less American tourists who forgot to go home."[2]

About six or seven thousand years ago, probably in what is now Ukraine, people took one of the most eventful turns in human history. They began to domesticate horses, and by four or five thousand years ago the first horse cultures were coming into focus.[3] A horse culture, as opposed to a people who sometimes ride horses, is a society that has adapted its essential means of living to the many advantages horses offer. Horseback people could travel farther and faster, trade more extensively, transport heavier burdens and in certain terrains hunt far more efficiently. They could also wage war more ferociously. All the changes might be summed up in a word: *power*, its physical expressions over space and animals and people and its spiritual expression of spirit and self-belief.[4]

This was a genuinely revolutionary development in the human story, but its true source was not horses but what they ate. The horse's essential stuff was grass. Power requires energy. A horse's power comes from the energy stored in the grasses it eats, and on vast pastures like those in Central Asia and the Great Plains, that energy, sunlight captured through photosynthesis, is available in unimaginable amounts. It is unavailable to people, however. They can digest grass seeds (wheat, corn, and rice) but not the rest. They have to wait for a bison, deer, or other grazer to take in the energy before they can confiscate it for their own by eating the grazer. Because grass uses most of the solar energy it takes in for its basic functioning—just, that is, by being grass—a grazer gets only a small part of the original solar gift to the plants, and a person who eats the grazer gets only a small part of that.

When a person eats a horse, he is acquiring that limited energy stored as meat and tissue. But when that person gets on a horse to hunt, or harnesses the horse to a wagon or a plow, or loads it with a burden to carry, that person is accessing the animal's living energy, its power. He is in effect acquiring the energy, previously closed off from him, stored in the grasses around his feet. That was the essence of the revolution begun five millennia ago. A horse with a person on its back became in effect a new creation, an animal with the strength, speed, and grace of a horse and the imagination, ambition, and arrogance of a human. No wonder this new creature conjured up fabulous visions. In Greek mythology it became the centaur. In reality it might be called by the Spanish word for "gentleman": *caballero*, literally a "horse-man." A horse culture was an entire society of them.

At the horse's birthplace of the Great Plains, however, none of this could happen. At the end of the most recent ice age horses were among dozens of species that went extinct. People there remained afoot as horse cultures spread across Central Asia to China and Egypt, North Africa and Europe, and then, when Spain made the leap to the new world, to the Indies and Mexico.[5] From there in 1540 a large column under Francisco Vásquez de Coronado entered today's Arizona and New Mexico and the next year he led a command mounted on eighty stallions to the southern plains in present south-central Kansas. After a million-year circumnavigation of the globe, the horse had come home.

The effects were largely delayed, however, until the Pueblo revolt of 1680 drove the Spanish out of New Mexico and let loose their horses, through trade and raid, into the American interior. As horses and horse cultures spread from the Pacific Northwest to Canada, the grassland of the plains, suddenly a source of enormous energy and power, became prime real estate. Virtually every Native group that whites later met on the plains—Comanches, Lakotas, Kiowas, Cheyennes, Arapahos, Blackfeet, Crows, Assiniboines, and others— were relatively late arrivals. Each acquired horses at some point in their migrations; each committed themselves to a way of life impossible without them.[6]

By 1780, a scant hundred years after they began to spread across the West and coincident with the other American revolution cresting in the East, horse cultures were in place wherever they would take hold.[7] What followed was an American version of a very old story. Its most obvious feature was a burst of affluence and a quickening pulse of life that by the time the United States expanded to the Pacific had spawned a standard of living that, two authorities suggest, was literally and visually rising. Plains equestrians stood taller than the soldiers they would fight, and Cheyennes may have been among the tallest people on earth.[8] By trading more widely and effusively, horseback tribes filled their larger lodges with New England carpets, African coffee, sugar from Haiti, and English knives from Sheffield. As the givers of this grace, horses were flaunted and revered. Men painted them gaudily, braided their tails, strung bright ribbons from their manes, and chewed certain roots to blow into their hair as sweet fragrance. The famous Lakota leader Sitting Bull (Tatanka Iyotake) composed a song for his favorite, Bloated Jaw:

> My horse,
> Take dauntless courage.
> My horse,
> The Tribes depend on you.
> Hence, my horse,
> Run.[9]

As had been true from China to Arabia, the rise of horse cultures set loose a reign of violence that was cresting in the 1850s as other bloodshed was unfolding on the Pacific coast. Here, however, it was not one of whites against Indians but Indians against Indians. Newly arrived peoples fought to control the suddenly valuable grasslands. Two great coalitions—Cheyennes, Arapahos, and Lakotas north of the Arkansas River and Comanches and Kiowas south of it—clashed bitterly until making peace in 1840, then both preyed on sedentary peoples on the fringes. Pawnees, Otoes, and Omahas along the Missouri River, especially vulnerable after smallpox epidemics in the 1830s, reeled under attacks from Cheyennes and Lakotas. An agent reported that they were "in danger of losing their scalps as soon as they put their heads outside their mud hovels."[10] Fighting intensified as tribes on the eastern plains gained greater access to rifles and their long-distance killing power. In a single engagement in 1853 well-armed Pawnees and Potawatomies killed twenty-three Cheyennes and taunted the survivors by stuffing the victims' hearts into their bullet pouches.[11]

Fighting was even fiercer to the south, where Comanches, Kiowas, and Apaches launched wolfish raids into the Mexican states of Tamaulipas, Nuevo Leon, Coahuila, Durango, Chihuahua, and Sonora to take horses, mules, and slaves. After their peace with the Cheyennes and Arapahos in 1840 their attacks soared, and as historian Brian DeLay shows, the numbers of Mexicans killed or captured increased at least tenfold. Any loss of warriors demanded raids of vengeance, on which of course more Comanches died (and more stock and people were stolen), which triggered more bloody retribution.[12]

Strangely and significantly, Americans in the East had virtually no sense of the extraordinary violence roiling the Great Plains and Southwest. Comanches did raid on the Texas frontier, though nothing close to the degree against the Mexicans, and in the 1850s the army and the Lakotas contended for the Platte

River Valley, but the intertribal conflicts in mid-America had no effect on the nearest American settlements in the Missouri Valley and, consequently, posed not the slightest discouragement to national expansion. In fact, by odd indirection, they promoted it. By the mid-1840s Comanche and Apache raids had left large swaths of northern Mexico all but depopulated. This fed the image of a barbarous Mexico incompetently governed, and once the war with Mexico was under way, the unpeopled towns and devastated rancheros left the sweep of country below the Rio Grande as an open gate for Yankee invaders. The swift American victory in turn fanned expansionist rhetoric, the racist spout that would encourage the eviction of Mexicans and the murder of Indians in California's second conquest.[13]

The grass revolution had its price. Besides the costs of a spiraling warfare, the closer connections to a wider world and easier movement within their own left tribes more vulnerable to disease. Smallpox had often struck Texas and the Southwest, but it had spared those from the Missouri River to the Pacific because infected victims heading north on foot would be dead or noncontagious before reaching fresh bodies for the pox to colonize. Then came horses. By effectively shrinking western spaces, horses allowed the injection of one of history's greatest killers. In 1779–80 smallpox arrived again in the Southwest, but this time it moved steadily northward across the plains, up the Missouri Valley and finally westward to the Pacific Northwest. A recent estimate puts the deaths at more than sixty thousand. Another epidemic struck around 1800.[14] It was only partly coincidence that the date of the West's first smallpox pandemic, 1780, also marked the point when horse cultures were firmly in place.

Just having horses posed problems. The horse-man bargain obliged people to provide the horse's fundamentals, starting with food. Comanches amassed such enormous herds, totaling up to 150,000 animals, that they ran short of prime pasturage, in part because the southern plains supported as well tens of thousands of wild horses. The raiding into Mexico, central Texas, and New Mexico became in part a sophisticated system of resource management. By waiting to pounce until others had used their own grasses and their own labor to raise their animals to maturity, Comanches in effect were outsourcing horse production. They then would further conserve their grasslands by trading those horses in distant markets.[15]

Another basic need, shelter, was a problem for nearly half of the year. Winter storms swept into the plains with a speed and ferocity that threatened anything warm-blooded and in the open. The only sanctuary was in wooded valleys of rivers and streams, where timber and the slightly lower elevation provided a buffer from the blast, as well as water during the driest time of year. Occupying such a place for 15 or 20 weeks of winter, a camp of only 25 persons in western Kansas would require up to 5 acres of pasture and more than 260 cords of firewood, enough to fill more than 8 of the largest moving vans, culled from the same trees needed as shelter from the winds.[16] There were scores of such smallish camps and some that were far larger. In November of 1848, in weather "cruelly, bitterly cold," an agent reported about six thousand Indians with twenty thousand horses camped in the "big timbers" of southeastern Kansas.[17] Altogether these essential winter refuges made up only about 5 percent of the plains. As the rising plains populations turned to them during the cold time, year after year, the camps wore down the very resources that gave those places their indispensable value.

The grass revolution ate away at another vital resource. The horse-man was the ultimate bison nightmare, something never encountered before: a grass-eating predator. Besides helping Indians hunt more effectively for their own uses, horses allowed an expanding trade in what was suddenly a hot item of commerce. Bison robes, laboriously processed from hides by Indian women, were bought by customers in the Northeast and in Europe for wintertime use in carriages and coaches and as exotic rugs and bed coverings. In effect, New Yorkers and Londoners were harnessing grass power to warm themselves in their beds and on their winter rides, with bison burned as fuel in the process. The numbers of robes sent eastward rose sharply after 1820, then still more after the great peace of 1840 opened much of the high plains to the full brunt of hunters. By most estimates more than a hundred thousand robes a year were being exported in the 1850s, but because of the timing and methods of hunting and processing, that number measured only part of the price.[18] One authority estimated that in 1857 the toll from hunting along the Upper Missouri alone was a million and a third buffaloes.[19] He almost surely overshot, but by mid-decade, twenty years before white buffalo hunters began their great slaughter, agents along the Arkansas River reported bands were "actually in a *starving state* . . . due to the rapid decrease of the buffalo."[20]

Like the Persians, Egyptians, Chinese, Arabs, and Spanish before them, western Indian peoples were discovering both the gifts and the costs of lives on horseback. Channeling grass energy into military command, sweeping over the footbound and the slightly horsed, they were caught up in spiraling warfare and suffered mounting deaths. Able suddenly to draw from a far wider world, they were devastated by diseases never known in their earlier, narrower lives. They found and flexed unprecedented power, then found themselves struggling to feed it.

People elsewhere were caught up in another energy revolution, one that would draw far more power from the world around them. Its power was expressed not through animals but machines, from locomotives to textile looms, driven by coal, steam, electricity, and later petroleum. Its energy also derived ultimately from sunlight, but its reservoirs were far deeper, and consequently the raw power they fueled was much greater. The nineteenth century had no better example of this new power regime than the nation born of that other revolution unfolding in the East as western horse cultures were coming into their own.

In the 1850s those two revolutions came together in the middle of the nation. On the plains the Lakotas to the north and the Comanches and Kiowas to the south were the two great poles of strength and influence. Each had ridden the grass revolution into new lives that inspired a confidence and sense of possibility as solid as that of the new nation born in the East scarcely a lifetime before. That nation had more than tripled its size in less than fifty years, and its last expansionist leap, plus the discovery of gold and its consequences, would bring it into direct confrontation with the Native revolutionary regime. At its base the conflict would come down to one of resources, in particular the control of grass, but its outward expression was of rawer power, the clash of arms on the plains and elsewhere, the start of a quarter century of warfare between ways of living and of using the land.

The War against Indian America

In August 1854 several thousand Lakotas had gathered near the army's Fort Laramie, on the North Platte River, in what is today southeastern Wyoming. At a council there in 1851, they had agreed not to interfere with overland travel and to cease warring with their old enemies, the Crows. In return they were to receive from the federal government an annual shipment of fifty thousand dollars' worth of goods.[21] They had come for those annuities, which were stored in a warehouse, but the agent had not arrived, so the bands waited, a bit impatiently. On August 18 a train of Mormon immigrants passed by the camp of the Brulé band near the post of a veteran trader, James Bordeaux.[22] A footsore cow lagging behind wandered into the camp, and a young visiting Miniconjou Sioux, High Forehead, killed it with an arrow and announced a hearty meal for his Brulé hosts.

The band's leader, Conquering Bear, rode to Fort Laramie and offered the young commander, Lt. Hugh Fleming, one of his horses as compensation for the cow. Fleming demurred, and the next day he demanded that the cow killer be surrendered. Conquering Bear said he had no authority to give up a guest, but Fleming stood firm. He had been braced into this stance by another, even greener junior officer, Lt. John L. Grattan, twenty-four, who swore he could bring back the guilty party. Astonishingly, Fleming agreed. Grattan set off with two field pieces and a squad of twenty-nine volunteers, including two musicians. They arrived at the Brulé camp between four and five in the afternoon of August 19, which in late summer left hours of daylight for Grattan to find a way to begin nearly twenty-five years of plains warfare in revenge of a cow.

Grattan's drunk interpreter began riding about and taunting warriors: they were women, he would dine on their livers and drink their blood. The trader Bordeaux tried to calm matters, but Grattan refused to back off: "I have come down here for that man and I'll have him or die."[23] As he led his men into the camp and lined them up with the two guns pointed at Conquering Bear's lodge, hundreds of warriors positioned themselves on either flank. Talk continued for another half hour until Conquering Bear turned away, disgusted. Then someone fired. Older Lakota leaders called frantically for a halt, but Grattan had his men let loose. Conquering Bear was hit several times, but there were few other Lakota casualties, and the shots from the field pieces flew harmlessly over the lodges. The Lakotas responded furiously. Grattan fell immediately, struck by two dozen arrows; he later was identified only by his pocket watch. One wounded private hid in some bushes and eventually made it to the fort, although he soon died. The rest of the troops and the interpreter were caught and killed as they fled. For hours warriors swarmed up and down the river, some calling for overrunning Fort Laramie, which had only ten men left, but elders persuaded them not to. They broke into the warehouse and took the annuity goods, and Bordeaux emptied his shelves to them in mollification. Over the next days the bands broke camp and scattered. Conquering Bear was taken north to the Niobrara River, where he died nine days after the fight. He was the sole Lakota fatality.

The Grattan incident serves as well as any as the opening in the western interior of the War against Indian America. The war was undeclared, at least in the sense of that against Mexico, and in fact treaties with Native peoples always included boilerplate assurances of friendship with the tribes in question. The war had no formally stated goal and was never pursued by an overarching strategy, and in fact the government had no one opponent to strategize against. It unfolded as a series of more or less independent conflicts, each with its particular triggering, and only rarely were there pitched battles of the sort in European warfare. Still, during the thirty years after 1848, there was no time when the United States military was not in active conflict with some Native people or on the verge of it, and at the end Washington had broken all meaningful resistance from western Indians. Set together, the events add up to a roughly effective definition of a war.

It began in California, with the military's participation in campaigns against Native peoples, but most campaigns and assaults there were by individuals, vigilantes, and state-supported militia. In much of the Pacific Northwest and in the Great Plains, Southwest, and Great Basin, the war was primarily conducted by the military. Its actions began in the early 1850s, continued through the last major engagements in 1876–77, then tapered off into the mid-1880s.

In the early stage, in the 1850s, results for both sides were definitely mixed. Indians took some severe blows, but in 1860 their power was largely unbroken, and in much of the West it was dominant. This onset of the war in the interior, after all, came as horseback tribes of the plains and Southwest were flexing the full power from the grass revolution, and the Lakotas were near the apogee of their influence and command over much of the northern plains. The army's overall performance was spotty. It was hampered by inexperience, inadequate support, its leaders' misperceptions, and the government's naive and stumbling efforts to bring the new country under control. The fighting nonetheless began to produce lessons fitting the peculiar demands of warfare beyond the Missouri River. Once the eastern crisis of union was resolved, the military would turn westward and apply those lessons and others to terrible effect.

The U.S. Army's ample experience fighting Indians was of limited use in the West. Eastern tribes were mostly agricultural peoples living in permanent towns; most western groups were hunters and gatherers, on the move for much of the year, living much of the time in smallish groups and often difficult to locate. The closest parallel in the East was against the Seminoles in the Florida swamps where, a veteran remembered, "the front is all around, the rear is nowhere."[24] Besides their sheer size, those homelands—from Arizona deserts to the glaciered high country of the Rockies and Sierra Nevada—posed prodigious problems in simply moving around, much less establishing anything close to control. The army facing those challenges was understaffed, ill trained, and poorly supplied.

The response to the Grattan disaster was a lesson in both the army's power and its limits. There was debate over how to respond. The Indian Bureau and some politicians blamed Grattan's arrogance in what U.S. Senator Sam Houston mocked as the "crippled cow transaction."[25] In Lieutenant Fleming's brief report he lied six times in ten sentences, posing the Lakotas as the aggressors with far wider mischief in mind, and Secretary of War Jefferson Davis made the baseless charge of a Lakota strategy to terrorize the overland road.[26] Washington's decision was to teach a lesson by hitting the Lakotas hard. Its chosen hammer was Col. William S. Harney. Tall, white-bearded, and bull-chested, he was a veteran of the Mexican War and of conflicts with the Sauk and Fox,

Seminoles, and Comanches. Morally, he was a mixed business. Violent and volcanic—as a young man he had fled Saint Louis under indictment for beating a woman servant to death—he was impulsive, stubborn, more than a tad paranoid, and unforgiving and vindictive toward perceived enemies.[27] His impetuosity, however, often paid off in the field. Of Harney in Florida, his rival Stephen Watts Kearny wrote that he had "no more brains than a Greyhound," yet in his "stupidity and repair in action" he had done more to intimidate the Seminoles than anyone else.[28] Recalled from leave in France with a brevet rank of brigadier general, Harney prepared carefully in Saint Louis and by July of 1855 had assembled at Fort Kearny a command of about six hundred dragoons and infantry, nearly a tenth of all forces in the West.

In early September he found a camp of Brulés and Miniconjous, the bands involved in the Grattan episode, on Blue Water Creek near the junction of the North and South Platte Rivers.[29] After a brief parlay Harney's infantry opened fire with newly issued Sharps rifles, and the panicked retreating villagers were met by the charging cavalry and perched riflemen hidden on the far side. In the most lopsided rout of the Plains Indian wars Harney lost five men, and the Lakotas at least eighty-five, with seventy women and children captured. Lt. Gouverneur Warren wrote afterward of "wounded women and children crying and moaning" and the "piteous load" he carried to the army surgeon of a girl shot through both feet, a boy through his calves and hams.[30] To press his point Harney led a command of 450 a few weeks later on a march squarely through the Lakota home country to the newly purchased Fort Pierre on the Missouri River. This was chancy. Even that early he risked a winter storm, but his luck held until he met bitter wind and sleet on the last day. At a council in March 1856 most Lakota bands foreswore misbehavior on the Platte road, even "lurking," and promised to enforce the ban with their own uniformed police.[31] The government would return all prisoners and resume annuities. Harney was sure the Lakotas had accepted the "irresistible conclusion" that their day had passed and that they must take up a new life as farmers.[32] It seemed a conclusive victory for federal power.

Except it wasn't. The treaty (if that's what it was; Harney had no authority to negotiate) aborted in Washington. The Brulés, so badly stung on Blue Water Creek, did remain at peace, but the other bands soon got their pride and martial legs back under them. They withdrew and regrouped to the north and west, toward the Black Hills, and in the summer of 1857 all but the Brulés met in a great council at Bear Butte, a place sacred to both them and the Cheyennes.[33] Leaders took a stance decidedly hostile and, more significant, much more unified. Their "hearts felt strong at seeing how numerous they were," a chief recalled. They believed they could "whip all the white men in the world."[34] Soon afterward Lt. Gouverneur Warren, who had carried his "piteous load" of wounded off the field at Blue Water Creek, approached the Black Hills to survey a military road. A large delegation met him. They had begun "to see they would never be let alone," Black Shield of the Blackfeet band told him. They had given up enough, and in fact were questioning the Fort Laramie treaty. If annuities meant allowing whites into what was left of their country, they wanted nothing from Washington. As for Warren's party, they must leave or die. Warren left.

The pattern of the Grattan-Harney episode anticipated a lot to come. There would be nagging conflicts, some low level and attritional, some with nasty flash points. When Washington put up the resources, and if conditions clicked, the army could do real damage; the Brulés never fought the Americans again. But the government's confident claims afterwards rarely matched the consequences. Besides Washington's lack of follow-up and its general ineptitude, there were men like Harney who misread reality, partly out of ego, but above all out of ignorance—of the Indians' cultural and political basics, of their resilience, and of how they read the world around them, including how they measured whites and their intrusion. The pattern would prove remarkably consistent across the West, with regional variations.

The greater Southwest, from west Texas to Southern California, was divided into two military districts, the Departments of Texas and New Mexico. In the former the roughly fifteen thousand Comanches and Kiowas were the main concern. For a few years a small contingent of southern Comanches tried farming on a reservation on the Brazos River, but most scorned any notion of lives suspended and behind a plow and continued to raid the frontier that was pushing outward from Austin and San Antonio. The army responded with a double rim of forts across west Texas, with infantry on the outer rim warning cavalry to repel raiders from the inner rim. The strategy worked to a degree, but the forts, spindly outposts with whitewashed jacales as living quarters, were easily skirted by smaller groups of Comanches, the West's masters of mobility.[35] In 1856 Frederick Law Olmsted, the future giant in landscape architecture, toured the area. Relying on posts and patrols to control the Comanches, he decided, was like "keeping a bulldog to chase mosquitoes."[36]

To the west, New Mexico was home to about forty thousand Indians. About half were sedentary Pueblos, most of them in the Rio Grande Valley. They posed no threat. The rest, however, the army would have to police—Comanches out of Texas, Southern Utes ranging down from the Great Basin and southern Rockies, the numerous and powerful Navajos, whose homeland, Dinétah, spraddled today's northwestern New Mexico and northeastern Arizona, and several subgroups of Apaches splayed across the region. The region's stony mountains, swallowing distances, aridity, relentless summer heat, and frigid winters in the high country made campaigning as difficult as anywhere on the continent. Of all parts of the West, besides, the Southwest had the most venerable and consistent history of being in a violent roil. Navajos and Apaches had long preyed on Pueblos and Hispanos, Apaches on Mexicans and Navajos, Utes on Navajos and Plains tribes, and Comanches on Pueblos, Hispanos, and Mexicans. Now all of them had new targets, Anglo travelers and settlers. The United States found itself trying to impose order in country where disorder and conflict were an economic asset and a mass ingrained habit. An early commander, frustrated by the situation and the territory's political squabbles, noted that the annual cost of a military presence was half that of all real property. He thought the government should buy out everyone not a "wild Indian," then tell the army to pack up and go.[37]

There were some successes. North of Santa Fe, raids quieted the Jicarilla Apaches and Utes (an officer found rifle flashes in a nighttime attack "beautiful to behold"), but away from the Rio Grande true control was like diminishing light made even less effective by ignorance of cultural fundamentals.[38] A reprisal assault in 1857 turned out to be on the wrong band—not Mogollon but White Mountain Apaches.[39] The latter had so far been peaceful. Now they weren't. Four years later some from the Aravaipa band stole some cattle and an eleven-year-old boy from a ranch. The rancher and pursuing troops concluded they were not Aravaipas but heretofore peaceful Chiricahuas under Cochise. An overconfident, Grattan-like lieutenant, George Bascom, persuaded Cochise to parlay, and when he denied involvement, Bascom's guards seized several of his party as hostages. Cochise escaped and grabbed hostages of his own. Bascom hanged six men and the Chiricahuas lanced four and roasted three alive. The incident began a quarter century of on-and-off warfare with the Chiricahuas. (The captive boy later took the name Mickey Free and figured prominently in the following generation of conflict.)[40]

New Mexico's most numerous group were the Navajos, with perhaps fifteen thousand persons. Relations with them vacillated through much of the decade. Their homeland of Dinétah was woven through with canyons that held their sheep herds, gardens, and peach orchards. It was ideal defensive terrain, as Brev. Col. Edwin Sumner discovered when he led seven companies there in 1851, pledging to chastise the Navajos once and for all, only to wind around in bewildered search of anyone to fight. The campaign was less than Caesarian, the *Santa Fe Gazette* wrote: "He came, he saw, and he left." Relations stayed relatively peaceful for the next several years, partly because the army established Fort Defiance in Dinétah and partly from an honest, sympathetic agent, Henry L. Dodge, son of a U.S. senator and brother of another. Then Dodge was killed by Apaches while deer hunting and events moved into a pattern common across the West. Some Navajos took to raiding; the army answered with raids that took sheep and destroyed food supplies; some leaders agreed to peace but had little real command over bands and factions; raiding picked up again; and the pattern repeated. At the outset of the Civil War, relations continued to pitch side-to-side.

In the Pacific Northwest the story was similar, but with two differences. Indians there lived much of the year in well-established villages, which left them more vulnerable when trouble arose. And there was plenty of trouble, because the region had drawn much more white settlement than the interior. The earliest significant far-western immigration had been to the rich farmlands of western Oregon, and by the early 1850s the California gold rush was spilling northward into the territory's heavily forested southwest. To police this volatile situation, the military was spread even thinner than elsewhere. "I am a commanding general without troops!" fumed Maj. Gen. John E. Wool, head of the Pacific Division in 1851.[41] He reported a total of 736 officers and enlisted men for all of California and Oregon. Oregon had 139; of those, 53 were "absent."[42] In any conflict, it would be locals, whether mobs or militias, who would be more likely to attack, complicating immeasurably the army's efforts at control.

The first fighting followed California's scenario. Gold strikes after 1850 in southwestern Oregon brought the usual rush into the home country of several groups that whites lumped together as Rogue River Indians, or just Rogues.[43] Rogues responded to the environmental assault on their tender economies with thefts of livestock, whereupon a typical miner, an agent wrote, became "peevish and angry" until he finally "would about as soon shoot an Indian as eat his supper."[44] In October 1855 a militia company fell upon a camp of Rogues, killing twenty-three children, women, and elderly, and the next day warriors killed twenty-seven settlers in retaliation. For nine months the army and volunteer commands crisscrossed the region, engaging Indians where they could and twice getting caught and barely avoiding disaster. By July 1856 virtually all Rogues had removed to a reservation on the coast under much-needed military protection. Losses approached or met those in genocidal California. In 1851 the Rogue population approached ten thousand. Agents counted fewer than two thousand in 1857.[45]

To the north and east, in the Columbia River basin, relations had been tense but mostly peaceful. That changed as a result of yet another anticipation of conflicts to come—an ambitious politician. In 1853 thirty-five-year-old Isaac I.

Stevens became governor of the new Washington Territory. Stevens's fortunes depended on Washington choosing a northern route for a transcontinental railroad—he had helped survey it—but there was no chance of that unless Indians surrendered lands for its passage. To that end he arranged a series of councils in 1854–55 to press pertinent tribes to stand aside and repair to reservations. In the largest of these meetings, with the Yakimas, Cayuses, Umatillas, Walla Wallas and Nez Perces, he got his treaty, but only through chicanery, threats, and playing groups against each other.[46] Then, in an act of astounding irresponsibility, Stevens declared the lands open for settlement, fully four years before the Senate approved anything. Next a gold strike high on the Columbia drew the usual rush of miners, and when Yakimas killed a party of them and slit an agent's throat in the fall of 1855, three years of intermittent war began. Wool tried to control matters from California, but Governors Stevens and George Curry of Oregon sent in large volunteer units that Wool railed were plundering the region and committing the most "savage barbarities." These included murdering the venerable peace chief Peopeo Moxmox of the Walla Wallas, then cutting off his scalp, ears, and hands.[47]

Wool's answer was to make his own show of force to establish military credibility, then keep all whites out of Indian lands. After all, he wrote, the country between the Cascades and the Columbia was legally theirs and, one of his officers added, was "not necessary to the white people." Stevens railed back that Wool was caving to savages, and Oregon's legislature resolved that "certain officers" were depriving honest citizens of their territorial due and imposing "the very worst form of martial law."[48]

Then Wool was replaced in commanding the Pacific coast by Brig. Gen. Newman Clarke, and stresses reemerged. By now a coalition of nearly every larger group in the interior, Spokanes, Palouses, Yakimas, Coeur d'Alenes and others, was emerging. When Lt. Col. Edward Steptoe led a column into their country in May 1858, he barely escaped disaster when more than a thousand warriors met and pursued him. In response Clarke ordered a full assault. In August the Northwest veteran Col. George Wright marched with more than six hundred troops into the center of resistance around the Spokane River. In a rare case of a massed faceoff, he twice met a force of several hundred warriors in open terrain, and once again newly acquired firearms—Springfield .58-caliber rifles against bows and arrows, lances, and Hudson's Bay muskets—gave the army an unbeatable advantage of distance. Wright's men killed around a hundred opponents. Their sole death was a horse. With that the demoralized coalition gave up the fight. Over the next few weeks dozens of their leaders came in to sue for peace. Wright hanged sixteen of them.[49]

The opening phase of the western War against Indian America was the official, state-directed side of the bloody 1850s. Outside the Pacific coast, it accomplished little. Much of the interior, especially where the grass revolution still worked its bloody magic, the military had only a feathery influence. Many Indians had likely never seen a soldier, and many who had could hardly have been impressed by the isolated knots of ill-provisioned, scurvy-ridden units scattered across the region.

A wider view, however, anticipated a different future, one with the army as the hammer of white American conquest. Native power was crippled in the Northwest and California when tens of thousands of gold-hunting, land-hungry civilians overwhelmed Indian groups or forced the military to take them on. The years after the Civil War would see that pattern expanded—quickening settlement, environmental convulsions, and migrating contagion followed by rising tensions, occasional crises, and, finally, crippling military blows. The army was starting to puzzle out the challenges of western topography. Harney's march through Lakota country in 1855 suggested a later telling tactic, campaigning in winter, when Indians were least mobile and most vulnerable.[50] Commanders in the arid Southwest learned the advantages of "scouts" of dragoons and foot soldiers against the supremely elusive Apaches and Navajos, while engagements at Blue Water Creek and in the Pacific Northwest showed the advantages of modern riflery in open terrain. The future Confederate officer Capt. Richard Ewell wrote that the Mescalero Apaches he caught "were not aware of musket range until they paid for the experience."[51] Others would as well.

Most telling, the army was feeling its way toward a hybrid strategy to meet the nagging problem of having so few troops to control so many Indians moving around such enormous spaces. If the army could find mobile opponents in their occasional congregation, it could concentrate what force it had to destroy everything they needed not only to resist but to survive, in particular their horses. "Nothing can more effectually cripple Indians than to deprive them of their animals," one of Wright's officers wrote.[52] Such gatherings were almost always domestic encampments, which made the assaults both brutal and intimate. Troops sent from Texas into Indian Territory in the late 1850s were told to "follow up the Comanches to the residences of their families." They killed as many as three hundred persons, destroyed all lodges and supplies, and left "nothing . . . to mark the site . . . but the ashes and the dead."[53] After trouncing the Spokane coalition, George Wright marched methodically through the area, burning grain fields and destroying stores of wheat, oats, vegetables, and camas roots and killing more than a thousand head of cattle and horses. Eight hundred horses were killed at one time, blood work that took more than thirty hours.

Wright had set out against the coalition "to impress them with our power." His means to do that—focused, even surgical, yet total—would be advanced during the Civil War and used again and again over the next twenty years. Its intended effects were psychological as well as physical, and at the end, looking back at his "route . . . marked by slaughter and devastation," Wright thought he had done his job: "They will remember it."[54]

As Wright's earth-scorching showed, the federal hand was being felt in some parts of the new country, in his case in terrible ways, but most of the upheavals and death-dealing of the 1850s—the appalling violence in California, the warfare among Indian peoples provoked by the rise of horse cultures, the environmental upheavals and scything of disease—happened well beyond federal direction or control. For the most part Washington's presence in the emerging West was most notable for its absence or ineptitude. If expansion and gold were in fact a divine assurance of America's command of the West, the good Lord was indeed working in ways mysterious, and not especially impressive.

Figs. 1–3. In the great coincidence, Nicholas Trist (*left*) signed the Treaty of Guada-
lupe Hidalgo, acquiring the Southwest and California, about two hundred hours
after James Marshall (*right*) discovered gold at Sutter's Mill. Trist and Sutter's Mill:
Library of Congress, Prints and Photographs Division. Brady-Handy Photograph
Collection, LC-BH82-5294; LC-USZ62-137164. Marshall: W. H. Pilliner, [James
Marshall Seated in Chair in Studio]. Grass Valley [Calif: W. H. Pilliner]. California
State Library, Digital Collections.

Fig. 4. With the news from California, earlier overland trails became busy passways as more than forty thousand goldseekers crossed the continent in 1849. Joseph Goldsborough Bruff, *Straggling Emigrants: fall of 1849*, mssHM 8044 (123), The Huntington Library, San Marino, California.

Fig. 5. Thousands more made the trip by sea, crossing between the Gulf of Mexico to the Pacific Ocean via an arduous traverse of Panama. *Prospectors traveling to the California gold regions crossing through jungles on the isthmus of Panama 1849 or 1850.* Hand-colored woodcut. North Wind Picture Archives / Alamy Stock Photo.

Fig. 6. In the 1850s the gold discovery spawned physical, environmental, and cultural assaults, including campaigns by state and federally financed militias, that devastated Indian peoples in California. *Protecting the Settlers*, illustration by J. R. Browne, *The Indians of California* (New York: Harpers, 1864). Wikimedia Commons.

Fig. 7. Meanwhile, following the rise of horse cultures in the eighteenth century, other tribes dominated much of the midcontinent from Canada to Mexico, an area larger than that of the original thirteen states. George Catlin, *Comanche Meeting the Dragoons*, Smithsonian American Art Museum, Gift of Mrs. Joseph Harrison, Jr.

Figs. 8–10. Between 1853 and 1855, four government surveys of possible rail routes to the Pacific coast included teams of scientists who gathered information in a range of fields and produced illustrations of animal, plant, and human life in the new West. Western lynx and prairie rattlesnake, courtesy New York Public Library Digital Collection; Mojave horsemen, "Mohave or Mojave Native American Indian People, Colorado, USA 1860 Engraving. With Body Scarification or Tattoos. Vintage Illustration or Engraving," Chris Hellier / Alamy Stock Photo.

Fig. 11. (*top*) Civil war, defined as Americans killing Americans over issues of sovereignty, began in the West in the 1850s. Indians and Mormons massacred overlanders at Mountain Meadows during Utah's putative bid for independence in 1857. T. B. H. Stenhouse, *The Rocky Mountain Saints: A Full and Complete History of the Mormons, from the First Vision of Joseph Smith to the Last Courtship of Brigham Young* (New York: D. Appleton, 1873).

Fig. 12. (*bottom*) Lethal clashes in Kansas were born of both sectional hostilities between pro-slave and free-soil groups and contests over command of land and resources. *Bleeding Kansas, Clash between proslavery and antislavery groups in Fort Scott, Kansas Territory, 1850s, Encyclopedia Britannica.* https://www.britannica.com /event/Bleeding-Kansas-United-States-history#/media/1/69220/96172.

Figs. 13–14. Finding them confined by the cold time in camp along Idaho's Bear River, the command of Patrick Edward Connor (*above*) defeated and massacred Western Shoshones in January 1863. In deep winter the next year the famous guide Kit Carson harassed Navajos into surrender and exile from their home country of Canyon de Chelly. Connor: Library of Congress Prints and Photographs Division, Civil War photographs, 1861–1865, LC-DIG-cwpb-06319. Carson: National Portrait Gallery, Smithsonian Institution, Washington DC.

Figs. 15–16. As James Carleton directed campaigns against Navajos, Apaches, and others, he oversaw the reservation at Bosque Redondo in eastern New Mexico, the destination of the Navajos' Long Walk of more than four hundred miles. It was an early attempt at transforming defeated Indian peoples for ultimate citizenship. Carleton: Library of Congress Prints and Photographs Division, Civil War photographs, 1861–1865, LC-DIG-cwpb-07382. Bosque Redondo: Photograph by the United States Army Signal Corps, courtesy of Palace of the Governors Photo Archives (NMHM/DCA), 044516.

5 ▷ Conquest in Stutter-Step

Imagine President James Polk standing by a map of his newly expanded nation. He wonders what part of it is farthest from his government and from most of those he governed. Had he thought through his question for even a moment, he would likely have put his thumb down on what he would soon learn was the nation's most rapidly growing population and one of the most valuable places on earth. The coincidence of expansion and gold was a stunning stroke of luck that brought with it problems of stunning complexity. The challenges can be summed up in one obvious word: control. Fundamental structures of governance had to be set in place. A vast new country, vastly different from the East and varied within itself, had to be roughly limned and some infrastructure provided for access and movement within it. Washington would have to challenge Native independence, decide whether and where and how Indian peoples were to fit into the national family, and hatch a strategy to make it all function. It was quite a job.

As with some of its efforts in the War against Indian America, Washington did manage some successes. Overall, however, its performance was one of blunders and misdirection, conflicting energies and breathtaking naiveté. Beginnings were made, but as the lefthand side of the new national map was wracked by extraordinary violence, the government moved there in stutter-step, and there were plenty of stumbles, enough to make it an open question whether the lands acquired on paper would ever be truly bound into the nation—whether the nation's new country would in fact become "the West," an extension of the authority and culture in the East.

Half a House, Divided

As 1848 opened, nearly half of the United States had no formal government. California and New Mexico were under temporary military rule, and the Oregon Country had an informal provisional government, but most of what the nation had acquired in 1846–48, plus all of the Louisiana Purchase north of the Missouri Compromise line, save Missouri, Iowa, and Minnesota, was beyond Washington's effective authority.[1]

The next six years was a time of political formation rivaled only by the stretch after the War of 1812, when six states and territories were added to the union between 1816 and 1821. The main cause of the frenzy was the gold rush. California's combination of wealth, instant population, and isolation called both for bridging its distances from the East and for some political structuring of the country to be crossed. Besides creating California as a state, the Compromise of 1850 established New Mexico and Utah Territories, one with a rooted Hispanic population and the other with newly arrived Mormons. Oregon Territory was created in August 1848, and Washington Territory was hived off in 1853. Three years later political fights around a preferred rail route to California created Kansas and Nebraska Territories. In six years, six states and territories.

Looking at the political map alone, it might seem that Washington was in firm command of the West by 1860, but control was often more apparent than real. There were two main reasons, even aside from the fact that the majority of the land was under Native control. At their most effective, state and territorial governments were often off-balance and uncertain in coping with challenges that had few precedents in the East. And the governments themselves were wracked by divisions—conflicting authorities, professional jealousies, and abrasions of local and national interests and of economic ambitions. Near the end of the decade, the rising politician Abraham Lincoln warned that a house divided against itself would ultimately fall. He referred to the sectional clash of Northeast and Southeast, but his warning applied continentally. Authority in the western half of the national house was as divided and uncertain as that of the eastern. If the question in the East was whether the republic of the past would survive, that in the West was whether country newly acquired would be truly brought into the nation or would follow its own, wholly different course.

Eastern officials, moving with desperate dispatch to carve out the first political units, knew little about the lands they were carving. They seem to have followed a simple formula. Begin with a significant center of population (the Rio Grande Valley for New Mexico, the area around the Great Salt Lake for Utah, the Willamette River Valley for Oregon). Now extend its political boundaries to the east and west until they bump against the boundaries of some other center. What was scarcely considered was the actual lay of the land. New Mexico Territory stretched eastward from the Rio Grande to Texas and hundreds of miles westward to California across deserts that were hard to cross and hardly known. Oregon and later Washington Territories stretched from the Pacific coast to what later became Yellowstone National Park. As each territory gained new residents, usually after some gold or silver strike, Congress would slice it apart and draw new borders by the same formula. Practicalities of governing and moving around the land seemed less of a worry than the need to set up some authority—and as was soon clear, to set the political games in motion.

Thus the modern West's odd political geography. States and territories were like topographical flea markets. Colorado had rearing mountains on its western slope and, to its east, the plains, grassy and hummocky. Washington and Oregon ran from their rocky Pacific coasts across the thick forests of the Cascades to the deserts beyond them. Idaho stretched from its rugged northern panhandle to the sagebrush drylands to the south. In place of topological sense many showed a striking rectangularity. The prime instance was at the southwestern Four Corners, where Colorado, Utah, New Mexico, and Arizona converged on one arid square inch, indistinguishable from the country around it yet as precise and markable on the grid as on a geometer's graph.[2]

Those boundaries were a metaphor for territories in operation. Political structures on paper seemed as clear in conception as the lines on the map, but their parts often were as much at odds as territorial geographies. Governments derived from a system born in 1787 under the Articles of Confederation. The president appointed a governor, secretary, and three judges, and Congress provided most of the support for creating the territory's infrastructure. This had always brought brawling over offices and federal contracts, but far-western conditions—so much money at stake in meeting such political and physical tasks—made for fights nastier than ever. The West's social and physical peculiarities brought their own complications.

Particulars varied. New Mexico attracted few Anglo settlers, which left it as the only place in the West where indigenous people (Hispanos, not Indians) played prominently in public life. In 1859 the territorial lower house still had only two Anglo-Americans.[3] The Hispano majority, however, was so fractured along old lines of family, economic interest, and religion that the simplest concerns could leave it stymied. An early session needed three ballots to elect a doorkeeper.[4] A new division pitted reformers, arguing for tighter connections with American interests, against traditionalists resistant to cultural and economic changes. Public schools had strong support in most territories, but here traditionalists saw them as tools of Americanization and a challenge to the Roman Catholic church. In 1856 a proposed school tax failed in a referendum by a vote of 5,016 to 37.[5]

Indian conflicts fed political factionalism. The military had the responsibility to control any troublesome Natives, yet until 1857 territorial governors were also superintendents of Indian affairs, charged with daily relations with tribes and authorized to raise their own militias. The resulting conflict of authority was predictable and common, and the stakes were all the higher because war was big business. An army officer in New Mexico estimated that an astounding eighty cents of every dollar in circulation came from the government, much of it from the army.[6] Everyone "from the professional man and the trader down to the beggar" relied on federal funds, an observer wrote, and much of that money went to supplying campaigns against Indians.[7] One result was a contradiction that would nag at events for thirty years. The army was there to protect citizens from Indians, yet because fighting could be profitable, the locals being protected sometimes encouraged "Indian troubles," or at least boosted rumors that provoked them.

The most dramatic clashes were where fighting was the bloodiest. In wars in the Columbia basin in the mid-1850s, Governors Isaac Stevens of Washington and George Curry of Oregon seemed sometimes more fiercely at odds with the commander of the Department of the Pacific, Maj. Gen. John Wool, than either of them were with the Indians. In New Mexico the civil and military authorities were "in hostile array," Gov. James Calhoun wrote Secretary of State Daniel Webster in 1851.[8] Navajos were raiding within seven and a half miles of Santa Fe, he added, yet Lt. Col. Edwin V. "Bull" Sumner refused to protect Indian agents and threatened to set his troops against any militias ("marauding parties") sent out by the governor.[9] Within a year Calhoun was so exhausted by the struggle and so wasted by scurvy that he headed home to Georgia, bearing the coffin he would fill before he reached Missouri. Sumner took the opportunity to seize the governor's office. Quickly rebuked, he backed off, but with a final flourish he confiscated the new governor's flag.[10]

The new, untested civilian governments often were divided within themselves, partly because power and responsibility were so ill defined. "We are compelled to grope in the dark in discharging our duties" one official wrote of this "strange state of things" that could bring all governing to a halt.[11] The situation reached its absurdist height in Washington Territory in 1856.[12] With his Indian campaigns going poorly, Governor Stevens declared martial law, called up militias, and arrested half a dozen mixed-bloods for rebellion and treason.[13] When a district judge, Edward Lander, challenged the edict, Stevens had his volunteers arrest Lander, kicking down the bolted door of his court. Stevens's Whig opponents condemned him as a "diminutive Napoleon," then, finally checking Oregon's constitution, discovered that only the legislature could declare martial law.[14] When Stevens backed down, Lander cited him for contempt, whereupon the governor pardoned himself. "What a fizzle!" a participant wrote, but the farce had its serious side. Stevens's opponents huffed that a "Governor . . . so ignorant" of his territory's law made him unfit for office, but in fact ignorance about governmental basics was pretty widely distributed, there and across the West.[15]

A final cause of division was politics itself. The usual jockeying among parties and factions was complicated by the decade's fevered mood and Washington's inordinate role in public affairs. With so much to be done so quickly, squabbling and intrigue had plenty of fuel, starting with where government would be. Oregon's especially bitter competition among Oregon City, Corvallis, and Salem fell along party lines. Salem, the center of the Democratic machine, won out over the Whig hopes for Oregon City. With the governor appointed by the president and the legislature elected by territorial voters, the two might owe allegiance to opposing parties. If so, ructions were guaranteed. "Everybody and everything in this . . . country appears at cross purposes," wrote a New Mexico official in 1851. American newcomers squared off against Hispanos, civil and military officers "are at war," the governor and his secretary "cannot hitch horses," and even the missionaries squabbled over religious turf—Baptists against Methodists and Presbyterians against everybody else.[16] The same tangling was true across the West.

In one area the federal government began tentatively to remake its new country. It set in motion the process of uniting its geographical diversity within a single legal arrangement. The essential means was the surveying of land by the system of ranges, townships, and sections first devised in 1785 as an ordinance under the Articles of Confederation. The job after 1848 was daunting. "Imagination can scarcely keep pace with the increase of the western country," the commissioner of the General Land Office wrote in 1851, and besides its extent, the "face of the country," as in California, posed special problems—the broken terrain of mountains and hills, the large swaths with little water or timber for stations, and the erratic swings of wet and dry seasons.[17] Nonetheless the work progressed. During the fifteen months between July 1, 1854, and September 30, 1855, well more than six million acres were surveyed in California, Oregon, and Washington and an equal part on the other side of the developing West in Minnesota and Iowa. Together they accounted for 86 percent of all land surveyed during those months. The focus shifted sharply toward Kansas and Nebraska, where more than twenty-four million acres had been surveyed by the end of September 1861.[18] Each acre of course had been Native land and was newly opened by treaties, typically coerced or manipulated or, in California's case, claimed to have been acquired as land previously ceded by tribes to Mexico.

By the government's formal position, the lands newly surveyed were meant for family farmers who would transform them and build better lives for themselves and, collectively, for the nation. This, the agrarian focus of the ideals of free labor, was expressed legislatively by the Preemption Act of 1841. By its terms, settlers could take up land ahead of its survey and, once the grid of townships and sections was laid down, purchase their land for $1.25 per acre. Coming on the eve of expansion, the law seemed to presage that where they were arable the millions of acres acquired would be a great gift of opportunity for families of the middling classes. Plenty was, in fact, taken up under preemption and under the even more generous terms of the later Homestead Act, but even before the Civil War it clear that the disposal of much of for farming. The official assumption here was that expansion's landed bounty would take a very different turn, one toward its concentration in a few hands.

As with so much, the most vivid examples were in California.[19] Congress had passed a land donation act for Oregon giving up to a full section free to families settling there early, but no such law was provided for California. Families did settle on unsurveyed land, expecting to file under preemption, but if titles were disputed, decisions were made under a confused system of an ineffective state land commission, district courts, and the U.S. Supreme Court. California's Mexican heritage played into the concentration of land. The Mexican government had bestowed hundreds of grants totaling nearly a tenth of all land in the state, and by the terms of the Treaty of Guadalupe Hidalgo the new regime was to respect those grants. Earlier grants were to Hispano rancheros, but on the eve of the war with Mexico, many new grants were bestowed on Anglos and many others were acquired from previous owners. As early as 1851 four out of ten grants were in Anglo hands, and many more were acquired over the next years through purchase, litigation, and foreclosure for indebtedness.

As relatively few Californians acquired more and more of the grants, many used wrinkles in the system to expand their holdings still more. New arrivals in California found, in Paul Gates's words, a "a maze of inchoate, incomplete, conditional, inexactly surveyed" grants.[20] A grant defined vaguely by its features, some hill or grove of trees, typically included far more land than what was supposedly given, and until it was surveyed the grantee could define it however he wished and could change it at will, stretching it around farmers or some mineral strike. Those claimants then might be tossed out or secure their places by paying off the grantee. A grant that changed like this was said to "float," taking different shapes as it absorbed desired locations. Henry George compared one—appropriately, he thought—to a tarantula.[21] Any challengers faced the expense and time of court cases drawn out often for years, which left the grantee in control of land far larger than the original donation for years.

More land was monopolized through federal grants to California. By 1852 Congress had turned over to the state lands that eventually totaled more than eight million acres. The grants were for internal improvements, public schools, and swamplands to be drained and made ready to open to farming families for the common good, but once again the delay in survey and legal definition, plus the lack of a coherent system to determine who owned what, opened the way for enormous land grabs. Under the Swamp Lands Act of 1850, places designated as so flooded as to be unusable would be turned over to the state and then sold at a dollar per acre to persons who were to drain them and bring them to flower. Cooperative county surveyors identified enormous stretches of land as swamps, in some cases at five thousand feet up in the Sierra Nevada. The depreciated warrants for those lands then were bought up by surrogates, "dummies" that the *Alta California* said included "shirtless vagrants," who for a pittance turned over the land to those who hired them.[22]

These efforts were not uncontested. The 1850s were years of legislative and courtroom jockeying between interests of the new landed barons and settlers that occasionally sparked into violence. The line between "squatter" and "speculator" was clear and stark in public rhetoric but much less clear in reality. Squatters called themselves independent landholders bringing the land to blossom. The intent often was honest enough, although as would be the case in the far larger movements onto the plains after the war, squatters and homesteaders often took up land as much to profit from its lift in value as to break it to the plow. Whatever the mix of goals, the cumulative effect was clear by the Civil War. A state legislative committee later found the means of distributing Mexican grants and public lands a "deadly curse" on the people, laws "cunningly converted to a fruitful course of fraud."[23] The effect on the course of the state's agricultural and ranching economies would be more than considerable, and the fights of the 1850s would evolve into the broad-based anti-monopoly movements later in the century.[24] More generally, it anticipated a theme unfolding as the West emerged—visions of democratic opportunity meeting the reality of near-monopolies with resources and enterprise widely commanded by a few.

Meanwhile another of Washington's new responsibilities, coping with scores of thousands of independent Native peoples, followed the pattern of its attempts to create the first governments. Its authority on paper seemed firm and its goals seemed clear, but in fact the first was gauzy and the second near fantastical. Washington's first efforts to act the master over Indian America were even more inadequate, conflicted, and unmoored from reality than its work at governing its own citizens.

Policy as Fantasy

Ten days after the first anniversary of the Treaty of Guadalupe Hidalgo, the federal government took one of its first steps in extending its authority into the West. Rep. Samuel F. Vinton's bill to create a Department of the Interior passed with little discussion and less opposition.[25] Federal functions dealing with earlier Wests had been scattered across the executive branch. The Bureau of Indian Affairs (often called the Indian Office) was under the War Department; the General Land Office was in the Treasury Department; the Department of State administered the territories. Vinton's bill answered a rising call for a single department to focus on domestic affairs, especially federal relations with the more thinly settled parts of the nation.[26] The Department of the Interior was born of western needs and in the West its focus would remain. In its early years that focus was mostly a study in misperception.

It was born from two ironies. Its immediate cause was the expansion of the 1840s, which in turn was an outgrowth of the American revolution seventy years earlier. That revolution began with colonists complaining of London's ignorance of local economic problems and needs, its failures to control Indians and its undue sympathy for them, its misunderstanding of the colonies' vastly different environments and their demands, and its appointment of officials based not on their abilities and local knowledge but on politics and patronage. Every one of those complaints would be heard in the West about the Department of the Interior and more generally about the federal government. Expansion led to an arrangement strikingly like the incommodious one that had helped birth the nation itself.

The second irony had to do with the new department's most immediate concern, Indian policy. It had been several years since the last Indian conflict, the sucking swamp war with the Seminoles. Congress reasoned with Sen. Jefferson Davis that with "war being the exception, [and] peace the ordinary condition," dealings with Indians no longer belonged in the Department of War. Instead, they should shift into the new agency.[27] In fact the War against Indian America would crank up within a few years, and while tribes at the time might not have been fighting the U.S. Army, relations were anything but peaceful. Whites were slaughtering Indians by the thousands in California, Comanches and Apaches were raiding deep into Mexico, and Plains Indians were warring against one another and dealing devastating blows against villagers on the plains fringe. So it was that during one of the most sanguinary periods of American Indian history, Washington was turning Indian relations over to a new department on the blithe assurance that out West a new era of peace was dawning.

Unsurprisingly, the first policies laid down were at best naive, at worst disastrously wrongheaded. One of the most consequential came quickly. Expansion cut the legs from under the strategy that had guided relations from the republic's beginnings. Washington had recognized Indian peoples' sovereignty and self-government and had given them separate territories, but the official goal also had been for agents and missionaries to convert them to the fundamentals of white mainstream culture—Christianity, the English language, monogamous and patrilineal families, individual landownership, monoculture farming, and social details ranging from dress and hair style to housing. Changes did come, but they came more slowly and more culturally garbled than hoped. Meanwhile the farming frontier had rolled over the Appalachians and around Indian lands far faster than any had anticipated. The strategic answer had been removal, conceived during Thomas Jefferson's presidency and executed with special vigor under Andrew Jackson. Indian peoples would be transplanted as far west as possible into country as similar as possible to what they had known, which in 1830 meant eastern Indian Territory, now Oklahoma, and eastern Kansas.

On its face it was a bald grab of land, given that prominent members especially of the Five "Civilized" Tribes of the Southeast were Christians who farmed by white methods and had formed governments modeled on that of Washington. The formal goal, however, was to buy the time needed to accomplish a full cultural conversion. By 1840 roughly a hundred thousand Indians had been removed, not only of the Five Tribes but of many others from Maine to Illinois. A "permanent Indian frontier" of military posts was established along the western borders of Arkansas and Missouri to seal off the removed tribes and to stand firm against pressures of white settlement.

Then came the expansionist burst. Removed Indians who were on the western fringe of the nation in 1845 were squarely in the middle in 1848, once again directly in the path of white settlement sure to come. The same expansion brought tens of thousands of far-western Indians onto the national map, and unlike the removed tribes, most of them had little or no acquaintance with national institutions and norms. Still other Indians, the seminomadic western Sioux, Cheyennes, Arapahos, Crows, Blackfeet, and others on the Great Plains, had been within national boundaries since 1803. Because they posed no threat to the closest white settlements, and because their semiarid, tree-poor homelands had no appeal to eastern farmers, the government could ignore them. Now, like the newly removed tribes, they found themselves not on the nation's western edge but in its middle, and now there would presumably be some sort of reckoning. The older answer, resettling them to the western fringe, was no option. The Pacific coast was attracting thousands of emigrants decidedly hostile to Indians. Washington would need an alternative if it was to meet its formal commitment of transforming Indians into Christian Anglophones who plowed fields in bib overalls.

The answer was the reservation system.[28] Reservations were a kind of internal removal. Rather than being sent to the nation's rim, Indians would be confined within spaces inside it. Each tribe would be assigned some clearly defined part of the West. An agent would be appointed. Whites would be kept out. The official goal remained the same—transmogrifying Indians into peoples culturally indistinct from those crowding in on them—but given that reservations were islands within what was assumed to be a rapid, enveloping invasion, the transformation would have to come fast. To hasten Indians into lives as farmers, Washington would provide tools and stock as well as the means of "intellectual, moral, and religious" education. In these crucibles of civilization, the commissioner of Indian Affairs wrote in 1850, Indians would remain until their "haughty pride can be subdued" and their "general improvement and good conduct" showed they were ready for society at large.[29]

This sunny vision jibed with Washington's assumption that a reign of peace and friendship was at hand, but like that assumption it badly misread reality and thus was bound for deep problems. Agents would apply the same crude cultural engineering that had made for such untidy results back East but now to a much wider splay of cultures that had virtually no previous exposure to the life they were told to adopt. The work would be overseen by an untested distant bureaucracy led by men largely ignorant of the people and places they were dealing with. Congress would give millions of dollars to political appointees who were to apply it on behalf of people both politically helpless and at the far edge of public concern—an ideal formula for corruption. Looking back, the reservation system seems destined to be what it in fact became: a frustration for its honest supporters and for those agents who tried to make it work, and for its critics a model of ineffectiveness, venality, and waste.

Other questions demanded immediate answers. The Great Plains and Rocky Mountains, now the nation's midsection, were also a geography of transit. The migration of overlanders, begun in the early 1840s and surging after 1848, passed through what would be Nebraska and Wyoming, home country to the horseback peoples thus far allowed full sway over the country. Commissioner of Indian Affairs Luke Lea of Tennessee reported in 1849 that Native peoples along the road had so far been peaceable, but "some have regarded with much jealousy" the mounting toll that the people, animals, and wagons were taking on game and resources.[30] The disruptions would likely spawn hostility toward the immigrants and worsen warfare among the tribes, unsettling the country still more. Some control was needed over what was now the nation's main pathway to El Dorado.

In 1849 the government had Forts Kearny, Laramie, and Hall along the main road in today's Nebraska, Wyoming, and Idaho, but the most expedient course to stabilize the transcontinental corridor, the commissioner of Indian Affairs advised, was prophylactic. Washington should call a council to "bring about a proper understanding" with the area's "wild" tribes and to "secure their good will." Congress approved a hundred thousand dollars for a grand council in September 1851 with tribes of the central and northern plains at Fort Laramie on the North Platte River in today's eastern Wyoming.[31] David D. Mitchell, head of the new Central Superintendency, and Thomas Fitzpatrick, a former trapper now an Indian agent, would meet with leaders of the Lakotas, Cheyennes, Arapahos, Assiniboines, Gros Ventres, Crows, Mandans, Arikaras, and Northern Shoshones. The gathering was the first formal meeting between the federal government and western Indians and the largest council in American history.

It was one of those moments of historical clarity that capture the state of things in a far larger arena and insinuate the trend of what lay ahead. Two points are clear. The perceptions of whites and Indians about their common world and their powers within it were starkly, fundamentally different, yet both left the council with those perceptions largely unchanged or even unchallenged. While the gathering was of only a handful of tribes in a small portion of the West, it suggested more widely how the cultural give-and-take would unfold over the next quarter century. The view was not reassuring.

Washington's goals were laid out by Commissioner Lea. Nothing illustrates better the government's glib confidence than his orders and their schoolmasterish tone. The Indians of the plains "are entirely ignorant of their position and relations toward the government," he wrote: "It is time they understood them." They were to behave themselves in their homelands, and should there be any trouble, either with passing whites or among themselves, they should look to federal authority to sort things out. They should know that "it is no less our disposition than our duty . . . to civilize them and improve their condition, and they should readily yield themselves to all the measures the Government may adopt for that purpose." Lea's agents were to tell some of the continent's master hunters, warriors riding the crest of the grass revolution, to dismount, forswear violence, and take up farming. As for particulars, they were to insist that overland travelers have unrestricted passage across the plains, and for that he would promise annual compensation, not in money, which "will be of no service" to such people, but in agricultural implements and other items to secure the tribes' cultural conversion. Finally, each tribe should agree to live within its fixed boundaries, precursors to reservations, and never intrude into those of others.[32]

The council convened for three weeks.[33] It was, at the least, grand theater. The assemblage of ten thousand persons had so many horses that the site was moved more than thirty miles downriver to the larger pastures at the mouth of Horse Creek. By the council's end the place was a grassless, dust-shrouded basin so fouled with offal and human and animal waste that troops decamped two miles away to escape the reek. As per custom in council, the tribes were determinedly amicable. In a solemn ceremony a Cheyenne warrior presented a Shoshone man with the dried scalp of the man's brother he had recently killed. The man looked at it sorrowfully before embracing his brother's killer. There were demonstrations of fabulous horsemanship and nearly constant drumming and dancing. Attendees dressed in their best, as colorful as hoopoes.[34] Women painted their faces with ocher and vermilion and wore their sleek hair braided and woven with eagle talons, snake skins, and strips of American flags.[35] Evening visits commonly featured feasts of dog stew. Pierre De Smet, a Jesuit priest who baptized 955 Indian and mixed-blood children, was served from a kettle full of "little fat dogs, skins and all." He doubted there had ever been "a greater massacre of the canine race" than during those three weeks.[36]

At nine on the morning of September 8, a cannon shot announced the start of the council. As thousands moved toward the meeting ground, an observer wrote, "each nation approached with its own peculiar song or demonstration, and such a combination of rude, wild, and fantastic manners and dresses, never was witnessed."[37] Mitchell and Fitzpatrick waited under an arbor at the center of a great semicircle of skin sheds opening to the east. The two sat with headmen at the center with warriors massed behind their leaders and women and children behind them.[38] Mitchell opened with the government's essentials: "Since the settling of districts West of you by the White men, your condition has changed, and your Great Father desires you will consider and prepare for the changes that await you." After intermittent meetings, and with food running low, a treaty was produced and signed on September 17. The first of eight articles pledged a "permanent and lasting peace" and a future of "good faith and fellowship" among the signatory tribes. In other articles the United States was given the right to establish roads and posts and tribes were to make "restitution or satisfaction" for any wrongs done to passing whites. Article 5, the longest, laid out boundaries around what the government defined as tribal homelands. In return for all this Washington promised to shield and protect tribes from white society massing to the east and passing through, and every year for ten years it would provide them with fifty thousand dollars in goods.

Three days later a caravan arrived with fifty thousand dollars in promised presents. The bands were arranged around them in a huge circle covering several acres. In a scene Father De Smet thought begged the satirical brush of a William Hogarth or a George Cruikshank, soldiers handed out bolts of cloth, bushels of beads and trinkets, hundreds of iron pots and other utensils. Then the huge assembly broke their camps and departed for their homes.[39]

The Fort Laramie Treaty appeared to confirm federal dominion over the region, secure peaceful passage westward, and stabilize the plains so American control could steadily advance. His Indian counterparts, Mitchell wrote, accepted that their future depended on faithfully embracing the vision presented them by the Great Father. Tribal boundaries seemed a firm step toward reservations, with tribes kept within limits and maneuvered toward assimilation through "improvement of [the Indians'] moral and social customs." One of its early historians declared the council a "great success" that "gave promise of a lasting peace."[40]

It wasn't, and it didn't. The Indians did understand that they were to allow some soldiers along the Platte route and were not to bother passing white immigrants. The federal government understood that it was to hand over annual shipments of goods. Beyond that, however, the council was a study in miscommunication, in particular about power. As non-literate people, Indians considered the final treaty only part, and not necessarily the most significant part, of a council's meaning. They paid at least as much attention to the tone of discussion and to details of how the parties engaged one another, and by that standard it seemed clear to the Indian participants that the dominant power on the plains was not the United States. It was the Lakotas and their Cheyenne and Arapaho allies.[41]

During the generation before the council the Lakotas had established themselves as lords of the region and, with the Comanches, the prime beneficiaries of the grass revolution.[42] Originally part of the Dakota people of Minnesota woodlands, they had moved with other Dakotas first to the Missouri River and then as the colonies were winning independence they migrated as seven bands to an area around the Black Hills (Paha Sapa). By 1840 they had risen through raw power, shrewd diplomacy, and luck to preeminence on the northern plains and, allied with the Cheyennes and Arapahos, had extended their command south of the Platte River.[43] Like the United States, they were newcomers to the region and consequently were determined and supremely confident in command of what they considered a world they had rightfully won.

The Lakotas made up the large majority of those attending the council and in exchanges were self-assured and brash. Mitchell's first draft of their territorial boundaries left them incredulous. It was entirely north of the Platte River with none of the country to the south that they and their allies had swept clean of Crows and Kiowas. Surely the government could understand their position, Black Hawk of the Oglala band said: "In [expelling their enemies] we did what the white men do when they want the lands of the Indians."[44] Mitchell backed down. Lakotas were free to hunt, fish, and travel outside of their boundaries, effectively recognizing the Native sense of territory defined by rights of use. In other words the Lakotas pledged to stay where the government put them, except when they didn't. The proviso added that they were in no way surrendering any claims to land beyond what Washington said was theirs—something easily read as barely veiled permission to consolidate the drive to power that had made them masters of the plains from Canada to Kansas. And in fact, despite the paper pledge of peace, they would soon turn against their rivals the Crows.[45]

A second mutual misperception involved the very nature of power on either side. Who had it, and how did they use it? Indians could not possibly have understood what the "Great Father" and United States were—a society with a population many thousands of times that of any tribe that a decade later would send men by the millions into battle. Conversely, the treaty's repeated reference to "Indian nations" assumed that a tribe's collective identity was in rough parallel to Mitchell's own, with a central authority similar to Congress and the president. In fact each tribe was composed of bands that shared a language, affinity, and some common interests but otherwise were wholly independent. In most cases behavior was controlled not by compulsion but personal suasion and group pressure. Authority over individuals, as whites understood it, was simply not there. And yet orders from Washington decreed a revolution in the tribes' social and political order: "Your Great Father will only treat with the whole nation or tribe when united, not with any band." Each tribe must select one "chief of the whole nation" who would represent and hold authority over them all.[46]

Indian leaders were baffled. The Lakotas as usual took the lead. "Father, we can't make one chief," explained the elderly Blue Earth. Well, Mitchell answered, then he would choose someone and the bands could approve or not. He selected a Brulé man, Mah-toe-wha-you-whey, translated as Conquering Bear or Scattering Bear, respected as courageous but otherwise not especially prominent. Mitchell's announcement "came upon him like a clap of thunder from a clear sky." He said he was in no sense "a *big chief*" of the sort Mitchell seemed to be talking about, but he finally agreed and said that he would "try to do right with the whites." Probably he saw his role as a go-between—"the voice of [the] Great Father," a chief told attendees—but in the final treaty he was much more.[47] Conquering Bear and six other men from attending tribes were now "principals" and "head chiefs" with the impossible responsibility of taking charge of "all national business" and enforcing the treaty's terms among all his tribe's bands. At the final gift-giving, agents formalized the appointments. They gave the six men gilt swords and uniforms of major generals in the army, bits of gaud as preposterous as their new titles.[48]

Mitchell would report that the leaders of these "ill fated tribes" left Horse Creek submitting to federal authority with an "honest solemnity." His superiors could believe that the United States, newly transcontinental, had taken a stride toward consolidating its power all the way to the Pacific. In turn the Lakotas, Cheyennes, and Arapahos could break their camps just as confident that the commissioners had recognized their rise to dominance and, with Comanches and Kiowas to the south, their command of a midcontinental empire as large as the republic at its birth. Each side, that is, could ride away believing that much had been settled, and settled in its favor, which meant that nothing of real consequence had been settled at all.

Two years later, at Fort Atkinson on the Arkansas River, Thomas Fitzpatrick presided over a council with Comanche, Kiowa, and Lipan Apache leaders designed to secure the Santa Fe Trail, just as the Fort Laramie Treaty had apparently secured the passage along the Platte. Tribal leaders agreed to allow roads, military posts, and unmolested passage along the roads. They agreed to remain at peace with each other (they were, in fact, allies) and to stop raiding into Mexico (a prospect far unlikelier). Washington agreed to protect them from white incursions and to provide eighteen thousand dollars in goods annually for a decade. As signatories, a "chief" was designated for each group, with subchiefs under each. As with the treaty at Fort Laramie, it appeared to bode well for harmonious relations, but an experienced sergeant at the treaty's signing knew better. Given the mutual distrust and miscommunication—the intricacies and subtleties of negotiations were conveyed mostly in sign language used for simple bartering—"nothing was more uncertain than [the Indians'] intention and action at the end."[49]

The Treaties of Forts Laramie and Atkinson set the pattern for the next decade. By 1861 more than twenty treaties had been signed, most with provisions, flaws, and misperceptions like the first two. Many provided for "head chiefs" or their equivalents among peoples with no basis or tradition for such authority. Virtually every one promised undying friendship, or at least an end to aggression, between the tribe in question and the American nation, and in virtually every case, that pledge did not hold. The treaties usually assured tribes of hunting rights and access to territory that usually was soon constricted and compromised by intrusion and settlement. Never in the history of national diplomacy was so much agreed among so many parties based on such elemental misunderstanding (and, often enough, on Washington's willful manipulation). To no surprise, things invariably came unstuck, and when they did, Washington would call upon another institution facing its own knotty challenges in new circumstances—the army.

After expansion the military was reorganized into three broad divisions, the Eastern, Western, and Pacific, with eleven numbered departments, four of them in the West: the Eighth (Texas), Ninth (New Mexico), Tenth (Pacific coast), and Eleventh (the rest of the country beyond the Rocky Mountains).[50] In 1848 there were eight western military posts, all of them along the eastern edge of the plains. By the mid-1850s there were fifty-two across the plains, mountains, deserts, and Pacific coast. By the end of the decade the military had become in effect a frontier army, with 82.1 percent of men in service (13,143 out of 16,006) in the West.[51] Looking strictly at numbers, it might appear that Washington had moved decisively to enforce its new order.

The particulars tell a very different story. The West still had nearly forty thousand square miles for each fort and more than 250 for each man. Many posts were shoddily built and their facilities primitive. An officer in 1878 could not recall a single bathhouse in thirty-six years of service.[52] Rates of disease, debilitation, and injuries were high, sometimes shockingly. In 1852 surgeons in California's northern district reported between three and four cases of significant illness for every soldier and nearly one death from disease for every ten men on duty.[53] Winters took an especially awful toll. At Fort Pierre on the upper Missouri River, where Harney met the Lakota chiefs in March of 1857, frostbite and frozen extremities led to several amputations in its first year. Three men lost their penises. Many posts were badly undermanned, sometimes with too few healthy troops even to send out patrols. Pay was abominable. Under pressure Congress in 1854 raised the monthly pay for an infantryman from seven to eleven dollars, and three years later officers finally got a bump, their first since 1798.[54] Especially in the remoter outposts, the weeks and months were grindingly, numbingly dull. A trooper at the bottom of the order, Secretary of War Jefferson Davis wrote, was essentially "a laborer without pay or promise of improvement in his condition." The results were predictable. As many as four in ten soldiers deserted during a typical year.[55]

Nor did the army present anything like a united presence. Not only was it at odds with the governors and agents supposedly in charge of Indian relations. It was also divided within itself, starting at the highest levels of command.

During the critical years of the mid-1850s, Jefferson Davis was secretary of war and Winfield Scott the commanding general of the army. The two men loathed one another. Scott publicly called Davis an "enraged imbecile" who practiced "random malevolence"; Davis huffed at Scott's "malignity and depravity."[56] Yet even with their knives in each other, Davis and Scott agreed that the present situation was both insufficient and unsustainable. Thomas Fitzpatrick, the veteran fur trader and agent who had presided over both the Fort Laramie and Fort Atkinson councils, summed up the situation. Washington might think the posts would "intimidate the red man," he wrote in 1853, but in fact they "create a belief in the feebleness of the white man." The only choice was to stifle raiding by giving Indians enough of what they wanted or to send and support enough troops to control them by force.[57]

Washington did neither. Ultimately it did not need to. Indians would be defeated and dispossessed primarily through the traumatic displacement and environmental havoc already playing out in California and Oregon. The military would refine its role to act in conjunction with those forces, and at critical points during and after the Civil War it would play its part to telling effect. During the 1850s, however, its western presence was one of inadequate force directed by confident illusion. The consequences were suggested by events following the Fort Laramie council. For two years federal agents delivered their annuities to Lakotas and others, who in turn allowed overlanders to pass untroubled. Then, in camp waiting for the third installment in August 1854, High Forehead killed his hobbling cow, and when Conquering Bear failed to turn him over for punishment—as he and others had tried to explain, no one had such authority—Lieutenant Grattan marched his twenty-nine troops to the Brulé camp and ordered them to fire. "Father, I am not afraid to die," Conquering Bear had told Mitchell: "I will try to do right to the whites, and hope they will do so to my people."[58] It was grimly apropos that the first man chosen as a formal liaison between peoples at peace would be the first fatality in the plains theater of the War against Indian America.

Roads and Knowledge

One reason that the federal government's control of its new country was so wobbly was its fundamental ignorance. Somehow, simultaneous with doing all it needed for some measure of command, Washington also had to establish just what it was supposed to be commanding—what the West was, what was in it, who all lived there, and how to get there and move around in it. Ultimately that work proved one of Washington's greater successes, one with implications that went far beyond the nation and its immediate concerns. In the short run, however, the effort would worsen the stresses that pulled at the seams of the older republic.

Exploration itself was hardly new, but the scale of work after 1848 was unprecedented, as fitting the needs at hand. For the moment traffic via the sea lanes largely sufficed to supply the far coast, but there was a clear need for better means of moving people and things from Missouri to the Pacific and among the settlements sure to come in the country in between. This was no small challenge. Traveling from Missouri to California meant crossing two cordilleras stretching north-to-south and between them several hundred miles of an arid catch basin lined like corduroy with other north-to-south dry and stony mountains. North and south of the Great Basin were two enormous plateaus. Much of the interior West was a showcase of geographical extremes. There were parts no larger than two counties of Virginia or New York that ranged more than ten thousand feet in elevation and contained every ecological zone but the arctic and the tropic. The challenge was somehow to link across those spaces and to begin to grasp them, both in understanding and control.

Much of the earliest work was done by a smallish but exceptional group created by Congress in 1838, the Corps of Topographical Engineers. All were army officers, most of them West Point graduates and all especially gifted as engineers. They began by surveying the nation's new southwestern boundary to resolve the fuzziness of the Treaty of Guadalupe Hidalgo. Overseen by William H. Emory, then a lieutenant but a major by the time the job was finished, that work took fully seven years (1848 to 1855) and produced a sprawling report in three volumes.[59]

The greatest concern was the politically loaded question of a rail connection to California. Whether or not a transcontinental railroad was necessary at this point is debatable, but the assumption was that a connection would be built sooner than later.[60] The discovery of gold brought a pressing need for "shackle bolts" to the Pacific, as a resolution to a Memphis convention put it in 1853, to insure that the whole nation "would enjoy the rich promise of the glorious future."[61] Quickening the interest in the 1850s were advocates of the slaveholding and non-slaveholding states who considered a connection to the Pacific essential to their respective futures.

Efforts began even before the full promise of Marshall's discovery was known.[62] Lt. John Charles Frémont's search for a route favoring Saint Louis through the mountains of southern Colorado in the fall of 1848 ended disastrously, with ten men dying after the party was caught in the San Juan Mountains by deep snow and bitter cold. (The episode led to a notable moment in political rhetoric when, in 1856, Frémont became the only presidential candidate in Amer-

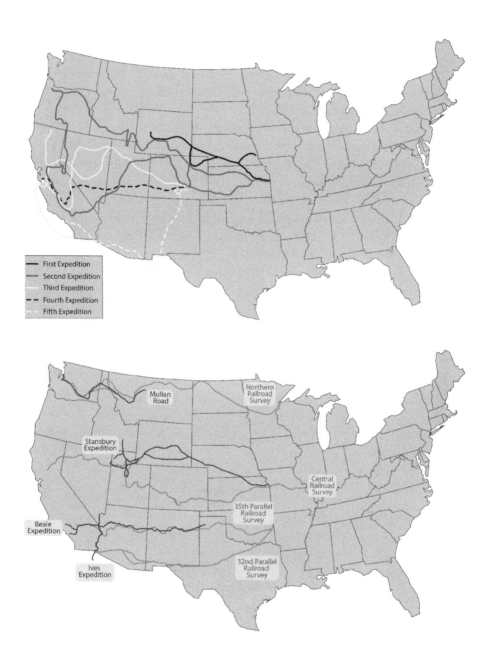

Mullan
Road

Northern
Railroad
Survey

Stansbury
Expedition

Central
Railroad
Survey

35th Parallel
Railroad
Survey

Beale
Expedition

Ives
Expedition

32nd Parallel
Railroad
Survey

MAP 2. After expansion, railroad surveys and ambitious explorations, including five by John C. Fremont (top map), began to fill in the knowledge of new lands that its new claimants had scarcely known when acquired. Maps by Maggie Rose Bridges.

ican history to be publicly implicated in cannibalism.)[63] The next year Capt. Howard Stansbury of the Topographical Corps followed the increasingly busy overland road to Fort Bridger and the Mormon settlements, and after exploring the great lake's western shore he found a feasible passage through the Rockies south of the emigrant route.[64]

In 1853 Secretary of War Davis created a Bureau of Explorations and Surveys to determine the best choice for a route. There were four candidates: a northern route from Saint Paul, Minnesota, to Puget Sound; a central route from Saint Louis, Missouri, to Sacramento via the southern Rockies, Great Salt Lake, and Great Basin; one from Fort Smith, Arkansas, to Southern California along the thirty-fifth parallel (see map 2); and the southernmost route from El Paso, Texas, to San Diego along the Gila River and thirty-second parallel. Among the most ambitious government efforts of the century, the Pacific Railroad Surveys were completed in less than two years.

The northern survey was under Isaac Ingalls Stevens, the new governor of Washington Territory. The ambitious Stevens predictably described the route as all but flawless, although a member of his party considered the weather and the latitudes and disagreed: "A road *might* be built over the tops of the Himaleyah mountains," but no sane man would try.[65] The central survey, led by Capt. John W. Gunnison, found promising routes through the southern Rockies and Wasatch Mountains and two over the Sierra Nevada and down to Sacramento, but the later deaths of Gunnison and several of his men at the hands of Pahvant Indians in western Utah conjured the fear of Indian resistance and chilled any enthusiasm.

The most vigorous efforts were in the Southwest. A rail link there would be economically luscious to the slaveholding Southeast, and these surveys were clearly favored by Davis. Lt. Amiel W. Whipple's ran west from Fort Smith then bent southward to the Colorado River and thence to San Bernadino. Whipple gushed that the route's first portion "seems formed by nature for the special object in view" and that the rest was "eminently advantageous."[66] For the southernmost route roughly along the thirty-second parallel, Lt. John G. Parke surveyed one variation through the rugged Chiricahua Mountains while Capt. John Pope mapped a way through the Guadalupe Mountains along the Texas–New Mexico border. This rail passage Pope predicted would facilitate army operations against Indians, open a vast and fertile region to settlement, "put an end forever to the dangers and privations" of Pacific-bound immigrants, and likely draw the commerce of northern Mexico into the new American network.[67] Unfortunately for southeastern interests, however, no practical pass was found to San Diego via the thirty-second parallel, which severely dampened prospects of a southernmost rail passway.[68]

The railroad surveys were part of a still-larger project. By 1860 the federal government had laid out and begun to improve a sprawling network of wagon roads across much of the region.[69] They included one improving the main immigrant road ending at Honey Lake on the eastern side of the Sierra Nevada. Another of a thousand miles, surveyed with the help of twenty-five Tunisian camels by Edward Fitzgerald Beale from Fort Defiance in New Mexico to the Colorado River, would soon attract considerable traffic to California. Other roads were laid out across west Texas and from the Missouri River into the Dakotas.[70] In 1858 Lt. John Mullan began laying out a long, looping road of 624 miles from Walla Walla in Washington across the northern Rockies to Fort Benton, the highest point on the Missouri River serviced by steamboats. Serving military and commercial needs, it accomplished (on paper at least) what Thomas Jefferson had asked of Lewis and Clark—establishing a usable route from the river traffic of the Missouri River to the Columbia.[71]

With that the prewar stage of western exploration and survey was finished. Never had anything close to a comparable portion of the republic been explored and described over such a span of time, a scant dozen years. Washington now had a remarkably detailed prospectus of how the era's newest technology of movement might link the East to the nation's Pacific edge by threading its way via one passway or another through country that had been largely a forbidding mystery just a few years before. Surveyors as well had laid out and begun to improve more than twenty thousand miles of road, an astounding weave that, if stretched out together, would have allowed more than six round trips between New York and San Francisco.

The work had its ironies. A prime provocation, choosing a route for a transcontinental railroad, yielded no answer. Competing constituencies could find nothing close to a consensus. Part of the reason was that Jefferson Davis was so set on the far southern route that he never maneuvered toward some workable compromise, the most likely candidate Whipple's survey along the thirty-fifth parallel. A deeper cause was the very nature of the surveys. They produced so much information, as historian William Goetzmann has pointed out, that those interested in a Pacific link, awash in facts, paging through so many reports with so many strong opinions, weighing one intricately detailed description against another and another and another, found themselves far better informed and even more confused. The grand reconnaissance failed in its purpose in part because it did its job so well.[72]

Meanwhile the practical project of connecting East to West was integrating the new country into a far broader realm. All the railroad surveys and many of the road makers brought along scientists to study the land and what lived on it. The result was a compilation of scientific intelligence—zoological, botanical, geological, and anthropological—that matched the geographical sweep of the mapmakers. Many thousands of specimens were sent back to the Smithsonian Institution, including more than 12,000 birds and more than 2,500 plants from the Mexican boundary survey alone. The published railroad surveys introduced 70 new species of animals and fishes and 232 avians and produced in three maps a geological overview of the entire West. John Strong Newberry, with Joseph Ives's expedition up the Colorado River in 1857, was the first geologist to see the Grand Canyon and the first to speculate that water erosion over an unimaginable unrolling of time had created it. Major finds in geology's sister discipline of paleontology revealed the ancient West as an extraordinary menagerie. As Edward Beale was introducing camels into the West, others were showing that the creatures in fact had evolved there and had roamed and grazed with ancestral elephants.

Human inhabitants got their own attention. Surveyors described the life ways of dozens of Indian peoples and began to fill in the cultural mosaic that others would elaborate after the Civil War. They stumbled on ancestral Pueblo ruins in Arizona's Canyon de Chelly. Listening to the Indians they met, they compiled twenty-one glossaries that then were analyzed and sorted into kinships that, again after the war, were refined into families still used to relate various groups to each other and to trace their historical trajectories. The practices of anthropology (the term was not yet in use) and zoology sometimes blurred together. Joseph Ives met a Hualapai Indian in the Grand Canyon, a man with "features like a toad's . . . the most villainous countenance I ever saw on a human being." His zoologist, Heinrich Balduin Möllhausen, who later parlayed his western time into a career writing dozens of potboilers as the "German Fenimore Cooper," suggested dispatching the man and sending him off, pickled in alcohol: one more exotic specimen.[73]

Taken together, the work was an unprecedented federal enterprise. Its geographical achievements were summed up in a magnificent map of 1857 by the twenty-six-year-old Lt. Gouverneur Kemble Warren, who two years earlier had been with Harney at Blue Water Creek. Warren consulted every reconnaissance report, survey, and travel account since Lewis and Clark, comparing his sources and weighing the methods used.[74] The General Map was a brilliant expression of current understanding and governmental purpose. Its most embellished portions were along major routes of expansion and in recently settled regions.

Other areas—much of the Rockies, western Texas's Llano Estacado, and the plains between the Platte and Arkansas Rivers—were sketchily traced. Finally there were islands of empty paper, notably the Colorado Plateau, southern Nevada, and portions of eastern Oregon and of the northern plains. These places, labeled "Unexplored," had two things in common. They were especially difficult to cross, but they were near other routes of passage. The push of an occupying society had flowed around these areas like a stream around its biggest rocks and nastiest sawyers. Scientific investigations produced sagging shelf-fulls of lavishly produced reports, sixteen from the railroad surveys alone. They made up the majority of scientific publications in the 1840s and 1850s that, by one estimate, accounted for between a fourth and a third of the entire national budget.[75]

As one result, a mass perception of the West was emerging. Overland forty-niners had found the country they crossed a continuing revelation. By 1860 stay-at-home easterners could muse among several ways to cross the new lands and, if they were willing to make the effort, could imagine in some detail what they would see along the way. They could learn how the Klamath people said "beard" (*smokl-smankl*) and ponder the elaborate dwellings of other Natives long dead. Planning a crossing via the Beale wagon road, they could imagine meeting a Mohave man, tall and muscular and "with a step as light as a deer's."[76] National preoccupations found their way west, too, in science as well as in territorial politics. As Oregonians were debating slavery and race, a zoologist with California's survey noted that the track of a grizzly bear's hind foot was "very like that made by the foot of a negro."[77]

Following the Civil War this work would expand into a project meant, in the word's fundamental meaning, to comprehend the West, to reach around it and draw it into a global geographical scheme and a single, infinitely detailed understanding of the world and its life. In so much else that it did, however, federal efforts to control the new country came down to indefinite commitments to gauzy goals that were pursued in unfamiliar conditions by persons thinly qualified. The West's divisions and incapacities were enough to question whether the government would ever truly command its new country—whether, that is, the expanded nation might hold together, East to West.

Expansion meanwhile was raising the same question, Northeast to Southeast. The question's most volatile particulars raised one more irony around the nation's remaking. Expansion's advocates promised both an ascent to national greatness and an enlargement of human freedom. The result instead was the growth of unfree labor in the West, an extraordinary effort to bring into it chattel slavery from the East, and, from that, an intensifying conflict from the political heights to parlors and taprooms that nearly destroyed the nation.

6 ▷ Carnal Property

The stuttering, scattershot efforts to bring the new country into a national embrace had one thing in common. They all began to turn the West into property. A few parts, notably Mexican land grants, had been under private ownership before, but now Washington began to unite everything west of the Missouri River within one system of legal definitions. The means was the same surveyed grid laid down across much of the East. Grasslands and forests became collections of legal parcels. Each was infinitely divisible, each a negotiable abstraction potentially marketed around the world. As a first step toward the country's its legal conversion, explorations mapped and catalogued it. Territorial governments established the means of recording, taxing, and adjudicating property. Treaties opened land to the transformation and confined Indians to reservations where they were to adjust to the new reality being constructed around them. All this was a given. It was an unquestioned impulse to remake into one entity what had been a mosaic of scores of authorities and perceptions of the land's meanings.

By another definition, however, property was the most debated and divisive question around the emerging West and, from that, around the survival of the republic. The issue behind this question was whether property could take the form of human bodies and spirit. The issue's focus was Black chattel slavery, the economic and social system well rooted in the Southeast. The question it provoked was whether that system would be allowed into lands acquired by expansion of the 1840s. The story of how that question was hashed out has much to say about the roles that the West was coming to play in national politics and life.

The Slavery Paradox

At the center of that story is a puzzle. At the opening of the Civil War there were African American slaves across the West. Slavery advocates devoted extraordinary energy to extending slaveowners' rights fully throughout the new country, and in some quarters, including parts of the federal government, they had considerable clout. The question of slavery's extension came to dominate political life in the 1850s, and at decade's end it triggered disunion. And yet as debates in the East grew increasingly shrill and their threats to the Union ever more dire, the substance behind them had less and less standing in reality. On the eve of Southern secession there seems to have been no realistic possibility of truly establishing the peculiar institution, as it was practiced in the Southeast, in the West. Teasing away at that apparent paradox reveals a lot about national politics and about its distinctive contours in the West.

Past historians (and prominent politicians of the time, like Daniel Webster) argued that slavery was naturally confined to the Southeast. They claimed that because enslaved people there labored mostly at producing cotton, and because cotton cultivation was mostly infeasible in the semiarid and arid West, slaveowners would have no reason to move in numbers with their bondsmen anywhere beyond the one-hundredth meridian.[1] That argument has long been debunked. In fact many on the ground dismissed it at the time. The claim was "*all apocryphal*," a New Mexican wrote Salmon Chase in 1851: "I don't believe there is one intelligent man in a hundred here who believes it."[2] Slaves in the Southeast worked at a wide range of occupations, including in the region's fledgling factories, and they presumably could have done the same in the West. Gang labor would have been particularly suited for western mining of all sorts, for the large-scale agriculture that developed early in California, and for the lumber industry in the Pacific Northwest. Enslaved people, vital to the flourishing cattle operations in the Southeast, would have fit nicely the labor needs of ranching in the Great Basin and California. Prior to the war they worked as Texas cowboys. Most slaves in the Southeast worked not on plantations but on family farms, and so they might have done so throughout the agrarian West. There were no "natural limits" to African slavery.

Its limits were human—that is, political and cultural. If the West were to have chattel slavery, southeastern style, a labor system with large numbers of African Americans engaged in large-scale agricultural, mining, and industrial enterprises and on family farms, it would need both legal authority and a respectable level of popular support.[3] Both ran against basic facts of life, starting with who was there. Most western immigrants were white workingmen and white families of middling means, those parts of American society that embraced earnestly free labor, the opposition to all systems of labor massed against independent workers by force or by contract. In the goldfields they saw the threat as gang labor by Hispanos ("péons") and Chinese ("coolies"). African American slavery would be a more obvious threat there and in the West at large. Slaves (or for that matter free Blacks), working in bands "under the direction of capitalists, . . . a monopoly of the worst character," would siphon the land's fabulous wealth from honest families into the pockets of the few.[4] Such economic hostility was always bonded to another of free labor's hallmarks—racism. A strong current of opinion among western whites, whether from Southeast or Northeast, was that Blacks, enslaved and free, were generally debased and debasing, unruly, naturally criminal, lazy, thriftless, and in general a drag on any society aiming at improvement. Free Blacks, restrained by no master, were an "evil . . . greater than that of slavery itself," a delegate to California's constitutional convention said. Another claimed that no population "could be more repugnant to the feelings of the people."[5]

Those sentiments undid the chances for slavery in the two places, Oregon and California, where it would otherwise have been best suited. In 1843, three years before the Pacific Northwest was even acquired, Oregon's provisional government forbid slavery and banned free Blacks, at first threatening any who remained with the lash. The first formal government confirmed both positions.[6] Anti-slavery feeling was strong enough to nudge the territory into statehood. Oregonians had rejected statehood in 1854, 1855 and 1856. Then, in 1857, the U.S. Supreme Court ruled in the *Dred Scott* decision that Congress could not bar slaveholders from taking their bondsmen into any federal territory. Whether a territory itself could deny slavery was hotly debated, but all agreed that a state could choose to be slave or free. In a hastily called convention, delegates drafted a constitution and submitted it as a referendum. Separate ballots posed an up-or-down question on both slavery and admission of free Blacks. Voters overwhelmingly approved the constitution, 7,195 to 3,215 (69 percent). They rejected slavery even more emphatically, 7,727 to 2,645 (75 percent), and the toleration of freedpeople more emphatically still, 8,640 to 1,081 (88 percent).[7] Campaign rhetoric made clear that free labor, not the slightest sympathy for enslaved Blacks, explained the vote.[8]

California had far and away the most Blacks in the West—more than four thousand in 1860—and of those probably a few hundred were enslaved.[9] And yet from its start, the state banned slavery, and for essentially the same reasons as in Oregon. Tradition has it that the catalyst had come in a camp on the Yuba River when Texans brought in fifteen slaves in July 1849. Immediately a committee of independent miners laid down an ultimatum: leave, or face the consequences. The slaves fled the next day, the Texans the day after. At the constitutional convention two months later it was the delegate from Yuba, William Shannon, who proposed slavery exclusion. Pro-slavery advocates acquiesced to the obvious. Shannon's motion was seconded by William Gwin, the owner of more than two hundred slaves in Mississippi who would become the leader of California's "Chivs," the pro-Southeast wing of the Democrats. The convention approved the measure without debate.[10] Anti-slavery opinion was not entirely hostile to Blacks. There were prominent abolition-ists in the business and legal communities, and Shannon, who introduced the article to deny slavery, fiercely opposed the ban on free Blacks and was described by an early historian as "more favorably inclined to the negro race than any other man in the Convention."[11] Delegates nonetheless came close to banning free African Americans but backed away, apparently out of worry that it might derail statehood. A look at the votes suggests the uniting power of free labor sentiment. Support for banning enslaved people and free Blacks was especially strong among delegates from the mining regions—and, signifi-cantly, those dominated by miners from slave as well as non-slave states in the East.[12] As Gwin would later explain, workingmen, wherever they came from, "do not wish to see the slaves of some wealthy planter . . . put in competition with their labor, side by side."[13]

The slim chances of slavery, southeastern style, dimmed steadily over the following years. While southeasterners at first made up a considerable portion of new Californians, the burst of railroad building and the consequent emigrant flow out of the Northeast quickly sent population numbers tilting in another direction. In 1860 fewer than 10 percent in the state had been born in the deep Southeast. A good portion of those were in the California's southern counties that were politically dominated by the more populous and staunchly free-soil northern mines and San Francisco.[14]

Slavery advocates nevertheless continued to pursue their interests, dog-gedly and with some effect. Their voice, through the Chiv Democrats, could be heard in a minor key throughout the decade. The first legislature, nick-named "the legislature of a thousand drinks," considered but rejected a bill to allow the bringing in of African American minors as apprentices and to hold them until the age of twenty-one. In the next session the Chivs maneuvered through the legislature a law allowing owners to recapture escaped bondsmen brought to the state before 1850. Pro-slave justices of the state supreme court upheld it.[15] The same year lawmakers received a petition from South Caroli-na's James Gadsden, who would soon negotiate a treaty to encourage a south-ern rail connection, to allow a slave colony in Southern California. Gadsden's vision, set down in a letter to Thomas Jefferson Green, was of the slave men working mines and fields while the women and boys provided their "food and raiment," but in his petition he stressed that slaveholders would be coming with their "*domestics* reared under their roofs," families of mutual "endearing associations, and sympathies."[16]

The efforts were persistent and nearly continuous, but they only nibbled around the edges of the constitutional ban on Black slavery. Free-soil advocates seemed willing to live with the sprinkling of slaves, as long as they posed no economic challenge, and to tolerate some rights of their owners, but the reality of the results was minimal. The fugitive slave law expired in two years and was never revived. Gadsden's petition died in committee. Ongoing moves to legalize Black apprentices came to nothing. The only effort to truly establish the peculiar institution came in 1859: a special bill to split the state in half around San Luis Obispo. While never mentioning slavery, justifying the split instead as breaking from the political domination of northern California, the bill would have left Southern California open to a slave-based agriculture and allowed southeastern allies access to the Pacific. The bill passed, but given the political turmoil of the time and the Republican strength in Congress, the measure was dead on arrival in Washington.[17] When the war came a year and a half later, the number of California's enslaved Blacks was several times that of those in all western states and territories outside of Indian Territory, yet they constituted less than a tenth of a percent of the state's population.[18]

Black slavery was legal in three territories, but as so often in western politics, what might seem apparent was not. In 1853 Washington Territory, north of the Columbia, was split from Oregon, which would shortly become a state. Initially governed under Oregon's constitution, it banned African slavery. When the Dred Scott decision raised the question of a territory's right to do so, the Democratic-dominated legislature endorsed the decision. Its resolution, however, stressed each territory's right to determine its own affairs. Black slavery itself was never mentioned, and in fact the question remained utterly moot.[19] Political leaders, as in California, often favored it—two of three governors before the Civil War owned slaves, though they left them back home—while studiously avoiding encouraging it in the territory itself. The 1860 census showed only thirty Black residents, and only one can be definitely identified as a slave—George Mitchell, a teenager brought by the territory's surveyor general, James Tilton of Maryland. And then there were none: with the help of free Blacks George escaped to Canada on the eve of Lincoln's election.[20]

In New Mexico a fruitless constitutional convention soon after the U.S. conquest unanimously declared slavery "a curse and a blight."[21] Then the Compromise of 1850 left open the possibility of slavery, the Dred Scott decision of 1857 declared it legal, and in 1859 the territorial legislature passed a slave code that apparently cemented the institution. Given its timing, the code caused something of a stir and inspired a debate in Congress, where the House narrowly passed a bill to annul it (it died in the Senate). The slave code might seem obvious evidence of sympathy for the institution, but one of the code's historians calls it something else—a "political gimmick" to court support of the slave states for a railroad through the territory.[22] In any case popular interest in Black slavery remained essentially nil. The census of 1860 listed no slaves, although perhaps two dozen or so were there, most or all of them servants of army officers.[23] In 1861, when the legislature first met after secession and the onset of war, its first actions were to pledge loyalty to the Union and then to repeal the slave code.[24]

In 1852 Utah became the only state or territory in the West to formally establish Black slavery, but again appearances deceive.[25] The gathering of Zion could serve as a profile of opponents of slavery—poorer and middling whites from free states and northern Europe. Nor did the peculiar institution have an obvious place in Deseret's economy and tight social structure. Although early church leaders showed some abolitionist sympathy, evolving Mormon theology situated Blacks steadily lower on the social scale. They were denied full church membership, and they could not vote, hold office, or serve in the militia. African Americans were declared descendants of the tribe of Ham, divinely cursed and relegated to servanthood, and Brigham Young declared that any white man of the "chosen seed" who should mix his blood with a Black woman ought to suffer "death on the spot."[26]

The legalization of slavery was likely something of a hedged bet. It did nod to a few prominent Mormon slave owners. Like New Mexico's slave code it might have been meant to court sympathy from southeastern Democrats, and by validating the patriarchal relation of master and servant it indirectly did the same for polygamy. And yet the brief, six-article law in its particulars was a grand mitigation.[27] It was as if a deep-southern slave code were turned on its head. Most restrictions were not on enslaved people but on their owners. An owner had to prove that his bondsmen had agreed to come to Utah, and he could neither sell nor leave with them without their consent. He was to provide them with comfortable housing, good clothes, sufficient food, "recreation," and at least eighteen months' public education for all between six and twenty. Sex with a slave would not bring "death on the spot," but it did mean forfeiting the sexual partner and facing up to five years in prison and a fine equal to more than $33,000 in 2020. This, the West's only statute specifically authorizing Black slavery, strongly discouraged the institution it permitted.[28] The results were revealing. In 1850, two years before the law's passage, Utah had twenty-six slaves. In 1860, eight years after slavery was legalized, it had twenty-nine.[29]

Western attitudes toward slavery can help in understanding otherwise puzzling wrinkles of western politics. Hostility was so widespread, and the hold of white supremacy was so strong, that familiar eastern political terms refracted, bent into new meanings. In the East the free-soil movement was scrambling the political order and reconstructing the party system, launching the Free Soil Party in 1848 and evolving into the Republican Party by 1856. Out west the Free Soil Party had almost no traction. Because its essential plank, opposition to western slavery, was such a given, the party was left with only its tepid strain of abolitionism to distinguish it, and the majority of westerners reviled abolitionists. The Republican Party was slow to take root for much the same reason. A second issue, popular sovereignty, was counterpoised to free soil in the East. Embodied in the Kansas-Nebraska Act of 1854, it called for territories to decide for themselves whether to permit African American slaves. Eastern free-soilers bitterly attacked the doctrine for potentially opening the West to slavery. Out West, however, voters strongly favored popular sovereignty. Precisely because slavery expansion was off the political table, they saw it as a hopeful move toward wider control generally over their own affairs. In 1858 Oregon Republicans began their first campaign by embracing the very principle their eastern colleagues were calling poisonous and by heartily endorsing the Kansas-Nebraska Act, the law their mother party had been born opposing.[30]

The strangeness came together in California politics. Fewer than one in ten voters were from the deep Southeast, yet the state was controlled for most of the 1850s by the Chivs, the wing of the Democratic Party dominated by southeastern slaveholders. Californians, that is, consistently elected politicians who favored and practiced what most voters were determined must never be part of their own lives. The Chivs got and kept their power, in part through patronage and organizational skill, but also by artfully dodging around racial issues. They persistently pushed to mitigate the ban on slavery, yet they never openly challenged it. Thus they pushed slaveholding interests where they could while defanging themselves as a threat to free labor and white supremacy.

There were odd consequences. When Congress admitted California as a non-slave state as part of the Compromise of 1850, southeastern leaders mourned that the Northeast would now control the U.S. Senate. California's admission did indeed upset the Senate's balance. Slave states now could often outvote the other side. For eight of the eleven years between statehood and the Civil War, both California senators were Chivs who in Washington voted consistently with their southeastern colleagues. It was a demonstration of how pro-slavery interests could insinuate their way to influence by brilliant maneuvering inside an otherwise hostile political world. They helped their way along by tarring Free-Soil Democrats as too sympathetic to Blacks and, the ultimate canard, as closeted abolitionists.

That tactic led to one of the most bizarre episodes of these troubled years, a fatal duel between two of California's highest officials. The duel was fought over the implications of the letter *s*. David Broderick, one of the state's U.S. senators, was leader of the Free-Soil Democrats. A former New York stonecutter, saloon bouncer, and firefighter, he was best known as a champion of workingmen and free labor. In 1859 his often bitter rivalry with the Chivs was at new heights. He warned that their support of pro-slavery forces in Kansas was a prelude to plans for California. If they had their way, Broderick predicted, "you, fellow citizens, who are laborers and have white faces, must have black competitors." On the stump he compared William Gwin, the Chiv leader, to Benedict Arnold, Pecksniff, Iago, and Hester Prynne. The Chivs pilloried Broderick in terms just as vicious, if less literary. In a particularly pointed attack David S. Terry, the Chiv chief justice of the state supreme court, railed at Broderick and his wing as posers. They claimed to be followers of the northern Democrats' best hope, Illinois senator Stephen A. Douglas. And they did "sail under the flag of that name," he said, but not the one they claimed. It was "the banner of the black Douglass," the escaped slave and prominent abolitionist Frederick Douglass. That extra *s*, and the taint of its racial slant, was enough for Broderick to call Terry out to the field of honor. On September 13, 1859, they met behind a barn at Lake Merced, south of San Francisco. Broderick fired into the ground, undone by a hair trigger. Terry shot Broderick in the lung. He died three days later.

It was a fitting end to a decade of strange and bitterly contentious western politics. What came closest to a common ground was, ironically, what was most divisive in the East. At the end of the 1850s, at least as things stood at that moment, questions around the extension of African American slavery into the West were hardly questions at all. Where it was permitted, in New Mexico, Utah, and Washington Territories, it showed not the slightest suggestion of truly taking root. The number of slaves was, at most, about fifty.[31] Where it might well have taken root, in California's and Oregon's mines and fields, it faced overwhelming popular opposition exactly because it could have taken root, which made it anathema to the bulk of voters determined to keep the West a home of free labor. That sentiment made dimmer still any support for abolition or the slightest tilt toward racial equity. After all, David Broderick died insisting furiously that he *agreed* with his killer on the rightness of white rule.

And yet slavery's national advocates worked, energetically and with at least bluff confidence, to establish it throughout the West, pushing with increasing vehemence the demands that would carry the republic to the brink of disaster, and then would carry it over. How they did has a lot to say about how the states of the future Confederacy saw themselves and their destiny. Why they did says much about the increasingly strange and perilous state of mind in national politics.

Iron Streams and "Terrors of the Slave Power"

Part of the answer to the slavery paradox has to do with the slave Southeast's vision of its future and its place in a larger world. Historians once portrayed the region as economically and culturally retrograde, inbred and inward looking, mired in outmoded agrarian ways being rapidly eclipsed by the modernizing states to the north. That portrait, like the "natural limits" thesis, is now dismissed. The view now is of a Southeast perceiving itself as having a vital hemispheric future—economically expansive and confidently committed to becoming an innovative commercial power. Black slavery was a crucial, irreplaceable part of this vision. Historians often address slavery in focused national terms, but in fact it was part of developments and debates across the Atlantic world. By that perspective, southeastern influence and power would expand only if slavery, or at least its acceptance in principle, would go with it. The newly won West was to be one, but only one, new realm hopefully to be brought into the Southeast's growing orbit.[32]

This dream had its fullest flower (and a strange bloom indeed) in the Knights of the Golden Circle, a secretive organization founded in the mid-1850s by George Bickley. A southern-born émigré to Ohio, Bickley had lied his way into a medical professorship before marrying into wealth and turning his attention southward. His vision was of a vast alliance of slaveholding nations centered in Cuba and enclosing the West Indies, Brazil, Central America, Mexico, and, in the United States, the upper and lower Southeast and the Southwest, plus a tad of Kansas.[33] Seizing Mexico would be step one in this new creation. It would be "Texasized," "Southernized," and divided into twenty-five slave states to gain a lasting control of the federal government. By late in the decade the dozens of local chapters ("castles") across the Southeast were promoting secession and the seizure of Washington DC, but once the war began Bickley's star did not ascend. After lobbying unsuccessfully for secession in Kentucky, he slipped into Indiana, posing as his own nephew, to organize resistance to the Union cause. He was arrested and imprisoned until after the war. He died in 1867.

Binkley's vision was only one of many that gave Mexico special attention. That country's northern states, stretching from the Gulf of Mexico to the Pacific, were especially alluring. Disordered and virtually ungoverned because of Comanche and Apache raids, they seemed easy pickings for those hoping to expand the border—and with it, Black slavery—to the south. Albert Sidney Johnston, soon to be one of the Confederacy's most brilliant generals, toyed with filibustering in the late 1850s, and Maj. James Longstreet, in 1860 the army's paymaster in Albuquerque, lobbied to raise volunteers to invade and seize Chihuahua and

Sonora. Sam Houston, a member of the Knights, hoped to create a protectorate there.[34] Grabbing northern Mexico in turn would make it part of a corridor from the Gulf states through Texas and the Southwest to California. Some saw a route farther south as a key connection. Matthew Maury, the great oceanographer and the superintendent of the U.S. Naval Observatory, called for a link across Panama to make New Orleans "the thoroughfare of travel between South America, California, and China." Tapped directly to three-fourths of the world's population, midway between Asia and Europe, the Gulf of Mexico would become "the centre of the world and the focus of the world's commerce."[35]

Increasingly, however, southeastern hopes focused on the railroad as a corridor to the Pacific coast and beyond. Senator William Gwin proposed a branching line of 5,116 miles, more than twice as long as the eventual transcontinental, that would run from Oregon through San Francisco to Los Angeles, then eastward to both New Orleans and Memphis. This vitalizing link would open the "States fronting the Gulf of Mexico" to California and the Northwest and, beyond them, to Hawaii, the riches of "Oceanica" and "the Japanese Islands, soon to be unsealed."[36]

The land itself was said to make the case. Ships leaving California for the Orient had to sail sharply southward to catch trade winds that carried them to Canton and "the great ports of Hindustan," the Arkansan Albert Pike told the Louisiana legislature. A rail link from ports of the Southeast would trim seven hundred to eight hundred miles from any trip from Boston, New York, or Philadelphia, shaving customers' costs and boosting their profits. Anyone with a nose for business and an eye for latitudes could see that "the world's route to the Indies is through the territory of the Southern States," Pike concluded: "The trade is ours, if we choose to take it."[37]

The vision, then, was of dual expansions, westward as well as southward. Together the two would situate the Southeast within a bi-oceanic trade arrangement across tens of thousands of miles of sea lanes and land transport. The point to note is that the vision's emphasis, as in so much else during the years of the West's creation, was on connections, which puts the expansion of African slavery in a slightly different, wider perspective. Establishing it in California and the West was certainly desired. But it was not required in order to fulfill the Southeast's future as a global player. What *was* required was linking to the Pacific and beyond. The essential link here was the revolutionary technology of the railroad, which as an abstraction, a Euclidian line of breadthless length, could take on a kind of magical binding power. As the rail revolution in the Ohio Valley and Great Lakes was shifting the thrust of expansion from south-to-west to north-to-west, tipping the balance of immigration in favor of free soil, southeastern slave interests were placing ever-greater faith in railroads to bring the West into their orbit.

They seemed to have good reason for the faith. They could count on the branch of the federal government that was best positioned to help: the executive. Presidents Franklin Pierce and James Buchanan, both northern "doughface" Democrats dependent on the support of the Southeast, worked steadfastly to extend its interests, most famously by trying to acquire Cuba or at least to prevent Spain from emancipating its slaves.[38] Less recognized was their support of acquiring northern Mexico. Pierce was ready to spend $50 million for four Mexican states, and in his 1859 message to Congress Buchanan asked permission to invade the Mexican borderlands, a derelict, "a wreck upon the ocean, drifting about" that a rival power might take if we did not.[39]

Both men appointed slavery advocates to positions key to controlling connections to the Pacific. Buchanan appointed Aaron V. Brown, formerly a congressman and governor of Tennessee, as postmaster general. For mail service to California Brown devised a route out of New Orleans and Memphis through southwestern deserts to Los Angeles. Six hundred miles longer than a central option, John Butterfield's oxbow was touted as the "pioneer route" for the first rail link to the Pacific that would connect to "Virginia, South Carolina, Georgia, Alabama, Tennessee and Kentucky" as well as New Orleans and Texas.[40] The prime case for presidential favor for a southeastern rail link was Pierce's appointment of Jefferson Davis as secretary of war in 1853, a post that had him overseeing the survey of the four possible routes for the first transcontinental railway.[41] Thus Washington's choice for the first iron road to the Pacific, the plum that slave interests considered the key to victory, was left up to the future president of the Confederacy. His final report, objective in tone and clinical in detail, boiled down to a nearly thirty-page denigration of the three alternatives to the southernmost route along the thirty-second parallel, which he found superior by climate, topography, distance, and, consequently, by cost.[42]

Unmentioned in the report was that his favored route ran through country acquired only the previous year with a treaty negotiated by the man who had petitioned the California legislature for a colony of two thousand "African domestics," the South Carolinian James Gadsden, ambassador to Mexico.[43] The boundary of 1848 had left a series of desert mountains blocking Davis's preferred rail pathway, and at his urging, Pierce had Gadsden approach Mexican president Antonio López de Santa Anna with an offer to buy more traversable land to the south—and hopefully much more. In a secret order Pierce sought most of the states of Chihuahua, Sonora, Coahuila, and Baja California or, failing that, the mouth of the Colorado River as a western port for the South.[44] Santa

Anna pared down the cession to a little less than thirty thousand square miles, today's southern Arizona plus a slice of New Mexico, for $10 million. While well less than the grand dreams of some, the Gadsden Purchase unblocked the way for a southern rail route that Davis would shortly declare the government's preference.[45]

When the nation's final addition to its contiguous states was engineered by southeastern slaveholders, when two consecutive presidents sympathized with them, and when the men most directly in charge of linking the older republic to the Pacific worked consistently in their interest, it is no surprise that advocates of Black slavery might speak so confidently of carrying their cause into the West. That cause seems focused on the long game with its first priority a rail connection to the Pacific which would expand, enliven, and sustain the slave economy and society of the Southeast. That vision did not rely on Black slavery in the West, at least at the time, but it by no means abandoned it, either. Connections might cultivate various possibilities in the years ahead. Most obviously a railroad out of the Southeast would funnel citizens as well as commerce to the far coast, and as their numbers grew, so would their political influence. Presumably elected officials with close bonds to the Gulf states would be more likely to look amicably toward their interests. That is, in fact, what happened in California and Oregon. Both were majority free soil, and yet Democratic officials in both, while only dancing around and nibbling at the question of slavery where they were, supported it in the East. In time, an Arkansas editor wrote in 1853, Californians with commercial connections to the slave states might first sympathize with and then join the Southeast "as a common community, contending for common rights."[46]

There were still other reasons to press for slaveholding rights. Even if Black slavery had little or no chance of taking hold in the present, the simple possibility of it expanding in the future, the economic historian Gavin Wright argues, would keep the long-term investment value of slaves in the East, and thus their worth to their owners, high and healthy. The market price of bondsmen bears him out. The price of a prime male slave rose precipitously during the three years after the *Dred Scott* decision, but then, between the nomination and election of Abraham Lincoln—with, that is, the political triumph of free soil in national politics—the price fell by about a third, back to where it had been before. The right to take slaves westward seems as well to have been a kind of psychological brace that answered what Wright calls the slaveowners' "craving for reassurance" that the institution was proper or at least legitimate.[47]

Reassurance was especially needed in light of fears that, if confined to the Southeast, Black slavery was destined to die. A Georgia congressman claimed that every slaveholding colleague knew that if slavery were kept within its present limits, "its existence is doomed."[48] Historian James Oakes finds this concern close to the heart of the impassioned demands for slavery extension. Arguments on both sides raised the direst alarms about slavery's growth or confinement (while, rather paradoxically, generally ignoring the question of whether the status quo might actually change). As early as 1850 North Carolina's congressman Thomas Clingman warned of plans to annex northern Mexico for free soil to further trap and isolate the slave Southeast, while the abolitionist Cassius Marcellus Clay was convinced that, after capturing Kansas, slavery expansionists would stack more slave states on top of it, all the way to the Canadian border, cutting off free-soil expansion to "the Great West and Mexico."[49]

The slavery paradox, then, is at least mitigated when the goals of the slave Southeast are set in a larger frame and a longer term—as a package with connections to the Pacific the paramount concern and with slaveholders' rights linked to that goal in hopes that the peculiar institution might be truly present in the future. From such a perspective, two facts at the end of the 1850s would have been especially encouraging. First, with the *Dred Scott* decision in 1857, slaveowners would be able to take their human property into any federal territory, both those already there and those yet to come. And in terms of non-Indian population, most of the West was largely empty. New territories were bound to appear as it was opened up—in fact six were organized over the next eight years—and if the decision held, African slavery would be legal in them all. Perhaps the long game might favor the slave Southeast.

Yet plenty of puzzlement remains. How much effect a southwestern rail link would have had is debatable. Events showed clearly that Black slavery had virtually no appeal in the Southwest, and while a line might bring slavery advocates to California, the state was overwhelmingly free soil, and via the well-used routes from the East and by sea it was becoming more so year by year. New territories might be open to slaveholding, but what, realistically, was its prospects? The places where those territories were most likely to appear were places least likely to support the institution. The case of Kansas would show that even the parts of the West most accessible from the Southeast were at least as open to floods of free-soilers, and most of the rest, the northern plains, Rocky Mountains, and the interior Northwest, was even more so. Colorado suggested how things were likely to go. Gold was found there in 1858. By the time Colorado became a territory, a month and a half before the war began, it was overwhelmingly free soil. *Dred Scott* or no *Dred Scott*, the odds against Black slavery, as practiced in the Southeast, being established in the West in the foreseeable future seem very long indeed.

Perhaps the answer lies less in *what* was argued than in *how* it was argued. Recent scholarship stresses that by the 1850s Black slavery, and more to the point the questions behind it of the natural rights of human freedom versus that of property, had become the key issue of the day. Slavery, whatever the context, "stalked through this hall like Banquo's ghost," as a Whig congressman put it, and to many it was the single greatest determinant of the American future.[50] In that context *Dred Scott* amplified basic questions around citizenship, and given the decision's specifics, it was all but impossible to engage those questions without invoking the West, realities aside. In such a mood, the abstract right to take Black bondsmen westward assumed a weight that had little to do with whether any of those bondsmen might actually be taken there, coffled and ready for work. Simply being permitted by law into the West would give Black slavery a standing that some found essential, and others found incompatible, to their vision of the Union.

Such arguments took on particular power because of the rhetoric they were couched in. Two trends were obvious. First, each side made increasingly extravagant claims about what the other was really up to. From 1850 on southeastern politicians warned that keeping Black slavery out of the West would be only the first step to breaking it down wherever it existed, "by fair means or foul." A congressional coup d'etat would make of the Southeast a "colonial vassalage."[51] In turn a New Mexican free-soiler warned Salmon Chase that allowing Black slavery there was the opening ploy of an intrigue, as monstrous as the Gunpowder Plot, to expand it to the Pacific and southward to Tierra del Fuego. Others feared the ambitions would not stop there. Most famously, Abraham Lincoln, who would see his opponents' offers of compromise in 1861 as a cynical move to forge a "high road to a slave empire," warned in his "House Divided" speech that the *Dred Scott* decision went well beyond positing perilous legal principles. Events strongly suggested a "common *plan* or *draft*," a "design and concert of action" among Stephen Douglas, doughface presidents Franklin Pierce and James Buchanan, and Supreme Court Chief Justice Roger Taney that intended nothing less than making Black slavery "lawful in *all* the states, *old* as well as *new—North* as well as *South*."[52]

A second trend was especially dangerous: both sides elevated the threats posed by the other toward ones of elemental evil and human worth. In their "Appeal of the Independent Democrats" in 1854 six prominent anti-slavery figures called slavery expansion a "plot against humanity" that threatened not only the nation but "liberty throughout the world." Southeastern interests were intent on binding the nation under what the *Albany Evening Journal* called the "organized Barbarism" of a despotic minority. On the other side, the *Richmond*

Enquirer wrote that the right to take even a single bondsman to New Mexico or California went beyond a mere legal point to (with unmissable irony) the universal "principal of equality." The denial of taking just one slave westward, it implied, would mean the denigration and humiliation of everyone (or, rather, all whites) in the slave states.[53] Questions of principle became increasingly ones of individual integrity. When collective rights were compromised, standing quiet was personally degrading. Submission to what Salmon Chase called "the terrors of the slave power," the Republican Party declared in its first platform, would be "too shameful to be contemplated."[54] As southeastern politicians defended their honor by hurling insults at slavery's opponents, three prominent anti-slavery congressmen in 1858 pledged to challenge any of the hurlers to duels. If needed they would fight "to the coffin." Anything less would threaten "their very manhood."[55] Two years later, on the first day in session after Lincoln's election, Senator Albert Gallatin Brown of Mississippi judged that accepting the principles behind his victory would be "the deepest degradation that a free people ever submitted to."[56]

Degradation, humiliation, barbarism, emasculation: couched that way, within what historian Joanne Freeman calls the *"emotional logic of disunion"* (her italics), the question of Black slavery in the West took on an evocative power that politicians of all parties in both sections seemed to find irresistible.[57] As political historian Michael Holt shows, they would summon that power again and again, invoking its strident rhetoric at each twist in the tortuous political course from the Wilmot Proviso to the Civil War, calling on its energy for whatever issue was right in front of them. Often enough the tactic worked. As it did the terms of the question became increasingly ones of mistrust, virtue, fear, and honor. By the end of the 1850s, Holt writes, the trend had grown "like a bad weed," invasive, noxious, and in time impossible to uproot.[58]

Ultimately the slavery paradox is, and will likely remain, an illustrative puzzle. Year by year the actual extension of slavery, southeastern style, became a question with less and less immediately at stake. It was not coming to California, to Oregon, or by 1857 to Kansas, while elsewhere it was only the dimmest presence. And year by year in the East the question was argued with growing vehemence in terms that were more and more ominous, lofty, and symbolic, which meant that, year by year, any resolution to the question became less and less possible. In the end the greatest bloodletting in the nation's history began over questions that, at least in their western particulars at the time, seemed already answered.

However anyone might try to unriddle the paradox, one thing is clear. At this critical moment of American history, the West was playing a role it would again and again as it found its distinctive character and place in the nation. The West was where others would project their values and beliefs, their needs and anxieties, and their visions of what they feared and hoped America might be. What the West actually was often mattered less, especially in times of great disquiet or aspiration. After the Civil War, many would project into the new country their hopes of unification, of common purpose, and of healing—in one historian's apt term, of a national convalescence.[59] Before the bloodletting, the West played the same role, but with the opposite tack. It became, in historian Stacey Smith's words, "a theater of the sectional crisis" as those in the halls of Congress, as Joanne Freeman puts it, were "performing sectional warfare."[60] The West served as the projecting ground of all sides among an increasingly contentious people, and by that it had its part in the dreadful wounding that, after 1865, it was called upon to heal. In 1860 Black slavery had virtually no place in the West of reality, but it did make of the envisioned West the battleground for America's future and, many would say, its soul.

Slavery by Different Names

The heightening conflict over the extension of Black slavery and the unmatched tragedy and ultimate triumph that followed have made it easy to miss a vital point. If slavery is defined as labor compelled by force or by law, there was plenty of it the West at the time of expansion, and within a few years there was much more. Once that is recognized, the view of the new country challenges what Michael Magliari calls the "three familiar polarities" of American slavery: "white vs. black, North vs. South, and free wage labor vs. chattel slavery."[61] Once those polarities are challenged, the familiar western narrative takes on a truer shape—and a far darker tone.

Western slavery was more de facto than de jure, and it took several forms. Long before the arrival of Europeans, unfree labor was well entrenched across the region. Intertribal slaving was central to many Indian cultures and economies. In the Southwest it was invigorated by new pulses of trade and by the surge of power among some Native peoples with the rise of horse cultures.[62] The Spanish became participants, in part by profession of Christian responsibility. The claim was to ransom captive Indians to save them from savage mistreatment and, by converting them, to save their souls. The captives were sold by Apaches, Comanches, Utes, and Navajos who preyed on Wichitas, Pawnees, and each other. Slavery had been prohibited in New Spain since 1542, but an exception allowed the taking of slaves in warfare against hostile and resistant tribes—in this case the same tribes who were selling captives to the Spanish. The Indians that were ransomed or seized, mostly women and especially children, were scattered among Spanish households to work as servants and laborers until they had paid off their ransoms. Called sometimes "children of the enemy," drawn from a stew of cultures, living on the lowest step of the colonial order and outside the orbit of the Pueblo peoples, they made up their own category. Once away from their adoptive families, they were known as *genízaros*, a collective hybrid. Born from a system of captivity and forced labor, the *genízaros* by one estimate composed more than a quarter of Albuquerque's population in the mid-eighteenth century.[63]

Indian captivity in turn was bound up with another well-rooted means of unfree labor—debt peonage.[64] The many impoverished of the borderlands lived a cash-poor life. Should they require some essential, they could often get it only through a loan. Even the familial basics of moving through the generations—baptisms, weddings, and funerals—were often paid for on credit. The one who incurred such a debt, and with no resources to repay it, was bound to work for the lender until the debt was satisfied. The terms of the loan, however, with wages low and expenses and interest rates high, often left the debtor in an ever-deepening financial hole. "The initial debt," a New Mexican priest wrote, "is truly the tie that binds him to servitude . . . for the rest of his life."[65]

The systems of Indian captivity and debt peonage were distinct yet woven together. An Indian purchased as a captive from Comanches or Utes, while freed from one sort of bondage, was usually bound anew to work for the buyer until the price was repaid (although it rarely was). The child of a woman in peonage was legally free but would often fall into debt and thus into his or her own forced labor. The systems were largely self-perpetuating. By the time the United States acquired the Southwest, captives and debt péons made up a large portion of the labor force, working especially as domestics, herders, and field hands. The new administration quickly drafted and passed a law meant to define the arrangement with legal particulars and, at least in part, to minimize abuses, but the practical result was instead to cement the near absolute control of a patrón. His debt péons were now formally required to respect their masters as "superior guardians."[66]

Meanwhile, the coming of the Americans was invigorating both debt peonage and Indian slaving. First the Santa Fe trade, born with Mexico's break with Spain in 1821, then American conquest twenty-five years later, drew New Mexico into the vibrant market economy of Missouri and the middle border. The accelerating trade, plus an inflow of U.S. capital increasingly concentrated in the hands of the wealthiest, heightened the need for labor and expanded the ranks of debt péons.[67] The same changes gave a boost to the slave trade, most of it done by the neighboring Navajos, or Diné. Not just the numbers but the dynamics of slaving changed, to lamentable effect. In the past both Nuevo-mexicanos and the Diné had used captives from each other as a type of diplomatic currency in negotiating a truce following their frequent conflicts. Now, as the need grew for Indian slaves as workers, New Mexicans grew less willing to return captives to pay for peace, even as the same motives inspired more raids, which brought more reprisals, which led to still more counterpunches and more Navajos captured. By 1850 hundreds of Navajo slaves were scattered among households across the territory.[68] As the pace of raiding grew in the next decade, so did Navajo frustration. More than two hundred of their children had been taken, a headman told an agent in 1852, and even though his people had returned the captives they had taken several times, only once were a few of theirs sent home: "Is it American justice that we must give up everything and receive nothing?"[69]

The tightening tension snapped in 1860 with a furious Navajo assault on the army's Fort Defiance, on the edge of Dinétah, and against the area's New Mexico settlements. In response volunteer forces, armed by the government, launched into Navajo country, killing some and capturing others they were allowed to sell on their return. Pueblos, New Mexicans, and especially Utes, ancestral enemies of the Diné, did the same. The deteriorating situation, worsened by divisions among the Diné, came coincident with the onset of the Civil War and in 1863 Col. Kit Carson's campaign against the Navajos. During their infamous Long Walk to the reservation in eastern New Mexico, Ute and New Mexican slavers harvested at least several hundred for their trade.[70] This was not wholly a bad thing, Carson thought. Sold as servants, the captives' tribal allegiance would fade and they would be cared for without government worry or expense.[71]

No one can know the extent of unfree labor in New Mexico by the 1860s, but a judge reported that the few thousand Americans were vastly outnumbered by "forty-four thousand peons."[72] As for Indians living in forced servitude, New Mexico's chief justice, testifying on Independence Day 1865, estimated between 1,500 and 3,000. They were mostly Navajos, dispersed across the territory but usually present in the homes of the well-to-do, including the governor and other federal officials. They were remnants of a custom reaching back deep in the region's past, he said, one rarely if ever questioned, with captives of various tribes marketed "as much as is a horse or an ox."[73] They were a small portion of the territorial population, but, assuming 2,000 of them, the enslaved would have represented perhaps 15 percent of all Navajos. If that percentage were applied to the United States at the time, as historian Andrés Reséndez points out, it was as if the citizens of New York and all of New England had been taken into bondage.[74]

In California, as in New Mexico, a culture of intertribal slaving preceded American conquest.[75] When missions were secularized in 1833, nearby ranchers absorbed many of the Indians released with advances of food, supplies, and alcohol that obligated them to indefinite labor to pay off the debts. Pre–gold rush Americans and Europeans who acquired land fell into the same practices. John Bidwell, who led the first overland party in 1841, kept "serflike bands of Indian retainers" until the Civil War. Another early overland arrival recalled that all large landholders had Indian slaves, some taken by vaqueros who rounded up children and killed what men resisted. "They never permitted [slaves] to walk, but made them go about on a trot all the time," she wrote, and added, "These Indians made good slaves, excellent."[76] Treatment by some, including Bidwell, was relatively benign. That by others was not. James Marshall's discovery took place where John Sutter's extensive grain production relied almost wholly on Indian workers he kept in thrall through debt dependence, supplying needful goods, and outright enslavement. Through alliances he drew on other groups as his own armed force to keep others under control, some of whom he farmed out to other rancheros.[77] Mountain man and guide James Clyman passed through in 1845 and found six to eight hundred Natives "in a complete state of Slavery." He watched in "mortification" as they were fed at "10 or 15 Troughs 3 or 4 feet long . . . brought out of the cook room and seated in the Broiling sun[.] all the Labourers grate and small ran to the troughs like so many pigs and feed themselves with their hands as long as the troughs contain even a moisture."[78]

Under American rule the arrangements of de facto slavery were quickly affirmed. The conquest was not yet complete when the commander of the northern department of California, Capt. John Montgomery, issued a proclamation in September 1846 that was a model of how, as one hand giveth, another might taketh away. He declared that Indians must not be viewed "in the light of slaves" and commanded the immediate release of any held to labor against their will. He followed with an order that Indians must find employment and, once employed, must continue to work until released by their "master" or the court. Any not working and "wander[ing] about in an idle and dissolute manner" would be arrested and drafted into "public works." When ranchers reported "wild" Indians stealing livestock, Lt. William Sherman, writing for the military governor Col. Richard Mason, urged locals to "pursue and kill" any trying to steal animals. He then added that there were new regulations requiring all Indians in pueblos or ranches to carry passports when abroad. Any without the papers would be "treated as horse-thieves and enemies."[79]

Such double-speak was repeated in 1850. On the last day of its first session, the state legislature passed the Act for the Government and Protection of Indians. One historian has compared it to a piñata that spilled forth something for all hoping to exploit California Indians.[80] Any who were "loitering or strolling about," which came down essentially to pursuing their usual lives, or were publicly intoxicated or practicing "lewd" behavior could be arrested and contracted to work for the highest bidder. The traditional practice of burning prairies, critical to the hunting and gathering economy, was outlawed, again with anyone convicted available to any white posting bond. White citizens were authorized to arrest "without process" any Natives they suspected of a crime, including trying to escape bondage by debt or force. Conviction brought terms of labor ranging from days to months to years.

What emerged was a system systematically drafting Indians into coerced labor through local courts. Horace Bell recalled one variant in Los Angeles. On most Monday mornings local whites, especially vineyard owners, gathered at the local court. Many had paid Indian workers at the end of the previous week with liquor, with the result a weekend bacchanalia. On Sunday afternoon the marshal would herd the crowd into a corral to spend the night. The next morning they would be formally convicted of public drunkenness and "bought up" for two or three dollars each, part to pay a fine and part to be paid in whiskey on Friday. "Los Angeles had its slave mart, as well as New Orleans and Constantinople," Bell wrote, "only the slave at Los Angeles was sold fifty-two times a year as long as he lived."[81]

The law of 1850 also began one of the most pernicious aspects of the new system. Under it whites could become custodians of Indian children with the consent of a child's "parents or friends," the latter being undefined, and could hold them as indentures until males turned eighteen and females fifteen. A decade later the law was amended to make seizure of children even easier and to extend the time they could be held.[82] A justice of the peace could grant custody of a boy or girl by permission of anyone having "care or charge" of the child. Child thieves now could, and did, murder parents, take the child, and, as the ones with "care or charge," convey custody to a paying customer. The Indian superintendent of the state's northern district in 1861 reported children "seized and carried into the lower counties and sold into virtual slavery." When Indians retaliated by killing livestock, troops and volunteers marched against them. Kidnapers followed "to seize the children when their parents are murdered and sell them to the best advantage."[83] The next year the superintendent wrote that a man arrested for kidnaping pled that he and his colleagues were performing an "act of charity" by finding homes for children. With their parents murdered, he argued, they would otherwise have starved. When pressed on how he knew the parents had been killed, he answered that he had "killed some of them myself."[84]

The 1860 law also expanded the means of seizing adults. Now they could be taken into forced indentures if they were "prisoners of war," which would fit hundreds in the turbulent counties wracked by genocidal raids by volunteers and the military. At a time when armed mobs were killing thousands of Indians, thousands more were taken into de facto slavery so that, a state assemblyman said, "whites might be provided with profitable and convenient servants" while Indians were protected in stable households.[85]

There were provisions to protect Indians—they could contest seizure or loss of children and excessive abuse was forbidden—but because another law forbade Indians (and Blacks and Chinese) from testifying against whites, chances of legal satisfaction were beyond remote. Even if complaints came to court, the constitutional ban on slavery allowed an out. The provision forbade "involuntary servitude" except for "punishment of crimes," which allowed practical enslavement of Indians convicted of anything from loitering to intoxication, while the servitude of child indentures, formally arranged by "friends" or those in "care or charge," was considered voluntary.

Estimating the numbers and extent of unfree labor again is an educated guess. A rare case of surviving indenture records in a single county shows 110 between 1860 and 1863, 49 of them between ages seven and twelve. One authority sets the number of all California's forced indentures between 1850 and 1863 at 10,000.[86] Later they played a critical role in California's spectacular rise in grain production. Despite the hungry demand for grain, the lure of the mines, plus the high price of free labor, kept a tight cap on its production early in the rush. Then, after 1850, a large supply of bound Indian labor was suddenly available, and just then grain production swooped upward. The census from the centers of production shows concentrations of Natives with high male-to-female ratios, almost surely the field workers who, writes an economic historian, were "probably the most important" advantage giving the state its edge in this major national enterprise.[87] As landed property in the Central Valley was massing into the hands of an elite, it was worked by the land's previous lords now bound to the land as human property.

In Utah Mormon leaders brought about a similar legal arrangement, although one mitigated by their beliefs.[88] The Book of Mormon described modern Indians as descendants of the Lamanites, one of the original tribes of Israel that had immigrated to North America, and predicted that at the end time they would join with the Saints in Christ's new kingdom on earth. Prior to that, Mormons were to welcome Native peoples and convert them to the faith.[89] Reality, however, interfered. In time some Indians responded, but many did not, and some of those the Saints met had customs unexpected and unpleasant. To play on their emotions Utes starved and tortured captive children they brought to trade for firearms. On one occasion they killed a girl when the prospective buyers balked. As in Spanish New Mexico, Brigham Young defended captives as the means of redemption, "buying the slaves into freedom," in this case to make of these Lamanites "a white and delightful people."[90] By an 1852 law "for the relief of Indian slaves and prisoners" a citizen could become guardian of a child for up to twenty years, longer than in California. How many were taken in is unclear; a careful study by two historians found more than four hundred in households between 1847 and 1900.[91] A large portion died young, and as the Native population at large plummeted and the gathering of Zion continued to fill the Great Basin, the survivors, despite the professed official intent of bringing them fully into the fold, apparently remained on the fringes of Mormon life.

Western systems of bound labor quickly became part of the ongoing, ever-vigorous conversation about work and society, freedom and bondage across the continent. With enslaved Blacks costing between $800 and $1,500 each, and given the strong sentiments against bringing any of them into California and Oregon, western boosters touted Indians as an attractive option. Lansford W. Hastings, whose popular emigrant guide to California included glowing descriptions of what awaited at journey's end, pointed especially to that opportunity: "Indians are readily employed, and, in any numbers," with only a "trifling expense" up front and the barest support afterwards. Should they try to leave, he added, employers could legally track them down and bring them back.[92] As in slave states, California had a pass system requiring Indians moving on their own to have documents showing they had permission to be abroad, and in 1851 New Mexico passed a fugitive péon law to apprehend runaways.[93] Not only that, an Indian agent wrote, Indians accepted their condition, thinking of themselves as property "as much as does the negro of the south to the owners of his cotton plantation." And besides, added another new arrival, Indians would "submit to flagellation with more humility than the negroes."[94] The picture, Hastings assured his readers, was rosy. For years to come California Indians, living in an "absolute vassalage," would be available "for a mere nominal consideration."[95]

White newcomers could dismiss those in the thrall of de facto slavery with the same smug disdain shown elsewhere toward Black bondsmen. Lt. Philip St. George Cooke shrugged off the "great mass" of New Mexicans, "reared in real slavery, called peonism," as "eighty thousand mongrels who cannot read—who are almost heathens." In California Lansford Hastings said the same about the Indians and Hispanics, with their "beastly habits and an entire want of moral principle, as well as perfect destitution of all intelligence."[96] Those at the top of the system defended it in terms mimicking the ripest of the Lost Cause after the Civil War. Salvador Vallejo, owner of a huge California ranch, said he considered his laborers part of his family: "We loved them and they loved us. Our intercourse was always pleasant: the Indians knew that our superior education gave us a right to command and rule over them." (In a raid on a ranchería in 1850, Vallejo's party burned half the men alive in a sweat lodge, then marched three hundred of the survivors to work on ranches in Napa Valley.)[97]

Peonage in fact became part of a continental conversation on racial ordering. Its opponents used comparisons to Black slavery to emphasize its inhumanities. After the Civil War an army officer who looked on Abraham Lincoln "as a second Christ, almost" found New Mexican péons far worse off than the slaves Lincoln had emancipated. Their masters "could punish them in any way," and "if a peon died his place was at once filled with no loss but the small debt he was working out." A péon who worked during his "*health and manhood*," another officer added, could be tossed aside by his patrón as he aged past his usefulness. As a result, the Southwest "had more beggars than any other division of North America."[98] Defenders of Black slavery turned the same observations around to put the peculiar institution in a better light. A former U.S. attorney in New Mexico thought that péons, with no financial commitment from their masters, did not "enjoy so many blessings and comforts of domestic life" as did chattel slaves. In a variation of their comparisons with factory workers of the Northeast, pro-slavery politicians claimed that péons "would be happy to change places" with their bondsmen.[99]

Chattel slavery and western systems differed considerably, of course, starting with the law. Péons and bound Indians were never formally defined as property, although in practical realities they were, and there was no principle of *partus sequitur ventrem* by which their status was passed along from mother to child, although in New Mexico others in the family could be required to stand in for a deceased péon if a debt remained.[100] Strictly by the text, effective slavery looked usually like contracted work or punishment for a crime or even benign protection and guardianship. Nor was western bondage encased within the elaborate codes and proscriptions found in the Southeast. Its terms and forms were "kaleidoscopic, shadowy, and ever-changing," writes Andrés Reséndez, and while life could be quite different for a Black slave in Mississippi and one in Delaware, such differences paled beside those among a Mexican child taken by Comanches, an indebted field hand near Santa Fe, a Shoshone domestic in a Mormon household, and a Pomo man tending cattle in California.[101]

For all the differences, however, it is just as clear that unfree labor was a continental fact of life, highly adaptive and as varied as the land and societies from Oregon to Alabama. In a report to the U.S. Senate in 1846 William

Gilpin, an especially overripe expansionist, wrote that as Americans fulfilled their "*untransacted* destiny" by expanding to the Pacific, they would "cheer . . . upward" its backward peoples, "set free the enslaved," and "change darkness into light."[102] In fact expansion increased considerably the numbers and the range of involuntary servitude in North America. The vigorous uptick of the southwestern economy brought hundreds more Indians into coerced labor, and the turmoil that came with the Civil War set loose "the greatest Indian slavery boom" in the territory's history.[103] In California the stroke of luck that fed both American ambition and the national economy sent many thousands more into famished confinement and outright bondage.

As the political establishment in the East was failing to slow the movement toward disunion, conflicts in the new country were bringing their own crises. As it had from the start, the federal government continued to flounder in efforts to command country that was both increasingly valuable and borderline ungovernable. As the decade drew to its end the stresses took bloody form in two episodes that, while distinctively western in their particulars, mirrored as well the gathering crisis in the East.

7 ▷ The Fluid West

Notions around Manifest Destiny predicted an era of collective national great-ness. Instead the very gifts of the opening country—its unsuspected riches and its grand social potentials—challenged the national order more dangerously than ever before. The emerging West's fluidity, its sheer up-for-grabness, brought a near-fatal continental disharmony. Some causes were inherent to the land itself. Others were imports. In two new territories, Utah and Kansas, disputes that had roiled affairs in the East took hold, and in the West's heady atmosphere of open possibilities they flared with a special intensity. One played out over the rights of individuals to worship the divine as they chose and, more spe-cifically, over how their faith might act as secular power. The other expressed the darkening contest between Black slavery and free labor in the national future. Each was a measure of midcentury America's volatility. Each showed how expansion gave the nation's divisions a perilous specificity. Together they were a grim premonition of what was soon to come.

A Western Dixie

Outside its Native population, Utah Territory was peopled almost entirely by members of the Church of Jesus Christ of Latter-day Saints, or Mormons. It was one of several religions arising during the first couple of generations of the new nation. Joseph Smith, its founder, claimed to have been visited by Christ and God in 1820 at age fourteen and three years later by a shining angel, Moroni, who told him that buried at a nearby hill were plates inscribed with a hitherto-unknown ancient history of America, one that revealed the true and full Chris-tian gospel. Smith said that, with the help of two "seer stones," he translated the plates' contents. The Book of Mormon, published in 1830, extended both the Old and New Testaments into the Americas. It told of a group of Israelites who sailed from the Holy Land six centuries before Christ, across the Indian and Pacific Oceans to America. There prophets revealed the Christian gos-pel, and later Christ himself visited after his resurrection. A peaceful era that followed ended with a terrible war between two groups, the Nephites and the Lamanites, and when the second destroyed the first, a Nephite general, Mormon, passed the record of those times to his son, Moroni, who revealed them to young Smith centuries later.

Mormonism was a paradox. On the one hand it embodied many of the nation's common values. Its birthplace was quintessentially American, the farms and hamlets of rural New York known as the "burned-over district" because of passions there around religious and political reforms. In an individualistic age of buoyant optimism, Mormons served up the ultimate self-advancement: God was a former mortal who had exalted Himself into divinity, and through determined spiritual effort any ordinary man might also "arrive at the station of a God."[1] Mormons foretold that Christ had chosen the United States for His second coming, specifically some sacred spot in America's region of new hopes, the West. The man who bore these revelations, Mormonism's founder and first prophet, had the most American of names: Joe Smith.

Yet Mormonism also offended and frightened and attracted a virulent hostility.[2] Non-Mormons (called "gentiles" by the church) found some beliefs both bizarre—the notion of humans as proto-gods suggested polytheism, for instance—and, given the thousands who embraced those beliefs, threatening. The threat seemed especially acute on four points. In the early 1840s stories first circulated that church leaders were taking more than one wife, a practice seeming to threaten the social and moral order and conjuring lurid visions of older, goatish Saints enticing gullible young women into degrading unions. A second fear spoke to the pervasive issue of free labor. In the church's top-down structure Mormon leaders dispatched platoons of laborers with a word to this task or that, which seemed to many little different from slave coffles and gangs of Hispanic péons and Chinese coolies. Deepening that threat was the Mormon practice of voting in lockstep for whatever candidate their leaders chose, "like following a bell sheep over a wall," a young Saint wrote.[3] A third suspicion was that Mormons were allying with two minorities, African Americans and Indians, to join in a common uprising against white gentile America.

The first three concerns came together in the fourth. At the heart of Mormon teaching was the vision of the Latter-day Saints as a people apart from all other society, bound together in preparation for an imminent return of Christ. There were other millennialist religions during these years, all of them sure that Christ's second coming was both at hand and in the neighborhood, and others, such as the prolifically successful Methodists, looked to the West as home of a new, purified Christian order.[4] Mormons were different. They were gathering by the thousands into a structured social and political order, commanded by determined leaders and defended by armed force. Mormons were both a separatist religion and a coherent physical presence, a bordered entity.

That raised questions, one above all. The church claimed it was commanded by God to prepare for a realm that would sweep all other power away. But were they saying that they were waiting until the return of Christ before establishing a new political order? Or, some wondered, were they gathering to do it now? Were they organizing and arming in militant cause to conquer and command the nation and have it prepared and ready at Christ's return?[5]

Popular suspicions led to a pernicious cycle. Wary Mormons stood in bristly defense against perceived outside threats; uneasy outsiders suspected that the defensive posture hid invidious, even treasonous, motives; Mormons reacted to mounting suspicions by becoming still more confrontive. The result was a dual withdrawal. Mormons pulled, and were pushed, progressively apart from gentile society around them. And as they did, they relocated steadily westward in search of security and independence.

After first settling his followers in Kirtland, Ohio, Smith called in 1831 for a new Jerusalem, the City of Zion (or just Zion), in western Missouri. Local attitudes quickly soured, and the Saints were driven from Jackson to Clay County and then to a thinly peopled part of northwestern Missouri.[6] Hostility followed, and Mormons in turn formed a secret militia, the Danites, and prepared for a showdown. With God behind them, one of Smith's closest aides proclaimed on Independence Day 1838, the Saints would meet threats from gentiles with "a war of extermination. . . . We will carry the seat of war to their own houses and their own families."[7] Instead it was the Mormons who were harried from their homes by mobs and state militiamen after Missouri's governor formally ordered them "exterminated or driven from the state." About fourteen thousand Saints surrendered all property and fled into Illinois, where Smith bought a small riverfront town, renamed it Nauvoo, and set about making it the newest Zion.

Illinois welcomed the Mormons as an economic boon. Nauvoo received a remarkable charter with a highly centralized local government and what was officially a militia but effectively an independent military force, the Nauvoo Legion. Smith was both mayor and legion commander. Soon enough, however, the cycle was spinning again. In a couple of years Nauvoo had more than twelve thousand persons, about as many as Chicago. The Nauvoo Legion, with nearly four thousand armed and gaudily uniformed men, was nearly half the size of the national army after the Mexican War. The Saints seemed poised to dominate the region, economically and politically, and some claimed their ambitions were much grander. In 1842 an apostate, John C. Bennett, published *The History of the Saints*, claiming, among much more, that church leaders planned a midwestern religious empire bound to trigger "armed collision" with loyal Americans. His charge, that is, was of Mormons plotting civil war.[8]

Smith meanwhile saw the second coming as ever closer. He created the semi-secret Council of Fifty, or "Living Constitution," to be the core government of the imminent Kingdom of God, and he assigned them the task of pulling yet farther away from corrupt gentile society. They were to find some place at a far-western remove, maybe Texas, or Oregon, or the Great Basin, where the Saints might go their own way unimpeded.[9]

The situation snapped in the summer of 1844. After Smith ordered the destruction of the offices of a dissident newspaper, the *Nauvoo Expositor*, he and his brother Hyrum were arrested and jailed in Carthage, Illinois. On June 27 a crowd in blackface stormed the jail and murdered both. After months of splintering and infighting, the Quorum of the Twelve Apostles and their leading figure, the masty Vermonter Brigham Young, were recognized as the church leadership. Meanwhile violent confrontations, including artillery exchanges, forced the majority of Saints to abandon Nauvoo. In the spring and summer of 1846 about ten thousand of them slogged their way across Iowa to set up ramshackle camps beside the Missouri River and at spots along the way.

From there they would head west to yet another gathering of Zion, this one outside the nation now considered the church's oppressor. Other options were ruled out in favor of settlement beyond the Rocky Mountains in the Great Basin. (Later traditions had it that Smith's vision was precise enough for him to map the exact location and the best routes to it, by one account chalking it all out on the floor of a Masonic lodge.)[10] Young, a brilliant organizer, used the winter of 1846–47 to lay down a structure of command, supply, and communication for the exodus, which he began on April 7 when he set out with 147 others. Young was so determined to sever all ties with the nation that he blazed a new overland route, one along the north bank of the Platte River, so his followers could keep the stream between them and gentile immigrants. Other parties followed that year, and by winter more than 1,700 persons had settled at the site Young chose in the valley of the Great Salt Lake. Another 2,400 came in 1848.[11]

Then, even as the Saints were raising their first crude cabins, their hopes were again frustrated. The Treaty of Guadalupe Hidalgo and the great coincidence remade the continent's power realities. The Mormons were back inside the United States. Just as expansion undid an Indian policy that assumed eastern tribes had been removed beyond the press of expansion, so it also knocked the legs from under the Mormons' imagined future of a people safely apart.

Young's response was to turn the situation to their advantage. The former blacksmith set out to forge within the nation's new country a separate state, Deseret (the word in the Book of Mormon meant "honeybee"), that would be a "Theo-democracy," with heavy emphasis on the "theo."[12] He declared boundaries from the continental divide to the Sierra Nevada and from present-day southern Idaho to San Bernardino, California. He sent out families to colonize, and within a decade more than 40,000 Saints had founded 95 settlements. When Congress instead created Utah Territory, whittling Deseret down to a mere 220,000 square miles (still larger than any contemporary state except Texas), Young created a shadow religious government, a job made far easier when President Millard Fillmore named him the first governor and superintendent of Indian affairs. An apparatus of church command was quickly in place. Election codes guaranteed control; over the next quarter century every church-backed candidate won election, usually by majorities above 95 percent.[13] Territorial law kept virtually all land in Mormon hands, and any Saint who left the church would forfeit his. Most civil and criminal matters were turned over to county probate courts staffed by the governor, and to clear the way for theocratic law all appeals to English common law and to precedent of past decisions elsewhere were expressly denied. Church doctrine shaped countless legal details. The teaching of "blood atonement" held that some grievous sins demanded the shedding of the sinner's blood. Capital punishment consequently included a truly capital option—beheading.

The Mormon exodus, with its opportunity to pursue their purposes in ways impossible back east, allowed the Saints a far greater independence and, by the same measure, deepened their tensions with the society they had left. The conflict now was between Washington and the Mormon West.[14] It was a variation of the conflict between Northeast and Southeast. Particulars differed, but the essentials were much the same. Expansion allowed the Mormons to develop a physical integrity, a bounded area of authority like that of the contiguous slave states—and in fact roughly the size of South Carolina, Georgia, Alabama, Mississippi, Louisiana, Tennessee, and Florida together. Within their settled spheres Deseret and the slave Southeast each cultivated institutions and visions of the American future quite at odds with the national majority's, and in pursuing them leaders of each bluntly challenged federal authority (and each invoked the Constitution to justify their challenge). Each challenge led ultimately to a clash of arms. The two conflicts deepened simultaneously during the 1850s, with the showdown in the West coming just eighteen months before that in the East.

The Mormon challenge was directly at odds with three of Washington's prime projects—gaining control over the West's Native peoples, physically binding the West into a national whole, and forging and securing connections to California and the Pacific coast. The Book of Mormon foretold that Indians, descendants of the original arrivals from Israel, would return to the true faith at the end time and help create the new kingdom. In those last days, when God's chosen struggled with nonbelievers, Native peoples, the "remnant of Jacob," would be as "a young lion among the flocks of sheep" and would "treadeth down and teareth in pieces" all gentiles who resisted. To reconnect with their spiritual kin, Mormon leaders sent out 21 missionaries in 1854 and 160 the next year. Indians reportedly were being told that federal surveyors were the advanced guard of an effort to steal the land by exterminating its inhabitants.[15] Authorities in Washington grew increasingly suspicious, especially after church authorities frustrated a government effort in 1854 to find and punish the Pahvant Indians who the year before had killed Capt. John W. Gunnison while surveying a rail route across Deseret.[16]

The Saints also resisted Washington's efforts at span and control. The survey of the territory into townships and sections was an assertion of federal control and, indirectly, an invitation to outsiders to come and settle. Both threatened the church's legal grip on all land. After trying to make a start, the new surveyor general reported "the most diabolical threats" against his life, while one of his deputies was beaten nearly to death with the butt end of a horsewhip. Local officials intercepted his letter of complaint and told him that "*the country was theirs.*"[17]

As for Washington's determined work of connections, the vigorous surveying of roads and possible rail routes promoted the very thing Mormons had come west to escape—being close and accessible to enemies and nonbelievers. The main overland route, passing just north of the Great Salt Lake, was particularly troubling. Although Mormons were in a "remote and almost inaccessible region" well beyond the easy reach of federal authority, wrote Secretary of War John Floyd, they were still astride "the great pathway" to the "new and flourishing communities growing up on our Pacific seaboard."[18] Young had nearly a dozen posts built and fortified there and along other routes through Deseret. All were positioned to cut off traffic to California if need be.[19]

As conflicts sharpened, a cycle of threat and response unwound, a repeat of those earlier in the East but far wider in extent and with far greater stakes. As other divisions were hardening between Northeast and Southeast, Deseret was becoming a western Dixie, pulling away, finally to the edge of full rebellion. The few federal appointees were stymied at every step. Trying to administer the law was "noonday madness," one judge wrote, and in February 1857 the surveyor general described the Mormons as "*in open rebellion against the general government*" (italics in original).[20] Four months earlier Mormon leaders had let loose a "Reformation," a campaign to recommit the Saints to the church's teachings. Individuals were grilled about behaviors ranging from theft and adultery, through drunkenness and broken promises, to nightly prayer and weekly bathing. (Young said he had tried the last but didn't care for it.) Believers also were to commit anew to leaders who formed "the chain that the Almighty has let down from heaven to earth." They were to be utterly compliant, "like clay in the hands of a potter."[21] It was a winnowing of Saints in anticipation of hard times ahead, and as one wrote in his diary: "The fire of the reformation is burning many out who flee from the Territory afraid for their lives."[22]

Some eastern opinion, meanwhile, was painting Deseret as something close to an alien, specifically oriental, entity. Even before the exodus some had cast Smith as an "American Mohamet" and his followers as exotic in habits and leaning toward perversities. Once polygamy was in the open, Mormon homes were compared to Turkish harems, while Salt Lake City became to some either an American Sodom or, from the *New York Daily Tribune*, "this our Mecca." A more immediate—and to many an especially alarming—Asian kinship was between the Saints and the Chinese arriving in California by the thousands coincident with rising tensions in Utah. The imagined threat was of a natural alliance between Mormons and other new westerners also given to strange beliefs and customs and a similar blind adherence to authority so jarring to free labor sensibilities.[23]

Matters came to a head in 1857. Young's appointment had expired the year before, but with no replacement appointed, he simply continued to run things. Then the newly elected president James Buchanan appointed Alfred Cumming, formerly Indian superintendent for the Upper Missouri, to replace Young as governor (without informing Young). He ordered the army's top commander, Gen. Winfield Scott, to raise a force to install Cumming and, if needed, enforce proper civil law. The slightly veiled purpose was to secure federal authority over the intermontane West. Even before Buchanan took office, however, Utah legislators had sent him a memorial promising they would resist any federal attempt to interfere with their laws or to enforce any congressional act they considered "inapplicable" or "not in force."[24] Utah in effect was reviving the doctrine of nullification that had taken South Carolina to the edge of rebellion in the 1830s and had laid a basis for the state's secession in 1860.

The confrontation that followed would be called the Utah War. Assembling more than two thousand infantry and dragoons (many unhorsed) delayed departure from Fort Leavenworth until mid-July, perilously late, and gave the Saints time to set themselves well at the two eminently defensible approaches to the Salt Lake area. Commanding the first units to arrive in September was the indecisive colonel Edmund Alexander. As he dithered, Mormon guerillas destroyed two months' worth of supplies, including forty-five tons of bacon.

Weeks passed. The temperature dropped. The tenor of command changed on November 3 with the arrival the brilliantly aggressive colonel Albert Sidney Johnston, but it was too late to do more than find refuge from early blizzards that killed dozens of the army's weakened horses.

Young, meanwhile, had dug in, actually and metaphorically. Insisting that he was still governor, Young pronounced that Utah was being "invaded by a hostile force," and "we have every Constitutional and legal right to send them to hell." He declared martial law and decreed that no one could "pass or repass into or through" Utah without a permit, thus officially closing the nation's main overland connection to the Pacific coast.[25] He mobilized and armed the Nauvoo Legion, at one point considering issuing them crossbows. A few months later he would create a new force of a thousand riflemen, the Standing Army of Israel. No pretense of a civil militia here but a formally independent military command, the first in American history to be arrayed against the government. The next would be the Confederacy's. To meet any assault on Salt Lake City, he set his forces at the only approach to the valley, the narrow defile of Echo Canyon. It had walls hundreds of feet high of reddish sandstone, in places with great outcroppings, tapered and tilted, like teeth of a giant saw.

Key to Young's strategy was support of the Saints' doctrinal kin, the Indians. Stress to them, he told his agents, that "they either got to help us, or the United States will kill us both." He made moves to reach out to the Plains Sioux and Cheyennes.[26] Over the past year he had established Fort Limhi in the valley of the Salmon River in present eastern Idaho near the Montana border and had made overtures to powerful groups there and to the west, the Bannocks, Salish, Shoshones, Nez Perces, and others who were uneasy over the pseudo-treaties recently bullied through and by the fighting that had followed. On the eve of Buchanan's mobilization, Young traveled with church officials and with converted Indians to this strategic cockpit and spent more than a month meeting with and gifting leaders from the area's tribes.

Back in Utah Young declared the new kingdom was at hand. Should the defenses at Echo Canyon fail, he ordered a mass exodus southward, with the city and settlements destroyed. To the north he strengthened his positions around Fort Limhi and made contingent plans to withdraw there. With other followers and with Native allies he would turn the area into a redoubt. It was time, he said, "to cut the thread between us and the world." Tempered by the fires of the reformation, the Saints responded with defiance. They drilled in the streets, learning "a few motions of the British infantry sword." They prepared to "burn and leave [Deseret] as much a wilderness as we found it." They composed bad poems:

Then come, ye hireling sons of Hell,
　　Your dues you'll quickly get
　　Whene'r you venture on the soil
　　　Of peaceful Deseret.[27]

In camp to the east Colonel Johnston was eager to bring down the federal hammer. Four years later he would die as the Confederate commander at Shiloh, but in 1858 he pledged to chastise those "in rebellion against the Union," intent on an "insane design" to establish a western despotism "utterly repugnant to our institutions."[28] Before he was thawed and set loose, however, the crisis was defused. Two events coincided to make it happen. Buchanan, burned by questions about the stuttering campaign, sent an offer through a prominent Democrat, Thomas Kane, a gentile friend and sympathizer to Young. While denouncing a rebellion "without just cause, without reason, without excuse," the president proposed to pardon all Mormons who would now step back and accept federal authority. Simultaneously word arrived among the Saints that a couple of hundred Shoshones and Bannocks had attacked and besieged Fort Limhi, killing three, wounding several more, and stealing most of the outpost's animals.[29] With Colonel Johnston poised to bulldog his way into the capital, and with Young's belief in an Indian alliance shaken and his plans for a northward withdrawal dashed, Young backed down. He sent Kane with a conciliatory message the day after he heard the news from the Limhi. The new governor Cumming responded in kind and on June 13 Young formally conceded. Colonel Johnston marched his command through the Salt Lake City, then established Camp Floyd an unobtrusive fifty miles to the south.

It was less a conquest than a compromise. Cumming was installed as governor, but given the territory's political realities Young remained Utah's de facto leader. The army's presence was a physical reminder of federal authority and an assurance of reprisal to any outright challenge, yet the Mormon leadership largely controlled legislative and judicial affairs. In future elections opposition votes were like rare exotic species. Young's hopes for an alliance with northwestern Indians had taken a beating, but the Saints remained in effective control of the Great Basin and a corridor through Southern California to the Pacific. The conflict between Salt Lake City and Washington would continue as a high simmer for another thirty years.

By the time confrontation came in Utah, the Mormon experiment was thoroughly entwined in national politics. The year before the war the newborn Republican Party condemned polygamy, with Black slavery, as one of the "twin relics of barbarism." The nation's leading Democrat, Stephen Douglas, called for the federal government to dissolve Utah Territory's organic act and to reassume total control of the area. This stance required him to twist his fundamental political position of popular sovereignty into an ideological pretzel, but the Saints, he said, were "alien enemies and outlaws" unfit for self-government. To permit their treason and "bestial" practices would disgrace humanity and threaten wider American interests across the West.[30]

The Utah conflict was not, as some have described it, bloodless. There were few casualties among combatants, but in the hysteria around Johnston's approaching army, attacks on gentiles claimed as many as 150 persons.[31] At the center of these killings was an atrocity that is still the cause of argument. A California-bound party of about 135, mostly farmers from northwestern Arkansas, found themselves the victims of the cruelest coincidence of circumstances. They arrived in Salt Lake City on August 3, 1857, just ten days after Young had revealed that an army had been raised against Zion and had called for the stiffest resistance to any intruders. From Salt Lake City the party, led by and composed of ardent Methodists, among the most frequent critics of Mormons, took the southern route to California, which ran through settlements that, if anything, regarded outsiders with even greater hair-trigger hostility.[32]

On September 6 the Arkansans stopped at a spot called Mountain Meadows, thirty-five miles beyond the town of Cedar City. It was flush with grasses for their draft animals and fed by a generous spring. It was also all but indefensible to attack. The next morning Indians from several area groups, encouraged by local Mormons, surrounded and opened fire on the camp. When the immigrants regrouped and held on, Mormon leaders promised to escort them to safety, and the Arkansans, nearly out of ammunition and with several killed or badly wounded, agreed. On September 11 they filed out of the camp, each disarmed man beside an armed Mormon "guard." On a command—"Halt. Do your duty."—the guards shot the men while Indians leaped from the underbrush and beat women and older children to death with stones or slashed them with knives and hatchets. Seventeen children, set apart in their own wagon, were spared. They were under six years, incapable of sin according to church doctrine. They were taken and given to Mormon families. The bodies of their families were left as they were. Nineteen months later a military command sent to investigate found the area strewn with cracked skulls, scraps of children's clothing, and women's hair clotted and still tangled in the sagebrush. Soldiers buried remains and erected a twenty-four-foot cross of red cedar and on the transverse inscribed "Vengeance is mine; I will repay, saith the Lord."[33]

Mormon involvement in the massacre was at first denied but later admitted, although debate continues about how far up the theocratic chain of responsibility it ran, in particular whether Young himself had a hand in the atrocity. The vigorous arguments tend to gloss over an inarguable point. On September 10 a courier brought Young word that the Arkansans had been attacked and laid siege by Indians. At the time Young was meeting with an officer of the advancing army command, Capt. Stewart Van Vliet, yet Young said nothing of the report he had just received. The man who claimed to be Washington's territorial governor and superintendent of Indian affairs, that is, made no effort to inform the nation's most elemental authority, its army, of the eminent danger to more than a hundred American citizens in the country he commanded. He did, however, demand an end for "all emigration across this continent" and warned that any advance on Utah would bring destruction to "their own homes" throughout the United States.[34] Claiming to be the rightful representative of the United States, Young was acting wholly independent of it. He was keeping the power he had entirely inside the church, and he was exercising it, not as the governor he claimed to be, but as Deseret's commander and the "Lion of the Lord."

In this sense the massacre in Utah's high desert anticipated the infinitely greater carnage soon to begin in the East. At issue was how far a portion of the populace, geographically bounded and with its own political structure and armed force, could assert effective independence from the Union. The essential question was that of the limits of federal authority. That question was an old one. Expansion ratcheted it to the edge of war when tens of thousands of converts to an eastern-born religion found the space in the new country to pursue their vision of God-granted autonomy far more fully than would have been otherwise possible. The result was the Utah crisis. It fell short of pitched, sustained conflict. It did, however, show how expansion was testing the bonds of union across the continent.

Much the same story, with different particulars, was unfolding in another part of the West. In another new territory there was also talk of the land and its promise, of how it would be worked and who would work it, of sovereignty and of race and Indians and the word of God. Mormons saw the connection. One poetized that the federal "invaders" might soon be called away from Deseret, for

> They've other fish to fry, sir.
> For Kansas is the battle ground
> Where men in deadly strife are found
> And Civil War's discordant sound
> Is echoing far and near, sir.[35]

Why Kansas Bled

The Mormon poet's "discordant sound" was of a clash of interests, sometimes violent and always confused, in the newly created territory of Kansas. At the time and ever since, some would claim that the Utah War was a sham meant to divert public attention from a devilish political problem President Buchanan had inherited with his office.[36] There was something to it. Virginia's Robert Tyler wrote Buchanan: "*I believe that we can supercede the Negro-Mania with the almost universal excitements of an Anti-Mormon Crusade*" (italics in original).[37] In any case, as every history of the era makes clear, the fight over whether Black slavery would be permitted in Kansas was enormously consequential in the political slide toward disaster. "Bleeding Kansas" was as clear an instance as we have of how the emerging West could interact with the East to shift the nation's course, in this case making national calamity far more likely.

The episode was about much more than that, however. Kansas sat as a hinge. It was at the western edge of settled white society, the gathering point of influences bearing toward the Pacific. It was at the eastern edge of the country and the peoples that were already feeling those influences and would feel them much more over the next couple of decades. What happened there in the 1850s is a story with distinct eastern and western sides, although the first has largely obscured the second. The story's eastern side is indeed essential to explaining the dire path toward disunion, but the other side is equally revealing of forces at work in the developing West, including those bearing down on the gravest victims of Bleeding Kansas, its Native peoples.

The Kansas crisis had its roots in the same challenge that helped bring on the troubles in Utah—connectivity, how to bind the new lands into the Union. On the contentious questions of which among the four surveyed rail routes to the Pacific would prevail, the two southern options had a definite edge. One of the two northern routes might seem a strong candidate. It would run across the Great Plains along the Platte River and through the wide opening between the northern and southern Rocky Mountains. A decade earlier Thomas Jefferson Farnham had predicted that migration to the Pacific would find in this broad and largely level valley "its great highway" of "unequal importance," and in fact the Platte corridor was the chosen way of the huge majority of overlanders.

As a rail route, however, it had problems. The key issue went back thirty years. In 1820 the Missouri Compromise had supposedly settled what was even then the thorny question of whether Black slavery would be allowed into the West. It established Missouri as a slave state (and Maine as non-slave) and divided what remained of the Louisiana Purchase into two disproportionate parts. Missouri's southern border, at the thirty-sixth parallel, thirty degrees, was projected westward to what was then the nation's far edge, the crest of the Rocky Mountains. Slavery would be allowed south of that line, in today's Arkansas and Oklahoma. It would be forever forbidden to the north, which included the Platte corridor. The northern, non-slave portion was by far the larger, but because it was semiarid and largely treeless, there was little prospect of white settlement. It would be set aside indefinitely as "Indian country," where "wild" and "roaming" tribes would live as they chose. This northwestern corner of the nation, about seven hundred thousand square miles, nearly a quarter of the republic, was essentially a national irrelevance. It would have no civil government whatsoever.

Then, in 1848, the nation was on the Pacific, and Marshall made his find. Now "Indian country" was in the middle of the nation, not on its edge, and like Deseret it sat astride the main thoroughfare to El Dorado. The 1851 council at Fort Laramie was meant to secure the corridor for the first wave of traffic, that of overland wagons, by getting tribal consent for travel and by building a few military posts. A railroad, however, demanded more. Land would have to be surveyed and a system of sale and ownership established, which meant, at the least, organizing the area as a territory.

That was the rub. Congressional action would require some support from southeastern lawmakers. With Secretary of War Jefferson Davis pushing the southernmost route and dismissing the others, the slave states seemed all but certain to get their connection to the far West and to the "ports of Hindustan." Holding all the political cards, their legislators had no reason to favor a law that would boost the opposition's chances. Without southern support, there would be no territory, and without a territory, no northern rail route. The man most bedeviled by this problem was the senior senator from Illinois, the Democrat Stephen A. Douglas, and he had his reasons. A railroad along the Platte corridor would start in Saint Louis, which would make it a delicious plum for neighboring Illinois, with its dense rail connections through the Ohio Valley and the East. Douglas set out to win the prize.

To buy southern support, he offered to repeal the Missouri Compromise. The Platte corridor would be organized into not one territory but two, Kansas and Nebraska. Kansas supposedly would be quickly settled by slaveholding, or at least slave-friendly, Missourians from next door and would move rapidly to statehood. (The law referred to Kansas as a "temporary" territory.) Nebraska presumably would be non-slave and linger much longer as a territory. Thus the South would gain a slave state and pull even with the North (sixteen states and thirty-two senators, each), and Douglas's central rail route would gain new life. With practiced skill Douglas maneuvered the Kansas-Nebraska bill through Congress and into law in May of 1854. So it was that one of the era's nonpareil politicians managed what has often been ranked as the costliest political miscalculation in American history.

The Kansas-Nebraska Act went beyond rendering the Missouri Compromise "inoperative and void" (which, slavery aside, outraged many as a betrayal of national commitment). It declared that the recent Compromise of 1850 had established a new principle, "non-intervention by Congress with slavery in the States *and Territories*" (italics added). Throughout the West voters would be "perfectly free" to allow or forbid slavery. The law was vague, probably intentionally vague, on a key question: just when would voters make their choice? At the earliest stages of political organization, or when they petitioned for statehood? The law in fact was on this point nonsensical. No territory could establish or forbid slavery by itself. Congress could reject its constitution and veto any law, whether allowing slavery or taxing prunes. Yet to many the Kansas-Nebraska Act appeared both to add a slave state and to leave all territories free to take the same path, unimpeded by federal authority. During debate over the bill an exasperated Douglas had claimed it would cool hostilities between Northeast and Southeast, not inflame them. Its passage would destroy "all sectional parties and sectional agitations."[38] If there were a contest for the most wrongheaded statement ever by an American politician, this would be an odds-on favorite. Douglas's law was perfectly designed both to rouse eastern passions and to give them a place to find their voice.

What followed is best understood by standing on the hinge of Kansas and looking at events from two directions—first from the East, looking into Kansas, and then, crossing knuckle and pin onto the other leaf, standing in Kansas, looking around, and considering events from the West eastward. From the East, Kansas became a projection of outside fears and fantasies that were being fanned ever more feverishly in the national debate. Southerners saw it as the key to expanding slavery across the new country. "We play for a mightly stake," Missouri senator David Atchison wrote the governor of Virginia: "If we win we carry slavery to the Pacific Ocean."[39] Losing Kansas, on the other hand, would confine and cage Black slavery at home. It would wither and die, and with it a way of life. Worse yet, it was commonly claimed, settlers from free states were mostly New England abolitionists who, if successful in Kansas, would turn next to Missouri, Arkansas, and Texas. Feelings ran white hot. A Missourian was "for tarring and feathering and gutting and hanging and drowning the scoundrels until not an abolition[ist] . . . shall be found in Kansas."[40]

Free-soil advocates, too, predicted the most sweeping consequences. Their view looked back over sixty years and traced steps, from certain Indian treaties to the Compromise of 1850, that added up to a well-laid plot to subvert the Constitution and raise a "slaveocracy" to national dominance. The final thrust of the "Slave Power" was at hand, and the Kansas-Nebraska Act was its opening maneuver. The stakes could not have been higher. The "power victorious" in Kansas, warned Eli Thayer, founder of the New England Emigrant Aid Company, the leading organization promoting free-soil settlement, "would, in due time, govern the country."[41] As southeastern leaders predicted an abolitionist assault if Kansas were lost, rising political stars among free-soilers like Abraham Lincoln and William Seward, warned that if Kansas fell to African slavery, the institution might well overwhelm white workingmen from Illinois to Maine.[42]

Early arrivals divided quickly into pro-slave and free-soil clusters, the former in Atchison and Lecompton and the latter in Lawrence and Topeka. Slavery's advocates made the first move. Up to five thousand Missourians crossed the border to elect the first territorial delegate and the first legislature. In July 1855 that legislature quickly expelled its few free-soil members, moved the capital to Shawnee Mission, snuggled against the Missouri border, and passed a slave code imposing the death penalty for giving the slightest encouragement to slave resistance, including possessing a pamphlet suggesting it. Simply stating publicly that slavery might be illegal could bring a punishment of two years of breaking rocks while bound to an iron ball with a six-foot chain of quarter-inch links.[43] The legislature had scarcely adjourned when a convocation near Lawrence formed the Free-State Party that condemned the legislature as a "foreign body" and a nest of demagogues. By year's end free-state advocates had formed a shadow government and had approved a state constitution that would close Kansas to both slavery and free Blacks.

Now President Franklin Pierce was in a bind. Protests to events in Kansas showed alarming strength in key states, while Pierce's own ranks were starting to splinter. He tried to quiet matters with a proclamation in February 1855 condemning the free-state government as "reprehensible" and warning that federal troops stood ready to insure order—"order" meaning full control by pro-slavery authorities. Pierce was essentially following Stephen Douglas's disastrous lead, trying to mollify southern Democrats while keeping the issue of slavery expansion confined in the territories. But, as Douglas had learned, the issue would not be shut in a Kansas closet. Instead it was set at the center of the national stage. Pierce's evasions only made politics more fractious. Eleven days after his proclamation the Republican Party was formally born at a convention in Pittsburgh.

In November 1855 the tension flashed into bloodshed when, after a pro-slavery settler shotgunned to death a free-soiler, 1,500 Missourians besieged Lawrence and killed one man. Among Lawrence's defenders was the ardent abolitionist John Brown, lately arrived with his sons from New York. Frustrated by free-state leaders he found "more talk than cider," Brown stewed during a frigid winter spent living in a lean-to on bear meat and johnnycake. In May 1856 the national and the local literally bled together in an extraordinary week of violence. On May 19 and 20, Charles Sumner of Massachusetts delivered to the Senate "The Crime against Kansas," a blistering indictment against the "Slave Power" flecked with metaphors of sexual depravity. Southerners were guilty of the "rape of a Virgin Territory"; his South Carolina colleague, Andrew Butler, had taken as his mistress the "polluted . . . harlot, slavery."[44] The next day a pro-slavery "posse" of several hundred seized Lawrence and razed the Free State Hotel and the offices of two newspapers.[45] Back in Washington on May 22, Preston Brooks, a South Carolina congressman and a cousin of Butler, responded to Sumner's speech by bludgeoning him into unconsciousness with a cane, eventually breaking it over his head and leaving him incapacitated for months. Scarcely thirty-six hours later, over the night of May 24–25, John Brown, his sons, and a few others pulled five supposed slavery sympathizers from three homes along Pottawatomie Creek and shot and hacked them to death with broadswords.

The three months that followed cemented the popular image of all Kansas unrest as a face-off over western slavery. President Pierce declared the free-soil resistance an insurrection and called in troops to disperse at gunpoint the free-state legislature, on Independence Day no less, even as Washington's own investigators found that eight of ten votes for the pro-slavery legislature were illegal.[46] Meanwhile, free-soilers had organized into an "army" that clashed with Missourians in August and September of 1856. They were led by James N. "Jim" Lane. Tall, stone faced, irredeemably rumpled, intense, and erratic on multiple levels—ten years later he shot himself in the head as he jumped from a carriage with a "Goodbye, Mac" to his brother-in-law—Lane suggested the sorts who might rise to power in those times. By the end of 1856 around three dozen persons had died in what was ostensibly slavery-inspired violence.

That was the worst of it. There were half a dozen deaths in 1857 as James Buchanan took office, and half that the year after. A new governor, John W. Geary, worked with the military to tamp down the violence with a firmer, more impartial hand. The contest became more formally political, centering on proposed state constitutions. The pro-slave Lecompton constitution was met with dueling boycotts. Free-soilers stayed away from the first vote, and when

Congress sent it back for another, pro-slavery advocates did the same. The first time it was approved by 92 percent, and the second time it lost by 98.5 percent. Meanwhile, northern immigration was adding steadily to opposition to slavery. Free-state supporters sent Congress their own constitution from a convention at Leavenworth. It was criticized as too racially tolerant, going so far as to offer a referendum on suffrage for free Blacks and generally, one editor huffed, suggesting that "Mr. N–– is as good as a white man."[47] Yet another convention in Wyandotte ("We have been Constitutioned to death," one man complained to his diary) allowed free Blacks to settle but not vote. It was approved by a two-thirds majority.[48] The House soon approved the constitution, but with the gathering sectional storm it was blocked in the Senate until January 21, 1861, the day the last southern senators abandoned the chamber. Eight days later a free-soil Kansas became the thirty-fourth state.

And so winds down the traditional narrative of Bleeding Kansas. Some political leaders in Washington tried to marginalize a dangerous debate by sending it to the territories. Instead they made slavery's expansion the central question of eastern politics. Maneuvers to keep the Democratic Party unified instead left it splintered, fouling Pierce's administration, crippling Buchanan's, and all but scuttling Stephen Douglas's once-shining hope for the White House. The law Douglas said would undo any sectional party instead created one that would dominate the federal government for more than seventy years. In Kansas, Americans first organized to kill each other over issues of race. Twelve days after Kansans approved the Wyandotte constitution, John Brown led his sons and a handful of followers against the armory at Harpers Ferry, Virginia, a tiny foretaste of a now-nationalized violence that eventually would take as many as three-quarters of a million lives. Expansion and its needs had amplified the most treacherous political issue of the day and set a course toward the nation's deepest tragedy.

All true enough. And yet what might seem a western narrative says little about the West. It is set in service to the East and to the event, the Civil War, that dominates the usual story of America at midcentury. It ignores almost entirely other Kansas realities and how they reflected an emerging region. For one thing, while blood indeed was shed over slavery, it was questionable whether, as across the West, the institution would ever have grabbed serious hold. Agriculture suitable for gang labor was possible only in the easternmost quarter or so of the territory. Much was made of Missouri as a slaveholding neighbor, but its portion of slaves had dropped considerably over thirty years. Only in Delaware was it smaller. Plenty of southerners were sure to come to Kansas, but plenty had gone to Oregon and to the California gold fields, both places fiercely anti-slave (and anti-Black). More than a year after it was opened to settlement, Kansas had fewer than two hundred slaves.

Most anti-slavery arrivals in Kansas were just that—opposed to establishing the peculiar institution. Again as elsewhere in the West, attitudes seem mostly a combination of free labor commitment and racism. Abolitionists were nearly as rare as slaves. The New England Emigrant Aid Company, called by southeasterners a great pump of abolitionism, sent at most two thousand persons, and many of those were not what they were charged with.[49] The company's founder, Eli Thayer, railed against abolitionists, especially William Lloyd Garrison, as irresponsible fanatics marked by "emotional insanity" and "chronic monomania."[50] Garrison himself wrote that "hardly a single abolitionist can be found" in Kansas.[51] There were a few. The future state's first governor, Charles Robinson, was one. He had been a prominent leader in the squatter rights movement in California. Now he worked with Thayer's group and defended its efforts by binding its call for free soil with the cause of free labor, and as with prevailing attitudes across most of the West, that translated into racial threats to white workers.[52] Jim Lane said it clearly. When a runaway slave tried to join his free-soil army in 1856, Lane sent him back to his owner. He and his men were "not fighting to free black men," he said, "but to free white men."[53]

From that view, Kansas is best seen as a variation of what was unfolding across the new country—transforming the West into property. As everywhere else, this raised the question of whether slaveholders would be permitted to bring along what they claimed was their human property, and as just about everywhere else they were blocked by a majority who were determined to work or manipulate the land unthreatened by chattel labor.

Beyond that contest was another one, also being acted out across the West, especially in California. The 1850s saw the most frenzied period of land speculation in American history, with western values driven skyward by California gold, globally high commodity prices, and high immigration. Kansas, easily accessible and suddenly available, was the sharp focus of that energy. Efforts to control the land took three general forms vaguely divided by blurry lines: squatting, speculating, and concentrating land among a moneyed elite.

Not a square foot of the territory had been surveyed when it was opened, and early efforts were so incompetent that a year and a half later not a single township had been laid out.[54] This meant that early settlement was under the preemption system, by which firstcomers, squatters, could claim land and, once it was surveyed, could buy it as a minimal price. As in California, much of the earliest occupation of unsurveyed lands was by squatters acting out a traditional vision of an American future of independent family landholders profiting by developing the country. From this perspective Kansas was what one historian calls the "frontier cockpit of laissez-faire capitalism."[55] As a capitalist enterprise, however, many squatters were not raising their landed investment through sweat equity. Because no land had been surveyed, none could be sold. A squatter might claim a prime location, do nothing to develop it, acquire title once it was surveyed, then sell it for a fine profit to a later arrival. Squatter speculation by its nature could set neighbor against neighbor. Especially given the sloppiness and confusion, "claiming" was an interpretive enterprise with, as one observer put it, "the revolver and bowie-knife [as] certificates of title."[56] A close study shows the majority of violent conflicts, said at the time and since then to be over slavery, were in fact about personal squabbles and "the scramble for property."[57]

Struggles over carnal and landed property had one thing in common. Both turned savagely on the greatest casualties of Bleeding Kansas and of the West at large, the resident Indians. Nearly all land immediately across the Missouri border, land bound to be the first grabbed, had been parceled into reserves for more than a dozen tribes, some from the region, like the Osages and Kansas, and several only recently removed from the East: Ottawas, Pottawatomies, Miamis, Shawnees, Delawares, Kickapoos, and others. All were "weak and dispirited" after steep declines in population, and now politicians and officials, Missouri senator Thomas Hart Benton first among them, moved quickly to ease them aside.[58] Tribal reserves were reduced, supposedly to establish safe enclaves, and some called for further removal, but if so, William Seward asked, "where will it stop—the Himalayas?"[59] The director of the Indian Bureau, George Washington Moneypenny, thought that dogged effort by a "union of good influences" would avert imminent destruction and secure the tribes' "complete and thorough civilization."[60]

Moneypenny's bluff optimism was undercut by the rapid settlement and, especially, by the third effort to control the land—aggressive speculation on a wider scale by political and moneyed elites. The focus here was on town lots, timber rights, rights of way, and more. Its actors included Kansas's first territorial and state governors (who were at ideological poles) and the territorial secretary, attorney, and two Supreme Court justices. Army officers charged with expelling intruders on Indian land instead jumped into the action, forming land associations and pursuing various schemes.[61] After a treaty granted nicely timbered land near Topeka to mixed-blood children of Kansa Indians, the recipients were caught in a crossfire between more than sixty squatters and territorial officials, including Gov. Andrew Reeder. When the Indian agent appealed to the army, they arrested him for arson.[62] As others jumped in, including some in Congress, the Indians lost most of the land.

Then the grab intensified through what was already shaping so much of western life: railroads. In another Kansas anticipation of what would follow war, rail corporations partnered with the federal government and well compensated political allies to push aside both Indians and hopeful smalltime white landowners. At the time tens of thousands of acres were at stake. Later it would be tens of millions. New towns jockeyed for position on rail lines projected west to the Rockies, north to Nebraska, southwest to New Mexico, and south to Texas. All required some Indian land, and many needed a lot, and the federal government moved to secure what was needed from tribal reserves, then distributed it to corporate railroaders. The experience of the Delawares sums up what typically followed. First a treaty in 1860 substantially reduced their reserve and opened land well positioned for a run to the west. The Leavenworth, Pawnee and Western Railroad bought it for $1.28 per acre, far below what it would charge when it sold it, and it paid that with its own bonds. It did pay a prominent lobbyist ten thousand dollars in real money for helping smooth the way. By 1866 the Delawares had lost the rest of their reserved land through similar manipulations.[63]

What seemed to outsiders a struggle over the nation's moral core became increasingly a story of all sides finding common cause. Speculation trumped ideology. "The almighty dollar melted away the iron of bitterness," a New York journalist reported. What conflicts there were, another from Saint Louis added, amounted to a "stock-jobbers war" with the slavery question serving as a "bugaboo . . . introduced to give character" to the contest. Both exaggerated, but the trend was clear. Gov. Robert Walker wrote President Buchanan that proslavery squatters switched allegiance as soon as they saw that a free-soil claim brought a higher price, and the clearer the tide of profits, the more pro- and anti-slavery leaders joined in a "revelry of speculation." Lawrence and Delaware, once bitterly at odds, now joined in pursuit of a rail connection, and an editor wrote of the free-state militia leader Jim Lane and Missouri fire-eaters John Stringfellow and David Atchison investing together in town lots and "growing fat in their purses."[64]

Kansas was, in fact, as it appears in every history text: a field where the battle over the limits of African American slavery was disordering national politics. The view from the East has much to teach about the West's role in the Union's descent into its greatest crisis. The view from inside Kansas—from the other leaf of the hinge—shows a different picture largely obscured by the first. It recalls another in California half a dozen years earlier, and together the two capture a lot about the emerging West. The picture is of an immigrant swell into country wholly unprepared for it, a federal presence near comically inept and authorities deeply at odds, thousands of Indians displaced and dispossessed, with fully a fourth of Kansas, "and by all odds the best fourth," passing from Native hands.[65] The story is of contests over landed property, fired by passions around race and free labor, with the balance shifting from hardscrabble squatters to politicians and business and corporate kingpins. Charles Robinson, the abolitionist and squatter rights champion in both California and Kansas, emerged from his governorship as a wealthy speculator.

The Kansas story also suggests what lay ahead. After the war that it helped bring on, Kansas and its neighbor to the north would become the most rapidly growing part of the West. A far greater wash of immigrants would bring a speculative frenzy spread just as fully across all groups involved. As before the war, those in the East, now including emancipated slaves, would project onto Kansas their hopes of the West as the stage of better possibilities. Kansas was a hinge in both space and time, bridging the East and West during the turmoil before the war and bridging the past of national fracturing and a future of the national rebinding.

Between 1848 and 1860 the federal government took a greater range of actions over a larger span of space than ever before, yet its command over its new country was barely tentative. On paper it had brought nearly a billion acres under legal authority—governments that were rickety, divided, and often baffled in their most basic tasks. Its new policies toward Native peoples were ones of deepening misapprehensions that wound tensions ever tighter. In the Great Basin Washington faced down the most direct threat to its authority before secession then left largely in control a putative theocratic state restive and resentful and double the size of Texas. As Washington sent out unprecedented explorations of lands it called the stuff of common destiny, those lands, as perceived, were dividing the nation as never before and fracturing its political order. The forces set loose by expansion were less unifying than centrifugal. As the 1850s ended the older America threatened to split apart and the newer one to fly apart.

Strangely, one of the few questions clearly answered in the West was the one that dominated the East—whether Black slavery would truly expand into the new country. Indigenous unfree labor was well established, but Black slavery was chimerical where it was allowed, and elsewhere, as an Oregon politician put it, the odds were better that it would take root on the moon.[66] And yet as national leaders tried to dodge disaster, they looked for answers, of all places, in the West, focusing on New Mexico as a bargaining chip. Extend the Missouri Compromise line to California, some said, or ram through a bill making New Mexico formally a slave state. Lawmakers argued and railed, bargained and backed away. They tried a series of knobs to locked doors. In the end, they failed to agree.

Southwesterners yawned. "There is no excitement" over what was rocking affairs in the East, New Mexico's governor Abraham Rencher, a pro-slavery North Carolinian, wrote to William Seward: "It can never be otherwise. . . . No efforts on the part of designing men can ever disturb the public by agitating the question of slavery."[67] He wrote on April 14, 1861, the day after Maj. Robert Anderson surrendered the shattered Fort Sumter to the recently seceded South Carolina.

8 ➤ Continental Reckoning

Between 1861 and 1865 the nation survived the gravest crisis of its history. The crisis was continental, and so were its consequences. That point is easy to miss if attention is kept where it usually is, in the East. From that perspective the West's primary significance in the 1850s—its raising the issue of Black slavery's expansion—was moot once the war began. Its influence on the military confrontation of the Union and Confederacy was slight from the start and was altogether gone within a year. The very definition of the West shifted. The "war in the west" migrated eastward from New Mexico to Tennessee.[1]

When the perspective is widened to one from coast to coast, the West takes on a far greater significance. The prime question in the East was whether the Union would prevail on the battlefield. That in the West was whether the Union, should it survive, would continue to expand its power across the continent. Thus far that process had moved at a limp and a lurch, but during the next four years Washington made considerable strides toward binding the new country into the nation. It would do so by a brief, successful military effort, by making more real the West's filmy political structures, by legislation to empower the West in making a modern nation, and by securing command of movement through the country by assaults on its Native peoples.[2]

A Poor Effort Turned Back

The Confederacy began with high hopes of expanding to the far coast.[3] Its president, Jefferson Davis, pursued expansion "with an eye that never winked and a wing that never tired," according to a western Unionist, and his attorney general, Judah Benjamin, wrote that New Mexico was their new nation's "natural appendage" that opened "a pathway to the Pacific." At a glance there appeared to be just such a developing southern corridor. Roughly the lower half of New Mexico Territory—today's southern New Mexico and Arizona—was home to recent arrivals from the Southeast, and this desert country became all the more alluring after strikes of gold at Pinos Altos and silver at Cerro Colorado near Tucson. In March 1861 a convention in Mesilla, in today's New Mexico along the Mexican border, voted to secede as a separate territory. Farther on

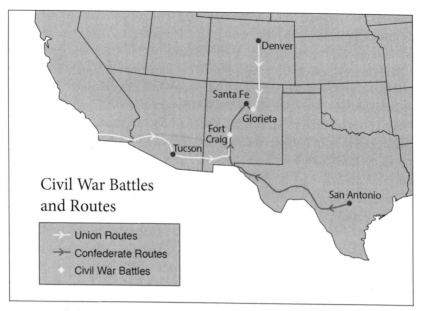

Civil War Battles and Routes

→ Union Routes
→ Confederate Routes
◆ Civil War Battles

MAP 3. An ill-fated incursion into New Mexico, turned back by mid-1862, ended any attempt by the Confederacy to control the West. Map by Maggie Rose Bridges.

in Southern California secessionist sympathy was strong in San Bernardino, Visalia, El Monte, and Los Angeles, where an editor called Lincoln a "driv-elling, idiotic, imbecile creature."[4] Gen. Edwin V. Sumner, commanding the Department of the Pacific early in the war, had no doubt of "deep scheming" in Southern California to create a "Republic of the Pacific" that would quickly join the Confederacy.[5]

In New Mexico the Union's Col. Edward R. S. Canby saw his command of fewer than 2,500 troops severely weakened when several key officers resigned to join the other side. Morale was low. Conditions seem to invite a Confederate invasion. It came in July 1861, when Lt. Col. John R. Baylor led a Texas regiment out of El Paso and occupied Mesilla after its panicked commander surrendered 500 veterans to 300 militia. An elated Baylor proclaimed on August 1 that all of New Mexico below the thirty-fourth parallel was now the new Confederate Territory of Arizona, with Mesilla its capital.[6] Canby responded by raising several volunteer companies in New Mexico and Colorado. As 1862 opened he had more than 5,000 men in arms.[7]

He would need them. In mid-December Confederate Brig. Gen. Henry H. Sibley arrived from San Antonio with a brigade of nearly 3,000 and took command from Baylor (see map 3). Once he controlled the Rio Grande, he would turn his aim toward the new gold fields to the north in Colorado. Its governor, William Gilpin, wrote that there were 7,500 Confederates in his territory and 64,500 men in arms in Indian Territory ready to attack.[8] This was delusion—Colorado was heavily Unionist—but Sibley might have thought the same, and more. After grabbing the gold fields, one of his officers wrote, "'On to San Francisco' would be the watchword" with thousands of western sympathizers. Once he added Utah to his bag, he would acquire northern Mexico by purchase or conquest.[9] In late January Sibley sent a cavalry company to Tucson to begin a link to Southern California and to ask Sonora's governor for access to northern Mexico—only to buy supplies and chase Indians, he assured him.[10]

First, however, Sibley had to defeat the Union troops at hand, and he got off to a good start.[11] In February he moved with 2,500 Texans up the Rio Grande and in a sharp engagement cut off Canby at Fort Craig from his support to the north.[12] This left him, too, with no line of supply, and he chose to press on and find what he needed in towns upriver. The gamble at first appeared to pay off. He occupied Albuquerque and sent Maj. Charles Pyron unopposed into Santa Fe. The capture of posts at Socorro and Cubero yielded badly needed arms (two Texas companies had carried only lances) and twenty-five wagonloads of supplies.[13] Now only Fort Union, northeast of Santa Fe, stood between him and full control of New Mexico. Sibley had served there. He knew that it had fewer than eight hundred troops and bulged with supplies he would need for his thrust at Colorado. The outlook seemed even rosier when Pyron reported that, remarkably, the enemy was coming to him. With about four hundred men Pyron went out to meet a column advancing from Fort Union.

It was not what he thought it was. Governor Gilpin had ordered the First Colorado Infantry from Forts Wise and Weld into New Mexico. Led by Col. John P. Slough and Maj. John M. Chivington, the regiment of mostly miners and Denver street toughs had left at the end of February and marched at "all possible and impossible speed" through snow and bitter winds. (In camp they huddled in tents warmed with Sibley stoves, patented in 1856 by the commander who waited for them in New Mexico.)[14] On March 11 the First Colorado reached Fort Union, having walked four hundred miles in thirteen days. After ten days' rest, Slough left with his volunteers and the fort's regulars and moved toward Santa Fe.

Fort Union sat along the "mountain route" of the Santa Fe Trail, which ran through the town of Las Vegas before curving around the southern tip of the Sangre de Cristo Mountains and up to Santa Fe. The key point on this stretch, commanding access in both directions, was the narrow and twisty Glorieta Pass at the base of the mountains. On March 26 Pyron was entering the pass from the west just as an advance group of Federals under Chivington entered from the east. After a hot skirmish both sides fell back to wait for reinforcement. Slough hurried in and Pyron was joined by Col. William Scurry. Now the sides were roughly equal. The showdown came on March 28, with Scurry commanding the rebels. The six-hour battle included charges and counter-charges, artillery duels and face-to-face fighting with pistols, fists, and knives, all in the narrow canyon bottom and the steep wooded slopes above it. Casualties were almost equal—110 Federals killed or wounded, 106 Confederates—but in the end Slough withdrew and Scurry held the field.

The decisive action took place elsewhere. Early that morning Chivington had led more than four hundred men in a wide arc, up out of the pass and across a rugged mesa thick with piñon pines, and four hours later, well behind Scurry's line, he was looking down on the thinly defended Confederate supply camp with more than sixty wagons of food, clothing, arms and ammunition, medicines, and forage for animals. On Chivington's order his men clambered two hundred feet down a canyon side so steep that some were lowered by ropes and leather straps, then charged and quickly dispersed the defenders. Confiscation was impractical, so Chivington ordered the wagons burned and virtually all of the more than five hundred horses and mules bayoneted.[15]

The animals' screams, the flames and the thunderous explosions from torched powder effectively marked the end for the Confederates. Having won every significant confrontation, the Confederates, stunningly, had no choice but to go home. Canby had come up from Fort Craig, and now he followed, far too timidly, his critics complained, but Sibley managed to bring his own disaster. Bottle fond and chronically over-tippling, he rode south in an ambulance with lots of whiskey and several women after ordering his men to avoid Fort Craig by a roadless hundred-mile bypass through desert mountains. As the Texans labored along on blistered feet through thick brushlands, with Apaches killing stragglers, the once-confident command unraveled. "Not a murmur escaped the lips of these brave boys," Sibley would claim, but in fact one of them wrote bitterly of knots of thirst-crazed men staggering leaderless, regretful that "the drunken individual who was the cause of all our misfortune" was not starving with them. Between twelve and seventeen hundred of the Texans, a third to a half of the command, died in the campaign. Sibley wrote that he was glad to leave New Mexico, "not worth a quarter of the blood and treasure" spent on it. No talk now of a conquered domain from San Francisco to Sonora.[16]

The invasion awakened Washington's concern about the West, with results that would shape the region profoundly. The shaping force came not out of Colorado but from California. While Confederate sentiment was strong in the state's southern counties, Unionists dominated the north, and news of Fort Sumter's fall brought a flood of enlistments. By 1865 California had raised 15,725 volunteers, a number roughly equal to the entire U.S. army at the outbreak of the war.[17] A sizable regiment was sent down to a new military district soon commanded by Col. James Henry Carleton. In early 1862, with Union control of Southern California reasonably secure, Gen. George Wright, head of the Department of the Pacific, ordered some of them to strike eastward, eventually to the Rio Grande, to short-circuit any connection between southeastern and Californian secessionists, secure gold and silver mines, man garrisons against Apaches, and hopefully reopen the stage route used before the war. By the time the expedition was being organized, a more pressing reason arose with the news that Texans were pushing into New Mexico.[18]

The command's leader, Carleton, would have an active role in the Southwest for the next five years. He cut quite a figure. Portraits show a forceful bearing and a rather fierce face with muttonchops, mustache, and features as firm and clean as a coin's. Carleton was a veteran of the Mexican War and of dragoon duty in the West. He had been among the first outsiders to see the grim remains of the Mountain Meadows Massacre and had reported, correctly, that Mormons had been behind the slaughter. He was an example of erudite officers often found in the service. He had literary aspirations—as a young man he exchanged letters with Charles Dickens—and in the field he wrote some dispatches in Greek and sent to the Smithsonian Institution minerals, scorpions, and a large meteorite he found being used as an anvil in a Tucson smithy.[19] Carleton could be stubborn, rigid, arrogant, and self-righteous, but he was brave, extraordinarily energetic, and utterly focused on whatever goal was before him.

The command, which came to be called the California column, began with 2,350 men in fifteen companies of infantry and cavalry and an artillery battery with four field pieces. They gathered in the spring of 1862 at Fort Yuma on the California border where the Gila River joined the Colorado. Carleton ordered his officers to "drill, drill, drill, until your men become perfect as soldiers, as skirmishers, as marksmen." The officers were to study tactics manuals until they could quote them verbatim.[20] Carleton himself began what was to be a long tutorial in desert campaigning. He dispatched the column not together but in groups that could find food, water, and forage more easily. The first set out in April. An advance patrol was captured by Confederate skirmishers, and in the Civil War's westernmost "battle" (only twenty-two men were involved) at Picacho Pass northeast of Tucson, three Federals were killed, but in Tucson the Confederate leader, Maj. Sherod Hunter, wisely withdrew his tiny command and headed for the Rio Grande to alert Sibley of the threat from the West. The first federal unit entered Tucson on May 20 with a small band playing "Yankee Doodle." Carleton arrived on June 6, soon after learning of his promotion to brigadier general.[21]

The Californians arrived in New Mexico well after the surviving Texans had limped away. Carleton soon took over the Department of New Mexico and occupied El Paso, Fort Davis, and other posts in west Texas. The Confederate Territory of Arizona persisted on paper until the end of the war although its capital was moved six hundred miles to the southeast to San Antonio.[22] Besides the scuffle at Picacho Pass, the California column had fought no rebels, but their crossing to the Rio Grande held a hint of what was ahead. Apaches killed and mutilated three troopers and fought two companies for four hours for control of a vital spring.[23]

The confederacy held out hopes in grabbing at least part of the West. Jefferson Davis authorized a soldier of fortune to clear a path through New Mexico to the Pacific and issued a letter of marque for a privateer to capture gold shipments out of San Francisco. Neither showed up. Rumors persisted of crafty rebel agents angling for gold mines in Idaho and courting allies among Indians and Mormons. All were baseless.[24] By the fall of 1862, as Robert E. Lee prepared for his first move into Union territory, the Civil War in the far West, insofar as its influence on the military balance in the East, was over.

It had never amounted to much. Sibley's campaign and defeat would be described grandly—the fight at Glorieta Pass was the "Gettysburg of the West"— but it is difficult to imagine how the Confederacy could have found any long-term purchase in the new country.[25] The only Confederate portal into the West was New Mexico. Despite Sibley's flush of victories, he would have been unlikely to hold onto it. Union forces had clear access to the staunchly Unionist Colorado, then a clear shot southward, while the Confederacy's support would have to come across six hundred tortured miles through Comanche country between San Antonio and El Paso. In one of his few credible statements toward the end, Sibley itemized the difficulties there: food was scarce, the Indians hostile, and New Mexicans loathed Texans. There were islands of Confederate sympathy in the larger West, but the great majority leaned the other way. On balance southern hopes of controlling the West were like prewar aspirations of planting Black slavery there: pipedreams.

The Political Dance

The near-death experience of the political order in the East had its positive consequences in the West. With southeastern legislators out of Congress, the way opened for measures they had blocked, in particular ones promoting western settlement by freeholding families, who would surely oppose introducing

Black slavery, and financing of a rail connection between the free states and California. Within forty-one days in late spring and early summer 1862, President Lincoln signed into law the Homestead and Pacific Railway Acts. The first offered 160 acres on the public domain not already committed to anyone twenty-one or older, including the foreign-born intending to become citizens, as long as they occupied the land for a designated time, made certain improvements, and paid nominal fees. The second set up an arrangement, anticipated in earlier federal support for the Illinois Central Railroad, by which Washington would donate enormous amounts of land and would loan as bonds the prodigious funds needed to construct a railroad that would follow some variation of the main overland trail to the Pacific.

Since 1848 a homestead law had been high on the platform of the Free Soil and then the Republican Parties, and the railway act was part of the continuing federal effort to forge connections from the older republic through and around the new country. Each law would influence considerably the settlement and economic course of the postwar West, and so doing each would illustrate the contributions, shortcomings, and contradictions of federal power. Both would be central to the ongoing issue of the distribution of the West as resources and property.

The question of African slavery in the West was put finally to rest in June 1862, between the homestead and railway acts, when Congress forbade it in all territories, present and future. The West did play a role in the question's national resolution. By the time the Thirteenth Amendment was before Congress, four western states were represented: California, Oregon, Kansas, and Nevada. A persistent tradition has President Lincoln maneuvering to have Nevada hastily admitted in time for its favorable vote in a crucial test in the House. The story is at least exaggerated and likely off the mark entirely. Lincoln may have pressed for admission for the state's electoral votes, but it was Radical Republicans, more than the president, who pushed for Nevada's admission as part of their reconstruction strategy.[26] The West's delegation did, however, support the amendment overwhelmingly, with only one of twelve, California senator James A. McDougall (by then a dysfunctional alcoholic who, in his rare appearances on the floor, often dressed as a vaquero) voting nay.[27] Thus the issue's ironies continued. Before the war the possibility of Black slavery truly taking root was remote to the point of vanishing. Then, although the West had opposed abolitionism nearly as much as slavery's expansion, in the war's final stages western support for killing the institution was stronger than in New England.

De facto slavery continued, however, as did the slaughter in California. As regular troops were transferred eastward, thousands of civilians answered the call to service. They were much the same elements that had formed the

Native American Conflicts and Massacres

- 1863 Punitive Expedition
- 1864 Punitive Expedition
- - Overland and Santa Fe Trails
- Long Walk
- ◆ Native American Conflicts

Fort Rice

Oregon City

Boise

Bear River

Fort Pierre

Dakota War

Sioux City

Overland Trail

Salt Lake City

Sacramento

Sand Creek ◆

Santa Fe Trail

Canyon de Chelley ◆

Santa Fe

MAP 4. More significant fighting was against Native peoples. New strategies were used to secure routes of movement around the West. By war's end the military defeat of Indian America was well under way. Map by Maggie Rose Bridges.

Indian-hunting militias, except now, instead of joining in hopes of future pay, they were assured of regular pay from Washington—a lure sweetened when the California legislature provided an extra five dollars per month. Some California volunteers would be sent into the interior, including into Utah to crush the Shoshone camp at Bear River, but nearly six thousand remained to take part in a strengthened "killing machine." From 1862 through 1864 hundreds among the Yana, Whilkut, Paiute-Shoshone, Lassik, and other groups were killed.[28] Congress continued its support; a bill providing $400,000 for militias was introduced the day after South Carolina seceded.[29] As for the reserves, an agent at Round Valley reported conditions far better than elsewhere, then reported that women and children, lacking hoes, were digging in the fields with their fingers. Three-quarters of the residents slept in the open and on the

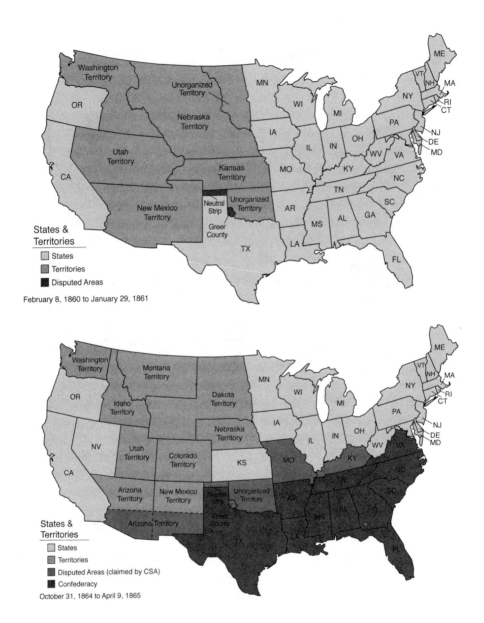

MAP 5. States and territories 1860–61 (*top map*) and 1864–65. As the fate of the nation's political order was being decided on eastern battlefields, its western side was being organized with extraordinary speed. Two states and five territories were created in five years. Maps by Maggie Rose Bridges.

ground, while "not a whole blanket could be found among 100 Indians." The daily ration was reportedly two or three ears of corn per person.[30] Anyone fleeing was subject to arrest and indenture. As Union forces fought a war in the East that would end Black slavery, troops on the far coast were helping to devastate Native populations, enslave many survivors, and leave others confined to reserves as grim as the Confederate prison camp at Andersonville.

The wartime Congress's most consequential impact on the West was in extending its most elemental means of control, political organization (see map 5). In 1860 the West (excluding Texas, which would soon secede) had six territories and a pair of states. Five years later there were ten territories and four states—an arrangement that would remain essentially in place for thirty-five years. Kansas was admitted as a state, and Dakota and Colorado were made territories in 1861. In 1863 Idaho and Arizona Territories were created, and the next year Montana became a territory and Nevada a state. Keeping track of the political map could be dizzying. Someone living in today's Helena, Montana, at the start of 1861 would have had to adjust his address three times in the next three years—to Dakota in March 1861 to Idaho in 1863, then Montana in 1864.

As before the war, creating territories was ad hoc and reactive. Colorado, Nevada, Idaho, and Montana came to life because gold and silver strikes created clusters of populations far from any formal authority; Dakota Territory was born because farmers moving in from Nebraska and the Midwest needed to secure title to land and to establish the civil basics, including public schools. Boundaries were as geographically nonsensical as ever. Colorado and Montana had rugged mountains in the west, rolling plains in the east. Southern Idaho was part of the Great Basin, its northern parts some of the least accessible portions of the Rocky Mountains.

The dance between national and western politics continued. In Utah Lincoln's victory left him with a conundrum. He inherited a tense relationship in wake of Buchanan's Utah War, and his party's platform had partnered polygamy with Black slavery as one of the "twin relics of barbarism," but he could not afford even to flirt with any confrontation with Deseret, and he desperately needed Brigham Young's cooperation in keeping open the overland lifeline to California. Lincoln's appointments of territorial governor and judges especially raised the Saints' ire. Lincoln's first governor, Stephen S. Harding, attacked polygamy, suggested the Saints were disloyal during the great crisis, and called for curtailing the church's role in government.[31] As before, judges provoked special hostility. At one point Young told his followers to refuse jury duty. Lincoln's response was typically pragmatic, and he explained it with typical folksiness. When Young sent an emissary to feel out the president's intentions, Lincoln recalled his boyhood days in helping to prepare fields for planting. Families sometimes faced a fallen tree that was too big to move, too tough to split, and too green to burn, "so we plowed around it. That's what I intend to do. . . . Tell Brigham Young that if he will let me alone, I will let him alone."[32]

The one consistent theme in western territories during the war was patronage and the political jockeying around it. The president had seven positions to fill in each territory: governor, secretary, three judges, a marshal, and commissioner of the land office. The positions were political currency used to repay party loyalists. Usually they were from the East; only fourteen of the first chosen by Lincoln, fewer than one in five, were from the territories where they would serve.[33] The predictable result was more fractious relations and heated competition for the posts among eastern factions, not to mention the frequent bafflement of appointees walking into alien circumstances. Concerned that New Mexicans might prove restive and even lean toward the Confederacy, the president first filled the posts with local Democrats, the party of the legislative majority and of Carleton, the autocratic military commander. Then, after the Confederate campaign into New Mexico collapsed, Lincoln named as territorial secretary W. F. M. "Alphabet" Arny, an ardent abolitionist and Radical Republican. The public was treated to accusations of drunkenness and bribery, inventive insults (the chief justice called Arny a "moronic maniac"), a writ of replevin to recover the territorial seal, and intense struggles over who was rightfully the Santa Fe postmaster and territorial librarian. (In the former spat Arny stormed the post office and demanded a count of the stamps.)[34]

Lincoln over time named Radical Republicans to many key offices—in the national administration the secretary of the interior and commissioner of the General Land Office, and in the territories nearly every governor as well as many judges, secretaries, and surveyors general. This left Republicans generally, and Radicals specifically, well placed to shape territorial policies, including disposal of lands, and an early historian suggested that radicals would use territories as "'pilot plants' for the later reconstruction of the South."[35] Western politics, however, was nowhere near as coherent as that might suggest. Republicans could be as rancorous with one another as with Democrats, who were themselves divided between a minority of Southern sympathizers and those supporting the Union. Everyone, whatever their political stripe, squared off over offices, contracts, and the many enticements of the developing region. In Oregon the governor and both senators were Unionist Democrats, opposing the Confederacy yet not all aboard with all Lincoln's policies, either, while Republicans maneuvered for advantage among themselves, blurring the party's focus on territorial issues.[36]

In California, too, Republicans with Unionist Democrat allies seemed in firm control. The first legislature elected during the war endorsed the Emancipation Proclamation, passed laws including death for anyone arming a ship against the Union, and removed the ban on Blacks and mulattoes testifying against whites in court. But here again the mix was unstable. Politics generally were what Gov. Frederick Low called "an infernal jumble." Congress's Legal Tender and National Banking Acts were unpopular in a state staunchly in favor of hard currency. The Emancipation Proclamation aroused furious protests; the Democratic Convention in 1863 resolved that it would prolong the bloody war and "close the door forever" on readmission of the seceded states. When war critics were briefly jailed, including the chair of the party's state committee, Democrats condemned a subversion of the freedom of speech and the press. Playing on such issues, Democrats steadily gained strength. After Appomattox they would again assume control.[37]

Politics reached their peak of testiness in the infant Montana Territory, created in the spring of 1864. As organized warfare wound down in Missouri and Arkansas, large numbers of southern veterans gravitated to gold strikes around Helena and Virginia City. Collectively nicknamed "General Price's left wing" after Missouri's best-known Confederate leader, they quickly made their mark, starting with Montana's first capital. Until a judge discreetly changed its name to Virginia City, it was "Varina City" in honor of Jefferson Davis's wife. With not two but three major factions, the others being Republicans and Unionist Democrats, and with the Republicans being both the smallest and the one with the closest ties in Washington, the first few years verged on political chaos. There were rhetorical salvos of "traitors" and "n--r lovers." Duels were proposed. Southern noses were thumbed and bloody shirts were waved. Otherwise, however, little was accomplished. The muddle continued after the war. Thomas Francis Meagher, an Irish revolutionary once exiled to Tasmania, was appointed governor after distinguished service from first Bull Run through Chancellorsville. He presided over bitter divisions before falling from a steamboat into the Missouri River, either by homicidal shove or accidental trip or drunken stumble. The second and third territorial assemblies were so caught up in wrangling with Washington that Congress declared both of them null and void.[38]

Somehow out of this brawling, new territorial governments had to set up the structural fundamentals and to cope with distinctive western problems. Finances presented a classic chicken-and-egg dilemma. Most income eventually would come from real-estate taxes, but no land could be taxed until it was owned, and none could be owned without surveys, which had barely started. In the meantime legislatures raised stopgap funds through general property taxes and licenses on most businesses, and with nothing to pay for roads or other public necessities, they chartered private companies to take up the slack. Charters in turn were one of many economic plums, including offices, suddenly up for grabs and, often enough, up for sale. Contracts for supplying reservations and building and supporting military posts were hungrily sought. Nearly everyone in the early governments was a lawyer, speculator, surveyor, or land agent, all jockeying for the best Washington connections and ever on the sniff for the main chance. W. W. Brookings, a leader in Dakota Territory's first council, hobbled around on stubs, his feet mostly amputated after he froze them in a blizzard while rushing to claim a townsite. In an age infamous for corruption, western states and territories set a standard of crassness rarely matched elsewhere. Dakota's assembly granted a lavish charter to a railroad, but only after every member had been made a partner.[39] Nevada's first legislature granted so many toll road franchises, Mark Twain wrote, that unless Congress gave the territory another degree or two of longitude, the roads would hang over its boundaries "like a fringe."[40] The infighting could seem a parody of western bluster. In the contest over locating Dakota's capital, the speaker of the house resigned after learning his colleagues planned to throw him through a second-story window. (The sergeant-at-arms later tossed him through a saloon window anyway.)[41]

And yet capitals *were* established, and with them the essentials of a legal and economic order. Between 1861 and 1865 an area a little less than half of all territory acquired in expansion of the 1840s, much of it previously beyond the federal reach, was organized politically. Even in Montana, before the two Legislatures That Never Were, the first one wrote criminal codes and probate regulations, passed laws governing mining claims, cattle brands, irrigation, and town charters, created counties, and provided for public schools.[42] Colorado did all that, plus authorizing a branch mint, creating a state militia, fixing interest rates, and providing for a university at Boulder (though it would be years before it opened).[43] The new order had its western wrinkles—in Colorado the minimum sentence for stealing a cow worth ten dollars or more was triple the maximum sentence for kidnapping—but the governments beginning to sputter into operation showed a profoundly conservative impulse.[44] They represented an unquestioned projection east to west, a replication of institutions rooted three centuries deep. They expressed a common polity, a collective past, and assumed values that lay beneath the flashier obvious—the corruption, the incompetence, and the occasional defenestration. The point is easy to miss, writes its clearest advocate, because it is so elemental and "so organic a part of national development."[45]

The very dysfunctional weirdness of early territories could make the point. In early 1864 Idaho's second territorial legislature voted to move the capital from Lewiston to Boise. Lewiston leaders issued an injunction forbidding removal of the state seal and archives and subpoenaed Gov. Caleb Lyon to explain himself. Saying he was off to hunt ducks, he fled to Washington Territory. To keep the territorial secretary in place the sheriff issued a writ of *ne exeat*, a court order originally used to keep feudal armies in the field and more recently to collect alimony. Meanwhile, the new government in Boise considered itself paralyzed without the imprimatur of the seal. The dustup was finally resolved after sixteen months when the new secretary, Clinton DeWitt Smith, helped by a military escort and a muscled bartender from San Francisco, departed for Boise with the seal. Furious Lewistonites locked the departed officials' furniture in the local jail, but their legal recourse was exhausted.[46]

Consider the context of this opéra-bouffe. Washington's true command of Idaho was years in the future. Living there and in the region were some of the West's most formidable Native peoples, whose power was mostly unfazed, the Nez Perces west of the Rockies and the Lakotas and Northern Cheyennes on the plains. It was isolated from much of the nation and divided within itself. A delegate from Virginia City could reach the first legislature in Lewiston, about five hundred miles away, only by traveling more than four times as far, via Salt Lake City, San Francisco, and Portland. Travel crudities and Indian troubles delayed Smith so long on the East Coast that he finally traveled via Panama. He was eight months coming to Idaho, long enough to cross the Atlantic half a dozen times. And yet, as the arcane maneuvering showed, laws were there, on the books but more importantly in the heads of men otherwise out to take full advantage of the place. A tissue of tradition reached across the continent and backward through centuries. The first politicos might jigger the rules and push against the boundaries, but they stayed inside them. That impulse was as much a part of making the West as anything else.

9 ▷ Civil War and the "Indian Problem"

The contest between Federals and Confederates in the West was over inside of a year, but the fighting was not. The nation's violent reordering that had begun more than a decade earlier continued after Fort Sumter (see map 4). Its focus stayed where it had been, in confrontations between newcomers who were trying, however imperfectly, to set a new order in place and the Indian peoples who were trying to maintain an ancient independence. In the war to preserve the continent-wide union, the military's prime contribution was to tip the balance in the West in its favor. That work was done pursuing another basic goal of unification, the control of movement across and around the western half of the new nation. In 1865 Indian resistance was far from fully broken, but the crippling was underway.

Some of its bloodiest particulars came along the seam between East and West. They brought to an end an earlier chapter of expansion and its failed effort to solve its ironically named "Indian problem."

An End and a Beginning

Territorial growth of the 1840s raised the question of what would happen to the tribes recently removed to present-day Oklahoma and Kansas. With other resident groups, they were now squarely in the path of expansion, not *out of* the way but *in* it. Kansas of the 1850s gave a hint of what they could expect. Delawares, Otoes, Pottawatomies, Pawnees, and others found their promised reserves reduced and invaded. Many were ousted entirely and sent to join removed tribes in the increasingly crowded Indian Territory to the south. Then the Civil War quickly caught them all in its jaws. Their experience, and another variant in Minnesota, made up one of the grimmest stories of those grim years.[1]

Outnumbered and open to attacks from Arkansas and Texas, federal troops withdrew from Indian Territory into Kansas almost immediately, and the Confederacy quickly moved to court support from the Cherokees, Creeks, Choctaws, Chickasaws, and Seminoles, the "Civilized" Tribes removed from the Southeast during the 1830s. There was Union support especially among the Creeks and Cherokee followers of the aging chief John Ross, and long-standing convoluted intertribal feuds refracted into conflicts over the sectional crisis, but with many slaveholders among the tribes and with no federal support, Confederate pressure was irresistible. First the Chickasaws and Choctaws signed treaties, then the wavering Creeks and Seminoles, and finally John Ross, feeling abandoned and vulnerable, fell into line in October of 1861.[2]

The treaties, however, could not paper over divisions, which flared into one of the least recognized tragedies of the war. The strongest Union supporter among tribal leaders was the elderly Creek chief Opothleyahola. As the diplomatic tide became clear, he withdrew with supporters to an encampment on the Canadian River in the fall of 1861. Many more Unionists from other groups had joined him when Confederate Indian troops moved toward them in late November. A long caravan, some afoot and others on horseback and in wagons, carriages, and buggies, retreated northward toward hopeful refuge in Kansas. When a larger force reinforced by Texas cavalry struck again, Opothleyahola's fatigued warriors were routed so quickly that the panicked camp left behind virtually all conveyances and most supplies and food as they fled over the Kansas line. Within hours a vicious winter storm struck the refugees, some of them shoeless and all thinly clothed and hungry.[3]

As more Union sympathizers stumbled in, conditions descended into horror. An army surgeon in late January found about 4,500 persons along the Verdigris River and heard of many more scattered along other streams. It was "impossible . . . to depict the wretchedness of their condition," he wrote. The clothes of most were worn to shreds. Some were wholly naked. It was bitterly cold, yet for shelter most had only "scraps and rags stretched upon switches." For relief of the several thousand refugees he received three dozen small quilts, forty pairs of socks, three pair of pants, and assorted other items.[4] The bacon sent later was "suitable only for soap grease." As the numbers kept growing—around 7,600 by April—another doctor reported amputating more than a hundred frozen limbs.[5] Warm weather brought its own problems. All camped along the Verdigris had to move to flee the stench from the thawed and rotting carcasses of about two hundred horses. Eventually most found temporary homes on lands of nearby Indians and at Forts Scott and Leavenworth.[6]

In 1863 Union forces regained control of the territory above the Arkansas River. From Fort Gibson they struck periodically against Confederates to the south, winning a signal victory at Honey Springs in July, but poorly supplied and hampered by squabbling commanders, they could not fully prevail. Neither could their opponents. The contest degenerated into two years of grinding guerilla attacks by Confederates, led finally by the Cherokee general Stand Watie (who in June of 1865 would be the last Confederate of that rank to surrender), and ineffectual federal response. In 1864 about five thousand survivors of the Kansas ordeal marched to Fort Gibson to join about ten thousand others already there. And there they stayed, penned up by the near anarchy in the country around and starved by the wholly inadequate support from distant authorities.

At war's end the Indian Territory, while on the far edge of military concern, was as devastated as the most ravaged parts of the Southeast. Where there had been flourishing cattle herds before the war, wrote an investigating army officer, "now scarcely a head can be seen in a ride of 200 miles." Many had been taken by rebels and bushwhackers, but most by far—one estimate was three hundred thousand head worth $4.5 million—had been rustled by white Kansans and sold at huge profits. The place had gone feral. Wild game dominated and "wolves howl dismally over the land."[7] The human toll was horrific. Diseases, especially malaria, dysentery, and venereal disorders, flourished among refugees. Many had fled southward into Texas, where some would stay as others trickled back to wasted homes. Between deaths and those who left the territory, the Cherokee population by one estimate dropped from twenty-one thousand to around fifteen thousand, and a census in 1863 showed a third of their adult women were widows and a fourth of their children orphans.[8]

Meanwhile another bloody episode was unfolding six hundred miles to the north.[9] Minnesota was originally the home of all the Sioux people. During the preceding century and a half many had moved westward, some (Nakotas or Yanktons) to settle close to the Missouri River. Others (Lakotas or Tetons) shifted farther west around the Black Hills and rode the grass revolution to become the dominant power of the northern plains. Those who remained, the Dakota or Santee Sioux, were feeling the pressure of one of the most rapidly growing frontiers in the nation. During the 1850s Minnesota's non-Indian population grew from just over 6,000 to more than 172,000. Most were farmers, and many were drawn to the rich woodlands and fertile prairies in the southwestern part of the state along the Minnesota River, home to the Dakotas. In 1851 the Dakotas agreed to live along a 150-mile stretch of the river, ten miles deep on each side, and seven years later they gave up half of that, the north side of the stream, in return for annual payments of money to buy supplies. Inefficiency and graft scandalous even by standards of the day, however, delayed and bled away the annuities; by one account the total provided by 1862 averaged fifteen dollars per person.[10]

Meanwhile the settlers' harvest of game and environmental transformations hobbled the work of hunting and gathering, while government programs to convert the Dakotas to agriculture had slim results and created a deep division between hunting and farming factions. By the summer of 1862 the Dakota economy was tottering, and in August it was brought to a crisis when traders refused to extend credit until current bills were paid, something impossible without annuities. Traders' attitudes did not help. "If they are hungry," one of them infamously said, "let them eat grass."[11] There are hints that the Dakotas saw the Civil War as an opening to strike back. "It began to be whispered about," Big Eagle recalled, that with so many whites away there could be little response to an uprising that might "clean out the country" of settlers. In a bizarre scrambling of current issues, the Dakotas were further alarmed by fears that "n--s" had seized control of the national capital and would take their annuity money for themselves.[12]

The tension snapped on August 17 when four young Dakotas killed three men, a woman, and a teenaged girl. Warriors of the anti-farming faction immediately argued for an all-out assault, and a prominent leader, Little Crow, after arguing against the plan, finally agreed to take the lead. He struck fast. The next morning warriors killed several men at the Redwood Agency, including the "eat grass" trader, and when a command of nearly fifty soldiers came in response from nearby Fort Ridgely, the Dakotas killed about half of them in an ambush.

Dakotas could probably have overrun Fort Ridgely, but most turned instead against nearby settlers, many of them recent German immigrants. In dozens of attacks over the next days warriors killed hundreds and took scores more as hostages. Thousands of others fled the region. The town of New Ulm, where hundreds of settlers had taken refuge, was nearly overrun and much of it burned during a daylong assault on August 23. By the time Fort Ridgely was finally reinforced on August 27 by 1,500 militia under a former Minnesota governor, Col. Henry Hastings Sibley (no relation to the Confederate commander in New Mexico), the main body of Dakotas had withdrawn toward the north end of the reservation. Sibley followed and on September 23 defeated them at Wood Lake. Soon 269 captives were freed, but the toll among settlers was huge, between 700 and 1,000. It was the heaviest loss of life among whites of any Indian conflict in the nation's history.

Sibley had all warriors who remained in Minnesota arrested. Although their trials were before a military tribunal, the offenses were treated as criminal acts, so simply firing a weapon in a battle brought a capital conviction. In hearings often lasting only minutes, 303 out of 392 tried were sentenced to death by hanging. At the urging of religious leaders, President Lincoln reviewed all trial materials and reduced to prison time the sentences of all but thirty-nine men he concluded were guilty of murder and rape. One sentence was later reduced. A little before ten in the morning on the day after Christmas, 1862, the condemned marched from their cells to a collective gallows in the town of

Mankato. Arms pinioned, some painted in bright ocher, they sang and swayed as they walked toward the gallows. As soldiers placed hoods over their heads one managed to bare and thrust his genitals at the crowd of about three thousand. At an officer's command a single rope then was cut to spring all the trap doors at once.[13] It was by far the largest mass execution in American history. Those convicted but spared hanging were sent to a prison in Davenport, Iowa, where a third of them died before survivors were released three years later.

Little Crow and a few hundred others had fled westward onto the plains, where he tried to enlist Yankton Sioux, other tribes, and even the British in Canada to continue the war. He returned to Minnesota with his son in early July of 1863 and was shot and killed by a farmer while the two were picking berries. His body was taken to a nearby town and defiled, with young boys exploding firecrackers in his nostrils on Independence Day, before being decapitated and tossed into an offal pit. His head was displayed for more than fifty years in the state historical society.[14]

Between the hangings and imprisonments, more than a thousand Dakota women, children, and elderly were left as unsupported dependents. White opinion overwhelmingly agreed with one editor on what to do with them: "Punishment and Expulsion!" He proposed exiling not only them but Minnesota's Chippewas, Winnebagoes, and Menominees, plus the Yankton and Lakota Sioux, on Isle Royale in Lake Superior.[15] Instead the Dakota remnant of 1,318 persons were taken by steamboat in May of 1863 to Crow Creek on the Missouri River in central South Dakota.[16] Soon several hundred Winnebagoes, who had no connection to the uprising, were sent to join them.[17] Conditions slid quickly toward crisis. The refugees planted corn on the barren river flats, but most of it never sprouted and drought destroyed what little did.[18] During the winter provisions amounted to about eight ounces per person a day, much of it in the form of a thin soup made from flour and some beans, pork, and beef, including heads and unemptied intestines. A missionary who came with the Dakotas estimated two hundred deaths in the first six months, and by the spring of 1864 a quarter had died.[19] To get by, women gathered wild plants (and, according to one, picked undigested grain from horse manure) and serviced nearby whites by cutting wood, washing clothes, and engaging in prostitution. In 1866 the survivors were moved to a somewhat more promising reservation downstream, where they were joined by their men who had survived imprisonment in Iowa.

Meanwhile the military used the occasion to expand its presence. There had been reports of Santee and Lakota bands uniting in opposition and even working on an alliance with Missouri River tribes.[20] In the summer of 1863 Maj. Gen. John Pope, commanding the new Department of the Northwest, sent Sibley and Brig. Gen. Alfred Sully into Dakota Territory in pursuit of those who had fled onto the plains. Sibley reported killing 150 Santee warriors in a fight, Sully claimed twice that as well as three hundred lodges and half a million pounds of bison meat burned.[21] The next summer Sully's men killed an undetermined number of warriors at a huge encampment at Killdeer Mountain on the Little Missouri River and spent the next day stacking and firing the skins and poles of hundreds of lodges and vast stores of supplies.

The campaigns clearly were meant for more than chastisement. Besides likely settlement under the Homestead Act, passed a few months before the uprising, the northern plains offered the most direct access to gold strikes in Washington Territory and Montana in 1862 and 1863. After Killdeer Mountain Sully marched westward through parched, grass-poor badlands between the Little Missouri and Yellowstone Rivers, territory never before challenged by the military.[22] With him were more than two hundred immigrants in 123 wagons bound for the gold fields. He left two companies at prominent trading posts, and Pope soon had three posts constructed. It was bound to cause trouble. This was heartland to the Lakotas and Northern Cheyennes, who knew from experience along the Platte what a passway for wagons, punctuated by posts, would mean. As early as 1862 even friendlier Lakota leaders spoke to their agent in "bitterness" against any further intrusion. They would brook no attempt at a route across the northern plains.[23]

The Minnesota uprising and removal and the disaster in Indian Territory ended an era begun more than six decades earlier. The dismal end of one policy overlapped with another. The formal goal of both was the integration of Native peoples, but the newer approach had to wait on the suppression of any resistance from western Indians. It was here, more than deflecting the Confederacy's weak and abortive jab, that the military would secure the Union's continental future. A critical step was fitting wartime strategies to the realities of the new country. Among the lessons was the usefulness of the weather.

The Winter of Native Power

A key to understanding what happened is in the western environment. As Indians in California were suffering the greatest calamity of Native history, the return of the horse had blessed thousands in the interior grasslands with unprecedented power and affluence. Their mounted elusiveness frustrated the federal military's efforts to find and confront them. The same environment that offered such freedom to move, however, periodically restrained it. That left horseback Indians vulnerable. During the Civil War the army began to learn how to exploit that vulnerability to lethal effect.

Command of the West in large part came down to controlling who could move around it, and how, and when, and on what terms. That meant that one of the government's first and most pressing roles was the surveying, building, and improving of roads. Once made, roads had to be kept open, all the more so during the crisis of disunion. That, it turned out, was the rub. Nearly all Indian conflicts between 1861 and 1865 were outgrowths of efforts to secure the systems of movement that had begun to tie the West together. The government's immediate concern was less to control Indians than to control roads, which meant not so much commanding Indians as keeping them out of the way. Staying away, however, was exactly what many groups could not do. Consequently, what might seem an unobtrusive job, maintaining the flow of people and things across the land, all but guaranteed conflict between Natives and newcomers.

The reason had to do with two geographical facts of life. First, the West is extraordinarily rugged. The lefthand third of a national topographical map is a mass of wrinkles, mountains rising up to fourteen thousand feet above sea level. Virtually all of them run north and south, so travelers moving toward the Pacific were forever coming up against massive stone walls blocking the way. They had to find ways across, and there were not many options. Second, outside the Pacific Northwest and the highest elevations elsewhere, most of the West is relatively arid. Anyone crossing it had to have access to enough water to finish the trip.

Mountains and aridity: both pointed toward the same thing—rivers. Flowing water and human immigrants both sought out the easiest ways through the wrinkled West. In particular a river running east or west off some saddle of a north-to-south mountain range offered both a rare path through an otherwise impenetrable barrier as well as water, trees for fuel, and forage for draft animals. As a result immigration and trade essentially moved via interlocking watersheds of the most eligible streams. The main overland route used the Platte, Clearwater, Humboldt, Carson, Truckee, Snake, and Columbia Rivers; that across the Southwest ran along the Rio Grande, San Pedro, Santa Cruz, Gila, and Colorado. Whenever some new part of the interior drew interest, typically through a gold or silver strike, the first impulse was to ask which river best opened the way to it.

The features that made rivers natural highways made them also natural places for Indians to live. Rivers gave them what they gave to overlanders, water, forage, and trees for fuel. Especially in the arid areas like the Great Basin, rivers provided irreplaceable food sources—bulbs, roots, berries, and the seeds of grasses that grew along the swards in the warm months. Rivers were especially valuable in winter. Horseback Indians would repair to carefully chosen spots with protective trees and slightly lower elevation as refuges from storms and cold. What were roads to whites, then, were to Indians homes and pantries.

The two sets of needs were hopelessly at odds. Returning in autumn from their summer progress of gathering and hunting, Indians found that the annual march of immigrants and their animals along rivers had cut the stands of cotton-woods for firewood and had devoured the forage crucial in the coming months, leaving them, as an agent wrote in 1855 along the Humboldt, with nothing to eat "but ground squirrels and pis-ants."[24] Direct contact with travelers risked exposure to a variety of diseases. A prime national imperative, making and maintaining a continental connection, was in catastrophic contradiction to lives of thousands of Native peoples. They responded accordingly.

The point was made early and bloodily along the California trail through Utah and Nevada Territories. Besides the toll taken by overland traffic, Mormons had settled on many of the Indians' best sites, including the Cache River Valley, home to the Northern Shoshones. With the war the trail became the mail route to California with dozens of stage stations and thousands of horses to provide "safe and speedy transportation of mail and treasure."[25] By the winter of 1861–62 Indians were starving along the Humboldt. On abortive experimental farms Goshutes were freezing to death and parents, unable to feed their babies, "*laid them by the stone*," an agent wrote, "which means that they had laid them on the ground to die and be eaten by the wolves."[26] Then, in 1862, came another blow. Miners heading for new gold strikes in Montana poured through the Cache Valley. Attacks rose sharply, and hundreds of Indians mobbed stage stations, "clamorous for food and threatening." Washington ordered more than a thousand volunteer cavalry and infantry from California to keep the trail open.[27]

Leading them was Col. Patrick Edward Connor. Irish-born (indeed, on Saint Patrick's Day), he had fought in the Mexican War, left the service for California gold, then reenlisted in 1861. He had a trim frame, a beard à la Souvaroff, courage, and an aggressive, self-promoting personality. Connor arrived in Utah in late summer 1862.[28] He despised Mormons—they were all "traitors, murderers, fanatics, and whores"—and established Fort Douglas at a commanding position overlooking Salt Lake City, but his primary call was to secure the overland road, and by mid-fall his command was "poised like a sledgehammer in midair." The blow followed a series of confrontations—twenty-four Shoshones killed in retaliation for an attack on immigrants, three miners killed on the new road to Montana, four Shoshone prisoners shot when stolen stock was not returned, another miner killed in revenge. At this point Connor made a presumptive leap. With no evidence he concluded that a band under a prominent Shoshone, Bear Hunter, was guilty not only of the recent attacks but "had been murdering Emigrants on the overland Mail route for the last fifteen years." Without consulting his superiors, he organized a major assault on the band's camp on Bear River, just over the line in Washington Territory.[29]

His timing was portentous—and essential to understanding the army's strategy from that point on. It was late January 1863. Although Connor called the season "unfavorable," it was precisely the season that gave him his edge.[30] The horse-men then were hunkered down in their protected enclaves, easier to find and, one of Connor's officers later explained, "least able to make resistance, as they are half famished."[31] The army, on the other hand, could draw on large stores of materials cached during the warm months and taken into the field in wagons pulled by well-fed draft horses. Conner's command of 220 infantry and cavalry set out from Camp Douglas with twenty days' supplies in fifteen wagons, along with two howitzers. It was so cold that troopers could scarcely open their mouths because their beards and mustaches were iced together. Rations of whiskey froze in canteens.[32]

At dawn on January 29 Connor approached Bear Hunter's camp. What followed was a battle that became a rout and then a massacre.[33] The Shoshones were in a deep ravine and firing behind stacked logs at the exposed soldiers. Connor's men attacked from three sides and at first took most of the casualties, but when troops flanked the camp and broke through, the ravine became a trap. All fled who could as soldiers used rifles and revolvers and finally axes to kill many of the wounded and those trying to swim the icy river. Women were killed when they refused to lie down to be raped, others raped "in the act of dying from their wounds." Probably between 250 and 300 died, though claims would run as high as 1,200. Bear Hunter was killed, and all but one leader, and about 90 women and children. The toll was highest of all engagements of the War against Indian America. Twenty-three of Connor's men were killed, including one officer.[34]

Within nine months Connor, now a brigadier general and increasingly a darling of the western military, and Utah's governor James Doty negotiated treaties with most bands along the overland route in Utah and Idaho. In exchange for annuities, including blankets and supplies as winter approached, they swore to leave all traffic and mail stations alone.[35] The troubled stretch of the main overland route west of South Pass was now secure.

But the road to the east, across the plains, was not. It had been generally open and safe since the Grattan debacle and Harney's campaign, but things came unstuck in 1859, when a gold rush brought about a hundred thousand persons over the trail to Colorado. Nowhere outside of California did Indians suffer such an erosion and loss of resources, and as always the worst was along rivers, the Platte and the Arkansas, that now were avenues of immigration and commerce, and the South Platte where the new settlements centered. Nonetheless the peace held because the tribes had options—the rich valleys to the north for the Lakotas, the rivers between the Platte and Arkansas for the Cheyennes and Arapahos, and those south of the Arkansas for the Comanches and Kiowas. The crisis came when the tribes' degenerating situation and the stresses of the war combined with two men's abandonment of responsibility and one man's rogue act.

The key figures were John Evans, appointed governor of Colorado Territory in 1863, and John Chivington, Colorado's military commander. Evans was a physician who had made a fortune in Chicago real estate, risen high in the Republican Party and Methodist church, and helped found Northwestern University. Its town of Evanston is named for him. As governor he hoped to ride with the growing territory to greater wealth and prominence. He had not a whisper of experience with Indians. Chivington, who had saved the battle of Glorieta Pass for the Union, was a Methodist minister, a large and thick-bodied bull-roarer. Ferociously ambitious, he hoped that another flashy victory in Colorado would open the way to military and political advancement. He was also openly disdainful of Indians. It was an unstable combination. The two men's authorities overlapped. Governor Evans was also the superintendent of Indian affairs; Chivington was charged with dealing with any military crisis, from Indians or rebels. The fuzzy lines of authority had made for confusion and conflict in New Mexico and the Pacific Northwest before the war. In Colorado the results would be especially terrible.

Evans at first tried honestly to mollify all sides, but the situation was tangled. After the sham Treaty of Fort Wise in 1861 some Cheyenne factions, notably the Dog Soldier band, were determined to resist every white encroachment, while "peace chiefs" like Black Kettle and Lean Bear counseled accommodation. Evans's mastery of Chicago real estate and Methodist theology did not well equip him for dealing within the snarl of tribal politics, and when a council he called among Plains bands aborted, his impressions of his Native counterparts soured. Chivington, meanwhile, ordered troops to "chastise" whatever camps they could find after reports of stolen livestock in the spring of 1864. An attack on a large camp killed Lean Bear as he showed the peace medal given him by Lincoln during a visit to Washington the previous spring. Dog Soldiers answered with raids into Kansas and along the Platte. In June Evans ordered all peaceful Indians to report to military posts, but few appeared—summer was the season for hunting bison—and in early August a lathered Evans authorized civilians to sally forth to "kill and destroy" any Indians encountered (none did). Coloradans faced "the largest Indian war this country ever had," Evans warned, and, even worse, the prime connector to the Pacific along the Platte was under siege.[36] On August 11 Secretary of War Henry Stanton agreed and authorized Evans to create the volunteer Third Colorado Cavalry to serve under Chivington. It was to disband after a hundred days.

At this point two events a few weeks apart turned the story toward one of the Indian Wars' most infamous episodes. In early September Evans reluctantly agreed to meet the peace chief Black Kettle and others at Fort Weld, outside Denver. There he essentially abdicated his duties as superintendent and turned the situation over to Chivington, who sent Black Kettle and his band to Fort Lyon on the Arkansas River. The commander there, Maj. Scott Anthony, was unable to feed them and sent them to a traditional camp along Big Sandy, or Sand Creek, to await further word. Meanwhile, the militant Dog Soldiers continued their attacks along the Platte until Ben Holladay, owner of the Overland Stage Company, wired Secretary of War Stanton in mid-October that without immediate action "the great overland mails must again be stopped." He knew the man to help—Patrick Connor. Two days later Connor was ordered to Colorado.[37] Now the ambitious Chivington was in a bind. Suddenly faced with being overshadowed by Connor, and with the term of his volunteer regiment ticking down to its final days, he ordered the Colorado Third into the field for his own campaign—not, however, against the Dog Soldiers in winter camps a hundred miles or so west of Denver but nearly twice as far to the south and east to Fort Lyon. With Anthony and his regulars he would strike against the Cheyennes and Arapahos at Sand Creek, ones who had obeyed the orders he himself had given at Camp Weld council.[38]

On a clear but frigid dawn on November 29, nearly 700 troops, about 450 from the Third and the rest regulars from Fort Lyon, approached the camp of about 120 lodges. When Black Kettle saw the cavalry approach he called out to his people "not to be afraid, that the soldiers would not hurt them," a survivor remembered: "Then the troops opened fire."[39] The outnumbered warriors put up brief resistance before all who could retreated upstream and dug pits in the sand as shelter. Two officers, Silas Soule and Joseph Cramer, refused to take part and commanded their companies not to fire. Each later described the massacre. The attackers became "a perfect mob—every man on his own hook." Children begging on their knees had their brains knocked out. A woman, shot in the thigh after pleading for her life, cut her two children's throats before killing herself. Two men, chased down afoot, "kneeled down, and clasped each other around the neck and both were shot together." The killing lasted more than eight hours and left about 130 dead, the majority women and children. Soldiers, including two officers, then mutilated the corpses. Most bodies were scalped, including that of an unborn child cut from its mother. Fingers were taken off for their rings and "Squaws snatches were cut out for trophies." A few women and children were taken as captives, including a baby of three months abandoned to die a day later.[40] Chivington led the volunteers back to Denver, where they were cheered on the streets and saluted in the press as having "covered themselves with glory."[41]

The predictable result was the opposite of what Holladay and the government had sought. In rare winter assaults, Cheyenne, Arapaho, and Lakota warriors sacked waystations, destroyed the town of Julesburg, stole hundreds of cattle, and killed between thirty and fifty freighters, soldiers, settlers, and travelers.[42] As bad as they were, the losses showed how overblown were the fears of the Indian threat. The annihilating total war that Evans had predicted killed fewer than a hundred persons and destroyed several thousand dollars in property. After a final sharp engagement west of Fort Laramie, the Platte was secure by the time Grant and Lee met at Appomattox Court House. Plains tribes were far from subdued, but the grand connector between the East and far West was open and safe, this time for good.

The Southwest had two essential routes of transit. One ran east and west, connecting Southern California and the head of the Gulf of California to Santa Fe and the Rio Grande via desert passes, springs, and the Colorado, Gila, and San Pedro Rivers. It was a lifeline for army posts and new gold strikes made in 1862 and 1863. The other route, running south and north, centered on the Rio Grande, one of the continent's most ancient roads that had carried travelers and trade between today's Mexico and the North American interior long before the Spanish used it as a path of conquest.

As with the overland trail to the north, immigrant travel on the arid road to California was caustic to the Indians—Yumas, Yavapais, Mohaves—living there. The "irruption of Americans" devastated game, fish, and other resources. Road merchants harvested mesquite beans, traditionally pounded into flour to make wintertime cakes, and sold them as livestock feed for a dime a pound.[43] James Carleton was responsible for keeping the road open, and he turned his unflagging vigor against Indians.

In the chaos around Sibley's campaign, Mescalero and Mimbres Apaches had struck hard at settlements and ranches in the Rio Grande Valley, and to the west gold strikes and the closing of the oxbow stage line encouraged western Apaches to raid ferociously across today's central and southern Arizona.[44] Carleton's answer was elemental. He had barely settled into Santa Fe before sending two of his colonels, Joseph R. West and Kit Carson, into areas he considered hostile. All men encountered, he ordered, "are to be killed whenever and wherever you can find them." Women and children were to be captured and held unharmed. Should any leaders "beg for peace," they should be sent to Santa Fe to talk, but "tell them fairly and frankly that you shall keep after their people and slay them until you receive orders to desist."[45] To the west, where the army's control was dimmest, groups of "twenties and forties and eighties" were to "radiate in all directions" and follow any trail and hope to "destroy or worry the Indians into submission." In 1864 Carleton took this approach a step farther. He asked the territorial governor and Mexican officials to whip up a "general rising of both citizens and soldiers" to clear the country of "these terrible savages." Any man with the good of Arizona at heart, whether in or out of uniform, "must put his shoulder not only to the wheel, but to the rifle."[46]

He called, that is, for civil war. Between 1862 and 1866 campaigns against western Apaches and Yavapais, as a recent historian writes, were "on a scale and with a ferocity unequaled before or after." Officers reported hundreds of men, women, and children killed.[47] They used the seasonal approach emerging elsewhere. Pimas, Maricopas, and Mexicans, long at odds with Apaches and Yavapais, were drafted into the Arizona Volunteers and paid to fight for long stretches, especially in the winter. Early in 1866 they killed eighty-three Yavapais, thirty of them caught while taking winter shelter in caves, then in summer they "destroyed the cornfields and everything that fell in their way." The supremely elusive Apaches were largely uncowed, but the Yavapais were on the lip of disaster, "completely demoralized," a prisoner reported, and "not knowing whither to flee for safety."[48]

Closer to Carleton's center of power, two converging columns quickly broke the Mescalero Apaches south and east of Santa Fe. "We have no more heart," one of their leaders told Carleton after traveling to supplicate in Santa Fe: "We have no provisions, no means to live; your troops are everywhere."[49] Carleton sent four hundred to a reservation he created on the Pecos River, Bosque Redondo, overseen by a post established in 1862, Fort Sumner. If they behaved, he told them, they would be fed and well cared for; if they tried to leave, they would be shot.[50] He turned next toward the Mimbres, Chiricahua, and other Apache groups in the Gila River basin, where a gold rush as usual had riled relations. By mid-spring of 1863, after the respected leader Mangas Coloradas was taken under a flag of truce and promptly murdered, the Gila bands had been harried from the area of the diggings.[51]

Carleton now felt he was in position to take on his greatest challenge, the numerous and formidable Diné. Writing that "the Navajos have got to be whipped," Carleton first ordered all Diné to report to Fort Canby, recently set on Navajo territory, and when none complied, he declared that "the whole tribe is a war party." All men were to be killed or taken, all women and children captured, and all fields destroyed before harvest.[52] To carry out the orders he tapped Kit Carson.

"Make *every* sting draw," he wrote Carson, who set off with nine companies into Dinétah, aided by Utes, Zunis, and Hopis.[53] He grabbed or killed any Navajos found, wasted crops and stores of food, burned hogans, cut down orchards, and captured or slaughtered sheep and horses. In the late fall he asked to pull back and rest his command, but Carleton answered that this was precisely when to strike hardest: "Now while the snow is deep is the true time to make an impression on the tribe." By the first of the year Carson estimated he had destroyed two million pounds of grain. The rousted Diné were so fearful that they rarely built warming fires, "[which] adds greatly to the horrors of their Situation."[54] Now Carleton sent Carson against the ultimate redoubt, Canyon de Chelly, whose red sandstone walls rose in some places 1,500 feet above its floor. Carson patrolled its rim with some troops while others marched through its fastnesses; the Navajos hid where they could, including atop an eight-hundred-foot tower with water only from pockets of snow.

Carson's forays between August and February killed only twenty-three persons and captured thirty-four, but the rest were "in a complete state of starvation," a captive reported, and "many of their women and children have already died from this cause."[55] Penetrating Canyon de Chelly, Carson wrote, showed the Navajos that "in no place, however formidable or inaccessible . . . are they safe." Many scattered into remote canyons and some continued raiding. The majority, however, capitulated. By early February the first freezing refugees were filing into Fort Canby to surrender. Ultimately several thousand gave themselves up.[56]

To cement his control over the Rio Grande Valley, Carleton ordered the Navajos sent to join the Mescaleros at Bosque Redondo, but he had far too few wagons to carry them. So most walked. Organized into groups ranging from a few score to more than two thousand, weak and hungry from the start, sickened by the unfamiliar rations and struck by spring snowstorms, the columns of captives plodded more than four hundred miles to the south and east, as far as from Washington DC to Augusta, Maine, along what they would call the Long Walk.[57] Many died on the way. Many more were taken by Utes and New Mexicans and sold as slaves, fattening still more the territory's number of unfree workers. By May more than six thousand Diné had arrived at Bosque Redondo.

The Civil War ended with the power of Indian peoples mostly broken on the Pacific coast, in the Great Basin, and on the eastern plains. Elsewhere there remained several centers of Native power. The Lakotas dominated a region never matched in size in the long history of the Dakota people. Even in the interior, however, the military made inroads. The Diné were in painful exile, and the Cheyennes and Arapahos had taken some severe blows. The military was laying the basis for future dominance in the West even as it was saving the Union in the East.

It did so by making the western environment a critical ally. Winter campaigns did more than reduce the Indians' ability to fight, a point made clear at Connor's bloodletting at Bear River. After tallying up the dead, he added that he had captured 175 horses, burned more than 70 lodges, and destroyed large amounts of wheat and other essentials. Then, an offhand note: he "left a small quantity of wheat for the sustenance of 160 captive squaws and children, whom I left on the field."[58] That image, of women and children standing homeless in subzero cold next to a pittance of grain, catches the wider message of the strategy that now was part of the western military canon: resist, and you will put your families on the line.

The twin lessons of wartime, the importance of roads and using weather as a weapon, were made dramatically, and with delicious irony, in a campaign by the architect of the strategy himself, Patrick Connor. At war's end Congress authorized a new road from Nebraska to the Montana gold fields, through the heart of Lakota and Northern Cheyenne country. The tribes had made clear that they would never accept such a thing, and when hundreds of warriors confronted surveyors, Connor was sent in to settle matters.[59] He built a new post on Montana's Tongue River, modestly named Fort Connor, and in late summer of 1865, he organized three commands under himself, Col. Nelson Cole, and Lt. Col. Samuel Walker to converge for a punishing strike near the Powder River.

Connor had some success, but not Cole and Walker. In country without "a particle of vegetation," they found Lakotas and Northern Cheyennes "thicker than fiddlers in hell," a trooper wrote, but the warriors were not the direst threat. An early winter storm turned a stifling day quickly Siberian, and in twenty-four hours Cole lost 225 horses and mules to "excessive heat, exhaustion, starvation and extreme cold." The temperature rose sharply, only to plunge again five days later, with rain and hail, then sleet and snow. Before Cole could find sheltering timber he lost four hundred more animals. Walker described a "scene of horror" at the end. As each horse dropped "20 men would pounce on [it] and in less time than I can tell it [the horse's] bones would be stripped and [the meat] devoured raw." When the survivors finally staggered into Fort

Connor on September 20, frozen and famished, "shoeless and ragged," they learned that Washington had canceled the roadbuilding and the campaign.[60]

Saving the Mastodons

In 1864 William Dole, commissioner of Indian Affairs, was well pleased with the "rapid settlement of the country" and the "constant prospecting expeditions in every direction." Every step forward, however, deepened a pressing problem. Immigrants, farmers, prospectors, and cattlemen were displacing Indians and leaving them increasingly destitute. The grim effects of the advancing settlement demanded that the government confront "that most difficult of all political problems, viz: Indian civilization."[61]

That term, "Indian civilization," opens onto a fuller view of how the nation was being remade during the middle of the century. Close to the heart of the remaking was a restructuring of America's racial and ethnic order that began in the 1840s when expansion brought more than 100,000 former Mexican citizens and roughly 350,000 Indian peoples inside the nation's borders. The Civil War ended with more than 4 million enslaved Africans freed and admitted tentatively to citizenship. Then there were immigrant arrivals from places barely represented before, a trend that also began in the West with more than 250,000 Chinese between 1850 and 1880.

All of it forced to the fore old, elemental questions: Who would be in, and who would be out, of the national family? Besides their unprecedented numbers, those in question differed greatly in how they had come to the moment. Former slaves had suddenly gained a freedom they had never known; Indians were losing independence they had always known. Immigrants had come voluntarily, southwestern Hispanos through the distant stroke of a pen. All differed from one another and among themselves. A Cantonese in the gold fields, a Black field hand or domestic or herder from Alabama, Virginia, or Arkansas, a Hispano merchant in New Mexico, and a Blackfoot bison hunter, a Pueblo villager, a Tlingit fisherman, and a Washoe rabbit hunter—they had as little in common as any random sampling of peoples from across the globe.

Integrating such numbers and diversity into society was one of the most complex challenges the nation would ever face. What is striking is how Washington approached them all with essentially the same strategy and demands. At the core of its policies of assimilation was an insistence that all occupy a common cultural ground. It started with English as the national tongue and a commitment to legal institutions, to private property and a capitalist marketplace, and to the European structure of the family. Christianity and its habits, especially Protestantism, were much preferred. Schooling of the young was both a virtue in itself and a means of cultivating all of the rest. The various parts came together as a floor of citizenship, of "being American."

Freed people's ancestors had come to America by force, but their descendants had been intimately part of its life for more than two centuries, albeit at the lowest rungs. They were cultural insiders. At the other extreme were the Chinese. They had come voluntarily but most had no interest in staying, and although they embraced the economic order and worked well enough within it to inspire jealousy, they had no families and were cultural outsiders in language, religion, and customs. In between were Hispanos, who differed in language and customs but were Christians (albeit Roman Catholics), lived in nuclear and extended families, and posed no threat to the economic order.

Western Indians were their own category. They had not come to America. America had come to them. Even more than the Chinese they were cultural outsiders with their own values, traditions, laws, languages, and cosmologies that were different from everyone else's and different from one another's. Another crucial point defined the "Indian problem." Indians' lifeways bound them intimately to particular places that together composed the great majority of new country. The new order presumed that country would be transformed into property and retooled to purposes usually incompatible with those of the Indians. Its laws held that Indians did not own those places in the sense that citizens of Maryland or Georgia owned theirs, but they had the right to occupy them and to deny occupation to anyone else unless they surrendered the land by treaty. Western Indians, that is, held a legal key to the future of the emerging West while posing the greatest challenges in bringing anomalous peoples onto the common floor of the national family. Indian removal had been the earlier plan to meet the need, but events in Indian Territory and Minnesota marked that policy's wretched end.

Here was the nub of Commissioner Dole's "problem." If "Indian civilization" meant its collective ways of living that were safely rooted in homelands, Dole's problem was how to end it as quickly and as thoroughly as possible so that the "rapid settlement" by farmers and townspeople and the "prospecting in every direction" by miners could proceed unresisted. Hopefully this would be done through persuasion, so Indians would regard "regard us as friends," but if that failed, the new order would come about at bayonet point, helped now by the strategies being sharpened even as he wrote.

The work relied on the twin mechanisms of treaties and reservations. Past treaties had typically promised mutual amity between encroaching settlements and Native peoples, then laid down some demarcation between them. Now, with no stark division possible, treaties became more direct, assertive, pointed, and particular. They would partner with the reservations that had emerged in the 1850s. There Indians would be set apart, not on the edge of an expanded nation, but inside of it, and the purpose was not to keep them apart from white society but ultimately to make them part of it.

As a measure of the change, compare the Treaty of Fort Laramie in 1851 with one with the Western Shoshones twelve years later. The first had drawn lines around tribal territories and guaranteed safe passage for whites westward. The second had done the same, but then: "Whenever the President of the United States shall deem it expedient," the Shoshones would "abandon the roaming life" and convert to lives as "herdsmen or agriculturists." For the next quarter century the government would provide five thousand dollars a year in articles needed for the new life.[62] On reservations, Dole wrote, Indians would be elevated to a "scale of social existence" where they might "live credibly amongst the most enlightened nations."[63] Lines would dissolve, first the cultural line between Natives and newcomers, then the physical line separating the two, as reservations, having done their job, were eliminated. The "problem" of "Indian civilization" would vanish.

The process, devised and begun during in the 1850s, cranked steadily ahead during the Civil War. Indians surrendered more land by treaty between 1861 and 1865 than in any other comparable period—half again as much, in fact, as the next greatest loss, more than enough to fit into Texas and New Mexico together.[64] The number of western superintendencies grew from 8 to 11, with 37 agencies. With them came new reservations. Some, like those in the Pacific Northwest, were born of the conflicts of the 1850s, but others followed campaigns during the war, among them Kit Carson's into Dinétah, which used the new methods to hound the Navajos into submission. To James Carleton the work was nothing less than the Almighty's dictate and a natural law of life. Just as "mastadons and the great sloths" had given way to higher life, so all Indians would pass away if they failed to become one with the superior peoples replacing them.[65] If the Navajos were to survive, they would have to change in their essence, which in turn called for their Long Walk to the Pecos River and Bosque Redondo.

The reservation there was one of the first full-tilt attempts at cultural conversion, and Carleton engaged the challenge as if "in a holy crusade." The forty-square-mile reservation eventually held nearly ten thousand Diné as well as the Mescalero Apaches previously sent there. As the Diné arrived in increasing numbers, Carleton ordered the hunters and herders to prepare fields and to dig ditches to irrigate them. He built a chapel and provided Christian services and instruction. To school children in English and the standard curriculum, classes were organized and teachers, mostly Roman Catholic priests, were brought in to staff them. Carleton's dictates ran to daily life: men would wear white trousers, women pleated skirts. He would employ both geographical and generational displacement. Adults were as wily as circling wolves, but they could at least be controlled by removing them from their familiar "haunts and hills, and hiding places." The young were a better bet. Schooled in educational basics, the farming life, the "arts of peace," and the "truths of Christianity," they would veer from their parents' ways into contented and peaceable adulthoods. The "latent longings for murdering and robbing" of the Diné would be left behind.[66]

Carleton immediately ran into problems, starting with basic needs. He had badly underestimated how many Diné he would have to support, and as the refugees stumbled in from the Long Walk (Carleton found it "not only an interesting, but a touching sight"), he cut his troops to half rations, limited each arrival to a pound each day of meat, or corn, or flour, or even kraut or pickles.[67] A shipment of flour, cattle, and other supplies averted disaster, but the troubles at Bosque Redondo were only beginning. In planning for the reservation to feed itself, Carleton miscalculated what the environment could do and how it would behave. The land probably could not have fed all who tilled it even if all had gone well, but as it was the corn was ravaged by plagues of worms and both stunted by drought and blighted by excessive rain. The timber that gave the place its name (Bosque Redondo translates as "Round Grove of Trees") was soon cut for fuel; within a couple of years residents had to walk miles to dig roots of mesquite trees. Hunger fed rampant prostitution—a soldier's standard payment for sex was a pint of cornmeal—and venereal diseases. Of 321 persons treated at the reservation hospital (a "tumble down concern" that the surgeon found "only fit to keep pigs in"), there were 235 cases of syphilis.[68] Carleton had his own "Indian problem," blurring Native divisions and identities and so missing crucial distinctions. The Navajos and Mescalero Apaches he penned up together, although related, were traditional enemies, and they were at bitter odds from the start, while the Navajos' intricate clan relations complicated his dealings with them.

Carleton misjudged another complication, relations with non-Natives. By buying great amounts of territorial produce to cover the reservation's shortfall, the army drove up prices for all consumers, with predictable results.[69] Then there was the corruption that would prove epidemic throughout the system. In a single shipment of blankets a special agent charged the government triple the usual price, for an overage of sixty thousand dollars.[70] Finally, complicating it all, was a confusion of responsibility, the clash between military and civilian authority that had snarled Indian relations from the start. Carleton said the

Navajos remained prisoners of war and so were under his control alone. The territorial superintendent of Indian affairs, Michael Steck, predictably disagreed. Arguing correctly that the reservation could not possibly support its numbers, he pushed for a reserve much closer to the Navajos' home country.[71] Carleton's autocratic temperament further fouled the relationship.

By the end of the war it was clear that Bosque Redondo was indeed a model—of how far short of official intent the system's lofty goals could fall. Diné were slipping away and heading home, harvests were as poor as ever, popular and administrative criticism was relentless, and the experiment had become a sucking hole for government funds. When Carleton was mustered out of service in 1867, the Interior Department took over Bosque Redondo, and the next year a treaty created a reservation back at Dinétah, far smaller than the tribal homeland. Those remaining on the Pecos made the Long Walk again, now in reverse.

As also true of most reservations, the original aims were not wholly unmet. The Diné never again posed anything like the threat they had for generations, and the crucial corridor of the Rio Grande was essentially secure. Survivors had integrated some useful elements of reservation life—wagons rather than travois, skills ranging from irrigation to smithing, a hybrid, roomier hogan.[72] The mixed consequences, weighted more toward failure than success, could apply to most reservations in these years and those ahead, as could the heritage of bitter memories. Diné would vilify Carson and Carleton and would look back on the Long Walk and Bosque Redondo as the bleakest and most painful time of their modern history.

After its faltering efforts of the 1850s, the federal government's power to control the new country sharpened considerably between 1861 and 1865. After Washington turned back the Confederate bid to invade, it began to solve the riddles of subduing Indians and to broaden its new means to confine and transform them. It was close to securing for good the control of movement across and around the continent, and Congress had established a mechanism to elaborate on it with a rail connection to the Pacific. Other legislation had widened access to public lands and had expanded and fleshed out the West's political apparatus.

In that last regard, Idaho's territorial secretary Clinton DeWitt Smith arrived in Boise from Lewiston with the territorial seal on April 14, 1865. That afternoon Abraham Lincoln and his wife, Mary, rode in an open carriage through the streets of the national capital. He was "supremely cheerful," she remembered. He had spoken earlier of heading west across the Rockies to watch ex-soldiers digging California gold, and in that spirit he told Mary of feeling that finally on *"this day,* the war, has come to a close."[73] As an awful punctuation, hours later John Wilkes Booth ended Lincoln's tortured time as president with a bullet to the back of his head.

The Civil War was not quite over—some say it still isn't—but as millions mourned the dead president, the nation was moving into a time when wounds would begin to scab over and the fundamental remaking of the nation, set in motion by expansion to the Pacific twenty years earlier, shifted from keeping the Union together toward consolidating it from coast to coast. In the East, the states of the former Confederacy would be reintegrated into the nation and millions of former bondsmen would begin to learn the ironic realities of emancipation. The West in turn would increasingly shape the new America as it continued its shift onto a new course and into new possibilities.

PART 2 ➤ Things Come Together

In 1865 the Union was preserved, but the nation was anything but unified. Some questions were resolved, but their resolution raised others. In the East secession was blocked and Black slavery abolished. That called for setting the terms for stitching Southeast and Northeast back together while defining what citizenship would mean for the emancipated. Out West a pair of new states and twice as many new territories were in operation. Native resistance was snuffed in key parts of the new country, treaties had acquired, at least on paper, just under four hundred thousand square miles of land, and more reservations were created for the displaced. Now there was a need for a fuller inventory of the country's resources and a further pursuit of how to work their promise toward reality. All that added up to bringing a geographical and human diversity more into something singular.

Consolidation moved steadily ahead during the next dozen or so years. It started with the basics. Sovereignty, as practical ownership, begins with the power over how and where people move. It comes down to the familiar call of a watchman in the night—"Who goes there?"—and whoever can truthfully answer "I do" wins. Union campaigns against Indian peoples had secured control of essential western passways. Washington now began to build them into a spreading infrastructure of roads, rails, and wires, which in turn sped the exploration of the land and its resources. That work in turn helped bind the West into the world through the enlargement of knowledge, not only of the lay and nature of the land but also of new scientific understandings in a variety of fields, the pursuit of which made the West one of the most productive laboratories on earth.

The postwar West was bound up with the nation in subtler but crucial ways. Acquiring it had brought on the nation's near fatal wounding. After the Union was saved America's thirty-year reconstruction entered a new phase. Now national consolidation inspired visions of national healing. Farmlands and pastures would be the raw stuff for all families to rebuild lives. The laying of track and the spanning of wires would be a common achievement assuring a common greatness. Resistant Indian peoples were pictured as aggressors and their defeat and dispossession as proof of America's ordained mastery of the continent. Western landscapes by their very differences from the East would be a source of unifying identity. An image emerged of a West that was, paradoxically, unique and apart and yet intimately bound to the nation's sense of itself.

Every unifying development after Appomattox—the rail-laying and wire-stringing, the scientific probing, the comprehension of the land and what it held—had its start in the 1850s, including the vision of the West as common national ground where Americans could transcend their older divisions. The vision had appeared in unexpected places.[1] On March 11, 1850, the New York abolitionist William Seward delivered as his maiden address to the Senate his famous invocation of a "higher law" that forbid the spread of Black slavery in the West. The speech is most often cited in tracing an irrepressible division between Southeast and Northeast, but deep into it Seward took a sudden turn. That division was now artificial, he said. Expansion had created a new, truer one, with the East on one side "and the boundless West . . . on the other." These two were not opposed but united by "nature and commerce" into one destiny.[2] If there was a higher law speaking to the crisis at hand, Seward was saying, the nation also had a higher purpose that bound all its parts in a future of continental promise.

Seward's views had something else in common with those after the war. His higher law was of a duty to seek the "highest attainable degree of happiness" for all mankind. As they set out to bind the "boundless West" into the nation and the world, however, he and others showed little evidence of interest in the "degree of happiness," or of life and liberty, of those, especially Indian peoples, who would be forced by the same vision to surrender independence and to join in that common future.

10 ▷ Iron Bands and Tongues of Fire

The West was acquired, conquered, and largely consolidated almost precisely coincident with the greatest advances in movement in human history until that time. The revolution's two prime means were the telegraph and the railroad. The Morse-Vail telegraph was formally tested on May 24, 1844, roughly six months before the election of the expansionist president James K. Polk. By the time the West was coming fully into focus its remotest corners were linked into a national and global webbing that moved information infinitely faster than anything before it. The nation's 4,377 miles of railroads in 1844 multiplied seven times by the Civil War, and at the end of 1877 it was nearly 100,000 miles. Nearly 2,000 of those miles, the longest rail line on earth, connected the East to the Pacific coast. Both spannings of the West were accomplished by cooperative arrangements with the federal government, partnerships of unprecedented scale and sophistication (and, often enough, corruption) that in the years ahead would be extended throughout the nation. Both would unite the West to the nation as well in the popular perception of a people bound for greatness via what one journalist called "iron bands and tongues of fire."[1]

The West and America's movement revolution grew up together. They were historical twins, and like many twins, neither can be truly understood without the other.

Wired to the World

Before the telegraph, most information moved no faster than people. There were a few exceptions—commands by bugle, semaphore, notes tied to pigeon legs—but a message of any length and subtlety had to be carried by a human being, either as a document or in someone's mind. News had to walk or ride. That made the transportation revolution also a communication revolution, with steamboats, better roads, and the railroad giving a giddy sense of acceleration.

Measured simply by speed, the telegraph's accomplishment was vastly more impressive. A railroad at full speed quickened the passage of information five or ten times over that by horseback or wagon. The telegraph carried information more than forty million times faster than anything before it. Once a western system was in place, an electrical jot of information could travel faster from Kansas City to Denver than the resulting click could move from the terminal to its operator's eardrum.[2]

The hope of sending messages electronically through wires had been around for generations, but inventors faced three practical obstacles—creating a reliable source of electricity, keeping it moving over long distances, and designing the mechanisms and methods of sending and receiving signals at each end.[3] Alessandro Volta's electric pile opened development of a power source and the New Yorker Joseph Henry's intensity battery could send currents much farther than before, but while many messaging devices were tried, employing rolling marbles, litmus paper, and hydrogen bubbles set loose by the current, the search continued for the simplest solution.[4]

The answer came from a painter. Samuel Finley Breese Morse was New England reared and Yale educated. By middle age he had won some critical success with his landscapes and portraits and had been chosen the first president of the National Academy of Design. In 1832, however, his career was sputtering when, sailing home from Europe, he took in a conversation about electromagnetism and how "intelligence" might be moved instantaneously over distance. Morse was immediately taken by the notion.[5] With Albert Vail he spent several years working on a telegraphic prototype and in 1843 secured $30 thousand from Congress to run an experimental line from Washington to Baltimore. In the system's first official test the next year, Morse sent Vail a message schoolchildren would memorize for generations: "What hath God wrought?"

The system's virtues were quickly clear. With periodic boosters, or "repeaters," telegraph wires could carry a signal enormous distances and over whatever terrain a crew could string them. The means of sending and receiving was elegantly simple. Rather than using the electrical current to do anything, the system kept it running continuously so when the sending device interrupted it, the receiver reacted with a click. This also allowed for Morse's crucial insight: information was best sent by code. Rather than the receiver translating a signals into letters, Morse's impulses—a quick click was a dot, a slightly longer one a dash—were the letters, coded into combinations with the commonest letters the quickest to send (the most frequently used, e, was a single dot). Eventually telegraphers communicated almost as rapidly as by speaking, and seasoned operators grew to know each other's styles as if they were hearing accents and inflections.

Construction naturally focused first in the East, but because the first successes coincided exactly with the acquisition of the far West, some immediately called what the editor of the Saint Louis New Era in 1848 pictured as a "streak of lightning" for "instantaneous and constant communication" with the far coast.[6] The telegraph was beautifully suited to western conditions. Running a line was relatively easy, even through the kind of rough country that frustrated efforts at road building and laying rail lines. It was cheap enough that local communities could provide their own connections to the wider web. The first need, however, was for a trunk line connecting the expanding eastern system with the Pacific coast, but the financial risks, technical difficulties, and costs—all, as it turned out, overestimated—dissuaded investors until the eve of civil war.

A telegraphic framework awaited in California. In November 1853 the California State Telegraph Company completed a line from San Francisco to San Jose and Stockton and then through rugged country to Marysville. Other efforts soon connected to Yreka in the north and Los Angeles to the south. Telegraph lines looped along poles and sometimes snaked over tree limbs and through bushes, one more startling intrusion during this time of frantic change. As everywhere, the telegraph was used almost wholly to coordinate business operations, and by 1858 the Placerville, Humboldt and Salt Lake Telegraph Company had crossed the Sierra to new gold strikes in Nevada, just in time for what would become the Comstock silver boom. Two years later it had reached Fort Churchill, 150 miles east of Virginia City, Nevada.

The same year Congress passed the Pacific Telegraph Act. Its chief proponent was Hiram Sibley, president of Western Union.[7] He had pressed for the project for years, and by 1860 the obvious need to close the communication gap to the Pacific had made a transcontinental line a priority. Under an arrangement with Sibley's company Washington would be both patron and guaranteed customer. It provided public land for a right of way and for repair stations, no more than one every fifteen miles, and it pledged $40 thousand annually for ten years once the line was finished. For that it would have priority use but would pay for any messages beyond what its subsidy would buy at reasonable rates. The government's scientific arms, the Smithsonian, Coast Survey, and National Observatory, would have free use. Otherwise, service would be open to the public.[8]

The law, scarcely recognized in the usual texts, is worth noting. It expanded and elaborated on business partnerships with the federal government spun off by expansion. Before this Washington had surveyed and improved roads that were quickly lined with private mercantiles, ferries, smithies, ranches, and other enterprises. Its military posts had supported woodcutters, laundries, and brothels. With its postal contracts it had subsidized stage lines and steamship companies, and in partnering with Wells Fargo it had effectively fed the West's most successful express and banking operation. Now, following a similar arrangement in 1851 to use land grants to finance the Illinois Central Railroad, Washington used what it had the most of in the West, land, to provide help in constructing a revolutionary innovation, then it took things another step by guaranteeing the private enterprise a base of income. That general impulse would be used over and again to help open the West, most obviously in laying out railroads.

Construction also anticipated that of railroads. Two companies contracted to run the line. The Pacific Telegraph Company would build west from Omaha, Nebraska, to Salt Lake City, Utah. Edward Creighton, experienced in construction in the East, would head its operation. The Overland Telegraph Company would build the line to Salt Lake City from the West, out of Carson City, Nevada, with the Californian James Gamble in charge. The law required the link to the Pacific to be finished by July 31, 1862, and each company began manic preparations in early summer of 1861. Creighton's crew raised their first pole in Omaha on July 4. It was an Independence Day of muddled meanings. As workers began to string a wire that would help bind the far West into the nation, Congress was authorizing President Lincoln to raise an army of half a million men to stop the South from leaving it.

Naysayers had predicted all sorts of difficulties. Few materialized. Indians posed little threat on the plains and none at all in Nevada and Utah, and worries about herds of bison knocking down poles proved groundless. Trees, or the lack of them, posed the most nagging problem. Law required at least twenty-five poles per mile—a demand that strained severely resources of the rain-poor midcontinent. Mormons contracted to provide poles for both companies on the approaches to their holy city, but otherwise crews had to find their own. The Overland company's most vexing problem was bringing in manufactured items. It had either to ship insulators, repeaters, and spools of iron wire around Cape Horn or float them up the Missouri and haul them overland and through the Rockies.

Nonetheless, construction went forward with remarkable ease and much faster than anyone had thought possible. By mid-October of 1861 both companies were nearing their goals. Creighton's men arrived at Salt Lake City on October 19, Gamble's on October 24. In the first message across the continent, California's Chief Justice Stephen Field assured President Lincoln of his state's loyalty to the Union, and the president of the Overland Telegraph Company followed with the hope that the electrical communication would prove "a bond of perpetuity between the states of the Atlantic and those of the Pacific." The government's deadline had been met with an astonishing nine months to spare.

Again as would be true of railroads, most business was at either end, among towns in California and between Missouri Valley towns and the East, but as new settlement came into the interior West, telegraphic connections soon sprouted off the main trunks. Virginia City, Montana, had its first connection in 1866, four years after the first flicker of its rush. Leadville, more than ten thousand feet up in the Colorado Rockies, was linked by a wire over Mosquito Pass only a year after silver was discovered.[9] The telegraph became a badge of status, a prerequisite for respectability, and in time there were dozens in operation.[10] These were hardly financial behemoths. When Nebraska's Beatrice Electric Company, chartered in 1880 with $2,000 in stock, was bought out two years later, its final balance sheet showed income of $1,269.12 against expenses of $1,279.34, leaving it $10.22 in the hole.[11] Whatever their size, they were part of an expanding mesh, and the farther it spread, the less the West could be called truly isolated.

Meanwhile Western Union hatched an audacious effort, backed enthusiastically by Secretary of State William Seward, to extend its system up through Russian America and under the Bering Strait to link with a Russian line to Saint Petersburg. The American West would be the middle relay of a global circuitry that would give the United States a connection to foreign centers of power unthreatened by blockage or censorship by Great Britain. As crews built up the Pacific coast others in Siberia made a considerable start before the project was undone by word that Cyrus Field had completed a transatlantic cable in the summer of 1866. Field managers sold wooden brackets as firewood and iron wire as snarework to Siberian Korak trappers. Glass insulators were marketed as distinctively American teacups.[12] By then the global system was increasingly elaborate. In 1869 Europe had 110,000 miles of line. The cable across the Atlantic was followed by others to Cuba, Malta, Aden, Singapore. By 1872 London was in telegraphic connection to Tokyo, which meant Tokyo—and Berlin, Stockholm, Philadelphia, and hundreds of other places—were in contact with Virginia City, Denver, and scores of western towns. The West was wired to the world, plugged into a global conversation moving at nearly the speed of light.

America's telegraphic network stood alone in one way. Other systems were state owned and state operated. Here the government sponsored and subsidized a system that stayed in the hands of Hiram Sibley's Western Union, which essentially monopolized western traffic. Profits were enormous. The principal owners of Western Union hired themselves for the construction. To build its line, the Pacific Telegraph Company issued $1 million in stock, seven times the actual costs. Western Union then bought the company with $2 million of its own stock, but since the two firms were essentially the same, their owners essentially doubled their own worth by buying themselves out. Paying dividends demanded a lot of revenue, but from the outset Western Union ignored the law's cap of $3 for ten words. A customer in San Francisco paid $0.8743 per word for a message to New York. Translated into 2019 dollars, this amounted to $153 to send "Happy Birthday Mother. Love you very much," or "All us customers are being badly overcharged."[13] The Western Union's swollen capitalization, a Senate committee concluded in 1884, "has created at one and the same time a cover, inducement, and in some cases a necessity for excessive charges for telegrams."[14] The maneuvering and chicanery was one more parallel to what would soon come in the building of the first Pacific railroad.

More broadly, the telegraph was a harbinger of a key development of the next twenty years, the corporatization of the West.[15] Three factors—the distinctive needs in developing the region, federal support in helping to meet them, and the emergence of the corporation as the dominant form of business organization—converged in the West to create concentrations of wealth and influence never imagined before. Western Union was among the first. At the end of the Civil War "its business was large, its outlook brilliant, its position impregnable, its influence immense," one historian writes: "It stood confessedly one of the vastest and most comprehensive of the private enterprises in the world."[16] When the United States Telegraph Company invaded California and began a line toward Missouri, Western Union absorbed it within a year and soon merged with its chief rival, the American Telegraph Company, owner of the transatlantic cable. The resulting combination was, and would remain, effectively a national monopoly. Of nearly thirty-two million telegraphic messages sent in the United States in 1880, more than twenty-nine million were through Western Union lines.[17]

The telegraph's role in creating the West had its limits. The high prices kept it well beyond reach of most individuals and families. They relied on the postal system, which expanded prodigiously via the West's new roads, rails, and stages. Most traffic by wire was in the realm of business and finance. Ranchers and cattle jobbers tracked the best options before moving herds to markets. Agricultural shippers used it to coordinate supply, transport, and destinations within the nation and across the Pacific and Atlantic worlds. Mines were financed by stock purchased by wire from Berlin, Edinburgh, New York, and Chicago. Their managers ordered equipment telegraphically and had it delivered by rail service coordinated by the same system.

The telegraph did touch westerners' day-to-day experience in one way— the transmission of news and, with that, the national consolidation of public information.[18] After the Civil War the Associated Press became the exclusive source of wired national and international news for hundreds of newspapers across the country, while Western Union required that the Associated Press use only its wires for news distribution. Under this, the nation's first "bilateral monopoly," a reader in Globe City, Arizona, formed the same picture in her head of what was happening in London or Cairo or Charleston or Chicago as did a reader in Augusta, Maine, or New Orleans. Among its other connections, the West was bound into the nation through a common awareness.

It is a legitimate question, in fact, whether it would have been possible to think of the West, in the singular instead of plural, without this technology. The telegraph changed the very nature of communication. By making information instantaneously available in innumerable settings far apart from one another, it played a pivotal role in perceptual history.[19] Someone in effect could be simultaneously in Tucson, Seattle, and Omaha, which meant that as the nation was expanding, it was effectively much smaller and compressed and unified. At the very moment that Washington was integrating what would become by far the largest and most varied of its regions, roughly one-half of the lower forty-eight states, land embracing Death Valley and a Pacific coastal rainforest, the Grand Canyon and the northern Great Plains, it was employing a technology that was collapsing distances and ignoring distinctions, which made it conceivable to call such a far-flung diversity by one name. Perhaps the telegraph allowed the West to be shrunk into existence.

Its impact was inseparable from the other revolution in movement, the railroad. If the telegraphic web was "a network of iron nerves," Oliver Wendell Holmes wrote, linking sensation and act as if in "a single living body," railroads were "a vast system of iron muscles" moving the limbs of the "mighty organism."[20] Holmes's metaphor was of the body militant. He wrote in 1861, when a New England regiment, ordered by wire to travel by rail, was "a clenched fist full of bayonets at the end of it" sent against the Confederacy. Once the Civil War was over, the body turned its fists toward the Union's recently acquired western half. Wires and rails would play vitally in the War against Indian America and, even more tellingly, in the settlement and environmental transformations that would undermine and overwhelm the Indians' means of living. Small wonder, then, that the speed and sweep of the technologies of movement fed a sense of national confidence that focused most sharply on the West, its conquest, and domestication.

The message of mastery and prerogative had been there from the start, embedded in the message Morse sent to Vail in May 1844: "What hath God wrought?" The message is from the biblical Book of Numbers (23:23). It is usually taken as gape-jawed wonder at mankind's transcendence of worldly constraints, but in light of Morse's early life it takes on a very different meaning. His father, the prominent Congregational minister Jedidiah Morse, was a distinguished biblical scholar and the earliest American geographer. His geographies went beyond physical description to foretell the inevitable expansion of America's superior institutions into the "wild and uncultivated" West. Native peoples "fast melting away" before the advance would accept the inevitable or face grim alternatives.[21] Samuel inherited that perspective and, as the preacher's son, surely knew the context of the passage he chose to telegraph. Near the end of the Hebrews' wilderness wandering they drew close to the Moabites, whose king, Balak, hired a holy man, Balaam, to implore God to repel the invaders. Alas, Balaam reported, it was hopeless. The Hebrews were God's chosen people. They marched with an irresistible authority to fulfill their destiny, and the world could only stand in wonder: "It shall be said of Jacob and Israel, What hath God wrought?" Should any resist, he went on, God's chosen will be like a great lion that "shall not lie down until he eat of the prey and drink of the blood of the slain."

Morse's inaugural message was not of awe at human invention. It was a divine blessing on the nation's destiny. Others preached the same lesson. Musing on the telegraph and its meaning, a New York editorialist effused that "steam and electricity," the combined miracle of rails and wires, had created the "most wonderful country the sun has ever shined upon." Its continental dominance was ordained, and any foolish enough to stand in the way "will be crushed . . . into impalpable powder."

Vision and Greed: Thinking across the Continent

The telegraph's corresponding story, that of the earliest rail connection to the Pacific, ranks high in the brisk competition for the most misrepresented in western history.[22] The connection is almost always called the first transcontinental railroad, but it wasn't transcontinental and it wasn't the first. Its length of about 1,900 miles, from Omaha, Nebraska, to San Francisco, was roughly two-thirds of that from coast to coast, and it was finished fourteen years after the forty-seven miles of the Panama Railroad first connected ocean to ocean. By the usual story the first Pacific rail line quickly transforms the country between the Missouri and the Pacific. "Feeder lines" spread off the main routes and aroused the interior into healthy growth. Spindly new settlements lean toward them, like plants toward sunlight. As they hasten new settlement of the West, railroads provide the means for the military to subdue and dispossess its Native peoples. In time all those images were true enough, but when it was first built the Pacific rail connection was largely unnecessary and of little use to most of the land it touched. It did absolutely nothing toward what many argued was its primary purpose, securing the Pacific coast for the Union. Eventually its influence was indeed expansive, but it was birthed from narrow localism, and, for all its high-minded rhetoric, it was accomplished through bluster, chicanery, inefficiency, and breathtaking corruption.

There had been calls for a rail link to the Pacific virtually from the moment the far West was acquired. The idea had a certain airy logic. Nearly a million square miles, what Indian Agent Thomas Fitzpatrick called a great "disconnecting wilderness," separated the bulk of Americans east of the Mississippi River from the growing population on the Pacific.[23] Railways, nicely adaptable to the West's great distances and variations of climate and terrain, seemed the obvious way to span it, and the government surveys of the 1850s presumed one would soon do just that. Like telegraphy, railroads fit the image of a vital America seizing the future. "No man can keep up with the spirit of this age," Stephen Douglas had written in 1853, "who travels on anything slower than the locomotive, and fails to receive intelligence by lightning."[24]

The West, however, was also where rail construction was least likely to occur. Taking on the job seemed financial suicide. The unthinkably large cost would be far more than any individual or corporation was willing to risk or even scratch together. All likely routes were partly unsurveyed and in some places unexplored. As for profits, the very reasons given for building the line—to bridge the unpeopled gap in the nation's middle—was another way of saying that, for the foreseeable future, there would be no people to pay for using it. Nearly all business would be at either end. Most of the miles between would drain income, not add to it.

The Civil War cracked open the door to the project. In the penultimate plank of its 1860 platform Republicans called for a Pacific railroad, and their new president strongly supported it. The departure of southeastern lawmakers broke the deadlock over which course the line would take, while supporters played on fears of Confederate schemes to seize California. The notion that a line would be finished in time to have any influence was beyond ludicrous, and in fact the Union Pacific let its first construction contract three days before Robert E. Lee's surrender, but in the alarm of the day calls to build a line garnered serious support. Some advocated a massive government project in the European fashion, but a reverence for private enterprise and a reluctance to levy taxes weighed against it. Thus the railroad riddle remained. A Pacific rail line was widely assumed to be of great ultimate benefit, yet its problems made it a project impossible to sell. What emerged was a blend of private and public approaches like what had sent the telegraph to the Pacific. The government would charter, assist, and oversee the enterprise, but this, one of the most ambitious undertakings ever proposed, would be done under what one politician called "the lynx eye of capital."[25]

The solution to the riddle seems conceptually brilliant. Its particulars were laid out in the Pacific Railway Act, passed by Congress on July 1, 1862. First, the government chartered a new corporation (something last done with the Second National Bank), the Union Pacific Company, and authorized it to issue a hundred thousand shares of stock at a thousand dollars each. Investors buying the stock presumably would fund the project, but few were likely to put their money into a railroad that did not yet exist and was prey to so many unknowns. So, second, the government would loan funds for construction to the Union Pacific and to the Central Pacific, a corporation created under California law to build from California eastward. The loans took the form of $50 million in bonds, handed out at the rate of $16,000 for every mile built over level terrain, twice that for hilly country, and $48,000 for each mountain mile. Bonds would be handed over only as rails were laid, not in advance, which proved to be a crucial point. To make the bonds a safe bet, Washington guaranteed their payment at maturity.

It was a staggering sum, more than had ever been given or even contemplated. But it was a *loan*. Given that western settlement would be gradual and erratic, how could the companies hope to repay it? The answer, the third part of the stratagem, was to give the companies what the government had in abundance—land, every other section along the route, five sections deep on each side, or 6,400 acres per mile. The land was worthless at the time, but the railroad supposedly would change that. The more the West was connected to the outside world, the more its value, as real estate, would grow, and the land closest to transportation, in this case the acres along the tracks gifted by the government, would appreciate the most and the quickest. As it did, the companies could sell it and apply the income to paying the loans. By selling land to pay their debts, the railroads would also be filling up the interior and creating customers for future business. It got better. Because the government kept every other section along the rails, the settlers buying the government parts of the checkerboard would be paying prices instantly elevated by the railroad that now was paying back its obligations. Washington's pot would be not only replenished but sweetened.

The scheme was ingenious—in theory. Congress would use what it had most of, land, to fund what it thought that land needed most, a railroad, and it would finance what seemed hopelessly expensive with what at the time was essentially worthless. Here was the quintessence of western dreaming, a vast corporate version of every squatter's hope. The Pacific Railway Act seemed to create something out of nothing.

In reality it was born not as a sweeping vision of continental connection but a jerry-rigged alliance of local interests. Southeastern contenders were out of the picture, but several towns from Missouri northward still contested for the eastern terminus. Since none would support a bill that gave the prize to a rival—or, as a critic groused, unless the proposed line "starts in the corner of every man's farm"—a bill from Rep. James Rollins of Missouri provided that three lines (involving six companies) be built from the Missouri Valley to the one-hundredth meridian in western Kansas. From there one new company, the Union Pacific, would build westward to meet another line built out of California by the Central Pacific. The Central Pacific also represented a coalition of local interests. Its lobbyist in Washington was its engineer Theodore Judah, speaking for Sacramento businessmen later called the Big Four, or the Associates—Collis Huntington, Leland Stanford, Charles Crocker, and Mark Hopkins. They in turn were allied with interests bound up in the Nevada Central Railroad in a move to control the route from Sacramento to the mines of the Comstock Lode. Those forging the law for a grand national enterprise, then, did so from a much narrower subregional focus, the middle Missouri Valley and key passes over the Sierra Nevada. It is questionable how much the principals cared at first about actually pushing a line across the continent. Those in the East focused on getting their hands on public lands in Kansas, Iowa, and Nebraska; the western Associates wanted to control traffic to Nevada mines by a wagon toll road over Donner Pass.[26]

That concentration on either end, with softer concern between, was in a sense appropriate. Historian Richard White has written that the trackage outside California, Nevada, and the eastern feeder lines was both a guaranteed financial drain and unnecessary for supplying California and the Pacific coast. For many years to come maritime traffic met that need more efficiently and economically than railroads would. Rail companies would sometimes pay ships to sail empty around Cape Horn to force shippers to use their boxcars instead. The Union and Central Pacific, as White puts it, "were from their beginning always running ahead of schedule," in this case claiming as their purpose the servicing of huge areas long before they needed it.[27]

Even where railroads were needed, building stalled for lack of funds. The builders would get money to lay tracks by selling land and bonds, but to get land and bonds they first had to lay tracks. Congress had expected owners to reach into their own pockets to provide that initial investment, but for good reasons they were unwilling. They might sell stock for the startup funds, but the law required the stock be sold at par, and no one was buying. During the wartime frenzy anyone with money to invest had far safer options for fast and hefty profits. Out in California directors of the Central Pacific used federal bonds as collateral on a loan, convinced San Francisco and Sacramento voters to buy its stock, and received a promise from the state to give them bonds, ten thousand dollars for every mile completed, in return for future free passage for state militia, convicts, and inmates of madhouses. Nonetheless workers laid the first rails only in October 1863, and by early 1864 the line was still shy of the forty-mile mark required for the first issue of government bonds. Back East the Union Pacific was yet to spike down its first rail.

During 1864 two developments finally got the project moving. Each was highly shady even by standards of the time. After aggressive lobbying and the gifting of a quarter million dollars in bonds to amenable legislators, a second Pacific Railroad Act was passed.[28] It authorized the Union Pacific to issue its own bonds as a first mortgage, meaning they were first in line to be paid off, shoving the government bonds back to second mortgage status. The law also allowed the company to issue up to another $50 million in stock, for a total of $100 million, with the minimum price reduced from $1,000 to a $100 and with no limits on how many shares any one person could buy. To enhance the project's long-term appeal, the government doubled the land grant, to 12,800 acres per mile, and released the mineral rights it had kept to itself in 1862, which proved to be highly profitable. Washington also loosened its reins to allow the release of bonds and to grant land in advance of construction.

The practical effect of it all was to ease the release of money to the companies while sweetening the opportunities and reducing the risks for investors. This also increased the chances that the government would end up paying if the arrangement should fail. Sloppy drafting of the bill also gave the rail companies a stunning windfall. By a later court ruling, the Union and Central Pacific were responsible for only simple annual interest on the bonds, not compounded interest, and they did not have to pay until the bonds matured. Instead of using money from bond sales to pay out the interest semiannually (payments the government was instead obliged to make), they could hold and invest the funds as they wished. The harvest came probably to more than $40 million.[29]

The second development in 1864 was the creation of two insider construction companies, the Crédit Mobilier and the Contract and Finance Company, the first for the Union Pacific, the second for the Central Pacific. This represented a shift in the ambitions of the companies' principals from constructing lines at either end to building across the continent. The purpose was neither lofty national purpose nor profits from traffic, which clearly would not be coming for quite a while. The profits, rather, would be grand and immediate and through the same device used to string the transcontinental telegraph—a construction company owned by the same people letting its contracts. The two corporations in effect would be paying themselves, and paying quite well. First, however, they had to overcome key obstacles. The plan's originator was the appropriately named George Francis Train, a wealthy eccentric whose public speeches flowed "like an embodied Niagara."[30] He convinced Union Pacific officers, in particular its vice president and main promoter, Thomas C. Durant, to try the scheme, which came to him, he wrote later, in a flash that "cleared the sky . . . [and] made the construction of the great line a certainty."[31]

The Union Pacific would use its unsellable stock, valued at par, to pay Crédit Mobilier. It paid it also with its own bonds and with those from the government, which, as of the new law, it could now acquire prior to construction. The bonds, at least, had a market, and as they were sold to the public the work could begin, which in turn would release more government bonds and land. But to produce enough money to pay for the road, plus other expenses (overhead, lobbying, and more) and especially the exorbitant profits the principals demanded, enormous amounts of stock and bonds were called for. Actual work that cost $10,000 might need $20,000, and since no one would buy the stock, getting the $20,000 required the issue of $40,000 in bonds—for $10,000 worth of work. Thus the total paid out was far, far greater than what the job would in fact cost. Union Pacific directors, however, had no reason to complain about being vastly overcharged, since ultimately they, as principals of the Crédit Mobilier, were the ones being vastly overpaid.

On the other end the Central Pacific granted itself bloated construction contracts through the Contract and Finance Company. The company's main advantage over the Crédit Mobilier, one historian remarked, was that it "was able to get its accounts into such shape that no one has ever quite been able to disentangle them."[32] And in fact when a government investigation later demanded to see the company's books, none were to be found. A later investigation concluded that owners of the Central Pacific cleared at least $10 million by building their own line, and they took in huge amounts as well from state and local subsidies.

At the end of the war the project was starting to lumber into life. Lee's surrender began to ease a national shortage of labor and equipment, and although it was a full eight months after Appomattox before the Union Pacific completed its first forty miles, by 1867 the grand project was well under way and (in a metaphor born from the industry) was gathering steam.

Certain particulars around the Pacific railroad naturally draw attention. There was the astonishing vault of some leading characters from modest merchantry into stratospheric wealth. Collis Huntington, physically and personally imposing, was a former watch salesman turned California hardware merchant in partnership with Mark Hopkins. Charles Crocker, portly and clean shaven but for a shrub of chin hair, had operated a forge before also moving into merchandising. Thick-witted Leland Stanford turned early from the law to rise in California's fluid politics. Oliver and Oakes Ames, Bostonian brothers who became major players in the Union Pacific, were nicknamed the "Kings of Spades" after prospering with a Massachusetts factory producing what could stand for the symbol of this age of remaking America—shovels. All had done well, but they were hardly members of the financial aristocracy. Huntington and Hopkins were among Sacramento's leading merchants, yet their business was valued in 1861 at only $21,401 and Huntington's personal property at $8,680. The funds that the principal figures personally invested were miniscule.[33] Yet in the end all were on trajectories to entering the ozone of the nation's wealthiest.

There was, too, the operation's unblushing corruption. It had its defenders. A participant of the day was asked whether the Crédit Mobilier had overcharged the Union Pacific. "It depends upon how you look at it," he answered: "If your right-hand pocket had more money than your left, and you took some from your right and put it in your left, you would be neither richer nor poorer."[34] The era's businesses did indeed run under far looser rules than even a generation or two later. Congress, however, passed the law of 1862 not to watch the Union Pacific owners jump over a hurdle but to ensure that the principals would risk their own capital, not create a financial structure resting wholly on government credit. But making an operation based on government credit is precisely what happened, and it was done not by a tactic widely winked at but by one, insider construction, that critics had warned about from the start. By a *conservative* estimate the Crédit Mobilier cleared 74 percent a year, or 370 percent by 1869. Economist Robert Fogel set the figure between 480 and 610 percent, translating into as much as $16.5 million between 1864 and 1869.[35]

A wider lesson concerned the financial arrangements that evolved with the project. For all its ethical rot, the Pacific line was a new level of partnering between government and capital that would become increasingly central to the economic landscape, not only in western enterprises of mining, ranching, and farming, but across the country, including the railroads meant to reknit Northeast and Southeast. The Pacific road, not its physical presence but in how it was created and paid for, was another sort of connector. It linked the years of prewar division and crisis to an era of new financial arrangements that, while abusive of public trust and productive of economic pain, would be used again and again to capture western resources and to remake and reunify the nation.

And more: the rail connection was among the earliest instances of colonizing powers extending their grasp by shrinking distances and mastering geographies. The Suez Canal opened for its first traffic 191 days after completion of the Pacific railway, and over the next forty years rail lines built into the interiors of Africa, India, and Indochina secured for European empires resources and military control. From this perspective the American project, for all its improvisational lurch from start to finish, turned out to be literally pathbreaking. Washington's commitment, however premature, and the seat-of-the-pants shenanigans of Huntington, the Ameses, Durant, Stanford, and others, however corrupt, coalesced into a modern imperial mechanism, an American invention born of expansion and gold that anticipated others that would span other continents and, like this one, would trigger the dispossession, subjugation, and cultural assault on their Native peoples.[36]

Pushing toward the Center over Mass and Space

The railroad's construction has a legacy as mixed as its conception. The financial chicanery continued, and many of its principals reaped enormous wealth by riding on the public's back. At the line's completion both the Union Pacific and Central Pacific were up to their corporate noses in debt that would only grow deeper, obligations that ultimately taxpayers were to pay. Much of the line's 1,900 miles was so poorly laid that it was in need of repair or replacement before the famous final spike was set. And yet from a loftier view the first Pacific railroad, as an engineering and organizational aesthetic, was extraordinary. It was by far the longest in the world. It produced numerous engineering innovations at a time of rapidly expanding global rail networks. Most impressive—and easiest to miss, knowing how things turned out—is that the project jelled at all. It began with its organizers not knowing how they would pay for it. Engineers did not know what challenges were ahead, much less how to meet them. They didn't even know *where* their problems would be, since there was no precision to the route. Field commanders did not know where they would get their workers and how they could keep them, where they would bed them and how they would feed them, how best to organize them and, since they didn't quite know what jobs they would be doing, how they might train them. Out of this great uncertainty emerged a coordination of forces and finally an operation of considerable scope and not a little grace. Surveyors, shovelers, drillers, blasters, tie-men, rail-layers, gaugers, spikers, drovers, teamsters, blacksmiths, lumberjacks, carpenters, cooks, bakers, and clerks all merged into what was, in both senses of the word, something singular.

Builders grappled with the West's two defining physical characteristics—mass and space. On the western end the Central Pacific faced the daunting Sierra Nevada. Shoved high by California's vigorous tectonics, deeply gorged by erosion and faulting, the Sierra was among the western hemisphere's most rugged cordilleras. Winter storms swept the high country with hurricane winds and dumped snow up to five or more feet in a day. There was no lucky gateway like the great saddle the Union Pacific would use to cross the continental divide. Theodore Judah, the initial chief engineer, had surveyed a route that rose from Sacramento past Dutch Flat, connecting there with the Big Four's profitable toll road, then on to the summit and down into Nevada's Truckee River Valley. This portion of the road was far and away the most difficult and costly of either company. It had a grim heritage. Twenty years earlier the starving Donner Party had been trapped and had fallen to cannibalism in the pass Judah had chosen for this first rail link.

Securing and paying for equipment, tools, and materials was almost as intimidating as topping the Sierra. From New York Collis Huntington organized funding and procurement and coordinated sending supplies around Cape Horn. From San Francisco they were shipped upriver to Sacramento and hauled by wagon and later by rail as close as possible to the work, then humped the rest of way by whatever means could be devised. Mark Hopkins, eldest and least involved of the four, kept the books, and Stanford, elected governor in 1861 and nominally head of the company, kept the political skids well greased.

Grading and bridge-building crews began in late October 1863, but by September 1865 only fifty-four miles of rails had been laid, and in the next hundred miles the line would have to ascend more than seven thousand feet. The greater problem was to make a smooth and steady incline out of topography as fractured and jumbled as any in America. Any given mile might require filling gullies and low points with thousands of tons of rock, building trestles over canyons as deep as a hundred feet, blasting cuts through hundreds of yards of towering rock, and eventually tunneling through granite. In the foothills the first stage required cutting through woodlands thick with trees up to a dozen stories tall and eight feet in diameter then clearing debris, grading, and laying track.[37] Rains in 1865–66, the heaviest in memory, turned potential roadbeds into a morass. Crews watched for slides of boulders and red mud as they blasted and pulled at gargantuan stumps. They built masonry culverts, some nearly thirty feet tall, to keep the runoff from washing out everything they had done. Higher up, well ahead of track-laying, others began the more laborious work of hacking a workable grade along sides of cliffs and drilling tunnels where there was no other option. They moved by an agonized inching. During 1866 the Central Pacific advanced less than six hundred feet a day. At $8 million total, the cost was about $211,000 per mile.[38]

Managers advertised for five thousand men; eight hundred showed up. Both the Union and Central Pacific faced the same dilemma. They needed huge amounts of grunt work done under harsh conditions and rigid discipline, yet on the frontier, defined as a place with plenty to do and too few to do it, workers usually had better options, and once hired many were balky and liable to bolt. The problem was compounded in the California mountains, where the work was hardest, the conditions most appalling, and the alternatives, dreams of gold in this case, the most seductive.

When Charles Crocker, who directed construction, suggested hiring Chinese, James Strobridge, a tall, profane Vermonter who oversaw the labor force with one eye (having lost the other in a powder explosion early in the work), at first refused. He invoked the usual canards—they were dirty weaklings, bizarre in habits, and repulsive at mealtime—but he relented, and Chinese laborers soon were handling even the more technical tasks of blasting and drilling.[39] Most of the roughly hundred thousand in California had been largely pressured out of mining, so there were plenty available. After drawing all the local Chinese they could, the company turned to jobbers in San Francisco whose agents in the Canton region recruited young men, mostly farmers in their twenties, who agreed to repay their passage in regular installments. The Central Pacific paid a lump sum to the recruiters, who took their own portion and distributed the rest to the recruited. Jobbers even provided the laborers' food. Each mess of up to twenty men had a cook who prepared vegetables, dried seaweed, cuttle-fish, pork, chicken, and rice. Tea was carried to the work site in powder kegs and served out of forty-gallon whiskey barrels. Eventually about twelve thousand Chinese, eight of ten workers, would labor along the line. Each terminus became a China camp crowded with small huts with wooden cots inside and outside small tubs for sponge baths at day's end.

The company was pleased. "Wherever we put them, we found them good," Crocker would testify, and in the crucial but grueling labor of tunneling, he wrote to Huntington, "they can't be beat." Besides their "quiet, peaceable, [and] patient" nature, Stanford found that they "have no strikes that amount to anything" and were contented with less than half the wages paid to a white man's.[40] The language was loaded. Its adjectives were positive variations of meek compliance and docility, precisely what critics of Chinese labor had long stressed in their hostility to "coolie" labor.

In fact the Chinese laborers were not as complacent as described. On June 25, 1867, along an especially arduous stretch, they tossed aside picks and shovels as if by common signal, returned to their camps, and insisted that their hours be shortened and their pay raised from thirty-five to forty dollars a month. "The truth is, they are getting smart," wrote an alarmed Crocker. When they held firm, he and Hopkins played on free labor's racial and economic anxieties by importing recently freed Blacks. They could not have been more explicit. "A Negro labor force would tend to keep the Chinese steady," Crocker wrote Huntington, "as the Chinese have kept the Irishmen quiet." The ultimate answer was to "inundate" California and Nevada with workers: "Freedmen, Chinese, Japanese, all kinds of laborers, so that men come to us for work instead of our hunting them up. . . . A surplus will keep wages low. It is our only remedy for strikers." The immediate remedy was more direct. The company pressed the contractors to withhold all food. After a week the famished workers were back on the job.[41]

The incident, which seemed to come from nowhere and ended obscurely, is a reminder of how the view of the Chinese experience remains opaque, starting with the basics. How many died punching the Central Pacific through the Sierra? One Sacramento press report in 1870 told of a single shipment of ten tons of bones arriving from the mountains to be sent home, remains of "perhaps 1,200 Chinamen." Another on the same day had the number of deceased at fifty.[42] As here, impressions are often mixed and the workers voiceless. Some impressions were surprisingly positive. Two days before the driving of the last spike, Edwin Crocker, Charles's brother and the company's attorney, toasted the "fidelity and industry" of "that poor, despised class of laborers called the Chinese."[43] In the public eye, however, Chinese workers remained alien and cartoonish, which left them uniquely vulnerable to changes in corporate need and popular mood. Once the Central Pacific was finished they faced a growing resentment and some intense local hostility. As one historian put it, the success of their work led to the expendability of their lives.[44]

By the summer of 1867 the push was on for the summit. The last twenty miles needed fifteen tunnels. The longest, a third of a mile long, took twenty months to bore. As many as four hundred kegs of powder were spent daily blasting through the metamorphic rock. The advance was typically less than a foot every twenty-four hours. Crocker turned to the promising menace of nitroglycerin, eight times as powerful as black powder. With that ("*Nitroclycerine tells*," Crocker exulted to Huntington) the pace doubled to a respectable creep of four yards a month.[45] There were forty-four storms the winter of 1866–67, two of them leaving ten feet of snow between February 18 and

March 3. A snowplow eleven feet tall and ten feet wide and mounted on a railcar kept the track partly open, and elsewhere gangs of men with ox sleds removed the accumulation a shovelful at a time. In the cuts, with no place else to shove it, snow was stuffed into cars and hauled to Sacramento, "to the infinite delight of snow-balling youth."[46] Workers abandoned traditional snowshoes and strapped on long thin strips of wood grooved on the bottoms, "Norwegian snowshoes," an early introduction of skiing to the West. Because tunneling had begun before the first snow, weather did not hinder the digging itself, "except," an engineer wrote, "as . . . avalanches sweep over the shanties of the laborers." Some operations dealt with the snow by staying under it. Tunnels up to two hundred feet long were extended out of the granite through the packed accumulation. Some had windows punched out for light and ventilation, and in one a flight of stairs was hacked deeper into the drift to a room for a subnivean smithy.[47]

On the far side crews graded and built bridges and trestles, so the summer of 1867 became a season of linking completed parts into a whole. Tunneling continued. The longest and highest, tunnel no. 6, was dug from each end and, after a shaft was sunk from 125 feet above it, from the center outward. Rock was lifted out with a steam hoist made by retooling the state's first locomotive, the Sacramento. Tunnel no. 6 was finished in August, and on the last day of November the first passengers arrived by train at the summit.

Meanwhile, construction of the Union Pacific had stopped for the winter at Cheyenne, a ramshackle tossed together to house essentials during the cold months. A little more than five hundred miles had been completed, less than halfway to where it eventually would join the Central Pacific, but the terrain was far easier than on the Pacific end. Forty years later one of the lead surveyors told an audience: "The Lord had so constructed the country that any engineer, who failed to take advantage of the great open road from here west to Salt Lake would not have been fit to belong to the profession."[48] The Union Pacific's main line ran out of Council Bluffs, Iowa, and Omaha, Nebraska, and followed the valley of the Platte River for the first four hundred miles to the junction of the North and South Platte. Ahead were the Rocky Mountains. Planners chose a route between options through Denver and the gold towns and across the overland crossing at South Pass. Theirs would go up the South Platte and then up Lodgepole Creek and over the Laramie Mountains, onto the Laramie plain, then west to Green River. It was more direct by seventy miles, and the wind patterns kept the snow from piling up as badly as at South Pass. Surveyors had also found great coal deposits along this route—a prime reason Union Pacific directors had made sure the 1864 law gave them mineral rights to their land grants. Even before the line was completed mining had begun at Rock Springs, Wyoming.

Finding an acceptable grade to cross the Laramie Mountains, mostly under 9,500 feet, was a greater puzzle than that for the Sierra Nevada. There seemed no way to meet the law's demand of a rise of no more than 2.2 percent, or 116 feet per mile. After considerable searching, engineers found a divide at what was later named Sherman Hill (elevation 8,471 feet). Once that particular lock was picked, the way opened across the Wyoming Basin and into Utah.[49]

In the construction itself, Grenville M. Dodge is usually given credit for both broad oversight and much of the week-by-week direction, a distortion arising from Dodge's autopuffery.[50] In fact the survey and building were much more a collaborative effort. Dodge, who had risen to a general's rank during the war before resigning in the spring of 1866 to join the project, had helped plot the route while stationed on the plains. Peter Dey, an engineering luminary who had worked with Dodge in the 1850s, surveyed the Platte Valley and tapped James Evans and Samuel Reed to find the best way from the Laramie Mountains westward. Dey left early in disgust over the corruption among the principals, but the other two remained deeply involved. Reed became superintendent of construction. In charge of track-laying were the brothers John S. "General Jack" and Dan Casement. While not as sweeping as he portrayed it, Dodge's role was considerable and varied. As chief engineer he had full command of ancillary construction and repairs after the road was finished. He took energetic part in the detailed survey of the established path. He directed the choosing (and promoted the business) of towns founded along the route, lobbied effectively with the government, and as much as anyone smoothed the choppy relations within the company and with others outside.[51]

Supplies and equipment were first carried up the Missouri or freighted overland, but once the Chicago, Rock Island and Pacific Railroad reached Council Bluffs, the railroad could feed its own construction. Crates and barrels of flour, sugar, coffee, beans, oats, dried fish, vegetables, bacon, rice, corn, and molasses rolled into camp daily, along with tents, candles, blankets, and other basics for this work force on the move. Organizers applied logistical experience from the recent war to what was in effect another campaign of conquest, this time of geographical challenges rather than secessionists. Workers, too, often came to the job out of the army and so were switching one form of disciplined, top-down mass labor for another. Recruiters also brought in newly arrived Irish to fill the ranks.

On the semiarid plains and even more so in the Great Basin finding wood for bridges and for ties, roughly 2,500 per mile, was a constant worry. Planners chose their route through the Rockies for its access to mountain timber as well as coal, but for long stretches the only source was cottonwood, soft and pulpy, that had to be burnettized, toughened by replacing its water with a zinc solution.[52] Water too was sometimes desperately short. Surveyors did their best to plot a course that took advantage of what was available—the modern town of Rawlins, Wyoming, is named for Brig. Gen. John A. Rawlins, Dodge's companion who discovered a clear spring on the site—but ultimately there was not much to be done.

As the Central Pacific crept forward by inches, construction of the Union Pacific proceeded in 100-mile increments. Out front engineers laid down the exact pathway within the broadly established route. Next came the largest part of the workforce, the graders. The basic job was to dig dirt from one place and haul it in barrows to where the rails would run to build a grade at least 2 feet up and about 12 feet wide, ballasted with sand and packed and smoothed enough to support rails and what they would carry. Teams hacked cuts into hills and hummocks that could not be bypassed. Some were manmade canyons 60 or more feet deep and hundreds of feet long. At each terminus carloads of rails disgorged their loads into fleets of wagons, with one rail hefted and dropped every 30 seconds, 40 rails to a wagon. At the newly raised grade men hustled each rail, 30 feet long and 560 pounds, to its place and dropped it to the ties. With a rod of precisely the correct length a gauger made sure the distance between the rails was what Abraham Lincoln had approved: 4 feet, 8½ inches. The spikers stepped up next. They pounded in each spike, usually with 3 blows, and it done: a 30-foot stretch of a 100-mile segment of ultimately more than 1,000 miles of track. Thus the road progressed, uncountable barrows of dirt dug and dumped and leveled, a tie every 2 feet, 350 to 400 rails every mile, 10 spikes per rail.

By 1867–68 the Union Pacific workforce numbered about 10,000. Close to 4,000 were graders, fewer than 500 were rail-layers, and only 100 were surveyors, with the rest divided among tie-cutters, shop workers, and support labor at the base camp. Whether an individual worker found any pride or significance in this cannot be said, but in the context of the day he had little to complain about. His wages were good, between $2.50 and $4.00 a day, less $5.00 a week for room and board. He would work at least as hard for less pay at many jobs elsewhere, and living conditions were better and the food superior and more dependable than on any campaign in the late war. For Confederate veterans this life was a long step upward. Workers close enough to the terminus lived out of a camp centering on 4 enormous cars 80 feet long and 10 wide used for offices, kitchen, dining, and bunks. Grazing nearby were 500 cattle to keep the rough plank tables (127 feet of them) heavy with the beef that General Jack Casement thought was the best diet for the men, with potatoes, beans, fresh bread, and coffee on the side. Some slept on flatcars, others in bunk cars, and during high summer many on the roofs. Graders working down the line were supplied from ranks of wagons and slept in the open or in crude dugouts with sheet metal roofs. There was an hour's break for lunch. Evenings were full of smoke and talk.

To pay for it all and to keep the profits coming, Union Pacific principals continued their dodgy maneuvers—and added others. As the bonds used to pay (or, rather, overpay) Crédit Mobilier were sold, the income was used for both laying rails and fattening the owners' profits. Once rails were laid, the company began to receive its alternate sections of land along the right-of-way. Some was sold, especially along the easternmost stretch where a railroad made actual economic sense, then some of the unsold land was mortgaged to produce more funds for more tracks, more land, and more profit. One asset, however, was dead weight. The stock that had been used to pay Crédit Mobilier remained largely unsellable and thus effectively worthless. That changed. Owners began using part of their borrowed funds to pay dividends, which conveyed an impression of viability and success. The stock began to sell. The Union Pacific owners had been forbidden to sell it below par, but once they had given it as payment to the Crédit Mobilier (that is, to themselves), they were free to market it at a far lower price. Stock worth $100 at face value—stock in an apparently going enterprise—was offered at $60, or $50, or $40. To an investor, making money by buying it appeared to be as sure as gravity. The transactions were indeed profitable—for the Union Pacific principals. Stock they had used only as a ruse to get things going now was suddenly worth something, and because their other maneuvers had already paid for expenses and their first round of profits, whatever they sold, whether at 90 percent of par, or 60 percent, or 30 percent, or 1 percent, was pure gravy.

In the world of bottom lines, however, the Union Pacific sank ever deeper in debt. The paper value of Union Pacific's bonds and stock had little resemblance to the railroad's reality. First its construction and then its operation relied on marketing an illusion. When the great national contraction of 1873 called its bluff, the Union Pacific would fold in upon itself, and its investors, and eventually the taxpayers, would bear the cost.

And so the great effort progressed. From above, it moved through financial contortion and obfuscation. On the ground, the two termini moved toward one another through organizational efforts as complex as in any campaign in the recent war. By 1868 any one day's combined muscle power surely surpassed anything given before to any one project in American history (at least since construction of the great pre-Columbian mounds). On April 16 crowds gathered and champagne corks popped at Sherman Summit as the first locomotive ascended to this highest point on the Union Pacific line. Ahead of them surveyors worked rapidly to chart the route into Utah. The Central Pacific was finally about to break out of the Sierra and was surveying eastward even more ambitiously. The two lines were now in competition for the miles remaining and the dollars and acres that came with them. Huntington hoped to race across Nevada and Utah well past the Great Salt Lake to the base of the Wasatch Mountains. They should grab and hold the right of way, he wrote Crocker, "as though it was held by the great I am." Coming at them, however, were General Jack Casement's crews on the downslope past the continental divide. "We are now *Sailing*," he wrote his wife.[53]

11 ➤ Connections Real and Imagined

Railroads and telegraph lines were the main strands of an increasingly dense web born of those revolutionary technologies. Surveyors and roadbuilders made their own connections, many of them branching off rail lines, that commercial firms used to circulate everything from people and billiard tables to gold dust and velvet trousers, all of it coordinated through the spreading net of wire. It all came together into a continental connective, built in scarcely a generation. It in turn played a part in an enduring influence of the West on American life. Whatever else it was and did, the West was an imaginative creation that from the start has served as a screen others have used to project how they perceived the nation. Here the maturing structure of movement and exchange fed a paradoxical vision. The West was the stage where actors performed the making of a new and unified America, yet the West as performed was also a land ever and dependably apart.

Myth and Consummation

No event in the West during these years commanded more public attention than the Pacific rail project. Journals and newspapers followed it in scores of articles, and few literary visitors resisted observing and writing about the spectacle. Its scale and visibility alone made it difficult to ignore, but it had more than that going for it. The simple fact of its being built, the particulars of how it was carried out, and imagined events and threats that in fact were not there were the ideal makings for myths around the emerging West and its meanings for a reconstructing America.

The most obvious theme was of western settlement as the unifying sequel to the Civil War's saving the Union. As if in relay, the Union Pacific's first rails were being laid simultaneous with the end of the war. Its most prominent field commanders came from high in the ranks in eastern campaigns. Maj. Gen. Grenville Dodge had served in Missouri, Tennessee, and Mississippi, and Brig. Gen. Jack Casement in engagements throughout the war, eventually marching through Georgia under William T. Sherman. Sherman himself would oversee protection along the route. Descriptions of construction evoked troops in mass array. Construction teams stood "like the grand reserve of an army" behind the graders, and once at work their spiking of rails sounded up close like a "hotly contested skirmish" and from a distance like the "roar of the wonderful advance."

In 1873 the popular *Croffut's Transcontinental Tourist Guide* recalled that in 1860 the nation had faced being riven, not into two, but into three parts—North, South, and West. It had taken the Civil War, that "carnival of blood," to convince naysayers into building the Pacific railroad that now joined all three into one.[1] The next year *Croffut's* would feature on its cover John Gast's *American Progress*, with its floating female figure leading the railroad westward while stringing a telegraph line. Politicians hailed the project as truly national. A "free and living Republic" would spring up along rail lines as "surely as grass and flowers follow in the spring," one promised.[2] His reference was not to Nevada or Oregon but to the former Confederacy. Railroads were called agents of both reconstruction and recommitment. They would fuse all sections into one by tapping their resources, easing the movement of their peoples, and overcoming a bloody past with a binding prosperity.[3]

In this, the shift in the railroad's message could not have been sharper. An especially illuminating irony of the Union Pacific is this: Crédit Mobilier, the corrupt engine that drove construction of what was now celebrated as the nation's great unifier, had been born in dedication to national division.[4] Before it was acquired and renamed by Thomas Durant and George Francis Train, it was the Pennsylvania Fiscal Agency, brainchild of Duff Green, an ardent slavery apologist from Georgia who hoped to fund lines from New Orleans through Texas and then both westward to Southern California and southwestward through Mexico to Mazatlán. His was one of many visions of a powerful bi-oceanic Southeast resting on the institution "intended by a wise Providence" for any civilized order—Black slavery.[5]

Now, with the Union preserved, the rhetoric of sectional dissonance gave way to one of railroads as agents of coalescence. As with the telegraph, bodily metaphors seemed irresistible. When the Pacific line was completed, Chicago celebrated with a hundred thousand persons in a seven-mile-long procession that ended with a windy oration by Vice President Schuyler Colfax. His imagery was both tangled and revealing. The nation had been literally reborn. Before the war it had been divided north-to-south but also, overall, had been a sprawling, inchoate body, what France's Charles-Maurice de Talleyrand had called "a giant without bones." In the war that body had found its strength and now, reaching westward, it had found its form. The new America lay toward the Pacific, the railroad its spine and with "iron ribs in every direction" and arms reaching for the commerce of Asia.[6]

This vision, of the railroad embodying a renewed nation, had distinctive western colorations. First among them was virility, a West of unbridled masculine energy. Its clearest description was in the towns, "Hell on Wheels," that served as supply and recreation points.[7] North Platte in Nebraska, Julesburg in Colorado, Benton, Laramie, Cheyenne, and Green River in Wyoming, and Bear River in Utah—some had been snoozing stage stops before being shaken awake. Others were built from nothing. All were collections of tents and flimsy plank buildings along dust-blown streets. Like other western working sites, notably mining camps and cattle towns, they were dominated by young men with spending money and glands at full throttle, on the loose from monotonous grunt work done under tight discipline. There was open, rampant vice. Visitors like Henry Morton Stanley wrote of the many hard cases, sharpers, and especially prostitutes, "expensive articles [who] come in for a large share of the money wasted."[8] A large, revolving population of over-liquored men translated into plenty of brawling and high-decibel disorder. There were a handful of homicides and in Bear River a riot that took at least a dozen lives. Cheyenne vigilantes hanged seven men in 1867 and 1868.[9]

That rough reality, however, was consistently overstressed. An eastern reporter claimed absurdly that Julesburg hosted 750 brothels and gambling houses. Samuel Bowles wrote that the towns, "congregation[s] of scum and wickedness," averaged a murder a day. Stanley agreed on the homicidal clip and noted that men walked the streets of Julesburg who had murdered for five dollars. The going rate in Cheyenne was ten, wrote a *Chicago Tribune* correspondent.[10] There is nothing to back up such claims, however. The *Frontier Index*, a newspaper that moved with the railroad, eagerly recorded the violence it witnessed from Laramie to Green River to Bear River, yet between March and November of 1868 it noted only a single murder and three lynchings (and dozens of arrests for public drunkenness and disorderly conduct).[11]

Even correcting for lively exaggeration, there seems something like a compulsive inflation of mayhem and dissipation that would be repeated over and again by visitors to the new country. The towns pictured at the tip of the railroad were expressions of expansion as national machismo. It was an image that would appear and prosper in various settings, a West of hairy chests and split lips.

Another theme, bloody as well, is of the railroad earning America's way westward through struggle and loss. The image here is of Native peoples as ferocious opponents. The most respected histories give the impression, as in the chapter titles of one: "If We Can Save Our Scalps," "Until They Are Severely Punished," and "They All Died in Their Boots."[12] Another wrote of bands of from twenty to two hundred warriors "but occasionally in the thousands" engaged in near-constant raids, it all adding up to "the agony of the Union Pacific."[13] The *Frontier Index* told of numerous rumored attacks on workers, none confirmed, and of horrific assaults on settlers that never happened, one with "copper-colored fiends" murdering seventeen women after raping them all, one of them forty times.[14] Grenville Dodge would write of multiple ferocious assaults, including one on himself that led to his discovery of the crucial pass that opened the gate to the far West—an attack that never happened and a pass someone else discovered eleven months later.[15]

There were certainly Indian attacks, mostly in-and-out raids to take horses and livestock and strikes at small groups of surveyors and woodcutters. Nothing in the record, however, suggests anything like a concerted resistance. There were many alarms from locals, "such Cowards and liars that it is impossible to place confidence in any story," one officer wrote. Military reports note plenty of scouting, escorting of stages, and occasional pursuit of suspicious groups but very few attacks.

The facts, as usual, are messier and revealing. The Union Pacific was entering a Native world of an evolving, adaptive strategy. By the time construction began in the Platte Valley, the Lakotas and Cheyennes had essentially conceded it and had largely withdrawn northward to the Powder River and southward between the Platte and the Arkansas. "We have no objection to this road [the Union Pacific]," a Lakota leader that summer told peace commissioners at a parlay in North Platte, "but we object to those along the Powder River and the Smoky Hill." Leave those areas alone, agreed a Cheyenne chief, and "your people can travel this road without being molested."[16] The had reason for concern. In 1863 John Bozeman and others had blazed a road, soon fortified by the military, that ran squarely through the Powder River country. Every summer from 1865 to 1867 had seen fighting there and to the east. Meanwhile the Union Pacific Eastern Division (soon to be the Kansas Pacific) was building out of Kansas City into the Cheyenne sanctuary south of the Platte. When the Cheyennes resisted, Gen. Winfield Scott Hancock sacked and burned one of their large villages on the Arkansas River after its people abandoned it.

This was the context for what violence did occur along the Union Pacific route. Serious incidents occurred in only two places. One was at Plum Creek, near the railroad's Ogallala Station in western Nebraska. It was the traditional crossing spot for Lakotas and Cheyennes, and violence there seems to have been chance encounters between younger warriors and whites. The other spot, where fighting was much more common, was around Lodgepole Creek, between the North and South Platte Rivers in southeastern Wyoming. Union Pacific engineers had deviated here from the Platte—that is, from the land the

Lakotas had conceded—to take advantage of topography and the timber that was also a vital resource for Indians. This area was the first accessible approach from the south for whites pointing northward to the Bozeman road. In effect it was a defensive extension of the Lakotas' prized country around the Powder River, and it was contested for the same reasons behind the fighting to the north. At least a dozen soldiers and civilians were killed here, well more than all deaths taken together elsewhere along hundreds of miles of construction. Violence along the Union Pacific's route, on the one hand, was far less than was usually portrayed and, on the other, was almost entirely where Lakotas and Cheyennes were simply crossing the line and where the railroad had swerved into country where they were determined to take their stand.

It is worth wondering, in fact, how much Indians considered the railroad at all. The episode most associated with the Plum Creek crossing came in August of 1867. There a group of Cheyennes saw their first train as it passed by. If they could "throw these wagons off the iron," one recalled thinking, they could learn what they carried. The men laid a log across the tracks and upset a handcar, scalping a passenger and leaving him for dead. Next they unspiked and moved a couple of rails. When an engine approached they tried to rope it like a horse, which did not work, but when the engine derailed they killed the engineer and brakeman and looted the boxcars of rifles, hatchets, whiskey, and bolts of bright calico, which they tied to their mounts' tails as flaring victory banners.[17] Four points are notable about the incident. Well into the progress of the Union Pacific across the plains, these Cheyennes looked on the train with bewildered curiosity. Their derailment of it was both successful and comically simple. The incident seems to have become widely and quickly known among Cheyennes and Lakotas. And they tried the tactic only once more, at the same spot, a bit more than a year later.

What was described as furious resistance comes down to opportunistic raids and occasional defensive thrusts from beleaguered people trying to hold fast to a shrinking homeland. That, however, did not fit the part the West was to play in remaking America. The railroad was called the forerunner of a great civilizing enterprise, and civilizing enterprises require savage barriers to meet and overcome. That was the Indians' role. Before the war, overland traffic along the Platte had introduced catastrophic diseases and brought environmental devastation to Native peoples along its way, yet the popular image had been of Native peoples terrorizing families heroized as carrying the seeds of a new and elevated order. Now, with the Union saved and projected toward the Pacific, the railroad reprised the role.

"Low and brutal" Natives were resisting it "inch by inch, foot by foot," wrote Silas Seymour, but the "laws of civilization" made the march of a superior people unstoppable. The view, absorbed in popular lore and most histories, was given substance by occasional artifactual spine-tinglers. The man scalped in the train attack in 1867 managed to retrieve his hair and walk to safety carrying it, a patch about four by nine inches, in a bucket of water. It reminded Stanley of a drowned rat. When doctors failed to reinstall it, he gave his scalp to history, a reminder of the days of an ever-present Indian threat to national progress. For generations it was displayed in the children's section of the Omaha Public Library.[18]

By the second half of 1868 the great project had entered its final phase. Once past the crest of the Sierra Nevada the Central Pacific engineers took advantage of a narrow break in the Carson Mountains, Truckee Canyon, and a fairly easy descent to the Great Basin. On June 19, less than seven months after the first train to the summit, they were finally out of the Sierra. The following month they added thirty-five miles and in the next month another forty-five. Soon they averaged more than two miles a day, and after slowing somewhat during the winter they reached that pace again in the spring. The route was nothing like the Union Pacific's easy slide up the Platte Valley—the Great Basin is not a smooth concavity but a washboard of alternating desert ranges and valleys— but the obstacles were not nearly as daunting as those of the first two years, and the seasoned Chinese and their bosses made excellent progress.

As the Central Pacific's job grew easier, the Union Pacific's toughened. Close to Sherman Hill the trickle of Dale Creek flowed through a canyon—deep, wide, and unavoidable—that required a bridge supported by an extraordinary latticework in turn held firm by guy wires. Beyond that was the arid stretch to Green River, with water sometimes hauled in more than fifty miles, and next the rise into the Wasatch Mountains and a tricky descent into Utah and the eastern side of the Great Basin. Unlike in previous years, the road's directors, ever eager for more miles and more bonds, did not stop the work for winter, and those on the ground discovered what life in the high country could be like. A ferocious blizzard halted shipments intermittently for more than three weeks. "Have seen a cut [through a hill] fill up in two hours which took 100 men 10 hours to shovel out," Jack Casement reported.[19] When the ground froze two feet deep, nitroglycerin was needed to loosen the soil enough for shoveling, and private woodcutting teams kept from freezing by burning ties they had cut to sell.[20] Sheets of ice made it treacherous simply to move around, much less keep at work. When a freight sled bogged at a crossing, a supply train struck and smashed it, spilling the cargo meant for the Mormon market: hundreds of pairs of baby shoes. Nonetheless by the end of January 1869 the Union Pacific had negotiated the difficult defile of Echo Canyon, where twelve years earlier the men of Deseret had set their defenses against Albert Sidney Johnston's advancing force, and was building toward Ogden.

By then any cooperation between the Union and Central Pacific had long given way to an increasingly tense rivalry. The original law of 1862 had a critical omission. It said nothing about where the two lines were to meet, or even if they *were* to meet. It effectively set up a race between the two corporations to determine which could cover more miles and thus reap the most land and the most money in bonds. This guaranteed that much of the headlong construction would be appallingly shoddy, and because nothing required the two lines to connect, the Central Pacific in theory could pull in its money-for-miles all the way to Omaha, the Union Pacific to Sacramento. At one point Central Pacific crews were grading parallel to Union Pacific tracks already laid in the opposite direction. After some jockeying the two compromised. The official meeting point would be near Ogden, north of Salt Lake City, which would leave each line with roughly the same amount paid in bonds.

The contact point would be near the northeastern edge of the Great Salt Lake at Promontory Summit. (Promontory Point, a stubby tongue of land on the lakeshore, often is misidentified as the juncture, perhaps because a congressional resolution used it in error and perhaps because of its alliterative appeal.) As with the entire project, the physical accomplishment of the final push from both ends redeemed somewhat the seedy stratagems and ugly bickering. The Union Pacific had built more than five hundred miles of road during the past year, and now its graders, working at double pay, labored night and day up switchbacks toward the summit. Excavation on the flats had cost about eighty cents a yard; here it was nearly four dollars.[21] The final approach required extensive rock-cutting and a trestle eighty-five feet high, "like a frame gossamer." The Central Pacific also lay track deep into each night by the light of sagebrush bonfires. It gathered momentum as it moved past Terrace, Matlin, Kelton, Monument Lake. On April 28, with elaborate preparations, a specially picked team received quadruple pay to lay an astounding ten miles of track. Chinese loaded and dumped the supply cars as eight Irish rail-lifters with names like Kenedy, McNamare, and Killeen hefted more than eleven tons per hour for eleven hours. The pace slowed toward the end because the *horses* pulling the wagons tired. Two days later the Central Pacific was at the summit. The Union Pacific arrived on May 9.

The ceremonial laying of the last two rails and driving the final spike is one of the most stylized moments of American history, in considerable part because of Andrew Russell's photograph of the two locomotives, the Central Pacific's Jupiter and the Union Pacific's No. 119, nose-to-nose on the afternoon of May 10, 1869. As with many historical images, it invites us to pick it apart and look for what is not there. The photo has not one Chinese face. The crowd seems tiny, given the numbers of men who had been at work, and in fact most of the force had already dispersed, perhaps sick of their jobs and suddenly without prospects. Of the workers who do look back at us, remarkably little is known of their on-the-ground experiences, starting with the most fundamental questions. The record of the Pacific railroad brims with statistics. At Promontory Summit the Central Pacific was at mile 690 from Sacramento; the Union Pacific ran 1,085 miles and 4,680 feet from its start to finish. To complete that distance, the latter required something between 11,400,000 and 13,000,000 sledge blows to drive its roughly 3,800,000 to 4,340,000 spikes. Figures for tunneling are especially precise. We know that the Central Pacific's Donner Peak tunnel was dug at an average of 1.26 feet per day, while the Union Pacific's tunnel no. 2 (772 feet long, 972 miles from Omaha) required 33,200 feet of fuse and 3,450 pounds of candles. On tunnel no. 3, gentile workers blasting with black powder progressed 2.62 times faster than Mormon laborers.[22] For one of the railroad's numbers, however, no one has ventured even a crude guess: how many people died building it.

But the job was done. Jupiter and No. 119 met, completing the longest railroad in the world and what was called one of the great engineering achievements of the age. Two decades after the great coincidence created its prodigious gulf, the long-discussed continental bond of iron was in place. In twenty more years three more main links would be run as well as major interior lines like the Denver and Rio Grande and Atchison, Topeka and Santa Fe, with smaller connecting and feeder railroads webbing into them all. Whatever its limits at the time, and they were considerable, the Union Pacific–Central Pacific was a stride toward a new level of western integration, both within the West and, as the region came into focus, into the newly continental nation.

A sense of that unification likely explains the iconic pull of Russell's photograph. Four years earlier the Civil War had resolved the crisis that had fractured the East. Now the West, so recently a sprawling disconnection, was bound symbolically into the whole. Russell's image is of both completion and possibility. Grenville Dodge and Samuel Montague, chief engineer of the Central Pacific, clasp hands in the foreground as a collection of dignitaries and workers stand among the sagebrush and perch on the engines. Two men lean across the gap between the smokestacks. They reach toward one another with bottles of champagne. It is a Sistine moment, Gilded Age American style, with dark-suited, slouch-hatted hardies instead of angels and cherubim but with the same tension of imminence, the undeniable feeling that with the clink of the bottles something is going to quicken into life. It is not God imbuing divinity with a finger's touch, but in the spirit of that day, given its faith in the mastery of machines, it is not much less.

As a bonus, the railroad's starkly simple imagery fit nicely a virile age and the need to see the West as masculine enterprise. The iron line over the land, and the locomotive thrust, were bringing together what had been apart but now was one, and as they did, they brought new life into it. It was penetration as conquest and, at its finish, as consummation. It was "a bridal day in America," Vice President Colfax would effuse on May 11 in Chicago, with the older East bound to its twenty-year-old western bride: "We clasp her as we never clasped her before." Out in Utah, the famous golden spike was dropped into its sheath and removed. At its tip was a small nugget that would be forged into five rings for President Grant and the lords of the line. On each ring was inscribed "The Mountain Wedding."[23]

Mules, Bullwhackers, and, Briefly, the Dromedary

On the eve of the culminating ceremony, Leland Stanford and friends spent a day at Monument Lake, twenty miles on the California side of the summit. As they lounged and enjoyed the scenery, a wagon company of California-bound emigrants appeared and rolled past the locomotive and cars. The photographer Alfred Hart's image of the scene became a popular stereograph, a glimpse of what the public took as a frozen moment of an age's passing. In fact railroads supplemented, rather than replaced, older means of transport that continued to expand with extraordinary vigor after the Civil War. Rail lines touched directly only the tiniest portion of budding settlements. The rest, scattered across the new national outback, would be connected to the larger world by roads. The transcontinental railroad may have been the era's showiest accomplishment, but more consequential for ordinary lives was the expanding network of roads and what rolled over them.

The prodigious federal project of roadmaking in the 1850s continued. After initial opposition from Lakotas and Cheyennes, James Sawyer managed to lay out a thousand-mile road connecting the Missouri River to gold strikes around Virginia City, Montana, and others punched through a route to the mines from the west across the Bitterroot Mountains.[24] Far more common, as the region filled up after the war, were ventures mixing governmental and private efforts. Private interests usually took the lead. The road to Montana blazed by John Bozeman and others and fortified by four army posts set loose the Lakota and

Cheyenne reprisals in the 1860s. Another mining boom around Tucson at first was supplied from Indianola on the Texas coast, 1,400 miles away. Then a link was built into Mexico to Guaymas on the Gulf of California. It was quickly used by the military. A cargo hauled before for four months at twenty cents a pound now arrived in a month at a fourth of the cost.[25]

Hundreds of toll roads interlaced the opening West, some wretchedly built but many good enough for a healthy flow of goods. In the 1870s the San Juan Mountains of southwestern Colorado had some of the richest strikes and roughest terrain in the West. Money first was raised from a tight, wealthy circle of outsiders, but as settlement thickened smaller companies sold shares at ten, even five dollars each, coffee-and-salt money a community could easily raise. In 1879 Gunnison County alone got forty-five new charters, and roads wormed their way up virtually every gulch worth climbing.[26] Besides roads there were dozens of toll bridges and private ferries. Those in the Platte Valley ranged from the bridge John Burke used to leverage his way to a small cattle empire to the ferry visited by Henry Morton Stanley, an operation run by a "classic ferryman of the Styx" who lived in a miserable hut plastered inside with a mix of sand and bison dung.[27] "Wagon road" could be a generous descriptor. Particularly where grades were steep and precipitation heavy, roads degenerated rapidly, and the most useful ones eroded the fastest from the wear of thousands of wheels, hooves, and boots. Alva Noyes once set out in a heavy rain on a trip from Utah to the Montana mines. "Before we got the length of a wagon," he remembered, "it would be down to the axle in mud." It took his three wagons of oranges and lemons nine and a half days to go a half mile.[28] Grander undertakings like the Mullan Road were no exceptions. John Mullan remained in the field for nearly two years after its opening, spending $230,000 to make improvements and repair damage. Even then the western stretch still was impassable by wagon.[29]

The crude conditions opened the way for another enterprise—mule trains. New mining camps, typically in some mountain remoteness, especially depended on them to service the sudden population of a rush. A pack train straining up some thin ribbon of a trail might have 50 or more mules. With each one carrying up to 400 pounds, a 50-mule team carried as much as 10 tons of freight. The acknowledged master muleteers were Mexicans whose craft ran generations deep in southwestern life. They "elevated packing and driving to a science," according to one writer, and their subtle understanding of the animal's character and of the physics of the load "gave their lowly occupation a luster and dignity."[30] Spanish-speaking mule drivers fanned out far to the north and eventually into Canada as new settlements demanded their skills. Their days were long, covering about fifteen miles and ending with unloading and pasturing the animals before seeing to their own needs. Depending on the intensity of business, the labor ranged from tough to brutal. A veteran muleteer in the Pacific Northwest, James Watt, was in charge of 15 mules when he started, but with steepening demand he and a partner eventually were handling between 36 and 40, which meant the two of them muscled as much as eight tons on and off the animals every day.[31]

The trade could be prodigious. From January to mid-November of 1866, 6,000 mules carried more than 2 million pounds of freight over the Mullan Road to Montana camps. Five thousand head of cattle, 1,500 horses, and 20,000 people also made the trip.[32] Extensions from the road fed into Idaho's Boise Basin, with its several thousand persons beyond wagon-reach. Some reached eventually into Canada. Unlikely cargoes tottered up the trails—caskets, mining equipment, and even pianos. One mule bore a 667-pound steel casting more than a hundred miles to a new camp. Among the commonest burdens was whiskey, or raw alcohol to be diluted later, that sloshed around in "8 casks," special kegs that held twenty-eight gallons each. Some trains were independent operations, others owned by merchants who ran their own goods to remote settlements to sell in impromptu local markets.

Rates, always erratic, were always far above that for wagon freight, and as usable roads multiplied, the mule trade dwindled to a pittance. Freighting boomed with the rushes to Colorado and the Comstock in 1859, then rose even more sharply between 1863 and 1867 as mining booms opened new areas and the end of the war brought waves of new economic activity. At that point freighting may have employed more men than any other single business. Overland commerce all the way to the Pacific coast was never practicable, but the main arteries to Colorado, Salt Lake City, and Santa Fe were thick with commercial wagons, "prairie schooners" that loomed ten or more feet tall and carried up to four tons. In 1865 the Missouri River depot of Nebraska City alone sent out 7,365 wagons pulled by more than 50,000 oxen and 7,000 mules and worked by 8,385 men. Freight to Colorado alone totaled more than 62,000 tons. The Santa Fe Trail, while not quite so busy, still carried an estimated 5,000–6,000 wagons in 1866.[33] Pacific coast freighters tapped deep into the interior. San Francisco suppliers opened overland trade to Idaho's Boise Basin and those in Los Angeles fed Arizona mines and army posts, Salt Lake City, and occasionally Montana camps, 1,100 miles away.[34]

The obvious need drew large players. Augustus Kountze of Omaha and Alexander Caldwell of Nebraska City hauled an astonishing thirty million pounds of supplies to military posts in 1867. The prime example, Russell, Majors and

Waddell, in the 1850s had used its three hundred wagons to try to corner both the army and private markets. By 1862, overextended, weighed down by vast debts, and battered by scandals, it was bankrupt.[35] Smaller operations were more flexible and suited to the frontier's flux of events. After just three trips from Leavenworth to Colorado, Percival Lowe and two others expanded from six to thirty-six wagons, plus a Denver store and a haying business.[36] This made freighting a fine arena for go-getters. During the bitter plains warfare of 1864–65 C. B. Hadley saw his opening: "When the news came . . . telling of the Indians burning the ranches and killing the ranchmen, killing the freighters, destroying their goods, driving off their teams and burning their freight wagons," he recalled, "I knew then that if a man could get to Denver with a load of apples he would make a big thing."[37]

A railroad could carry more apples, and carry them more cheaply, and once one arrived in an area the snuffing of freighters was stunning and swift. "The shriek of the iron horse has silenced the lowing of the panting ox," a reporter wrote when the Atchison, Topeka and Santa Fe arrived in New Mexico: "The old trail looks desolate."[38] Away from a new railroad's immediate market, however, the effect was the opposite. Every stop along the tracks was potentially a new distribution point, so railroads that choked off the freighter's flow along longer hauls fed it along the shorter ones. During the year after the Union Pacific arrived in Corinne, Utah, freighters left there for Helena and Montana gold camps with as much as a quarter million pounds a week.[39] Freighting, not railroading, remained the West's economic lifeblood throughout the rest of the century, and it continued to supply huge parts of the region well into the next one.

Freighting was a craft, and hard work. Each wagon was pulled by 5 or 6 pairs of oxen and carried up to 7,000 pounds. Besides repairing a wagon's minor breaks and keeping its canvas taught and trim, a teamster yoked and unyoked oxen twice a day, handled the straining animals with a 15-foot lash, and drove them to and from their grazing ground. He had to know a diversity of equipment nearly as great as on a small ship and become familiar with the oxen's collective psychology and individual quirks. To cover 15–18 miles a day, with a three-hour layover at midday, a seasoned crew worked like a clock. Alexander Majors once timed one of his best crews as they yoked and hitched 300 oxen to 25 wagons. The job was done in 16 minutes.[40] When fresh recruits worked with unbroken animals, the story was different. "Had lots of fun," a newcomer wrote in his diary at the end of his first day: "One [ox] got so cross we had to shoot him." After weeks of floundering he turned sarcastic: "Not much bad luck. Only broke 2 wagons."[41]

Freighters were a public display of mastery over beasts and, apart from locomotives, over the biggest things moving. No wonder, then, that there flourished the cult of the bullwhacker. Their work and its gritty realities made them
seem a breed apart, an impression some teamsters undoubtedly cultivated.
They "would not shine in a drawing room, any of them," a New Yorker wrote
of ones he met on the road to Colorado. James Rusling agreed: "A harder or
rougher set . . . it would be difficult to find, or even imagine. . . . With the inseparable bowie-knife and revolver buckled around their waists, they swung and
cracked their great whips like fiends." Their "many-headed oaths . . . [left] the
whole Mountains corruscated with sulphur!"[42] Indians along the road showed
their frequent contact with freighters by greeting emigrants with "Gee, Whoa,
Haw. God damn you." The portrait has persisted: men aloof and above the
immigrants who ate their dust, larger and wilder, tougher and gamier, profane
demigods of the road.

But look closer and the image quickly fuzzes out. There was little to distinguish freighters from the crowds they moved through. William Chandless's
crew included army deserters, a graduate of Dublin College, a French silver-
smith, and a doctor's son trained in medicine as well as cooking, painting,
acting, and tailoring. Among Thomas Creigh's fellow teamsters was William
H. Jackson, who would become the century's most famous photographer of
the West. They called one of their wagons the "Reading Room" because it
carried so many books as well as hairbrushes and a violin. A collective biography of more than a hundred Nebraska-based freighters shows many turning later to farming, ranching, merchandising, and jobs higher up the scale.
Francis White rose to head the Midland Pacific Railroad Company; Eugene
Munn, who worked the trail for nine years, was later president of an insur-
ance company. Englishman John Bratt survived a shipwreck to arrive broke
in Nebraska City in 1866, took up bullwhacking, and eventually became one
of western Nebraska's most successful ranchers. Mark Coad was another from
the British Isles who turned from freighting to stock raising, selling out for a
fortune before dying in rancherly fashion: shot by a sheepman in a Cheyenne
hotel lobby.[43] Freighters were another case, like the denizens of the "Hells on
Wheels" along the Union Pacific, of cultivated machismo along the entry-
ways into the West.

In binding the West one innovation was tried but failed—camels. They
seemed an obvious fit in the arid Southwest. Their splayed feet and pads stayed
atop the shiftiest sand under loads several times anything borne by a mule.
They could go without drinking for stretches that could drive a horse or mule
mad. In sandstorms they could clamp shut their nostrils and double sets of

eyelashes. Their milk could be drunk (but not churned into butter), their meat resembled veal, and their thick hair might be made into clothing. As proof a Texas housewife in 1856 knit a pair of socks for President Franklin Pierce.[44]

Camels had several advocates, including the eminent naturalist George Perkins Marsh and the would-be ruler of Afghanistan Josiah Harlan, the inspiration for Rudyard Kipling's "The Man Who Would Be King."[45] All were full of bold predictions. A Californian asked his state legislature for five quarter-sections to anchor a "speedy and secure" service to carry mail and goods from New Orleans to Los Angeles in eight to ten days, and Armenian Joseph Hekekyan Bey proposed a stitching of caravans to create a domain greater than "the pretended conquests of Alexanders and Tamerlanes."[46] Jefferson Davis used part of his final day as U.S. senator to argue for bringing in fifty camels for use of the army. He was greeted by guffaws, but as secretary of war he had seventy-six dromedaries brought through Texas. In their first test helping survey a wagon road along the thirty-fifth parallel they earned high praise from the expedition's leader Lt. Edward Fitzgerald Beale.[47]

By 1860 there were a couple of hundred on the ground, most in California and Texas. With the Civil War Confederates in Texas sold some and released most of the rest. One, "Old Douglas," fell to a Union sharpshooter near the end of the siege of Vicksburg. In 1866 the army sold off the last of those left, but some private interest continued.[48] Camels worked in mines from the Southwest to British Columbia and on trails in the Pacific Northwest and Montana. But there were problems. Camels could kick, bite viciously, and regurgitate, violently and at will, a large and unpleasant cud. During rut males turned cranky and stubborn. Their appearance and powerful odor panicked horses and mules and led to stampedes and scattered loads. By 1875, when the Nevada legislature outlawed camels running loose on public highways, owners had sold most of them to zoos and circuses and had released the rest into the wild. The last survivor, Topsy, caught in the Arizona desert in 1905, lived in a Los Angeles zoo until 1934.[49]

In the end the episode is most intriguing when set into the deep history of the West. Camels had evolved out of the North American midlands, migrated into the Arctic and across Beringia to fan out through Asia and into Africa. Camelids died out in North America during the late Pleistocene but flourished elsewhere, and around five thousand years ago, probably in what is now Somalia, they were domesticated.[50]

The parallel is obvious. Horses, too, evolved on the Great Plains, crossed into Asia before vanishing from their homeland, were domesticated about five millennia ago, and finally came home to the Americas. But the camel's return was as disappointing as the horse's was successful. That was partly because they came late. There were brief experiments in the Spanish colonies and even in early Virginia, but only when the army brought its seventy-six imports did camels truly complete their global circuit. They came in numbers far too small to establish a natural breeding population, and they were poorly suited to the denser settlements of mining towns and army posts. The most obvious difference, and most insightful lesson, was in the historical role of the cultural bond between people and domesticates. Horses returned home in rooted symbiosis with the culture that brought them, a society of horse-men, and they came early enough for Indian peoples to cultivate the same bond. Camels arrived late as cultural aliens, and there was as well something in the western character that never warmed to their misbehavior, flashy temper, foul odor, and projectile vomiting. Camels in the West were a case of a homecoming that did not take.

The Splendid Misery of Stagecoaching

Imagine movement in the West along a sliding scale among speed, value, and materiality. Information, so crucial to the creation and operation of the new country, could move at nearly the speed of light through the telegraph, but it had no material substance. Anything physical had to be carried, and the greater its bulk, the slower and more challenging its delivery. Mules and freight wagons answered that call by carrying many millions of pounds of goods every year. That left a gap. There remained a need to move some physical things, ones of modest bulk and high value, more rapidly than via teamsters or muleskinners. Railroads eventually did that, but they serviced directly only part of the West, and at first only a tiny part. Otherwise something else met the need—stagecoaches.

Long the standard means of rapid land travel in the East, stagecoaches appeared with the earliest western roads and continued to service some places into the next century. Stages were especially valued for three payloads. While money to a point could be transferred as shifts of bookkeeping, ultimately wealth had to be physically moved, either as currency or as its basic stuff, gold dust and bullion. For that gold producers and banks relied heavily on ships and coaches. Another item, the mail, was considered by some nearly as valuable as gold. Besides the government's constitutional obligation, for economic and personal reasons there was tremendous public pressure to provide reliable postal service to the opening West.

The third item was people. As long as coaches were carrying bills, letters, and bullion, paying passengers were an obvious addition, but they were something more than remoras. From the start stagecoaches were the default travel of the politically, economically, and socially prominent, and as tickets cheapened they connected middling families across the continent. Stagecoaches also played prominently in creating the imagined West. Every author of every one of the long shelf of books describing the new country had traveled through it at some point by stage. The absent public viewed the West largely through the windows of a swaying, jolting coach. It was a view that colored the new country in ways both revealing and not immediately apparent.

Transcontinental stage service, like that for the telegraph and railroad, was private enterprise propped up by the government. Washington's early commitment to eat considerable financial losses to provide postal service continued during and after the war. In 1860 the expenses for the connection from Saint Joseph to Sacramento were more than $200,000. Its receipts were $5,284.14.[51] This route, via the main overland road, and its contracts became the prize in an elaborate financial chess game. The colorful and canny Benjamin Holladay by 1866 had parlayed control of the Platte Valley into an empire connecting Saint Joseph and Atchison to Denver and Salt Lake City and both of them to the Columbia River and to mining towns of Montana and Idaho—more than three thousand miles of stage lines in all.[52] His reward was nearly $2 million in mail contracts. Holladay's system was considered the invaluable connective network of East and West. In 1864 it took only a couple of telegrams from Holladay, warning that Indian raids might disrupt his system, for Washington to send Patrick Connor from Utah to Colorado and set in motion events that led to the Sand Creek Massacre and the bitter fighting that followed. Holladay still lacked the westernmost connection from Salt Lake City to Sacramento, however. That was held by the Pioneer Stage Company, which in 1864 was bought out by Wells, Fargo and Company. Then, in a stunning move two years later, Holladay sold all his interests to Wells, Fargo for just under $2 million and a place high in the new structure.

With that, Wells, Fargo had grown from its early days of express and banking in California to become the primary distributor of mail, raw wealth, and financial paper for the entire West. It did so, however, knowing that soon—only three years, as it happened—a rail connection to the Pacific would instantly take away its role. (Wells, Fargo squeezed the maximum out of that connection by contracting to run between the converging termini of the Union and Central Pacific. Its final run of a few miles came the day before the last spike was driven.) Buying out Holladay might seem a shortsighted investment, but in fact it was shrewd positioning. The more people and goods that moved in and out of the West on the main rail lines, the more traffic there was on the roads radiating out from them. With its connections, stock, and equipment, Wells, Fargo could now play off the main trunks to carry whatever was desired to anywhere any usable roads ran.

As settlement spread after the war, new roads were laid, which brought stage traffic and commercial connections and postal service. The last of these offered a vivid means of tracking what was happening. By 1880 the nation's postal system was the most extensive in the world. Its hundreds of offices in the West were fed via both overland traffic and maritime links. Washington paid shippers ten million dollars between 1866 and 1876 to carry mail, hauled over the isthmian link, to the Pacific coast. From there stages carried it into the interior.[53] To map post offices as they appeared is to follow the course of western development and national integration as an ongoing partnership of the federal government and business, the process begun hard on the discovery of gold and the surge of overland traffic.[54]

Where letters, currency, and orders for merchandise could be carried, so could people. For travelers with a ticket, their introductory capsule to the West was the Concord coach built by the New Hampshire firm of Abbot, Downing and Company. Made from seasoned ash, white oak, elm, and poplar, upholstered in ox hide, trimmed out in brass, and painted vermilion or dark green, with landscapes painted on its doors and the faces and figures of famous actresses on the sides of the driver's footboards, the Concord was a rolling elegance. It weighed more than a ton and carried nine passengers inside, two more seated beside the driver, and if need be as many as a dozen up top. Besides appearance, the Concord's appeal lay in its strong and durable wheels and its suspension of the cab on broad leather straps, or thorough-braces. Together they allowed for maximum speed with minimal jolting or tilting, since the body could swing and naturally seek its own level. About six hundred Concords were made between 1858 and 1900, most of them for the West. Depending on weight and terrain, from four to eight horses usually pulled a coach. They were not the only ones on the road. Lighter "mud wagons" were faster and more maneuverable and thus preferred for tricky mountain routes. The "celerity wagon" was also engineered for speed, but being lighter it was less stable than the Concord.

The stage driver was another figure, like bullwhackers and railroad workers in Hell on Wheels towns, who became a living emblem for the coarse, hard-living West. To a point the image was rooted in fact. The first of his drivers was "in plain English drunk," wrote Richard Francis Burton (who knew something about drinking), and the profanity of others, he thought, would "crimson the face of an Isis bargee."[55] A life out of doors, working through all weather but the impossibly cruel, sometimes for two or three days straight, certainly toughened these men and their characters, but many observers were more impressed by their skills and concentration. One marveled at his driver's "riveted attention" and command over his "little game horses." Another described as "perfectly artistic" his driver's encyclopedic knowledge of every turn and dip of the road, knowledge that was crucial in the mountains where the tiniest error could be calamitous. A veteran ranked as most dangerous the moments high on a mountain pass when a cloud suddenly enveloped the road in the darkness of freezing mist. Only a precise foot-by-foot memory of what was ahead could get the coach through.[56]

The ride itself was among the most written-about experiences of the day. In part, of course, that was because any literary tourist at some point would take a coach, but there seemed also an obligation to give readers a feel for something distinctively western, and nothing fit that category better than several lurching days on the road over distances and across terrain that had no parallel in the East. A typical account emphasized its mortifying discomfort. The coach was "a most ingenious torture chamber" and the ride "simply horrible,—the heat, the dust, the jolting, awful!" For four days and nights, the Earl of Dunraven wrote, he and his fellow passengers were "shot about like shuttles in a loom." Time dragged. Muscles cramped. Children turned cranky and infants wailed. In the sway and stuffiness, motion-sick passengers hung from the windows to "cast out Jonah."[57]

The stops were nearly as bad as the ride. Most stations were described as filthy hovels. As for the food, one veteran recalled "milkless coffee, rancid bacon, stale beans, and green bread," another wrote of "various abominations," "rusty bacon and gravelolent antelope," and "milk not more than one quarter flies." On longer journeys the physical and mental toll was high. There were stories of men during stops wandering into the desert deranged, never to be seen again, and a group that had ridden from California to Kansas was described in a "deplorable state of despair and defacultization." Some "seemed merely hanging on to life by the neck of a pocket-flask."[58]

Something in the nightmarish accounts, however, rings another note. Descriptions of land and people along the way were of admiration and wonder. In the same paragraph that he wrote of the misery, the exhaustion, the "grunt of torture . . . [and] deep groan of pain" that typified a trip, John Mortimer Murphy praised the expansive views, vivifying atmosphere, and especially "the sensation of travelling through a country almost as primeval as it was thousands of years ago."[59] Like his, many accounts are of transport not so much to a different place as to another category of experience. They are akin to magical journeys in which ordeal and trauma are rewarded with a leap into another realm. After awful days of little sleep on the southwestern oxbow route Raphael Pumpelly wrote of waking from delirious dreams to a pistol shot out of a crowd of quarreling gamblers. He was in Tucson. Stage narratives are full of such moments of breaking through. A hundred or so hours in some horse-drawn hell was the price to see what few on earth had seen or, as with Fitz Hugh Ludlow, to be given some secret knowledge. Battered by his ride across the plains and blistered by wind "like a hot blast of the Cyclops' furnace," his first view of the Rocky Mountains was "a sudden revelation of the truth" that "the eternal things of the universe are which afar off seem dim and faint."[60]

Stagecoaching brought close the West's most isolated settlements, yet readers could believe that if they rode fast and far and uncomfortably enough they could cross a mythic line and outrun history itself to find an American primeval that promised things as terrible and as wonderful as in Africa's Mountains of the Moon. As such it embodied a paradox of the emerging region. The very means of connection most responsible for drawing the West into the nation were the means as well of portraying the West as a land enduringly apart, the "American elsewhere."[61]

At 10:00 a.m. on October 26, 1825, the Erie Canal officially opened when the *Seneca Chief,* carrying Gov. George Clinton and other dignitaries, set off from Lake Erie to New York City. A relay of cannons had been strung along the route, and as the boat floated its first foot, the first cannon, a thirty-two-pounder, was fired. When a cannoneer at the second heard the faint boom, he fired his, and so on until the crowd at New York harbor, more than four hundred miles away, heard the final concussion, eighty-one minutes after the first.[62] At the time it was the fastest communication in American history.

Forty-four years later, the official completion of the Pacific railroad in Utah was signaled by a single telegraphic impulse from the final sledge blow by Leland Stanford. It traveled throughout the nation in the tiniest fraction of a second.

More land in the nation was pulled into connection with other places during the mid-1800s than during the previous two and a half centuries, much of it during the fifteen years after the onset of civil war. The most impressive accomplishments were in the lands added to the nation just as those transformations were underway. The process redefined topology itself, at least in its practical realities. North America's western half lies naturally north-and-south. Its cordilleras run up and down on a standard map, and so do its plains and open spaces and most of its greatest rivers. The new systems of rails, wires, and roads took that orientation and wrenched it ninety degrees around. Now the dominant flow of people, things, and information was east-to-west. The continental American state was made in defiance of the continental grain.

It would be difficult to overstate the consequences. New technologies created a kind of endoskeleton that permitted every broad change that followed while giving shape to both an emerging region and an idea, the West. As they did, they would help bind its plains, mountains, and deserts even more broadly into a global pursuit of new understandings of the world, of its peoples, and of life itself.

12 ▷ Maps

Discovery is not as simple as the word says it is. A discoverer does not merely register information, as if uncovering (*dis* + *covering*) a pot on the stove to see what's for dinner. Discovery is a creative act. People who enter a place for the first time bring to it attitudes, values, intentions, and presumptions about how things work. They fit what they see into this mental framework. Whatever the discoverer then reports is a description, not only of the place encountered, but also of the reporter's mind and of the culture where that mind matured. Usually the discoverer claims in all honesty that the report is objective, but it is only one among countless possible versions of accuracy. As similar reports multiply and as people absorb them, a widely held view takes shape. There is now an established impression (exactly so: a pattern imposed by pressure), and as people act according to it, that impression deepens. By living into the world as we see it, we make it into the world we see. The discoverer's original view becomes increasingly real. A place has been created. The word *invent* (from the Latin *in* + *venire*) originally meant "to come in to." To enter new country is always to invent it.

That process was well under way in the West by 1861, and after the war it expanded prodigiously. Federally funded exploration and scientific pursuits went far beyond the considerable efforts of the 1850s. Four ambitious surveys compiled a vast inventory of the West and its resources. There and in other efforts, with and without federal support, scientists mapped the West in the word's broadest sense, probing its land, its animals, and peoples through the lens of sciences ranging from geology and paleontology to anthropology and ethnology to meteorology, botany, and zoology. The effort was in one sense global. It included the study of the world as a colossal machine, fitting western peoples into a single human family, and probing the mechanisms within life itself. The work was also distinctly national, stamping the West as uniquely American, its character marked by physical grandeur, a racial ordering, some deep contradictions, and an enduring oddness.

"The Great Unknown"

On May 11, 1869, the day after the ritual sinking of the Pacific railroad's final spike, Maj. John Wesley Powell stepped off a Union Pacific passenger car at Green River, Wyoming.[1] He came to lead an expedition into one of the last geographical mysteries of North America, the inner gorge of the Grand Canyon of the Colorado River. While the particular day was coincidence, the larger timing was not. The railroad inaugurated a new stage of western exploration. Its result would be a tightening grip on the country, both directly, in muscling control over resources and Native peoples, and more subtly as an imaginative grasp. Exploration helped create a West that was in part a reservoir of riches that would be the stuff of national greatness, in part a scientific laboratory for unlocking elemental mysteries, and in part an aesthetic expression of adventure and wild wonder.

Only seventy years earlier the West had been a land of almost pure speculation—a place where Thomas Jefferson, probably the most widely read American, could expect to find wooly mammoths and descendants of ancient Welsh immigrants. By 1860 much of the country west of the one-hundredth meridian had been at least roughly described. No mammoths or wandering Welshmen, it turned out, but, as the General Map of Governeur Kemble Warren showed, easterners looking west now could know at least the West's broad contours and landforms and, most clearly, the most promising pathways across it to the Pacific.

Now exploration turned to two purposes. The first was the penetration of the last blank spaces on the map that Warren had labeled "Unexplored." The second was a great survey of the West, piece by massive piece. Its goal was a descriptive inventory, partly an international scientific inquiry but always with an eye to how the country might best be controlled and used. A subtler and surely less conscious impulse was also at work. As more of the West became familiar, the very remoteness of its last enclaves took on new value. Inaccessibility, especially if it took on the coloration of the sublime, became its own resource. The paradox of western transportation was that more efficient connections to the outside world triggered fantasies of escape and separation. Exploration had its own variant. In its search for the stuff of national greatness, it expressed as well the need to believe that Americans could still move beyond the familiar to the unknown—and in the future could count on such wild places being always available.

Powell's western career bridged those two purposes. The Grand Canyon expedition of 1869, which William Goetzmann called "the climactic event of late-nineteenth century exploration," was into one of Warren's last cartographic blanks.[2] The innermost gorge of the canyon was the most inaccessible part of a forbidding region, the fractured, deeply eroded Colorado Plateau, blistering hot in summer and lashed by winter storms. The Spanish explorer Francisco Garcés described the plateau in 1776 as "a prison of cliffs and canyons." He was "astonished at the roughness of this country, and at the barrier which nature has fixed therein."[3] That barrier, the canyon itself, two hundred miles long and up to a mile deep, was approached from its lower end in 1857 by Lt. Joseph Christmas Ives, who had made the first descent to the canyon floor at Diamond Creek.[4] No non-Indian had ever ventured into canyon above this spot, and at the upper end none had seen anything below what is usually regarded as the start of the inner gorge, the entry of the Little Colorado River into the Colorado. From there downstream to Diamond Creek was 164 river miles. This was the stretch that John Wesley Powell set out to float.

As his given names suggest, Powell was the product of a devoutly Methodist home, but his passions ran to the natural sciences. By the time he volunteered in the Civil War he had developed a reputation for intellect and aggressive field work. In the war he showed his other defining traits, courage and determination. After losing his lower right arm at Shiloh—it was shattered as he raised it to command his artillery unit to fire—he remained in service until the end and preferred ever afterward to be called by his rank: "the Major." As a college instructor Powell scrabbled together funds to lead students and fellow enthusiasts on a geological tour of the Colorado Rockies in 1867 and 1868.[5] It was his life's turning point. From these forays he hatched a plan to descend the Green River, which rose in Wyoming's Wind River Mountains, into the Colorado, formed when the Green joined the Grand River, and thence downstream to the Grand Canyon. He assembled a crew of nine others, most of them Civil War veterans and none trained in science, and gathered funds from railroads, Illinois colleges, the Chicago Academy of Sciences, and his own pocket. The federal government gave encouragement and some rations but no money. Powell had four wooden dories specially designed and tested on Lake Michigan, then he loaded them on the Union Pacific and sent them to Wyoming. He followed close behind to join his crew.

On May 24 Powell and his men shoved away into the current of the Green River. They learned the basics of river running on the first and longest portion of the voyage, through a thinly peopled country with deep canyons and treacherous rapids. They flirted with disaster, which sometimes flirted back. One boat was lost in a rapid, but the precious barometers (and a smuggled keg of whiskey) were saved. After five weeks they paused briefly at a Ute reservation, where one of the men who had been dunked with the lost boat chose to remain. Powell climbed often to observe the surrounding country, sometimes up cliffs of more than two thousand feet. Once he was saved from a narrow ledge when his companion removed his long underwear for use as a rescue rope. In the clear air he identified distant ranges, but the terrain around him was "but a wilderness of rocks,—deep gorges where the rivers are lost below cliffs and towers and pinnacles, and ten thousand strangely carved forms in every direction."[6]

Only on July 18, after more than five hundred miles, did they reach the junction with the Grand and the start of the Colorado, and it was nearly four more weeks before they camped at the turquoise inflow of the Little Colorado. Ahead, Powell wrote in his journal, was "the Great Unknown," the deep belly of the gorge. After a short rest it was into the void. At this depth the ancient hardened granite—later called Vishnu schist, aptly named for the Hindu creator at the heart of things—was so resistant of erosion that for miles the river tumbled through sheer walls that offered no chance of landing. At other points the men used lines to lower the boats through the worst rapids or portaged around them. They knew roughly how much altitude the river would lose by the other end of the canyon, but there was no way to predict its drop mile-to-mile. Passing around some blind turn might send them over a southwestern Niagara. The tension shimmers in the crew's terse journal entries: "August 21. Made a portage to begin with, then ran 6 rapids; there came to a very dangerous rapid fall of 20 ft. in 300 yds; made portage on south side. Made 14 miles today. Passed 27 rapids. Average width of river 60 yds. Course northwest. Walls 4000 ft."[7] Sometimes the only sleeping spots were wide cracks and narrow ledges above the torrent. The bacon turned rancid and was tossed away and the saleratus was lost, leaving rations of unleavened bread, dried apples, and coffee.

On August 27, when they stopped at the head of a horrific rapid with no way around it and no end in sight, three of the crew announced they had had enough. They would scale the walls and walk their way out. After a breakfast the next day "as solemn as a funeral" and final goodbyes, the three climbed to a crag and, after watching the rest push into the rapid to run it blind, climbed out. Soon they were killed by Shivwits Indians who mistook them for miners who had assaulted one of their women. For Powell and the remaining crew, the gamble to run the rapid paid off. The five faced barely a minute's danger in what turned out to be the last rough water of the voyage. Two days later they met a man, his two sons, and an Indian seining fish. The man and his sons were Mormons who had been told to watch for debris, "fragments or relics" of an expedition most assumed had ended fatally.

Powell's feat was hailed in the press, partly because he had carefully cultivated public attention. At the Ute reservation he had left letters describing the
trip to that point, a hairsbreadth account telegraphed to the East and drib-
bled out to newspaper readers through the *Chicago Tribune*, so when the men
emerged from the void it was to an accumulated imagination of what might
have happened. His new national stature gave the support needed for a second expedition down the Green and through the canyon in 1871–72. Powell
would write that "I had no interest in that work as an adventure," only for its
scientific pursuits, but when he testified before a congressional panel in 1874,
Rep. James Garfield, a future president, told him "in a pleasant manner" that
he could expect no federal funds for his future work unless he published an
account of the journey.

He did, and when serialized in *Scribner's Magazine* it drew a huge audience
and generated public calls for a more accessible version.[8] In 1895 Powell published his "fuller account in popular form," *The Exploration of the Colorado
River of the West*, ostensibly an account of the first trip but in fact somewhat
of a collapsing of the two into one.[9] It quickly became what it remains, a classic of exploratory adventure. It was part of an emerging global literature of
outsiders' probing of the mysteries of Africa, Asia, and the South Pacific, and
it stands with the best of them.

It is also fundamentally different. Powell explored within his own nation at a
turning point in its understanding of itself, and his account catches something
about what the West was coming to mean between his time on the river and
the publication of *Exploration*. As science, Powell's narrative helped shape the
study of geology and provided basic insights into the West's arid heartland,
how it was formed, and what could and could not be expected of it. At its heart,
however, *Exploration* was an exploit and an encounter with the sublime—that
is, with what inspires both awe and terror. Geologic descriptions of hogbacks
and side canyons slide often into a prose of ironic heroism ("It is curious how
a little obstacle becomes a great obstruction when a misstep would land a man
in the bottom of a deep chasm") and enthusiastic romance ("What a chamber
for a resting place is this! . . . The heavens for a ceiling . . . , clear lakelets for
a refreshing bath.")[10] *Exploration* is a narrative of immersion—in danger, in
immensity, in a magnificent, swallowing wild. This vision would persist. To
geologists, the Grand Canyon would be the ultimate laboratory. To many Americans, it became an essential untamed landscape, an adventure forever waiting,
uniquely theirs precisely because it could never be truly grasped.

As all discoveries must, Powell's imposed some meanings over others. This
made it also an act of conquest, not only of physical possession but also of

perception. His own journal, when read closely, reminds us that the canyon was the "Great Unknown" only to its newcomers. He wrote of ruins along the walls, and at the canyon's deepest cut he found grinding stones, broken pottery, a globular basket, and knapped flint at "the home of an old arrow-maker." Five days before their emergence his hungry crew found a flourishing garden and hurried away with a dozen squash, "not willing to be caught in the robbery."[11] Havasupais lived up one of the Colorado's tributaries. Paiutes and Shivwits lived just to the north and Hopis and Navajos to the south. To them the country Powell traversed had meanings based on practiced use, including growing the squash that Powell stole, on historical identity, and on spiritual connection.

The very place where Powell wrote of "the Great Unknown" is a case in point. That spot, where the Little Colorado entered the Colorado, was and is immeasurably sacred to the Hopis. Nearby is a spring. It is the Hopis' sipapu, the opening from which their ancestors first climbed into this present reality. Each year around the winter solstice reviving spirits, kachinas, reemerge there and remain for half a year. If ceremonies are properly done to keep the world well tuned, rain clouds come from there to bring life's most essential blessing. For many generations a trio of men, two elders and a novice, made pilgrimages to that spot. They went ostensibly to gather salt. More centrally they were reenacting a defining historical episode, the primal journey of the Hopis' heroic figures, the War Twins. The pilgrimage consisted of a series of meticulous rituals. If done improperly or without due regard, the year ahead would go badly awry. Doing them well and respectfully insured the proper functioning of life's forces. In a cave the men played a gambling game with the Twins, cheating to be sure they won. They feigned copulation with a stone formation believed to be the frozen form of the Twins' grandmother. The pilgrimage was both a veneration of their origin and a liturgy necessary to the continuing order of things.[12]

To the Hopis, Powell's campsite was literally at the center of the world. Powell made it, and the West at large, into the world's rim, a frontier of science and a romantic horizon, an edge to be looked over with brave trepidation: "We have an unknown distance yet to run, an unknown river to explore. What falls there are, we know not; what rocks beset the channel, we know not; what walls rise over the river, we know not. Ah, well!"[13]

Siting the West

Powell next embarked on one of four grand surveys sponsored by the federal government between 1867 and 1879. They were both an inheritance and expansion of the railroad and road surveys of the 1850s. Those after the war were sometimes at odds but the intent of all was to comprehend the West in two senses—to understand the West through describing it and to bring the country under full command. Knowing the West would bring it more fully into the national embrace.

A summary of the surveys gives a sense of their geographical and topical scope, and a glance at their principal figures tells us something of the spirit behind them.[14] Powell parlayed his Grand Canyon fame into government sponsorship of both a second run at the river and a survey of its larger environs, the Colorado Plateau.[15] In 1871–72 his brother-in-law, self-taught topographer Almon H. Thompson, mapped the Kaibab Plateau north and east of the Grand Canyon and on a spring reconnaissance brought back the first descriptions of the Escalante River and Henry Mountains.[16] These were the nation's last river and range undiscovered (by whites). Powell explored southern Utah, including the spectacular landscapes of what would become Zion National Park, and mapped the Shivwits Plateau west of the Kaibab. By 1875 he had assembled a scientific team that would work this arid heartland of the West until 1879. They included Grove Karl Gilbert, considered by some the century's greatest geologist, and the remarkable Clarence Dutton. A divinity school dropout, largely self-taught in a dozen fields, elsewhere an innovator in the study of earthquakes and volcanoes, Dutton was also a superb stylist who composed lengthy passages in his head (once dictating eleven thousand words that required only two minor corrections). Besides the Kaibab and Shivwits, Powell's team mapped the Uinkaret, Kanab, and Paria Plateaus on the north side of the canyon and on the south the Colorado Plateau, the term given later to the entire region drained by the river. Their work also extended northward to the eastern Great Basin and western Colorado. Some seasons Powell was in the field, others he spent in Washington, but he remained the survey's unifying spirit. "Gathering about him the ablest men he could secure, he was yet always the intellectual leader," Gilbert wrote of Powell, "and few of his colleagues could withstand the master influence of his mind."[17] Of the four surveys this one came closest to exploration in the classic sense, description of extensive areas unseen before by non-Indians.

At the head of a second survey was Clarence King, Yale graduate and darling of eastern intellectuals.[18] With support from the scientific establishment he secured government funding for the U.S. Geological Exploration of the Fortieth Parallel. Even at a time of youthful energy in such enterprises, his appointment was unusual—he was only twenty-five. The survey's name told its location but only part of its goal. Its focus was indeed the 40th parallel from the 105th to the 120th meridians—the reader might picture a line westward from Denver across the Rockies and the southern end of the Great Salt Lake to the eastern slopes of the Sierra Nevada—but its interest went beyond geology.[19] King recruited botanists, ornithologists, and the photographer Timothy O'Sullivan, former colleague of the Civil War's famous Matthew Brady. Technically King was under army command, although he staffed his team entirely with civilians trained mostly at Yale and in Europe. In the summer of 1867 they began working west-to-east across the northern Great Basin and through the suffocating valley of the Humboldt River. King's compatriot James Gardner used new surveying techniques to compile a topography far more detailed than anything before it. Meanwhile, King, Samuel Emmons, and James and Arnold Hague studied the geology of the silver mines in Nevada's Comstock and in southwestern Idaho. Sullivan was with them, and with bursts of magnesium powder produced the first American images from underground—the claustrophobic shafts and tunnels, cave-ins, and pick-wielding workers of an emerging subterranean industry. By 1871 and 1872 the survey was working its way eastward over the Wasatch Range, through the Green River basin and eventually to Colorado's Front Range, following roughly along the Union Pacific's route and ranging a hundred miles on either side. Then they retraced their work across fifteen degrees of longitude from Cheyenne to the peaks of the Sierra. Of the four surveys, King's covered the most familiar territory, but it did so with unique rigor and level of analysis.

Ferdinand V. Hayden, like Powell, was largely self-taught and expansive in his interests.[20] Before the Civil War he had fallen in with leading lights of scientific exploration, including John Newberry, early geologist of the Grand Canyon, and Lt. Gouverneur K. Warren, author of the General Map of the West. His work had been mostly in Nebraska, Kansas, and the Dakotas, and 1867 he won a government assignment to survey Nebraska's geology and resources. So successful was this season and the next, and so popular with politicians was his positive reading of this area's future, that in 1869 Congress funded the grandly named U.S. Geographical and Geological Survey of the Territories with Hayden as director. Money and the survey's personnel increased steadily after that. Hayden's teams studied Colorado's Front Range and the high country and mountain parks immediately to the west, then turned to the general vicinity of the Union Pacific route in Wyoming and country to its south.

Much of Hayden's surveys so far were of country already worked by Powell and King, but in 1871 and 1872 Hayden led forays into a place that, like the Grand Canyon's inner gorge, had remained remarkably elusive to outsiders—the upper reaches of the Yellowstone River. It was a fantastic landscape of gorges, geysers, giant waterfalls, boiling springs, and bubbling, sulfurous mud pots.

Hayden understood well his campaign's potential visual impact, and he took along two men destined to be among the West's most famous landscape artists and photographers, Thomas Moran and William Henry Jackson.[21] Their images and his descriptions quickly began to establish the area as another alien island, a western place apart. Hayden next turned southward and from 1873 to 1875, joined by James Gardner lately of the King survey, he conducted a topographical survey and resource studies of the Colorado high country. Of the four surveys Hayden's was the most scientifically eclectic (critics would call it scattershot and ill-disciplined) and partly for that reason it enjoyed the widest public attention.

The fourth survey, led by Lt. George M. Wheeler, was in one sense a throwback to an earlier era when the army had conducted most exploration.[22] Wheeler entered the field in 1867 and in 1871 his expanding effort took the name the U.S. Geographical Survey West of the One Hundredth Meridian. As the title suggests, its scope was enormous. In time Wheeler's survey covered roughly a third of all land west of the one-hundredth meridian. Most important in the survey's early years was Wheeler's expedition through the Great Basin. Several parties fanned out through southern Nevada, braving its hammering summer temperatures, then joined to drop into and across Death Valley ("The stifling heat, great radiation, and constant glare from the sand were almost overpowering").[23] In 1872, the year after Powell finished his second voyage down the Colorado, Wheeler led an assault upriver from its mouth to determine finally how far navigation might go and to scout possible routes for army supply roads. It took more than a month, in a harrowing, hungry pull past huge standing waves, before he reached Diamond Creek, the spot where the Ives expedition had descended to the canyon floor in 1857. After 1874 Wheeler turned more systematic. Up to seven teams worked from California to Colorado, mapping and probing the country's geological and natural histories. By 1879 the government had spent just under half a million dollars on Wheeler's survey, the most geographically extensive of the four.

Summing up the surveys is not easy. They varied among themselves, and each shifted in its own emphasis. Still, their work fell roughly into four categories. First, there was some true exploration of areas never seen or barely glimpsed by non-Indians, notably in Powell's early work in the Colorado Plateau and Hayden's in the Yellowstone Valley and in parts of the Colorado Rockies. A second, more common purpose was mapping, although it itself was never a single enterprise. Wheeler's early work was mostly reconnaissance, close observation, and descriptive sketching done especially for military routes and sites for outposts. But in 1873 Wheeler advised a shift "to a thorough survey that shall build up . . . and fortify our knowledge of the structural relationship of the whole."[24] He called, that is, for a consistent topographical mapping eventually covering the entire West, not reconnaissance but a geodetic survey to reproduce meticulously the region's landforms. The result was scores of hachure maps that used triangulation and astronomical observations to show topography through lines and shading. Eventually all four surveys drafted such maps that would blend later into the nation's checkerboard of ranges, townships, and sections now working its way to the Pacific.

The third purpose was to gather scientific intelligence. The accumulated information sprawled across disciplines. The surveys' field staffs and contributors included many of the era's leading scientists: Edward Drinker Cope, Othniel C. Marsh, Joseph Leidy, and Fielding B. Meek (all in paleontology), Grove Karl Gilbert, John Strong Newberry, Clarence Dutton, and Powell himself (geology), Elliott Coues and John A. Allen (zoology), and Leo Lesquereux (paleobotany), among others. All the surveys, and especially Powell's, emphasized geology, the science closest to the goal of mapping, but those of Wheeler and King and particularly Hayden took a remarkable scientific range. The expeditions were a platform for some of the century's most important discoveries in paleontology. They gathered enormous numbers of plants and animals—Wheeler's survey alone sent more than forty thousand specimens to the Smithsonian Institution—and their observations on bird and insect life were especially productive.[25] From 1869 on, Hayden's annual reports contained a series of scientific bulletins, some based on his teams' work in the field but others on independent contributions from other scientists, essentially an alternative scientific journal, uneven in quality but remarkably diverse in scope.[26] They included articles on New Mexico butterflies, Montana snakes, Texas birds, Rocky Mountain vegetation, and aboriginal language and burial practices.[27] The surveys pioneered the visual representation of nature with the photography of William Henry Jackson and Timothy O'Sullivan, the landscapes of Thomas Moran, and the extraordinary drawings of the greatest topographical artist of that age, William Henry Holmes.[28] The expeditions had their blind spots and crackpot ideas, but together they represented a massive assault by modern scientific curiosity.

Always, however, that curiosity, as well as the goals of mapping and exploration, were weighted toward the surveys' fourth purpose, evaluating the region's economic potential. A precursor of the expeditions had been California's Geological Survey of the 1860s, led by Josiah Dwight Whitney.[29] Several survey notables trained there, including Clarence King and William Henry Brewer, who left a vivid personal record of his experiences.[30] Whitney devised the basic techniques of triangulation used in geodetic mapping. The author of the standard work on the nation's mineral resources, Whitney had been expected to sniff out new gold fields and other ready resources. This he did, to a point, but he saw as his prime purpose the nation's first methodical geological mapping of a region. Whitney's refusal to make his survey more devotedly developmental, plus his conservationist tendencies and his deflation of promoters' extravagant puffery, in the end were his undoing. By 1870 the California Survey was dead.[31]

Perhaps with Whitney's problems in mind, the heads of the federal surveys focused more sharply on western development. King's work in the Comstock advanced both the search for silver and, in experiments with chemical ore reduction, its extraction, while in the Wasatch Mountains he boasted of "a most satisfactory estimate of the *unopened* [coal] *fields*."[32] Wheeler scouted out Nevada mining sites and evaluated the Southwest for irrigated farming. Hayden and his companions were the most avidly developmental. "Never has my faith in the grand future that awaits the entire West been so strong as it is at the present time," he wrote as introduction to his fourth annual report in 1870. When John Strong Newberry wrote of the "irremediably sterile" Colorado Plateau, he hurried into the next paragraph about the "green and flowery mountain valleys," temperate climate, and mineral treasures of its neighboring country.[33] In surveying unsettled areas Hayden chose first "those sections which appeared . . . to be the chief objective points of emigration and improvement."[34] Scientific descriptions were shot through with boosterish commentaries, including early appeals to tourists. One of Hayden's geologists tipped off sportsmen to the abundance of grizzlies, moose, mountain sheep, and game birds around Wyoming's Teton Mountains. He predicted that "when the region becomes more accessible by means of already projected railroads, this must become a favorite resort for tourists."[35]

The explorations did expose some of the more bloated claims of the time. In 1867 Whitney's California Survey had punctured the state's "oil bubble," a speculation pumped up by no less than Professor Benjamin Silliman of Yale, whose chemical experiments had inspired the first oil well in Titusville, Pennsylvania.[36] After two prospectors with a handful of diamonds reported in 1872 a vast field of gems at a secret spot somewhere in the western interior, King and a few companions found the spot through clever deduction and proved it had been salted. Instantly the "great diamond hoax" collapsed.[37]

But when claims were only a little subtler, science and boosterism could fuse, sometimes with unfortunate results. The most flagrant case was Hayden's endorsement of the theory that "rain follows the plow." This theory held that by planting crops and trees on the semiarid plains, settlers would increase the area's rainfall. It might be too dry to farm at the moment, this argument ran, but the climate would turn wetter once farming started. It was likely the most blithely confident idea in the long history of frontier optimism. The notion had been folk wisdom for years, but Hayden cited German authorities on the beneficent effects of planting trees: "As the lightning-rod abstracts the electric fluid from the stormy sky, so the forest abstracts to itself the rain from the clouds." Settlers supposedly would bring this happy change as they planted their way to the base of the Rockies. Ten or fifteen acres of new trees per quarter section ought to do the job, Hayden thought.[38] Richard Smith Elliott added his own assurances to Hayden's. He failed to note that he had been hired by the Kansas Pacific Railroad to sell its land to wary farmers.[39]

The great surveyors were by no means in lockstep. On one point Powell's vision of the West could not have differed more from Hayden's. His years of tramping the arid interior convinced him that, plows or no plows, rainfall would always be sparse and erratic. He would later argue that the rain-poor realities called for a fundamental shift in federal policies toward the public domain and in conceiving the West's political arrangement.[40] Within that reality, however, Powell's faith in national destiny and development was as firm as Hayden's. People could adjust. Much of the drier West could support great herds of cattle and sheep to feed the growing republic. In some places, with the right manipulation, arid lands could be *more* suited to agriculture. If mountain rain and snowfall were captured in reservoirs and delivered to dry but fertile areas, presently barren and unyielding lands would be "ultimately one of the great agricultural regions of the country," he wrote in 1889: "Sage-brush plains, sand-dune deserts, and alkaline valleys will be covered by gardens, fields, and groves, all perennially fertilized by thousands of mountain lakes."[41]

Before the war the federal government had begun the job of describing and detailing what was now the western third of the nation. Because most was bound up with the contentious work of the four railroad surveys, that effort to unify America's geographical portrait paradoxically nearly tore the nation in two. After the war, with the Union confirmed and its powers grown, the four surveys of Powell, King, Hayden, and Wheeler went beyond connecting the West to siting it, placing its parts inside a national grid, and linking their particulars into one grand promise of prosperity for the now-reunited states.

The same work was binding the West into another expanding community— that of scientific understanding. Quickly the West assumed a role as one of the era's great laboratories in pursuit of answers to the most pressing questions of the day.

Bones from the Well

In August of 1868, nine months before Powell disembarked at Green River to begin his foray down the Colorado, Othniel C. Marsh stepped off the Union Pacific at Antelope Station, Nebraska, just east of the Wyoming line. He was looking for bones. In Chicago for a professional meeting, the young Yale professor of paleontology had taken advantage of the new rail line to investigate rumors of ancient human and animal remains seen along the route. He was not disappointed. Beside a newly dug well were piles of fossils Marsh quickly identified as mammalian and, in several cases, previously unknown. He gathered up what he could and hired the station master to save the rest. Back on the train, he found eleven creatures represented in his "hatful of bones." The implication was obvious: he had to come back.

The postwar surveys were only one of many platforms of exploration. A small army of scientists, including many skilled amateurs, fanned across the country, measuring, collecting, cataloguing. As when Marsh pulled fossils from the station well, these scientists probed the West quite literally to its depths. They explored its deep antiquity, its forms of life present and long-gone, and the formative forces that had shaped the land they were crisscrossing. These years were one of the most vibrant and contentious periods of modern scientific engagement, and those working the West took what they found, applied it to questions of the day, speculated on what it all meant, and helped transform long-held assumptions about the basic nature of the physical world.

Their work was especially vigorous in what has been called the prince of sciences in the nineteenth century, geology. The field has two main branches, historical and structural. Historical geology is the recreation of the earth's story. An essential tool is stratigraphy, the study of the strata laid down beneath our feet. To geologists, these are chapters in the book of the world, and by cataloguing and studying those layers they piece those ancient texts into a whole. For this, the deeply eroded Colorado Plateau was "to the geologist a paradise. Nowhere on the earth's surface, so far as we know, are the secrets of its structure so fully revealed as here."[42] That opinion was from John Strong Newberry, who in 1857 was the first geologist to work in what he called "the Great Canyon." Stratigraphy's graphic expression is the geologic column, a drawing and labeling of the earth's layers. Newberry produced the canyon's first, showing a sequence of limestones, sandstones, shales, and grits piled a mile deep over a granite base. It was a remarkable first vision of how the West had come to be.[43] As surveys gathered more and more evidence farther and farther afield, a geologic narrative gradually emerged.

Its culmination was Clarence King's *Systematic Geology* (1878). It told a fabulous story of mountains rearing up higher than Everest and replaced by oceans that came and went, the Great Plains rising as a dome and the Uinta and Wasatch Ranges thrust upward forty thousand feet, then eroding as the plains tilted and dumped huge freshwater lakes into the Gulf of Mexico. Meanwhile the Pacific coast blazed with volcanoes and the Great Basin buckled and filled with gigantic lakes that dried to the comparatively puddle-like Great Salt Lake. The year before King's masterwork, his colleagues Samuel F. Emmons and Arnold Hague had produced *Descriptive Geology* massively detailing the fortieth parallel at present. Thirty years earlier this portion of the West had been a sprawling between. Now it was arguably the most fully comprehended place on earth.

Western contributions were even greater in structural geology, the study of forces behind the events described in historical geology. Both fields see the earth as alive, one as an ancient story, the other as processes always at work. Structural geology, or geomorphology, if anything is more distinctively American in its origins. The fantastic landscapes of the western interior raised fundamental questions and inspired tentative answers that gave form to this emerging international field.

Powell used the Grand Canyon and surrounding plateaus to posit basic shaping processes, one in particular—the erosional force of water running over time. His most famous argument answered the riddle of why the Green River flowed through the Uinta Mountains instead of around them. The key to grasping his ideas is looking back through a near-incomprehensible length of time. The river, he said, had come first, and so it "had the right of way." The mountains had risen from beneath it, but so slowly and gradually that the river could slice downward as fast as the rock could rise up. Powell compared the corrosive flow of water to a circular saw and the mountains to a log pushed up against it.[44] It was a dramatic illustration of fluvialism, the power of rivers to mold the landscape, that was becoming closely associated with an "American school" of geology.

Fluvialism, however, did not explain the endless writhing of the earth itself. Rivers might saw through rising mountains, but why and how had the Uintas risen against the Green River in the first place? This discussion in turn contributed to the more general principle of isostasy, the term coined only later, in 1889, by Clarence Dutton. He theorized that the earth's surface tends always toward an equilibrium as gravity acts on material moved from one place to another. Mountains might rise up as gravity presses sediments downward next door, but gravity also will immediately start wearing the mountains down. Dutton's colleague Grove Karl Gilbert took a similar approach to his brilliant study of Utah's Henry Mountains.[45] Besides describing the Henrys as a distinct type of mountain—a laccolith, a kind of immense unburst volcanic blister—Gilbert used the wearing-down of this dome to expand on Newberry's, Powell's, and Dutton's discussions of erosion. For all its complexity and variety, he wrote, erosion worked by three laws unified under one principle—a tension between, on the one hand, water's relentless desire to wear away slopes and irregularities to a level plain and, on the other hand, differences in rock's density and its ability to resist that watery desire.[46]

Gilbert's ideas seem commonsensical, lessons learned by anyone who has tried to sand something smooth, but his analysis of the Henry Mountains provided the basis for joining the insights of his colleagues into an overarching means of thinking about structural geology. Its general approach was to see the present shape of things as a momentary result of endless processes always at odds, the earth in motion, the earth seeking equilibrium.[47] The consequent narrative, the emergence and balance and collapse of every place on earth, could be understood as an engineer understood the making and the ultimate fate of a building or a bridge. This way of observing was the chief characteristic of the American school that profoundly influenced international geology. The school's busy classroom was the interior West.

Geology got such attention in large part because it related directly to the most volatile scientific, theological, and moral issue of the day—Charles Darwin's ideas on evolution by natural selection. The adaptive mechanism of natural selection requires what to most people was (and is) an unimaginable stretch of time, and structural geologists revealed a chronological depth, Powell's "slow, patient" agencies of nature, that could easily accommodate Darwin's claims.[48] With enough millennia to work with, geological and biological forces could have equally outlandish results—the Grand Canyon, giraffes, flying squirrels. Darwinism was more obviously the turf of historical geologists. One means of identifying geologic strata was by what fossils each layer might hold. Fossils "are labels written by the Creator" for the rocks around them, Newberry wrote in 1870.[49] And one way to order those layers into a sequence was to arrange the fossils into their own lines of development. This led to a natural partnership of historical geologists and paleontologists. Together they wrote a common narrative of a restless earth and its evolving species.

By chance the explosive growth of American paleontology coincided with far-western expansion. Until the 1840s most digs had been in Alabama, Virginia, South Carolina, New Jersey, and elsewhere in the East. Then in 1846 molars of a giant Tertiary tapir dug from the Dakota Badlands provided the first hint of western possibilities.[50] The lead was aggressively followed over the next twenty years by Joseph Leidy of the University of Pennsylvania, who soon realized that he was excavating a display of life distinct from Europe's.[51] His *Extinct Mammalian Fauna of Dakota and Nebraska . . . with a Synopsis of the Mammalian Remains of North America* was a declaration of independence for American paleontology.[52] It appeared in 1869, the year after a young Othniel C. Marsh of Yale had stepped off the Union Pacific and gathered his "hatful of bones." The next year Marsh led the first of many expeditions of students to the area. Soon a small army of bone hunters were scouring the interior West. The most notable figure besides Marsh was Edward Drinker Cope, a student of Leidy whose bitter rivalry with Marsh provided incentive for them both and added public drama to their efforts. Both men drew on considerable family fortunes, and Marsh had support from his position at Yale. The federal government was much involved. Material gathered from the field was turned over to, and sometimes gathered through, the great surveys, and western troops provided protection for Marsh's university field trips.

To a remarkable degree, however, it was a genuinely western effort by self-taught amateurs who recognized the wonders around them. The fossilized teeth that triggered the great hunt had been sent to Saint Louis in 1846 by trappers with the American Fur Company. Charles Sternberg was a teenager homesteading in Kansas when he amassed a prodigious collection of fossilized plants and, after crashing a reception at a nearby army post, began a twenty-year collaboration with Leo Lesquereux, the greatest paleobotanist of the century.[53] The most productive boneyard of the day, at Como Bluffs in Wyoming, came to light when a station agent and meat hunter for the Union Pacific, W. E. Carlin and W. H. "Bill" Reed, wrote Marsh of finding a vertebrae and scapula they speculated was from a Megatherium of the Tertiary period.

Fossils in fact became a minor variation of a western extractive business with freelancers like these offering specific finds and, as in prospecting for gold and silver, information to outside buyers and investors. Reed and Carlin, writing under pseudonyms to cover their trail, were willing to show Marsh "the secret of the fossil bed"—for a nice price. "We are working men," they explained, "and are not able to present them as a gift."[54] Arthur Lakes, an Oxford-trained clergyman who found fossil beds at Morrilton and Canyon City, Colorado, felt the same: "My circumstances oblige me to sell the specimens to the highest bidder." Reed and Lakes proved to be good enough to become Marsh's top field men. Reed helped to unearth and assemble the *Diplodocus carnegii* that would fill a hall and dazzle millions of visitors to Pittsburgh's Carnegie Museum. He left Marsh in 1883 to take up sheepherding.

The results, simply in numbers, transformed international paleontology. Before 1847 just under 100 genera and species of North American fossil vertebrates had been described. Fifty years later there were more than 2,200, including nearly 250 dinosaurs from late Jurassic and Cretaceous periods, some the size of chickens, and others, like Diplodacus and Allosaurus, larger than boxcars. No place on earth came even close to the American West in yielding that abundance from such a stretch of time.[55] The pace was dizzying. "In two days [I] have found 25 or 30 species of which 10 are new," Cope wrote his father from one camp.[56] New insights quickly began to accumulate. In the relatively unglamorous field of paleobotany, the study of fossilized plants, the Swiss émigré Leo Lesquereux noted in Hayden's fifth annual report that the early flora of North America were clearly akin to that of Greenland and Iceland.[57] Here was an early hint that the Americas and Europe were once connected, a point that in turn would lead a century later to understanding plate tectonics and continental drift. The weaving together of new fossils with the deep mapping of formations here and in Europe established the (more or less) agreed-upon eras, periods, and epochs that remain geology's basic sequential structure.

All this made the West the center of global attention in questions around evolution by natural selection. Two of the debate's most significant contributions occurred there. Both came from Marsh, although both were built partly on evidence gathered by on-the-ground western bone hunters. Darwin had argued that all species, living and long dead, had descended from others before them, but he had provided no examples of such a step-by-step evolution, a point his critics were quick to seize upon. On his several Yale expeditions, Marsh and his students had collected fossil remains of the modern horse and arranged them into five equine species from the Eocene to the Pliocene. This proved conclusively that horses were of New World origin, something Leidy and others had suspected but had not shown. Much more impressive, however, was how he showed those species clicking together as links of the field's first evolutionary chain.[58]

Marsh's second revelation came with his monograph *Odontornithes* (1880).[59] Evolutionists had long argued that modern birds had evolved from reptiles, but their critics answered that, as usual, they were building theoretical castles without proof. *Odontornithes*, or "toothed birds," was Marsh's answer. Sumptuously illustrated and thick with details from thousands of fossils gathered over nearly a decade from Cretaceous chalk beds in Kansas, it made a powerful case for the reptile-to-bird link, most dramatically by introducing a six-foot avian that had swum penguin-like through America's old inland seas, snapping up its meals with its ninety-four sharp teeth that, like its brain case and leg bones, clearly harkened back to reptilian ancestors. Marsh named the creature *Hesperornis regalis*, the "royal bird of the West."[60]

Marsh's two studies, the genealogy of horses and his analysis of toothed birds, showed natural selection at work at the micro and macro levels. The one focused tightly on the twigging of a single evolutionary bush to show how one of the most familiar creatures of the day had come into being out of a five-toed ancestor the size of a collie. The other linked two great clusters of species, making it plausible that rattlesnakes and hawks were distant kin.

Odontornithes was published as the seventh and final volume of the fortieth parallel survey reports. This made it something of a bookend, actually and figuratively, to the extraordinary scientific labors during the quarter century after the Civil War. The first volume of the survey's reports was King's *Systematic Geology*, with its mind-twirling account of the come-and-go of mountain ranges and inland oceans over hundreds of millions of years. Together the two, and all the work between and around them, established the West as the age's ideal place to tell the oldest stories in the world. The eroded plains and plateaus became as well the focus of the most important argument of the nineteenth century. Marsh in 1877 told the American Association for the Advancement of Science that his bird teeth and horse toes would soon be "the stepping stones by which the evolutionist of today leads the doubting brother across the shallow remnant of the gulf once thought impassable."[61] Darwin thought so. The day after he received *Odontornithes* he wrote Marsh to praise the work as "the best support for the theory of evolution, which has appeared within the last 20 years"—that is, since publication of *On the Origin of Species*.[62]

The debate was far from over, of course, and in some quarters it still isn't, but western geologists and paleontologists gave Darwinists a credibility increasingly difficult to challenge, and through the sheer wealth and density of their evidence they gave substance to a new view of life itself. Oliver Wendell Holmes wrote Marsh that when he read of birds with teeth he was as startled "as the midwife who first looked into the mouth of Richard Third."[63] Plenty of other Victorians had trouble swallowing Darwin's prophetic vision that environment, chance, and time, through the endlessly inventive machine of natural selection, could produce the most astounding results. As if on cue Leidy, Cope, Marsh, and their cohorts, including meat hunters, preachers, and farm boys, reached into western chalks and sandstones and pulled out flying lizards, piggish grazers the size of farm wagons, sea serpents, fish with body armor, and waddling monsters with bills like ducks. Life is an improbable lottery, Darwin said. The West gave the world examples no lunatic would have guessed.

13 ➤ The "Science of Man" and the American Sublime

The great reconnaissance that began with expansion always had a human dimension. Railroad surveys of the 1850s described the West's Native peoples in their physical traits, cultures, and material life. That work continued in far greater scope after the war, and like that before, it served the goals of both science and a national inventory. By then, however, it had a weightier purpose. The middle third of the nineteenth century saw an invigorated interest in the study of the world's peoples and how they related to one another. That interest was pursued with special energy in the West. Expansion and war meanwhile were raising a fundamental question around American identity—just who should be, and who shouldn't be, welcome into the national embrace? The interest and the question worked together, resonating between East and West, and their answers helped shape a new perception of America as an ordered human community.

Besides that ordering, western science, from geologizing to chasing birds and bugs, fed a new sensibility to the land, which itself helped shape a changing America and its sense of national self.

Potfinders, Storycatchers, and Headhunters

Late on the afternoon of October 9, 1874, a small party, an offshoot of the Hayden survey, made camp and cooked supper along the Mancos River in southwestern Colorado. After studying landforms and silver mining in the San Juan Mountains, they had detoured into an area known as Mesa Verde to check out rumors of crumbling ruins of ancient civilizations. So far the search had been frustrating. Now, in a campfire tease, the photographer William Henry Jackson, the journalist Ernest Ingersoll, and the party's guide told a young colleague that he had a steep climb in store the next day to reach a ruin high on the cliff that rose hundreds of feet above the campsite. What ruin? the man asked. The guide gestured vaguely upward and told the man to look:

"Gee," says he. "I see it." I beheld upon my close observation [Jackson wrote] there was something that appeared very like a house, the doors and windows could be seen. We all started at once to investigate. . . . One house was [about eight hundred feet up]. . . . Found a tree and a series of crevices by which, with a little trouble, we reached the plateau upon which the houses stood. Then, perched away in a crevice like a swallow's or a bat's nest, [there] it was, a marvel and a puzzle.[1]

In the gathering dark, with their campfire blinking below "like a far away little red star," Jackson and Ingersoll looked over the canyon with a view that to others, centuries earlier, had been not a span of mystery but a prospect of home.[2]

Jackson's trip up the Mancos River was part of a survey of ancient and contemporary peoples what was, like the plotting of lands, resources, and animal and plant life, also an act of national conquest and reconstruction. When the surveys were consolidated into United States Geological Survey in 1879, several of the most experienced field operatives went to work for another agency created simultaneously—the Bureau of Ethnology. Ethnology was another youthful field inspiring vigorous international debate, and as with geology and paleontology its pursuit in the federal surveys was part of siting the West within a larger intellectual setting. All the searching, collecting, asking, describing, recording, and cataloguing among Indian peoples was also openly directed to the postwar enterprise of expanding and redefining the national family and American citizenship. The prevailing assumption was that everyone must stand on some common cultural ground in pursuit of a common good—with both the ground and the good defined by those in charge of the project. The study of Indians was always set to that goal. Once they had been mined for the good of scholarship, would be made over and brought into the national embrace, willingly or not.

The bureau's first head was John Wesley Powell. The men who mapped and studied the West's landforms could not miss that they were well inhabited, and had been for quite a while, and some like Powell moved from a general interest to personal involvement. As Kapurats (He Who Has One Arm), he counted as companions several Utes, Paiutes, and their families, and while never questioning that their way of life was doomed, as a special commissioner he called for greater government support and protection. George Bird Grinnell, who eventually was his day's leading student of Cheyenne history and culture, first came west as a Yale student with Marsh's first bone-hunting expedition.[3] Marsh developed close ties with the Lakotas, and when he returned from a fossil hunt in 1874 with examples of the rotting rations given them on their reservation, he triggered a political scandal that drove the secretary of the interior and commissioner of Indian affairs from their jobs. Marsh remained lifelong friends with the leader Red Cloud, whose portrait hung in Marsh's New Haven home.

The men who gathered information on western peoples' basketry, dances, dress, and languages were not so different from those describing geology, resources, flora, and fauna. Historical geologists reconstructed the land's deep narrative, and paleontologists revived on paper animals vanished for millions of years, and the search for ruins like those in the Southwest filled in the human dimension over time. As the geological story gave a distinctive depth to an American identity, so its ancient peoples were the closest claim to a human antiquity. But, as with the study of the earth, this was also in quest for the arching idea. In his bureau's first report, Powell pledged to look at Indian peoples in their social entirety—their "customs, laws, governments, institutions, mythologies, religions, and even their arts."[4] He would bind what was found with investigations elsewhere to unlock the dynamics of human society. Geologists were after the whole earth's mechanics, paleontologists the universal scheme behind life's diversity. The bureau's purpose, Powell said, was pursuit of "the Science of Man."[5]

The information gathered was extraordinary in scope and volume. Two years after Jackson's finds along the Mancos River, he and the artist William H. Holmes photographed, sketched, and described major ruins in the region, including Canyon de Chelly and Chaco Canyon. In Wheeler's survey were superb illustrations of bone and wood implements and funerary textiles from Southern California and descriptions of the Ácoma, San Juan, and Taos Pueblos and of the Zuni "Cachina" [Kachina] dance.[6] Among the topics of the eight-volume *Contributions to North American Ethnology*, published under the aegis of the Powell survey, were lapidarian sculpture and a continental survey of Native "houses and house life" that included southwestern ruins.[7] Scattered through the bulletins of the Hayden survey were reports on Ute dialects, a calendar of Dakota winter counts, and much more. There was special attention to Native languages, individually and comparatively—a chart of more than two hundred words spoken by forty groups from the Southwest and California and lengthy dictionaries of Klamath and Dakota.[8] More about Native antiquity and contemporary life was documented during the three decades after the Civil War, and arguably in any five-year increment of that time, than during the three centuries since European contact.

Together the reports picture a splay of cultures. To cross the West would be to live in pyramidish tule lodges and earthen domes (California), multistory adobes (New Mexico), bermed pit houses (Missouri Valley), skin tipis (Great Plains), and wicker arbors (Mohave Desert). Each people might tell visitors stories of beginnings, wars, natural forces, human nature: how coyote made the moon, how primordial lightning left a spark in wood so fire might be rubbed to life, the migration of dead souls into fish. And life rituals: Every day a grieving Ukiah mother would visit where her dead baby had played, swaying and chanting while milking her breasts into the air. A newly widowed Klamath man would fast and walk the woods for five days and nights dressed in old blankets cinched with serviceberry branches.[9] The recorded voices speak of universal impulses expressed in unique vernaculars, as when Modoc youths chanted at each other on the conflict of the sexes:

> Girls: Young man, I will not love you, for you run around with no blanket on. . . .
> Boys: And I do not like a frog-shaped woman with swollen eyes.

There were occasional hints of white influence, as in this girl's song to a pestering lover:

> Shake your head! you son of a bitch, and go South.[10]

The guiding purpose was to bring this motley into one great understanding, and for that, languages were crucial. Ethnologists held that languages, like evolving species, over time send out limbs that fork into branches that send out sprigs. The strategy, pioneered by Powell, was to collect vocabularies of the same words (e.g., "man," "child," "tree," "water") from different languages and dialects, then look for patterns of similarity. Those patterns would reveal clusters of related languages—families grown from the same linguistic trunks, like Europe's Romance and Germanic tongues. The Sioux language turned out to be related to that of the Osages and the Catawbas of North Carolina; the Comanches' was related to the Utes' and the Aztecs'. Tribes of the same language family presumably had descended from the same stock, and by plotting the locations of linguistic relatives, ethnologists believed they could rough out the routes that each tribe had probably followed to its present place. Indian words and how they were spoken could be translated into an atlas of group relations and historic movement.

Customs had more to say. How the many peoples worked the land and fed themselves, how they organized themselves, how they worshiped and, in particular, how they defined their kinship fell into repeating patterns. Ethnologists like Lewis Henry Morgan argued that such customs, once entrenched, stubbornly persisted, and in fact he believed they were (before the term had appeared) genetic, passed down "with the streams of the blood, from the same common source."[11] Recurring patterns, like languages, could join different peoples into larger groupings that, when mapped and compared, could reveal how their histories had intertwined and diverged. That in turn would contribute to a global understanding of the human family.

The accomplishments were impressive. Powell devised a basic categorization of language families, and through that a tree of tribal kinship, still generally accepted today. Customs could not be studied as precisely as languages and so could lead in strange directions. Morgan concluded that Inuits and Plains Indians were kin because they both wore breechcloths and slept in the nude.[12] Still, the study of lifeways became the basis of broad patterns full of insights into how societies related to each other and to their physical settings. This vigorous categorization of distinctly human traits set the American cohort apart to the point that Powell could claim to have created the field of anthropology itself. Their efforts to "demark mankind from the lower animals," a work rooted in the American West, "raise[d] ethnic research to a higher plane," he wrote, distinguishing his Science of Man as "an essentially distinct science."[13]

Always, however, there was darker side. From the start, Powell wrote, the "immediate purpose" of this human inventory had been to make more likely that "amicable groups might be gathered on reservations."[14] That gathering in turn was key to opening the West to settlement and development. What Powell claimed was the emergence of a new science was born of the nation's commitment to occupy Native homelands and to command their resources. Its impulse combined ferocious curiosity with belief in national destiny and in setting Indian peoples properly within it with as little disruption and conflict as possible.

Fitting Indians into one scheme or another was an act of domination in a broader sense. It was attempted identity theft. Tribes typically called themselves by some variant of "the People," often qualified as "People of This Place." If one could imagine a map of western Indians as they saw themselves, it would appear as scores of dots flung across two million square miles. Each dot would be one people who looked outward from their particular homeland. Contrary to popular impressions, none were frozen in the past. Each had evolved over time, and many had been shaped by changes that had come with Europeans and, more recently, by invaders from the East. But for most, identities were rooted in their particular places, homelands that were the centers of their worlds. From each one—each dot—would radiate a series of ever-larger circles, each one reaching farther into country that was, for each people, increasingly alien. All tribes, of course, had relations with others—trade, alliances, and conflicts as their expanding circles overlapped and interacted with those of their neighbors—but each people's world still sat on its own center. Each had learned in its bones that its way of life, its stories, beliefs, and most of all its understanding of who they were, made sense only from that perspective, looking outward.

Ethnology meant to decenter all such circles. It would set each "People of This Place" within one overarching arrangement. To do that ethnologists first would disassemble each way of life and then reassemble its parts into patterns that matched those of other peoples whose lives others had dis- and reassembled into the same patterns, from Arizona to Borneo. Each of those patterns, they said, was transitory, evolving, and each could be located within one universal process of human culture evolving over time. The evolution was most famously summarized in Lewis Henry Morgan's *Ancient Society* (1877). The process was one of universal progress. Every society was advancing from savagery through barbarism to civilization, each phase with its own substages.[15] Western geologists were telling their far more ancient universal stories of the earth and its evolution. Morgan and his fellow ethnologists were plotting the deep history of Indians and how it fit inside the encompassing story of human cultures across the world. Their old narrative, however, was given a current meaning. While all societies were marching along the same route, Morgan wrote, some were lagging behind and others were pulling ahead. Africans were well to the rear, Caucasians at the foremost, Europeans and Euro-Americans in the lead.[16]

To categorize, that is, was to rank, and in this single scheme western Indians were always poking along toward the rear. Morgan concluded that they ranged upward from tribes in California and the Columbia Valley, now in the third stage of savagery, to the village peoples of New Mexico, well advanced into the middle status of barbarism but still "one entire ethnical period" shy of civilization.[17] Stephen Powers found California Natives well formed and blessed with white teeth and sweet breath, but he agreed that they were morally feeble, thieving, morbid, avaricious, revengeful, cunning, rancorous, oversexed, and, at least so far, utterly lacking in poetic ability, breadth of character, and capacity for conceiving the divine. The linguist Albert Gatschet, ranking languages downward from civilized inflective ones to the mostly agglutinative ones of Indians, concluded that his Klamath subjects, while morally "not better and not worse" than whites, had "no real human culture."[18]

Conclusions like these related directly to Washington's Indian policy. Men like Morgan and Powell believed that Indians, while culturally retrograde, were definitely improvable, but given the course of western development, they would have to pick up the cultural pace. They would have to be set apart in places akin to social laboratories and workshops where benevolent directors would conduct them up a ramp of progress through those "ethnical periods." Reservations would fill that role. Thus Powell's link between his field work and national vision: the reservation system would smooth this process by housing the most "amicable" tribes together. That rationale, and reservations generally, were undergirded by a full-blown cultural assault. Ethnologists fanned out across the West, describing life ways and collecting artifacts, precisely because they assumed the cultures they studied were, and should be, doomed.

They applied what they learned to speed the process. Powell well understood the intimate bond between Native groups and particular places. An Indian in the Great Basin meeting a stranger, he wrote, never asked the stranger's tribe "but to 'what land do you belong and how are you and your land named.'" To leave one's place was to surrender "everything most sacred" in a particular culture. And the lesson? Each of those scores of tribes should be picked up and taken somewhere else. Each should be knocked off its particular dot. This would be "the first step to be taken in their civilization," followed by forced adoption of white lifeways and economies.[19] So, too, with languages. Language expressed and conserved a people's cultural essence. The lesson? Take it away from them. A prime need for Indians, wrote the Peace Commission of 1868, was to blot out their "barbarous dialects." The ultimate goal was to obliterate tribal identities and "fuse them into one homogenous mass," and "uniformity of language will do this—nothing else will." And besides, Powell wrote, Native speech was so thickly woven with "sorcery" and "baneful superstitions" and so inadequate in expressing "the ideas and thoughts of civilized life" that Indians could never be brought up to cultural snuff without adopting an advanced language—namely, English.[20]

The intrusion into Indian life had a more gruesome dimension—the collection of human remains, especially skulls. This, too, had roots before the Civil War. The definitive individual bone-collector was Samuel George Morton, a respected Philadelphia physician who by 1849 had recorded 1,035 human crania. Nearly half were of Indians of the Americas. Only eight were "Anglo-Americans."[21] After the Civil War the new Army Medical Museum asked officers across the West to send Indian crania "to aid in the progress of anthropological science."[22] One in the Dakotas boasted of his cleverness after an elderly Lakota was laid to rest: "Believing that they would hardly think I would steal his head before he was cold in his grave, I early in the evening with two of my hospital attendants secured this specimen."[23] By 1880 the museum had taken 1,115 crania from 83 different tribes.[24]

The postwar surveys and private expeditions pitched in. When the students on Marsh's first expedition came across bodies of two Lakotas on funerary platforms, they stood in awe until Marsh brought them around: "Well, boys . . . we can't study the origin the Indian race unless we have those skulls!"[25] As with ancient fossils sold to Cope and Marsh, Indian bones were marketed to the Smithsonian, Peabody, and Field Museums. The great anthropologist Franz Boas trafficked in skeletons to finance his early work in the Pacific Northwest. "It is most unpleasant work to steal bones from a grave," he wrote his wife, "but what is the use, someone has to do it."[26]

Bone collection and craniometry, the measurement of a skull's dimensions and shape, were other means to establish Indians' relationships among others around the globe. But there was a much larger game in play. The remaking of America after 1848 raised a fundamental question: Who should be allowed into its social embrace, and who should be kept out? The issue behind the question hinged on new notions about race.[27]

Traditionally the word's meaning was rough and vague, as in "the Italian race" or "a race of nobility." Now *race* increasingly referred to a human group with clearly defined biological and cultural traits.[28] Skull collectors believed that craniometry held the key to grouping the world's peoples cleanly into a handful of races. Samuel Morton decided there were five: Caucasian, Mongolian, Malay, American (that is, American Indian), and Ethiopian. They differed not only physically but also intellectually and culturally. And they were not simply different. They were independent biological species with separate origins, unchanged and presumably unchanging. There was no human race, Morton argued. There were human races.

The theory here, polygenesis ("many beginnings"), had prominent supporters, among them Harvard's Louis Agassiz.[29] Its two masterworks were Morton's *Crania Americana* (1839) and *Types of Mankind* (1855) by his two leading disciples, Josiah Nott and George Gliddon. They appeared just before and right after expansion brought tens of thousands of Hispanos and Indian peoples within the nation's borders, and they coincided as well with sharpening arguments over Black slavery and, after the war, with emancipation and questions around citizenship for freedpeople. Given the timing, the polygenists' arguments naturally came to bear on America's evolving human composition.

Polygenists invoked science to call for firm and permanent ranks of power and privilege. Caucasians alone, Morton wrote, were graced with "the highest intellectual endowments." Indians, far slower on the mental uptake, were "restless, revengeful, and fond of war." Africans, "joyous, flexible, and indolent," occupied "the lowest grade of humanity." The obvious conclusion: Whites should rule. African slavery should remain because, Nott and Gliddon wrote, "the Negro thrives [only] under his white master." As for Indians, the "Red American" was an "untameable, carnivorous animal" destined to fade away before the "onward march of the [white] frontier-man."[30] Thus the dimensions of occipital and nasal bones and the volume of brain cases were inflated into a continental racial order. Indian skulls supported African slavery. Enslaved Africans predicted the end of Indians.

The alternative view was that of monogenesis ("one beginning"). Besides its biblical grounding in humanity's descent from a single set of parents, it was the guiding principle of Powell's Science of Man and the assumptions of Indian policies. Morgan and Powell and their cohort certainly recognized that the world's peoples differed greatly in cultural qualities. They agreed that those qualities could rightly be ranked as superior and inferior and, so, that some were more fit for social and political leadership and should be given some authority over others. Still, they held that all peoples were part of a single human framework, that all were advancing through cultural stages toward the same end, and that at some unstated future all would unite in a common American identity.

This view, in broad strokes and as formal policy, carried the day. Black slavery was ended and freedpeople were given citizenship, and the government persisted on its course with Native peoples. "Can any man who knows anything about the present condition of Indians . . . propose a scheme for their improvement, which would offer the least prospect of success?" Josiah Nott had asked in 1847.[31] "Yes," Washington answered, and gestured to reservations as its means to guide them along the upward road, even as it sowed the South with schools for freedpeople and invited them to become economic and political actors.

The decades ahead would show how unready and unwilling the federal government and the white public were to pursue those goals to anything close to accomplishment. There was vague commitment to common citizenship in the future but also a wide agreement that old-stock Anglos, Blacks, Hopis, Irish, and Hispanics were rankable in how they lived, spoke, and behaved, and in that ranking few in the majority questioned white superiority in the here and now.

The questions around the study of ancient and present Native peoples were being asked globally, but, like the theories of how mountains were made and the discovery of toothed birds, the answers came in an American accent and they helped define a new America. Vigorously imagined and pursued with prodigious energy, the work produced an enormous body of knowledge of indigenous peoples. It was also a collective act of breathtaking arrogance. It presumed to tell other peoples who they really were, where they had come from, and where they truly fit into the world around them, including just how far they were below their betters.

For all their eclectic curiosity, the men on the hunt for heads, artifacts, stories, languages, and bits of an ancient past showed little interest in one topic—the Indians' own thoughts on their present lives. Nevertheless Native voices sometimes sift through. To illustrate speech patterns, linguists published letters dictated to them by tribal leaders. An Omaha pled to the commissioner of Indian Affairs in 1878: "To deprive us of our land would be just like killing us. . . . Now, my friend . . . , having God in mind, have pity on us who are Indians!" And another to a friend planning a visit: "Do not come! The sickness is continually bad! And, moreover, we have not received money; we are very poor." Even the relentlessly contemptuous Stephen Powers occasionally let California's Natives speak out. One group practiced infanticide because "they say they do not wish to rear any more children among the whites." Pushed inexorably from their "fine broad valleys" and oak forests, "pursued and shot unto death like jackals," watching themselves "swiftly dwindling, dwindling, melting away before some mysterious pathless power," they seemed to have fallen into "a great and bitter despair," Powers thought, "so far as their natures are capable of entertaining any profound emotion."[32]

An American Aesthetic

Integrating the West into the world of knowledge also helped create the West as distinctive. As with the movement revolution, the work of scientists found in the new country connections in the widest sense—to the history and machinery of the earth we all share and to the fabulous narrative of life itself—yet also the chance to separate the West from the world of others and to portray it as a realm uniquely American.

The link between western science and this emerging perception was helped along by the popular appeal of the explorations' driving interest, geology. *The Knickerbocker* in 1835 called it "the fashionable science of the day . . . , a necessary part of a practical and ornamental education," and six years later a speaker at the first anniversary meeting of the Association of American Geologists noted that its emerging wonders were "the theme of discussion in the drawing-rooms of taste and fashion."[33] Popular curiosity grew after Darwin's bombshell in 1859. The extraordinarily ambitious western geological expeditions naturally drew special attention, enough to invite parody. In "A Geological Madrigal," Bret Harte made a paleontology dig into a lover's seduction:

Then come, love, and never say nay,
But calm all your maidenly fears;
We'll note, love, in one summer's day
The record of millions of years.[34]

Field scientists played to that interest to scare up money for future projects. Powell, Hayden, Marsh, and others consistently invited journalists to tag along, and some of their articles in turn grew into full-blown western travelogues.[35] The accounts describe the science conducted, often in impressive detail, but most are also occasions of gentlemanly adventure, bluff heroism, and pursuit of western fantasies. The future lawyers and corporate leaders with Marsh's Yale expeditions passed time with Mexican guides, cavalrymen, and William F. "Buffalo Bill" Cody. (Cody took Marsh's tutorials on ancient creatures to be great western stretchers, "mighty tough yarns.") Their time discovering mosasaurs was scrambled with encounters with grizzlies, prairie fires, horse thieves, and twenty-two of Brigham Young's daughters. They worked amid swarms of rattlesnakes, but the rattlers' "humming soon became an old tune" and shooting them a dull chore for all but one who was "collecting their rattles as a necklace for his lady-love."[36] One of Wheeler's parties thrilled to their first hearing of coyotes, "loud and demoniac as the glee of an escaped madman."[37] Marsh himself wrote breathlessly of interrupting his work to chase and kill a bison from a racing army ambulance: "As we drew closer, I singled him out as my victim. . . . I fired, and down he came. . . . [In the end I was] covered in blood . . . , with my hunting knife in my hand."[38]

Such hypermasculinity was common at the field's loftiest levels. The clearest expression was in the well-known rivalry between John Muir and Clarence King. Muir, a native Scot who grew up impoverished in Wisconsin, would go on to found the Sierra Club and be the founding spirit of the modern environmentalist movement. While King was an institutional insider, Muir's first research in the Sierra Nevada was done while herding sheep. Muir's and King's clash was partly rooted in science, specifically whether the spectacular Yosemite Valley had been formed, as Muir argued, through the slow grinding of glaciers or, as Whitney thought, by a cataclysmic event, its bottom literally dropping out.[39] The debate, part of the larger clash between the schools of uniformitarianism and catastrophism, in time would tip in Muir's favor, but not before King in *Systematic Geology* slapped at his "hopeless floundering" and condescendingly wished that this "ambitious amateur" would someday find a useful channel for his enthusiasm, "if there is one." In the book's index King allowed his rival one punning entry: "Muir, John, his glacial blunders."[40] King's commitment to catastrophism also colored his ideas around evolution. He accepted the basics of natural selection and took pride in Marsh's work, but he rejected Darwin's claims of slow, tiny incremental changes in species in favor of dramatic, radical developments that mirrored those of the earth.[41]

Muir, besides publishing articles arguing for gradual geological change via glaciers, slapped back with tougher-than-thou rhetoric. After King wrote lengthily on his arduous conquest of Mount Tyndall, Muir sniffed that "when I climbed Tyndall I ran up and back before breakfast."[42] The descent into the upper canyon of the Tuolumne River defeated King, but not Muir, who wrote pointedly that the job was easily within the grasp of "mountaineers of ordinary nerve and skill."[43] This must have stung. "I care very little about my reputation as a geologist," King wrote privately, "but a good deal as being a fellow not easily scared."[44]

A courageous self-image did indeed seem vital to both, and they were in the right place and business to cultivate it. Mountaineering was emerging among genteel Europeans and Americans as manly recreation, which made the West, with its dozens of peaks above fourteen thousand feet, a great proving ground. Tiffs aside, King and Muir both laced their scientific writings with testimonials to their manhood, and for both geological knowledge seems often to be earned through risk and endurance. Scaling a mountainside for a better view of a glacier, Muir found himself at "a dead stop, with arms outspread, clinging close to the face of the rock. . . . My doom appeared fixed. I *must* fall." He escaped and at the top had his reward: "How truly glorious the landscape circles around this noble summit!" There followed a treatise on glaciation and the imagined scene when a "wrinkled ocean of ice" covered the land.[45] He and a companion ascended Mount Shasta and described its trachytic and basaltic lavas and a few tuffaceous and brecciated laval beds. They were also caught in a snowstorm and survived only by hunkering close to volcanic vents, risking poisonous gases and suffering "the pains of a Scandinavian hell, at once frozen and burned."[46] King called himself a "pioneer" in probing the Sierra under Josiah Whitney, and in his classic *Mountaineering in the Sierra Nevada* he described personal perils equal to Muir's. He survived his own Sierra snowstorm, huddling against hurricane winds and dodging falling trees and rockslides, and when stranded on a sheer face as Muir had been, he answered less with Muir's outright fear ("I *must* fall") than with bluff irony: "It was not pleasant to consider at what velocity a slip would send me to the bottom."[47]

Just as fundamental to their writing and that of others was a fusion of feeling and reason, emotion and deduction, scientific rigor and Victorian romanticism. The most professional accounts might shift in a few sentences to some visceral response to the wild and its uplift to the human soul.[48] Within two pages King wrote of Yosemite Valley's "misty brightness," "charm of pearl and emerald," "cold naked strength," "stern sublimity" and "geological terribleness." When "scientific labor" demanded time in the "savage element" of the highest reaches, returning to the gentler flanks unbound his soul, "leaving it free, joyous, grateful!" As others swooned, Dutton could laugh. In the Grand Canyon's "isolated freaks of carving" he found raw humor, "nature's art mingled with nonsense."[49] Whatever the response, aesthetic nerve endings seemed always aquiver, and descriptions were above all passionate, even erotic. Muir described an earthquake as the "fervid throbbings" of the earth, and when he asked two violets what the quake was all about, they answered, "It's all love." King enjoyed letters from Dutton in the field depicting rock formations in orgasm and "faults *in flagrante delicto*."[50]

The geology of Dutton, Muir, and King had to be *felt* to be understood, and while the West could be partially grasped through its long formative story, that story was only half alive without the emotional wash called up by King's "geological terribleness" behind the lifts, fractures, and compressions that transcended mortal realities. Out of this emotive loop—geology was romance and romance geology—images of the western country and experience took shape, and through them a kind of American aesthetic. The values were of the mother culture of the East and Europe—impassioned science and its debates, alpine mountaineering, the Romantic reach of Ruskin toward lofty truths of towering peaks—and to that degree the images were projections from eastern and European parlors.

Two elements set this imagined West apart, however. The first was an especially strong current of heroism and virility that, if not the sibling, was at least first cousin to the raw and unwashed machismo of bullwhackers and tracklayers. It was there at its simplest with Yale fossil hunters bored with the buzz of rattlesnakes but rose to Muir and King confronting the Sierra at its most formidable. "It was as if King were testing himself against those archaic cataclysms which had sundered the earth," Kevin Starr writes: "In Clarence King, mountaineer, the American in California made symbolic contact with the lost life of the continent itself."[51]

That "lost life" gets at the second element. Earth and life science were revolutionizing the public's view of time and its passage. "Geology . . . has had the effect to throw an air of novelty and mushroom speed over entire history," Ralph Waldo Emerson wrote in 1867: "The oldest empires,—what we called venerable antiquity,—now that we have true measures of duration, show like creations of yesterday."[52] Dinosaurs brought Emerson's point to life: 150 million years before, the place that now hosted millions of bison had been home to predators that walked on their hind legs and dispatched victims with skulls a yard long and dozens of serrated teeth, and fifty million years later reptiles longer than the locomotives that met at Promontory Summit swam in shallow seas fringed by ancient magnolias.

All this allowed the United States bragging rights. In an echo from seven decades earlier, when Thomas Jefferson sent a large stuffed moose to France as proof that his country's animals could hold their own with Europe's in their size, his descendant scientists brought from the nation's deep past monsters dwarfing anything found thus far in the Old World, ones whose ferocity symbolized the nation's emerging power. To play on this national pride, Andrew Carnegie, Marshall Field, and other philanthropist tycoons funded museums and displays of wonders from the ancient West (and, as with corporate command of other western resources, increasingly controlled and directed West's outflow of fossil remains).[53] The United States may have been short on the "oldest empires," but nowhere in Europe or anywhere else was the earth's true antiquity so stunningly revealed. If the first distinctive element was about the individual, or more specifically the heroic man, the other was how nature at work in the West dwarfed all human effort and presence.

That theme was most fully developed in Clarence Dutton's masterpiece, *The Tertiary History of the Grand Cañon District*. The title is both stuffy and ironic, since the district was missing virtually all evidence of the Tertiary period and much of the Mesozoic before it. Dutton's history was of how the Tertiary had come and gone, and once the reader was aware of the astonishing prelude to what was now seen, no sight on earth could be more telling of the power of time. Dutton described first the layering of rock under ancient seas and lakes, then its titanic uplift, sometimes eighteen thousand feet, then its slicing, fracturing, and abrasion, and finally its washing away—three hundred million years erased by temperature, wind, and the flow of sandy water. To the West's defining traits of mass and space, literary geologists like Dutton added time so beyond human scale that its merest residue was overwhelming. The leavings of the "great denudation," gigantic amphitheaters, abysmal gorges, and soaring spires and turrets, left visitors feeling "like mere insects crawling along the streets of a city."[54]

America Down the Rabbit Hole

The invention of the West included the creation of the world's first national park. On March 1, 1872, President Ulysses Grant signed into law the Yellowstone Act. It withdrew from development more than 2.2 million acres of public domain, land mostly in northwestern Wyoming but lapping over into Idaho and Montana. The land was to be "set apart as a public park or pleasuring-ground for the benefit and enjoyment of the people."[55] How and why it came about reveals plenty about the constellation of influences at work in the new country, about the West's paradoxical role in reconstructing the nation, and, like the work of ethnologists and anthropologists, about how both were helping make a distinctive racial order.

Yellowstone Park took its name from the river, today the longest undammed stream in the lower forty-eight states, that rises on a volcanic plateau in today's northwestern Wyoming. Lake Yellowstone, three hundred feet deep and shaped "like the print of a great, maimed hand," sits near the plateau's center.[56] The plateau was created by one of the earth's most active hydrothermal areas. Water seeping into this cauldron returns to the surface as vented steam, mud pots, about 150 geysers, and more than 5,000 hot springs. There are spectacular canyons, most notably the Yellowstone River's with its pair of waterfalls, one of them 100 yards high. Then and now, the area has teemed with wildlife drawn especially in winter to zones kept clear of snow by Yellowstone's natural furnaces.[57]

Mountain men had worked the area and others had wandered through after them, but after the Civil War general knowledge of the place remained fuzzy. When three respected Montanans brought back one of the first detailed descriptions in 1869, dubious editors of *Scribner's* magazine and the *New York Tribune* declined their story, fearing for their credibility.[58] The next year a larger party with Henry Washburn, Montana's territorial surveyor, and Nathaniel Langford, former territorial revenue collector, as well as lawyers, merchants, a bank president, and the son of a U.S. senator, toured Yellowstone with a military escort led by Lt. Gustavus Doane. Their account was above doubt and established for good Yellowstone's credentials for flabbergast. In the summer of 1871 Ferdinand Hayden surveyed the area and returned with scientific reports, gushing commentary, photographs by William Henry Jackson, and sketches by Thomas Moran. In mid-December bills were introduced in both the Senate and House to create a park, forty by fifty miles, off limits to homestead, preemption, sale, or congressional grants and protected from commercial hunting. By the end of February the Senate version had passed both houses and been sent to the White House. When Hayden arrived for his second season of surveying, Yellowstone National Park was a reality—at least on paper.

These bare facts might imply that Congress made a forthright decision to set aside a place of unique beauty, scientific value, and natural wonder. But not so. Yellowstone Park was born and shaped by varied visions often in tension with one another. They raised basic questions about the West—whom it was to serve, who was in charge, and how it expressed an American identity.

The park's most immediate inspiration was yet another partnership between the federal government and private capital, expressed once again through railroads. The route of Jay Cooke's Northern Pacific Railroad was plotted across southern Montana barely fifty miles north of the park-to-be. Cooke needed badly to sell bonds, and he hired Nathaniel Langford to drum up business by publicizing Montana. Langford apparently thought that exposing Yellowstone's mysteries might pique popular interest. Thus the tour led by him and Washburn. Cooke then booked Langford into eastern lecture halls to fan an interest in future visits to this western marvel—via, of course, the Northern Pacific. After attending a lecture Ferdinand Hayden quickly shifted his survey of the summer of 1871 to the area. On his return he found a letter waiting from Cooke's office manager, A. B. Nettleton:

> Dear Doctor:
> Judge Kelley [William Darrah Kelley, a Pennsylvania congressman, longtime railroad advocate and Cooke's close ally] has made a suggestion which strikes me as being an excellent one, viz.: Let Congress pass a bill reserving the Great Geyser Basin as a public park forever—just as it has reserved that far inferior wonder the Yosemite valley and big trees. If you approve this would such a recommendation be appropriate in your official report?

Hayden, ever the booster, complied. His article in *Scribner's Monthly* ended in an almost word-for-word mimic of Nettleton: "Why will not Congress at once pass a law setting it apart as a great public park for all time to come, as has been done with that not more remarkable wonder, Yosemite Valley?"[59] To illustrate his points Hayden laid out in the Capitol Rotunda photographs and sketches from Jackson and Moran, and Langford supplied his own articles predicting that easterners would soon be only three days away from the mud pots, geysers, and waterfalls.[60] A soaring report from Lieutenant Doane was handed to legislators a few days before their vote.[61]

Created as a corporate promotion, Yellowstone was also linked to the promise of the land around it. On their approach to the park, the *Helena Herald* assured visitors, they would see an area "as large as one of the larger New England states . . . one of the continent's finest farming regions just waiting for the railroad to bring a full scale boom."[62] Montana guidebooks called the park the aesthetic clincher to the territory's "wonderful treasure houses" and "fertile and verdure-clad valleys."[63] Washington did its promotional part. Capt. William Ludlow's lengthy geological, zoological, and paleontological inventories and awestruck descriptions went on to predict that the land just outside the park was sure to bloom into a major stock-raising and irrigated farming region.[64] The government published a gilt-edged edition of Gen. William E. Strong's trip journal with its paeans to the falls and canyons and the view from Mount Washburn ("No pen can write it—no words describe it").[65]

Nevertheless, the park languished for a decade. The problem was the one facing nearly every aspect of creating the West—connections. The panic and depression of 1873 stalled the Northern Pacific well to the east in the Dakotas, which left all trips to the park expensive and physically grueling. A survivor of the final four-hundred-mile approach by stage wrote of being coated by clouds of stinging alkaline dust and of staying at an inn called Hotel de Starvation.[66] Then the Utah and Northern Railroad connected the Union Pacific to the western side of the park in the late 1870s and in 1883the Northern Pacific completed its continental link and built the Park Branch Line from Livingston, Montana, to the park's northern boundary. Now a ninety-dollar ticket would take a passenger round trip from Saint Paul, Minnesota, to the glories of geyserland, all in a Pullman Palace Car. The Northern Pacific picked up the promotional pace.[67]

One historian has called 1883 Yellowstone's "first vintage year," with well-publicized excursions by President Chester Arthur and a collection of European investors and journalists. Bozeman and towns along the rail lines enjoyed a burst of business, and just outside the park, Gardiner, with about two hundred residents, had twenty-one saloons and four brothels.[68] The park was entering a new phase that required answers to questions avoided thus far. If Yellowstone, in the words of its organic act, was to be a "pleasuring-ground for the benefit and enjoyment of the people," then who were "the people" and what was their pleasure?

"The people" initially were distant sojourners. There had been grand plans along the way—a national observatory, zoos, racetracks, a swimming school, and a hydropathy institute—but until the Northern Pacific rails approached, there were only a few crude accommodations, all squatters without leases.[69] In 1882 Washington granted a lease to the Yellowstone National Park Improvement Company, whose large red-roofed lodge at Mammoth Hot Springs had a Steinway, two billiard tables, electric lights, good champagne, and a French chef. Four years later Congress switched the lease to the Yellowstone Park Association, controlled by the Northern Pacific.[70] Visitors stayed in its hotels and experienced Yellowstone by its orchestrated stage tours. Besides the rail ticket there were supplies, wagons, and guides to be secured, mostly offered as Northern Pacific excursion packages. With a minimal outlay of $200–$250 per person (equivalent in 2019 to $5,700–$7,200 each), and with three weeks or so needed for a visit, the nation's "public park" was mostly for those in or near the economic ozone.[71]

Others among "the people," Montana locals, had far cheaper access, but they seemed most interested in carousing in what seemed a strange part of the neighborhood. Captain Ludlow reported ragged collections of grogshops, liveries, and bathhouses, and William Sherman's son found the "glaciers covered with chicken bones and eggshells."[72] Visitors hacked off and hauled away large chunks from formations around hot springs and geysers, and one early party tried to silence Old Faithful by stuffing its mouth with more than a thousand pounds of rocks, trees, and stumps. (At its next spouting the geyser blew the plug eighty feet into the air.)[73] The problem was serious enough by 1877 that the American Association for the Advancement of Science warned of "irreparable injury to natural accumulations of the highest value in scientific investigation" unless someone put a collar on local visitors.[74] Hunting the park's prolific game posed at least as great a problem. Locals killed game virtually at will for personal use and for sale. Captain Ludlow claimed in 1875 that between 1,500 and 2,000 elk had been shot during the previous winter for meat and hides that sold from $2.50 to $3.00 each. "In the name of humanity let this kind of hunting be stopped," General Strong pleaded, after his own party shot a grizzly, bagged dozens of dusky grouse, and landed hundreds of trout.[75]

Nobody, however, had authority to stop much of anything. Yellowstone had a staff of one, a superintendent. Its first, Nathaniel Langford, served five years without pay, and he gave the government its money's worth, spending his last two years in Minnesota as a bank examiner.[76] When Congress finally appropriated ten thousand dollars in 1878 to bring some measure of control, the wardens hired were dismissed by a critic as "a herd of irresponsible imbeciles."[77] Congress finally turned the job over to the army. In August 1886 fifty cavalrymen arrived under Captain Moses Harris, appointed superintendent of the park. Yellowstone remained under military rule for thirty-two years. Only in 1894, twenty-two years after the park was created, did legislation outlaw hunting and capturing animals and damaging "natural curiosities, or wonderful objects."[78] Vandalism declined, but poaching was tougher to control.[79] There was a vigorous trophy market for bison heads and later for the incisors, or "tusks," of bull elks, sold as cufflinks, watch fobs, rings, and hatpins to eastern members of the Benevolent and Protective Order of Elk.[80]

Yet another category of "the people," Indians, would have found the notion of Yellowstone as a wildlife preserve especially bizarre.[81] They had used the territory of the park well for millennia. White "explorers" had followed Indian trails and, as had Powell in the Grand Canyon, found plenty that told of a Native presence. Yellowstone had been a major production site for obsidian that for centuries had been traded across much of the continent.[82] Only a small number of Tukudika ("Sheepeater") Shoshones lived there year-round, but as large numbers of animals congregated there in response to intense hunting in surrounding areas, it had become a kind of reservoir of game that Bannocks, Crows, Lakotas, and Blackfeet hunted in summer and fall. In all, at least a few thousand Indians in the region relied on Yellowstone for subsistence and trade.[83]

Like white hunters, Indians found the formal uses of the park much at odds with their enjoyment and pleasure. The most dramatic collision came in the summer of 1877, when several hundred Nez Perces with about two thousand horses fled through the park trying to reach the plains and eventually Canada. At one point they nearly stumbled on a vacationing Gen. William T. Sherman, the nation's highest-ranking military officer. They killed two tourists, wounded others, and captured and released several more before continuing their flight.[84] The park superintendent used the widely publicized episode to orchestrate a "cleansing" of Indians from Yellowstone.[85] Bannocks, Crows, and others came nonetheless, but they kept far from tourists, who stayed in their own tight groove of standard stops.

Now Indians could be read entirely out of Yellowstone's past.[86] The preposterous story in periodicals and guidebooks was that tribes believed the basin's "rumbling and hissing sulphur fumes" were the "wails and groans" of departed warriors in agony for their earthly sins. The only residents, the "pygmy tribe" of Sheepeaters, "timid and harmless," were just the sort to give way to civilization without a ripple.[87] The park's official history now began with a geological summary and accounts of the gradual revelation of this "mountain-girt land of wonders," starting with mountain men and moving through the explorations by the military and intrepid scientists.[88] As in Powell's account twenty years earlier of the Grand Canyon, that other sublime place apart, the invented Yellowstone was essentially unhistoried, a timeless landscape with only the briefest, thinnest human presence and somehow exempt from the forces of change and development.

That invention would play an especially needful role in a changing America. As a national unifier, the postwar West provided images and experiences that rose beyond sectional differences. These included islands of country that were set radically apart from the land around them—places of such unusual scope, form, and natural beauty that they invited veneration. These places were distinctive within the nation, and they were distinctively ours. They became sacred spaces of the new America.

California again had led the way. On June 30, 1864, as Union forces in Virginia were locked in the siege of Petersburg, President Lincoln granted to the state of California the valley of Yosemite to be set aside forever for public use and enjoyment. First seen by non-Indians only thirteen years earlier, Yosemite's extraordinary sights were quickly recognized. The Merced River flowed through a sinuous valley bound by sheer and soaring walls. Scale alone set it apart. Yosemite Falls was more than fourteen times taller than Niagara Falls.[89] Yosemite contained the perfect makings for an ecstatic romanticism. Samuel Bowles's first view was a "confrontal of God face to face. . . . All that was mortal shrank back, all that was immortal swept to the front and bent down in awe." Albert Richardson called Yosemite a "stupendous roofless cathedral" inspiring "a profound sense of Divine power."[90] When Frederick Law Olmsted, later the designer of Manhattan's Central Park, was tapped to make of Yosemite a public space, he wrote that this "greatest glory of nature" would be a natural antidote to the baneful stresses of modern life now producing a people overly excited, melancholic, cranky, and morally hobbled.[91]

An American Eden had no place for residents, however. Indians would have to go. Of at least several hundred Ahwahnechees who had lived there when whites first invaded the valley in 1851, only a small remnant remained.[92] Writers from John Muir to Thomas Starr King and even the prominent "friend of the Indian" Helen Hunt Jackson looked on them with disdain and called for their removal. Jackson was repulsed by a woman, "dirty beyond words" and with "soulless eyes," she saw near her hotel. Echoing the views of ethnologists, she and Olmsted thought that, among their many shortcomings, Yosemite's Indians were not advanced enough to appreciate their home's transcendent beauty.[93] The few allowed to remain worked as wood-choppers and guides and, later, posing for photographs with tourists.[94] With removal of its Native peoples, Yosemite could be well seated in the popular mind as an incomparable natural wonder, a people's park, and a national boast.

So it was natural for A. B. Nettleton, Jay Cooke's agent, to reference Yosemite ("that far inferior wonder") when he prompted Hayden to call for making Yellowstone a national park. Together the two would be the fullest expressions of a common theme of the invented West—a region at once bound in purpose to a remade America and offering the chance to break away into other spheres. Early guides often called Yellowstone "Wonderland," taken from Lewis Carroll's *Alice's Adventures in Wonderland*, first published in the United States in 1866. The term fit well a place where travelers could pass in a moment from ordinary life to a land that was awesome in scale and terrible in behavior and where beauty was both transporting and unnerving.[95] Well-to-do infatuates were struck silent—and said so in the lushest prose. The Earl of Dunraven was "possessed with the feeling of utter littleness" and "sublime terror" as he gazed on the lower falls. All human concerns became only "the slight creaking of machinery" within an "all-pervading Something, . . . a great awful Oneness."[96]

That awful Something was put to national purpose. In a final meaning of "a pleasuring-ground . . . for the people," Hayden predicted that intelligent Americans would point to Yellowstone in "the conscious pride that it has not its parallel on the face of the globe." Americans might lack Europe's historical depth, but, like the dwarfing geology of Dutton's and Powell's Southwest, the geysers, peaks, and falls were America's answer to the Old World's buttresses and spires, "only loftier and sublimer," a visitor wrote.[97] Another champion was more specific:

> The towering Alps, the castled Rhine,
>   Cathedrals, all as one,
> Speak not in language so sublime
>   As our own Yellowstone.[98]

The park was Wonderland in another, unintended sense. Besides an entertainment for his young friend, Lewis Carroll's story was a caricature of England and its oddities. And so Yellowstone caught some of the illogic of an emerging West. Three of the nation's most powerful forces—the federal government, railroads, and territorial boosters—joined to integrate into the nation what had been one of the continent's most isolated areas. They proclaimed it a fair land ready for capture and cultivation. Then they set aside, in the middle of it, a place they sold as an otherworldly escape, immune to the very changes they were aggressively promoting. Now pilgrims could walk away from "little, old, antiquated Europe," the park's superintendent Philetus Norris told the Scientific Association, and travel a new "national highway" past fertile valleys and productive mines before passing through a "fairy glen" into "nature's crowning temple . . . Wonder Land." All should thank God, "who created it for His own wise purpose [and] preserves it for our enjoyment and benefit."[99]

Things did indeed seem curiouser and curiouser. Yellowstone Park and Yellowstone Valley—geysers and farms, Wonderland and Arcadia—were two parts of a fused image. Something similar could be said of the new country as a whole, with its twinned promises for a reunited America. Heading West, one should always be ready both to build a better life and to tumble down a rabbit hole.

As the West was being bound together and mapped into a region and an imagined realm, the "new" country was also being re-peopled. Its population increased fivefold between 1860 and 1880. Re-peopling involved de-peopling. Native populations were dropping, both from outright assaults and even more from the environmental and social disorder brought on by the in-flooding of others from the East and around the world.

In raw numbers, of course, the West lagged far behind the older republic. In size it comprised about half the nation in 1880, but only about 1 in 13 Americans lived there. That, however, was up from about 1 in 40 in 1860, and the difference measured the nation's steepening westward tilt. The Census Bureau followed the drift of its people by siting on a map the mean center of them all—that moving point where there are as many persons on one side as on the other. The movement had always been toward the Pacific, but between 1850 and 1880 the mean center moved farther than it ever had or ever would again in a comparable period, 213 miles, from Wirt County, West Virginia, to just beyond Cincinnati.

Just because the nation was leaning toward the West, however, did not mean that the western population looked like that in the East. In fact it could be startlingly different, and yet, as in so much else, those very differences could anticipate the course of the new America over the decades ahead.

14 ▷ The World's Convention

Looking back on how the West was being probed, categorized, imagined and reimagined, secured by rails and woven by wires; and then thinking ahead on how its plains, deserts, and mountains would be plowed and cropped, mined and pastured; and through all of it following how its Native peoples were seeing their lands taken, their numbers diminished, their cultures assaulted, and their identities publicly redefined and pegged low into the world's "civilized" order, it is important also to ask: Who was there? More particularly, as the number of non-Indians in the emerging West grew from about 179,000 to more than 3,384,000, how did they fall out? What pasts did they bring with them? When they came together, how did they cluster and gel, or not, into societies and communities forming a new human fabric over the left half of the national map?

The answers reveal a human makeup that was in some ways jarringly apart from that of the nation to the East—differences that gave their own cultural flavoring and generated distinctive tensions. And in yet another paradox, these very differences in some ways reflected the nation's tidal changes and its course toward a modern America.

One thing would likely have struck visiting outsiders immediately about the people they met in western towns and farmlands: they were from all over the place.

America Speaks in Tongues

Of all Greenlanders reported in the 1870 census, fully two-thirds were in the West. One was in California, another in Kansas, the third in Pennsylvania.[1] It was a national profile writ small (see map 6). In 1848 the nation's new country was already among the most ethnically and culturally mixed places of its size in the hemisphere, with about a hundred thousand Hispanos and dozens of distinct Native peoples brought into the national embrace. Events following the great coincidence would make for an even richer stew of cultures.

This struck an ironic note. Among its several common impressions, the West was celebrated as a refuge for old-stock Americans from a rising tide of immigrants arriving in Atlantic ports in the decades after the Civil War.[2] The

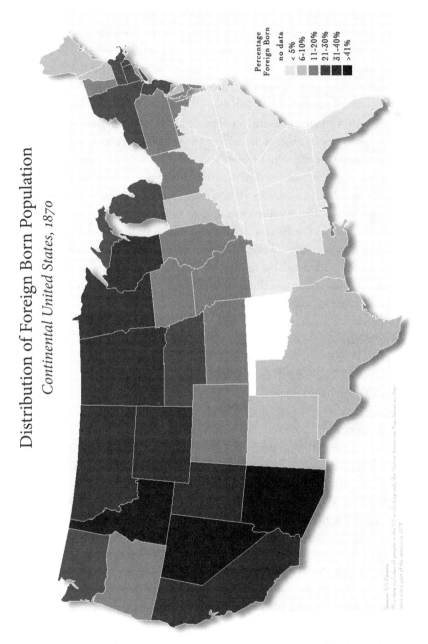

Distribution of Foreign Born Population
Continental United States, 1870

Percentage Foreign Born

no data
< 5%
6-10%
11-20%
21-30%
31-40%
>41%

MAP 6. Distribution of foreign-born population, 1870. In the years after the Civil War, the West, measured by its portion of those born elsewhere, was by far the most ethnically mixed and polyglot part of the expanded nation. Map by Maggie Rose Bridges.

anxiety could be open and rhetorically violent. Frederic Remington, among the most successful artists and illustrators of the late century, lashed out: "Jews, Injuns, Chinamen, Italians, Huns—the rubbish of the Earth I hate. I've got some Winchesters and when the massacring begins, I can get my share of 'em, and what's more, I will." These, "the rinsins, the scourins, and the Devil's lavings" of humanity, were corrupting the true American stock, and as Remington set his eye on the East, the corruption seemed unstoppable.[3] The West, however, "Injuns [and] Chinamen" aside, could provide a national cleansing. Ambitious and energetic descendants of those from the British Isles and northern Europe would naturally gravitate to the new country. There the challenges, opportunities, and even the bracing climate would bring out the best of their inborn qualities, and Indians, Mexicans, and other lesser peoples would somehow fade away before the superior newcomers.[4] William Jackson Palmer, kingpin of both the Kansas Pacific and Denver and Rio Grande Railroads, envisioned the East Coast as a filter to hold the "foreign swarms" away from "the inner temple of Americanism." He founded Colorado Springs as a hopeful model for an ethnically and culturally cleansed future. He wrote his wife: "Isn't that a logical as well as unique notion?"[5]

It was certainly not unique; many thought as Palmer did. As for logic, he got it exactly backward. Of all states on the Atlantic coast in 1870, New York had the highest portion of foreign-born persons—26 percent. If ranked among the fifteen western states and territories, New York would have come in ninth, behind Arizona (60 percent), Idaho (53 percent), Nevada (44 percent), Wyoming (39 percent), Montana (39 percent), California (37 percent), Utah (35 percent), and Dakota (34 percent), and it would have been barely ahead of Nebraska (25 percent) and Washington (21 percent).[6] [See map 6] Zooming in to smaller units only stresses the point. The percentage of immigrants in five Idaho mining towns (68.1 percent) was nearly twice that of Boston and Brooklyn (35.1 percent and 36.5 percent). Of fifty cities listed separately in the census, only one, San Francisco, was in the West. Nearly half of its people had been born outside the United States (49.3 percent), which placed it first in the tally of immigrants, slightly ahead of Chicago (48.3 percent) and far ahead of nearly all others. The city on the bay had 10,428 more foreigners than females.[7] The pattern persisted. Of the nine states or territories in 1880 with the highest portion of those born outside the nation, eight were in the West.[8] If Palmer hoped to avoid the "foreign swarms," he should have headed back to New York or Massachusetts.

A confluence of forces created this cosmopolitan West. It began with California gold. A woman described the soundscape in such a "perambulating picture gallery": "You will hear in the same day, almost at the same time, the lofty melody of the Spanish language, the piquant polish of the French, . . . the silver, changing clearness of the Italian, the harsh gangle of the German, the hissing precision of the English, the liquid sweetness of the Kanaka [Hawaiian], and the sleep-inspiring languor of the East Indian. To complete the catalogue, there is the *native* Indian, with his guttural vocabulary of twenty words!"[9] The pattern continued with later rushes. Of the six states or territories with the highest portion of foreign-born in 1870, five (California, Nevada, Idaho, Montana, and Arizona) had major mining centers. The most polyglot assemblages in American history, they were "emphatically the world's convention," a journalist wrote, convened as tens of thousands chased "the wild delusion of glittering sands full of golden eggs."[10]

So many people from so many places could travel from so far away because of the other force, the movement revolution, that with gold and its mesmerism was binding the new country quickly together. The perceptual experience of westering took a sudden turn. Prewar travelers on the trails, fascinated, frightened, and often dumbstruck by what they saw, filled their diaries and letters with descriptions of the vistas, weather, plants, creatures, and peoples they encountered. Now, in three days of dozing passage by train, a New Orleans lawyer crossing to San Francisco spent seven words on the Great Plains: "Passing a poor, sandy and stoney country." By the 1870s the midcontinent was on its way to becoming what many would later call it in the age of air travel: the American flyover.

Railroads did more than provide the means of travel. Although they found ways around selling outright the tens of millions of acres given them by Congress, they still needed to create a market for their services, and for millions of persons abroad cheap land was the ultimate lure. "HOMES FOR ALL!" the Burlington Northern promised Swedes in one poster: "MORE FARMS THAN FARMERS! MORE LANDLORDS THAN TENANTS!"[11] The Northern Pacific's modest prices in 1871–72 ranged from $2.50 to $8.00 per acre, depending on how close property was to the railroad, and a buyer need put down only 10 percent with the rest mortgaged for seven years at 7 percent. Other lines offered similar deals, some with credit for a decade or more.[12] Promoters learned cultural subtleties. A German pamphlet described a prospective site as *Ein Gut*, implying a manor, where a middling farmer might instantly become a lordly proprietor (*Gutsherr*).[13] Agents struck deals with companies like the Cunard Steamship Line, guaranteeing to fill passenger berths in exchange for inexpensive fares. Once in America immigrants bought discounted rail tickets, and when they paused at jumping-off places like Duluth, Minnesota, to ponder where to settle, they could live free in well-fitted company quarters, buy groceries at cost, and send their sick to company hospitals.[14]

By the late 1870s railroads were competing sharply for immigrant families.[15] The Burlington sponsored an English tour of a "Sylphorama," eighty-five giant paintings, each on more than 250 square feet of canvas. The Northern Pacific in 1883 employed more than 800 agents in Great Britain and 124 in Scandinavia, Germany, and Switzerland. A Burlington agent planned to board every departing ship, visit every emigrant hotel, and distribute maps and pamphlets in every public building and railway station. The Northern Pacific alone placed ads in nearly 4,000 newspapers, and for 10 years the Union Pacific published its own, *The Pioneer*, in English, German, and several Scandinavian languages. The cost was substantial—in 1871 the Burlington laid out $500,000 and the Union Pacific $300,000—but so was the response. In a single year the Northern Pacific received more than 60,000 letters of inquiry and mailed back 2.5 million pieces of promotional literature.[16]

The federal government, having partnered with corporations in construction of western railroads, indirectly encouraged the foreign immigrants who would use them. To Europeans, photographer William Henry Jackson recalled, the Homestead Act "was sheer miracle." An agent in Germany wrote that "it was with difficulty that I could get [audiences] to believe that they could get 160 acres of land FREE in Nebraska."[17] Once the point was made the draw was terrific. Washington brought in more immigrants through the military. Nearly half of all recruits in the West had been born abroad, mostly in Ireland, Germany, and England, with a scattering from other nations. The last Little Big Horn survivor to see George Custer alive, his bugler, Sgt. John Martin (Giovanni Martini), had fought for Garibaldi in Italy. Capt. Miles Keogh, an Irishman who died with Custer, had fought for the Pope on the other side. Foreign enlistees saw in the army temporary security in an uncertain new life. "It was either the soup house, starve, or the recruiting depot," recalled a Dane who landed in New York during the depression of 1873.[18] Because recruits knew they would almost certainly be posted somewhere beyond the Mississippi, many used the army as a free ticket to the new country, where they soon deserted to find work in labor-starved markets. The military thus was an inadvertent immigration agent pumping foreign-born into the developing West.

State and territorial governments did their own recruitment, urging Europeans to follow "our first Great Emigrant, Columbus," to the West's fertile lands. Those on the plains were the most active.[19] Farmers across the Atlantic learned that Nebraska, where native grasses were "rank and thick as a jungle" and where newly planted trees grew ten feet a year, was essentially disease-free: "Sickness is rather an accident of life than an expected incident of living." The plains, at the center of the rising nation that itself was centered between

Europe and Asia, were destined for global leadership. Kansas alone would soon support thirty-three million persons (nearly twelve times its population in 2010).[20] So best to hurry. This stretch of the West was "about to be wisely chosen by the Nations of Mankind as the last grand gathering place for the Tribes of Humanity."[21]

But not all tribes were equally welcomed. Railroads and governments recruited mostly from England, northern Europe, and Scandinavia, reaching also into Russia for ethnic Germans.[22] In 1876 immigrants buying Burlington land included 545 from Germany, Russia, England, Sweden, and Holland but only nine French, four Hungarians, and a lone Italian.[23] The claim was that the preferred farmers were especially progressive, but there were hints of other motives. An early Dakota booster wrote confidently that the man who would dominate its future would "have Norse, Celtic and Saxon blood in his veins." Railroads ignored experienced farmers much closer at hand, southeastern freedpeople, some of whom were making their own heroic efforts to find farms on the plains.[24] The selective efforts helped give the plains West its distinct human profile. Of all foreign-born in Nebraska in 1870 and 1880, nearly six in ten were Germans, English, Swedes, or Danes. In Nevada, by contrast, it was about one in four.

Religion helped diversify the West. The Mormon church recruited in England and Europe as vigorously as any railroad or territory, and secular boosters courted German Russians by promising relief from religious pressures from the czarist regimes. Jews fleeing persecutions in eastern Europe and Russia came first to eastern communities before opting for western opportunities. In a random sampling of thirty entries in a collective biography of prominent California Jews, every one had been born abroad.[25] Many of them, often related to one another, rose into positions of mercantile and financial prominence, and their descendants into political leadership. Abraham Ruef, son of Jewish immigrants from France, dominated San Francisco turn-of-the-century politics. Bernard Seligman and Michael Goldwasser left Germany and Poland and became wealthy merchants in New Mexico and Arizona. Seligman's son Arthur became mayor of Santa Fe and governor of New Mexico. Barry Goldwater, Michael's grandson, served as Arizona's U.S. senator and ran for president in 1964.

Western immigration, whatever the source, worked by a dynamic common across the country—the siphon principle. Ethnic newcomers called out for relatives and acquaintances to follow, and once a critical mass was in place, flow followed flow. The result was a puddling-up of distinctive ethnic communities. Tin miners in Cornwall were recruited to work in gold and silver mines of California, Nevada, and Idaho, and once there they pestered employers to offer work to relatives back home. This earned them their nickname of "Cousin

Jacks" (as in: "You really should hire my cousin Jack.")[26] In Montana, Butte's staggeringly rich gold and copper mines, largely controlled by Irish-born Marcus Daly, had a welcoming reputation for his countrymen. Its percentage of Irish in 1880 approached Boston's.[27] That year California accounted for nearly 60 percent of the nation's Portuguese; kin back in the Azores had come to join relatives at work at fishing, whale hunting, sheepherding, and farming along the coast.[28] Siphon immigration created many such ethnic pockets—Basque sheepherders in the Great Basin, Italian coal miners later in Colorado, German and Czech farmers clustering in certain counties of the Great Plains.[29]

Whatever the origin or the motive or the process, the global gathering gave the emerging West a character distinctive even within the diversifying nation. The stories left by the Basques, Germans, Portuguese, Danes, French, Italians, Albanians, and more are a seldom-heard part of the American experience. Jens Storm Schmidt, a Danish son of a miller, was riding across southern New Mexico as a forty-niner when he met Mexican soldiers fresh from an Indian raid. He wrote home of stolen babies hung in baskets from saddle horns, black scalps on the points of lances, and long strings of ears draped over a cannon.[30] At twenty, Carl Hendricks of Sweden threw in with three buffalo hunters out of Dodge City in 1872. Within weeks, he boasted, he could skin a carcass in eight minutes. He gave it up after a season, well paid but malodorous in clothes he had not taken off in a year. His first purchase back in Dodge City was a bar of soap.[31] The new country always had its traumas, but the voices, like those of the earliest overlanders to Oregon farms and California goldfields, were mostly of hope that bled easily into cockiness. Heading West later in the century, a Finn poetized:

> Although as hoboes on a boxcar roof
> We sing our many songs,
> One day in a Pullman we shall ride,
> Drawing great puffs of smoke.[32]

Like him, most immigrants came to the West from across the Atlantic, through the fabled golden door. Some, however, entered from the Pacific, through the Golden Gate. Among them was group with a story distinctive enough to deserve a separate look.

Jinshan

Expansion and gold quickly invigorated traffic around the Pacific along routes plotted during the thirty years before Marshall's discovery. One result was first substantial Chinese immigration to the United States. The customs house in

San Francisco recorded 14 arriving Chinese before 1849. In 1852 authorities estimated 25,000 were living in California. Ten years later it was double that. Hong Kong quickly emerged as the dominant departure point. At least 86 ships with more than 17,000 passengers left there for San Francisco in 1852.[33]

They were a small part of a far larger diaspora during the mid-nineteenth century. Most went to Southeast Asia and others to spots around the globe, including Africa. The Chinese population in Java alone in 1860 was four times that in the United States. Traditionally the outflow has been explained through "push" factors—a population explosion, rising unemployment, social upheavals that included the devastating Taiping Rebellion (1850–64), and various natural disasters. Most Chinese who flocked to Jinshan (Cantonese for "Gold Mountain"), however, were not dirt-poor Asian rubes but outward-looking, upwardly mobile sojourners from the relatively prosperous Cantonese province of Guangdong.[34] Their motives seem little different from others'. A Cantonese song composed in San Francisco's Chinatown caught the spirit of the Finnish hobo atop his boxcar:

> At the moment, I hardly have enough grub to eat.
> But I won't take it as my fate, my final destiny.
> I don't believe I will live like this till my hair turns white;
> It's only the low ebb in my life.
> When luck strikes,
> With the whole world behind me,
> I will be rich in a few years' turn.
> And then, I will buy property and build a Western mansion.[35]

During the first years of modest immigration the response in California was a generally positive curiosity. Timothy Osborn's intelligent and polite neighbors along the Merced River wrote out for him Chinese characters for "gold," "brandy," "church," "cigar," "rice," "Stockton," and "if you please." Other miners praised them. "Of their morrals, they are very exemplary," one wrote his wife. The Chinese in Weaverville were "among our best customers," wrote a storekeeper, "and certainly the best foreigners we have."[36] In 1852 California's governor John McDougall recommended using land grants to lure more Chinese, among "the most worthy of our newly adopted citizens."[37]

Then Chinese did show up in far greater numbers, and attitudes in some quarters shifted sharply. The year McDougall made his proposal the number of arrivals was seven times that of the year before, with twenty thousand more coming by 1855. The timing could not have been worse. Just as the diggings had been mostly cleansed of Californios, Indians, Chileans, Sonorans, and other foreign forty-eighters, this new group of non-whites came flooding in, and just as they did, gold output dropped dramatically. New finds became increasingly rare, and competition for what was left sharpened considerably.[38]

Chinese were the most anomalous immigrants in the American experience until that time. They differed substantially in everything from language and religion to dress, appearance, and foodways. They usually lived apart from others and showed virtually no inclination to bring in families. Apart from a small merchant community in San Francisco, they had no established population to speak for them. With Native peoples, Chinese were the ultimate "others." That appealed to Christian evangelists, who predicted that California converts would carry back the Word "ten thousand times faster than all the missionarys of Christendom could do."[39] A far commoner response was a rising hostility that burned hottest among independent white miners to whom the sight of Chinese squeezing out a living on supposedly exhausted sites seemed both a threat and a rebuke.[40] In April of 1852, four months after his predecessor had encouraged Chinese immigration, Gov. John Bigler raised the specter of a massive invasion of Chinese "coolies" contracted to work for three or four dollars a month while sending every ounce of gold they gathered back to bosses in the old country. That term, "coolie," applied before this to Chinese workers in the Caribbean, would be marvelously malleable. Here and for decades ahead it would be used to paint all Chinese laborers, whatever their situation, as robotic enemies of free white workingmen and their families. Bigler urged federal intervention and heavy state taxes to check the tide before it bled California of its wealth.[41] The response was immediate—and divided. Prominent Chinese and white merchants stressed the vigorous commerce in "China goods" and praised the immigrants for their hard work. But in the diggings around the Yuba and American Rivers miners took up Bigler's lead, expelled Chinese, and destroyed their camps and tools.[42]

This economic division would persist. Where merchants and employers saw ambitious risk-takers freely working for the main chance, white miners and other workers saw docile coolies bullied by grasping capitalists into "a strange system of slavery, obnoxious to our institutions."[43] Such free labor fears after the Civil War shifted away from enslaved Blacks to this alternate threat. Go into the California hills, a legislator warned his colleagues, and you will see the "China serf working side by side with the American freeman" whose father had fought with Washington to found the republic now threatened by the Asiatic tide.[44]

Out of the debate came an 1852 law levying a tax on all foreign miners, though the Chinese were clearly its focus. Tax collectors, who would get one dollar in ten, had authority to seize and auction off with an hour's notice the property of anyone not complying. The law revived one in 1850 directed at foreign-born forty-eighters, but while that tax had been a prohibitive twenty dollars a month, the new one was only three. It was meant to milk the Chinese, not drive them out. With rising anti-Chinese feeling in the legislature—a report called them "a disgusting scab upon the fair face of society"—the tax was raised by a dollar, then two dollars more, with annual boosts to come.[45] As immigration slumped and a few thousand fled the state, merchants and local governments felt the pinch and pushed back. A balance was struck in 1856 that set the monthly levy at four dollars, a hefty but manageable load that presumably dampened enthusiasm while maximizing public revenues. By 1870, when the law was declared unconstitutional, Chinese miners had paid nearly $5 million, roughly equal to half the state's income from all sources.[46] Another law in 1852 taxed arrivals from Asia to help fund California hospitals, though Chinese were allowed only in San Francisco's pesthouse and lunatic asylum.[47]

A more direct threat was the state supreme court's ruling that Chinese could not testify in court. An 1850 law had forbid any "black or mulatto person, or Indian" from taking the stand. Because Indians had apparently migrated from Asia, Chief Justice Hugh Murray argued, and because Columbus had called them Indians on the assumption that he was in Asia, a Cantonese was as much an Indian as a Navajo, Sioux, Yahi, or Pomo. Using "black" instead of "Negro" also meant that legislators intended to ban all non-white persons. After declaring Chinese both Indian and Black, Murray got to the nub of his reasoning. Grant them the right to testify, he wrote, and the door would open to their voting, sitting on juries, becoming legislators and (what must have been truly frightening) judges. Allowing such a thing for these people—mendacious, racially inferior, incapable of intellectual growth or cultural progress, naturally separated by an "impassable difference" from whites—would result in "actual and present danger" to society.[48]

The true danger, however, was to the Chinese denied the shelter of courts. An editor in Nevada City found them "at the mercy of every thief and cut-throat" and "prey to every vagabond who prefers a life of plunder to one of honest toil," and in nearby Shasta County a public notice gave them ten days to leave or be run out after suffering the biblical thirty-nine lashes.[49] Agents, unworried about any legal challenge, collected multiple times in a month and overcharged at that. "I took all the dust the rascal had," one wrote in his notebook.[50] The journal of a young collector in Yuba County, Charles DeLong, suggests how it went. He collected up to eighty taxes a day, some obviously shakedowns: "had a China fight knocked down some and drawed our tools [pistols] on the rest and they put out." On October 23, 1855, referring to their traditional long braided hair, or queues, he wrote: "Chinamen tails cut off." And on another occasion: "shot a Chinaman had a hell of a time."[51] DeLong later was elected to both houses of the state legislature, ran for the U.S. Senate, and from 1869 to 1874 was the nation's minister to Japan.[52]

The great majority of Chinese remained in California, but with mining rushes elsewhere and the need for labor to build railroads, some filtered into the western interior. Most landed in Idaho, Oregon, and Nevada where, as in California, they mainly worked placer claims that whites no longer found interesting. Of the 6,579 miners in Idaho in 1870, nearly six in ten (3,853, or 58 percent) were Chinese. For every well-paying claim operated by whites, there were half a dozen "which return profits only to Chinamen."[53] Relations there, while sometimes tense, were generally placid and even mutually respectful.[54] Elsewhere, however, hostility kept the number of Chinese low or kept them out altogether. In Colorado, a major mining region in 1870, the census reported seven Chinese, none of them miners. Arizona had twenty, Dakota and New Mexico none.[55]

In California and Nevada hostility did not abate. In the former, a legislative investigation in 1862 found at least eighty-eight Chinese murdered, many by tax collectors. Their treatment "would disgrace the most barbarous nation on earth."[56] Virginia City newspapers had almost daily accounts of abuses, including a man police dropped repeatedly from a derrick with a rope around his neck to encourage him confess to robbery. (He didn't.)[57] A hint of daily life is found in a pair of language phrase books from the 1870s. One offered English speakers useful expressions in addressing Chinese, the other gave Chinese the same in the other direction. While some choices are puzzling ("Have I no ape?"), most suggest the gist of ordinary conversations. Among the phrases for white housewives hiring a domestic are these:

> Can you get me a good boy?
> I think he is very stupid.
> I want to cut his wages.
> Wash the windows.
> Sweep the stairs.
> Light the fire.
> Wash the clothes.
> Brush my hat.
> Trim the lamps.
> Take care of the baby.

Come at seven every morning.
Go home at eight every night.
Go to bed just now.

Nearly two hundred pages long, the phrase book does not include "How are you?" or "Thank you."[58] What Chinese would need to say in English included:

He took it from me by violence.
He claimed my mine.
He assaulted me without provocation.
He tries to extort money from me.
I only mind my own business.

And for speaking about other Chinese:

He was choked to death with a lasso.
He was smothered in his room.
He was flogged publickly twice in the streets.
He was starved to death in prison.
He committed suicide.[59]

For twenty years after their arrival in numbers, the Chinese economic threat was largely fantasized. In mining they worked smaller, least productive placer claims. By 1870, as whites turned to other work, Chinese made up nearly 60 percent of California's independent miners.[60] In an ambitious effort to reclaim San Francisco's tidelands at least a few thousand were hired through contractors to do the grunt labor of levee building. "I do not think we could get white men to do the work," an owner testified of the men who suffered heat and malaria during twelve-hour workdays.[61] Elsewhere they worked as cooks and domestics and operated laundries feeding "nearly every branch of human industry," a legislative committee reported in 1861, and spending nearly $14 million in services and taxes.[62] By the 1870s, however, they were adapting and moving upward in the maturing economy. They made and sold everything from clothing and cigars to whiskey and whips.[63] They were advancing through the very system of enterprise and free labor that a few years before they were said to reject and threaten, which brought a growing alarm among white laborers, which in turn made them ideal targets of dark suspicions and popular unease.

Take, as a case in point, opium smoking.[64] Opiates were nothing new. Physicians had long administered them orally, as pills and as laudanum, and starting in the 1860s they injected morphine hypodermically. Patent medicines heavily laced with opiates promised cures for everything from cholera to bedwetting. But if using opiates via mouth or needle was pervasive across the West and nation, opium *smoking* arrived only with Chinese immigrants. Practiced in China since the seventeenth century, after England and other powers forcefully imposed traffic in opium to bolster their own trading profits, smoking was offered in "dens," facilities with bunks for lounging when stuporous. The practice filled a variety of roles—male socializing, relief from fatigue and ennui, and, when a user bought higher grades, establishing status. The male sojourners in California created an instant and hungry market that exporters in Hong Kong quickly fed. Walk any block in San Francisco's Chinatown, a visitor reported, and "from basement and open doorway pours forth the sickening odor" of opium fumes. What portion of the Chinese partook of the drug is only a guess—an early investigator thought 20 percent smoked occasionally, and 15 percent daily—but the extent of the trade was formidable. On the eve of the Civil War an importer estimated that one and two-thirds tons of the drug were being consumed every month.[65]

It would be nearly twenty years after the first puffs on America shores, however, before the habit spread much beyond the Chinese, and then it was primarily among white prostitutes, gamblers, and others of the western underworld. A user told the journalist Dan DeQuille that about fifty whites in Virginia City and maybe five hundred in San Francisco visited the dens regularly—if true, well under a single percent in places where it was easily available.[66] Quickly, however, there were shrill alarms of the habit's baleful effects. *Atlantic*, *Harper's*, and other popular periodicals warned that smokers were prone to a long list of diseases as they slid down a slope to moral decay. The dens lured curious youth of both sexes into degeneracy, adults to infidelities and miscegenation. As for that pillar of the home, American manhood, smoking first produced sexual promiscuity ("venereal fury") and then impotence. Opium was a feminizing vice, leaving its male users meek, submissive, and silent. Its grip on the user was immediate and unbreakable. As prohibitionists wrote of the first "fatal glass of beer" taken in a saloon, a critic of the dens warned that "it is utter ruin to smoke the first pipe." After that only the "walls of an asylum" could keep the instant addict from the drug.[67]

Every supposed effect of smoking—disease, effeminacy, sexual deviance, and docility—was in other contexts called natural to the Chinese character, which meant that native-born Americans who fell to the habit would become one with the alien invaders. One theory in fact held that a Caucasian who took up the pipe would develop Chinese coloring, behaviors, and mentality—a condition, "Orientalness," that in turn would be passed to others by simple contact, like the flu.[68]

Such an idea, that the Chinese were a kind of cultural infection, highlights how they stood starkly apart in the popular mind from others outside the white majority. Mexicans and Indians, as irredeemably inferior, were predicted somehow to vanish before a superior Anglo population. But not the Chinese. Not only would their vile cultural traits seep through the society around them. Despite having virtually no women among them, their numbers were also said to be growing like compound interest, and with them their chest of corruptions.[69] Vested in such power, the Chinese, as the perfect cultural others, became avatars of anxieties around changes in the new America—threats to the economy, the family, civic virtue, and political order.

Anti-Chinese sentiment, born in prewar California, became increasingly strident and increasingly continental. A special joint congressional committee in 1876 interviewed scores of white officials, businessmen, laborers, policemen, and farmers in San Francisco as well as prominent native Chinese.[70] Its report of more than 1,200 pages had some sympathetic testimony, especially by clergy, but it was mostly thick with warnings. The filthy, crowded conditions of western Chinatowns would render any eastern city diseased and uninhabitable. Leprous and syphilitic, congenitally dishonest, spreaders of opium and its horrors, both polygamous and given to buggery, the Chinese were called morally and mentally deficient and wholly incapable of taking a responsible role in political life. As their numbers exploded, the report concluded, the Pacific coast "must in time become either American or Mongolian."[71] The clear implication was that the nation at large would soon face the same choice. As a Nevadan put it, "Celestials" would soon be pouring over the Rockies like stampeding bison, and "then you may look for other means to support your families."[72]

That charge was at the heart of the Workingmen's Party of California, formed by Dennis Kearney in 1877 in the wake of the financial panic of 1873 and the subsequent depression. Its slogan: "The Chinese Must Go!" The party soon collapsed, but the sentiment remained, and earlier allies to the Chinese were largely falling away. Most of California's Protestant clergy, disappointed by tepid success among both Chinese and Indians, now backed Chinese exclusion and embraced what Joshua Paddison has termed "white Christian nationalism."[73] A referendum in 1879 asked California voters whether they approved of ending Chinese immigration. It passed by 99.4 percent (150,000 to 900).[74] That year a new constitution forbid corporations and municipalities from hiring Chinese and authorized cities to eject them entirely—moves a federal court soon declared unconstitutional.

Hostility and its reactions now were national. The Burlingame Treaty (1868) had guaranteed free movement between China and the United States, but in 1880 Washington renegotiated it to limit acceptance of Chinese workers if they appeared to threaten the nation's interest or "good order." Two years later the Chinese Exclusion Act suspended immigration of laborers, skilled and unskilled, for a decade. The door later was shut indefinitely and reopened only in 1943, when China became an ally in World War II.

Chinese were drawn to the West by its earliest and most enduring image, that of a field of opportunity. They became victims of another image that emerged after the Civil War—the West as national reconciler, the common ground for a Union remade. In this the Chinese played a unique role. As America's most anomalous newcomers, they became the raw stuff of imagined threats to the new nation. A Cantonese arriving in San Francisco in search of the main chance ("When luck strikes, / With the whole world behind me, / I will be rich in a few years' turn") found himself a walking parable for a nervous nation. Once the Chinese were saddled with fears of the future, the West could serve them up and symbolically and actually cancel them out.

Something similar happened with another group of westerners. Unlike the Chinese, however, they had been part of American society, albeit most of them as slaves, for more than two and a half centuries.

The Barely Black West

The most ethnically diverse part of the nation was also the whitest, in the sense that, excluding Indian Territory and Texas east of the ninety-eighth merid-ian, the West had the nation's smallest portion of African Americans.[75] This set it starkly apart from the East and even more from the Southeast, and yet exactly because of that difference, the West and the former Confederacy were in illuminating conversation about race and society at this vital turning point in American history.

In Indian Territory Black slaves among the Five "Civilized" Tribes, the Cher-okees, Creeks, Seminoles, Chickasaws, and Choctaws, made up between 10 and 18 percent of tribal populations in 1860.[76] Demographically, it was as if a portion of southeastern society had been picked up and dropped into the near edge of the West. After the war the federal government imposed new treaties that severely reduced tribal holdings, abolished slavery, and pressed the tribes to allot lands to their former bondsmen. Within those parameters treatment varied dramatically from tribe to tribe. Creeks and Seminoles granted full cit-izenship, and freedpeople took prominent parts in tribal governments. Choc-taw and Chickasaw leaders refused citizenship, enacted Black codes to regulate behavior, and pressed former slaves to leave. The Cherokee response fell between the other two. They provided freedpeople land and full access to citizenship but only to those present in the Cherokee nation six months after approval of the treaty of 1866. Many slaveholders had fled the wartime anarchy, and many of their bondsmen were slow to straggle back. Dubbed "intruders," those arriving after 1867 agitated for land and tribal rights with limited success. The issue of citizenship festered for generations. As the Five Tribes began to rebuild after the disasters of the war and the treaties that followed, the African Americans who had long been part of their societies would play varying roles.[77]

Elsewhere, measured only by statistics, African Americans barely registered. Only Kansas and Wyoming had populations exceeding one percent in 1870 and 1880, and in every western state and territory but two the ratio of Blacks to whites, already stunningly low in 1870, declined over the next decade. In Arizona and Idaho, which had the nation's highest portion of foreign-born in 1870 (60 and 53 percent), Blacks were 0.06 and 0.3 percent of the population. In Idaho's Idaho County in 1880 nearly six of ten persons were Chinese, but there was not a single Black American.[78]

Some reasons were obvious. There were so few African Americans after the war because there were very few before it. Hostility to both Black slavery and to free Blacks kept their numbers to a smidgen; in 1860 the Mississippi county where Jefferson Davis grew up had three times as many African Americans as all of the West outside of Indian Territory.[79] After the war laws banning of free Blacks were stuck down or languished (although Oregon's ban on free Blacks was on the books until 1926), but prewar hostility persisted, and African Americans often found their working lives as constricted as back east. In Oregon in 1870 Black Americans or mulattoes accounted for three-quarters of domestics and all cooks and waiters but none of the mechanics and 3 out of 9,750 farmers. The state had four hundred hotel and restaurant operators, three of them Black. Blacks did, however, service whites at each end of the body. They made up all the bootblacks and thirteen out of thirty-five barbers.[80]

The few genuine niches were in cities where there was a demand for labor.[81] A handful began the climb into the middle class as merchants, hostlers, restaurateurs, and editors, and eventually as lawyers and doctors. George Washington Dennis began as a San Francisco saloon janitor in 1849, bought his freedom, and went on to run several businesses and speculate successfully in real estate. By the 1870s urban Blacks were forming a variety of institutions, from fraternal groups to literary societies. Those in Portland sponsored a well-attended Ratification Jubilee celebrating passage of the Fifteenth Amendment. Several prominent white orators addressed the crowd.[82]

Blacks in three lines of work—cowboying, soldiering, and plains farming—have drawn a lot of popular and scholarly attention. Cattle raising was an important part of the deep southeastern economy, and enslaved people brought by their owners into Texas naturally moved also into its new methods of cowboying.[83] Once free, they kept at it. They applied their skills to all parts of ranching—by some accounts they were especially adept at the dangerous work of breaking wild horses—and the mutual dependence and common rigors of range work apparently blurred almost wholly racial distinctions in day-to-day labors.[84] Some white ranchers gave Black cowboys their highest esteem and trust. The most famous tribute was by the legendary Texas rancher Charles Goodnight to Bose Ikard (the model for the character Joshua Deets in Larry McMurtry's novel *Lonesome Dove*). Goodnight wrote that Ikard was the "most skilled and trustworthy man I had," and on a grave marker praised his "splendid behavior."[85]

Perhaps twenty-five thousand Black cavalrymen and infantrymen served in the West during the decades after the war, a significant part of the drastically reduced military there.[86] Like young white immigrants, Buffalo Soldiers enlisted to break out of otherwise dismal prospects. "I got tired of looking mules in the face from sunrise to sunset," as one put it, and another: "I Thought there must be a better livin' in this world."[87] Their four regiments, two cavalry (Ninth and Tenth) and two infantry (Twenty-Fourth and Twenty-Fifth, combined from four originally authorized in 1866), were attached to some of the most contentious Indian campaigns, against the Cheyennes on the central plains, the Apaches, Kiowas, and Comanches in the Southwest, and the Lakotas on the northern plains, including the 1890 campaign leading up to the massacre at Wounded Knee. They patrolled Yosemite National Park, and later some in Montana left their horses to form a bicycle corps.[88] More than twenty-five Black soldiers received the Congressional Medal of Honor, and they later fought prominently in the Spanish-American War, including at San Juan (Kettle) Hill.[89]

Freedpeople, to state the obvious, were also experienced farmers, having worked the fields of white owners for more than two centuries. After the war some began to make their way to the central plains, especially Kansas, where their numbers ballooned from 625 in 1860 to 17,108 in 1870 to 43,107 in 1880.[90] In 1860, 80 percent of Blacks in the West were in California, 12 percent in Kansas; Kansas held 70 percent in 1870, and 75 percent in 1880. Geography helped—Kansas was easily accessible from the upper South—and its free-soil past gave it a congenial (but exaggerated) image. Southeastern Blacks had reasons to leave their homes. Whatever hope that had flared after emancipation was dimming as Democrats regained control of state after state, and by 1876, according to an advocate of Liberian resettlement, there had been 2,141 murders and 2,115 serious assaults in the former Confederacy.[91] "Confidence is perished and faded away," a Black leader said. The blood of martyrs, another wrote, "calls from the ground and arouses us to action."[92]

Some of the aroused turned to Kansas. The migration of "exodusters," a term combining the biblical flight from Egypt with the dusty plains, focused on several towns founded on the Kansas plains in 1877–78. The best known, Nicodemus, was organized by Kentuckians, while Benjamin "Pap" Singleton founded two others.[93] Singleton was a Tennessee carpenter and coffin-maker who considered himself "an instrument of God" and claimed to have "fetched out" 7,432 Blacks into Kansas. Estimates of this initial migration run as high as ten thousand. The second wave was more spontaneous. On the frigid morning of March 11, 1879, Saint Louis residents were astounded when nearly three hundred former slaves arrived on the steamer *Colorado*, followed by nearly double that number on the *Grand Tower* five days later. For three months, there was a steady traffic of freed-people, borne by rumors of free land and free plows: a "Kansas fever" drawing thousands to levees in Louisiana and Mississippi.[94] Saint Louis officials suddenly had to provide for the destitute dream-seekers. A Colored Refugee Relief Board and Topeka's Freedman Relief Association, largely Black-staffed, raised money for food and housing and bought tickets for some to go upriver to Wyandotte (present Kansas City). Kansas governor John P. St. John was especially adept at exporting new arrivals to Nebraska, where some optimistic boosters thought enough might come to earn the young state an additional congressman.[95] Then in early summer, as the temperature rose downriver, the fever cooled. Steamboats refused to stop to pick up crowds waving frantically from levees. They "cast themselves on the ground in despair" as the boats chugged on and left them "without shelter, without food, with no hope of escaping . . . and hardly a chance of returning whence they came."[96] Vessels began stopping for migrants again after several weeks, but although the movement continued for another year, it never approached the vigor of that remarkable spring.

Exodusters found nothing close to a true deliverance. A brief time of radical and moderate influence among whites after the war was followed by a return of the racial anxiety and antagonism so virulent during the 1850s. Between 1865 and 1880 there were at least seventy-five cases of murders, mobbings, race riots, and lynchings, threatened and accomplished. Nicodemus survived (barely), but other colonies did not. No other part of the plains felt the touch of exodusters. Only in Wyoming and parts of eastern Montana did the percentage of Black Americans rise above a single percent.[97] Few Black immigrants returned to their former homes. Most seem to have looked on Kansas disappointments as Russian Germans looked on droughty Nebraska as they read about kinsmen back home starving on wood chip tea: as bad as things were at present, they had known much worse. In a typically biblical referent, one elder said that his people would "jine hands and walk into Jordan's tide" rather than "go back to Egypt."[98]

As in farming, the Black presence in cowboying and soldiering is also easily overstressed. By early estimates up to nine thousand African Americans worked western trails and ranches, but more recent research suggests they made up only 2 percent of the ranching work force, which in turn was only 2 percent of western working men.[99] Buffalo Soldiers accounted for as many as one in five western enlistees, yet by one study they figured in only one in twenty Indian engagements.[100] As for opportunity, there was a genuine racial leveling among working cowboys, yet Blacks only rarely rose to become managers. "If it weren't for my damned old black face I'd have been the boss of one of these divisions long ago," claimed Jim Perry, a longtime employee of Texas's XIT Ranch.[101] Most Buffalo Soldiers initially were stationed in Texas, where they drew such venomous hostility from former Confederates that by 1869 all twenty-one companies had been sent to the Comanche fringe, beyond the one-hundredth meridian.[102] Even there the tensions were raw. Some were murdered by men who were invariably acquitted or never arrested. Sentiments were little different elsewhere. A New Mexico editor advised the government to send the Ninth Cavalry back to picking cotton, hoeing corn, and entertaining whites as minstrels.[103]

Black Americans did play two important roles. One was in the West as imaginative playground in changing times. Some freedmen argued that, exactly because they had been enslaved, they had earned a place in the new country. Give his people land in the West, promised J. H. Williamson, a Black North Carolina state legislator, and they would civilize the wilderness as whites had from Jamestown to the present. It was manifest destiny: "The Indians are savage and will not work," Williamson said, while "we, the negro race, are a working people" who, like the white pioneers before them, would bring the land to blossom.[104] Frederick Douglass generally urged freedpeople to remain to claim their future in the Southeast, but addressing the American Anti-Slavery Society in 1869 he stood with Williamson. The African American slave had been spared the fate of Indians because "he is so close under your arm, that you cannot get at him." Now "the Negro is more like the white man than the Indian. . . . You do not see him wearing a blanket, but coats cut in the latest European fashion."[105]

The notion of freedpeople moving west, well dressed or not, in turn roused the fears of southeastern whites. A special Senate committee spent much of 1880 investigating the "causes of the removal of the Negroes" after the war. Democrats charged "wild and misdirected" philanthropists with fanning the "embers of hatred" in the former Confederacy. Republicans pointed to three thick volumes of persecutions, "whippings, maimings, and murders" after emancipation and explained the exodus as the pursuit of free labor's dream of "peace and happiness by [their] own fireside the earning of [their] daily toil."[106] Some southeastern whites took a "good riddance" position and urged recruitment of Europeans to replace Black labor altogether. An alternative was to court those causing such alarm in the West, "the teeming population of Asia."[107] Chinese labor had long been used on sugar plantations in Cuba and the British West Indies, and after the war Louisiana planters recruited them, and later others from China and California, in hopes of reviving an enterprise on the edge of bankruptcy. At least a couple of thousand worked the fields into the 1870s.[108] Moves to develop a significant Chinese labor force went nowhere, however. Wages were generally better in California, and cane workers in Louisiana were caught up in the ever-shifting politics of class and race. The usual bugaboos raised the usual frights. Bearing loathsome diseases, Chinese would multiply prolifically and soon "suffocate European civilization." One writer added that this "race of Oriental Yankees" was so thrifty and hardworking that they might end up owning all the South's plantations.[109]

As for their second role, African Americans, even confined by numbers and prejudice, wrestled out considerable legal gains. Some resonated through the nation at large. Before the war free Blacks in California cities had won key cases challenging slaveowners who brought bondsmen into the state. When the teenaged Archy Lee ran from his Mississippian owner, he was caught and re-enslaved on the novel grounds that the owner was young and poorly informed, but after months of legal maneuvering Lee was freed—and promptly took off for Canadian goldfields.[110] After emancipation, activists, including two sons of Frederick Douglass in Denver, turned hard toward two issues pressed as well in the Southeast, education and suffrage. Results for the former were spotty. Kansas segregated schools in its constitution of 1859, desegregated them in 1874, then resegregated them five years later. So they remained until the watershed decision of *Brown v. Board of Education of Topeka* in 1954.[111]

In 1867 Blacks could vote only in parts of New England and, ironically, in states of the former Confederacy required to allow it in their new constitutions. Western activists did have one promising angle. Because territories were under federal authority, they could work with sympathetic national leaders like

Charles Sumner. In 1864 three Denver barbers launched an effort to reverse Colorado's ban on Black suffrage. Local opinion was clear. In a constitutional referendum the next year white voters rejected equal suffrage by nearly nine to one. The group pressed on. When they petitioned Congress to deny Colorado statehood until it met the standard demanded of readmitted southern states, congressional radicals took up the cause and expanded it. In January 1867 the Territorial Suffrage Act became law without President Andrew Johnson's signature. It forbade all territories from denying the vote on the basis of race. It would be three years before the Fifteenth Amendment granted the vote to Black Americans in the nation at large.[112]

While only a tiny minority of the western population, Blacks still shaped the social and political life in their communities and eventually in the nation. What is striking is that, given that they *were* such a minority, they had so much to struggle against—that in the whitest part of America Blacks were considered even the slightest threat. Like the Chinese, African Americans posed no discernible challenge to white interests, yet they drew deep, often frantic, anxiety and hostility. As the remade nation struggled over questions of the scope of its citizenship, the West, as before the war, remained the projecting ground of both its loftier aspirations and, literally, its darker fears.

Fig. 17. Built with elaborate latticework, the bridge at Dale
Creek in southeastern Wyoming was the longest on the
Union Pacific, the eastern portion of the longest railroad on
earth. Andrew J. Russell, "Engine on Great Trestle," Oakland
Museum of California, H69.459.538.

Fig. 18. (*above*) An artist's rather fanciful impression of mix of Chinese and European workers on Central Pacific blasting through the Sierra Nevada. *Work on the Last Mile of the Pacific Railroad*, sketch by A. R. Waud. Library of Congress Prints and Photographs Division, LC-USZ62-127764.

Fig.19. (*opposite top*) The completion of the Union Pacific–Central Pacific would speed the conquest of the West and its Native peoples. Mythically, it was seen as a moment of national reunification and the sparking to life of a new westward-facing era. Andrew J. Russell, *East and West Shaking Hands at Laying Last Rail*. Oakland Museum of California, H69.459.2030.

Fig. 20. (*opposite bottom*) Looking formidably prepared for trouble, O. C. Marsh and graduate students embark on a western field trip in 1871. Yale University Library Manuscripts and Archives Digital Library, Wikimedia Commons.

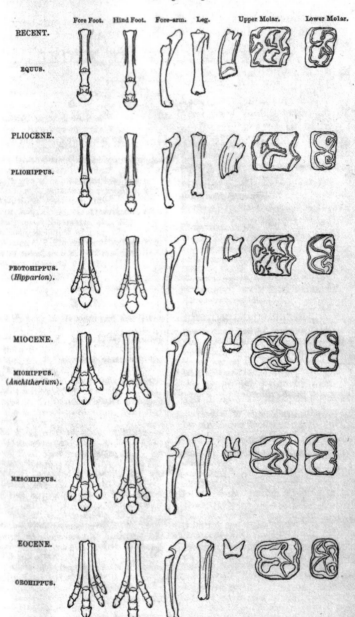

GENEALOGY OF THE HORSE.

Fig. 21. (*opposite*) Marsh's tracing of the evolution of the horse, shown through fossil toes taken from shales and sandstone of the Great Plains, was the first illustration of natural selection through a linkage of species over time. O. C. Marsh, *Polydactyle Horses, Recent and Extinct, American Journal of Science*, 3rd ser. 17 (1879): 499–505. New York Academy of Medicine. https://nyamcenterforhistory.org/tag/evolution/.

Fig 22. (*above*) Charles Darwin called Marsh's ancient toothed avian, *Hesperornis regalis* (the "Royal Bird of the West"), the "best support for the theory of evolution" since his *On the Origin of Species*. O. C. Marsh, *Odontornithes: A Monograph on the Extinct Toothed Birds of North America* (Washington DC: Government Printing Office, 1880).

Fig. 23. (*top*) Ferdinand Hayden, encouraged by a lecturer hired by the Northern Pacific Railroad, led his federal survey on the first formal exploration and description of the Yellowstone basin in 1871. W. H. Jackson Collection, U.S. Geological Survey Denver Library Photographic Collection.

Fig. 24. (*bottom*) In a promotional effort pushed by the railroad, spectacular photographs like this of the lower falls of the Yellowstone River were displayed in the Capitol rotunda in the spring of 1872. Congress speedily created Yellowstone National Park. William Henry Jackson, *Great Falls of the Yellowstone*, Library of Congress Prints and Photographs Division, LC-DIG-ppmsca-68717.

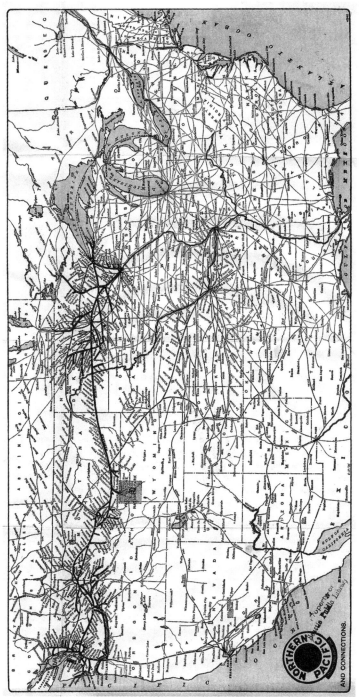

Fig. 25. The world's first national park became a star feature for the Northern Pacific's tourist trade for decades. From materials for the Alaska-Yukon-Pacific Exposition, 1909, scanned by the Seattle Public Library. Wikimedia Commons.

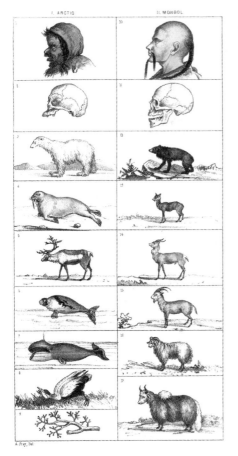

A. Frey, Del.

Tableau to accompany Prof. Agassiz's "Sketch"

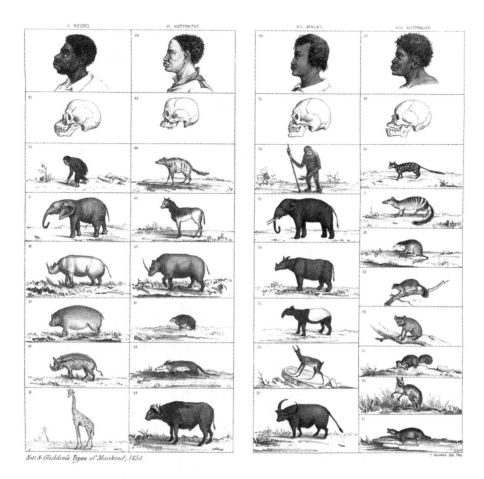

Fig. 26. Polygenists Josiah Nott and George Gliddon classified
human races, including Native and African Americans, as their
own species, as distinct and separate as rhinoceroses and whales.
From Josiah C. Nott and George R. Gliddon, *Types of Mankind*
(1854) via Science History Images / Alamy stock photo.

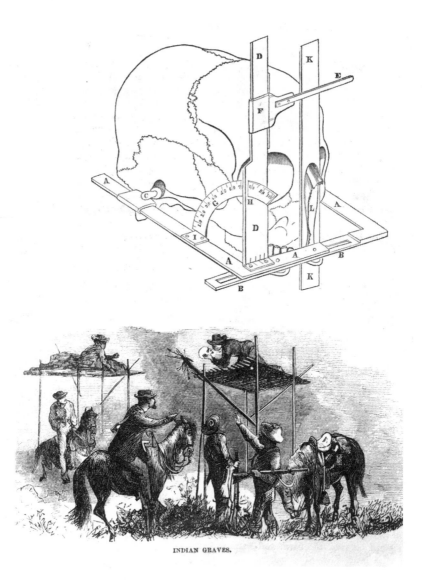

INDIAN GRAVES.

Fig. 27. (*top*) Polygenists based their claims heavily on craniometry, the measurement of skulls pioneered by Samuel George Morton through his collections of remains taken from earlier Native mounds. From Morton, *Crania Americana* (Philadelphia: J. Dobson, 1839), 252; New York Public Library Digital Collection.

Fig. 28. (*bottom*) "We can't study the origins of the Indian race unless we have those skulls!" Yale geologists steal skulls from Plains Indian burial platforms. *Harper's New Monthly Magazine*, vol. 43, 1871.

GTOWN-1849, NOW PLACERVILLE, CALIF.   5734

Fig. 29. Gold mining towns like Placerville, California,
were "the world's convention," likely the most ethnically
diverse gatherings in American history. Fritz-Metcalf
Photograph Collection, University of California–
Berkeley, Bioscience and Natural Resources Library.

A ROAD SCENE IN CALIFORNIA.

Fig. 30. (*top*) Chinese efficiency in working California's placer gold diggings inspired violent opposition from Anglo neighbors and the marginalization of Chinese into feminized occupations. Oakland Museum of California.

Fig. 31. (*bottom*) In this "road scene" from gold rush California, a forty-niner from the East mingles with Chinese and Indians, all set in motion by the Great Coincidence. Charles Christian Nahl, *A road scene in California* (1856). BANC PIC 1963.002:0118-B. Courtesy of the Bancroft Library, University of California–Berkeley online.

Fig. 32. As the West bulked up with men, to in some places more than 90 percent of the population, the demands for women in the workplace shifted. This schoolteacher in Custer Bonanza school in Idaho was one of many who filled the changing needs. Idaho State Historical Society.

Fig. 33. The same demographic reality across the male-dominated
West stimulated prostitution, with its occasional chance of
economic advancement but its far more frequent exploitation.
San Francisco History Center, San Francisco Public Library.

15 ▷ Crew Cultures, Cribs and Schoolhouses, Women on the Fringe

While the West's people were a promiscuous mix of origins and cultures, in their gendered makeup they were strikingly, sometimes bizarrely, weighted in one direction. The predominance of men, like the ethnic stew, was a lesson in how a transforming America was giving the West a nature and tone essentially different from earlier expansions, and yet the scrambled roles of its men and women in turn could suggest how it could both reflect and lead the way in changes in the gender dynamics of the nation at large. And as always, the West played its new mythic role. Outsiders' perceptions of its peoples and their behaviors, in this case hell-roaring cowboys and women homesteaders, could say as much about what others needed the West to be as about what was, in fact, there.

The Testosterone West

The West was full of men, in some places overwhelmingly so (see map 7). In 1870 and 1880 the United States was, by a whisker, majority male (50.5 and 50.8 percent). In the West's fifteen states and territories non-Native males made up 56.8 percent and 56.1 percent of the population. Ten western states and territories in 1880 had fewer than eight women for every ten men. In five of them there were fewer than five women for every ten men, a truly bizarre skew. Some mining camps in Idaho in 1870 had nine men for every woman, and in Nevada City, California, in 1850, the ratio was forty-four to one. In the thirty years after 1848 the gendered profile of one-third of the United States, an area larger than that east of the Mississippi, was an aberration found in few other places in the world. The nation had never seen anything remotely like it, and it never would again.

That bulking of men on half the map said five things about how America was changing in the wake of expansion. It teaches something about the effects of the Civil War and how economic and technological forces were reshaping the surviving nation. It reminds us how western changes fit into wider global patterns. It shows parts of the new western society as especially fluid and inventive,

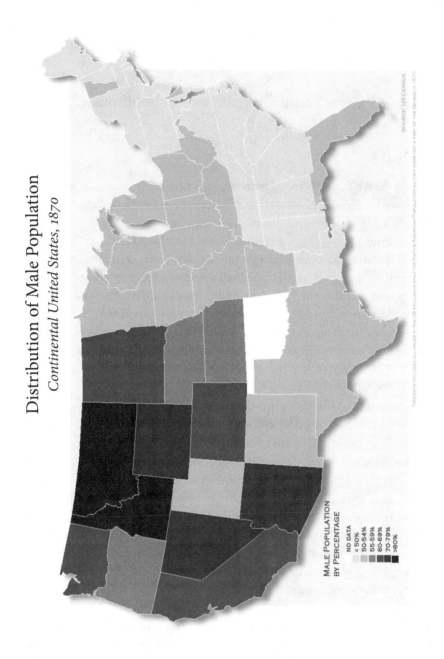

Distribution of Male Population
Continental United States, 1870

MALE POPULATION
BY PERCENTAGE

NO DATA
< 50%
50-54%
55-59%
60-69%
70-79%
>80%

SOURCE: US CENSUS

THIS DATA INCLUDES ALL MALES IN THE US EXCLUDING ONLY THE NATIVE AMERICAN POPULATION AS THEY WERE NOT A PART OF THE CENSUS IN 1870

MAP 7. Distribution of male population, 1870. Well connected by new technologies of movement and demanding the heavy labor of an industrializing economy, the postwar West bulked up with large majorities of men. Map by Maggie Rose Bridges.

taking turns and shapes unseen before. The new shapes in turn became part of perceptions of how the nation and world saw the emerging West. Finally, the West, with its swarming of men behaving strangely, could also show how stubbornly tradition and prevailing values persisted in the new country.

The gendered imbalance of East and West was one more case of the twinned effects of the Civil War and expansion. Wartime deaths took about three-quarters of a million men out of the population, the overwhelming majority in the East.[1] In 1870 males were a minority in eighteen states. All but four were east of the Appalachians. The primary reason was the deaths on battlefields and in hospital tents, but the numbers also show that a lot of survivors of the bloody fields in the East were drawn to western opportunities and jobs.[2] The West can be imagined as a collage of masculine subcultures at work in seizing and transforming the land. Cowboys drove herds to plains towns that had grown up beside tracks laid down by thousands of railroaders. Those lines ran also to northwestern forests with their dozens of camps of lumberjacks, the more remote supplied by some of the many thousands of freighters moving goods to new settlements, including army posts with their barracks full of cavalrymen and infantry. It all was bound together by a telegraphic grid operated almost exclusively by young men. The closest balance of the sexes was in agricultural country, with its thousands of family farms, but even there, with so many men homesteading on their own, tending to livestock, and filling jobs in the fledgling towns, the male portion of the population was well above the national average.[3]

The movement revolution that helps explain the new country's cultural variety does the same for the masculinized West. Work on previous frontiers was almost wholly related to farming, which demanded families. Reaching those frontiers was difficult, slow, and expensive, so households most often saved their resources and headed there together. As a result the balance between men and women was relatively close from the start. That was still the case when farmers first made their jump to Oregon and California in the mid-1840s.[4] A quarter century later a traveler could move back and forth and around the West with an ease unimaginable just a generation earlier. Tens of thousands of men, mostly young and single but with a minority of husbands and fathers, did just that, reasonably sure they could sojourn for a while before sending for families or, more likely, going home. The same systems that were knitting the new country into the world were helping to throw the West's human profile wildly out of whack.

The technological revolution was bringing changes from France to China to Brazil. One result was a second lesson of the masculinized West. Cowboys, freighters, miners, and railroad workers were part of a worldwide phenomenon of groups of men working at the sweaty particulars of establishing colonial systems, especially in British and Anglophone empires. Examples ranged from New Zealand to India and across the oceans between them—teams of sheep shearers, riverboat men, canal builders, whalers and sealers, and, prototypically, sailors. What historian James Belich calls "crew cultures" had distinctive identities. Each had its own dress, patois, code of behavior, and even body type and grooming (hair styles, tattoos, walking gaits). All, however, whether featuring bowlegs or braided hair, sombreros or hobnail boots, joined in a few traits.[5] They were members of "*prefabricated* communities." Veterans trained newcomers, who in turn became veterans with moveable identities nicely suited for transient lives lived over vast spaces. A freighter or cowboy could float from Montana to Arizona and slip into his workaday slot as easily as a British limey moving from ship to ship. This helped make crew cultures the "shock troops" of expansion. Together they formed an essential workforce that could shift where needed to take and control new lands and peoples. They were the muscle of what Belich calls the "progress industry"—the military and railroads that seized the country and, in a second wave, the extractive economies that brought resources under the new command.[6]

Most of their work was the child of private capital, which made crew cultures cogs in some of the world's most powerful and encompassing corporations. Freighters, cowboys, and the others were, in fact, ideal wage laborers. They worked cheap. They got by on grunt grub like beans, salt pork, and coffee. They trained each other. They did their work with consummate skill and often under hardships and at some personal risk. It was a combination any factory owner in New York or Massachusetts would have hungered for. These romanticized figures of later western fiction, pictured as paragons of a vanished time, in fact were prime players in the making of a new age.

The hairy-chested West offered up a third lesson: how expansion, with its demographic twisting, could make for societies that were twisted, too, into new arrangements with a new feel and tone. Heavily male gatherings were usually also highly transient, and one of the few things that bound them together was the fact that they had few women with them. Quickly they learned how much they had relied on wives, mothers, and sisters for life's basics. It began on the way out. Day after day a diarist on the road to Colorado wrote of eating crackers, raw bacon, and coffee "strong enough to float a four-pound wedge." Then he got ambitious: "Burned my hand on the spider [a skillet]—got mad at the potatoes and wouldn't eat them." On arrival many goldseekers parceled out cooking among themselves, which led to culinary spottiness. One campmate made fabulous apple pudding and turned squirrel meat into a "Beautiful Stew," a miner wrote, while others could barely light a fire.[7] Washing and mending clothes, essential chores given the rough and grubby work of mining, were at least as much a test.

Men fell quickly into homosocial activities. Barrooms and fraternal lodges—the Independent Order of Odd Fellows, Freemasons, Grand Army of the Republic, and others—offered instantly recognizable structures, rituals, and specialized languages that together allowed the quick bonding of men, however disparate their backgrounds.[8] Most occasions were informal. "Like the ladies at home, we often take our sewing with us," the Rev. Daniel Woods wrote of one: "While we plied our needles, our tongues were equally busy speaking of mutual friends and hopes."[9] A California diarist wrote of miners dressing up to look "fascinating" to one another.[10] Dances were special favorites. J. D. Borthwick attended one with the "ladies" determined by which men "had a patch on a certain part of his inexpressibles" (presumably underwear). The literary tourist Frederick Gerstäcker thought men in the camps he visited formed "a perfect social body" and "a little world of ourselves, in closest neighborhood and amity, eating, working and sleeping together."[11]

Scenes like these are a short step away from popular images that speak to the fourth lesson—how the testosterone West contributed to the stylized impressions emerging into a wider world. From the start literary tourists described hell-roaring, brawling, whoring, hard-drinking cowtowns and other moral sinks. This West was a land both rootin' and tootin'. Once again mining camps stood out. Hinton Helper found in California a "shameful depravity and unexampled turpitude" that was beyond the reach of his words.[12] Young Californian Edward Austin played to such images. "You ask me what temptations I had," he wrote his sister. "I did not have any. If I wanted anything, I had it. It I wanted to do anything, I did it."[13] An early account of San Francisco explained the lack of constraint: "[Gold] dust was plentier than pleasure, pleasure more enticing than virtue. Fortune was the horse, youth in the saddle, dissipation the track, and desire the spur."[14]

More than most cliches, this one had roots in reality. Most men in his camp, a miner wrote, "roll sin around as a sweet morsel under their tongues."[15] The sweetnesses were many. Prostitution was the most common occupation among women in Virginia City, Nevada, in 1870.[16] Loosened impulses and the easy availability of liquor made many western towns, and mining rushes above all, the most alcohol-sodden places in the nation. The pace could be feverish. A Montana editor kept tabs at a barroom revel of an hour and a half. Its thirty men averaged two beers and one whiskey every three minutes. With drinking at such a clip, another journalist thought that sobriety itself needed redefining. "No man should be considered drunk," he proposed, "as long as he can make a noise."[17] The Rev. William Goode was sure of the cause. Women were society's natural "restraining, elevating influence," and when men were left on their own, they "degenerate rapidly and become rough, harsh, slovenly—almost brutish."[18] A Californian wrote of neighbors who, once apart from their "pure and virtuous families," soon slid down a "fearful precipice of dissipation."[19]

This, what might be called the "men are pigs" thesis, has scholarly support. The "underside of American history" has been mostly peopled by young single men, one writes, and the western frontier, the most "youthful and masculine" part of America, was also "the one most prone to violence and disorder."[20] As with all western life, however, the hellraising images deserve their context. There was nothing distinctively western—or American—about the prodigality. Crew cultures of cowboys, freighters, miners, and track-layers drank and rutted and brawled pretty much like sheep shearers in New Zealand and whalers in Honolulu. All took part in "binge economies," splurging on food and clothing ranked otherwise as luxuries. While "orderly on the job," they were "disorderly off of it," quick to fight and spending their pay lavishly on alcohol, gambling, and sex.[21] Montana gold camps and French ports both had their riotous nights and their mornings of flat wallets and tired mattresses.

A Killing Field?

At the heart of those familiar scenes are images of male-on-male violence that was frequently fatal. By many outsiders' accounts at the time and in films and pulp fiction since then, a cattle or mining town and a hell-on-wheels could count on its "man for breakfast," a corpse awaiting collection each morning.[22] Hinton Helper estimated 4,200 murders in California during its first six years. If he were correct, a man living through that time had survived odds just slightly better than those of a Union soldier fighting at Antietam.[23] Impressions like that are vastly overdone, at least their raw numbers. As already noted, accounts of killings in railroad construction towns were wildly exaggerated. During their legendary boom years, 5 Kansas cattle towns averaged 1.7 murders annually inside their town limits, almost exactly the same (1.6 annually over 10 years) as in 3 booming Colorado mining towns.[24] These towns, that is, had their "man for breakfast" only if they had breakfast once every eight months.

At a closer, careful look, the story is more complicated—and revealing. A truer measure of lethality is the homicide rate—the number of killings in relation to the number of people available to kill. Figuring calls for a special caution. As historian Robert Dykstra points out, when the base population is small, as in most western towns, tiny changes in the number of homicides can cause the murder rates to surge or sag dramatically.[25] When the population is at least modest, however, and when numbers are collected over a number of years and then projected out to the number of homicides per hundred thousand persons, the rates do offer a crude measure of the frequency of murders. To no surprise, the rates varied.[26] For California's Tuolumne County in the 1850s it was 129; for Los Angeles from 1847 to 1870 it was 158. The rate for part of the Nebraska panhandle in the later nineteenth century was a stunning 260; those for California's Aurora (1861–65) and Bodie (1877–82) were 64 and 116.[27] Here, and in virtually every place measured, the figures were much higher than in eastern cities. Homicide rates in New York City, Boston, and Philadelphia in the 1870s and 1880s were, respectively, 6, 3.8, and 3.7.[28]

The numbers feel more than a bit obscure and algebraic, but they might be personalized. Most of us know a hundred persons wherever we live—close family and kin, good friends, acquaintances at work and at church and in stores. By this means of reckoning, using figures from 2020, if you live in Chicago (rate: 18) you will live 55 years before the god of averages rules that someone you know is murdered. In Saint Louis (87), the nation's grim leader in homicides, it would be 11 years, in Memphis (44) 23 years, in Phoenix (7.5) 133 years, and in Fargo (4) 250 years. Statistically the present writer, at home in Fayetteville, Arkansas, has until 2815 before he suffers a friend being killed. Once again, the figures from the early West are strikingly different. In Los Angeles (1847–70) the average time between murdered friends or acquaintances would have been 6 years and 4 months, in Tuolumne County (1850s) 7 years and 9 months, and in the Nebraska panhandle 3 years and 10 months.

Some reasons are pretty clear. Most homicides everywhere are committed by adult males, so where men predominate, more murders are all but guaranteed. Tuolumne County, with its rate of 129, was 95 percent male.[29] They also had the tools for murder. The West was born as the national firearms market was flooded by mass-produced revolvers; Smith and Wesson began selling theirs in 1857, and Colt introduced its famous "Peacemaker" in 1873. Handguns were the weapons of choice in the great majority of murders in these years, and the West bristled with them. While pistols were facilitators, ever-present alcohol was a dis-inhibitor.[30] The law was not much of a deterrent. Most lawmen were inexperienced and as transient as the crowds around them.[31] Fewer than one in six murders in one study led to a conviction, in part because of public tolerance of macho behavior. When a Confederate sympathizer in Oregon shot and killed a man who insisted he raise a glass to Abraham Lincoln, a jury acquitted him on the grounds of self-defense.[32]

Most to the point, the killing rates reflect what was not there. Violence is discouraged by family-dominated populations, reliable and visible law enforcement, institutions of cohesion such as churches and schools, and effective community leadership. Each was conspicuously absent in much of the new West. People who were inclined to do the worst to those around them were less constrained in doing their worst because there was so little collective identity and concern, so little to provide the "common" in "community."[33]

That throws into relief a final lesson from the testosterone West. As unruly and violent as it was, within a few years much of it shifted toward an equilibrium common to the nation. Women and families came west via the new modes of transportation. Populations stabilized. Churches and schools were established. Homicide rates dropped (but stayed higher than in the East). Towns with the wildest reputations tried to burnish images of Victorian respectability, and with that came social divisions little different from others in Indiana or Virginia. Cowboys might still fight and carouse, but the men who paid them now were founding churches, cultivating images of rectitude and self-control, and backing reforms and curfews. As town fathers, these cattle*men* raised a paternal hand to curtail the rowdier amusements of their workers, the cow*boys*.[34]

Larger towns divided spatially along lines familiar in the East. Germans and Irish had their own neighborhoods. Engineers, professionals, and better off merchants lived apart; those in Leadville, Colorado, perched comfortably on hillsides, looking down "on that life that twilight covered."[35] They sorted themselves out morally as well. Abilene exiled its prostitutes to its "devil's addition," a plot just outside its limits. Larger mining towns had their "dead lines" that separated respectable blocks of restaurants, theaters, and flashier saloons from the brothels, cribs, low groggeries, and the poorest hovels. Public sin continued, but, in Victorian mimic of the East, open vice was cordoned off and official eyes averted. As in Boston and Philadelphia, the division had a class coloration. Working-class men cavorted easily on the sin-side of the line. Middle-class men stayed mostly on the other.

But not entirely. As for how it worked, Alfred Doten, a handsome editor in Virginia City, Nevada, left us a moral map. He wrote in a secret diary of passing evenings with daughters of the elite, chatting in their parlors, then repairing to a favorite bordello in Chinatown to lie and smoke opium with the madam before attending a "big whore ball" and finally heading home. There he conducted a vigorous affair with his married landlady, Eunice Morton. He faithfully recorded and rated the copulations, each noted and numbered with an "ok" (526 in under two years), but these passages, and only these, he wrote in code, even in his secret journal. On this moral turf, on the proper side of the "dead line," Doten was properly discreet. For May 10, 1867: "ok 33—Evening

Mrs. Morton and I attended Rev. A B Earl's meeting at Presbyterian church. . . . Sermon on 'Prepare to die, be ready.'"[36]

Doten was acting the Victorian male. He recognized society's formal rules while hedging and outflanking them. His cavorting was in metaphor of the maturing West. Its earlier hell-roaring days were at once a departure from the eastern ways and a projection of them. It was as if in the cattle towns and mining camps middle-class American men were off on one of their usual toots, not to wilder precincts within an eastern city, but across the nation's "dead line" to California, Kansas, Montana, or Idaho. There for a while they engaged in open, even celebrated misbehavior, rolling sin "as a sweet morsel under their tongues," before returning to respectable homes, not in the East, but in the evolving West, as raw towns matured and sorted themselves out, building schools, opera houses, and lyceums, cultivating a familiar moral order that soon snapped into place.[37]

Look past the lurid descriptions of the time, and from the start there are stories of men who carried in traditional values rooted in community and family. As Victorian husbands their duty was to pursue the family good by going forth into the competitive marketplace, and after 1848 half a nation beckoned them to go manfully into the fray. "It is one thing to be a fireside warrior—entirely another to go into actual battle," Addison Crane wrote on his way to California: "But a good soldier will not shrink when the contest thickens."[38] Some used the occasion to cut loose from responsibilities or unhappy marriages. Their letters home could be ludicrous, feigned. A man pictured his church-bound children, a "rosy cheeked tribe of urchens racing on to the House of God," but cut it short: "but I must stop—my heart—oh dear!"[39]

Many others seem honestly determined to help their families by putting their homes behind them for a while, but, once out the door, they found themselves feeling not manly but miserable. They pined for their wives. "O, Why did I Leave Molly and the Baby!" a Colorado-bound goldseeker wrote on the side of his wagon. They longed to hear their voices and missed their touch. "My virtue is all right," one assured his wife, "for I do not care to meddle with any of the women that I see here." He would gladly welcome a reunion: "I look forward to something nice soon." (His wife, seeing that he "had not gotten out of the old way of 'wanting it' at night," reciprocated: "I do want to come to you *so so* bad & do little things for my love that I know he wants done.")[40] Fathers worried about their children's health and education and were haunted by the fear, as one man wrote home, that "being gone so long I will not appear natural to them again." Forty-niner David DeWolf wrote his wife: "I drempt last night I was home. I thought I was mighty happy. I thought little Sis [his daughter] was standing in the door. I thought she had grown tremendous but I knew her. I was enjoying myself fine when I awoke and behold it was all a dream. . . . When little Sis begins to talk, learn her to call me, won't you? My God, how I want to see you both."[41]

Women in Waiting, Women Who Went

DeWolf's wife, Matilda, back home in Springfield, Ohio, was one of many who remained behind as husbands set off for the gold fields, first to the Pacific coast and then, over the next twenty years, to other strikes in the interior. As their husbands were adapting to life without women, thousands of these "gold rush widows" were shouldering the work and responsibilities that had been mostly handled by their spouses, all the while rearing children and meeting social obligations on their own. These were the other forty-niners, and with them were more whose husbands drawn west by other enticements. Mostly absent from the usual histories, they were also vital actors in the transformations following the great coincidence.

Many of them had families and friends to help, but ultimately the job of running a household, and often a business, was up to them. Sara Pierce of New York handled the family farm and collected on her husband's loans (and avoided his creditors) while rearing seven children. "I am my own tinker[,] have set nine fruit trees[,] kleened house [and] Maria's help mend fence[,] set glass[,] mend my own stove grate in the oven, moved the front room stove out alone," she wrote, ending with understatement: "I am kept very busy here."[42]

Emotional responses of these "women in waiting" ran the usual range of human feeling. "I miss you so much," Harriet Godfrey wrote her husband, Ard, after battling mortgage payments, dismantling a failed mill, and nursing children through epidemics of measles and whooping cough: "Rich or poor come home so we can fare alike."[43] As their husbands were worrying about families at home, wives feared for spouses in the imagined wild. Like their distant mates, they allowed some reveries. "Oh if we could kiss," one wrote, and added that when intimate in her dreams, "you may depend I have fine times." Some turned deeply unhappy and depressed. After losing their two sons ("those precious children") to cholera soon after her husband, Cornelius, left, Margaret La Tourette wrote him that "every prospect seemed blasted, every hope crushed." Others developed a justifiable pride in what they accomplished and a fondness for an independence and sense of power they had never known. "I guess you will begin to think I am getting to be quite a business *caracter*," Sara Pierce wrote husband Hiram, adding coyly, "I get along very well concidering what [a] weak vessel I am."[44]

As vessels go, however, Hiram was the weaker. He failed in the diggings, drifted to San Francisco for wage work, and returned home after a year. Theirs was one of many separations that ended very differently from what was planned. Mary Warner managed well at home in Wisconsin before her husband, Leon, finally returned, broke and badly injured and mentally unhinged. She continued to run the household. He spent his last years panning for gold on a stream on the grounds of an asylum.[45] Other partings ended well or roughly in an economic wash. For all their differences, however, the paired stories all shook the established roles of the sexes. The same could be said of the other transforming event of the mid-nineteenth century, the Civil War, which took men out of their homes and pressed women into novel roles on an even greater scale than the opening of the West.[46] Together these two episodes temporarily (and often enough permanently) unsettled what it commonly meant to be man or woman in America. How the paired forces of expansion and war might have influenced the social contours of national life can only be speculated, but it seems more than coincidence that the years immediately ahead saw the emergence of a new feminism and rising demands for greater political rights and social opportunities for women.

Women who went west also found their family roles expanded. Accounts of remaking the West usually focus on men's work, but starting a new life relied at least as much on the work of women.[47] Before a new farm could make a dime the land required at least a year of preparation and planting. Keeping the family afloat required cash, and that often came from women's extra household production. During the first nine months on their Kansas farm, the Davies family got by on the twenty dollars the wife, Anne, earned by marketing fifty-five pounds of butter and forty dozen eggs.[48] Women and children took a hand in the heavier work. Men typically plowed, but that left unbroken clods and thick mats of grassroots, and if no harrow was available, things could get basic. With each parent taking an ax and each child a large knife, the Rauck family chewed the way through several acres, breaking down the soil for a garden and first crop.[49] Wives gathered wild plants and weeds that could make up much of the diet before a garden was producing. Suddenly widowed, with twelve children and no money, one mother learned the basics from an itinerant preacher, then fed her brood for weeks on bear grass, wild plums, and a variety of weeds found around their West Texas dugout.[50]

Where the imbalance of men to women was greatest, women's economic opportunity was as well. So was their burden of work. Both differed by class. Shasta, California, was drawing more families when Priscilla Sheldon arrived as wife of the town's Methodist minister. She taught private school, gave piano and guitar lessons, and took in donations from a Sunday school exhibition. Her income for a month quintupled her husband's take from his church's collection plate. Farther down the economic scale, a saloon owner's wife "earnt her *old man* . . . nine hundred dollars in nine weeks, clear of all expenses, by washing," which made her, by general impression, a "wife of the right sort."[51] Across the West, the most common income boost was by boarding unattached men. "Tell Alice I have not forgotten her," a Nebraska farm wife wrote of her sister: "She must remember that she has no one but herself, husband, and baby to look after, while I have the same, and two or three [other] men some of the time, and one all the time, washing and everything to do for him. I have butter and milk to look after, and [am] my own dressmaker and milliner. So it makes me pretty busy."[52]

Boarding was most common and most lucrative in mining towns, but the same economic logic made it the most grueling. Ellen Elizabeth Hunt, twenty-four and a mother of two, came to Denver with the rush of 1859. Her husband and a partner opened a boarding house, charging each lodger twelve dollars a week, but Ellen did all the work, plus selling butter, eggs, milk, and balls of "smeargrease" (cottage cheese). In her diary she summed up three weeks in July: "Weary days of labor and pain. I have made 175 loaves of bread and 450 pies. Taken care of the children and done all the house work but the washing. Ho hum." Ellen brought in the family's entire income, yet with stratospheric prices, and with broke boarders stiffing the Hunts, the "eating house" went under. Her husband, Alexander Cameron Hunt, went on to be governor. Ellen died at forty-four.[53]

Especially in towns women found their opportunities somewhat expanded—but only somewhat. The census showed the great majority of women "keeping house." Of fifteen western states and territories in 1870, only in Arizona and Wyoming were more than 10 percent of women over the age of ten "gainfully employed." Most who worked for pay clustered inside traditional roles. Nebraska's domestic servants doubled the number of women in all other categories together, and when those taking in boarders, working in hotels and restaurants, and making and servicing clothes are added, they made up 86 percent of the female work force. Still, the range of work done outside the usual lines was impressive: cigar-makers, barkeepers, photographers, clerks, gunsmiths, umbrella-makers, ragpickers, journalists, and even hunters and teamsters.[54]

One area offered better odds of independence and advancement. The West was born as public education was expanding in the nation at large, and the new country followed suit. Lots of schools were needed where much of the population was scattered over large areas—the majority of western states and territories in 1870 and 1880 had more schools per capita than the rest of the nation—and the demand for teachers also kept the salaries higher than average. Because men often had better-paying options, and because teaching was seen as an extension of childrearing, most teachers were women. State and territorial governments promoted the profession with normal schools—California and Oregon each had four—and in time women rose to the highest positions in the educational systems.[55] Nearly seven thousand women in fifteen western states and territories found work as teachers in 1870. As always, realities on the ground varied. In Oregon and Washington, settled heavily by families from the Midwest, about 1 in 5 working women was a teacher. In the male-heavy mining country of Idaho and Montana, it was 1 in 10. In New Mexico, where the Hispano population distrusted public education, it was 1 in 250. Arizona's census didn't have a one.[56]

In one more way women worked by taking on a wifely role—sexual in this case, as prostitutes.[57] Perhaps fifty thousand western sex workers, a rough guess, were found in every sort of setting but, predictably, most commonly where men most outnumbered women. Of all women fifteen and older on the Comstock Lode in 1870, there was one sex worker for every nine women keeping house, and nine sex workers for every schoolmistress.[58] They were grouped into classes. Those up top worked in brothels, a few quite finely fitted. Ida Hamilton's plush Hall of Mirrors, a two-story brick bordello in Cheyenne, opened with engraved invitations to many of the town's leading men.[59] Most, however, were essentially rooming houses with rapidly revolving tenants. A step down were sex workers in cribs, small shacks behind brothels or set apart in shadier neighborhoods. Although not all women in saloons and dance halls were in the business, some took customers to adjacent rooms for a fee. At the bottom were streetwalkers, who serviced clients in some dark spot or, more often, in a hotel room. A soldier at Utah's Fort Douglas recalled one who used a pigpen as a bedroom for weeks at a time. Where any one fit in the order depended on age and appearance. Most were between fifteen and thirty. A customer at a brothel in Atchison, Kansas, could have chosen among six between 15 and 19, five up to 29, and one 59.[60]

Even more transient than other westerners and often changing their names, sex workers left little to tell of their lives, only what can be gleaned from public records and the often lurid and romanticized impressions of others. Most apparently were single, divorced, or widowed, but a surprising number were married with children.[61] The most careful study suggests that most came from rural backgrounds of poverty and hard labor (and, if contemporary research is a guide, of sexual abuse). Perhaps they saw in the sex trade a life no more demanding, and possibly more lucrative, than what they had known. Some were Hispanic or Indian, but most had come into the West from elsewhere. How that came about—already in the trade and looking for a better market; suddenly desperate after divorced, abandoned, or widowed; or lured and duped in some nefarious network—remains, like most of their lives, in the shadows.[62]

By timing, acumen, and luck, some managed to become madams and found a measure of prosperity and security, but the lives of most were bleak.[63] No firm estimates are possible, but to pay for rent, bribes, and general upkeep a working girl would have to labor athletically just to keep even. If in a crib, charging a common rate of a half dollar per customer, she would manage what one called a "decent living" only by servicing ten men a day, six days a week.[64] In the process the women faced violence from tricks, pimps, and other women in the business, as well as frequent theft, venereal diseases, and unwanted pregnancies often answered with crudely performed abortions. A crib-lined backstreet in Leadville, Colorado, was called Stillborn Alley. Drug addiction was common, and for many it was a final departure from the trade. Alfred Doten, he of the 526 OKs with Mrs. Morton, wrote one evening: "Little Ida, that I used to [word erased] some 2 yrs ago was found dead in her bed at the 'Bow Windows.'" The thirty-two-year-old had lately taken to opium, and one of her customers awoke with her corpse next to him.[65]

The class layering of sex workers mirrored that of women generally. As others were spending waking hours washing, mending, cooking, and sewing for their families and male solitaires, Rachael Haskell in Aurora, Nevada, told her diary of "comfortable and cozy" evenings in her family's book-lined sitting room fitted with easy chairs and piano, and Elizabeth Fisk, wife of an editor and politician, oversaw her children's play, schoolwork, and recitations in their four bedroom house in Helena, Montana.[66] Such families had teams of servants. Those for Priscilla Hamill, wife of a British mining investor, lived in granite quarters behind her Victorian mansion in the Colorado silver town of Georgetown. In the grand house, including its solarium with a large fountain, they mopped its maple floors and dusted its gilded doorknobs and diamond-dust mirrors. Out back, marking the line between classes, was a gingerbread-trimmed two-entrance six-seater outhouse. The family sat on walnut, the help on pine.[67]

Whatever else the West did and did not offer women, its legal structures offered somewhat greater opportunity. Single women had an option unavailable before the Civil War—homesteading.[68] The law was gender-irrelevant. Any person who was a head of a family or who had reached twenty-one could file (as could any noncitizen, male or female, intending to become a citizen). Homesteading was available in several eastern states, but the amount of land available out West opened far greater possibilities. The acreage eventually proved up in Colorado alone was nearly 1,500 times that in Ohio, Indiana, and Illinois combined. Women seem to have made about one out of every ten claims on the central and northern plains and received their final patents at about the same rate as men.[69]

On their face, the numbers appear to show a remarkable stride toward female independence, and a generation or so ahead, with the celebration of the "new woman" around and after World War I, a flurry of memoirs of women home-steaders told of an irresistible independence and freedom. "Nothing could make me go back," one wrote: "I love it." Others boasted of "riotous health," economic security, and gravitas in local affairs.[70] The best-known example was Elinore Pruitt Stewart, who preached that "tired, worried" women in the East would find out west a sense of pride and full dinner tables inside their own warm and comfortable homes. They need only take the leap and take up a claim.[71]

The facts are muddier, as they are with everything to do with homesteading. A single woman filing a claim might simply be expanding the holdings of a father or other male relative. Some filed fully intending to marry. Elinor Pruitt wed her employer, Clyde Stewart, a week after filing a claim next to his. To keep it in the family, she later relinquished her claim to Clyde's seventy-three-year-old mother, who lived several hundred miles away.[72] Many set out to make new lives, not by working the land, but by investing in it, making minimal improvements while working nearby as milliners or teachers before selling the patented land and moving on to other ambitions. Whatever their motives, single women homesteaders usually did not fare as well as others; they brought far fewer acres under the plow than did couples and widows with children.[73] As across the opening West, the best hedge toward survival and success was to settle as a family, especially among other relatives. Westering did not so much foster individualism, as the popular images would have it, as it did familialism. From this angle the tributes to independent women homesteaders were another case of looking westward out of mythic faith in American opportunity, here refracted during years of an expanding feminism to show women finding possibilities outside the usual domestic margins.

Admitting all the messiness in figuring just what happened in homesteading, the law of May 20, 1862, birthed by expansion and the war that ended southern opposition, might well have done more than any single federal action of the era to loosen restraints on women without men and to open life paths closed before. In other ways women moving west found expanded rights and shrinking restraints. By the common law principle of coverture, a married woman lost all rights to property she brought with her, to any she acquired during the marriage, and to any income she might earn on her own. Nor could she enter into contracts without her husband's consent. Blackstone's *Commentaries* put it succinctly: "The very being or legal existence of the woman is suspended during the marriage." Coverture was facing challenges in the East, and in the West, by what one writer calls a "frontier effect," a large majority of new states and territories by 1881 gave married women control over their estates and of any independent earnings while also guaranteeing their right to engage in contracts and business.[74] Although it was not uncontested—one delegate warned that ensuring a woman's property rights would make her as unlovable as if she had "a masculine arm and a strong beard"—California's constitution adopted the Spanish Mexican principle that all real and personal property brought to her marriage remained the wife's "separate property," as did everything she acquired on her own.[75] The provision, copied exactly from that in Texas, in turn was adopted almost verbatim by Nevada, Arizona, Washington, and Idaho.[76]

Western divorce laws were generally more amenable to women than back home. The divorce rate in the West in 1870 in fact was double that of the Northeast, triple that of the deeper Southeast, and seven times that of the south Atlantic states. That could reflect women cutting loose from unhappy or violent marriages or, especially where they were a small minority, the chance to cut a better marital deal. "It is all the go here, for Ladys to leave there Husbands," wrote a Californian who left hers to hunt for a richer one: "Two out of three do it." And in fact almost exactly that portion of divorce decrees granted to husbands, 64 percent, were on grounds of desertion, although the number is misleading. If a wife should refuse to move west or, once there, to move again and again and again, the law in most states held that *she* had deserted *him*.[77] Of all California suits brought by women, on the other hand, eight in ten claimed desertion by husbands who likely drifted off in search of work and never returned or, like Edwin Bennett's father, decided to pick up and go one too many times. When he announced that the family would be leaving Creede, Colorado, the ninth move in the young boy's lifetime, his wife demurred. "Ernest," she told him, "you can move on if you have to, but I've dragged two boys and a houseful of furniture just as far as I'm going to. . . . Right here I'm going to stay."[78]

Whatever new opportunities and challenges women found in the West, they were always in an unsteady balance with the strong pull of custom and tradition. The grip could be seen most clearly in what sits at the center of every society, the family. Tradition could be a comfort, as with the solace of religion and letters from home, but it could also be a cage. Flora Hunter was in her twenties when she moved with husband Lyle and infant daughter Berna to a homestead in western Nebraska in 1879. They came with little money and no livestock and lived in a dugout, a hole carved into the side of a hill with a sod extension on its front. She had few neighbors and little contact with them. She wrote home of the "awful silence" when left often alone as Lyle searched for work elsewhere: "Would you think you could be so lonesome it could make you sick?" With little to eat but turnips and boiled wheat, Flora had trouble nursing ("Berna gets tired of dry eating"), and when Berna fell badly ill she told of watching over her:

> As I sat beside my sick baby a bull snake fell [out of the ceiling] beside her on a flour sack. I killed it. A few minutes after I almost stepped on a rattlesnake by the bed in my bare feet. I killed it. An hour ago, a great long striped one darted out of the corner. I killed it. A few minutes ago an enormous bull snake got away from me and ran into the dirt [of the wall].

"I . . . have stood everything but death," she wrote five months later. She pined for home in Pennsylvania but knew it was pointless. "Lyle . . . has told me from the first that I never could take Berna back, and that alone is enough to keep me here. . . . So you see there is but the one way—stay here and grub."[79]

Women of the Fringe

Three groups, Native, Hispanic, and Chinese women, are the ultimate outliers in the usual narratives, and their lives are indeed difficult to resurrect from the record. They came to the story from different backgrounds and moved through it in their own directions, yet the patterns were in many ways similar to one another, and as in western society generally their lives were an amalgam of new roles and relationships with traditions that persist and evolve.

Among Native peoples of the plains, the grass revolution opened the way to unprecedented affluence, but the results for women were mixed. A horseback hunter could kill bison at a far faster clip than a woman could skin them and process the carcass, and if the animal was taken for a robe, producing one was at least a week's labor. The resulting bottleneck both heightened the workload of women and encouraged polygyny. To add to the family workforce Blackfeet girls in the 1880s usually married around the age of twelve, four or five years before girls had a century before.[80] The Cheyennes had lived before in villages on the Missouri River, where women controlled vital economic resources of the gardens, but on the plains they lost that role and with it some status and spiritual heft. In their new lives, however, they still controlled the possessions of the household, and as the Cheyennes became more militaristic, women took on new roles. They were prime motivators, inspiring young warriors by publicly praising their successes and ridiculing their failures. By the skillful making of war shirts, shields, and other objects thought to bring protection and victory, they bestowed spiritual power on their men. A small number took active parts in warfare and some joined men's military societies.[81]

Where overwhelmed by the white invasion, Native women's lives ranged from horrific to sharply constricted. At the worst, as in California, they found themselves on a "rapists' frontier," subject to assault, sexual slavery, and forced labor as domestics.[82] Those who turned to prostitution to survive might find themselves in a double bind, risking punishment by their own, including, as in California tribes, having an eye plucked out.[83] At best some might find a marginal place in town life. Northern Paiute women in Virginia City, Nevada, collected scraps from restaurants and hired out to wash, clean, and cook in homes and hotels for a pittance of pay as well as food to take back to families camped by a mine dump. In a sense they adapted traditional roles to reduced circumstances, gathering castoff fruits and vegetables instead of pine nuts and roots. At work as domestics, they wore traditional dress and painted chin and cheeks with white, blue, and red lines.[84]

From the earliest contact, some Native women had married white men.[85] In the interior West intermarriage had played a critical role in the fur trade that was both vital to tribal economies and the opening wedge of white influence and power. By marrying into prominent families, trappers gained protection and commercial access; their wives got status and privilege. Here was what John Mack Faragher calls a "frontier of inclusion," an arrangement of cultural interpenetration and mutual benefit. Then the tables flipped. Expansion, strikes in the interior, and the full white invasion, with its families and Victorian values and racial presumptions, remade society into a "frontier of exclusion" that drew hard cultural lines and scorned any who crossed them. Men who had been well positioned through intermarriage now were "squaw men," a term that carried "a little whiff of dirty blanket and boiled dog." Now their wives were on the nether edge of the social margin, their children at best an embarrassment and their marriage bond, as the overlander Sarah Hively put it, "a shame and disgrace to our country."[86] In the California rush some white men took Native wives, or at least ongoing partners, but as with everything else, the changes there came even faster than elsewhere. A young Californian wrote home of a sudden need: a white wife, "for Squaw time is about over."[87]

On reservations Native women found their traditional roles under assault. An insistence on monogamous and patriarchal families reduced authority they had had in previous matrilineal and matrilocal systems. The government pre-empted the roles of both parents by pressing for sons and daughters to attend schools on and off reservations, where education combined the "three r's" with cultural transformation, an attempted identity hijacking. The effort was occasionally more direct. Of three orphaned Cheyennes taken after the Sand Creek Massacre, a boy was displayed on tour in a circus, a young girl soon died, and her six-year-old sister, renamed Minnehaha, was adopted by Col. Samuel F. Tappan, bitter critic of the massacre and member of a prominent abolitionist family. Cheyenne leaders begged for her return (they "wanted the children more than anything else"), but Tappan took her to Boston, where she joined the Tappans in Christian spiritualism, attending seances to consult departed Indians as spirit guides, and joined the movement to save her original people through their conversion to Christianity and white lifeways. In preparation she enrolled in Howard University, founded to raise up children of freedpeople. There, at sixteen, she died of tuberculosis.[88]

The Indians' new world had effects not so obvious. Native societies often allowed and even celebrated a gendered ambivalence. Some men dressed as women and adopted feminine behaviors, including sexual roles, and some women played masculine roles, including that of warriors, and took on wives and adopted children. Mohaves in the Southwest schooled cross-gendered women (*hwames*) in masculine roles and work, gave them masculine names upon puberty, and recognized their marriages to other women. Missionaries and the insinuation of white cultural norms changed that. Openly choosing a life different from one's sex became increasingly rare. The last known Mohave *hwame* was eventually shunned and killed as a witch.[89]

Hispanic women also found their social position eroded and their most intimate lives redefined by law and custom.[90] The Anglo presence was almost entirely male; in 1870 Hispanic women made up 98 percent of Santa Fe's female population. They continued to fill traditional roles in the workplace. In Santa Fe about two in ten Hispanic females over the age of fifteen were seamstresses, about six in ten laundresses or domestic servants. Yet a seamstress or laundress received a third less pay than the rare Anglo competitor, a domestic less than half.[91] Women better positioned might maneuver their way to influence and some wealth within the new order. The best known was Maria Gertrudis Barceló. In her Santa Fe gambling saloon Anglo traders and émigrés from before the war with Mexico were joined by the territory's new business and governmental leaders. Known as La Tules, she was sometimes described by visiting Anglos as a wanton, but in Santa Fe she was well respected. Her mastery as a monte dealer made her rich, her *sala* provided a laboratory of lifeways for newcomers, and her personal appeal and her instincts for cultural brokerage eased the passage of power after 1846.[92]

The wider picture, however, was different. Before conquest New Mexican women had enjoyed the considerable legal autonomy of the Spanish system, keeping all they brought to a marriage and earned during it. La Tules acquired and sold property, including real estate, made her own will, and loaned money, all independent of her husband. But the new regime was largely ambivalent on such rights, and only in 1901 did the territory pass a community property law. The practical effect was to leave the question to courts that decidedly favored the Anglo tradition of leaving authority with the husbands. Women of means could jockey to protect their interests, but even as more and more states in the East assured married women greater rights, and even as those rights were granted elsewhere in the West where most women were Anglo, in New Mexico, a rare case where Hispanic women predominated, the opposite happened. There a wife's previous independence under the law was effectively taken away.

The lives of Hispanic women outside the elite are mostly hidden in the historical weeds. New laws supposedly protected a woman in debt peonage from corporal punishment, but the arrangement itself was voluntary—that is, as free labor—which left female *péones* largely as vulnerable as ever to abuses. New laws and customs around marriage could also push them down in the social order. Couples without nearby clergy in the past had often lived in unions that were informal but respected, with the men providing security and economic support to the women and their families. When mining rushes brought in crowds of Anglo men, they took up the women, but not necessarily the obligations, and when Anglo women arrived in numbers, the previous Hispanic women majority was caught in the changing gears. Like Indians who had married fur traders on the eve of the onslaught, they found themselves abandoned and on society's fringe. Arizona lawmakers took things further, outlawing interracial marriage—but not miscegenation. In a striking parallel to the Southeast, an Anglo man siring children with an Indian woman, or with a Hispanic woman deemed to be one, had no legal obligation to them or her, although he often bound a son or daughter to him as an indenture.[93]

The pattern was consistent across the West. Anglo women found a range of trials and opportunities. Wherever they landed, however, and whatever lives they lived out, it was inside their own society, the one taking hold of the country. Its raw contours were ones they knew, its values familiar, and whatever their situation those contours and values placed them and their kind above the women who had lived on the land before them. Those women found themselves near or at the bottom of the economic and social order and living within a cultural structure that redefined their most intimate identities.

Much the same could be said of another group, these not native but new to the country. While women were in a minority across most of the West, among the Chinese women were something like a rare species. The ratio of all women to men in San Francisco in 1852 was 1 to 3. Among Chinese it was 1 to a 155 (19 females and 2,954 males). Twenty years later women still made up only 4.4 percent of the nation's Chinese population.[94] The reasons were cultural and, with time, increasingly political. Because Chinese men had even less intention than others to stay, they virtually never brought wives. Deeply patriarchal traditions back home insisted women remain there to serve in-laws and to maintain respectful connection to ancestors. There was fear as well that women abroad were bound for moral corruption.[95] As a consequence China had its own large community of gold rush widows. A Cantonese folk song suggested feelings that a wife in Pennsylvania or Indiana might have recognized:

> Right after we were wed, Husband, you set out on a journey.
> How was I to tell you how I felt?
> Wandering around a foreign country, when will you ever come home?
>
> . . .
>
> I only wish that you would have good fortune,
> In three years you would be home again.[96]

The gender gap stayed wide in part because hostility toward Chinese came to focus on their women. They were assumed to be mostly prostitutes, a corrupting influence on a West reaching toward respectability. When the Page Act of 1875 forbade immigration of Chinese prostitutes, women trying to immigrate faced a series of humiliating interviews about their moral fiber by the American consul and British harbormaster, another on board, yet more on arrival.

If the law's purpose was to reduce the presence of women, it succeeded, although not necessarily on the terms intended. By 1875 a maturing Chinese community was bringing wives and brides. Some came as concubines or secondary wives, accepted parts of respectable households in the old country, yet census enumerators, whether from reflex or explicit bias, listed virtually all Chinese women as prostitutes. The 1870 census recorded just under 1,500 Chinese sex workers in San Francisco. If all were indeed in the trade, they would have accommodated 60,000 men each week, six times the number of Chinese men.[97] Even with repeat clients and non-Asian customers, and considering the roughly five hundred non-Asian sex workers, such a copulative frenzy seems pretty improbable.

Without a doubt, however, most women arrivals, then and before, were sex workers.[98] Funneled out of south China through Hong Kong, they were usually bought by contracts that were resold on arrival. The price for a contract during the early years was $250 to $350, a cost the women would work off on their backs. Others were simply bought as chattel, then used until they died or were tossed aside. At the top of the business, attractive "sing song girls" provided entertainment and conversation as well as sex. Those at the bottom walked the streets or worked out of cribs or cheap brothels, "salt pork shops," in scarcely furnished rooms as small as four by six feet. San Francisco's 159 Chinese brothels in 1870 housed an average of 9 women each. A lower-class prostitute charged on average $0.38 each for 7 customers a day, 6 days a week. As degraded as the picture is, the average take would have been several times that of a common male laborer, and some were able to retire their contracts. Brothel owners made substantial profits—one with nine women might net $6,000 a year, or $115,000 in 2019 dollars.[99] Where Chinese men moved into the interior, especially in the northern Rockies, so did the sex trade. Silver City, Idaho, had 14 Chinese sex workers in 1870, the Boise basin 35, and if the census is accurate, fully 1 in 10 Chinese in Montana's Deer Lodge County was a sex worker (130 among 1,053 men).[100]

The Page Act, whatever its complex of motives, quickly strangled the already small influx of Chinese women.[101] During the first three months after the law's passage, 161 Chinese women arrived in San Francisco. The figure for the same period the next year was 15. The Chinese Exclusion Act of 1882 allowed a few months before the door was shut for virtually all Chinese, male or female. Just under 40,000 rushed in through the opening. Of them, 136 were women.[102] The ratio of sexes remained at least as wildly out of joint as ever. The ironic result was the flourishing of prostitution, the supposed target of the Page Act, among the hormonal stew of many young men and very few women. Then, in 1889, fourteen years after the law passed, the very imbalance it perpetuated was cited by the Supreme Court in upholding the Chinese Exclusion Act. Justice Stephen Field, a Californian, justified the law in part because Chinese men, living on the cheap with no families to feed, had an unbeatable edge when competing with native-born men with wives and children.[103]

The connection of the Page and Chinese Exclusion Acts was more direct than that. Never before the law of 1875 had Washington restricted the immigration of a particular ethnic group. The following year Congress appointed its special committee that made Chinese immigration a national issue, and four years later came the revised Burlingame Treaty. Two years after that Congress closed the nation's borders to Chinese.

Thus a tiny part of the West's minority of women became the indirect goad for the first federal effort to shape the nation's ethnic composition by controlling who to let in. Over the following decades the nation would follow the West's lead in becoming, continentally, more and more "the world's convention," and as it did Americans would follow as well in trying to manage the nation's human fabric by policing who would be permitted through its golden doors and golden gates.

It is always easy to miss the obvious. In sorting through its human makeup, one revelation is a defining character of the new West—its sheer energy and fluidity, movement and change of a degree that set it apart at the time and, arguably, from any time before or since. Gold and then a range of opportunities were the drivers. New systems of roads, rails, wires, steamships, mule trains and coaches were the means. The surveys, the scientific gathering and probing, and the racial ordering gave it meaning in an evolving national story and a global setting. This made the West, paradoxically, both starkly different yet reflective of America at large and its arc toward the next century.

Another obvious but easily missed point is this: just about every person, whatever their origin, was a newcomer, which meant that expansion's first consequence, a profound continental unsettling, persisted. Whether they had come from Pennsylvania or Romania, all were in some measure cut off from their pasts and so also, to some degree, were their descendants two or three generations on. Outside Indian and Hispanic peoples, the West would remain America's special place of scrambled origins and shallow roots.

The human splay had something else in common. They all worked. So did just about everybody everywhere, of course, but the particulars of that common ground reveal a lot about how the new country was becoming the West by the time of America's centennial. Rarely in modern history was such a span of land transformed so thoroughly and so rapidly. The land's repurposing was well under way before the Civil War, but after it the changes took on a terrific momentum. With the older republic preserved in the East, attention turned toward binding the full nation, coast to coast, into a whole. That process might be imagined as a single labor, and as it unfolded the West was worked into existence.

PART 3 ➤ Worked into Being

In April 1880 young New Englander Clarence Mayo was working on a ranch in northeastern New Mexico, funded by a family friend in his search for a future in the opening West. He was restless. Too many people, he thought. He had heard good things about Wyoming, so on April 27 he set out by rail to Cheyenne, then west to Rock Springs, where he headed north and east by stage on May 5. Three days and two hundred miles later he wrote his parents from Crazy Woman Creek, disappointed again: too many cattle on the way. Now soured on ranching, he learned that "there are some good things about wheat farming," so it was back through Rock Springs and then by rail to Saint Paul. His bankroller had recently bought land in Dakota Territory, west of Fargo, and Mayo wrote next from there, confident of success (not wheat now but potatoes) by cultivating land "as level as a floor and black and rich as a manure heap." It took him a full eight days to discover that plains farming had three serious drawbacks. It required machinery he could not afford; it was very hard work; there were lots of mosquitoes. "Now is the time to go to Montana," he wrote home, his interest in the cattle business suddenly revived. On July 14 he headed west.

A month of silence followed. On August 15 he wrote his mother of making it as far as Bismarck before switching course. Word was that Montana was badly overdone—once again too many people and cattle—and besides he heard that its winters were awfully rough, so he had turned south and now was in the mining town of Saguache at the top of Colorado's San Luis valley. "Are you surprised?" he asked his mother. She probably wasn't, nor by his letter of September 9 and its menu of possible career paths: a hardware merchant, a grocer, raising hay, raising sheep, raising oats, raising mules. None, however, seemed to fit, and on October 3 he wrote to announce the final decision for his life's calling. He had founded the Saguache brass band. He would be a professional musician.[1]

Mayo's occupational browsing was a measure of how thoroughly the lefthand side of the national map had been reworked, and by that utterly remade, during the three decades before 1880. A young man heading west in 1848 could have chosen from a handful of lines of work in a few spots in the country's expanse— farming in Oregon's Willamette Valley or on Sutter's land, working wharves in

San Francisco, modest merchandising in New Mexico, various tasks in Utah if he were a Mormon, or soldiering in some out-of-the-way post. In 1880 he could have picked from a smorgasbord of opportunities well beyond those of Mayo's wandering attention.

As historian Richard White has reminded us, work has been the primary means by which people have involved themselves with the world.[2] Anyone looking for a vivid example could do worse than looking back on the creation of the American West. It was born as half of the contiguous United States was made over and applied to new needs by new muscling, all of it tied together in laboring kinship and bound into a common marketplace with the nation and the world. That in turn was inseparable from the national reconstruction during the thirty or so years after expansion and the discovery of gold that set it all into hyperdrive.

California's telescoped development after the great coincidence was repeated in varied, evolving patterns. Ranchers showed up around mining towns and in country newly cleared of Indian peoples after white hunters slaughtered bison and shipped their green hides to eastern tanneries. All new developments relied on Kansas homesteads, irrigated fields in Utah, Arizona, and Colorado, mega-farms in California, and the machine-heavy, mosquito-ridden ones that Mayo found in the Dakotas. Mining rushes brought their blooms of population to isolated spots and stimulated ranching, farming, lumbering, new foundries, and machine works. It was all knit together by the rails and roads that Mayo used to travel nearly four thousand miles before ending up about two hundred miles from where he'd started. He was part of a floating labor force able to flit from job to job across the West and beyond. Ernest Ingersoll found that "you can hardly enter into a conversation with a working-man who cannot give you some account of every settled district west of the Rocky Mountains, often including the Sandwich Islands, Australia, and the Chinese ports."[3]

Workers passed through towns and cities that fed and financed the work in and around them, hosted seats of government, and provided the basics of cultural life. Had Mayo not stopped at Rock Springs but kept going and stayed awhile in Ogden, Utah, he could have chosen among four hotels, refreshed his wardrobe at one of seven tailors, browsed among many eateries, and afterward lounged among ten saloons, smoking a cigar bought at one of two tobacco-nists. Had he felt poorly there were fifteen physicians to consult, and had things gone badly, there were two undertakers.[4] The new laboring had a major role in pressing forward the West's vigorous work in global science, in particular in the questions raised by new development—how to work the land in new ways, how to respond to plagues of insects and animals' lethal diseases, and more. The answers turned out to speak to the mechanics of the earth as a single organism, to basic causes of human suffering, and even to the spread of modern empires.

Reworking the land was always a work of conquest. In its broadest sense work is the act of people applying their energy to the world around them in order to get a surplus of energy back. A hunter assumes that the calories he spends stalking, killing, and butchering a deer will be nicely offset by the calories he gains when he eats it. That basic principle applied to Nebraska homesteaders, cattlemen and cowboys, miners and mine owners. But tapping into the land's energy through plowing or herding or tunneling meant redirecting it away from those who were using it to hunt or gather their own crops. Farmers, ranchers, and miners did not intend to cut the legs from under Native economies, but they were doing exactly that, and in the process they were knocking the props from under the entire cultural apparatus the other work had supported—structures of authority, religions, understandings of the world.

New workways in turn became the ground for new cultural elaborations. Starting with the first explorers, all newcomers were projecting and implanting their own visions of the new country. Sweaty overlanders brought Bibles and ingrained ideas about how families operated. Everyone after them, cowboys and gravediggers, homemakers, stevedores, and laundresses, at some remove were nourishing religious cosmologies, legal institutions, and teatime niceties and were cultivating productions of Shakespeare and Marlowe and performances of the Saguache brass band, Clarence Mayo on the cornet.

16 ▷ Cattle and the New America

For many people across the world, the cowboy *is* the American West. His imagined virtues sum up the region's best qualities, his work seems the essence of frontier skills and self-reliance, and his supposed hard-living ways embody the West's rough, appealing edge. The cowboy's notoriety came late, only as episodes associated with him—the cattle drives and the beginning and rise of plains ranching—were over or coming to an end, but during the twentieth century he became the preeminent figure in Westerns, the distillations of the region's evolving mythic meanings that had begun to take form with expansion. The cowboy of celluloid and pulp paperbacks, the lone rider and habitué of saloons, has been a great boon to global amusement.

But for history, not so much. The mythic cowpuncher has blinkered our understanding of one of the most revealing episodes of its age. He is usually pictured as facing challenges alone or with a few companions (and their horses) in a setting, generally the plains or Southwest, with little sense of connection to anywhere else. The lens's perspective is close in, tight. The cattle industry, however, can be truly seen only with the lens opened to the widest aperture. It was above all relational, a prime illustration of how the West was being sewn into a larger national and global framework. No enterprise showed more clearly the traits and forces transforming American business. None offers a more striking example of the era's volatility—a modern industry born, evolved, and poleaxed inside of thirty years.[1]

Pacific Beginnings

California's story again was an anticipation. From early in the gold rush through the Civil War years, ranching there expanded and evolved much as it would elsewhere after 1865. It also suffered, foundered, and managed to persist through troubles that would later plague the industry from Mexico to Montana.

Spanish cattle came into Southern California with the first missions established in the late eighteenth century. There they found a climate and generous grasslands near perfectly suited to their needs. As horses had spread and multiplied through the interior West during the previous century, these first herds expanded at an astounding clip. In 1773 five missions had 205 head. Thirty-two years later there were about 95,000.[2] The multiplying grazers were agents of Native disaster. Their spreading numbers and their devouring of indigenous grasses and disruption of habitats undermined the economies of local Indians and helped drive them into the missions, where they suffered further from cultural assaults and devastating contact diseases.[3] With secularization of the missions in the early 1830s, control of animals shifted to masters of large ranchos, an economic and social elite of Californios, the Spanish-speaking and California-born members of long-tailed families. The trade was much less in meat, which quickly saturated local markets and could not be practically sent to distant ones, than with the more easily shipped cattle hides and tallow made from hooves, horns, and body fat. Income went largely to support a self-contained, closely knit cultural order of interlocking Californio families joined, by the 1830s, by Anglo émigrés.

The eruption of population to the north undid this old order. A cow's main value instantly shifted from its hide to the meat inside of it. Reports of cattle sold in Sacramento for $500 a head were surely cousins to tall stories of men sitting guard on 500-pound nuggets and offering $10,000 for a plate of beans, but verifiable prices of up to $75 would produce prodigious profits. Over the next few years tens of thousands of cattle were driven as much as 400 miles from the southern *ranchos* and slaughtered in the diggings. Still more came from the Midwest, upper South, and Texas on drives considerably longer than the more famous ones out of Texas after the Civil War. One left San Antonio in early June and, after dipping into northern Mexico, arrived in Southern California five months later. Gov. John Bigler estimated that at least 62,000 head arrived from the East in 1853 alone.[4]

Meanwhile, the center of California ranching moved steadily northward, drawn by growing demand and driven by a severe drought in the south. By the eve of the Civil War four out of ten head grazed in the Central Valley, and even with the hearty consumption, the cattle population ballooned. A dozen years after the rush California's three hundred thousand head had increased tenfold.[5] Then the boom busted, the work of both Adam Smith's invisible hand and nature's clenched fist. The spectacular surge in cattle began to match demand just as the increase in hungry humans started to slacken. When prices peaked around 1856 cattlemen responded by playing the market, waiting to sell until late in the season in hopes of catching a late upswing, but a special census at the end of the decade found the supply far above demand and the cattle business "profitless and ruinous."[6] Many cattlemen now held their herds off market for the entire season; by one estimate one animal out of three went unslaughtered.[7] The result was to pump the numbers still higher, which pushed prices still lower, which edged cattlemen still closer to disaster.

By then the essential resources of the industry were under considerable stress. A close study suggests that California could have supported up to eighteen million cattle.[8] That, however, would have depended on careful management and relatively stable conditions. Instead the changes in the range environment were at least as tumultuous as others across the region. Herds expanded into new grasslands and crowded too tightly into old ones. Ranchers from the East arrived with practices at odds with the new setting. California gets most of its rain in the winter, eastern states in the summer, and grasses in both regions had adapted accordingly, so a cattleman from Illinois or Texas was likely to pasture his animals according to a grazing cycle essentially opposite to what the land called for.[9] Disruption and overgrazing led to a massive invasion from outside grasses and forbs. Some new species, bur clover, wild oats, and a few others, fed cattle well, but others much less. The introduction of hundreds of thousands of sheep deepened the melancholy trend.[10]

Then, from 1861 through 1864, two dramatic swings of weather dealt the cattle business a terrific blow. First, heavy rains from late 1861 through the following spring brought massive flooding through most of the state. Houses, horses, and pianos floated down Sacramento's main streets when its levee breached. "*The tops of the [telegraph] poles are under water!*" a diarist wrote.[11] In the Central Valley farmhouses were beaten apart by wind-whipped waves. To the south tens of thousands of cattle drowned—estimates for the whole state ran as high as two hundred thousand dead. In the spring the soaked pastures came up greener and lusher than any could recall, but it was a tease.[12] A two-year drought parched the whole state but especially the centers of cattle raising, the San Joaquin Valley and among the ranchos of Southern California. In June 1864 William H. Brewer of the state geological survey counted three hundred cattle dead beside a "miserable water hole" and around Los Angeles reported that the few surviving cattle "appear like skeletons" searching for sustenance around hills and plains as hard as baked brick.[13] Owners tried to shed their cattle at plummeting prices and even reverted to the old economy of hides and tallow, but even so there were few takers. By one report five thousand cattle were sold in Santa Barbara at thirty-seven cents apiece. "We poor Rancheros have had a damned bad string of luck," wrote one large landowner: "I don't know what will become of us."[14]

In fact the fate of that old order was already sealed. The 1870 census showed under twenty thousand head in Los Angeles County, a drop of 70 percent from 1860. Many large ranchos, "stately but leaky economic vessels," went deeper into debt during the boom, usually at usurious interest. Earlier obligations had been through informal personal networks, but the new arrangements were rigid and unforgiving, and when market forces and natural calamities turned on the rancheros they lost everything.[15] Beyond the economic battering, these years were psychologically devastating, dimming the shine of both boom-time fantasies and traditional lifeways. Southern California moved toward a more diversified economy that mixed some ranching with farming, vineyards, orchards, and sheepherding.

California ranching, however, was far from finished. As the Central Valley south and east of San Francisco emerged as the center of the business, eight of the ten largest ranches in the state were owned by those outside the old California elite. Increasingly they stocked their lands with midwestern breeds, first purebred shorthorns, then Devons, Jerseys, Ayrshires, Holsteins and, by 1878, Herefords that interbred with resident Mexican cattle to produce a distinctive sort, "American." In that, and in their economic strategies and the relations they forged with the environment, the new white majority foretold the story of ranching across the West over the next twenty years.[16]

The prime case was the firm of Henry Miller and Charles Lux, which within a generation emerged as one of the West's most powerful and economically sophisticated enterprises.[17] The German-born Miller and Lux both made their way to California after working as butchers in New York City. Their first common venture, butchering and selling 1,600 Texas cattle in 1854, matured into a decades-long partnership.[18] The socially adept Lux lived on ultra-fashionable Nob Hill, moved among the city's tycoons and leading politicos, and married prominently. Miller married Lux's sister-in-law, then his niece. As Lux greased the financial and legal skids in the city, the rough-edged Miller, described by John Clay as "a nervous little German who possessed some fairy's wand" that turned whatever he touched into gold, preferred living and running operations in the Central Valley.[19]

The partners made their fortunes by consolidating space, function, and capital. They linked city and countryside most obviously by selling San Franciscans slaughtered beef raised on interior grasslands; they drew on capital that pooled in the bay city as it emerged as the hub of a huge western and Pacific market; they deployed its legal establishment to expand their power and reach. In the process they re-engineered the region's ecologies. They bought and used some of the San Joaquin Valley for raising their cattle, some to fatten them, and some close to the city to hold them to time their arrival for the best price on the streets. To adapt to normal cycles and to hedge against drought, they bought summertime pastures in the hills and developed extensive haying operations. They acquired sections along the San Joaquin River and fenced them off to squeeze out competitors. One fence ran forty-five miles. To expand on that they helped to build and later wholly controlled the largest irrigation system on the Pacific coast.

The became masters in the land monopolization begun in the 1850s. They stepped in during the disasters of 1861–64 to buy land and cattle on the cheap from the old elite, eventually acquiring a quarter million acres of former ranchos, and they added another 120,000 acres by boodling from swamp, school, and agricultural college grants.[20] In this they had a hand in the continuing deterioration Native life. The close of the missions in the 1830s had offered Indians a measure of opportunity in the hide and tallow trade, but the new definitions of property and new economic regimes pushed them to the margins and beyond.[21] Some worked as vaqueros. Miller and Lux hired them among their more than a thousand workers who included Mexicans, Portuguese, Chinese, and Italians assigned to specialized niches to create a fluid compartmentalized labor force that kept wages low and inhibited strikes.

It all coalesced into a hallmark of the age. Miller and Lux was an early case of industries that expanded in terms of raw space and yet, in practical terms, compressed distances by integrating scattered resources and functions under a single command. Cattle were driven more than two hundred miles to San Francisco via exclusive trails and feedlots where cattle were fattened and held in coordination with marketers. In San Francisco's Butchertown the firm had its own slaughtering plant, the largest west of Chicago. By the 1880s more than eighty-three thousand cattle, pigs, and sheep annually were divided into marketable parts that were sent out for sale in scores of shops, many of them owned or controlled by Miller and Lux. In one arrangement covering thousands of square miles, resources—vegetal, liquid, carnal—were brought together, channeled, processed, and distributed, all of it in a single flow, virtually from pasture to skillet.

The rise and expansion of sheep ranching roughly mimicked that of cattle.[22] Just as ranchers had driven cattle from Texas to the gold fields, so others did with sheep from New Mexico to California, where their number grew until the state was second only to Ohio in its number of sheep. As also with cattle, sheep ranching expanded first into eastern Oregon, and in the 1870s California and Oregon sheep raisers began sending their animals eastward in response to droughts at home and opportunities in the interior. Between 1877 and 1880 about three hundred thousand made their way out, some along a southern route to Arizona, New Mexico, and even Texas and more via trails to the north to Nevada, Idaho, and Montana.[23] Sheep ranching took hold especially in the

Great Basin and on the northern plains, where the business would expand dramatically later in the century. The industry played its role in the West's human diversity by drawing especially Basques and immigrants from the Azores.[24]

The expansion of California ranching ran parallel to more familiar events after the Civil War in the Great Plains and Southwest. It is there, where cowboys of popular culture strut their stuff, that the usual histories mark the birth of modern ranching. And yet everything seen there, every trait that would appear on the famous ranches from the Texas coast to Montana, could have been found on the far side of the continent years before the first cattle drives to Abilene. More broadly, firms like Miller and Lux in the 1850s exhibited most traits, from vertical and horizontal integration to new technologies and muscular capitalization, typical of the nation's emerging industrial order during the Gilded Age.

Beefsteak and the Marriage of Regions

As in California, the plains cattle industry was born from a classic match of demand and supply. At the end of the Civil War the northeastern quadrant of the United States was hungry for beef and was getting hungrier. Americans have always been enthusiastic carnivores. From colonial times they had dined on mutton, fish, chicken, and a variety of game, flying and furred, but beef was considered particularly toothsome, with steak "the symbolic pinnacle of American meat." Practical matters, however, put a brake on its consumption.[25] Most families lived on farms and did their own slaughtering. A cow was cumbersome to butcher, and the excess beyond a few fresh meals was unappealing when cured. Pigs were easier to slaughter and, once disassembled, were perfectly palatable when smoked or salted.

Then, in the mid-nineteenth century, developments encouraged a steady rise in beef consumption. Growing cities were a natural market for fresh, uncured beef, as San Francisco proved in the 1850s. During the war enormous numbers of cattle were shipped and trailed to the field to feed Union troops. Expanded stockyards provided centralized sites where cattle were gathered before being processed by new technologies, including the tin can and the earliest can openers, and dispatched over ever-wider regions. By the latter years of the century middling families might eat beef at every meal—fried, baked, boiled, corned, chopped, and stewed, and served with tripe soup and pickled tongues on the side.

In 1865, however, beef was in short supply where it was most desired. Feeding Union armies and "the waste of the war" had reduced the number of cattle by 7 percent nationwide since 1860 (and pigs by nearly 22 percent), the commissioner of agriculture reported. Losses were especially heavy in midwestern states that had been the main suppliers and, even worse, in the South, which closed off the option of finding cattle there to take up the slack.[26] The price of northern cattle consequently soared. In 1866 it was more than 200 percent higher than before the war. The next year a typical cow sold for nearly forty dollars in New York and nearly forty-five in Massachusetts. Swine prices were just as high.[27]

There was a crucial difference between meeting demands for the two animals, however. Pig raising remained largely decentralized. Pigs required relatively little space, so thousands of farmers could devote bits of property to them even though land prices were rising steeply. Moving them to some central location for slaughter was impractical. Fatter, squattier, smarter, and crankier than cattle, pigs resisted herding and did not travel well. Instead, around November, as the weather turned cold enough to slow the meat's corruption, farmers slaughtered their own pigs or drove them a short way to some slapdash facility. By the 1850s the first pork-packing centers had appeared—Cincinnati was exporting seventy million pounds annually on the eve of the Civil War—where salted pork and bacon were crammed into barrels and hams and roasts readied for the tables of the elite.[28] From those hubs the various forms of transformed pigs traveled by boat, wagon, and rail to markets across the Northeast and even the South.

As those final steps were being centralized, however, production and the initial processing of pigs remained fragmented and dispersed, which was fine with consumers who sat happily down to meals of smoked and salted pork. The upshot was that the search for more pork remained where it had been, in the Midwest. The paradox of the pig was that customers assumed their pork would be raised and slaughtered at some unknown site far from their tables— just how far away made little difference—but practical economics kept the raising and slaughtering within the region, relatively close at hand.

That was in stark contrast to the situation for beef. Because there was no palatable means of preserving it, customers insisted that every cow be slaughtered nearby so they could buy their beef fresh. That arrangement was increasingly impractical. Grazing cattle required a lot of room, and as land in the northeastern quadrant rose in its price and its load of taxes, the devotion of large sweeps to pasture became a losing proposition. The result was to shift the search for pasture farther away, where cheaper land made grazing profitable. That, however, raised the question of how to move cattle from there to spots near customers so beef could be sold fresh.[29] The paradox of the cow was that consumers expected their beef to be butchered close at hand, while economics was pushing the cattle farther and farther away.

Out of this peculiar combination of mass preference, shifting land values, creaturely attributes, and the technology of slaughter, the pressure was on to devise a new system for raising and marketing this familiar domestic animal, the cow. An answer was quickly found. The results and implications went far beyond putting more beef on tables, however. How the cattle business was restructured showed how regions might be connected in new and dynamic ways and how such new economic arrangements were binding the West into existence.

It was common knowledge that plenty of cattle were available. They were in southern and central Texas and northern Mexico, more than a thousand crow-flying, cow-walking miles southwest of Chicago and 1,500 from New York. The 1860 census showed three and half million head in Texas; a leading authority placed the figure at a million more than that.[30] The situation was precisely the opposite from the Northeast's. In New York and Ohio there were two persons for every cow, in Massachusetts seven persons. In Texas there were about four cows per person, and where cattle were concentrated, along parts of the southern coast, they outnumbered humans by forty to one.[31] An animal that would bring $40–$45 in the Northeast could be had for $5 in Texas markets and a dollar or two on the range. "Then dawned a time in Texas," a contemporary wrote, "that a man's poverty was estimated by the number of cattle he possessed."[32]

The problem was connecting that supply with northeastern demand. Cattle could be driven to New Orleans then shipped up the Mississippi by steamboat, but the cost in money and wear on the animals was considerable. Another option was to drive cattle to the nearest rail connection, which in 1866 was at Sedalia, Missouri, but the route took them through wooded, hilly, rough terrain and across parts of eastern Kansas, northwestern Arkansas, and southwestern Missouri that in these years were violent and bandit-ridden to the edge of anarchy. The drives also brought along with them a mysterious malady, dubbed "Texas fever," that devastated any northern herds they mingled with.

Looking back, the answer seems obvious. By 1867 railroads were building out onto the plains from the Missouri Valley. Why not drive cattle directly north out of Texas to the nearest terminus in Kansas or Nebraska? Such drives would have to cross Indian Territory, but land north and south of the territory was largely open and unsettled and with plenty of grass and reasonable water. From Kansas and Nebraska cattle could be sent eastward to be fattened in Iowa and Illinois and then on to slaughter. The Union Pacific's Eastern Division (later the Kansas Pacific) had reached the ninety-eighth meridian by the summer of 1867 on the way to Denver, and an Illinois farmer and stock-raiser, Joseph G. McCoy, reasoned that Texas cattle could be plugged in to the eastern system through Kansas City to Chicago. Most rail officials dismissed him, as he recalled, as a fool with an idea as his only asset, but he finally secured connections, and for a loading point he paid $2,400 for land adjoining Abilene,

Kansas, a "small, dead place" of a dozen dirt-roofed hovels and few businesses, including a saloon whose owner sold prairie dogs to eastern visitors.[33] For two months McCoy oversaw the installation of scales and the construction of penning and loading facilities and a hotel.

All he needed now were cattle. McCoy sent out flyers and dispatched another Illinoisan as a roaming agent to meet herds bumping uncertainly around southern Kansas and Indian Territory for want of a destination. Doubtful, but with few alternatives, drovers shifted their eyes to Abilene. Equally dubious rail officials waited until thousands of cattle had arrived before building a switch and siding for cars. On September 5, 1867, the first twenty cars loaded with Texas cattle left for Chicago, and by the end of the season more than a thousand cars had rolled off eastward. McCoy estimated the number of cattle driven to Abilene that summer at thirty-five thousand. Profits were modest, but most owners made money. They would make more as this slapped-together arrangement was refined and expanded.

In his classic *The Great Plains*, Walter Prescott Webb explained Abilene in terms of postwar Reconstruction. Northern and southern businessmen found in this dusty Kansas burg a rare common ground in the bitter shadow of war, he wrote, and in its saloons the working stiffs of the two regions, "rough characters of the plain and of the forest," came together over the common cup. "Who can say that Abilene was less significant than Appomattox?" Webb asked.[34] Abilene, however, was more than a touching point of Union-Confederate rowdiness and reconciliation. As earlier in California, when ranchers repositioned the state's ecology, Abilene was part of a far wider process that reshaped the essential nature of one of the earth's greatest grasslands, and by that it bound East and West as much as reconciling Southeast and Northeast.

A good portion of the Great Plains was both valuable and essentially free. That around Abilene McCoy described as "entirely unsettled, well watered, excellent grass, and . . . adapted to holding cattle." It was of course very well settled by Indian peoples, and the ranches would be their final unsettling, but from the white developmental perspective, with the Kansas prewar rush well to the east, his view was true enough. Much of the land was public domain that advancing railroads would link to parts of the Midwest nicely suited to transforming for market what western grass made incarnate, beef on the hoof. Like Miller and Lux, McCoy grasped how complementary needs might be united, here by combining older and newer means of movement. By moving to the right place at the right moment, he accomplished the linkage in a matter of weeks. At Abilene, that "small, dead place," West and East clicked together, as a tab into a slot.

The bawling cattle crammed into those first twenty cars marked the first of two phases in the birth of the midcontinental cattle industry. It centered on the cattle drive, a practice with roots deep in the British Isles and Spain. Before the war there were drives to New Orleans, California, and a few to the Midwest. A thousand head made it all the way to Ohio.[35] Now they pointed north along several routes to plains railheads. On the earliest and most famous, several feeders braided together into a trail to Abilene and then to Wichita named for Jesse Chisholm, a half-Cherokee, half-Scot trader and interpreter. In 1872 the terminus of cattle drives began shifting westward, first to Ellsworth, Kansas (also on the Kansas Pacific), then to Dodge City, Kansas (on the Atchison, Topeka and Santa Fe), and Ogallala, Nebraska (on the Union Pacific). The Western Trail, running parallel to and a couple of hundred miles west of the Chisholm, fed Dodge City and Ogallala.[36] All passed through some part of Indian Territory, where tribes posed no danger except to tight budgets. Recently removed tribes levied tolls and taxes and required herds to remain on clearly delineated trails. The Cherokees in 1867 charged a dime per head (cut by half in 1871), the Creeks 27.5 cents per head, plus a quarter each for any that stopped long to graze. This led some drovers to bend the routes westward through lands of Cheyennes, Arapahos, and other Plains tribes, where tolls were lower and collection more sporadic.[37]

Between 1868 and 1872, the number of cattle driven to Abilene first doubled, then quadrupled, then doubled again for a total of more than a million and a half head. Over the next three years another million trudged to Wichita and Ellsworth, then at least a million more to Dodge City and other termini. Other tens of thousands traveled to markets in New Mexico and Colorado along the Goodnight-Loving and other trails.[38]

Cattle drives rose out of what the historical geographer Terry Jordan calls ranching's "hearth," the coastal prairie from the Louisiana border to southern Texas.[39] There two traditions of ranching techniques, tools, and language had met and melded. One, essentially Celtic, came from the Carolinas and deep South, and the other, Hispanic, from the Tamaulipas region of northern Mexico. Prelude to a drive was a spring roundup, a collective wild cow hunt by several ranchers over several thousand acres of mesquite and cactus where, a veteran recalled, "everything that grows has thorns on it except the willows."[40] Calves were branded, mavericks (unbranded adults and calves without mothers) were assigned to owners, and most males were castrated to control population and to breed selectively. A portion of animals were chosen for the drive north. The cattle themselves were a stroke of adaptive luck. Known collectively as "longhorns," they were a mix of Spanish and southern breeds.

In design a longhorn was a kind of anti-pig. It had the opposite of every trait that made porkers unsuitable for travel. It carried its weight high on a thinnish body that tapered to slim flanks. It might better have been called a longleg. With an easy shambling stride, its great hammerhead lolling in front, it moved with an unlikely grace. Longhorns were near wild. A writer for the for the *American Agriculturalist* thought them defined by their "long horns, fierce and savage looks, and their apparent dislike of mankind." But they had the supreme advantage of surviving the trek with most of their original weight, delivering maximum pounds and profit at the end of the long walk.

Herds of between one thousand and three thousand animals took off from mid-spring to early summer. A crew consisted of a trail boss, eight or so horse-back workers, called "drovers," a cook, and a wrangler charged with handling a considerable herd of horses—at least three or four were needed for every drover. The boss got a hundred dollars a month, the rest about a dollar a day. In time the business drew from both Texas and the thousands of young men floating westward after the war, Minnesota farm boys, newly arrived Irish and Germans, and Bostonians in derbies.[41] Some African Americans and Mexican Americans rode with the herds, but prejudice seems to have kept most of them in south and central Texas.[42] A drive's first days were crucial. A few tested drovers were needed to establish control over the uncivil animals. If handled properly and kept firmly in a daily pattern, however, a herd turned habitual, and with luck a trip was blessedly uneventful, ending with losses countable on one or two hands.

The workday began with breakfast at four or five and by full daylight the herd was on the move. Cattle were strung out a mile or so in a thin column, four or five abreast, widening somewhat from front to rear so the shape resembled a tornado with its stinger to the fore. Drovers at front rode "point" and farther back "swing" and "flank." Those riding "drag" at the rear ate the dirt kicked up by ten thousand hooves and ended the day with dust on eyebrows and mustaches "as thick as fur."[43] After a midday break, a long afternoon drive would bring the herd to its bed ground, chosen for adequate water and grass. After supper, around eight or nine, each hand would spend two hours of the short night in the saddle in watch over the (hopefully) sleeping animals, then pass the rest rolled in a blanket, fully clothed except for boots and hat. A day's drive covered usually twelve to fifteen miles.

A cattle drive would be among the most romanticized episodes of the day, but the rare firsthand accounts, as in one diary, tell a different story: "Wet cold morning," "These are dark days for me," "Lots of trouble," "Everything discouraging," "nothing to eat," "Almost starved not having had a bite for 60 hours,"

"Am not homesick but heart sick," and "Have *not* got the *Blues* but am in a *Hel of a fix*."[44] There were some dangers—falling from a horse while crossing a river, caught under the flailing hooves of swimming cattle, rarely turned out well— but stampedes were more irritant than danger. Coming typically at night they deprived men of precious sleep and left them spending a day or more retrieving any scattered animals. A strong approaching nighttime storm increased the odds. The air turned still and humid, almost palpable, and electricity might shimmer on the animals' horns and roll as pea-sized balls of light on a rider's hat brim. The first sizzle and thunderclap, or any sharp noise, could have the restless herd up and running. That imminence made a prominent part of cowboy folklore, singing in the saddle at night, an important drovers' tool. Some trail songs were mutated transplants, some born of the day:

> Come all you Texas cow-boys
> And warning take of me
> And do not go to Montana
> To spend your money free.[45]

The point was not content but sound. A song stayed within a narrow range of notes, a steady audible presence with the feel of a keen, "a hybrid between the weirdness of an Indian cry and the croon of a dark mammy," that would soften the startle of a sudden noise.[46]

In August and September the herds arrived at their railheads, and the population of Abilene, Dodge City, or Ellsworth multiplied spectacularly before shrinking within weeks. After a brief carouse, some drovers found short work around the railheads but sooner than later they headed elsewhere in another reminder of how America was coalescing. Some bought a horse and saddle and rode south to look for steady ranch work or to "ride the line," getting fed for brief labor, while others used a shrunken roll of bills to buy a rail ticket to Kansas City or Denver, there to shift around for work during the winter slack, perhaps then to head to Texas for another drive or to float into work as a hod-carrier, freighter, apprentice brickmaker, or any of innumerable options there from New Jersey to Oregon.

Expansion, Collapse

Cattle drives kicked modern plains ranching into life. Carrying a volume of hoofed traffic that dwarfed anything seen before, they connected what had been a fairly constricted regional enterprise into a rapidly evolving international economy. Ranching immediately showed a dynamism typical to America's innovating industrial culture, and within a decade it adopted that culture's traits, forms, and strategies. In another decade it would suffer one of its typical disasters.

Industrializing America produced spinoff businesses—producers of bolts and gaskets for factories and flywheels and retorts for mines. Ranching's spinoff was cattle droving (or cattle trailing). Because cattle drives came during a ranch's busiest months, ranchers typically turned their longhorns over to others, ambitious but ranchless and relatively cash-poor, to deliver herds to market. Cattle trailers were middle operatives, businessmen providing the connective tissue within an expanding, transforming economy. Some bought animals on speculation, such as Eugene Millett, who bought and drove a modest herd in 1867, doubled down the next year and by 1875 had made enough to buy a ranch.[47] Many contracted for a drive, usually for $1.00 to $1.50 per head. With overhead of about $500 a month, a herd of three thousand head would clear from $2,000 to $3,500. Profits rose headily for those managing several herds.[48] As across the economy, the business consolidated into the hands of a relative few. Only four agents controlled roughly half of all cattle driven north from Texas in 1875, and the firm of Lytle, McDaniel, Schreiner and Light alone accounted for an astounding 450,000 to 600,000 head taken north between 1871 and 1887.[49]

Droving agents were typically young. The average age of twenty-two contractors in 1866 was twenty-seven years. George Saunders got his first taste when a neighbor hired him to drive twenty cattle to Mexico to exchange for supplies. He was ten. Some operated with a western twist to Gilded Age flamboyance. The Rhode Islander Abel Head "Shanghai" Pierce, who carried a girth befitting the era, would ride into a cow camp on a large white horse and open his bargaining by heaping money on a blanket spread by an African American servant.[50] Droving required skills of the new business culture. An organizer of several herds was overseeing a small bureaucracy, monitoring performances up and down many food chains, moving among levels of status and responsibility and balancing control with delegation.

Meanwhile, Texas ranching was jolted into rapid change. During the 1850s it had spread from the Gulf Coast into the state's north central pastures of big bluestem grass, where cattle outnumbered people by between 25 and 150 to 1.[51] From there some of western ranching's most famous figures—George Webb Slaughter and his son, Christopher Columbus Slaughter, and the Illinois-born Charles Goodnight, arguably Texas's most legendary cattleman—were poised at the war's end to connect with other developments that were rapidly transforming the region.[52] In 1866 Goodnight and his partner, Oliver Loving, drove herds from the Brazos River basin to the Pecos River in eastern New Mexico to feed soldiers at Fort Sumner and the Navajos and Apaches recently penned up at Bosque Redondo, then from there to supply the gold fields in Colorado. After Comanches killed Loving in 1867, Goodnight used the trail to provide stock for ranchers like John W. Iliff along the Platte River to begin one of the earliest cattle empires on the western plains. Others sent cattle up John Bozeman's road to Montana gold strikes.[53]

By then a far wider expansion was afoot. Three developments sped the process. By the late 1870s the military and commercial hunters had confined Native peoples on reservations and cleared the plains almost entirely of bison. New railroads—the Missouri, Kansas and Texas reaching into north central Texas; the Atchison, Topeka and Santa Fe along the Arkansas River and south into New Mexico; the Northern Pacific across the Dakotas and toward Montana; and the Denver and Rio Grande up the Arkansas River—provided plains ranchers with more connections to distant markets. Finally, there were more markets to connect to. With new mining strikes and other settlements, railroads were shipping nearly as many cattle to the Rockies and elsewhere in the interior as eastward. Meanwhile diseases, anthrax especially, devastated cattle raising in England and Ireland as the first refrigerated shipping in the late 1870s allowed slaughtered beef to cross the Atlantic with minimal spoilage. As its popularity grew, with endorsements from Queen Victoria, the Prince of Wales, and the Lord Mayor of London, between 80 and 90 percent of imported meat in the British Isles came from the United States.[54]

The results were stunning. Between 1870 and 1880 the cattle population of six plains states and territories grew by nearly 8 times, from 584,966 to 4,594,147, with the numbers tilting heavily toward Canada. Those in Kansas grew 4 times over, in Dakota nearly 17 times, in Wyoming 46 (from 11,130 to 521,213).[55] The Great Basin, too, began to fill. As drovers like the Texas kingpin J. J. Myers organized drives to Utah, Mormons reached out on their own. In 1871 Joseph Roe and two friends borrowed $30,000, won $17,000 more at faro tables in Salt Lake City, rode to Abilene, and over a hundred exhausting days of heat and dust, sore eyes and peeled ears, returned with 3,600 "wild Texas cattle." They cleared $30,000. As early as 1873 Deseret was exporting cattle to the plains and eastern markets.[56]

It was the greatest short-term shift of domestic herd animals in the history of the world, and it created something like a single economic creature, stretching across fifteen meridians and twenty-five parallels, all of it bound together by the new latticework of movement.[57] How it worked in human terms is best shown by following men on the ground. In 1869 W. A. Peril, twenty-four, agreed to deliver about 1,700 "old, wild longhorns, from five to fifteen years old," from north of Austin to Montana. His crew drove the herd to Abilene, then north to the Platte and up that river and over Bridger Pass before wintering along Wyoming's Green River. The next spring the contractors changed the destination, presumably notifying Peril by wire, to western Nevada. There, with plans changed again, he shipped the fattest animals by rail to San Francisco and drove the remaining five hundred nearly to Oregon to join herds arriving from California. Gone now for two years, Peril rode a train back through Winnemucca, Cheyenne, Denver, and Kansas City to Saint Louis, took a steamboat to New Orleans and a ship to Galveston, then another train to Columbia and a stage to San Antonio, where he bought a horse and rode home to Gillespie County.[58]

Peril's odyssey took place within a classic Gilded Age industrial boom, one encouraged by a long shelf of books and pamphlets with the usual western promise: the sure bet. Calves supposedly could be bought cheap and in a few years sold dear to meet an unfillable hunger on both sides of the Atlantic. Ranchers had free access to more than a billion acres of public domain, "one immense pasture ground," nicely watered and moderately climed, "boundless, endless, gateless." And the bottom line? By one claim an investment of fifteen thousand dollars had more than quadrupled in five years, by another profits of 25 percent per year were typical and 45–50 percent not unknown.[59] High authority backed up the claims. The Great Plains offered "land for nothing and abundance of it," a special British commission reported in 1879, a cattleman's paradise covered with natural winter forage (*"self-made hay"*).[60] With such heady visions came the usual question, rhetorical, confident, naive: What could go wrong?

And so the money poured in. Some veterans of the earlier phase built home-grown empires, but much more common was a new creation—corporate mega-ranches, which proliferated during the 1880s. Most of those based in the United States were financed from the Northeast and Midwest. More than half of ninety-three prominent American investors were from New York City and Boston, with Chicago not far behind. Only four were from the South. Most investors were bankers, financiers, large-volume merchants, and industrialists, with a smattering of professionals scattering profits made elsewhere across the West, confident of ever-tastier gains.[61] The largest ranch ever in the lower forty-eight states, the XIT, was formed when Chicago businessmen who had made their fortunes rebuilding after the great fire of 1871 accepted three million acres in the Texas panhandle in return for constructing a new state capital. None had an hour's experience in ranching among them, but within a few years 150,000 head of cattle were at home there.[62]

To buy those cattle the XIT owners floated bonds in the British Isles, increasingly a source of ranching capital. Scots were especially eager. Among the Edinburgh financial elite "the ranch pot was boiling over," an agent there wrote: "Drawing rooms buzzed with stories of this last of the bonanzas; staid old gentlemen who scarcely knew the difference between a steer and a heifer discussed it over their port and nuts."[63] By 1883 there were several giant Scot firms, capitalized with more than £3 million, operating from Texas to Montana, including the famous Matador Land and Cattle Company and the Swan Land and Cattle Company, soon to be the largest in Wyoming.[64] A colorful subgroup were members of the eastern and European social ozone buying into frontierish fantasies. Most famous was Theodore Roosevelt, who in 1884 started and worked the Elkhorn Ranch in North Dakota.[65] Moreton Frewen, son of Sussex gentry and Winston Churchill's uncle, built a ranch "castle" with imported woodwork and a "minstrel's gallery" for serenading up to twenty guests in his dining parlor.[66] Walter Baron von Richtofen ranched in Colorado. He published his own tract, crowing that "no business in the world has brighter prospects" than cattle raising on the plains, an area sure to become "the meat producing center of the world."[67]

Now ranching was one of the most corporatized businesses in the nation. By 1886 Montana, Wyoming, Colorado, and New Mexico alone hosted 439 corporate ranches capitalized at nearly $170 million.[68] Hundreds more smaller individual operations joined them. In the twenty years since the Civil War, the industry had spread over much of the midcontinent, reached out across the rest and across the Atlantic, and adopted the most advanced financial forms and methods of the day. Few if any postwar enterprises could match it in the scope of its spread and its speed of evolution.

But no system can spread that far and evolve that fast without miscalculations, and western ranching had plenty of them. It was widely assumed that ranching as developed in southern Texas, with cattle fending largely for themselves year-round on an open range, would apply across the region. Conditions and demands of the interior West, however, varied hugely. The new cattle center of Miles City, Montana, was farther north from Kingsville, Texas, than Helsinki is from Rome. Kingsville is eighteen feet above sea level; ranches around Elko, Nevada, were at five thousand feet. Blithe assurances of boosters aside ("There is little difference between the climate of the Plains and the Atlantic Coast," one wrote), weather on the plains is some of the most erratic on earth, with especially vicious winter storms.[69] It was assumed as well that various breeds of cattle would fare more or less alike—that essentially a cow was a cow was a cow—but the new breeds being brought in, with fattier meat more palatable to eastern and English customers, were adapted to different climates, and none were necessarily suited for where they landed.

Most dangerous of all, the grasslands that had been puffed as inexhaustible by the early 1880s were becoming overstocked. Granville Stuart explained it as a simple equation. Take ranges that were "free to all," add men bound "to take big chances for the hope of large returns," and you end up with too many cattle on too little land.[70] To make it worse, fattening centers in Iowa and Illinois sent "pilgrims," many steers of new breeds, to graze in Dakota and Wyoming before returning to meals of corn and to their eventual demise. Then a tumble in swine production in the early 1880s pulled still more cattle up from Texas.[71] By mid-decade, as the new industry connecting raw source to development to processing to delivery to market was coming fully into focus, its most vulnerable part, the great midcontinent pasture, was increasingly overstressed.

Ranchers with the foresight and the money maneuvered to gain a competitive edge. A favored tactic was one used earlier by Miller and Lux, grabbing land along watercourses to shut competitors out of an essential asset. The Matador ranch's hundred thousand acres of "selected watered lands" gave it effective control of an area fifteen times that.[72] Controlling land usually meant fencing it, a problem on the tree-poor plains, but in 1874 J. F. Glidden patented the first practicable barbed wire—two long wires braided together with short pieces, sharpened at each end, twisted and secured every several inches along them. Strung between posts, three or four lines could contain all but the largest and most determined animals. Supposedly pitched by one promoter as "light as air, stronger than whiskey, cheap as dirt," barbed wire was as ideally conceived and as perfectly timed as any invention in modern history. In just six years its production increased from five thousand to forty thousand tons.[73] Many fences could have perfectly benign uses, but ranchers with the muscle and money used them to seal off water sources or to enclose the best of the public domain or to diddle with the law to create "barbed wire principalities" on railroad grants.[74] Ranchers also built east-to-west "drift fences" to stop cattle that instinctively plodded southward during winter storms. When cattle in western Kansas and eastern Colorado drifted deep into Texas and New Mexico, Texas ranchers in 1885 cooperatively ran a single fence for 250 miles from Indian Territory across the panhandle and into New Mexico.[75]

Barbed wire was delineating a new regime—economic, ecological, cultural. A world of semi-nomadic hunters had given way to one of businessmen, large and small, intent on rationalizing nature. They replaced millions of indigenous animals with millions of an alien species. They then used new technologies, including billions of pieces of sharpened metal in partnership with railroads and telegraphs and slaughterhouses, to redesign an incomparably complex natural system eight times the size of New England. They partitioned that system into artificial parts shaped not according to practiced use but by bottom lines of ledger sheets. They did all this, and more, to turn the land toward purposes never tried there, those of a modern pastoralism. This was a wholly imagined ideal, one unfettered from experience and inspired by claims of the purest gas. Many of the men in charge directed affairs from a distance with as much understanding of local realities as a chicken has of a warranty deed. In an audacious era, this was audacity of a rare order, made from sudden opportunity amplified by western dreaming. Its regime could hardly have been better positioned for disaster.

By the early 1880s the supply of cattle had met and passed demand, which sent eastern prices into such a slide that many ranchers held on to their animals in hopes of pushing the market back up, exactly as others had in California a quarter century earlier. By 1885 the boom's illusions were so increasingly, unavoidably clear that plains cattlemen were sending thousands of animals as short-term boarders on distant farms.[76] Then the weather made its play. Well away from the seacoast's moderating influence, situated where northerly and southerly systems meet and froth, the midcontinent from November to March experiences arctic fronts that will freeze anything warm-blooded and outside of shelter. An ordinary winter was "nothing less than slow starvation" for cattle left on their own, an agent explained, with tougher years all the more terrible.[77] This made ranching always a gamble, with, as Granville Stuart would write, "the trump cards in the hands of the elements."[78]

Winters since 1881 had been relatively mild, but droughty summers in 1884 and 1885 left the overtaxed grasses withery and the animals grazing them even thinner than otherwise going into December. In the first week of 1886 a system of frigid, dry air moving rapidly out of Canada met a wet low-pressure system formed in the Rio Grande Valley.[79] From western Kansas to the Texas Panhandle a lovely January 6 turned nasty within hours. Stiff, cold winds, blowing sand, and sleet turned into a ferocious blizzard followed by cold so deep and extensive that it left ice three inches thick on Galveston Bay on the Texas coast. Drift fences built to protect the range became death traps. Tens of thousands of cattle died where they stood, most freezing, some suffocating, leaving carcasses stretching up to a mile back from some spots. Cattle died trapped in coulees and draws. Something between 150,000 and 200,000 were lost in the Texas Panhandle, perhaps another 150,000 between Dodge City and Pueblo, Colorado. One ranch reported 182 survivors from a herd of 6,000.

The northern plains suffered less than the south, but the reprieve there was brief.[80] A desperately dry summer and fall in 1886 left grasses dangerously thin as winter approached, an equation for disaster under the best of conditions.

What followed were the worst. A heavy snow in November left cattle further weakened, and then, after a warming in January, one of the worst blizzards in plains history struck on January 28, raged for three days, and was followed by a frigid stretch longer and deeper than any on record. It was "hell without the heat," "Teddy Blue" Abbott wrote.[81] Only in the spring did ranchers begin to gauge the catastrophe. Estimates are shifty, if for nothing else because holdings often were based on notoriously inflated "book counts," but some points are clear. Longhorns from the south and "pilgrims" brought recently from the Midwest fared the worst, with some herds essentially annihilated. Of the 5,500 Texas cattle he had set out to graze in the fall, a rancher found a hundred alive in the spring.[82] Animals bred there for a few generations fared better, but many survivors were in wretched shape, and especially heavy losses among calves bit into future hopes.[83]

"There is not the slightest element of uncertainty in cattle raising," Baron von Richtofen wrote in 1885.[84] Two years later the structure that had built up so quickly and confidently had folded in upon itself. It was a classic of Gilded Age panic and collapse. As creditors read the news and called in loans, ranchers shipped tens of thousands of cattle to market, not a few of them half-starved, which sent already low prices plummeting, which triggered more desperate selling. Larger firms, many bloated and poorly managed and distantly overseen, were most likely to fail. The behemoth Swan Land and Cattle Company went under in May, and eight of ten major Scot corporations suspended dividends.[85] Moreton Frewen abandoned Wyoming and his ranch "castle." The *Cheyenne Daily Sun* heard he had moved to India to become financial advisor to a "Hindoo rajah."[86] Theodore Roosevelt headed east for what must have seemed a comparatively predictable future in New York politics.

The lessons of the "big die-up" of 1885–87 turned the business away from rank incaution toward more sustainable systems. The free-roaming open-range system gave way to midwestern strategies of moving animals by season to where and when grass could support them. Sheep ranchers moved in with flocks needing less water and willing to graze on forbs that cattle scorned. In 1880 Montana hosted fewer than three hundred thousand sheep; twenty years later there were 5.2 million.[87] In one more echo of California's Miller and Lux, haying for winter feed, often in irrigated fields, now played a central role. The connective tissue thickened between the grass and corn kingdoms. Meat-heavy animals of newcomer breeds, Devons and Herefords and shorthorns, shuttled between Dakota pastures and Iowa feed lots on their way to their stockyard doom.[88] And so the range cattle industry, as an economic evolution and a consolidation of national regions, continued.

The mythic and the real were blurring together as well. A twenty-one-year-old Missourian, Charles M. Russell, was a cowboy on a ranch in Montana's Judith Basin. When the owners wrote to ask how their herd was faring, the foreman sent a postcard, cut from the bottom of a box of paper collars, on which Russell had watercolored a starving, slat-ribbed cow, head lowered and shank-deep in snow as coyotes circled it, waiting for a meal. Russell named the sketch "Waiting for a Chinook" (a Chinook is a powerful westerly wind that in winter brings a rapid warming) and later "The Last of the 5,000." The postcard brought Charlie Russell the first offers that began a career as arguably the most popular artist of the West. He would paint explorers, Indians, and outlaws, but his favorites were cowboys—range-riding, hunting, fighting, pranking with greenhorns, taming horses, and hellraising on a toot. No one would cement more in the popular mind the image of western ranching as an American exotic than the man whose career began with a sketch of plains ranching as one of its era's classic business busts.

17 ➤ Wind, Fever, and Indians Unhorsed

The "big die-up" of 1885–87 is a stark reminder that western ranching in many ways was the Gilded Age on display, in all its creative, integrative, and destructive power. Measured by geographic reach, it was also the most striking example of how new western enterprises were transforming the continental environment and rechanneling its capacities. That ecological revolution undid another one that only few generations earlier had created a Native empire from Texas to Canada. Ranching imposed both an economic and a cultural order on the national heartland.

An enterprise that developed so quickly on such a scale and over such an area was bound to face devilish problems, and given the new industry's economic heft, the government was bound to use its expanded power to address them. To do so, Washington turned to new fields of science, and as it had since expansion, it used the West as a laboratory for their study. The result was to solve some problems and to find that others were unsolvable, but in all cases to illuminate what had been enduring mysteries about elemental forces and the harsh realities of ordinary life.

Rivers of Air

Some of the most provocative of that work was on an ancient and ubiquitous human concern—the weather. The ranchers and farmers moving onto the plains found that the land they hoped would welcome them instead could be especially resistant and cranky. The farther they went, the more obvious the problem. Such basics as rainfall and temperature were different from what was expected in the East, different from one part of the West to another, and in any one part different from one season—and one week or one moment—to the next. The growing realization pressed the federal government to gain a better grasp of the western climate and what it meant for settling and using the country. This was practical work, but its implications, meshing with investigations from Patagonia to Siberia, helped reveal the earth as a single unimaginably complex climatic engine.

The work began from a dead stop. Meteorologically, the interior West was one of the most uncharted regions on earth. In his magisterial *Winds of the Northern Hemisphere* (1853), James H. Coffin mapped the prevailing direction, speed, and annual variability of winds across most of the globe north of the equator.[1] He drew on reports from 579 stations around the world. There were 88 in New York, 21 in Maine, 17 in Ohio, 9 above the Arctic Circle, and 8 in Siberia. Between the Missouri River and the Sierra Nevada there was just one, at Fort Laramie in Wyoming. Coffin's maps folded out to a gorgeous panorama of the moving atmosphere above the entire Northern Hemisphere, save one portion. The American West was nowhere to be seen.

These were years when there was less and less tolerance for blank maps, even ones about how and where the wind blew. Wind, after all, was about weather, and in an increasingly integrated nation, weather was increasingly about money. A special concern was the threat of sudden storms on the Great Lakes and Atlantic coast, and to address it Congress in 1870 created the Weather Bureau under the War Department's Signal Service. In January 1873 it began issuing the *Monthly Weather Review*, with maps and discussion, but the bureau had so few stations in the West that for its first ten years the *Review* showed no data beyond the hundredth meridian.[2]

An effort to fill in the blank space had begun, however. In the 1850s Joseph Henry of the Smithsonian Institution began collecting and collating data from western military posts and other volunteers. More than five hundred sites were participating by the Civil War, and by the time the Weather Bureau began its work, the Smithsonian was sketching the first continental view of weather. It started with rain. In 1872 Charles Schott published tables and maps of month-to-month precipitation the Smithsonian had gathered from stations coast to coast. Dots were plotted for nearly eight hundred weather stations, and each was labeled with its average annual rainfall and snowmelt to the nearest inch. Dots with the same number then were connected. The result was a series of "isohedral lines" curving mostly north and south across the map; the spaces between them resembled waves and eddies, each wave an area with roughly the same precipitation. The map offered an instant impression of how much precipitation typically fell where.

Two lessons were immediately clear. Patterns of precipitation in any one area were remarkably consistent over stretches of time, and those patterns showed remarkable, even extraordinary, differences among the nation's parts.[3] The Gulf Coast, for instance, received the most rain in the East, from 50 to 60 inches annually. The Northeast and interior South received from the low to upper 40s, and most of the Midwest from the 30s to low 40s. The differences were considerable, but then, to move beyond the Missouri River, was to sink quickly down the rain gauge. Annual rainfall in Fort Scott, Kansas and Omaha, Nebraska, on the eastern plains (42 and 35 inches) was not so different from Marion, Ohio (43 inches), or Harrisburg, Pennsylvania (41 inches). A little over four hundred miles to the west, Fort Lyon in southeastern Colorado received 12 inches. Arizona's Fort Defiance got 14 inches; Albuquerque, New Mexico, 8 inches; and Fort Bridger, Utah, 6 inches. The map is coded from darker to lighter. Areas with more than 56 inches a year are in dark blue, with areas with less precipitation progressively lighter. Those with 20 to 32 inches are lightly striped. Virtually the entire western interior, plus Southern California, has no coloring at all, meaning it received fewer than 20 inches annually. Then, at the top lefthand corner, the map goes dark again. Precipitation there equaled and surpassed that of the Gulf Coast. Neah Bay, on the northwestern tip of Washington Territory's coast, reported a mean annual rainfall of 123 inches.

Schott's was the first full compilation of the nation's most essential resource, water from the sky. Like the surveys before and after the war, it was done with an eye both to science and turning the West to national development and private profit. Given that about half of American workers were farmers, the map raised fundamental questions about both farmers' opportunities and what western society would look like. Farmers had to have enough rain to work the land by the methods they knew. Without it, logic said, they would either have to stay away or adjust their work and lives to fit the new country. One of the four postwar surveys led to just that conclusion—and produced one of the most significant statements ever made on the nature of the far West.

When John Wesley Powell turned from geologizing to leading the new Bureau of Ethnology, he used the occasion to take Schott's data, combine it with what he had learned on his Geographical Survey of the Rocky Mountain Region, and reenvision what course western development should, and shouldn't, take. Powell's *Report of the Lands of the Arid Regions of the United States* made its essential point in its third sentence. Agriculture, as currently practiced, was possible only on "a very small fraction" of western public lands.[4] He was not questioning national destiny. He presumed it. But he did argue that America's presence in the West would have to take a different shape. On eastern plains, "beautiful prairie country," farmers might prosper, but beyond the hundredth meridian they would have to settle only in those rare areas where streams could irrigate enough to quicken their crops. There they would need to develop a more communal culture, and the federal government should recast its basic job of state-making and lay them out by river systems, the life arteries of an arid and "sub-humid" land. Laws like the Homestead Act, based on eastern realities, made little sense in the West, but more to the point most of the West was unsuited for farming of any sort. Change the laws to offer a generous twenty or thirty or fifty acres for every animal set upon the land. Leave the western Great Plains and virtually all the deep interior to pastoralism. That was all the land could support.

Powell was envisioning a West with social and economic contours as different as the ones of rainfall on the Smithsonian map. In time federal policies would bend toward his views, nudged by environmental calamities of the 1930s and 1950s, and a century after it appeared Powell's *Report* would become something of a sacred text among those calling for more sensible and sustainable environmental relations. At the time, however, he was badly out of jibe with popular optimism—he was "using bear language in a bull market," Wallace Stegner wrote—as well as with the plans of powerful interests, in particular railroads determined to sell western lands as small-scale freeholds.[5]

As science, Powell's *Report* was much longer on description of the continental climate than it was on the mechanics behind it. Elsewhere, however, that work was proceeding, and once more the West became an active laboratory. The results soon would start to coalesce into a basic understanding of how weather worked. They would confirm Powell's read on what the future West should look like.

By midcentury meteorology had its basic instruments in modern form: the thermometer, barometer, wind vane and wind gauge (anemometer), and rain gauge. As empires expanded ever more widely across the globe, scientists used those tools to gather ever-greater mountains of information into a single fabric.[6] A rough descriptive portrait of global weather began to gel. But if meteorologists were to move beyond the "what" of weather and climate to questions of "how" and "why," they would have to begin with sequencing. They would have to synchronize information on changing conditions over large areas to show how those conditions flowed and fit together in real time. The tool that made that possible was the same one that was doing so much to create and connect the West.

With the telegraph a station could report virtually instantaneously temperature, wind speed and direction, and barometric pressure even as others were reporting from thousands of other points across the continent at the same moment. When the same was done a few hours later, then the next day and the day after that, the effect was a holistic, seraphic view of conditions as they evolved over millions of square miles. The product was the modern weather map that gathered the "full harvest of facts" and applied them to the "full dynamical treatment" of weather.[7] By the turn of the century the Weather

Bureau had access within an hour to observations taken simultaneously from across a quarter of the earth's surface.[8]

Meanwhile, the understanding of weather dynamics was expanding rapidly. By around 1830 it was accepted that storms occurred when cyclonic systems (areas of relatively lower barometric pressure) encountered anticyclonic ones (higher pressure), and the next forty or so years saw the rapid advance of the understanding of how those systems developed and how and why they moved as they did. Of particular importance was the work of a pathologically shy mathematical genius, William Ferrel, in describing and explaining the movement of air from the tropics to the poles as made by the interactions of the atmosphere, global temperatures, and the spin of the earth.[9] The emerging patterns took on depth as students fit particulars from the past into what they saw unfolding on their own maps, month to month.

Once again new streams of knowledge converged in the far West. The bureau's agents mapped and tracked in growing detail western weather's fluctuations— its fronts and snaps, its dry spells and sleet storms—while others were learning to set it into hemispheric and global context. From that they began to grasp the mechanisms behind it all. One point quickly became clear. The West's most consistent export to the rest of the nation was not gold or cattle or wheat. It was storms.

Folk knowledge had long seen storms moving west to east, but now maps laid out far more fully the routes and the predictors of direction, speed and intensity, especially of winter storms. Of ninety-four tracked between 1885 and 1895, seventy-three followed three patterns. Some carried dry polar air out of Canada's Saskatchewan Valley through the Ohio Valley to the Atlantic coast. Others moved out of the Pacific Northwest and across the Rockies, then followed the first route. The third group arose in the Southwest and moved on a broad front through most of the eastern U.S., including much of the South. The first two sorts, and especially the first, brought frigid temperatures. The heart-stoppers of 1886 and 1887 were of this type.[10] The second type, out of the Pacific Northwest, were especially powerful and showed "greater vitality than any other class of storms traced over the Northern Hemisphere."[11] They could barrel across the nation in just three days.

Here was one more way that the West fit into the nation: it was America's great weather-maker, the generator of fronts that consistently shaped daily life across much of the Midwest and East. More broadly the work on western meteorology showed that climates everywhere were the creatures of primal forces, from the planet's spin and ocean currents to the play of airflow and landform. It was left to a member of one of western history's most influential families to bring theory and practice together and to report the news to ranchers and farmers.

Silas Bent was the eleventh child of Silas and Martha Bent and the youngest sibling of Charles and William Bent, who as much or more than any others had opened the southern Great Plains and the Southwest to American influence. Silas entered the navy at sixteen and sixteen years later sailed with Matthew Perry to Japan. There he mapped the Japanese current, known then as the Kuro Siwo, the Pacific equivalent of the Atlantic's Gulf Stream.[12] He resigned in 1861 in sympathy for the Confederacy and after the war took up ranching along the Arkansas River, near where brother William had presided over Bent's Fort.[13] There he learned the same sobering realities as his neighbors and applied to them his expertise in ocean currents and the emerging picture of atmospheric movements. He delivered his conclusions in 1884 before the first national convention of the Cattle Growers of the United States.[14] His canvas was big. He followed the atmospheric flow from Asia to the Pacific Northwest, where it picked up enormous amounts of moisture, then it carried some to the continent's "Water Dome" that fed the Columbia, Missouri and Mackenzie Rivers. It carried the rest to the south, where most fell on the Sierra Nevada and Rockies. Winds out of the Rockies were now wrung so dry that they were unable to "give forth even a mountain dew." The mountains cast eastward a metaphorical shade of aridity that gradually lightened as the river of air drew up moisture from below and began to give it back.

Silas Bent was describing the natural machinery behind the waves, swirls, colorations, and blank spaces on Schott's rainfall map—why in his case the average precipitation dropped from forty-eight to twelve inches between his one home in Saint Louis and his other along the Arkansas River, and why the same would be true for all who headed west into the rain shadow and beyond. His conclusion, delivered to the cattlemen in his audience and to any who would listen, was the same as Powell's in his *Report*: Live with it. The high plains and intermontane West "will forever stand" as they are, he wrote, rain-poor by "the immutable laws of Nature" that "no human intervention can . . . alleviate."

Bent's was the ultimate integration of the West into the world, and one done through yet another meeting of western and global science. Meanwhile, the contrary impression of a West apart continued to flourish. It was fed ironically through another Bent family connection. The fourth sibling in the Saint Louis household was Lucy, who admired her eldest brother enough to name her second son Charles, who in turn passed the name along to his son, Charles Marion Russell. This was Charlie Russell, the Montana cowboy whose career as a romanticizing artist of the plains West began with his watercolor postcard,

"Waiting for a Chinook," two years after his great-uncle laid out the hard realities about why the wait could be a long one.

Tickpickers

Plains ranching arose how and where it did partly because of disease. When Texas cattle after the Civil War were driven to Missouri or taken by steamboat up the Mississippi to Iowa and Illinois, they passed a mysterious fever to local animals. No one knew what the illness was, or how it was passed, or how to cure it, so a temporary fix was needed. Experience showed that after the first hard freeze in autumn, Texas cattle were no longer a threat. The obvious fix was to keep immigrant and local cattle apart until after the cold time. The only practical way to do that was to draw quarantine lines north to south across Kansas and Nebraska and hold Texas cattle west of them to overwinter before heading east.[15] The practical effect was to expand ranching westward. Fear of a fever helped open the high plains to an economic arrangement that coupled pastures to boardrooms, brought capital from Edinburgh to Texas, and sent cattle from Montana to Liverpool.

That wasn't the only connection. The killing fever, like the puzzles around plains weather, occasioned another case of the West a laboratory of global science. It began as an effort to solve a straightforward economic problem: how to reduce the penalty for moving around a resource, walking meat. Solving the problem was a long stride toward answering one of humanity's oldest questions: Why do people get sick?

The mysterious fever was found across the South, but it was usually called "Texas fever" or "Spanish fever" because its most common flash point came when longhorns walked northward into a national market. Anyone watching its effects would have understood the panic. After mingling with immigrants for three to four weeks, local cattle turned lethargic and feverish. They lost their appetite. An affected animal often stood off alone, back arched and head drooping, breathing at close to twice its normal rate, trembling, staggering, moaning, suffering first from constipation and then diarrhea, its urine bloody, its skin dry and its hair bristly.[16] Most of those stricken would mercifully die within seventy-two to ninety-six hours. Dissection showed organ damage, especially to the spleen.

That the disease passed from southern to northern cattle was undeniable, but the particulars were maddeningly elusive. As Texas ranchers were quick to ask, if their cattle were passing the malady along, why were longhorns unaffected? Why did the fever appear, not immediately, but weeks after southern cattle consorted with northern? In fact, northern animals might fall ill and die in fields that longhorns had left weeks before, not where longhorns *were* but where they *had been*. Why?

Beyond the temporary quarantine, the ultimate solution was to first identify the disease and from that find its cure and prevention. In 1884 Congress created the Bureau of Animal Industry (BAI) within the Department of Agriculture to confront animal maladies especially threatening to international trade. Texas fever was high on the list. One man is often given credit for cracking its riddles—Theobald Smith, the son of German immigrants who joined the Bureau of Animal Industry in 1885 and who would go on to found nation's first academic program of bacteriology at Columbian (later Georgetown) University.[17] The work, however, was a collaboration among Smith, F. L. Kilbourne, Cooper Curtice, and director of the BAI Daniel E. Salmon.[18]

As with geology and paleontology, their investigations took place during one of the most fertile generations of study in their field of epidemiology. In the 1860s continental scientists, most notably Louis Pasteur, Joseph Lister, John Snow, and Robert Koch, had proved that microscopic organisms, "animalcules," were the causes of many diseases. Smith schooled himself in that research and introduced Koch's methods of identifying the tiny culprits in the blood and tissues of victims. In 1889 he discovered in the victim's red blood cells a parasitic protozoa (named *Piroplasma bigeminem* and now known as *Babesia bigemina*) he correctly guessed was the cause of Texas fever. The real puzzler, however, was how this agent moved from cow to cow. Everyone presumed that the microorganisms passed directly from one victim to the next, but Smith and his colleagues could find no way that the protozoa got from the blood of an infected longhorn to that of a northern cow standing next to it.

Frustrated, they tried a radical methodology. To discover what was killing cattle, they listened to cattlemen. Texas ranchers had long argued that in some strange way the cattle tick (*Boöphilus bovis*) was responsible for the fever. By the learning of the day, this was absurd. Nonetheless Salmon urged Smith, Kilbourne, and Curtice to test the proposition. They began with two groups of cattle, one of tick-infested southerners and the other of tick-free northerners. They penned some northern cattle with some of the tick-heavy southerners. Next they took the remaining southern animals and meticulously, tediously picked off every tick, then they isolated the now-tickless cattle with the remaining northerners. Then they waited. After the standard time lapse, the northern cattle that had passed their days with the tick-covered animals sickened and died, while those consorting with the tick-free southerners grazed contentedly on, in good health (until they arrived at a slaughterhouse). Other northern cattle died after pasturing on fields simply strewn with ticks, with no contact with southern cattle at all.

So there was indeed some connection between ticks and the fever, but how the two connected was still a mystery. The assumption was that a tick first took in the parasite from a sick cow and then, after falling off the animal and dying, left it in some form, a spoor perhaps, for a new victim to ingest with contaminated grasses. But when Smith and Kilbourne tested that guess, feeding healthy cattle with hay full of ticks live and dead, nothing untoward followed. The breakthrough was accidental. Curtice had cultivated quantities of ticks a couple or more generations removed from an infected cow or field and thus, presumably, free of the pathogen. To test a longshot—that anemia caused by massive blood-sucking was somehow involved—the men took "clean" infants, released them onto a healthy northern cow, and checked daily for signs of anemia. They found not anemia but something else, a stunner: "Symptoms of Texas fever appeared and the parasite was detected in the blood."[19] It was an "Aha!" moment. Ticks were not passing along the parasite by leaving it lying around. They were a direct delivery mechanism. Such a thing had never appeared in medical literature.

The cycle of contamination began when a mature female tick, gravid and swollen with blood holding the parasite, fell to the ground and laid up to three thousand eggs. She passed the parasite along in eggs, which hatched into six-legged larvae that swarmed up the legs of uninfected cattle, latched on, and began to draw blood. At that point, or later as nymphs and adults, they could transmit their inherited protozoa to the cow, which was now a reservoir of pathogens ready to be taken in by a new wave of seed ticks. The mature ticks then mated and the fertilized female dropped off, starting the cycle again. The cycle answered nagging questions. The time lag between exposure and onset was that between a mature female taking in the parasite and her next generation gestating, hatching, advancing, and delivering it to a new host. The reason that northern cattle sickened on fields vacated by longhorns was because those fields had been broadcast with tens of thousands of eggs. The longhorns had left, but the disease hadn't. As for why longhorns did not sicken, later work showed that in the deeply infested Southeast and Southwest, calves exposed to the parasite handled it quite well for the rest of their lives, so as they matured they became carriers—and death-bearers as they moved into uninfested regions. Quickly the disease took on the name of "tick fever."

The next step was obvious. Get rid of the ticks. If cattle were dipped and treated consistently to kill the parasites, there would be no new infants to pass the fever along. The land they occupied would soon be free of contagion as freezing temperatures killed the ticks. Predictably, controlling the fever proved not so easy—an authority soon after the turn of the century estimated direct and indirect losses to southern and western cattlemen remained a staggering $63 million per year—but in time control was largely established.[20] A quarantine line remains today, not through Kansas but along the Texas-Mexico border.

The tick war had effects far beyond ranching and longhorn economics. In 1893 the Bureau of Animal Industry issued a 301-page report under the names of Smith and Kilbourne on "The Nature, Causation, and Prevention of Texas or Southern Cattle Fever."[21] Its description of the team's elegant, iron-logic methodology has been called a masterpiece of scientific literature. One historian compared it to Beethoven's Eighth Symphony.[22] It was the content, however, that was most notable. One authority has called it "one of those fundamental steps forward that alter the entire course of a science," with consequences "of inestimable and permanent importance."[23] Until then, it was assumed that all pathogens, "germs," passed directly from one body to another via touch or sneeze or, as Smith and company wrongly guessed, as a spoor that was eaten. That is the case with "contact" or "crowd" diseases like influenza, measles, or whooping cough. Smith and his colleagues found a second pathway. A disease also can move from creature to creature indirectly via an intermediary "vector"—and equally important, *only* through that vector. It cannot pass, flu-like, straight from one animal or person to another. Its connections are enormously complex, involving the entangled life cycles of host, vector, and pathogen.

The tickpickers had done more than solve a costly economic riddle. They had discovered an entirely unsuspected category of diseases. Others quickly pursued the implications to crack the mysteries of some of the worst scourges that had so far frustrated them. In 1895 David Bruce, a Scot pathologist working in South Africa, identified a parasitic protozoa as the agent of trypanosomiasis ("sleeping sickness"), a vicious form of encephalitis that ravaged both humans and livestock, and seven years later he proved that the tsetse fly was its vector. In 1897 Ronald Ross in India traced the complex life cycle of the parasite earlier identified by Alphonse Laveran as the cause of malaria and proved that anopheline mosquitoes passed the disease to birds. The next year others showed the same in humans. Ross, not one to share the limelight, would credit Smith and Kilbourne's "remarkable discovery in connection with the disease called Texas cattle-fever" as a crucial breakthrough.[24]

Yellow fever had plagued the southern United States for decades. In 1878 it had taken more than five thousand lives in Memphis, Tennessee, the worst epidemic in American history, and during and after the Spanish-American War it assaulted American troops in Cuba. In 1900 the nation's surgeon general was Brig. Gen. George M. Sternberg, who in 1867 had invited his younger brother

Charles Sternberg to join him at Fort Harker in Kansas, setting Charles on his course as a major figure in paleontology. When his new wife died there of cholera, George devoted his life to the study and prevention of disease, and by 1900 he was the nation's leading bacteriologist. To unpuzzle the cause of yellow fever he dispatched to Cuba a brilliant young army physician, Maj. Walter Reed. (Reed had begun his career in New Mexico, at one point doctoring the Apache leader Geronimo.)[25] Despite his boss's confidence that direct contact with bacteria caused the fever, Reed listened to a local doctor, Carlos Finlay, who argued that a particular mosquito species (*Aedes aegypti*, it turned out) carried the disease. Reed, who corresponded with Smith, at least on other matters, devised an experiment mimicking Smith's and Kilbourne's.[26] He divided volunteers free of the disease into two small barracks with bug-proof screens. One he kept free of mosquitoes and in the other, holding one volunteer, he released Finlay's mosquitoes that had fed on blood from fever victims. When that man sickened, and only that man, the point was proved.

There is a clear pattern to vector diseases. Most are in hot countries. Most vectors are insects or arthropods, so most vector diseases are most firmly entrenched where such bugs thrive year-round, in the tropics, and because it took dozens of millennia for the extraordinarily complex relationships among pathogens, vectors, and people to develop, vector diseases are most common where humans and their ancestors have spent the most time, in Sub-Saharan Africa. People indigenous to those regions evolved some innate resistance and acquired immunities by surviving diseases as children, much as longhorns handled tick fever better because they had contracted it when calves. The upshot was that the tropical world had an environmental edge in resisting colonization by outlanders who were largely unexposed to tropical plagues. In the 1870s, nearly four centuries after the first contact by their expansionist forebearers, Europeans were still confined to a few feverish outposts on the west coast of Sub-Saharan Africa.

Then came Smith and Kilbourne's discovery—and Bruce's, Ross's, and Reed's. It was no coincidence that they coincided with the rapid colonization of tropical Africa. Other factors were obviously at work, including those displayed against Indians in the West—modern military organization and technologies of warfare and movement—but the unriddling of hot country diseases played its role. Along with the vigorous use of quinine for malaria, colonizers could now confine tropical diseases simply by separating people and vectors, as with mosquito netting and screens, and by quarantining the sick to shrink the pathogen reservoirs. The obvious American case was construction of the Panama Canal. A French effort in the 1880s foundered after more than twenty thousand workers and engineers died from yellow fever and malaria, but by the time the United States took on the challenge in 1904, Gen. William Gorgas, who had worked with Reed and Finlay in Cuba, could apply the new understanding to succeed where the French had failed.[27]

A decade or so earlier Othniel C. Marsh had tied the ancient West's toothed birds and proto-horses into life's evolution, Clarence Dutton had revealed the Colorado Plateau as a text of how an unthinkably old planet had unfolded, John Wesley Powell and his minions had begun fitting Navajos and Umpquas into a single Family of Man, and Powell, Bent, and others had situated western weather into the planet-wide machinery of climate. Now Theobald Smith, F. L. Kilbourne, and their colleagues, by solving a costly puzzle of one of the West's new, vibrant industries, helped bind the West into a global community. This community was not one of flows of meat but of knowledge gained as a war against mankind's oldest enemies. And as with some of those other efforts, like the positioning of Indians well down the ramp of human progress, theirs was structured and applied to the work of empire and subjugation. The West was created through links engaged. The links here connected cattle ticks and rancher lore with the saving of millions of lives, a spreading misery to countless others, and America's expansion into the Pacific world.

The Grass Revolution, II

Ranching consolidated the nation in yet another way. In a single generation an expanding cattle pastoralism wrested control of millions of acres of Native lands and tied them into a national and international economy. The seizure went deeper than that. Partnered interests—on-the-ground cattlemen, distant investors, fantasizing aristocrats, military field commanders, and government agents—made an ecological revolution that ended a global epoch and helped introduce a new age.

When western Indian peoples in the eighteenth century swung astride horses, they harnessed sunlight and tapped into the energy stored up in the grass around their feet. They found new homelands, expanded old economies and fashioned new ones, and flexed far greater command over their world and their enemies. It was a reprise of a cultural revolution that had begun five thousand years earlier. It spawned new regimes of power, including a midcontinental empire the size of western Europe. It was an extraordinary liberation, and for Native horse-men it lasted scarcely a hundred years. Ranching was an outgrowth of another revolution, also cresting in the 1780s. The colonies' break with their mother country had made a new nation and by the mid-nineteenth century had birthed an expansionist culture that drew increasingly on new, far deeper sources of energy, fossil fuels in particular, to power new technologies from spinners of thread to locomotives and ore-crushing stamp mills.

The two revolutions met in the West, and within a lifetime the horse cultures that had remade the region from the Columbia Basin to southern Texas were left with only the most compromised remains of the life they had briefly known. That story was most apparent on the Great Plains after the Civil War. There the eastern revolution took the potential power in the vast midcontinent pasturelands as its own, which made the rise of modern ranching both an economic innovation and an act of conquest.

With one exception, the conquest followed a particular sequence. Ranching took root immediately as Indian power was broken. Two forces were at work. Between 1872 and 1882 Native economies were crippled as the numbers of bison, which had been declining for a quarter century, plunged to nearly nothing when hundreds of white hunters cleared the plains of shaggies and fed their raw hides to an industrial market. Simultaneously, the federal military turned against the horseback superpowers and by 1877 had confined them, however imperfectly, to reservations. The ranching invasion came right behind each Native defeat, "like a classic military envelopment," writes one historian, first into eastern Colorado, Kansas, and southern Nebraska in the 1860s and early 1870s, and by the end of the decade on the northern plains of Montana and the Dakotas.[28]

The one exception was in the heartland of the Comanches and Kiowas, on the southern high plains of west Texas and eastern New Mexico. There the ranching frontier did not follow the Indians' horseback empire. It met it. What happened reveals a lot about both the adaptive gifts of Indian peoples and about the forces that would overcome them.

During the 1850s, when plains ranching pushed onto the southern fringes of Comancheria, Comanche power was a shadow of what it had been. Drought, their own overhunting, and other stresses had cut deeply into the bison population, and their prodigious horse herds had shrunk dramatically. Their sprawling system of trade was unraveling. All this, plus smallpox and cholera, cut the Comanches' numbers from an estimated 20,000 in the late 1840s to 10,000 in 1855 and about 5,000 in 1865.[29] Some tried withdrawing to reservations in the Brazos Valley and, after harassment from paramilitary units (a "vile and worthless set," wrote an agent), in Indian Territory, but most pulled back to their heartland core in the Texas Panhandle where, a leader pled as early as 1852, "we might bury our people in quiet." The first expansion of plains ranching seemed poised to follow the sequence of later ones: Indian withdrawal, then ranchers' occupation.[30]

Then a stunning turn of fortune. Rains returned in 1865, and bison and horse populations rebounded. Washington helped. Concerned mostly with controlling defeated Confederates and blocking French ambitions in Mexico, Washington withdrew its forces well to the east and south, and in the Treaty of Medicine Lodge Creek it created a reservation in southwestern Indian Territory but recognized hunting rights in the Comanches' heartland as long as bison remained. Comanches took this to mean that the government would allow them to live just as they had, only now with access to government annuities on the reservation. Washington, that is, gave the Comanches and Kiowas some slack, and they eagerly took it up. They roared back in 1867. Nothing showed better the explosive potential of grassfed horse cultures than this resurgence. Warriors struck into western Indian Territory, eastern New Mexico, and especially northern Mexico and Texas. Raids approached the state capital itself. The new white settlements of the 1850s reeled into reverse.

It was a reprise of the Comanches' spectacular drive to power a half century before, but this surge had a new element. Cattle suffused it. During the chaos of the Civil War the herds on the Comanche fringe had proliferated, easy pickings for the suddenly invigorated raiders. One report had ranchers losing thirty thousand head (and four thousand horses) during the two years after Appomattox, and of the cattle trails like the one Charles Goodnight and Oliver Loving blazed to New Mexico, "nearly every drove . . . are captured by the Indians," a Texas official wrote.[31] Loving died at the hands of Comanches in 1867. Comanches amassed herds in the thousands of head. They drove some, along with horses, mules, human captives, and loads of bison meat, to trade fairs and to rendezvous with comancheros, the New Mexican cartsmen who for decades had journeyed onto the southern plains for bartering. Army officers at Bosque Redondo apparently invested in the growing trade, and a former agent to the Kiowas was trading whiskey and firearms for cattle in western Indian Territory.[32]

The ever-adaptive Comanches were experimenting with a modified, diversified pastoralism. To the horse, the key to their power, they added another domestic herbivore, the cow, and they made it a complement to a third form of incarnate grass energy, the bison. They did not become ranchers in the fullest sense, raising cattle over time. Instead they used the same strategy for cattle that they had devised for horses thirty or so years earlier. They waited for others to spend their own energy and pastures in raising the animals they wanted—that is, they outsourced the breeding and the feeding—before stepping in to steal the meaty results. There are just the slightest hints of Comanches feeling their way toward subtler, more calibrated arrangements. Should the bison population falter, one leader told an agent, his hunters "would allow them to breed a year or two without molestation" and instead "rely on Texas cattle for subsistence."[33] Meanwhile, they raided more intensely than ever and used the reservations only as a depot for annuities and occasional winter refuge.

After giving the Comanches and Kiowas some considerable slack in 1867, the government took it back in 1871. It was sparked into action in May by an attack on an army supply train, which General of the Army William Sherman missed by a half hour. Sherman answered by turning all the force he could muster against Comancheria, sending Colonel Ranald Mackenzie on cavalry forays over the next year and a half that destroyed supplies, captured horses, killed some warriors and captured women and children. Another command, with Texas cattlemen as paramilitaries, struck the comanchero system and effectively shut down that critical commercial outlet. Pressed first by the army from the south, then cut off from support to the west, Comanches next faced an even more elemental threat out of the north—a market-driven assault on the heart of their economy. In 1873 white hide hunters turned from the depleted central plains to the Texas Panhandle, the irreducible core of the bands' livelihood. The army did nothing to stop them.

Staggering from military attacks and stunned by the ferocity of the hunt, Comanches and Kiowas responded to a young holy man, Isatai (Wolf Vagina), who claimed divine power to reverse the disaster, restore Native dominance, and resurrect the slaughtered bison. He could freeze enemy bullets as they flew and could vomit forth thousands of his own to fire back. On June 27, 1874, he and the mixed-blood leader Quanah Parker led several hundred warriors against an outpost of buffalo runners at Adobe Walls near the Canadian River. The hunters, however, used their powerful, long-barreled rifles nearly as effectively against the Indians as against the bison. The bullets did not halt in midair but killed perhaps two dozen warriors, wounded Quanah Parker, and shot Isatai's horse from under him. The demoralized attackers dispersed and the great hunt continued.

At summer's end the army command ordered a full assault out of seven posts in Texas, Indian Territory, New Mexico, and Kansas. On September 28 Mackenzie and the Fourth Cavalry fell on a camp of more than two hundred lodges along the Prairie Dog Town branch of the Red River in Palo Duro Canyon, south of modern Amarillo. Comanches and Kiowas fled with minimal losses, but Mackenzie fired the lodges and everything inside them: the dried meat, blankets, flour, clothing, robes, coffee, and everything else the bands would need to survive the coming winter. They also captured more than 1,300 horses and mules. Two days later they herded more than a thousand to the head of a feeder canyon and shot them all. For decades afterward mounds of bones marked the spot and stories of whinnying ghost herds chilled the dreams of Texas ranch children.[34]

The episode was both unique and revealing. The Comanche resurgence must have seemed a rekindling of glory—the leader Ten Bears told agents in 1867 that his people were no longer "weak and blind as puppies" but strong again, "like grown horses"—but in fact it was a sobering lesson in a new reality.[35] An international market, reaching out through the bloody hands of white hide hunters, devastated the resource that fed and housed the bands. Then, after briefly looking away, Washington turned its attention back on Comancheria and sent in its own warriors, positioned and provisioned via train, coordinated via wire, and applied by what was now a well-tested strategy of denying winter refuge. The Comanches and Kiowas were certainly not "weak and blind," but they were fatally vulnerable. In the end their interlude of reborn power measured the weight—of the market's scope and might, of military force, and of sheer numbers of people—now leaning against all former masters of the plains.

To seal the Indians' defeat, Washington took a two-step approach. The first could not have been more basic. To destroy Native horse cultures, Washington would destroy or seize the cultures' horses. By the time Mackenzie turned his men's guns against those screaming animals, he was following a well-grounded military policy. In 1858 Col. George Wright had followed his victory over the coalition of tribes in eastern Washington with the slaughter of more than 800 horses. Five years later Col. Patrick Connor had sealed the crushing of the Shoshone village at Bear River by taking at least 175 horses from survivors who had fled afoot into the frozen countryside. In another five years, on November 27, 1868, Lt. Col. George Custer ordered 875 horses shot after routing a peace camp of Cheyennes on the Washita River, and the next year, on July 11, 1869, Gen. Eugene Carr seized about 400 horses and mules after sending the last resistant Southern Cheyennes into flight from Summit Springs along the South Platte River.[36] Two years after Palo Duro, after Custer's crushing on the Little Big Horn, Ranald Mackenzie caught the Northern Cheyenne band under Morning Star (or Dull Knife) along Wyoming's Powder River and took 500 horses as the Cheyennes fled on foot into the winter cold. In late September of the next year, Col. Nelson Miles caught resistant bands of the Nez Perces at Snake Creek in north central Montana, and in the battle's opening moments his men captured or dispersed the camp's several hundred horses. The surrendered Nez Perces were taken to Bismarck, Dakota Territory, by boat or on foot. They were allowed a single horse, ridden by Chief Joseph (Heinmot Tooyalakekt).[37]

The second step, usually hard on the heels of the first, was to replace remaining horses with cattle. In the fall of 1876, as some cavalry pursued the Lakota and Cheyenne victors at the Little Bighorn, more than a thousand others seized most horses on the Standing Rock and Cheyenne River Reservations and drove them to Saint Paul, Minnesota, for sale. Hundreds were lost along the way to distemper, frigid storms, exhaustion, and theft, and the rest, worth nearly twenty thousand dollars, were exchanged for 450 cows.[38] The next summer the surrendered Northern Cheyennes were given back some of their mounts for the trip to Indian Territory. One leader claimed they were promised "presents of horses" on arrival, but Ranald Mackenzie allowed one horse per lodge and sold the rest to buy 51 cows for 933 men, women, and children to begin a new life.[39] Two years earlier, Mackenzie had used a "pony fund" from selling horses he had not slaughtered at Palo Duro Canyon to buy 3,600 New Mexican sheep for surrendered Comanches and Kiowas. Three years later a Comanche reported that 30 survived.[40]

Officials always justified the swap as serving the Indians. The Brulé Lakotas would ever remain "a horde of painted savages" as long as they were in the saddle, their agent wrote in 1876, but unhorse them and he could begin their transformation, dressing them as whites, turning them to farming and "productive industry."[41] The rhetorical puff is easy to dismiss, but beneath it was a pragmatic strategy of ecological politics. By decoupling Indians from horses and recoupling them to cattle, Washington was securing its power by realigning the endless movement of sunlight.

Follow its flow, and consider the cow. From one angle the arrival of cattle was a variation of the coming of horses. A cow was another shortcut to the energy waiting in grasses, in its case turning it into readily available food. But a cow's advantages stopped there. An Indian cattleman could never be a cattle-man, a fusion of two species into a new form with possibilities that just kept unfolding. No Indian ever chased a bison or rode into battle on a Hereford. Washington was taking away grass power that was transcendent and liberating and giving back grass power that was dinner. And it was *giving* that power—providing cattle of its choosing and giving them on its own terms.[42]

The disconnect with horse power was essentially complete by 1877. Attention then turned more to what Indian-cow relations would be. Gen. Alfred Terry was one who suggested giving a nod to Indians' "savage love of freedom" by making them horseback herders as a step toward farming. Their pride in ownership each year would be "the great peacemaker."[43] Indian ranching would develop with considerable success late in the century, but at the time it posed two problems. Herding on horseback would be "too much like the old life," wrote the longtime agent James McLaughlin, and besides it would be expensive.[44] The Whirlwind, a Southern Cheyenne, thought each family would need six to eight cows to get underway, an investment far beyond what Washington was willing to provide.[45] Some agencies gave it a cautious try, but when government rations were late or short, as they typically were, and "when their children [are] crying for something to eat," the Kiowa agent wrote, "should any one be surprised . . . [that] they should kill and eat one of their breeding cattle?"[46]

Instead cattle would be a more direct tool of control. As novitiate farmers Indians would initially need support, and in Carnivorous America cattle were an obvious source. By distributing the beef themselves, not through heads of bands, agents undercut the old systems of authority, and the ways they handed it out made it clear where power now rested. A Cheyenne-Arapaho agent divided everyone into groups of up to forty-two persons. Each group got one cow a week along with some wet sugar, corrupted flour, and doubtful coffee. The beef was usually gone in two or three days. The issue to his Lakotas, White Thunder testified, was "just like giving chickens a few grains of corn."[47] Some openly saw this as a motivator: "You should keep the Indian hungry if you wish him to do anything for himself." Others opposed this "starving process" and pled, sometimes desperately, for more beef, but still others, like James McLaughlin, agreed that "you must reach the stomach of an Indian in order to civilize him."[48]

The system did work well for some—white ranchers and suppliers. Government contracts for nearly ninety million pounds between 1876 and 1880 offered guaranteed sales at favorable prices in an increasingly unstable industry.[49] Ranchers often skimmed off the least marketable animals and diddled the contracts to still better advantage.[50] Some reservations had plenty of cattle, but they belonged to other people. The Cheyenne and Arapaho and the Comanche and Kiowa reservations bordered Texas ranchlands. Only an "immense skirmish line" could expel the fifty thousand or so cattle that had drifted over the unprotected boundary, an agent thought.[51] The tribes tried to step into the game. They would be landlords. For annual payments in cash and cattle the Cheyennes and Arapahos by 1884 leased 90 percent of the reservation to a quarter of a million head, and the Comanches and Kiowas opened a million and a half acres.[52] The arrangements quickly fell apart. Government lawyers argued that the leases were invalid because the tribes did not own their land. Left-out ranchers complained, and some in the tribes opposed the system and fought over how to distribute the income.[53] Restive younger men and older soldier societies among the Cheyennes and Arapahos threatened herders and killed cattle, by one estimate a hundred thousand dollars' worth.[54]

In 1885 and 1890 President Grover Cleveland ordered all non-Indian stock off the Cheyenne, Arapaho, Kiowa, and Comanche reserves. The tribes lost income and ranchers lost their investment. More than two hundred thousand cattle expelled in the fall of 1885 were crowded onto overgrazed, drought-blighted land just in time for the ravaging winter of 1885–86. Many staggering survivors were driven northward into overstressed pastures in the Dakotas and Montana, straight into the teeth of the "big die-up" of 1886–87.

Reservation Indians, like the Comanches and Kiowas in their resurgence after 1865, were maneuvering for leverage inside a new reality. None of it worked. They were undone by their own factionalism, by bureaucratic snarl, and by the usual vagaries of the plains climate, but ultimately all promising options were blocked because, in the end, they had no power to force any of them. The rise of the cattle industry was a massive energy theft. Denied the free rein of grass power turned equine, Indians were bound into a world where others had turned it bovine, then those others made of that world what they chose, down to telling Indians where to live, how to work, and what and when to eat. With essentially one maneuver Indian power was crippled, plains energy was commodified, and a national market satisfied. The move was obvious. "If the grass on the preserves can be converted into cattle," the agent to the Comanches and Kiowas asked rhetorically, "why not do it?"[55]

With that the American grass revolution, part of an historical epoch five thousand years old, was over. Two things set it apart. It ended where that epoch had felt its first dim stirring, millions of years earlier, on the savannah where the earliest *Equus* had galloped and grazed. And it was the last time it would ever happen. In the new age of steam, no others anywhere would follow western Indians on their brief but heady path to greatness.

Indians had their own mythic responses to the new age. The fortnightly beef issue on the Pine Ridge agency began with hundreds of Lakotas gathered before a large corral packed with longhorns. One by one steers were released and prodded into a run. Two or three mounted men raced after each one, whooping and spurring their horses as they raised and aimed their rifles. Women descended on each still-warm carcass to skin, gut, and dismember it. It was "a good imitation of an old time buffalo hunt," Charles Eastman wrote of his first witness of the show.[56] In 1892, however, the agent decided that the spectacle both "incited the younger element" and inflicted "barbarous cruelty" on the cattle. Thereafter, agency police killed the animals, "one by one," and distributed them at the agent's direction.[57]

Thank goodness, wrote an early California historian, that the first Spanish fathers brought cattle to their missions. Forty-niners could never have done their state-making work on the Indians' thin diet of acorn cakes and clam chowder: "It required plenty of roasted and boiled beef to start California on her career."[58] Ranching more generally was considered an essential step on the nation's march toward continental mastery and future global prominence. History held no example of a "great and dominant race of people" without abundant supplies of animal flesh, wrote a western booster in 1871, "vegetable food alone degenerating people to the condition of the Maccaroni Eaters of Italy."[59]

Always, however, pastoralism was envisioned as a partner to a West full of sturdy farmers. The same view insisted that Indians dismount and turn to the plow. The thought was that our civilization, as with all peoples who had advanced to the fore, was necessarily agrarian at its heart. America might be turning toward a grand future of cities and factories, but workers would need to fuel the inner fires with both beeves from western pastures and the fruits of western fields. Agriculture's story, however, was no simple cultural progression. It was as interwoven and revealing as that of that of ranching and the mythic cowboy.

18 ▷ Breaking the Land

Begin with a paradox: American agriculture had its greatest expansion as Americans were turning away from it. Up to the Civil War, the nation had been overwhelmingly one of farmers and those directly servicing them. Hunger for farmland had been the prime force behind westward expansion. By 1860, however, the balance was tilting away from the countryside toward the city, yet it was just then that agricultural expansion turned by far the most vigorous. From the founding of Jamestown in 1607 until 1870, roughly 407 million acres were settled, and of that, 189 million were brought under cultivation. Between 1870 and 1900, 430 million acres were settled and 225 million acres improved. More land was converted to farms during the thirty years when Americans were shifting away from agriculture than during the previous 263 years of full-tilt agrarian absorption.

The paradox is more apparent than real. The same forces that pushed the nation toward an industrial culture—a technological revolution, corporate expansion, the integration of the nation's parts into an economic whole, and the ever-tighter connection of that economy into an international market—go a long way toward explaining the explosive increase in land occupied and farmed, nowhere more so than in the West.

A sister paradox: during the greatest agrarian expansion in the nation's history, the majority of that expansion was happening in the part of the nation that, taken as a whole, was least suited to farming. The West, defined as country beyond the Missouri River, accounted for nearly six out of every ten acres brought to the plow between 1860 and 1900, and yet, as science and experience were making clear, most of that country had too little rain to allow farming as it was usually practiced. Agricultural expansion was clustered on its edges and in islands like Mormon country. In the thirty years after 1870 the new acreage of Kansas and California alone exceeded that of the twenty-two states comprising the Northeast, South Atlantic, and East and North Central regions of the census.[1] In the interior West, farming certainly played its role in seizing the land and remaking the nation, but as the West at large led the way in agricultural growth, it became the first region without a majority of its people tilling the land.

Spillover and Speculation

Western agriculture fell roughly into three patterns. Its most dramatic expansion was in Kansas, Nebraska, and the Dakotas east of the ninety-eighth meridian, country where midwestern prairies gradually morphed into the Great Plains. It was "beautiful prairie country," John Wesley Powell wrote in his report on arid lands, fertile and swamp-less, with softly rolling hills and, especially in its eastern portion, usually with adequate rainfall.[2] In 1865 this country was on the dim edge of white expansion. By 1880 its farms increased from under twenty thousand to nearly a quarter million.

This was the only part of the emerging West that was an economic and cultural spillover. It was an extension of the country immediately to its east, the booming and bountiful farmlands between the eightieth and ninetieth meridians. Its soils were a continuum of the fertile loess deposits of the lower Ohio River Valley, exceptionally fertile, air-blown silts picked up from glacial runoff and laid down over the previous ten millennia. The prairie West was also one of the West's supreme speculative landscapes. Only a few generations before, these grasslands had spawned the rise of horseback empires. Now they were both an agrarian boomland and an arena where distant capitalists and scrabbling newcomers were betting on the land and playing the odds as vigorously as in any mountain mining rush.

Any study of agriculture can seem like a blizzard of numbers, but in the emerging West statistics can be both revealing and striking. A few suggest the speed and scope of the spillover being converted to property. During the 1870s Kansas farm acreage quadrupled, Nebraska's grew by nearly five times, that in the Dakotas more than ten times (from 302,000 to 3,801,000 acres). Between 1860 and 1880 the land value of the prairie West grew from about $16 million to $364 million.[3] An area equal to all of New England, plus Pennsylvania and most of Virginia, was converted in less than a generation to uses and methods it had never known.

This boom was part of another one, wider in space and longer in time. Imagine the increase of American farms after 1850 as a physical upwelling that rose to different degrees in different parts of the country. The rise was most vigorous in the Midwest, and it followed a distinctive pattern. It began in Ohio, Illinois, Indiana, Michigan, and Wisconsin, the subregion the census labeled the East North Central. In the 1850s more farms by far were opened there than anywhere else, and by 1860 it held more than the entire Southeast. Beyond was the

West North Central subregion: Minnesota, Iowa, Missouri, Kansas, Nebraska and the Dakotas. The number of farms was growing there, too, but at only half the clip. The upwelling, however, was moving westward. During the 1860s the number of farms in the East North Central and West North Central grew at almost exactly the same pace (175,000 and 178,000, respectively), and while the former still solidly led the nation in total acreage, the latter was catching up. In the 1870s, the agrarian wave crossed the Mississippi and Missouri, into the prairie West, and crested about three hundred miles farther on. The number of farms in Kansas and Nebraska alone grew by well more than in Ohio, Indiana, and Illinois combined. The West North Central shot up in ranking from fifth to second.[4] Now the Midwest and the spillover were the nation's agrarian heart. They contained fewer than one out of ten of the nation's acres, yet they held more than one out of five of its farms.

Powell's "beautiful prairie country" boomed also because it was more accessible. The rail networks that had knit the Ohio Valley to the Northeast in the 1850s, and by that had helped to people much of California with immigrants from the free states, had spread vigorously after the war. Eight of the ten states with the most trackage in 1877 were those adding the most farms, and again the action built westward into the spillover. Between 1865 and 1877, trackage in Kansas and Nebraska increased from 168 to 4,138 miles.[5] With that there was a tessellation of rails across Iowa, Missouri, and Minnesota and into eastern Kansas, Nebraska, and the Dakotas, all of them well connected to a consolidated system to the east. Fueling it all was a boom in wheat and corn. Between 1866 and 1880, the nation's output of wheat tripled and that of corn more than doubled. Most corn was consumed here, primarily by livestock, but wheat exports grew more than twenty-seven times over.[6] The prairie West followed the pattern. Kansas's wheat output grew from 1.3 million bushels in 1866 to 13.2 million in 1875.[7]

At work here, too, was the partnership of government and business that had driven western conquest from the time of the California gold rush. State and territorial immigration bureaus published books and pamphlets as hyperbolic as anything out of the gold fields.[8] The prairies were somehow both virgin and familiar, their graceful contours easily plowed, like "some region of Europe from which the wave has swept away the inhabitants."[9] Railroads did their part. There was a genuine demand for their acres in the spillover, so selling land both generated income and created customers. "He who buildeth a railroad west of the Mississippi," wrote an official of the Burlington Railroad, "must also find a population and build up business," and to do that he must "blow as loud a trumpet" as possible. There was lots of tooting. The Rock Island Railroad assured that any crop could grow in Kansas "because it rains . . . more than in any other place, and at just the right time." The Northern Pacific reported that doctors were paupers in the healthful Dakotas, although abundant crops and invigorating atmosphere sometimes led to painful overeating.[10]

The federal government's most obvious encouragement came as three laws passed between 1862 and 1877. They had two things in common. On their face all seemed to ease the way for small-scale farmers to take up western lands. And although all to varying degrees did so, each had fundamental flaws, was open to abuse, and encouraged an often-vigorous speculation.

Best known of the three was the 1862 Homestead Act, which to many symbolized western possibility itself. It was the culmination of a process, begun at the nation's birth, that centered on a crucial question: What to do with public lands? The initial answer was to treat them as a source of revenue when there were few other options, but over the next sixty years federal policy shifted in favor of those who actually worked the land, partly to cater to the voting majority of farmers but was also as a shift in its guiding purpose. Public lands were still an economic asset, but not as a source of immediate income. Now the public domain, which by 1848 was of imperial proportions, was an asset whose long-term development would cultivate the nation's economic health and global power. After opening more land offices, steadily reducing the minimum amount of land for sale and the minimum bidding price to $1.25 per acre, Congress took a critical step in 1841. The actual settlement of new lands typically ran well ahead of the land's survey. The Preemption Act of 1841 gave these ahead-of-the-curve settlers, "squatters," first shot at buying up to 160 acres at the base price of $1.25 an acre. Symbolically at least, the law declared the government now favored dirt farmers and meant to use them to make of the expanding West an agrarian empire. The next obvious step was to give the land away to those willing to work it.

The new Republican Party in 1856 made homesteading a key plank in its platform, but southern politicians, who had well-grounded fears that such a law would send waves of non-slaveholding families into the West, blocked it until secession and their departure cleared the way. On May 20, 1862, President Lincoln signed the Homestead Act. It offered 160 acres of unclaimed public land to any adult, either a citizen or planning to be, provided only that he or she live on the land part of the year for five years, improve it, and pay a nominal filing fee. The federal turnabout seemed complete. The Homestead Act officially enshrined an agrarian version of the ideal of free labor. "Originally and distinctively American," according to one government report, it would fill the continent with homes, cultivate communities, and diminish the inequities that led to social unrest.[11] Or so Washington claimed.

In fact homesteaders quickly found that the new country had its special challenges. There were fewer trees to build homes and fence their land by the practiced manner. Congress's answer was the second of the three laws, the Timber Culture Act of 1873. Now a quarter section could be had by planting and cultivating forty of its acres with trees.[12] Partly the hope was to block the famous midcontinent winds, anticipating the shelterbelt programs of the 1930s, but the act also expressed the theory that "rain follows the plow," the idea that by planting wind-stopping, dew-dropping trees, farmers moving farther onto the plains would drag along with them the precipitation they would need to cultivate the crops and employ the methods they had used to the east. To further deal with the lack of water, Congress in 1877 passed a third law, the Desert Land Act. For twenty-five cents per acre up front and another dollar later, homesteaders could file on a full section of desert land, defined as that which needed irrigation to "produce some agricultural crop," provided that they irrigate it within three years. Under the bundle of laws, filing could be frenzied. Over fifteen months in 1871 and 1872 the Concordia, Kansas, land office averaged a homestead or preemption claim every fourteen minutes.[13]

Experience quickly showed the system's flaws. The reason there were no forests was the climate, not a lack of planting effort. The plains, that is, were not rain-poor because there were not enough trees. The plains were tree-poor because there was not enough rain. Similarly, the purpose of the Desert Land Act, to make the arid West blossom by irrigating it, ignored the fact that most of the land it was offering was desert precisely because there was little or no water to irrigate *with*. The two laws were among the clearest examples of how Congress and federal officials, ignorant and naive, often applied eastern experience to western realities, with predictable effects.

Something similar could be said of the Homestead Act, though that picture was more mixed. The law fit well enough the opening country in Minnesota and much of the eastern plains, but in one of western history's uglier jokes, the ideal of free land matured just as agricultural expansion approached the point, roughly halfway across Kansas and Nebraska, where the government's terms of giving it away would not work. Lawmakers presumed that 160 acres would be ample for a family farm. And it was—on the wetter side of the line. But not on the other, drier, side. Land there could produce plenty as long as a farmer could follow the instructions for many modern processed foods— just add water—but as families entered the deepening "rain shadow," annual rainfall dropped steadily and the soil's yield per acre dropped with it. What rain did come was less predictable. A farm might go decades without its year's precipitation coming close to the annual average. Paradoxically, rainfall was almost never normal. The farther west from the spillover that a family moved, the more land it needed and the less its chances of making a go through the Homestead Act's offer of a quarter section.[14]

Homesteaders also found that much of the land was unavailable. The act of 1862 was part of what historian Paul Gates called in understatement an "incongruous" land system, a layering of laws and practices at clamorous cross-purposes.[15] Under the Morrill Act, signed into law on July 2, 1862, Congress granted public land to every state, thirty thousand acres for each congressman and senator, to support agricultural and technical colleges, all of it off-limits to homesteaders. Most land released by Indian treaties was available only by sale. By far the greatest amount held back was related to building transcontinental rail lines. In those massive checkerboards along a railroad's course, the railroad got half of the land, while the government hoped to sell the other half, and because some lands in the grants had already been claimed, Washington withheld still more "indemnity" or "lieu" lands to make up the difference. Lieu lands essentially doubled the acreage taken out of homesteaders' reach through the grants.

It added up. More than 180 million acres were eventually granted to railroads by federal and state governments, the majority in the West, with millions more for wagon roads.[16] Grants to the Northern Pacific alone would have held all of New England, and if all grants were put in one place, even without the lieu lands, and formed into a fifty-first state (historian Richard White would name it Railroadiana), it would be the third largest in the nation today.[17] Of the land that was available, much was taken up before homesteaders got to it—squatters' land entered through preemption and that taken with scrip issued in the East to veterans and to states under the Morrill Act. The combined result was that in some parts of the West homesteaders were left with the leavings from other laws, crumbs from the public table.

The vague and generous terms of all three laws, plus their misalignment with western facts of life, also made them a fine fit for a grand American tradition—land speculation. If speculation is defined as acquiring property, not to develop it, but simply to turn the acquisition itself to profit or some gain or advantage, then the laws were among our history's most splendid speculative vehicles.[18]

Especially in rain-poor country across the ninety-eighth meridian, better-heeled ranchers, sometimes using "armed riders, . . . espionage, and intimidation," had their hired hands file homestead and especially timber claims along streams to control water for their herds and to deny it to any others. They could hold the land for five and three years, respectively, then give it up for someone to file on it again. A close study of eight Nebraska townships found 202 out of 272 timber claims were eventually canceled, many of them reentered and recanceled as many as half a dozen times.[19] Investors bought up veterans' land warrants and scrip from the Morrill Act—a single Ohioan acquired five million acres' worth—and held it for later sale, sometimes to settlers but often to speculators.[20] In Pierce County, Nebraska, fertile country scarcely fifty miles west of Iowa, 179,920 acres were bought through scrip and warrants, ten times what was taken up as homesteads. In 1880 the county still had only 184 farms.[21]

Claims became commodities. The key to the arrangement was the relinquishment, the document a claimant signed to surrender his rights to the land he had filed on. Relinquishments became the currency of the claims-as-commodities business. On a larger scale investigations found that "monied corporations and wealthy speculators" hired "gangs" of ten to fifty men who took up choice lands, committed perjury en masse, and signed and turned over relinquishments to land agents who sold them to later land-seekers for from fifty to five hundred dollars "and upward."[22] On a micro scale what one historian has called "professional first-comers" took up newly opened land to sell, through relinquishments, to families showing up later. "The curse of this country is land-grabbing," a legitimate homesteader fumed. He was referring to his neighbors.[23]

Mortgages, while a sensible way to finance improvements, could be another speculative temptation. Eastern capital flooded into the farming West during these years, lured by the same naive prospects for ranching and mining.[24] As investors bought mortgages "regardless of whether those acres were good ground or stony ground, swamp land or sand hill," a homesteader could "commute" his claim by paying $1.25 per acre, mortgage it in the hungry market, then simply walk away.[25] Honest homesteaders often waded into debt up to their nostrils. When the weather turned or prices sagged, they might find themselves chasing solvency and agreeing with a song from the 1890s:

> We worked through spring and winter,
> Through summer and through fall,
> But the mortgage worked the hardest
> And the steadiest of all.[26]

Past a point, posing farming against speculation is a false contrast. Land speculation had always been woven into western expansion; interests and motives of the government, business and common settlers had long been garbled together.[27] As with squatters earlier in California, plains homesteaders, settling on classic terms of a republic of freeholders, could manipulate the legal apparatus as artfully as deep-pocket speculators. Washington was open-handedly offering them a fresh start through laws that were vague, ill conceived, and out of jibe with local realities. Could they really be expected to play strictly by the rules? Men "who would scorn to commit a dishonest act to an individual," an investigator wrote, quickly embraced any scheme to jigger the system to make it work.[28] A homesteader might take up a timber claim to hold it for future sale, or he might sell a relinquishment to pad what he needed for another farm, or he might cobble together maneuvers to buy a better situation farther on. He might, that is, violate a law's letter to pursue its essential purpose—the actual development of the country by family farmers.

Given such muddling of motives, plus so much taken under the smudge of deceit, historians often highlight the system's shortcomings and inspired chicaneries, but a recent study gives the Homestead Act a much healthier grade. Up to two out of three western farms begun between 1860 and 1900 were started at least in part as a homestead. The majority of homesteaders "proved up"—saw their claims through to a final patent. Based on a close reading of a few counties, fraudulent use of the law was pretty rare, in part because of the beady eyes of settlers keeping their neighbors honest.[29] Weighed against that are the enormous swaths handed to western railroads—the land given to only four of them surpassed that of all homesteads proved up before 1900—and the millions of acres that outside speculators took up by varied methods, plus the indeterminable amount that settlers themselves turned to profit by playing the system.[30] The numbers defy a clear balancing.

Yet sometimes a few points come into focus. Kansas and Nebraska, squarely in the spillover, were the classic setting for the promise of free land. About sixty million acres there were available only under the Homestead and Timber Culture Acts and preemption. Nearly half of that at some point was surrendered in failure or sold as relinquishments, then perhaps resold in a speculative shuffle, but in the end about forty-four million acres eventually were proved up or commuted. Roughly three-quarters of that public land, that is, ended up playing the part the laws meant it to play—giving smalltime farmers the chance to start a new life in what was, to them, a new country.[31]

The prairie West, properly so as the agrarian spillover, was a mix of past and future, East and West. It was both a true land of opportunity, land offered to anyone who would stick with it, grub, and make it crop, and a grand speculative carnival. In time and space, it was a passway into an expanded America.

On the Other Side

California was no spillover. Agriculture there followed the trajectory set by gold rush realities—a large, near-instant demand, the money to satisfy it, and isolation from the stuff to feed it. With virtually nothing to build upon, California agriculture almost from the start applied modern arrangements and methods, moving into a new agrarian era well before most did in the more settled East, and its speculative enthusiasms were at least as boisterous as anywhere in the nation. Within a decade of Marshall's discovery, farming was also directing the state's economic interests outward, into the Pacific world and beyond, expanding the nation's global reach well beyond anything before it.

The trigger of California's agrarian growth was simple. Tens of thousands of persons were suddenly there. Each one was hungry every day. Few of them had any interest in producing the food to feed themselves. Some wheat, fruit, and other staples were carried to the gold fields up from the mission country to the south, but most at first had to come from the outside. Oregon was the closest. Farmers who did not toss aside their plows and head for the gold fields found a fine market for whatever they produced. Other foodstuffs arrived from Chile and Peru, Hawaii and Australia. The obvious implication was the sure profits to be had from local production. "Plant your lands and reap," a Californio father reportedly advised his sons, "these be your best gold fields, for all must eat while they live."[32]

"The farming interest in our country has increased wonderful," another father wrote his son from near San Francisco in 1853. He had planted a vineyard, 1,000 fruit trees, 125 acres in wheat and barley, 4 in onions, and 20 in potatoes, an expansion of an operation that already was grossing between $200 and $400 a day.[33] A miner wrote his wife that he and a few friends ate 25 pounds of local potatoes a week: "We are pretty good Irishmen." Reports of crop profits were as fevered as those for mining claims and, 20 years ahead, for plains ranching. California's fertility, a man wrote his mother, was "far ahead" of anything on the Atlantic coast or even in the "rich bottom lands" of Illinois, Missouri, and the spillover country. A man bought a 100-acre farm for $1,100, cleared $21,000 from its produce, then sold the place for another $10,000.[34]

Climate and natural conditions demanded adjustments. To newcomers the seasons were out of whack, with most rain coming in the winter while dry summers could leave soil baked and fissured. Soil types varied widely, and some of them were wholly new. The Mediterranean climate of the south had no parallel in the East. Even so, the prodigious demand, potential returns, and the promiscuous mix of newcomers' backgrounds and experiences produced a rapid, telescoped agrarian development.

The early supply of fruits from Southern California were quickly replaced by orchards near the northern mines and cities. G. G. Briggs, a New York forty-niner, parlayed $20 in seeds into $5,000 in watermelons in one summer, then expanded his 5 acres to 26 and quadrupled his profit the next. Disappointed miners, turning to raising fruit and wheat along the Sacramento River and in its delta, pioneered methods soon adopted elsewhere—large landholdings and irrigation.[35] Viticulture flourished as well. Established wineries in the south, notably that of the ex–mountain man William Wolfskill, soon were supplemented by new ones in the north. Hungarian Agoston Haraszthy served as San Diego's first town marshal and head of the San Francisco Mint before starting a vineyard in Sonoma, north of San Francisco. In 1861 he spent six months in Europe and returned with more than 100,000 grapevines of 1,400 varieties as well as cuttings for olives, figs, lemons, oranges, and almonds. The next year he published a manual that guided the state's viticulture for decades. By 1880 California vineyards were producing about 12 million gallons a year, with about 1.5 million being shipped overland to the east.[36] (In 1868 Haraszthy's apparently short attention span shifted once more, this time to starting a sugar plantation in Nicaragua. There he vanished, apparently falling into a river to be eaten by caimans.)[37]

Most remarkable was the boom in wheat grown in the state's Central Valley. Grain production had a lot going for it. It was the traditional opening of an agrarian regime, the first market crop grown earlier in colonies like New York and Pennsylvania. Fruits required a lead time of at least a few years to produce, but wheat brought in money its first season. It was especially suited for growing in large units of land, which made it ideal where acreage was leased or bought from sprawling Mexican land grants.

Serious production began in 1852. During the next three years wheat yields in Yolo County shot up from 1,497 to 600,000 bushels. By the end of the decade the state's cereal harvest, mostly wheat and barley, was just over 12 million bushels and growing. By 1870 California stood eighth in wheat output. Ten years later, having risen one notch, its yield of just under 30 million bushels roughly equaled that of Kansas and Nebraska together. The total for cereals was nearly 45 million bushels.[38] In an era of unparalleled agrarian growth this expansion was unsurpassed anywhere in the nation.

Grain production in fact was a bellwether of California's economic evolution and that of the Pacific coast. By 1875 the value of wheat and wheat flour sent abroad from California—not all that was produced, only *exported*—was just below that of all gold and silver taken from its mines, and five years later their worth had taken a substantial lead. The gap only widened. California's gold and silver output from 1868 to 1889 was just under $400 million. The value of its wheat harvests for those same years was $647 million.[39] By then California's common moniker, the Golden State, more appropriately referred not to its mines but its fields of grain.

Soon enough the valley's fields were sewn into a network of trade across 150 meridians. Nothing, in fact, illustrates better the power of the gold rush and coastal settlement, coming coincident with the revolutions of rails and wires, to shrink the world. It was partly luck. The drought and floods of 1861–64, with their kiln heat and surfable waves, were followed by a string of lovely years of bountiful crops. They coincided with seasonal failures in the East and desperate demand in a devastated South, then a string of wretched European harvests that left the continent, and especially Great Britain, scraping reserves down to their bottom. New England supplied the means to connect supply and demand. Its shipbuilders were offering the last of the great clipper ships, the broad-bottomed and many-sailed downeaster, that combined its predecessors' speed with a far greater capacity for bulk cargoes.

And so the flow began. Wheat exports grew from just under twenty thousand tons in 1860 to more than half a million in 1880 and to an astonishing 1.2 million tons carried in 559 ships in the bumper year of 1882.[40] By 1868 one out of every three bushels of wheat sent out from the nation's ports was leaving through the Golden Gate. Nine years later it was four out of ten.[41] In another parallel to the Southeast, California's grain cultivators now kept their eyes abroad, just as Dixie's did for their cotton. Nearly 80 percent of all their harvest was exported during the late 1870s and early1880s. Nationwide, Americans exported 2.3 bushels of wheat per person. The figure for California was 30.7 bushels.[42]

In its means of production California again was showing the way. While some farms were modest shirttail operations, unfenced and haphazardly sown by clueless beginners, more were sprawling and worked on an industrial scale. The *Pacific Rural Press* in 1872 reported that three farms together contained seventy-six thousand acres. The largest produced enough to fill forty medium sized ships. Its season began with four gang plows, pulling four blades each, setting off in early morning and proceeding down the field lengthwise. They stopped at midday for dinner, then kept going, ending seventeen miles from their start. The next day they turned around and set off plowing the second set of furrows.[43]

As with this one, most of these megafarms were mechanized to the point that "nineteenth century observers watched in awe."[44] Both environment and economics encouraged it. The Central Valley, flat and relatively stone-free, was ideal for large horse-drawn gang plows. California's chronic labor shortage—the proportion of wages to value of farm production was nearly twice the national average in 1870, nearly triple in 1900—put the highest premium on cutting the number of workers.[45] Because there was so little summer rain, grain could be left to cure in the fields. After stalks were bound into sheaves, headers took only the grain, which was hauled to a central point to be processed by large steam-driven threshers.[46] As with mining equipment, production of machines was increasingly local. An operation in Stockton turned out twenty thousand gang plows between 1852 and 1886.[47] An eastern prototype of a combine, which both harvested and threshed, arrived in 1854. A model improved by machinists in Stockton, harvesting twenty to thirty acres a day, was called by one historian the "final development in the heroic age of animal power."[48]

"Alas for the romance of the harvest," a journalist wrote from the Central Valley in 1868: "The sickle, the cradle and the flail—Boaz and Ruth—all are gone!"[49] As California helped usher in a new age, the greatest challenge was in putting the entire arrangement together. In this the key figure was Isaac Friedlander, a towering German immigrant who by the late 1860s was already known as the "Grain King."[50] His operations ranked with the most sophisticated among global markets of the day, and none showed better how the revolutions in movement and finance and the corrupt consolidation of land were redefining space itself.

Friedlander grasped that in the new age the prime commodity was information and its coordination over great distances. From San Francisco he gathered remarkably accurate early estimates of the year's wheat production, then worked with British importers through the telegraph and transatlantic cable. He was selling dependability. By guaranteeing early in the season sales to growers and delivery to consumers, he locked in excellent rates on both ends, and he used the same networks to coordinate ships from around two oceans. To finance it all he turned to personal contacts in the bay city. It paid. By one estimate Friedlander controlled three-quarters of all wheat exported from San Francisco from 1867 to 1876.[51] Using mostly agricultural college scrip, he also bought on the cheap a half million acres of opening farmland in the San Joaquin Basin and then helped construct what was then the largest irrigation project on the coast.[52] Luck finally turned on the Grain King in 1877. When his typically reliable sources failed him, he failed to meet obligations and declared bankruptcy. The next year he died of a heart attack at fifty-five. Leland Stanford was a pallbearer.[53]

If California stood as a modern agrarian paragon, Friedlander was its epitome. He was history as biped. He lived by the western economy's speculative essence, fashioning a career that was one great wager, eventually on a global scale. By employing circuits of communication undreamt of a generation earlier, he became the grand integrator of his state's major enterprise. He was a model of the land monopolists denounced by Henry George, parlaying capital, positioning, and manipulation of land laws to close off the emerging agrarian domain to farmers of ordinary means. Friedlander led another of the new West's key developments. He turned it outward. By the time his chartered downeasters were shuttling 15,793 nautical miles to Liverpool, San Francisco had emerged as one of the nation's widest doors onto the world's ports. And when Friedlander finally paid the price, his economic end foreshadowed the implosion of California's grain empire in the 1890s.

California's system spread up the Pacific coast. Wheat produced in Oregon's Willamette Valley, the first settlement site of incoming farmers, was shipped early from Portland, and in the late 1860s it was joined by that of a boom in the Walla Walla and Palouse country up the Columbia River. Harvests from the prodigiously rich upcountry fields were first carried from a benchland two thousand feet down a canyon to the Columbia, leaving teamsters with their "vocabulary of cussing pumped dry," then grain was poured down a system of wooden pipes and chutes from rim to river. From there the sacks moved downstream via barges, steamboats and rail, finally landing at Portland and shipped abroad, mostly to Liverpool, usually by way of San Francisco.[54] In 1880 Walla Walla was Washington Territory's largest town, and The Dalles, the transition point for the burgeoning traffic in food and stock, was "a whirlpool" of humanity, "traders, land-hunters, cow-boys, speculators, saloonkeepers, Indians, Chinamen and cayuse ponies."[55] Oregon's wheat output that year, 7,480,000 bushels, was triple that a decade before, while Washington's had grown nearly nine times over, from 217,000 to 1,921,000 bushels.[56]

Well before that the Pacific coast, led by San Francisco, had captured a hefty portion of the nation's export trade. During the 1870s the city on the bay moved ahead of all eastern ports except New York and New Orleans in the worth of its trade, and the value of goods leaving through the Golden Gate stood at roughly 7 percent of all the nation's exports. With New York out of the picture, its portion was closer to 13 percent.[57] The process began with gold, but then agriculture—industrial in its production, thoroughly modern in its financial and ecological arrangements, and unique in the reach of its international markets—built on the beginnings to direct the coastal West increasingly outward.

In that it anticipated as well the nation's turn even farther to the west. Imagine all foreign imports and exports moving into and out of every port up and down the Pacific coast in 1880, from Puget Sound to Southern California. Now follow their trails. Most was being traded, not to and from Europe, but around the Pacific rim. A decade later the gap between the two was even greater.[58] Gold and wheat partnered in the making of, literally, America's new Orientation.

Between the spillover and the Pacific coast stretched an enormous expanse of plains and deserts and a cordillera made of several mountain ranges. In 1848 much of it was yet to be mapped and some had scarcely been explored by non-Indians. Agriculture there followed three patterns. None was like those of the eastern plains or the Pacific coast, and even when combined their output was tiny in comparison to either of the others. But their impact was as great—and their role in controlling the West and in ultimately breaking the land was as weighty—as any across the region.

The first pattern was in the Southwest. Agriculturally, it was a national laggard. New Mexico enjoyed a modest boom with America occupation, but the Civil War put an end to that. Among all states and territories between 1860 and 1880, New Mexico, Arizona, and Nevada ranked dead last in their increase of farms, and in the latter year the value of farms in the first two was 2 percent of the West's.[59] Some reasons were obvious. An arid, erratic climate discouraged or forbid farming except in islands where water for irrigation was dependable. The population of local consumers was small and slow growing. Raiding by Apaches, Comanches, Navajos, and Utes raised the prospect of losing everything, including life, while hoeing or scything. Altogether it was a notable disincentive. As other parts of the West were coming into rampant flower, the Southwest crept along, far behind.

Some production was propped up by the federal government, not through generous land laws but more directly. The army was far and away the major customer of commercial farmers. Half of all Anglos in New Mexico in 1860 were in the military, and while some posts made desultory efforts to produce their own food and forage, most came from outside the territory or from farms that popped up near every new post. This set up a frustrating dynamic. A post was established to control "wild" Indians. Farmers settled nearby to feed the post. Soon they were also feeding Indians who drew on their fields. Farmers then petitioned for yet more military protection. "It seems rather absurd," Gen. John Pope thought, "that a military post, once established, must be forever kept up for the protection of a few settlers who live by trading with it." The army bought as well from more established areas on the Rio Grande and Mesilla Valleys. Two firms in 1869 delivered to Fort Stanton 630,000 pounds of corn and 364,000 pounds of hay and fodder as well as 275,000 board feet of lumber.[60]

There were a few hints of changes in echo of what was happening elsewhere. The number of flour mills increased from three to thirty-six between 1850 and 1870, five of them steam powered. By then larger landowners had introduced some gang plows and threshers in the Salt River Valley. Still, land under cultivation in 1880 was barely half of that on the eve of the Civil War. "The wooden plow of the Mexican fathers holds preference with the majority of farmers," Gov. Lew Wallace lamented.[61] In a West characterized by seismic change, Southwestern agriculture in 1880 was not so different from thirty years earlier, save in being propped up by a federal presence that was itself stretched thin and under stress.

The second pattern was among Utah's Mormons. They, to say the least, did not hope for a military presence as a trusty market. The Utah War of 1857 had only deepened their determination to be as far and as isolated as feasible from the nation and its armed might. "We have been kicked out of the frying pan into the fire, out of the fire into the middle of the floor," Brigham Young thundered, "and here we are and here we will stay." The immediate commandment was for the saints to avoid the vulnerability of importing food by feeding themselves: "We will cultivate the soil. . . . Then, brethren, plow your land and sow wheat, plant your potatoes."[62]

The first challenge, however, was avoiding starvation. Many of the first settlers were farmers unschooled in the arid climate or English and European city dwellers who knew nothing of plowing and harvesting. During the hot, droughty summer of 1855 clouds of grasshoppers descended on fields "like snowflakes in a storm." Harvests dropped by as much as two-thirds. There followed the coldest and harshest winter since the first immigration. As snows came early and stayed late farmers ate frozen cattle from their devastated herds and in the spring, as in the first years, fed on what edibles they could find—pigweed, thistle roots, and rare vegetables lengthened with bran. Some ate crow, and not metaphorically.[63]

By the 1860s Mormon agriculture was finding its legs. It did so in part by famously adopting an irrigation regime attuned both to regional geography and the structure of the church. Stories of its birth often have a mythic feel suggesting destiny's blessing—one straight-faced account from Idaho has beavers working the night shift in helping construct dams—but the early efforts drew on much older traditions.[64] Members of the Mormon Battalion in the war with Mexico were in Deseret even before Young arrived. With methods they had seen among Pueblo and Pima Indians they immediately began building dams and diverting streams to irrigate late-summer crops meant to feed other immigrants soon to arrive.[65] Irrigation became the lifeblood of the Saints' agriculture. By 1865 there were more than thousand miles of canals feeding farms covering sixty thousand acres in 1870. Ten years later farms had grown to a quarter of a million acres.[66]

The form was unique.[67] It drew on a deep winter snowpack in the Wasatch Range and on the Jordan, Ogden, Weber, and Timpanogos Rivers. A series of relatively narrow valleys fit nicely Young's vision of smallish, tight-knit communities. Somewhat like Puritans in early New England, families lived in modest villages and tilled their farms a short distance away.[68] The valley contours also made it relatively easy to connect and collectively irrigate individual farms through a series of small canals. It all was organized and prosecuted through the church's hierarchy, with wider decisions made at the top and applied via a descending system of authority.[69] The result was paradoxical. Agriculture was on the one hand fragmented—the average size of farms in Utah was by far the smallest in the nation—and yet with its top-down direction and elaborate coordination it was conducted on a scale far greater than the largest Pacific coastal megafarms.

In the reach toward self-sufficiency the Deseret Agricultural and Manufacturing Society experimented with a long list of items, from molasses and flax to hemp and sugarcane, solicited seeds from around the world—squash and "curious nuts" from Japan, ornamental trees from Batavia, and sea island cotton and "a new climbing bean" from England.[70] Some of the first farmers had fashioned plows from the iron rims of wagon wheels, but within a few years threshers appeared and in the 1870s more advanced machinery was in operation. By then Utah was moving toward export. The newly built Utah Central Railroad was sending out two and a half million pounds of produce in 1873.[71] Young tied the effort to his promotion of immigration. From 1861 to 1868 he dispatched nearly two thousand ox-drawn wagons on annual "down and back" trips of 2,200 miles from Salt Lake City to the Missouri Valley. Going down they carried some export goods and supplies for immigrants; going back they carried new settlers and manufactured goods that Utahans could not yet make for themselves. More than twenty thousand immigrants arrived under the system.[72] Meanwhile, church leaders were broadcasting colonies across much of the intermontane region, from Idaho to Arizona, each of them following the approach taken by the first settlements, with families living in small villages, cultivating crops on the outskirts, and organizing it all collectively.[73]

Mormons would see their accomplishments as a divine promise fulfilled. God would "rebuke the frost and the sterility . . . and the land shall become fruitful," Young had assured them.[74] The achievements were undeniable, notable if nothing else for the brash effort to bring into fruit country known mostly for its main feature, a dead lake. In larger context, the Mormon enterprise was anomalous. As a survival of a common prewar impulse to find in the West independent loyalties and arrangements of power, its vision was glaringly at odds with the postwar impulse to make of the West a national unifier. With its "down and back" wagon trains and centered villages, its communalism and top-down direction, Mormon Utah kept its focus inward, part of a separatist vision meant to ready the world for a Christ who was due any day. Even as it began to bend toward national compliance, Deseret's vision, unique and persistent, was putting its distinct stamp on the western heartland.

The third pattern was not concentrated but scattered around the western between-land. Its engine was a series of gold and silver strikes from the eve of the Civil War until well into the 1880s. Its pattern mimicked California's. Scores or hundreds or thousands flocked to each site. Farms soon appeared. Some were a speckling of settlements in the high country's sheltered valleys, called "holes," that had good enough soils and a permissible climate for oats and hardier vegetables and even wheat. More consequential were regions a bit farther away but in places where, with experience, farmers could supply the mines, then expand and diversify to sustain wider settlement.

Colorado was a prime case. Gold was discovered in 1858 on Cherry Creek in what would soon be Denver. Quickly the South Platte River and its several feeders were hosting commercial gardens and fields to supply Denver and fresh strikes in the mountains. The first threshers were at work within a couple of years. Then came ambitious agricultural colonies farther down the South Platte, most notably Union Colony, later called Greeley after the New York editor and former boss of the founder, Nathan C. Meeker.[75] Begun as a collection of sad shanties amid prickly pears and prairie dogs—"Don't go to Greeley," a visitor warned—it soon had a twenty-seven-mile canal and, with two other colonies, was contributing to the 1.3 million bushels of grain coming out of the South Platte valley by 1867.[76]

The same pattern unfolded elsewhere. California farms met the needs of the booming silver mines around Virginia City, Nevada, but still during the next decade there were more farm and ranch towns founded in the territory than mining towns.[77] Northern Idaho's strikes brought farming along the Clearwater River and tapped into the supply down the Columbia around Walla Walla. Gold finds farther south, at Idaho City, Atlanta, and other spots, found their own sources below the mountains in the valleys of the Boise, Payette, and Weiser Rivers and among Mormon settlers sent up from Salt Lake City.[78] Brigham Young had shooed the saints away from dreams of gold and silver—"Let others seek them, and we will cultivate the soil"—but he was fine with profiting from mines to the north.[79] In Montana virtually all farming was not on the eastern plains, later the site of a great homesteading boom, but near the mines of its mountainous west. By the early 1880s the wide and well-watered Gallatin

River Valley alone held nearly a quarter of the sprawling territory's improved land. By one breathless report a "volunteer crop," coming to harvest without plowing, sowing, or irrigation, yielded a thousand bushels of superior wheat.[80]

In all cases farming and mining towns seeped one into another. Disappointed miners hired out to farmers; farmers worked periodically in the mines. One historian calls them "agriminers." Many shared the same plunging spirit, "already capitalists when their plows first broke the sod," and the same "get-it-and-get-out" attitude as in the camps.[81] They set their farming apart in tone as well as pattern.

Farming in western between-land has to be kept in perspective. Its eight states and territories were about the size of the dozen states from Ohio to the Dakotas, Nebraska, and Kansas, an area that held 38.5 percent of the nation's farm acreage. The between-land held 7 percent, and even that was concentrated in a few places. Wyoming had only 175 more farmers than the District of Columbia. Seen only in those terms, however, it is easy to miss the significance. The western interior posed the most elemental challenge to consolidating the nation. Its distances were enormous, its climate forbidding, its Native peoples stubbornly independent. The challenge was met through a variety of means—military commands, Mormon settlements, mining booms, ranches, and more. All relied to some degree on the farms that made up less than a single percent of the cultivated nation. Very few tried to export what they grew, but they made possible the extractive industries, mining and ranching, that, with expanding settlement, were binding the West together and into the nation. These farmers had a continental and international impact by keeping their eyes on the neighborhood.

In this, between-land agriculture fit neatly into a pattern across the West. Typically, before, farmers in newly occupied country had reverted to earlier methods, then over time had moved toward more advanced styles. That was not the case now. Starting in California, land suddenly acquired was put to fundamentally new uses and worked with modern methods and tools. In time the new arrangements spread to part of the spillover. Part of the Northern Pacific's massive land grant was bought on the cheap and organized into "bonanza farms," many of them tens of thousands of acres, that were worked with gang plows and reapers by migrant workers.

Look, yet again, at some numbers. In 1880 the average size of a farm across the West (313 acres) was more than twice the nation's average (134 acres), and California's was more than three and a half times greater (462 acres). Because modern field machines were designed to be pulled by horses, not by the slower plod of traditional oxen, one crude measure of modernization is the ratio

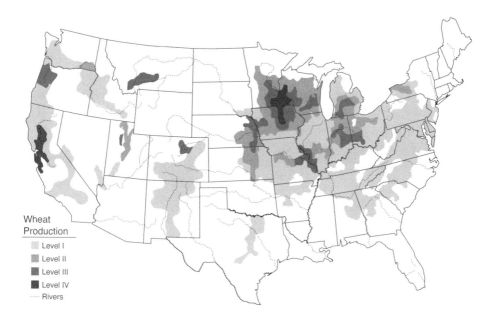

MAP 8. U.S. wheat production, 1870. As this map from the 1870 census shows, some of the nation's most efficient production of wheat was in the newly developed West, areas that were effectively born modern in their agriculture. The darker shadings are where the most wheat was produced with the least labor. Map by Maggie Rose Bridges.

between the two animals. In 1870 the ratio of horses to oxen in California was six times that of the nation, and twenty years later it was thirty times. New methods required fewer workers. In the older agrarian America, east of the Ohio Valley, one worker plowed on average an acre and a half a day. In the prairie country, including the spillover, it was two and a half acres. In California, with its gang plows drawn by eight or more horses, the average jumped to six to ten acres per worker per day.[82] At least by a statistical gauge, the West was leading the way into a new agrarian order, and even in the between-land, which held a tiny fraction of the West's farms, the pattern held.[83]

The point is made through a map in the 1870 census (see map 8). It shows wheat output coast to coast as ranked by the "productive power [or] productive capacity." Counties were graded on an ascending scale of I to IV. Those harvesting more wheat with fewer people (and presumably workers) on less improved land received a higher grade. Most of the Midwest, the most productive region in terms of total output, ranked only a I or II. Parts of Michigan and the Ohio and Mississippi Valleys ranked at III and a newly settled slice of Minnesota earned a top grade. Most of the West was blank: no wheat at all.

Of those parts that did show up, production had been underway twenty years or less, yet five areas were in the top two categories, and three of the four areas earning a III were in the between-land: Montana's Yellowstone and Gallatin River Valleys, the South Platte Valley along the Colorado Front Range, and the farmland south of the Great Salt Lake. The fourth was the Willamette Valley of coastal Oregon. California's Central Valley, the Grain King's domain, got the highest grade of IV.[84]

As with pastoralism, visitors to the new country often would have found not earlier, simpler means of working the land, as on past frontiers, but ones with forms and functions of a new age. In other indirect ways, agriculture was carrying the West into a modernizing nation and world.

19 ▷ Domination and Extinction

Agriculture, whether spillover, far side, or between, was not only establishing a new order. It was also ending an older one. By taking grasslands for their crops and cattle, farmers and ranchers undid the lives of Indian peoples and broke their hold on their homelands. Most did so unintentionally—they meant simply to make money and to make new lives—but in this agriculture did differ from ranching on one respect. At the level of official policy, far above the sweaty work of plowmen and their families, farming was meant as a tool with a dual purpose. It would open Native lands to white settlement, and it would transform Native peoples into citizens, content and prosperous, who would blend smoothly into the reconstructed America. The policy succeeded well in its first purpose. Gauging the second is a much trickier business that has a lot to teach us.

Repurposing the land also required the dispossession of other, nonhuman inhabitants. Outlanders saw both the horse-men and the America bison as lords of the continental center. Theirs was in fact a kind of joint rule, and as lords they fell together, both as victims of the changes that were uniting the West with the nation and world. At the time and ever since, the bison's near demise has been seen as an appalling marvel of the destructive power of those changes. It was that, but it was hardly alone. One other was even more impressive, the extinction of one of the most prolific animals not only of North America but of planet earth.

"God Damn a Potato!"

Since the early republic Washington's formal Indian policy rested on the sunny assumption behind Powell's Science of Man and Morgan's ethical stages: Native peoples were lagging behind their conquerors on the same road of human progress. The government's task was to help them draw even by escorting them "over the first rough places on the 'white man's road.'"[1] The nation then would be unified—economically, ideologically, culturally, and morally. The prime measure of a people's advance was how they fed and supported themselves, and the loftiest level was by farming by modern methods.[2] The implication was obvious. To bring Indians up to cultural par, they would have to turn from the hunting life to working furrowed fields.[3]

It was an old idea justified by practical arguments. More than a century earlier the legal theorist Emer de Vattel wrote that human progress demanded agrarian societies to feed a growing population. Any who resisted should have no complaint if others took their lands, and any who preyed on farmers should be exterminated "as savage and pernicious beasts."[4] A natural side effect would be to embrace an economic individualism considered a pillar of national character. Communal land holdings were "the seat of barbarism," an agent wrote, while an individual farm was "the door to civilization."[5] The transition would require instruction in the mechanical arts and the farming life, especially among the young. All was suffused with Christian uplift which, one reformer wrote, was inseparable from lessons in how "to till the soil, shove the plane, strike the anvil, and drive the peg."[6] Helping Indians up the rungs of the human ladder in turn would open tens of millions of acres of their homelands to white settlement. To civilize was to confiscate. Some would naturally resist, but because everybody would ultimately win, for everybody's sake the government would have to be strong, benevolent, and unbending. Its duty was "to conquer by kindness."[7]

That phrase came out of a thoroughgoing review of Indian relations at the end of the Civil War. Shocked by the Sand Creek Massacre and by mounting reports of corruption, Congress created two groups to investigate the situation. A committee chaired by Wisconsin senator James R. Doolittle, an ardent Baptist who considered July 4 "the birthday of God's republic," in 1867 toured much of the West and corresponded with dozens of agents and army officers.[8] The next year a "Peace Commission," with commissioner of Indian Affairs Nathaniel G. Taylor and six others, including William T. Sherman, then commanding the army in the West, met with many tribal leaders and negotiated two major treaties with plains tribes. Each group issued a report.[9]

Their conclusion: Indian relations were a mess. Outside Indian Territory all groups were shrinking in numbers due to disease, dissipation, fighting among themselves and with whites, depredations by lawless whites, and destruction of traditional economies. As a group, agents were inefficient, lazy, faithless, and corrupt. The government had broken promise after promise, leaving Indians understandably jaded. "Have we been uniformly unjust?" the Peace Commission asked rhetorically, and answered, "Unhesitatingly, yes!"[10] The twin reports might seem to challenge Indian policies down to their roots. But not so. Washington's guiding assumptions remained undoubted. The problems were not in the policies but in their botched prosecution, and the answer was to find the true path to the proper end, starting with a pledge "to do no act of injustice."[11]

The upshot was the "Peace Policy" adopted by the newly elected president, Ulysses S. Grant. Often considered a dramatic shift in Indian affairs, it was more a case of well-rooted ideas made suddenly specific and formal. Two points stand out. The president would divide agencies among several Christian denominations that would appoint "upright, faithful, moral and religious" men to oversee them. Episcopalians got the Sioux; Presbyterians the Nez Perces and Navajos; the Quakers, who had first proposed the idea, got the Cheyennes and Arapahos; and Roman Catholics the Flatheads (Salish). Even the Unitarians got an agency, Warm Springs in Oregon. Now the union of Indian policy with Christianity was official.

Second, Washington bore down with much greater detail on the labors of conversion, as shown in two treaties negotiated during and after the Peace Commission—that of Medicine Lodge Creek with the Southern Cheyennes, Arapahos, Comanches, Kiowas, and Kiowa-Apaches and of Fort Laramie with the Sioux, Northern Cheyennes, and Arapahos.[12] They specified what buildings would be constructed (warehouses, schools and churches, sawmills and shingle factories, housing for agents, doctors, carpenters, millers, and engineers). Schooling for children between six and sixteen would be compulsory, and annuities would come as supplies detailed down to proper clothing: men would receive coats, pants, flannel shirts, hats and homemade socks. At the treaties' heart was the push toward farming. They stipulated how much land families would get, how they would choose it, and how they would get seeds and tools to begin the work. Particulars included inducements for the conversion. The Fort Laramie Treaty provided twenty dollars a year for each person on a farm but only ten dollars per "Indian roaming." The ten persons raising the most valuable crops would get special presents.

The Peace Policy's formal promise was clear. It would fulfill what had always been Washington's prime goal: opening new country to the settlement and profit of non-Indian peoples. It would further the work of unifying the West by uplifting its Native peoples, educating them, and awakening them spiritually. And it would bring the two together in pursuit of the enduring national vision of breaking the land and bringing it to bloom.

It was a promise blindly made. Two factors worked against it, starting with the land and the weather. The president was pressing western Indians into godly cultivation where, as an agent on the northern plains would later concede, such work was "a waste of time, labor, and money, for the simple reason that this is not an agricultural country."[13] Indians were not stuck in an early stage of human progress. They had adapted to what their homes would best allow them to do—hunting large and small game, gathering from a huge catalogue of wild plants, fishing western streams, and harvesting seafood and shellfish along its coasts. When they had met plant domesticates that did fit the land and their needs, they eagerly took to them, as when southwestern peoples adopted watermelons that had arrived from northern Africa through Iberia and Spanish settlements in the Southeast. But with few exceptions—the Spokanes and Walla Wallas in the Columbia Basin had grown fields of oats and potatoes that Col. George Wright destroyed to cripple them into submission—no western Indians had freely retooled their economy to European-style farming. The reason was obvious. They knew the land better than Congress did.

When other European introductions did fit the land, Indians were quick to respond, which leads to the second factor—recent history. Horses were like watermelons. They spread into the interior West because, while farming defied the environment, a horse culture fit it beautifully. This willing adoption of a new relation to the land, an equine life, over and again would undercut every effort to impose another relation, the agrarian life. The Peace Commission reported that the "old Indians" were stubbornly holding to the antique habits of roving, hunting, and warring. They got it backward. Indians were not clinging to old lives. They were trying to continue and expand new ones they had fashioned from what the whites themselves had provided and what fit the world they knew well.

Those who did try taking up the new life were usually met by a dash of cold reality. Washakie, a prominent chief of the Eastern Shoshones, told commissioners at the 1868 Fort Laramie council that he was "desirous to settle down to farming and stockraising."[14] Eight years later the agent on their reservation in western Wyoming reported some progress but added, with no apparent irony, that they "would be self-subsisting . . . were it not for grasshoppers annually destroying the most of their crops." The news in another eight years was that weather and pests had left the Shoshones in such "a starving condition" that they were eating seed. In another few years Washakie had had enough. When told yet again of the need to farm, he reportedly erupted: "God damn a potato!"[15]

Most reports were similar litanies of failure. Washington rarely came close to providing what had been pledged. Nine years after the Nez Perces had surrendered the majority of their homeland, their spokesman told a delegation that they still had no school, no church, no teacher, no doctor, no gunsmith, and no blacksmith.[16] Floods had destroyed all crops on his reservation's lowlands, the Crow agent wrote in 1873, and the ripening grain above them did well until an "army of grasshoppers" devoured it. For the Gila River Apaches and Wichitas two years later it was drought and prairie fires.[17] The essential problem was the environmental reality that science was confirming and John

Wesley Powell and Silas Bent were articulating. A Lakota agent wrote in 1881 that on his reservation even a small army of skilled white farmers with plenty of seed and good equipment "would die of starvation."[18]

The year before, the commissioner of Indian Affairs summed up tribal progress outside Indian Territory. Cultivated reservation land across the West totaled 168,340 acres, barely enough for a thousand homesteads. Their wheat production, 408,812 bushels, was roughly a third of the harvest of one California megafarm. The 27,105 acres broken to plow that year was a tenth of the farm acreage in Saline County, Nebraska.[19]

By then the Peace Policy was foundering. Religious groups could bicker and maneuver as much as congressional factions, and their appointments often were as political, and their agents as corrupt, as any had been before. Denominations varied in their commitment; Quakers and Episcopalians performed well and Methodists poorly.[20] Some of the most dedicated agents were also the most rigid. Any agent who tolerated any "heathen customs," one wrote the secretary of the interior, had both "degraded [Indians] and lowered our own dignity."[21] The problem at base was that men who typically had neither administrative experience nor contact with Indians were asked to achieve goals that were inherently difficult, if not intractable, and were asked to do it in situations poisoned by decades of fraud and neglect. For that, as a special inquiry in 1878 wrote in understatement, "the bible and a creed" were not enough.[22] By 1881 the government's formal partnership with churches had been abandoned.

By then the reservation system faced other assaults. Whites in counties adjacent to the White Mountain Apache Reservation in Arizona doubled in number between 1880 and 1890, those neighboring the Shoshone Wind River reservation quadrupled, and those in lands southwest of the Great Sioux Reservation grew a remarkable thirteen times over. In the 1870s Indians in the Dakotas were a majority. Ten years later whites outnumbered them six to one. Meanwhile the "new" reformers, notably leaders of the Indian Rights Association, founded in 1882, and those attending the Lake Mohonk Conference of Friends of the Indian, which met annually in upstate New York beginning in 1883, condemned the agencies' inefficiencies and corruptions. Reservations were hopeless, wrote Lyman Abbot, who had never been to one. The whole business "could only be uprooted, root, trunk, branch and leaf" and a new system put in its place. As always, however, the uprooting spade never touched the assumption that Indians would have to turn to the farming life and surrender most of their land. What was needed, the Indian commissioner declared in 1880, was yet another new strategy fit for the "progressive age in which we live."[23]

That new answer was "allotment in severalty." Reservations would be surveyed and authorities would allot parcels of land to families and individuals ("in severalty"), thus ending the traditional communal ownership of homeland, and whatever was left would be sold for settlement by others. Some treaties already had provisions for allotments, but the call now was to make it a blanket policy with no options.

By the early 1880s an allotment bill was introduced annually, and after being stalled for several years, once by a debate over a tax on oleomargarine, a version proposed by Senator Henry Laurens Dawes of Massachusetts passed in 1887 and was signed by President Cleveland.[24] The Dawes, or General Allotment, Act gave the president authority to set the system in motion. Agents would compile a census of tribal members. Reservations would be surveyed and each head of household would receive a quarter section, single adults and orphans would get half that, and single persons under eighteen half of that. Tribal members had four years to choose their lands, after which allotments would simply be assigned to them. The government would hold allotments in trust for twenty-five years. Landholders then would receive full title, become citizens, and live under the laws of their particular state or territory. Land left over after allotment would be sold and opened to settlement, and the proceeds would also be held in trust and used for tribal benefit. The Five "Civilized" Tribes of Indian Territory and some others in New York state were exempted, and where there was less pressure to open reservations, as with the Navajos in the Southwest, allotment was not pushed. But elsewhere the policy proceeded.

The Dawes Act was backed by honest idealists and monied interests, respected scholars and the most cynical land-grabbers.[25] Critics like Grant's Indian Commissioner Ely S. Parker, a Seneca, embraced assimilation but with recognition of some Native rights and tribal integrity. A very few, like Thomas Bland, founder of the National Indian Defense Association, argued for tribes keeping their communal ownership and many of their traditional life ways. (A scandalized "new" reformer wrote that the association apparently was intent on "defending the Indian's right to be an Indian.")[26] As sympathetic supporters clashed over how best to reach common goals, self-serving interests worked so persistently to pry lands out of Native hands that eight years after his law's passage Dawes told the Lake Mohonk Conference that the law had "fallen among thieves."[27]

The story around the law was no simple morality tale, but its role in speeding Native America's deteriorating place in national life is undeniable.[28] By the time the policy was reversed in 1934, tribal lands had shrunk by about two-thirds, from around 133 million to 48 million acres. As with other assaults on Native lifeways, the loss of communal lands undercut tribal identities and social structures. True to its own traditions, the federal government failed to provide the most basic promised material and instructional support even as western agriculture was becoming increasingly modernized and more costly. Efforts to defy geography and climate were no more successful on allotments than they had been on reservations. The consequence was another parallel between West and Southeast. As southeastern Blacks were confined increasingly to sharecropping, western Indians were marginalized as scratch farmers.

The Dawes Act offers a point of reckoning. It was one of those events that, when turned this way and that, can suggest the different meanings we can find in some especially revealing story. The story here is that of the government's policies toward, and intentions for, Indian peoples and how those policies and intentions played out during the first century of their history.

As officially promoted, the Dawes Act was an old aspiration finally fulfilled. Seen this way it was a victory of policies from Emer de Vattel to post–Civil War reformers, with Indians taking a long step along the path of human progress and into full membership in the national family. Turn it another way and it was a case of aspirational need trumping reality. The strategy for transforming Indians supposedly was to first train them to be farmers, and thus civilized, and then to give them individual farms. That was not happening, at least at nearly the pace needed. So Washington simply flipped its strategy and goals. Instead of training Indians to be civilized farmers and then issuing them their own lands, it issued them their own lands and then declared them to be civilized farmers. The end became the means, and vice versa. Read this way, the law was legislating illusion—"manufactur[ing] [the Indian] into a white man by act of Congress."[29]

Twist the Dawes Act a third time, and it is something else again. It becomes a final step in a shift of power—power rooted in the land itself—and, more widely, in the process of domesticating western America. Indians had begun that process. When they acquired horses they forged a more direct connection to the land's energy in the wild grasses around them. Then whites stepped in and took control of the shift that Indians had begun. They forged their own connections, switching out domestic cattle for bison and domestic grasses, wheat, corn, and barley, for wild grama and bluestem. In doing that they unhorsed the Indians and left them dependent and reservation-bound. The logical last step was, in Washington's own terms, to domesticate the "wild tribes" on the reservations. Realities aside, it would declare them to be farmers, smoothly bound into the new order.

To follow the process, from the onset of the grass revolution to the firming of the new western pastoralism and agriculture, is to trace the rise, tilt, and fall of

Native power. To follow official policy is to see it as unwavering in its original goal, turning Indian lands over to others, while steadily adjusting particulars and redefining Indians to fit the goal's needs of the moment.

Thirty years before the Dawes Act, Lakota leaders reportedly were saying that farming was merely the means to confine them to "a small tract of country." Then, when their crops failed, as they surely would, Indians "would starve unless they should eat their own children."[30] That last was not happening, but the rest was pretty close to the truth. By the 1880s Indians had effectively lost most of their homelands and were left to find a way on "small tract[s] of country" to live by means and customs that laws had long declared to be their true badge of civilization.

In the same council the Lakota spokesmen had called farming a ploy to give "all the buffalo to the whites" and by that to end the tribes' "hunt[ing] game on the prairies." Washington certainly meant to end the hunting life, and whites did in fact take the bison, but the story is less straightforward than the one the Lakotas told—and much more revealing of the changes afoot.

Bison and Bugs

In late June of 1820, as the expedition of Stephen H. Long ascended the Platte River in present-day Nebraska, it passed through herds of bison "blackening the whole surface of the country." Night was full of the bulls' guttural bellowing. Sentries had to drive back animals that came close to sniff at the horses and to press against the wagons. During the day, as Long's men rode along the south bank, the wind occasionally sprang up behind them and carried their scent across the river into the massed animals. "We could distinctively note every step of its progress through a distance of eight or ten miles," the diarist Edwin James wrote. As the "tainted gale" made its way over the herd, whatever animals it touched bolted and surged against the crowd around them. Long's men were watching their own smell move over the plains to the horizon, a current of agitation passing through the bison like wind through tall grass.[31]

Thirty-five years later virtually no bison could be found there or anywhere within a hundred miles of east of the Rockies, and other parts of the plains were similarly empty of shaggies. After another twenty-five years the herds that had left observers gape-jawed from southern Canada to central Texas had dwindled to nearly nothing. The best estimates today put the population of the plains bison at its height, around the time of Long's expedition, at about twenty-eight million. A close count in 1889 found 1,091, a decline of 99.999965 percent.[32]

The near extinction of the animal later inscribed on our nickels and state flags is a contender for the most striking case of the environmental convulsions of the market and industrial revolutions remaking the West. The bison's story, however, was hardly alone. Another western creature, nearly a million times smaller but far more prolific, was also driven to the edge, and then pushed over it.

The collapse of the bison population came in two phases. Both were related to the new commercial order that was linking the West to a larger world. Whites had some role in the first—the overland migration destroyed the bison's habitats and the millions of oxen, cattle, horses, and sheep may have passed along new diseases—but the Indians were more responsible, mainly from trade. The grass revolution peaked as a global market opened for bison robes. Plains horse-men and the women who turned hides into robes sent many hundreds of thousands of processed hides into a global market, then drew on that market for an unprecedented array of goods. By the eve of the Civil War the number of bison had dropped as much as half.

Whites dominated the second phase. After the war professional hunters shot thousands to feed railroad work crews, and farmers on the eastern plains hunted bison to feed their families, but their impact was nothing compared what followed. In the early 1870s there was a global shortage in leather brought on by a surge in demand in factories for belts and gaskets. The prime source, cowhide from Argentina, could not keep up, and as prices rose steeply, tanneries looked desperately for alternatives. In 1871 at least three—in Philadelphia, England, and Germany—discovered that after soaking in a lime solution bison hides could indeed supply the need.[33] The moment the news arrived back on the plains, a bison hide, as a prospect circulating through a worldwide market, became something entirely different. What had been an exotic source of comfort for distant, well-to-do consumers now was a vital component in factories that were remaking the world. What had taken up to a week of steady labor to turn it into a marketable robe now could be shipped to tanneries by the thousands after being taken "green" from the animal's back. A bloody and untreated hide would bring up to $3.50.

The "great hunt" began in 1872.[34] Using powerful single-shot .45- or .50-caliber rifles—Sharps were a favorite—hidemen would position themselves several hundred yards downwind from a herd. After killing a group's protective bull, they would turn methodically to the rest, working from the outside in. Slaughtering twenty or more of the animals in a single stand was common.[35] One hunter claimed 121 killed with a bit over 300 shots; a companion killed 46 with 47 shots.[36] Skinners then would flay the carcasses, scrape off the remnants of meat on the hides, and stake them out to dry into stiff "flint" hides that could be stacked into wagons and hauled to the nearest rail stop. The entire operation—the killing shot by shot by shot, the coordinated skinning and drying, the dispatching—had an industrial feel, much as in a hide's likely destination, a factory.

In 1872 a few thousand men converged on western Kansas and eastern Colorado, centering around Dodge City, Kansas, on the Atchison, Topeka and Santa Fe rail line. One estimate, adding in hides wasted and taken by Indians and settlers, sets the total bison lost in 1872–74 at around 3.7 million.[37] The hunt then turned southward onto the high plains of western Texas. This was the shift that brought on the "buffalo war," the confrontation between army and the Comanches and Kiowas, already beset by the ranching frontier. Within a couple of years the bison population south of the Platte River had fallen well below what was worth hunting. The great hunt's focus turned to the northern plains. Herds there had long faced aggressive Indian hunting and, across the Canadian line, killing to produce enormous amounts of pemmican to supply British fur trading companies.[38] That toll was dwarfed by what came now. Hides were shipped out on the Northern Pacific Railroad and via steamboats down the Missouri River. Those stacked on one "hid every part of the boat, barring only the pilot house and the smokestacks." A single buyer in Miles City shipped out 50,000 in 1881, 200,000 the following year, and 40,000 the next. In 1885 the hides needed a single car. The herds were gone.[39]

The carcasses were left mostly as a bounty to wolves, coyotes, and vultures. The remaining bones also had industrial uses, ground into fertilizer (another connection to agrarian expansion and a global market) and fashioned into corset staves and playing dice. Cash-poor farmers, "bone pilgrims," gathered them up and stacked them like hay at railheads. The Atchison, Topeka and Santa Fe alone carried out nearly eleven million pounds over three years.[40]

A persistent impression holds that the western military organized and directed the great hunt to subdue resistant Indians by destroying their economic mainstay.[41] Military leaders certainly approved of the killing, but the hunters' motives were summed up by hideman Frank Mayer. Firing a cartridge that cost a quarter, he could obtain a hide he could sell for up to five dollars. If he killed a hundred a day, he would net six thousand dollars a month, triple the salary of the president of the United States: "Was I not lucky that I discovered this quick and easy way to fortune? I thought I was."[42] The plains bison's problem was not the military. It was that, starting in the 1820s, it became an increasingly desirable commodity. It became a numerical value within a global calculation of evolving needs and satisfactions. That number, as a robe, first clicked up, then, as industrial leather, it shot up, which meant that bison, as commodities, were quickly gathered up. The Plains Indians' problem in turn was that their livelihood was tied to the bison, and thus to its market number, so as that number went up, their fortunes went down. They became like one of several baubles suspended in a mobile of the sort that later hung above innumerable cribs for infants to wonder at. Each bauble on a mobile appears to float independently, but that is an illusion. If any one of them is even slightly jiggled, by a touch or breath of air, every other one moves. In 1871 something moved in a few tanneries on either side of the Atlantic, and halfway across North America the life of Plains Indians jiggled, and not for the better.

As with western extractive enterprises, the hide trade soon collapsed. The slaughter was so rapid that it depressed prices while eliminating its shaggy resource. Frank Mayer soon learned that his calculations ("Was I not lucky?") were preposterously overblown.[43] As was also commonly the case, the episode quickly took on a mythic sheen. The mythic hideman had two faces. At the time one was a predictable cousin of bullwhackers and cowboys, men in a rollicking fraternity drawn to the free life and facing elemental threats with the now-familiar squared masculine jaw. The other, more familiar face came after the slaughter, with a growing outrage over the loss of what had become an American icon. Hide hunters now appeared as filthy, gore-covered, greed-driven degenerates, "butchers drawn from the dregs of border towns," stinking and flyblown, men who were "conscious of their own unfitness for civilized society."[44]

In fact, as with other mythic types, buffalo runners had stepped out of the common crowd and, their bloody work done, they stepped back in. They went on to lives as merchants, druggists, candy salesmen, and tax assessors. James Mead founded Wichita, Kansas, and presided over the state historical society and Kansas Academy of Science. Bill Tilghman held the record for bison killed in a season, more than six thousand. He went on to be police chief of Oklahoma City, an early filmmaker, a delegate to the 1904 Democratic national convention, and a breeder of racehorses. His favorite, Chance, won the 1894 Kentucky Derby.[45]

This was myth as hand-washing. The critics who deplored the "indiscriminate, improvident, and wanton slaughter" would usually call it a needed step in the passing of an old life toward the new one of farm and ranch. The rotting carcasses were eggs broken for the national omelet. Still, the grotesque particulars and a growing sense of losing the wild made the truth uncomfortable. To show the hideman for what *he* was, a dollar-chasing westerner no different from millions of his countrymen coast to coast, was to show the butchery for what *it* was: the natural consequence of forces creating the West and remaking the nation. Thus the mythic buffalo runner. He was made into an outlier and misfit, a stinking exile. Now Americans could turn up their noses, or rather hold them, and walk away from what had happened while embracing the consequences.

The bison, individually, was the largest land animal in the western hemisphere. Collectively, however, it was not the heaviest even on the Great Plains. In the mid-1870s Rocky Mountain locusts appeared there in unimaginable numbers. A single flying swarm, a quarter to half a mile deep, covered about 200,000 square miles, an area equal to all of New England plus New York, New Jersey, and Pennsylvania. A conservative estimate sets the total number of swarming locusts at 15 trillion, more than 2,000 for every human alive in 2015. One way of measuring the extent of a creature's presence is its biomass, the total weight of a species' population in a particular place. The plains bison's biomass at its peak was about 7 million tons. At half a gram each, the locusts added up to 8.5 million tons.[46]

As the locusts were massing in swarms "larger than any known biological phenomenon on earth," the bison's numbers were collapsing, but the locust's dying time was just ahead.[47] During the 1890s the periodic swarming subsided, then stopped. Although it took a while for the country to be sure, or even to notice, the Rocky Mountain locust was extinct soon after the turn of the century. The story of how and why it vanished is both ironic and revelatory, and like that of the bison it demonstrates vividly the forces that were making the West.

The Rocky Mountain locust, *Melanoplus spretus* (roughly translated as "despised creature in dark armor") had its essential home, or "permanent zone," in the northern Rockies of Colorado, Wyoming, and Montana. Most of the time locusts appeared to be ordinary grasshoppers and lived scattered and dispersed and so drew no special attention.[48] When certain conditions coincided, however, they underwent quite a change. Counterintuitively, drought sent them into reproductive overdrive. By shrinking the supply of edible plants, it brought locusts together in increasingly dense concentrations until females began laying eggs chemically designed to encourage offspring to aggregate still more. As their numbers grew exponentially their wings grew longer and they darkened in color. The evolutionary purpose became clear. Sometime, usually in early summer, they would rise up in enormous masses and migrate in search for more food.

The swarms moved with the prevailing wind patterns, those rivers of air that even then meteorologists were exploring and mapping, and thus headed south and southeast. An outbreak usually lasted three to five years, with the normal population multiplying between a thousand and a million times over. First generation migrants would lay eggs after several hundred miles; those eggs would hatch the next spring and the next generation would move farther, and so on, until the migration reached its natural limits in Texas, Arkansas, Missouri, Iowa, and Minnesota. Succeeding generations may have retraced the route on a lower level of the jet stream, but whether returnees or stay-behinds or both, locusts would live as usual back in the permanent zone until conditions brought the next outbreak.

The legendary swarming of 1873–77 moved like a weather front, anticipating the horrific blizzards of the big "die-off" a decade later, but its advance was much slower and its wreckage was not over weeks but over forty months. On July 28, 1875, a Kansas professor of biology, Francis Huntington Snow, stood on the summit of Pikes Peak and watched a winged cloud, "as high up in the air as the eye could reach," riding the wind due east. Later that day an observer more than three hundred miles to the east watched a swarm, probably the same one, settle into local fields. It stayed for a week until the wind shifted from the north and the insects rose and flew with it. "Happy we were!" he wrote, but then: "Vain delusion." At four that afternoon another cloud rose out of the north and west, "more dense, more terrible, more numerous," and an hour later a final swarm came down "like huge flakes of snow" to cover the land. The next morning, sun-warmed, they marched into the cornfields and in a few hours devoured "every leaf, ear, and in many places the stalks" before they lifted up and flew southward.[49]

How this looked and felt on the ground became part of plains lore. Locusts devoured a man's linen coat as he walked through them and ate some roasting ears from the arms of a woman before she could reach her house. The day turned so dark as the swarm neared that the chickens roosted, Katherine Wooden remembered. The movement of the chewing insects through the dry vegetation, numberless, unstopping, sounded "like a train of cars on a railroad." Her parents tried to save some tomatoes, but it was hopeless. Soon everything was gone. Onions were eaten from the inside so the outermost skins sat like empty cups. "People in the east have often smiled incredulously," investigators wrote later, at stories of locomotives stalled on their course by the insects, but it happened often when the sheen of oil from crushed locusts left an engine's wheels spinning helplessly.[50]

The only defense was against the crawling newly hatched nymphs. A mini-industry appeared of contraptions meant to roll over and crush them, lure them into basins of poisons, suck them up and bag them, incinerate them with a reflected fire, and suffocate them with sulfurous fumes.[51] All were at best erratically useful. Plainspeople set out to whack at the millions of nymphs with cloth sacks, and as they bent their backs they hedged their bets by bending their knees. Missouri, Minnesota, and Dakota Territories all invoked the divine with days of fasting and prayer, which proved no more effective than rolling vacuums and locust-roasters.[52] By the outbreak's third year, the loss to plains agriculture was estimated at $200 million.

The result was another case of the West pushing Washington into new responsibilities. Congress in 1877 provided eighteen thousand dollars to fund the United States Entomological Commission charged with both reporting on the crisis, its extent and losses and—the key phrase—to discover "the practical means of preventing its recurrence or guarding against invasions."[53] This was the first time Washington had enlisted the scientific community on a focused, particularized mission. Countless other cases would follow, in the near future Theobald Smith's and F. L. Kilbourne's puzzling over Texas fever. The ultimate impact of federally sponsored research in solving thousands of specific problems would be incalculable.

The commission's head was Missouri's former state entomologist, Charles Valentine Riley. Brilliant, insatiably ambitious, and more than a tad eccentric (an insomniac, he sometimes would rent a nightly chair in a barbershop to lengthen his sleeping odds), Riley worked with two other skilled veterans of insect wars, Alpheus Packard and Cyrus Thomas, both veterans of the Hayden survey. The trio produced two reports that totaled more than a thousand pages.[54] They documented *M. spretus*'s anatomy, life cycle, and habits and showed it was a separate species. They plotted out its home country, where it nested and bred during outbreaks. They exhaustively described those outbreaks and documented them through dozens of interviews. Most impressive, the commissioners recommended or anticipated defenses that future specialists would term "integrated pest management"—multipronged programs that combined using natural enemies, manipulating the environment through tree planting and irrigation, and diversifying crops into combinations that locusts would find less tasty.

The report placed little faith in new contraptions and called instead to use forces already at work. It called on the federal government to step up. The Signal and Postal Services and the Weather Bureau could gather information on any outbreaks, and the western military could battle the swarms, two-legged warriors against the six-legged. More sponsored research could improve understanding and add to the weapons in the struggle. Washington should also continue to promote development—financing railroads and opening lands to farmers, assisting both irrigation and selective burning—that would transform the western environment and destroy the enemy's habitat. Washington, in short, should encourage the same rapid command of the country that was driving the near total destruction of the bison.

More specifically, in fact, they suggested doing to the locusts what was being done to the bison: sell them—commodify them, give them a number in the world market, and hope it would rise so their population would sink. Their remains might be used as fertilizer or to feed poultry. Pickled, salted, dried, and pressed into cakes, they might be sold as Atlantic fish bait. The oil that slickened railroad tracks could be processed for its formic acid and sold to laboratories at sixty cents an ounce. They might also be eaten, and not only by chickens.[55] Riley found locusts quite palatable when boiled into a broth, pureed, fricasseed, and fried or roasted in their own oil (although their spiny legs bothered his throat). He had them tested by a leading Saint Louis caterer, and he sent a box of them, well fried, to a society of French entomologists. Reviews were restrained.[56]

In the end, the commission's story is above all ironic. Its reports appeared in 1877 and 1880. *M. spretus* swarmed a few times afterward on a smaller scale, but although irruptions of grasshoppers persist until today, those of the Rocky Mountain locusts ended in the 1890s. They were soon extinct. Two specimens were collected in 1902. They rest today in the Smithsonian Institution. Given the timing, with the pouring of funds and their prodigious results, it was natural to associate the locusts' demise with the commission's remarkable work.

In fact there was no connection at all. The locusts' extinction was a matter of mathematics and location. The trillions of locusts in their swarming would have sprung from a relatively small number, ten million to ten billion. All could have lived comfortably in a circle of land sixty miles in diameter, tops. Those breeding grounds were focused sharply along Montana's Yellowstone River and the three forks that formed the Missouri—the Jefferson, Madison, and Gallatin Rivers, as well as their tributaries. There females laid their eggs, up to 150 of them in every square inch of the sandy soil of the river swards. To survive, the locusts had to keep access to those riversides as they had, presumably, for eons.

But those same places were under environmental assault. They comprised one of those few islands in the western between-land being aggressively, thoroughly farmed. Gallatin County had more than twice the improved acreage of any other Montana county, save one, and 98 percent of its cultivation was along the Gallatin, Madison, and Jefferson Rivers—precisely in the locusts' egg beds.[57] The area rated a next-to-best rank of III in that measurement of efficient wheat production in the 1870 census (see map 8). This country and that along the Yellowstone was also one of the first regions to feel the northward spread of ranching, which also concentrated along streams, with thousands of cattle grazing and churning the soil with their hooves. All this—the plowing, harrowing, irrigating, and grazing, with occasional flooding from those very changes—bore suddenly down on the micro-environments that were the cradle of *M. spretus*. Every year more of its eggs were uprooted, exposed, eaten, crushed, and flooded. The creatures that a short time before had risen up in their trillions rapidly dwindled and vanished.

As Riley, Packard, and Thomas were calling for the government to do whatever possible to protect embattled farmers from the locusts' aggressions, it was the locusts that were being victimized and the farmers who were, unwittingly, the aggressors, wreaking the ultimate devastation on the most prolific visible life form in North America. It was another western anticipation. The next century and a half would witness similar, far wider extinctions as spreading development destroyed vital habitats of species across the globe.[58]

The true destroyer of *M. spretus* and near annihilator of *B. americanus* was a new economic and cultural order. It remade much of the land and redefined its plants and animals and minerals into fluctuating values that moved around much of the world via new systems of connection. Those values swung up and down with the new order's needs, and the fates of creatures, grasses, and stones swung with them.

Western agriculture should be seen in those terms. It broke the land far more profoundly than as the phrase is usually taken. It broke and realigned ancient flows of energy, which set parts of the West on course to become one of the most productive regions on earth while setting loose unintended physical changes beyond control or calculation. It broke the sod and planted a good part of it with domestic grass to send to hog pens, feed lots, and dinner tables from Connecticut to London. That broke the reign of wild flora and began to send grama grass, pigweed, and lamb's quarters, along with the bison and the locusts, toward the nether places. Because the Indians' grip on the land's energies ultimately rested on that floral regime, agriculture, along with ranching, finally broke their independence in its most elemental meaning, their ability to choose how to feed themselves.

It was part of a still-wider process. On their faces farming and mining seem fundamentally different. Both do involve digging in the dirt, but men blasting quartz half a mile into the earth would appear to have little in common with men plowing and harrowing on the surface. The differences deceive. In their larger consequences and their roles in making the West, agriculture and mining were far more alike than not.

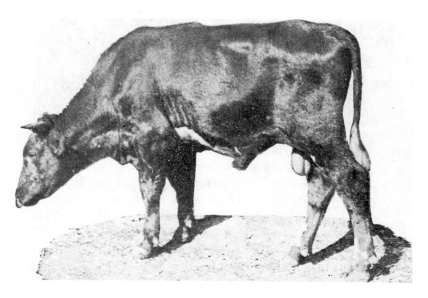

Fig. 34. (*top*) The romanticized cattle drives out of Texas spread a deadly fever to north-ern cattle and threatened the emerging national cattle trade and beef industry. *Cowboy with Steers*. Nineteenth-century engraving. Pictorial Press Ltd / Alamy stock photo.

Fig. 35. (*bottom*) A dying cow infected with Texas fever. The Bookworm Collection / Alamy stock photo.

Fig. 36. (*above*) Young animal scientist Theobald Smith, partnered with F. L. Kilbourne, solved the puzzle of Texas fever. Their discovery that ticks transferred the disease from one animal to another led to breakthroughs in understanding malaria, yellow fever, and other global maladies, indirectly helping to open Africa to colonization and allowing the construction of the Panama Canal. Library of Congress Prints and Photographs Division, George Grantham Bain Collection, LC-DIG-ggbain-06111.

Fig. 37. (*opposite top*) The grass revolution and rise of horse cultures fueled a bison-based economy that helped carry Plains Indians to an unprecedented power and affluence before the great ungulate swap replaced bison with cattle. George Catlin, Plate No. 6 Buffalo Hunt, 1844. Wikimedia Commons.

Fig. 38. (*opposite bottom*) Meat rationing on Pine Ridge Reservation in South Dakota. The bison's near demise and the rapid rise of plains ranching quickly left Indians reliant on federal agents for their basic needs. Library of Congress Prints and Photographs Division, John C. H. Grabill Collection, LC-DIG-ppmsc-02683.

SKINNING BEEF, NO 332.

Fig. 39. Born modern. Wheat farming in California's Central Valley was from the start done by methods modernizing agriculture across the nation. *The Graphic*, July 14, 1883.

Fig. 40. (*top*) Western agriculture developed by a splay of methods in a variety of economic and social contexts. In the Great Basin Mormons pursued collective irrigated cultivation. *Method of fencing irrigated fields, near Salt Lake City, Utah, about 1860–1865, Harper's Weekly, No. 3405.*

Fig. 41. (*bottom*) Across the West, and especially on the eastern plains, there was homesteading, with its accompanying speculation and manipulations. [J. D. Semler, near Woods Park, Custer County, Nebraska], Solomon D. Butcher, 1886. Library of Congress Prints and Photographs Division, LC-DIG-ppmsca-08370.

Fig. 42. On the northern plains, it was mechanized industrial-style "bonanza farms" worked by gang labor. Institute for Regional Studies, North Dakota State University–Fargo (Folio 102.AGB66.4a).

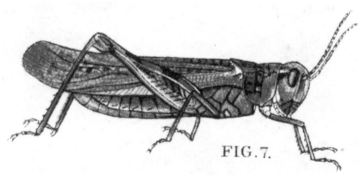

FIG. 7.

Fig. 43. (*top*) A sudden global demand for industrial leather spawned the factory-like hunt and processing of bison and their hides, nearly exterminating one of the West's totemic animals.*Curing Hides and Bones, Harper's Weekly,* April 4, 1874, suppl., p. 307. Library of Congress Prints and Photographs Division, LC-USZ62-100250.

Fig. 44. (*bottom*) The rapid development of market agriculture and ranching in western Montana drove to extinction one of the most prolific life forms on earth, the Rocky Mountain locust. Annual Report of the Agricultural Experiment Station of the University of Minnesota, 1902–3. Wikimedia Commons.

Figs. 45–46. (*opposite*) Placer mining, the pursuit of gold eroded from its original deposits, evolved rapidly from simple devices like rockers and long toms (*above*) into hydraulic mining (*below*), an industrial operation that took an enormous environmental toll and reengineering of entire ecosystems. Long tom: *Le Tour du monde* 5, no. 1 (January 1, 1862), Wikimedia Commons; Hydraulic: Library of Congress Prints and Photographs Division, Lawrence & Houseworth Collection, LC-USZ62-9889.

Fig. 47. (*above*) Lode mining, the pursuit of gold and silver in their original veins, from the start was typically as complex and heavily capitalized as any industrial enterprise in Gilded Age America. It required hauling workers and ore from thousands of feet underground. National Archives and Records Administration, War Department, Office of the Chief of Engineers, U.S. Geological Exploration of the Fortieth Parallel (1867–1881), NWDNS-77-KS-1-13.

Fig. 48. On the surface mills also transformed the environment while process-ing tens of thousands of tons of ore. The Gould and Curry Mill in Virginia City, Nevada, had its own reservoir as well as Victorian-style terraces and statuary. Timothy H. O'Sullivan, Plate 94 from Geological Exploration of the Fortieth Parallel / United States Army Corps of Engineers. Library of Congress Prints and Photographs Division, LC-DIG-ppmsca-11880.

Fig. 49. A ritual drummer in the peyote religion, later the
Native American Church. Like the more widespread Ghost
Dance religion, peyotism continued Native religious traditions and beliefs while adapting some elements of Christian
theology. *Peyote Drummer*. Atomic / Alamy stock photo.

Fig. 50. Wohaw (Kiowa) seeks to fashion a place in his new world by drawing on the power of past and present, tipis and houses, bison and cattle. *A Man Receiving Power from Two Spirit Animals* (1877). Courtesy of the Missouri Historical Society, Saint Louis. http://collections.mohistory.org/resource/502917.

20 ➤ When the West Turned Inside Out

Think of flashes on a map. The first to flare are on the eastern slopes of the Sierra Nevada and in the Front Range of the Rocky Mountains just before the Civil War. Others pop and brighten from the northern Rockies southward almost to Mexico. Each flare and glimmer was a discovery of gold or silver following California's great coincidence of 1848 (see map 9). Each set in motion changes of a speed and scale unique in westward expansion. They built together into one of the great transformations of American history.

The flashes seem random, and they were in the sense of specific discoveries made through luck and studied hunches, but the larger lesson was not randomness but coherence.[1] Most broadly, each rush was part of a planet-wide boom. California's led soon to others in Australia, New Zealand, and British Columbia. By 1888 the world's annual output of gold was twenty times what it had been in 1848.[2] Nationally, California's strike brought a quickening pace of federal action—construction of roads, coping with Indian resistance, and surveying rail routes—that opened the western interior to more strikes that brought their own changes. The enormous wealth taken from the earth fed an expanding economy as new operations changed one of humanity's oldest enterprises into an industry that rivaled any others in its scope and complexity. Their methods of financing, including the most fantastic chicanery, pioneered the mechanics and psychology of marketing mass desire. The stifling, stinking, disaster-bent tunnels of western deep mines rivaled the worst industrial hells. Mining's gifts of wealth and national cohesion also levied a price of atrocities against land, air, and soundscape matched by few if any new industries across the world.

As usual the popular view has told it differently: raw camps, burbling creeks, barroom carousing, and "Eureka!" The color and oddities were certainly there, but mining regions from the start were in close conversation with the rest of the evolving nation. Shipyard owners and housekeepers in Philadelphia and Cleveland invested in cutting-edge mines and mills in Nevada and Colorado that produced wealth that helped pay for factories and business blocks in New Orleans, Chicago, San Francisco, and New York City. What was true in general was true in the details. The new cables of braided steel that hauled miners from a thousand feet underground also supported the suspension bridge that connected Manhattan to Brooklyn. Thomas Edison formed a corporation to produce electromagnets to extract gold from mining tailings. He predicted profits of up to $50 million. The scheme went belly-up.[3]

The West Gathers Dust

Gold and silver discoveries after California's came in three periods. After a few gold strikes in Oregon in the mid-1850s, prospectors in 1858 found gold in Nevada just over the Sierra and along Colorado's Front Range. Silver found in Nevada's gold country grew into the massive Comstock Lode. More gold and silver was discovered in the Colorado Rockies, along Idaho's Clearwater River and in the Boise Basin, and in western Montana around Virginia City and Helena. After a hiatus in the early 1870s the second period began with spectacular finds of gold in the Black Hills and of silver in far southern Arizona at Tombstone and at Leadville, high in the Colorado Rockies. Silver was found in the all-but-defunct gold camp at Butte, Montana, and in along the Wood River in Idaho. In the final period, in the 1890s, a major gold deposit was found at Cripple Creek a day west of Colorado Springs and soon afterwards in the state's south-central mountains at Creede. All of the big surprises had been uncovered by the end of the century. Plotted together, they all formed a connective peppering across much of the interior West.

Western mining proceeded by two broad methods, placer and lode mining. The first is the gathering of gold that has been eroded out of its original deposits and has migrated as small pebbles and dust to some part of the deposit's watershed. The second takes a step backward to extract gold and silver still in their homes in the earth. Both had been practiced for centuries in the Americas, Europe, Asia, and Africa, but both were moving in new directions that reflected the changes in the industrializing nation.

All placer mining was for gold (though plenty of gold mining was not in placers). Placer gold has risen with erosion to the surface of mountains and hills and has been washed out of its buried veins. Gold combines with very little else, so as it travels down streams and crumbling slopes it remains essentially pure. Because it is also very heavy, it collects in streambeds and other low places, and because it is shiny it is easily spotted by those who know what to look for. Miners occasionally found placer gold in small nuggets and very rarely as rocks of several ounces, but typically its descent had ground it into dust, sometimes as fine as flour. Some was found in active streams but much of it lay in deep dry gravels that had been the beds of ancient rivers.

MAP 9. Gold and silver mining rushes, 1848–80. During the thirty years after the great coincidence, boom after boom in gold and silver across the West pumped money into a growing economy and triggered rapid settlement and political organization of the interior. Map by Maggie Rose Bridges.

Of all western work, placer mining in its earliest stage came closest to matching the democratic myth of common men finding wealth by just looking around and picking it up. A Californian in 1848 watched "the happiest set of men on earth" digging gold from the dirt with knives and weighing it on scales fashioned from sardine boxes.[4] The first step was to locate a stretch of a stream that promised to pay. Thus the familiar sourdough: A man squatting by a stream with a shallow pan, scooping up some sand, gravel and water, then swirling it so the lighter material would wash away. If gold were present, flecks of it would remain on the pan's bottom. Panning was the means of finding placer gold, not mining it. That often began with a rocker, which resembled a baby cradle open at each end. As one man rocked it back and forth, another poured buckets of gravel onto a screen at one end and a third poured water through it. As the filtered and agitated gravel washed through, the gold settled and was caught on crosswise pieces of wood called riffles or cleats. A long tom, a wooden chute twenty or thirty feet long, carried a continuous flow of diverted water as its cleats and perhaps a sheepskin at the end gathered gold dust washed from gravel filtered at its head by a perforated metal sheet, or riddle. A rocker processed about three hundred buckets a day, a long tom between three and four thousand.[5] In the next evolution, sluicing, a series of wooden troughs with riffled bottoms were strung together, some for hundreds of yards, with miners working alongside shoveling dirt and gravel into a continuous flow of water.

A pattern now was evident. The more lucrative a site proved to be, the more elaborate the means of gathering placer gold, the costlier the operations, and the greater the call for coordinated labor. The trend continued. The enormous demand for water led to construction of wooden flumes, artificial canals that carried water from some distant stream. As some miners were moving water to where they needed it, others were removing it from where they didn't want it. In "river mining," some obstruction, usually a "wing dam" of rock, brush, and dirt, diverted the stream enough to expose the streambed. More ambitious systems sent the water into flumes as much as forty feet wide and six deep with pumps removing what water remained. On California's American River in 1858, 250 Chinese drained their claim with a flume three-quarters of a mile long and with twenty-five waterwheels.[6]

All this was meant to take eroded gold from living watercourses, but everyone understood that there was probably much more nearby. Streams meander. A stream of the moment held only the most recently arrived gold. In the area around it there were gravel deposits, some in ridges a hundred feet tall, left by a river's ancient incarnations. Inside those deposits were hundreds of millennia worth of powdered wealth. Digging and sifting gold from these "dead rivers" became the next stage. The goal was to dig to bedrock, the solid layer that caught the gold dust that had filtered the deepest. Bedrock might be a few feet down, or twenty, or two hundred, and concentrations of gold at the bottom of deep gravels could easily be 1,000 percent more valuable than up top.[7] In "coyoting," or drift mining, miners dug tunnels up to a mile long and carried promising rock to the surface, but burrowing through the unstable gravels was dangerous. Cave-ins crushed and suffocated the burrowers, and the use of blasting powder could have the grimmest results. A witness wrote his wife of a fellow worker with "one arm completely Cucked [cooked] . . . Hand torn to pieces . . . His face . . . filled with powder and rock . . . and eye blowed out."[8] Coyoting was also costly and work intensive—one writer guessed that the energy spent could have rebuilt San Francisco twice over—and the returns were iffy. One prominent site yielded an ounce of gold for each 55 tons of gravel, while for another it was 375 tons.[9]

Here was a riddle. The plentiful gold in these old gravel beds was so erratically dispersed, in effect millions of dollars scattered as pennies, that it was often not worth it to pick it up. The solution was hydraulic mining.[10] Hydraulicking can be seen as one more step in elaborated, expensive, and tightly choreographed ways to gather displaced gold. This step was such a long stride, however, that it took the process into a new order. It made placer mining industrial.

Near Nevada City, California, in 1853, a New Englander named Edward Mattison, having barely escaped being crushed in a collapsing tunnel, wondered how water might be applied to keep men out of harm's way. This former tinsmith fashioned a large crude nozzle into the end of a canvas hose that carried water from a stream above. Compressed into this small outlet, the water shot out with fabulous force and tore at a gravel bank more thoroughly in moments than human labor could in hours.[11] His experiment in safety introduced a new method that flourished especially in California and played prominently in Colorado, Oregon, Idaho, and Montana.

Quickly hydraulicking expanded to a terrific scale. Water was channeled downward from a reservoir to a mining site through flumes, pipes, and hoses and was fed into a monitor, a specially designed cast-iron nozzle. With four hundred feet of fall behind it, water exploded from a seven-inch barrel at three hundred gallons each second.[12] A single monitor in one hour could shoot out enough water to fill two modern Olympic pools. As operators raked their targets, hillsides would "crumble down . . . as if they were but piles of cloud blown away by a breath of wind."[13] The "melt" was sent through sluices and the gold extracted through expanded versions of the usual methods. In some operations deep gashes were blasted and dug on a steep slant downward and away from the hydraulic pits. Sluices were placed periodically along the cuts, paved with large wooden blocks. As thousands of tons of gravel tumbled through the cuts, gold was caught by spaces among the blocks.[14]

Such an operation was more expensive by magnitudes from placer mining before. Besides the costs of facilities and of disposing of the tens of millions of cubic yards of residue, the amount of water needed strains imagination. The daily supply of the North Bloomfield mine would have more than met the needs of London.[15] As placers expanded they birthed ever-larger operations. At the Big Canyon reservoir a ninety-foot dam held back a lake covering 537 acres. Some mining companies built their own reservoirs, while others drew on corporate enterprises like the Tuolumne County Water Company and the Eureka Lake and Yuba Canal Company. Reservoirs of the latter held more than a billion cubic feet of water. By the late 1850s more than four hundred water companies had been formed with some of the largest generating profits of up to 12 percent a month. California reservoirs held an estimated 7.6 billion cubic feet of water.[16]

Hydraulicking fed another spin-off enterprise. Gold does combine with a few elements. Mercury, or quicksilver, was one. In yet another stroke of luck, California had one of the world's largest deposits of the raw stuff of mercury, cinnabar (mercuric sulfide).[17] The New Almaden mine, near San Jose, had just begun operations when gold was discovered fewer than two hundred miles away.[18] Within a couple of years it was producing between 1.5 and 2.25 million pounds of quicksilver annually.[19] Cinnabar miners wormed their way steadily deeper as *tenateros* (carriers) bore leather bags, each with two hundred pounds of ore, up hundreds of feet of ladders and steep steps. By the mid-1870s Mexicans and Cornishmen were working twenty-seven miles of tunnels.[20]

Mercury was shipped to the mines in flasks, each holding about seventy-five pounds. When dumped into the sluices it bonded with gold. The combination was heated, the gold extracted, and some of the mercury saved to be used again. The demand was enormous. By one estimate a hydraulic used between twenty and thirty pounds of mercury for every pound of gold retrieved.[21] In 1874 California mines used nineteen thousand flasks, or about 1.4 million pounds. Because mercury combines with silver as well, it became essential to processing the ore that began pouring from western mountains after the strike at the Comstock in 1859. A hungry foreign market added even more demand. What began as a subsidiary to gold mining became a major industry itself, producing nearly 120 million pounds of mercury by 1890.[22]

The great commitment of capital earned its way through the algebra of scale. All mining profits depended on the ratio between what was gotten and the effort and expense to get it. A rocker demanded a lot of effort, so to earn a few dollars a day the few men operating it needed a claim with at least $0.50 in gold in every cubic yard of gravel. A long tom, handling more gravel with less effort, could make a profit with $0.13 a cubic yard. When the prodigious energy of water was applied in an ever-greater scale, the minimum amount of gold per unit of earth fell drastically.[23] A cubic yard of gravel at the North Bloomfield averaged only about $0.07 worth of gold, but with eighteen thousand cubic yards processed in a day, the yield was still $765, or about $23,000 a month, even after subtracting costs of water and labor. The yield per yard for other companies was far greater than that, from $0.20 to $0.60.[24]

A few implications were obvious, starting with the investment up front. For its first eleven years the Blue Gravel mine in Yuba County used all of its gross income, about $2,400 a month, to operate and dig its main tunnel. Then expenses plummeted and output shot up nearly ten times over.[25] Once the advantages kicked in, a hydraulic's unbeatable edge drove smaller independent operations toward the margins. Only four years after Edward Mattison's experiment, at least half of all California gold was coming from hydraulic placers, most of them corporate enterprises.[26]

The same advantage reduced the need for human beings to make it work. As a hydraulic took the energy of gravity applied to water, funneled it, and spit it out of a nozzle, the human role was reduced to directing the blast and dealing with the aftermath. "No such labor-saving power has ever been introduced to assist the miner," wrote the *Sacramento Valley Union*.[27] Hydraulics did indeed reduce dramatically the required effort, but the work now done was for wages from a corporate paymaster. If "labor" here refers to the hallowed term of the day, "free labor," the promise of opportunity for independent workers, then hydraulicking was not labor-saving. It was labor-killing.

The West yielded about $1.6 billion in placer gold between 1848 and 1931. Most by far, about $1.175 billion, came from the California Sierra.[28] The richest placers in the interior were in Idaho, on the Clearwater River and in the Boise basin, and in Montana at Virginia City and Helena. Arizona and New Mexico were full of promising rumors, but nearly all were mostly or wholly promotional bluster. In 1861 New Mexico governor Henry Connelly and partners formed a hydraulicking and ditch company to work a claim they said held $350 million in gold, roughly three times that year's national debt. It didn't.[29]

Placering's limits punctuated, once again, the common key to so much of western development, or the lack of it: connectivity, the ability to get to the West and to get around in it. California was nicely plugged into maritime networks and was bound inside itself by roads and rails. That system fed placer sites with people, equipment, and money that kept the operations, rich to begin with, going for years. The rich strikes in the Northern Rockies were so isolated that one authority marveled that "anyone should come there or stay there at all."[30] Connections in the Southwest were so tenuous and roads "so heavy or rough" that sites as rich as California's were "utterly neglected."[31] They were also cut off from what was, besides paydirt, placering's essential stuff: water. Arizona's Vulture Mine simply leased out its dirt at fifteen dollars a ton to anyone who would haul it to where there was enough water to work it.[32]

Conditions in the interior differed, place to place, and they flavored life differently. Chinese in California and Colorado faced legal, social, and sometimes physical assaults, but whites in Idaho happily turned over the declining placers to Chinese, who were happy to squeeze their livings out of anemic sites. In 1870 virtually no Colorado miners were Chinese. In Idaho six in ten were.[33] One result was a rare cultural cross-pollination. Chinese in towns like Idaho City mingled with white neighbors and shared in social occasions. Leading the July 4 parade in 1875, processing before the Goddess of Liberty, was a Chinese band with horn, drum, gong, and cymbals. For Chinese funeral processions an Irish brass band provided requiems, including Mozart's Twelfth Mass.[34]

Underground Factories

Placer gold is orphaned gold. Natural weathering has taken it from its mother deposit and broadcast it over a widening erosional fan. Other gold remains at home, in deposits often in the shape of veins woven through mountain rock, typically running through quartz. The generic term for such a deposit is a lode, and the pursuit of it is lode mining. Silver, the West's other precious metal, is accessible only through lode mining. It erodes like everything else, but unlike gold it bonds eagerly with materials it meets on its wandering, and the resulting combinations are either elusive or too expensive to process. All silver and much of the West's gold has been accessible only by locating and working a lode.

Even more than placering, lode mining tended toward large-scale, complex, corporate-financed enterprises. Almost from the start, it took on an industrial and corporate cast, and meeting the demands of western lode mining led to new understandings, methods, technologies, and applications that revolutionized one of humanity's most ancient lines of work. As generally in the West, mining was an inventive, modernizing force that coalesced knowledge and practice across much of the world.

Like placering, lode mining often began with the work of small-timers who found some substance of the western dream. As California's independent gold-seekers bumped against closed doors to the main chance, a small army smitten with the fever, "yon-siders," turned their practiced eyes to the interior in search for promising signs and formations. The prospector was the mythic equivalent of placering's sourdough. In popular imagination he wanders the hinterlands leading a burro loaded with tools and daily needs, picking at some promising rock, hoping for a smile from fate. Their stories feature mining's essential allure, the stroke of luck. Two of the West's richest finds, at Virginia City, Nevada, and Leadville, Colorado, began with placer miners grousing about meddlesome bluish sand that turned out to be silver in breathtaking amounts. A variation involved "burro dowsing." By legend the silver mines of northern Idaho were revealed when Noah Kellogg found his donkey with "his ears set forward, his eyes . . . set upon some object" that turned out to be an outcropping of high-grade ore.[35] The stories, with grizzled dream-drunk veterans wandering to their last, are the purest expression of western opportunity as crapshoot.

One of the most famous prospectors, Ed Schieffelin, came to embrace the myth himself. Born in Pennsylvania the year of Marshall's discovery, he claimed to have begun prospecting in California at age nine. By 1876 he was roaming Arizona's desert borderlands, a John the Baptist of mining capitalism—"the queerest specimen of human flesh I ever saw," a friend remembered: tall with long black hair and a matted beard, weatherworn and clothed in a motley of corduroy, flannel, and rabbit and deer hide. He later said he went twenty months without taking off his clothes. By the common story, his friends told him that the only rock he would find would be his own tombstone, so when he found his vein of silver, he named the claim the Tombstone, and the town that sprang up nearby took that name too. After winning a lawsuit around his claim, Schieffelin was rich. He spent time in the East, living and dining sumptuously and meeting President Rutherford B. Hayes, presumably after bathing and changing his underwear, but he returned West and for the rest of his days reveled in the image of a prospector as ever hopeful and a little "crazzy." It was "natural for me to be wild," he wrote, but for a man of "good grit," he found it quite a life. At his death in 1895 the wealthy Schieffelin was prospecting in Oregon. The dirt in the pan beside his body was said to assay at two thousand dollars a ton. In fact it was seven dollars.[36]

Like Schieffelin, some lucky strikers ended up well enough, and a few better than that. John Mackay, an early Comstock claimant, parlayed his first earnings into one of the largest fortunes in the nation. Many others added a note of pathos to the myth by squandering their luck and dropping toward the gutter. By tradition three prominent discoverers of the Comstock, James Finney, Peter O'Riley, and Pat McLaughlin, ended up, respectively, buried by public subscription, dying in a lunatic asylum, and cooking on a sheep ranch.[37] A broke Henry Comstock killed himself. Eilley Bowers, who with her husband, Sandy, had first worked the Comstock, lost it all and, as the "Washoe Seeress," squeezed out an ironic living predicting the future.[38]

Perhaps these stories—"a marbled mix of myth and reality," one student calls them—have such a folkloric appeal because they reflect a wider shift in thinking about success, from a faith in steady work, in frugality, and in gradual accumulation, values rooted on the farm, toward ones set in the new marketplace that embraced risk-taking and luck.[39] The mining West was the ultimate setting for that shift, and the prospector myth spoke to both sides of it, the dizzying stumble onto western jackpots that could just as quickly drain to nothing. Stories of prospectors surrendering claims for a nonce that would then make millions for corporations also said something about how quickly lode mining was commanded by big money. As with placer mining, the reasons had much to do with the technical challenges and how they were met.

Nevada's Comstock Lode offers the best examples of both.[40] It was among the deepest of all western lodes and was hands down the richest, so it offered both great difficulties and the motivation to overcome them. It developed in two stages. From the discovery of silver in 1859 until the mid-1860s, the initial surface deposits were pursued until they gradually played out. A small coterie of investors pushed deeper, eventually more than three thousand feet. The gamble paid off. After 1870 the search revealed what early historian Eliot Lord called a "wonderful ore-casket," by far the richest silver deposits in history until that time.[41] In the "big bonanza" two mines, the Consolidated Virginia and the California Mining Company, produced more than $100 million in the decade after 1873. At one point the former was turning out $50,000 daily. By the time production peaked in 1876–77 the Comstock held more than two hundred miles of underground shafts, drifts, and galleries. Then it quickly declined, from $38 million in 1876 to just over $1 million in 1881.[42]

The costs were staggering. They began with the paradox of the lode: you might know it was there, but then again you didn't. A vein exposed on the surface obviously had come from somewhere, but a mountain is in a constant inner roil, and its movements can shift and scramble whatever it holds. A vein can rise, dip, drift. A promising lead on the surface might continue into a true bonanza, but it might quickly dwindle to nothing, or veer away, or break off and resume elsewhere. Wealth was fractured, stuttering, deeply hidden, and so a lode in the abstract might or might not be a lode of workable reality. To find out which it was required both a lot of money and the willingness to risk it.

Other problems threatened to close these, the richest holes on earth. An early puzzler was especially ironic. The problem was the sheer size of the silver deposit and the ease of its extraction. A vein that might be more than forty feet across was made of crushed ore nearly soft enough to remove with a shovel. It was like digging through money. To complicate matters the soft clay just beyond swelled rapidly when exposed to air, generating what Clarence King judged an "almost incalculable force" on the expanding tunnels.[43] The usual timber supports could not hold back the earth around them. The solution, one that revolutionized mining across the world, was developed in an astounding one month by a young German engineer, Philip Deidesheimer. By his "square-set timbering," stout wooden beams were milled and notched uniformly so that one joined to another at their ends. They were fit together into hollow cells that in turn could be joined to other cells and put into place as miners moved farther into a lode. The result was a hive-like structure that could expand into cavernous spaces. The sight reminded visitors of "buried cathedrals."[44]

There was also the problem of going down and getting out. Increasingly powerful steam-driven machinery had to be developed to lower miners into the deepening shafts and to lift them, and the ore they dug, to the surface. One gargantuan hoist unspooled a four-thousand-foot cable weighing more than twenty-five thousand pounds. Eventually ore could be hauled from three thousand feet at close to sixty miles per hour.[45] To carry the miners, "cages" ran up and down vertical shafts, held in wooden grooves by I-beams on their sides. Rope of such lengths would break under its own weight, and if iron chains snapped, the result would be instantaneous and catastrophic. The answer was "wire rope," strands of iron (later steel) braided into a helix. It had considerable tensile strength, and if one strand broke, the others were likely to hold long enough to miss calamity.[46]

The Comstock had a peculiar problem.[47] As its mines deepened, their temperature rose rapidly, by various estimates at one degree Fahrenheit every twenty-eight to fifty feet. Was it a chemical reaction between water and certain rocks or superheated water extruded from below? No one was sure, but the practical consequences were obvious. The rock itself was like a well-heated stove, up to 160 degrees, and a miner's punch with a pick into a wall might spring loose a chamber of water at just 40 degrees below boiling. The ambient air temperature often ranged between 108 and 116 degrees, sometimes higher. In a rare case of cooperation, the viciously competitive operators linked their vertical shafts with horizontal tunnels that with the help of large fans moved the fetid, torrid, water-thick air out and fresher air in. Here was an odd reversal in the age's quest for power. As industries across the western world hungered for energy, Comstock engineers worked to get shed of it. By one estimate the heat that the mines expelled annually from the earth's natural furnaces equaled that produced by burning fifty-five thousand tons of the best anthracite coal.[48] Companies showered workers with water out of perforated pipes, provided "cooling rooms" with air pumped from up top, and supplied an expensive prophylactic for heat stroke—ice, ninety-five pounds per man per day in the Consolidated Virginia in 1878.[49]

Another opponent, water, was more formidable even than heat. The challenge of advanced placer mining was how to find enough of the stuff. The Comstock's problem was how to get rid of it. Within a few hundred feet, mines reached the table where surface water had percolated down to be caught in pockets. Breaking into one of them would turn the connected shafts into a honeycombed underground lake. The main answer was to pump it out, and the standard tool was the Cornish pump. A steam engine on the surface, with a large flywheel for balance and torque, used pine pump rods to suck up as much as five thousand gallons per minute. As early as 1865 three San Francisco foundries were turning out more than three thousand tons of pumping equipment a year, and as mines drove deeper the production rose and the pumps got larger. One in 1879 had a flywheel weighing close to a quarter of a million pounds.[50]

The alternative to pumping was draining. It spawned one of the most audacious engineering and financial enterprises of the century. A local mill owner, Adolph Sutro, proposed digging a tunnel from three miles down slope in the Carson River Valley to tap into one of the mines at 1,663 feet below its opening and would potentially drain virtually all the lode's operations.[51] The estimated cost was $3 million. Mine owners would pay two dollars per ton of ore taken from mines serviced by the massive drain. Financing was caught up in the speculative tangles that plagued the Comstock, but construction began in late 1869. The project proved technically ferocious and demanded vast resources—every five feet of the tunnel required a thousand board feet of lumber—but with the help of pneumatic drills developed in the East Sutro pushed ahead until finally connecting to the mines in July 1875. By then many mines had pushed below the tunnel entrance, leaving it useless to them, so in the end the project, one of the industry's true marvels, came nowhere near meeting its promise. Sutro meanwhile had cashed in his part and retired to San Francisco and a life of successful investments and public philanthropy, building a public aquarium and a complex of seven public baths.

New technologies had created a subterranean nether land. It had its beauty. Quartz with a mix of silver and chlorides had a crystalline look. With miners working with thousands of candles and walking with lanterns, "like so many Diogeneses searching for Truth," the walls threw back the flickering light in a dazzle "worthy of a fairy palace in some Arabian Wonderland."[52] T. H. Watkins used a different allusion. The Comstock held "a catalogue of horrors to challenge Dante's tour through the Inferno." "View their work!" Eliot Lord commanded his readers.[53] Heat made the mines "a place for salamanders rather than men." Some were carried out when they fell to raving. Speeding upward in an open cage, rising from the hellish heat into a frigid winter day, exhausted miners might fall to the side and be swept against the stone walls, smeared like butter before falling to the scorching sump hundreds of feet below. Fires could feed on the millions of board feet of timbers and, fanned through the elaborate system of ventilation, could turn a mine into a furnace. The most catastrophic fire started in the Yellow Jacket one April morning in 1869 and spread to the neighboring Kentuck and Crown Point. The flames, smoke, poisonous gases, and collapsing ceilings killed between thirty-four and forty-five men.[54]

As with surface mining, lode mining quickly measured the widening gap between the West's early promise of free labor and its increasingly clear reality of corporate regimes. Wage workers had as little command over their work-places, and as little a share of their income, as the shovelers and sluice-tenders of a large hydraulic. The most obvious difference between work above and that below was the level of discomforts and dangers of the latter. A tally of serious accidents in the Comstock, almost certainly incomplete, showed 901 between 1863 and 1880, roughly one a week. Of them, 295 were fatal.[55]

All this—the labyrinthine work hives, the clamorous traffic in shafts and tunnels, the earth's artificial breathing, and the stifling, nightmarish labors—was underground. Above it was another industrial world with its own sprawl, innovations, and dangers. Once operators got the ore out of the ground, they had to get the silver and gold out of the ore. The first step was to crush the raw rock in a "stamp mill." Five or six iron stamps, each up to a thousand pounds, rose and fell, piston-like, on a revolving cam in an alternating hammering pat-tern. Workers shoveled ore into a bed below to be pounded almost to powder. The first mill appeared in California in 1850. Eight years later there were 280. California machinists once again took a standard form, here the Cornish "grav-ity" mill, and soon improved it. Simple in form, easily built and taken apart, the California quartz mill became the standard around the world, starting with the interior West. They were carried across the plains in wagons to Colorado, where two hundred were operating only a year after the 1859 rush.[56]

The Comstock again was the great innovator, now in ore processing. To slash the expenses of hauling ore over the Sierra, a California mill owner, Almarin Paul, in 1860 contracted to do the work for several owners within sixty days of the first handshake. It was a brassy move. San Francisco foundries began working around the clock to turn out the mill makings that were carried over the mountains by dozens of mule-drawn wagons, and on the sixtieth day Paul's mill began operation. A competitor opened a few hours later. By the end of 1861 seventy-six mills were operating within a radius of sixteen miles of the mines. Together they could crush 1,200 tons of quartz daily. Stamping, however, was only the first of two steps. The gold and silver next had to be extracted from the pulverized ore, and Paul's mill did that as well. His promise was even brassier. "None of us knew anything about milling silver ores," he later admitted.

Geology smiled on him. Silver is typically bound up with baser metals, notably lead and copper, which requires sophisticated smelting to unlock the bond. Comstock silver, however, was bound with gold. Besides making for extraordinarily rich ore—one geologist guessed that at first the Comstock produce nearly as much gold as silver—extraction was simpler and cheaper.[57] Because both silver and gold bond with mercury, Paul could adapt established methods to new needs. Pulverized rock was mixed with water and shoveled into an "amalgamation pan" with mercury, salt, and copper sulfate. The heavy combination of gold, silver, and mercury was extruded through a hole at the bottom and retorted to separate the three.[58]

As with farming and ranching, the innovations' repercussions were global. Paul's "Washoe pan process" became the standard around the world wherever a strike's geology and chemistry allowed it. Lode mining fed regional growth, especially San Francisco's rise as the West's great metropolis. By the late 1860s its foundries were unrivaled in the nation, and arguably in the world, in production of mining equipment. Their market reached across the western interior and to Canada, Mexico, Australia, New Zealand, Japan, China, and Russia. San Francisco's *Mining and Scientific Press* became a global journal for mining engineering.[59]

As a workplace, a mill did not approach the hellish conditions of the mines, but it was bad enough, starting with the aural assault of dozens of stamps slamming iron against iron. An observer compared this to "truckloads of iron nails being hauled along a cobbled street."[60] The pace was relentless. Samuel Clemens (Mark Twain), after a short stint in a mill, thought it "a pity that Adam could not have gone straight out of Eden into a quartz mill, in order to understand the full force of his doom to 'earn his bread by the sweat of his brow.'" During lulls workers would "screen the tailings," shoveling what was washed from the pans in a try to recapture what had escaped. Doing this under a Nevada sun was "the most undesirable . . . of all recreations in the world."[61] There was the boredom of industrial work everywhere. When asked about such ennui, a man measuring out the incoming ore managed a literary pun: "They also serve who only stand and weigh it."[62]

No lode in the interior matched the Comstock, but some were contenders. The West's role as innovator continued. Colorado offered the best examples. The ore in strikes west of Denver around Central City was refractory (or in local slang, "rebellious"), with complex combinations of gold, silver, copper, zinc, and iron in the form of sulfides that the Washoe method could not break down to free the bullion. Various processes were pitched to solve the puzzle—"*Desulphurization*," wrote one expert, "became the Abracadabra of the new alchemists"—but mining was stymied until an ivy league chemistry professor, Nathaniel P. Hill, solved the problem.[63] It was a vivid use of shrinking distances. Hill took seventy tons of local ore across the plains, down the Mississippi, and across the Atlantic to Welsh smelters at Swansea. He then built a similar plant in Black Hawk, neighbor to Central City, hired a metallurgist trained in Freiberg, Europe's finest mining school, and a practiced manager from Cornwall.[64]

Colorado mining then took an upswing, especially with new silver strikes in the years ahead. The greatest was at Leadville, more than ten thousand feet above sea level at the headwaters of the Arkansas River.[65] As at the Comstock, gold miners in 1877 found that the bluish sand that fouled their placers was silver. Three years later the camp of 200 had become a city of nearly 15,000 with 28 miles of streets, 13 schools, 3 hospitals, and 114 saloons. Silver output grew from well under $1 million in 1877 to $11.5 million in 1880, more than that of any other country except Mexico. The first smelter opened even before the town was named; fourteen were there by 1880, again devising new techniques quickly employed across the world.[66]

Mining, milling, and smelting were bound increasingly into a single network. Silver mines in Butte, Montana, sent ore to Colorado and some as far as Germany. In 1878 William Andrews Clark of Butte partnered with Hill to form the Colorado and Montana Smelting Company to take advantage of the growing portion of copper in the ores taken from its silver mines. Within a decade Butte was the world's largest producer of copper, one of global industry's most essential metals.[67] Railroads as usual were key. Rails fed Hill's smelters with the fuel it used to transform ore carried in from Arizona, New Mexico, Montana, and northern Mexico.[68] As booms birthed towns tucked into the high country, rails brought them everything from groceries to billiard tables. Anheuser-Busch had seven rail cars with their own crews to keep its beer flowing to Leadville.[69]

Mills and smelters above ground had become an industrial expanse that matched that below. By 1880 the Comstock's mills had treated more than 6.2 million tons of ore. To do it they consumed bluestone, salt, iron, mercury, and, in one year, thirty thousand pounds of "lard oil," animal fats that prior to petroleum were used to lubricate factory machinery.[70] Some were emblems of the age. The Gould and Curry Mill appeared less a factory than a Gilded Age chateau. Built of hewn stone and finished wood, rising from an artificial plateau in the shape of an enormous cross, it had its own reservoir and stately terraces and verandas. Livestock grazed its lawns. In front was a large pool with statuary of cavorting nymphs and a water-spouting swan.[71]

Taken together, the mines below ground and the clanking machinery above were an industrial plant that rivaled in expanse and impact any others across the world. They reached miles across and thousands of feet downward. They grappled with vexing puzzles around an expanding worldwide enterprise, and by doing that they wrestled with the primal forces air, fire, and water. It was high industrial drama that played out through scenes of the land defiled, of ghastly human tragedies, and of near-unimaginable conditions for those whose daily labor made every accomplishment real.

Behind it all was capital. In its scope, audacity, inventiveness, and wreckage, its story rivaled that of the mines and mills that it brought to life.

21 ▷ Legal Wrestling, the Land Convulsed

Gold and silver mining, especially lode mining, brought into some remote continental corner an advanced version of the industrial economy that was rapidly transforming other parts of the nation.[1] It brought this change faster and more fully than any other western episode. A town like Leadville, sprung up like some urban toadstool at a lung-testing altitude, was as finished a version of industrial culture as in many manufacturing centers of the East. All was a gamble. Every structure and service, from a boarding house to a bank, sat on the presumption that ready wealth would soon pour from the earth. "Men walked the streets of Virginia City as if pacing the roof of a fabulous treasure house," Eliot Lord wrote of the Nevada boomtown.[2] A Dakota ranch, California megafarm, and every honest homestead was at its heart a stride of hope, but lode mines were different. Potential profits were greater by magnitudes, yet it all would come from something that was hidden, and might not be there at all. Simply finding out whether there was any money to be made demanded an investment of far more capital than for any ranch or farm.

The combination—greater potential wealth, more money needed, and greater risks—made mining more economically volatile than any other western enterprise. It also left it marvelously open to the baldest manipulation and the wildest chicanery. As such it was arguably the nation's clearest instance of the plunging spirit so much a part of late nineteenth century America.

Global Gambling, Courtroom Wars

Before 1866 every mining claim in the West was illegal, at least in the eyes of Washington.[3] On the eve of far-western expansion, the federal government reserved all mineral rights on public lands. Every placer miner and lode operator was the equivalent of a squatter farming on an unopened public domain, except a squatter knew that a legal path to ownership would soon open. A miner didn't. At the end of the Civil War tens of thousands of persons were working claims in the far West. Investors had lavished tens of millions of dollars on developing the claims and on building vast infrastructures to operate and support them. Whole societies had appeared to service these operations.

And yet everyone knew that a real possibility existed that the legal foundation might be snatched out from under every bit of it. It was the ultimate expression of western risk-taking, inspired by the ultimate western dreamscape.

Mining did have an extralegal basis. Firstcomers had established rules that courts would partly uphold. A placer miner would have free access to public lands but could make a claim of limited size only if there was gold there, and he could keep it only by working it.[4] This brought some shaky order. Thousands of districts across the West produced thousands of codes with near-infinite variations. Resolving any dispute relied on accurate records of who had claimed what and when, but, if they survived, records could be comically vague.

Lode claims were by nature even fuzzier. A miner would lay out dimensions on the surface above what he suspected was a vein, or "ledge," and project them downward. Imagine a loaf of bread two hundred feet long and seventy-five feet wide, then sink it into the earth to an indefinite depth. A lode claim included whatever minerals were in that enormous cube. Early California districts made a crucial change to this rule. A claim's owner could pursue the "dips, spurs, angles, and variations" of his ledge beyond the sides of his claim's subterranean boundaries. If that took a miner beneath someone else's claim, assuming he had made his claim first, the ore was still his.[5] The change seemed to reward a prospector's savvy and good luck, but, in fact it was absurdly naive. Veins of ore fragment over time. Connecting something close to the surface to something farther down is often conjecture at best. Some ore was not in veins but in pooled deposits. While placer claims could be confusing, this was confusion squared and cubed and beautifully designed for a carnival of litigation.

Consequently, the mining West became the new country's most vigorous speculative playground—and the competition was stiff. Initially the speculation was remarkable for its scope, from the well-heeled to ordinary dreamers and hucksters off the streets. Charles Shinn described "the chattering, half-dazed, wild-eyed" crowds drawn to Virginia City, ragged men "wonderfully childlike" in their faith that riches waited within anyone's grasp. Rumors ballooned into stories of deposits not only of silver and gold but of platinum, iridium, plumbago (a flowering tropical plant), and ambergis (the valuable digestive secretion of sperm whales). One group dug for a subterranean lake of kerosene.[6] By one estimate 5,000 claims were made within thirty miles of Virginia City in the rush's first year and about 16,000 by 1879. Only a small portion, however, were actual mines—maybe 300 during that first year, with 20 of those "well established" and only 8 or 9 paying dividends.

The rest produced not ore but visions. Unlike the rules for placer claims, there was no requirement to work a lode. A small group of speculators instead would obtain a claim, form a corporation and offer shares (often called "feet" because the number equaled the length of the claim) for sale. To push up the price they would puff the prospects with breathless rumors and sometimes with "experting," hiring an alleged specialist to testify of a sure bonanza. Once inflated shares were sold, the organizers might just walk away, or they might levy assessments on stockholders, allegedly to meet new expenses (and their own salaries). Shareholders who did not pay lost their shares, which could be resold.

The frenzy of trade required a clearinghouse. The result was one of the defining institutions of the mineral West. The San Francisco Mining and Stock Exchange opened in 1862, with a few members buying seats for fifty dollars each. Within a year 1,300 companies, mostly mining concerns, were trading there. During silver's heyday this was the busiest stock exchange on earth, and soon others sprang up "like beer-booths about a military parade."[7] Sales read as a barometer of illusion, collapsing and soaring with imagined tomorrows, "fluctuat[ing] with the pulse-beats of the public."[8] In 1863, at the height of its first boom, the Comstock's four thousand or so companies had $1.5 billion in shares for sale, nearly seventy times the value of all bullion produced thus far.[9] Then came a great slump. On the eve of news of the great bonanza in 1874 the value of Comstock shares on the exchange had sunk to about $93 million. Two weeks later it was more than $300 million, half again the assessed value of all San Francisco real estate. The number of a company's shares changing hands in one day might be double those in circulation.

The exchange showed the West once again bound outward by new technologies. "From whence came our orders?" one of its founders later asked, and answered: "Wherever the telegraph wire extended, our orders would roll in on us," not only from California and Nevada but "Eastern cities also, New York in particular. . . . London, Paris, Berlin and Frankfort sent us orders." Funds flowed to the exchange "from the kitchen to the pulpit, from every shade of life, and from every nationality," a founder wrote.[10] The copper net tapped a universal gullibility, with investors in Boston, Denver, Milan, and Amsterdam, "the millionaire and the mendicant, the modest matron and the brazen courtesan" buying into discoveries never made and mines that would never feel a shovel.[11] It was a grand democratization of suckerdom.

Before, some in settled regions had pursued imagined opportunities by buying into distant land or some enterprise, but practicalities kept the numbers low. Then the telegraph collapsed the distance, while corporations and mass marketing gave nearly everyone a chance to take a hand. The terms used were revealing. Selling shares as "feet" concretized the illusion of being there. An investor could pace off a personal bonanza in his head. It was all invisible, units of capital riding on electricity, an economy of the ether. Corporate finance and new technologies had made possible a kind of vicarious immigration, a means of moving via a new medium into an imagined West. Many variations would follow.

The financing had its solid side that also found its footing in stock exchanges. Corporations were usually the only practical means to gather the prodigious capital needed for deep mines and their risks. These efforts had their own speculative variations, this time acted out in courtrooms. The method of claiming, said a California congressman, was guaranteed to "promote litigation, create controversy, and occasion difficulties" for generations.[12] In 1880 there was a single lawsuit over a land title in the rich iron and copper region around Lake Superior. Prior to 1867 twelve Comstock companies alone were involved in 245 suits at district court.[13] The basic reason was simple. Congress had abdicated the job of conveying title to local customs that were varied, vague, and rooted in dubious beginnings. A title ultimately worth millions of dollars, the Public Land Commission wrote, might be traced back to a couple or three prospectors off in the hills forming a district and with one recording its rules and claims with a "stub of a lead pencil . . . on the back of an envelope or on the ace of spades, grudgingly spared from his pack."[14]

A district map could show dozens of overlapping claims laid out like a handful of twigs tossed onto the ground. Owners of a "fighting claim" never intended to dig into the earth. Like "floating" Mexican land grants in California, they would use the rules' ambiguities to put the tap into owners willing to buy them off as nuisances. The California code that allowed the pursuit of a vein into a neighbor's claim made fighting claims and their maneuverings all but irresistible. Owners of the Grass Valley Silver Mining Company grandly promoted its prospects, marketed stock, then filed a series of suits while levying assessments of $70,000. Of that at least $34,000 went toward litigation, $13,000 of it as lawyer fees and $21,000 as "loans" to witnesses and others, possibly judges. Owners and officers received $15,000 as salaries and "loans," while more than $11,000 was simply unaccounted for. Less than $6,000 went toward mining.[15]

The contests soon provoked an argument that shot to the core of the entire subterranean enterprise. The question was fought among the Comstock's leviathans. In 1861 the Chollar Mining Company filed suits against a neighbor, the Potosi, and two years later the Ophir Mining Company sued the Burning Moscow. Both plaintiffs argued that they had followed ledges from their prior claims to those of the defendants and thus had rights to keep going and to pull out the wealth that their neighbors were, illegally, mining. The issues were fought out partly on the ground—or rather under it. When one tunnel poked through into a rival's, workers could swarm together and go at it, like soldier ants from warring nests.[16] The true contests were in the courtroom. They addressed the essential nature of underground wealth itself. The assumption had been that deposits of gold or silver were discrete clumps of richness continuous within themselves but unconnected with others. Gradually, however, a second view came into focus. By it the precious ore was united in one or a very few fabulous formations.

The two views were known respectively as the many-ledge and single-ledge theories. Their implications were staggering. Under the first theory a claimant with first rights might follow a dip, spur, or angle of a vein in his discrete ledge into a neighbor's and claim its ore. Under the second, that early claimant might pursue this dip or that angle or spur and, under the single-ledge view, eventually possess much or all of the Comstock's gold and silver. The claim could be not of a few choice slices but of the whole cheese. The issue went beyond any one case to the very perception of lode mining as an American opportunity. The notion of a mining region as a single body of ore, owned by whoever controlled its first claims, seemed what one historian calls "a door slammed shut" to hopeful prospectors and men on the make, yet a door swung wide for those with the money and the clout to gain its command.[17]

All sides consequently brought in their high-caliber legal artillery. The attorney for the Ophir and Chollar, champions of the single-ledge argument, was veteran Yale-trained mining attorney William Stewart. Tall and prodigiously bearded, he was arrogant, indefatigable, relentless, a master of detail, plain-spoken to juries and merciless to opponents. He rarely lost a case and was only rarely bested in repartee. "You little shrimp, you interrupt me again I'll eat you," he supposedly once told an opponent, who replied: "If you do you'll have more brains in your belly than you ever had in your head."[18]

The question was resolved out of a swirl of developments in 1862–64. Courts first favored the many-ledge argument, to popular applause. Then came the slump in production and onset of depression, which tilted opinion toward whatever was most likely to encourage discoveries and bring back jobs. That meant digging deeper into the earth, something affordable only from the deep pockets of bigger companies. Meanwhile a months-long study by a court-ordered referee provided a detailed geological analysis that concluded that the Comstock Lode was essentially a single fissure between two wholly different bodies of rock. Within it were concentrations of ore, scattered, as John Mackay put it, like "plums in a charity pudding," apart from each other yet all part of the same general formation.[19] In August 1864 a court ruled in favor of the Chollar Mine and the single ledge.

The legal circus ended murmurously. The Chollar and Potosi agreed to merge the following spring. The Ophir and Burning Moscow came to terms soon afterwards, the first paying the second $70,000 for eight hundred feet of rock that the two sides had spent $800,000 fighting over. The Chollar and Potosi had paid out between $1.3 and $1.5 million in legal expenses. That was enough to pay the new joint company's operating expenses—all its wages, new machinery, timber, freighting, and even taxes—three and a half times over.[20] Estimates set the costs for all the Comstock's litigation through 1865 at between $9 million and $10 million, which equaled fully a fifth of the value of all ore taken from its mines during those years.[21]

On its face this seems lunacy, bald men wrestling over a comb. To a point it reflected the overblown expectations in this, the nation's greatest lode adventure, and the mining attorneys' orgiastic pursuit of their own bonanza. Kingpin William Stewart reportedly commanded two hundred thousand dollars a year in fees. Another lawyer was deeded $4 million in property.[22] There were other hidden profits in the court fights. The stocks of the litigants naturally mounted and fell during the trials. The Burning Moscow's at one point multiplied five times in a day.[23] Savvy speculators manipulated rumor and fact by exaggerating the swings and playing them to great advantage.

Two points were clear at the end. Control of the underground wealth gravitated to those with the pools of capital needed to stay in the legal games that quickly became as much a part of the business as sinking shafts and pumping water. And that litigation brought a decision—the triumph of the single-ledge view—that by its essence gave the nod to concentrated control of whatever wealth was, in fact, there. In courtrooms, as in the mechanics of mining, whether of placer gravels or the deep sleeping veins and depositions, a single reality emerged: capital ruled.

California's great coincidence had begun the whole business, and its consequences continued to feed the state and its position. At home production of gold and silver slumped badly after 1852, but in the next decade the Comstock boom picked up the slack. Economically, it was largely an extension of California. Of 97 of the larger deep mines in Nevada in 1880, 68 were California-owned. Only 16 were based in Nevada. Of 94 California mines, all but 7 were owned in-state.[24] The initial rush, with its potent combination of wealth, demand, and relative isolation, had kicked a new economy to life, and the industries spun off in support of mining generated their own energies and demands. Just as agriculture matured from feeding locals and turned increasingly outward in its markets, so the state's industrial plant expanded. As its mining foundries and machine shops increased from 42 to 994 between 1850 and 1880, other operations appeared to service other industries. By the 1880s California combines were working its megafarms, and Hawaiians were processing their sugar cane with California-made presses. The company that invented a wire rope for hauling ore and miners provided the means for powering San Francisco's first cable cars.[25]

Mining set loose California as a financial center.[26] The state's banks, most of them in San Francisco, served first as depositories and sites of transfer, then as pools of investment for development. From the start manufacturing drew on home-grown capital, much of it moving indirectly from mining as wages, savings, and other investment. Mining capital was also sown back into extractive industries, merchandising and commercial systems, the infrastructure of railroads and telegraphs, and real estate. Over time the financial system reached throughout the far West and into Mexico and Canada.[27]

Banking and its effects were inextricably bound with stock exchanges and the ephemeral economy of speculation. Some of the millions entering the exchanges came in studied investments but much of it in purchase of illusion. An observer of the early Comstock boom wondered what would happen should people actually try to buy all the shares being offered, since their price exceeded all "the coined metals of the world." Some investment returned as dividends and profits to modest investors, but much was harvested by wit and subterfuge to financial elites, who set much of that to other work. The San Francisco Exchange, one economist writes, was the "eye of the vortex of [capital] accumulation" that profit-takers turned back into a remarkably diverse set of investments.[28]

As the West came into focus, California far surpassed in raw wealth any of its other states and territories. Its exports dwarfed in volume and value all others from along the coast. Its manufacturing output in 1870 surpassed that of all other thirteen western states and territories together, and in 1880 the difference was even greater. Its production then roughly equaled that of seven states of the deep South and ranked twelfth out of the forty-one states. Its agricultural production that year far exceeded everywhere west of the spillover; the value of its farms was double that of the rest of the West together and four and a half times that of the western interior.[29]

California's financial harvest was, to say the least, spread unevenly. This made the critical role of mining supremely ironic. The gold rush began as the ultimate expression of the dream of free labor, the hope that persons of ordinary means could find in the West the chance freely to work their way to independence, reasonable prosperity, and security for their families. Its mythic images of the sourdough and prospector embodied the vision. Free labor's most notable champion, Abraham Lincoln, spoke in the last hours of his life of hoping to visit California and its independent miners, whom he saw as one of the battered Union's great assets. Yet within a decade the rush had evolved into the epitome of the nation's rapid tilt toward industrialization, its concentration of both capital and economic control, and the shrinking realm of independent labor.

The imbalance was true among the corporations, too. Only 40 of the 212 mining corporations trading on the San Francisco Exchange in 1880 had ever turned a profit, and of the 109 on the Comstock, 5 accounted for 98.3 percent of the profits. Two alone, the California and the Consolidated Virginia, took in 75 percent. As for the speculative circus, "dollars [coming] from the servant girl and the farm labourer" mostly ended up elsewhere. Robert Louis Stevenson, who came to the city on the bay in the successful pursuit of a wife, called the exchange "the heart of San Francisco" that was continually "pumping up the savings of the lower quarters into the pockets of the millionaires."[30]

The California that emerged, while prodigiously productive and manically innovative, took the lead as well in snuffing the hopes of free labor that had fueled its beginnings. More generally the story of western mining was one of fabulous attainment at awful costs. The costs, while certainly high in the violent racial and ethnic ordering that came in California and the interior, were at least as impressive and appalling in the economies of nature, the world beneath and around the human realm.

Convulsion

Of the many environmental unsettlings during the creation of the West, none matched those of mining. They were three-dimensional. Miners made over the surface of the earth, bored thousands of feet into it, and sent clouds of smoke and gases thousands of feet into the air. They harnessed the forces that shaped the land itself, accelerating by thousands-fold the powers of flood and erosion and setting them to their needs. If we think of the environment as a dwelling place of people and fellow creatures, all western newcomers were barging in, refunctioning the rooms, and switching out the furniture. Mining regimes altered nature's very architecture. They played with basement and beam, remaking the region's very topology.

The impact of placer mining can be imagined as three concentric circles.[31] The first concentrated on the original find. When streams seemed fleeced of their obvious dust, miners used dams, sluices, canals, and pumps to move them, as with the American and Tuolumne Rivers in the mid-1850s, and dug tunnels to drain them from their bottoms. The Big Bend Tunnel, 16 feet wide, 13 feet tall, and more than 2 miles long, emptied more than 13 miles of the Feather River.[32] The second, wider circle encompassed nearby "dead rivers," ridges and hills of gravel like the one where the French consul in 1848 watched men "swarming like so many ants" as they hacked at the earth with picks and carried it up to several miles away for others to wash.[33] Coyoting pulled gravel out from the inside. California's Table Mountain was wormed through with forty thousand feet of tunnels, with tens of thousands of tons of earth disgorged.[34] "The whole valley has been literally dug and washed over," a miner wrote of the aptly named Coyoteville, California. In the process a thick forest of huge trees had been entirely undermined and toppled.[35]

Inside that second circle was probably an aborning town, with the usual crudities and discomforts vastly amplified by the work that had brought it there in the first place. A newcomer to Placerville (Hangtown), California, found parties of miners at work all along the creek, in the middle of the main street, and "even in some of the houses," shoveling, hauling, and rolling larger rocks as "mud, dirt, stones, and water were thrown about in all directions." With nearby trees taken for cabins and sluices—Hangtown's visitor saw nothing but "bare stumps . . . of gigantic pine trees" on the hills around—erosion sent rainfall, mud, and debris surging through the streets. A hurdy-gurdy girl in Helena, Montana, stepped from a saloon's rear door for a breath of air and tumbled twenty-five feet down the washed-out bank of a ditch.[36] The scarred hillsides and rubbish-filled streets of Central City, Colorado, turned English poet James Thomson metaphorical: "So ferociously does little man scratch at the breasts of his great calm mother when he thinks that jewels are there hidden."[37]

The profanation paled beside placering's next stage, hydraulic mining. Its third circle of shock was far larger, hundreds of square miles. To satisfy its demand for water—by one estimate more than a million and a half gallons were needed to extract a single ounce of gold—new lakes were created and old ones expanded. Reservoirs on the Yuba, Bear, American, and Feather Rivers held six billion cubic feet of water.[38] To channel the water a goodly part of California's riparian system was remade. Creeks and rivers were diverted into systems of canals and flumes. The state's largest stretched 247 miles. By the end of the 1850s California had 5,726 miles of artificial main watercourses, plus another thousand miles of connectors, more than enough to move water to Boston and back.[39] Blasted against the small mountains of gravel, this water in turn remade the land. Hydraulics carved canyons up to seven hundred feet deep and whittled whole valleys into pillars and obliques that left a visitor thinking of "a battlefield of the antediluvian giants and monsters." The pit of the North Bloomfield "could contain a whole settlement and [was] so deep that a high church steeple could hardly reach to the ledge." The "seamed, torn, scarified" earth struck a visitor as a theater of "the cruel war against the Great Mother."[40]

A hydraulic's advantage, its ability to process vastly greater amounts of gravel, left it with thousands upon thousands of tons of slickens, worthless rock, sand, and clay, to get rid of. Some mines disposed of it through tunnels. The North Bloomfield sank eight vertical shafts more than twenty stories down to bedrock, then connected them into a single sloping horizontal tunnel eight thousand feet long. Monitors sent gravel into the shafts, where it tumbled and fell over a series of steps to shake loose the gold missed in the process above, then it passed over a series of sluices to extract the gold. The debris finally exploded from the tunnel's mouth into Humbug Creek, which carried it into the Yuba River basin.[41]

Others could not ignore the mess. The steeper flow in the mountains kept much of the slickens moving, but where the streams left the hills and the current slowed, it settled thickly. On the lower Yuba River about half a billion cubic yards of debris created a fan-shaped apron of twenty-five square miles. These sites, bordering rivers and on the edge of the hills, were the same ones favored for market towns. As sludge settled in the rivers, their beds steadily rose, and towns soon were building levees as protection. Now a town was not conveniently on a river but inconveniently under it. When Marysville, California, was founded in 1850 it was twenty-five feet above the Yuba and Feather Rivers, but eventually the streams flowed behind levees a full twenty feet above Marysville streets.[42] Sacramento, located where the American and Sacramento Rivers joined, was especially vulnerable to flooding. A massive project between 1864 and 1868 moved the junction a mile downstream, handing their problem to neighbors farther along.

The rivers carried more than slickens. The mercury that mine operators used in millions of pounds has another trait besides its rare ability to bond with gold. It poisons people. Easily absorbed by the body, it brings the shakes, slobbering, vomiting, fatigue, memory loss, and in time insanity and death. An engineer working in a retort wrote his father of becoming so weak he could hardly stand. So severe was his salivation that he rarely ate, which worsened his nerves: "I was all in a tremble."[43] The fumes from the ore roasted at the New Almaden mines killed all nearby vegetation and sickened local cows. Gold watches and coins turned white. Residents in a mountain village a few hundred feet above the furnaces tied heavy bandages across their faces to filter the air, but they still salivated heavily. They had "pale cadaverous faces and leaden eyes," a journalist wrote: "One would seem to inhale death with every respiration."[44] Mine operators tried to save what mercury they could, but their crude methods washed away much of it. Stretches below the larger operations held up to twenty tons per mile. The Northfield mine alone lost 21,512 pounds between 1876 and 1881. As it flowed along, mercury degraded into a poisonous organic compound that was eaten by fish and grew more concentrated as it moved upward through the food chain. In larger fish, the ones that people ate, it could be a hundred thousand times that of the water they swam in.[45]

As hydraulics were scouring surface rock, lode mining was taking more out of the earth and scattering it around as loose debris. Mills added their smoldering slag. Their coal smoke and sulfurous fumes joined the superheated fetor sent into the atmosphere by the giant blowers in deeper mines. More advanced milling and refining used cyanide and arsenic—gold, silver, and copper mining seemed oddly bonded to elements most deadly to humans—which made their way into streams, groundwater, soil, and air. The geological uplift that brought wealth to the surface created steep hillsides and slopes that trapped much of the polluted air. So wretched were a smelter's fumes in Eureka, Nevada, that the company sent them via a smokestack fully up a canyon wall, then vertically even farther away.[46]

One of the greatest environmental consequences was, at a slight glance, unexpected. Mining was the West's leading expression of the new industrial age of iron, steel, and coal, yet its growth relied on the earlier age of wood. The loss of timber, in fact, was the environmental effect people noticed first. An editor thought two-thirds of the woodlands around Denver had vanished after barely two years of mining. The manmade watercourses that fed the hydraulics required vast amounts of lumber, and in lode mines wood was usually the greatest expense apart from wages. Timber, lumber, and wood fuel for the Comstock's Savage mine in 1868 accounted for 62 percent of the cost of all materials.[47] Mills and smelters consumed yet more, both in their construction and for the charcoal they used in furnaces. Suppliers had to reach ever farther away, floating huge rafts of wood down the Carson River, about 150,000 cords in a season. All told, the great silver boom there consumed an estimated 800 million board feet, enough to build fifty thousand modern houses, each with a double garage.[48] Meanwhile the artificial lakes that fed the hydraulics submerged thousands of acres of virgin timber, while sparks from mills, grassfires that prospectors set to expose promising rock, and simple carelessness triggered forest fires. Colorado's frequency of fires quadrupled during the sixty years after its gold rush.[49]

A mine was the cash cow of its neighborhood, so it was rare for a neighborhood or region to challenge the environmental consequences—until, that is, other interests rose high enough in their own worth and power to be heard. As the value of agricultural production was passing that of mining, it was becoming undeniably clear that hydraulic mining was irreconcilable with the farming inside its wide circle of shock. The showdown came where the effects of the West's largest hydraulics, on the upper Sacramento River watershed, met some of California's more prosperous farms downstream.[50] Complaints centered on Marysville, born to feed the mines upriver but matured into a regional market town and center of agricultural development. In 1880 the state engineer reported that clay and "slimes and sands" flushing down the Yuba, Feather, and American Rivers had covered fields, landmarks, whole orchards. Lands had lost 95 percent of their value ($2,738,200 to $130,665). He recommended tax-supported dams, built with nearby trees and brush, to hold back the worst of the debris. They proved worthless. High water in 1881 and 1883 slapped them down, and the buildup of slickens continued. Of one farmer's 1,275 acres, all but 75 was under 3 to 5 feet of sand.[51]

Still, the legislature's dedication to mining blocked any effort to intervene. The two sides organized for battle, the Anti-Debris Association versus the Hydraulic Miners Association. The first, in addition to forming an Anti-Debris Guard with uniforms and bright blue sashes to symbolize the rightful color of local streams, filed suit in state courts for an injunction.[52] They got it, but mine owners kept blasting defiantly away. With that, the Anti-Debris Association turned to federal court. Edward Woodruff, who owned flooded property both outside and in Marysville, took the lead and sued the hydraulic behemoth, the North Bloomfield mine. The case, which everyone knew would set the course of California mining, went to the Ninth Circuit Court.

Presiding was Judge Lorenzo Sawyer. He had come to California as a prospector in forty-nine, which of course buoyed the hydraulic hopes. Over sixteen months he heard more than two hundred witnesses, visited the area several times, and commissioned detailed studies of the situation. The case's testimony, notes, and data ran to more than twenty thousand pages. Mining attorneys maneuvered imaginatively. Because no one could say what sand and mud came from exactly where, they reasoned, no one could sue any particular mine. When that didn't fly, they argued that because so much of the North Bloomfield's debris had settled on Woodruff's land, it was now *the mine's* property, not Woodruff's.

In January 1884 Sawyer issued his opinion. The mines' accomplishments were undeniable, he concluded, but the damage to those lower on the rivers was colossal and irrefutable, and the future promised more of it. More than 700 million cubic yards of rich gravel remained to be washed on the Yuba River alone. The hydraulics were a nuisance: "*destructive, continuous, increasing, and threatening to continue, increase, and be still more destructive.*" Sawyer ended his sixty-page ruling, as well as the state's most productive era of gold mining, almost offhandedly: "I think the plaintiff is entitled to the relief asked." He then issued a permanent injunction. Mines could continue operations only if they compensated farmers for their losses, which was obviously financially unsustainable. Hydraulic mining in California was over.[53]

Operators elsewhere occasionally faced some opposition—a battle over Butte's wretched air brought some control of its smelters' smoke—but serious efforts to cope with mining's environmental damage were decades ahead.[54] *Woodruff v. North Bloomfield* did, however, suggest how across the West societies and how they supported themselves were maturing into a kind of balance. "Where once the temporary convenience and individual will of the miner was the only law," Judge Sawyer wrote in his opinion, now other interests and communities were having their say.[55]

By then mining had wrought stunning changes on the land. Seen from one eye, those changes were among the most impressive feats of the emerging West. The deep mines were deeper than any in history, and the technologies of gutting the earth and keeping miners alive far surpassed any before them. Thousands of miles of riparian California were re-engineered. Some sights were truly wondrous. One six-mile flume clung by brackets to a cliff a thousand feet above its foot. A system along the Feather River carried water across a chasm via an eight-thousand-foot siphon made of boiler pipe.[56] Turned loose, water from such systems washed entire surface formations away and back into the earth, there to race down newly dug tunnels, plunging over and through manmade waterfalls and cataracts. If the Pacific railroad showed the human ability to overcome topography, western mining showed its power to transform it. An awed Karl Hewitt wrote that "the mountain torrents of the Sierra, caught on their way to the Pacific, have been forced to pause and do the work of man."[57]

Seen from the other eye, the view is of man spectacularly fouling his nest. On the Comstock, a town was eating itself. The mines under Mount Davidson spread outward until tunnels ran under Virginia City, some so near the surface, a woman remembered, that when a friend visited for tea, they had to speak over the workers' voices just beneath their feet: "You could hear them as plainly as if they were in the yard." Buildings sagged and tilted until a two-story structure folded into a pit and burned. It was "completely swallowed up, not even the chimney being visible."[58] Mine builders poisoned the water they drank and the air they breathed and lived among great scrap heaps from mountains that seemed to be hollowed out. Each was soon to be "a huge nutshell, emptied of its kernel," wrote Mary Hallock Foote.[59] Mining spokesmen tried hard to spin it their way. One compared the dead muck that covered farms, houses, and graveyards on the lower Yuba and Feather Rivers to silt from the Nile, a great vitalizing blanket. An editor called "unbearable" the smoke that hung over the copper town of Butte. Not so, answered the city's kingpin William Clark. It was not only a disinfectant, slaying microbes and reducing illness, but also a cosmetic. The women of Butte were "very fond of this smoky city" because its air had "just enough arsenic . . . to give them a beautiful complexion."[60]

There were critics, especially outsiders. New Yorker Isabella Bird saw mining as "turning the earth inside out, making it hideous, blighting every green thing" as well as men's hearts and souls. But another visitor, Helen Hunt Jackson, understood that as long as mining was the life blood of a place, the "market [whose] stock in aster fields and brooks" would see no action.[61] The sack of the environment in fact fed a sense of prowess and conquest in line with the postwar celebration of railroads and ranches, a vision of the West raising the nation to greatness. "The hills have been cut and scalped," a writer observed of Calaveras County, California, "and every gorge and gulch and broad valley have been fairly torn to pieces and disemboweled." Appearing in a company prospectus, this was meant as *praise*. The author was advertising the "spade work" already done by the "fierce and desperate energy" of industrious miners as they claimed the new country for themselves and for America's future.[62]

That "desperate energy" might have been most apparent in gold and silver rushes, but it was at work across the region, and across the West its effects were evident, nowhere more so than in the lives of Native peoples. As the West was worked into being, its arrangements of power and the relations of its peoples were turned over and remade as much as was the land itself, and the two of course were intimately connected. The lamentable consequences for the West's original inhabitants, as well as their persistence and their inventiveness in the face of loss, is as essential as the making of ranches and the sinking of mines to understanding the birth of the West.

22 ▷ The Final Undoing

"Gold! Gold from the American River!" So, the story goes, the Mormon editor and merchant Sam Brannan called out along the streets of San Francisco on May 12, 1848, to set loose the rush to Sutter's Mill (and to make a killing selling grotesquely overpriced picks and pans). Inside of a year California Indians were in crisis and spiraling toward catastrophe. In late August 1858 headlines in Kansas City's *Journal of Commerce*—"The New Eldorado!!! Gold in Kansas Territory!! The Pike's Peak Mines!"—sent the first dash of fortune seekers across the plains to Colorado. Scarcely a year later William Bent, agent along the Arkansas River, reported Indians there driven desperate by "the failure of food, the encircling encroachment of the white population, and the exasperating sense of decay and impending extinction."[1]

Mining rushes were the most dependable triggers of Native disaster. With a few exceptions—the 1874 "buffalo war" with the Comanches and Kiowas was a notable one—every far-western Indian war began, sometimes at a slight remove, with a gold or silver discovery. The overlap was only part of the story. Every change brought by the unsettling after 1848 challenged, and most often undercut, Indian independence and ways of living, but the effects of western mining offer a magnified view of what was happening more generally. They also throw into equally stark relief the innovation and persistence of tribal peoples in preserving and cultivating their identities as the land's first peoples.

The Military and Its Limits

Understanding the outward defeat of western Indians ought to begin with what was *not* playing as much a role as is usually told. Nothing in the West's mythic image plays more prominently than the western military and its struggles with Native America. Library shelves sag with histories of campaigns and clashes. The New York Public Library has significantly more entries for the Battle of the Little Bighorn than for the entire Pacific theater during World War II, and only a true obsessive would try to count the literary and filmic treatments. Perhaps the fascination with Indian wars reflects the need to imagine terrible barriers to national destiny, and thus the grand heroism in overcoming them. Certainly the images of warriors and cavalry, warbonnets and sabers, all against back-drops of buttes and desert distances, have their universal appeal.

Whatever the reason, the enchantment raises a central puzzle of the emerging West. While Washington's hand seemed to be on so much, creating governments and institutions, exploring the land and cataloguing what was on and within it, legislating the means of exploitation, and much more, its main mechanism of physical control, the military so often pictured as mastering the new country, was scarcely there at all. The entire army in 1867 stood at 57,000 men, nearly all deployed in the former Confederacy and the West. As western settlements spread, the army just as steadily shrank, down to 25,000 men and 2,000 officers in 1874.[2] As before the war, low pay, discomforts, boredom, and abusive officers made it difficult to recruit and keep a force in the field. The desertion rate in 1871 was one out of three. Companies commonly were at half strength or less. As a result the western military, writes its leading historian, was "not so much a small army as a big police force."[3]

As also before the war, those supposedly in control of Indian-white relations were acidly at odds. The Department of War, charged with protecting settlers, said it could not do so unless it had control over Indians, who, it added, would never change their ways unless forced. The Department of Interior, charged with schooling Indians toward a civilized life, said forced conversion was like "the Mohammadean motto . . . , 'Death or the Koran!'" Commissioner of Indian Affairs Nathaniel Taylor claimed the army's real goal was Native annihilation, which he figured would take twenty-five thousand years and cost $300 billion.[4] The mix of skeletal support and bureaucratic bickering resulted in what historians Gregory Downs and Kate Masur have rightly termed a "Stockade State." In much of the West (and postwar South) outposts often had only the slightest influence beyond their immediate environs.[5]

And yet—the other half of the puzzle—western Indians were defeated, dispossessed, and largely deprived of independence far more rapidly than in the East. There the first conflicts between newcomers and Natives came in the 1620s, and Washington had established full control only around 1840. During the early decades, of course, Indians outnumbered the new arrivals, but that had reversed and begun to tilt heavily the other way by the mid-seventeenth century, yet final defeat east of the Mississippi still took about eight decades more. By contrast the contest for control west of the Mississippi, called here the War against Indian America, began around 1850 and was effectively over by 1880.

With an understaffed, overstretched, and ill-supplied military, the government needed only a fraction of the time to wrestle control over country that was more than twice the size of that to the east, that was far more challenging in terrain and climate, and that was home to peoples resisting in ways fundamentally unlike what the military had ever faced before.

A puzzle indeed. Answering it might begin with a hypothetical. If Indian America had ever posed a true threat of controlling indefinitely a significant part of the West, how would Washington have responded? No question calls more for setting western events in the full continental context of the thirty or so years after 1845. Three wars were fought in remaking the nation—the U.S.-Mexico War, the Civil War, and the War against Indian America. That last and longest of these was a far distant third in its number of national combatants and their number of deaths in battle.[6] In two years, 1846–48, Washington spent nearly as many lives taking much of the West from Mexico than it would spend during the next forty years securing it from Indians. The bloody bill to keep the Southeast in the Union was nearly a hundred times that of all warfare against western Native peoples. At Antietam, an engagement of about nine hours over two square miles, the Union's outlay of lives was more than half again what it spent over four decades in a theater a million times larger.

Given the costs of those first and second wars, surely no one could argue that Washington would not have done what it needed to win the third—to crush any genuine possibility that Indians might finally and truly control any significant part of country that, month by month, was proving of greater and greater value. Washington didn't do more because it didn't need to. The military was, on the one hand, wholly inadequate for controlling the lands assigned to it, and, on the other hand, it was all the government required. The War against Indian America must hold the record for the nation meeting its military goals on the cheap. Why?

Begin with the limitations of its opponents. "Indian America" is a collective noun. It included dozens of tribes, each with its own identity defined against those of its neighbors. Any tribe might be bound into alliances and semi-kinship with some and posed in rooted hostility toward others. In the majority of engagements against western Indian peoples, the military was aided by and sometimes fought beside members of tribes rival to the ones they were attacking. Pimas and Maricopas fought against the Apaches and Yavapais during the Civil War, Pawnees against the Southern Cheyennes (1869), Tohono O'odhams against Apaches at the Camp Grant massacre (1871), Tonkawas against the Comanches and Kiowas at Palo Duro Canyon (1874), and Crows with Custer at the Little Bighorn (1876).[7] The army used tribal members to scout against their own. Apaches were especially effective, both for their tracking skills and in demoralizing resisters. Gen. George Crook commended the tactic: "To polish a diamond there is nothing like its own dust."[8]

Most tribes in turn were divided within themselves into bands, clans, or other subgroups—such units in fact were typically the core identity of their members—and while tribes and bands had leaders recognized for skills in warfare, spirituality, hunting, negotiation, and reconciling conflicts, those leaders typically exercised authority only through persuasion and collective respect. Usually no one had any ultimate control over anyone else. As their situation worsened, furthermore, some leaders decided physical resistance was futile, even fatal, while others vowed to resist to the end. Washington played on those divisions. It invited delegations to the East to cow them through the sensory overload of cities and technologies. P. T. Barnum, treating one group to a "*coup d'oiel*" of Manhattan magnificence, promised the impression would stay with them "to the latest hour of their lives." (For one visitor, Cheyenne Lean Bear, that hour came only a year later, when he was shot and killed while wearing a peace medal given by Abraham Lincoln.)[9]

The divisions and diffuse authority worked doubly in the government's favor. Its diplomats operated by the fiction that Indian America was composed of tribal units with structures of authority essentially like that of a nation, as at the Fort Laramie council of 1851, when Commissioner David Mitchell had handed the role of "head chief" of all Lakotas to Conquering Bear. Whether done by ignorance or ploy, the maneuver was a useful tool. Once some accommodating leader (who wasn't a leader at all in the government's sense) was tapped as one who spoke for some tribal unit (that wasn't really there), Washington would hold all inside that unit accountable to the agreement's terms—terms as the government declared them. Now the agreement was a lever. Once some person or group broke some of those terms, as they usually did simply by following their cultural noses, acting as they always had within independent bands and by their own inclinations, agents could demand that some leader exercise authority he never had. When no satisfaction was forthcoming, a potential crisis was at hand.

Should it turn violent, the second advantage came into play. For the same reason a tribe could not put up a common front in diplomacy, it could usually offer no common front in warfare. Not even the most powerful could put anything close to the full complement of its warriors into the field or direct them by some coherent strategy.[10] Different factions and interests in Washington and in the federal territories might snipe and gouge at each other, and the conflicts certainly complicated and blunted the exercise of federal power, but ultimately the system was under a single authority that could act decisively when it had to. This basic cultural difference—relative unity and focus versus elemental divisions—would have given the expanding nation an unbeatable edge against Indian America even if all other factors had been roughly equal.

But the match was nothing close to even. In 1850 non-Indians in the United States outnumbered Indians 60 to 1. In 1870 it was 140 to 1. Only a small portion of those moved to the West, but even they quickly overwhelmed the number of Natives in their neighborhoods. Oregon's white population grew from a few dozen in the early 1840s to more than twelve thousand in 1850. By 1860 they had doubled the number of Indians, and in another ten years they had quadrupled it. A Walla Walla leader summed it up: "In one day the Americans become as numerous as the grass."[11] Behind every such surge was the population on the righthand side of the map, multiplying like yeast, leaning heavily westward.

The impact went beyond numbers to what the numbers were doing. Just by being who they were the newcomers commandeered resources Indians needed to be who *they* were. Ranchers set cattle on grasses that had fed bison and elk; timbermen harvested whole forests where Indians had gathered and hunted; town builders erected stores and houses at prime locations for seasonal encampments; farmers turned vital streams to irrigation and replaced prairie turnips and wild squash with wheat, corn, and barley. As when they planted elm trees and built Methodist churches, white plowmen and herders were simply replicating lives they had known, but they were doing it in country where others had long lived by their own means and visions. When the two ways of life came together, one almost always would have to give way.

This was the essential story of conquest. Cut through the smug rhetoric, the racist presumptions, and the patriotic goo and what remained was the collision of two cultural worlds that in their material particulars, in how they made their homes and fed their children, could only rarely occupy the same space. When one of them was vastly outnumbered, and when the other was propelled and fed by revolutionary global changes, the odds were heavily stacked.

War's End

It was here that a gold or silver strike really showed its stuff. Nothing could match its sheer convulsive power. Happening usually isolated in some mountain chain, it drew a booming population that set loose changes that rippled outward, spreading not linearly but exponentially, transforming ecologies and drawing in connecting roads and rails, then ranches and farms. A mining strike, any one of those flashes on a map, might be imagined as an artillery shell lobbed into the backcountry, the richer the find the greater the charge. Its jolt shook or flattened all before it in every direction, and in nothing more than in the lives of those at home when the shell arrived. As Native life unraveled, some groups essentially capitulated. Some resisted, and when they did, the military stepped in.

The military drew on the same technologies that drove the spread of mines, ranches, and the rest. Some of the pursuers of the Nez Perces in 1877 had come by rail from Georgia, and some who died at the Little Bighorn had recently been with the dwindling federal occupation of Louisiana. The army used the telegraph to coordinate divided commands and to track those they were chasing, and between fights it adapted the telegraph into a remarkably modern means of mobile communication. In the Southwest, with its arid distances and maddening terrain, even the smallest parties carried telegraphic keys and tie-ins to report locations and movements of Indians of interest. By the 1870s scouts were tapping out messages from remote waterholes and desert trails that someone in the national capital was reading within hours. In "holding a frontier, or protecting the first steps of advancing civilization," wrote the chief signal officer, nothing was more useful than this telegraphic system.[12]

The most telling adaptation combined tactics and environment. During the Civil War the military learned that the grassfed power of the horse-men had a weak spot. The same country that gave them their freedom and mobility demanded that during deep winter they remain in microhabitats along streams where grassbeds, water, timber, and lower terrain offered sustenance and shelter. Such spots were relatively rare and, thus, relatively well known. If a command could locate one of those camps, and especially if it could draw support from some entrepôt on the new networks of access, it could use its superior punching power to deliver a telling blow, an expression of total war that was also a psychological shock. The four most devastating attacks on Native power between 1863 and 1868 took place within about nine weeks in their respective years, between late November and the end of January.[13]

The upshot was a recurring pattern during the dozen or so years after the Civil War. Pressure from white development pushed tribe after tribe toward crisis. Calming treaties were soon broken by both sides and often contested by intratribal divisions. Resentment deepened, often by some heavy-handed action by the military. Then came flash points, lashing out, retaliations. An order went down for the army to act, and at some point it found its opponent exposed and delivered a crippling blow.

Most action after the Civil War was on the Great Plains. On the central plains the furious responses by Cheyennes and Lakotas after Sand Creek brought the Treaty of the Little Arkansas (October 1865) and a brief respite until Winfield Scott Hancock, sent to council with chiefs, instead destroyed a large camp after its bands, fearing another attack, had fled. After more raids and another restive calm after the Treaty of Medicine Lodge Creek (October 1867), further settlement brought rising tensions and more raids until Sherman ordered a winter campaign against Cheyennes and Kiowas.[14] On November 27, 1868, four years almost to the day after Sand Creek, Lt. Col. George A. Custer caught the band of Black Kettle—the one attacked at Sand Creek—killed around sixty, took many captives, destroyed all lodges, and killed more than eight hundred horses.[15] Divisions deepened among the Cheyennes, with some withdrawing to Indian Territory while others, concentrated in the Dog Soldier band, kept up resistance until July 1869, when a column under Col. Eugene Carr and guided by Pawnee scouts found the Dog Soldiers at Summit Springs along the South Platte River and crushed them.[16] The central plains were cleared of Indians. To the south the great hunt for bison below the Arkansas River led to splits among Comanche and Kiowa leaders, sloppy treaties poorly kept, increasing clashes, and finally Col. Ranald Mackenzie's campaign into the heart of Comancheria and his attack on the assembled bands in Palo Duro Canyon in September 1874. The southern plains were pacified.[17]

The pattern's clearest expression was to the north. It included the most famous episode of the War against Indian America, the battle along Montana's Little Bighorn River.[18] As late as the early 1870s the Lakotas and their Northern Cheyenne allies appeared secure. Since pulling away northward from the Platte River in the mid-1850s, they had resisted ferociously the Bozeman Road to the Montana gold fields, including annihilation of eighty-one troops outside Fort Phil Kearny. In the second Treaty of Fort Laramie in 1868 Washington abandoned the road, promised annuities, and agreed that certain unceded lands, including the sacred Black Hills, would be closed to civilian whites. The Lakotas agreed to the Great Sioux Reservation, roughly the western half of present South Dakota.

Their security was illusory. In the six peaceful years following, white development closed in. An alternative route out of Utah fed the mining towns to the west. As the great hunt of bison shifted to the northern plains after 1874, other development grew apace. Between 1870 and 1880 the number of farms in the Dakotas grew from 2,000 to 18,000, their acreage from 302,000 to nearly 4 million.[19] Rifts within the Lakotas widened. Some, like the former militants Red Cloud, Spotted Tail, and Young Man Afraid of His Horses, found the reservation the only real option, while others tilted more toward horseback resistance, among them the warrior and holy man Sitting Bull (Tatanka Iyotake), Crazy Horse, Gall, and Touch the Clouds. The now-familiar tensions tightened.

Then another gold discovery. In 1874 prospectors with a column led by George Custer, ostensibly to locate sites for an army post, found promising dust in the Black Hills, part of the unceded land west of the reservation.[20] Newspapers proclaimed (yet another) new El Dorado, and the familiar unraveling began.

President Grant, hoping to lift the nation out of the awful depression of 1873, tried to buy the Black Hills. When even the reservation bands refused, Grant in November 1875 secretly set out to force the issue with a manufactured crisis. The army had been evicting miners, but now it was told to let them be. Agents sent unfounded reports of "wild" Lakotas threatening mayhem.[21]

Now Washington tried to play its normally reliable winter card. Everyone living off the reservation was told to report there by late February 1876, obviously impossible in that season. Sheridan then ordered a campaign against the winter camps. Gen. Alfred Terry would strike west from Fort Abraham Lincoln, near Bismarck, and would meet along the Powder and Tongue Rivers with George Crook coming out of the south. A blizzard kept Terry penned up, however, and Crook's campaign misfired. Col. Joseph Reynold, in bitter weather in mid-March, destroyed a village along the Powder and captured more than five hundred horses, but within hours the Lakotas stole them back, and the Indians, far from cowed, were infuriated and alerted to the government's intent. Sheridan later claimed to have known that "unless [his enemies] are caught before the early spring, they can not be caught at all."[22] If he did think that, he was right. By early June many younger men had left the agencies to join the others, as they usually did for the summer hunt, but now, aware of the looming threat, Lakotas and Northern Cheyennes joined in an enormous moving encampment, their huge horse herds fat and full of grass power from the springtime pastures.

Here the military made its crucial error. It stuck with its wintertime battle plan at the height of the summer. As Crook stalled after a spirited fight with Crazy Horse's Oglalas on Rosebud Creek, Terry moved westward up the Yellowstone River. On June 25 George Custer, on reconnoiter with eleven companies of the Seventh Cavalry, located the huge main camp along the Little Bighorn (Greasy Grass) River. In a standard maneuver that had succeeded against the Cheyennes along the Washita eight years before, he divided his command and attacked from opposite ends. But this was not late November. It was two days after the summer solstice, and the village he found was several times that of Black Kettle's peace village. Custer and all in the five companies with him were quickly routed and killed. The rest, under Maj. Marcus Reno and Capt. Frederick Benteen, survived a hilltop siege until the victors left and a column under Col. John Gibbon arrived from the west to tend their wounds and bury the dead.

Custer's demise, usually portrayed as the ultimate flex of Native power, in fact showed just the opposite. The victorious bands scattered. A humiliated government used its maturing infrastructure to send in troops and the supplies to keep them in the field. The army turned back to its seasonal strategy. "I don't think [the Lakotas] can stand the winter if kept stirred up," an officer wrote.[23] They couldn't. As the bands searched as usual for bison while keeping to riverine shelters, troops ranging out from Fort Peck and a new post on the Tongue River kept them off-balance, striking when they could, forcing the separated bands to keep on the move, many afoot and others on horses "thin as shadows." The Northern Cheyennes had the bloodiest time. On November 25 (within three calendar days of Sand Creek and the Washita), Col. Ranald Mackenzie, in a reprise from his time at Palo Duro Canyon, surprised a village under Dull Knife (Morning Star) along the Powder River.[24] Warriors covered the escape of their families but left behind thirty or forty dead and virtually all belongings and hundreds of horses that soldiers and Pawnee scouts took or destroyed. For three weeks survivors stumbled toward a friendly camp in temperatures down to thirty below zero. More than a dozen infants froze to death over the first two nights, and the men occasionally killed a precious horse and split it open for some elders to warm their arms and feet in the steaming entrails.[25]

By the first of the year some already were surrendering or crossing into Canada. The pace quickened over the next weeks and culminated in early May. On May 6 Crazy Horse and hundreds more gave up at Fort Robinson in Nebraska, the day before Col. Nelson Miles struck a Northern Cheyenne village, scattering its people and killing its leader, Lame Deer. That week Sitting Bull led his dwindling followers crossed the line into Canada. Led by gifted commanders, the army maximized what power it had and, using strategies learned over the past twenty years, crushed its opponents. Less than a year after the most celebrated victory of western Indians, the Native superpowers of the northern plains, princelings of the grass revolution, posed not the slightest threat.

Native resistance was not quite over. Thirty-nine days after Crazy Horse surrendered, several young Nez Perce men killed a few whites along the Salmon River in central Idaho. The men were members of bands that the next day were to be forced onto a reservation created by a fraudulent treaty fourteen years before. The killings triggered a war lasting until early October. Looking back, there seems no obvious reason for it. The Nez Perces had been loyal allies of the United States since meeting Lewis and Clark in 1805. The bands being forced onto the reservation had been living amicably on land that had drawn little interest from white newcomers. Apparently the humiliation on the Little Big Horn stung Washington into clamping down and resolving all unsettled relations, including untroubling ones, and cementing its control. After fighting in their home country, several hundred Nez Perces of all ages headed east in search of sanctuary before they were finally caught in northern Montana, just shy of the Canadian border. A couple of hundred others made it across the line to stay for a time with Sitting Bull and his Lakotas before giving up and returning.[26]

Raiding by Apaches in the Southwest continued until 1886, but for the army this was less a war than an extensive police action.[27] The War against Indian America essentially began when John Marshall's discovery set loose the devastation and slaughter of California's Native peoples, and it effectively ended when the rush into the Black Hills triggered the Sioux and, indirectly, the Nez Perce conflicts. The bookends are reminders of the unsettling power of western mining. The War's prosecution between them shows the army's adaptations in the face of formidable challenges.

From a wider view, however, the army did not defeat the Lakotas or any other Native power. Cultural concussion defeated Indian America. In well less than a normal lifetime, between the great coincidence and the Sioux War, a confluence of accelerating changes and revolutionary technologies transformed the emerging West and ended Native independence, at least in its outward forms. In the western "Stockade State," the army's role was simply to be there if needed as other forces took command. If a need arose, the military focused a tiny portion of the nation's power on an overmatched opponent at some vulnerable point. Celebrated episodes like the Sioux War were essentially punctuations, like an exclamation mark ending the last sentence of a long, complex paragraph.

Tightening the Federal Grip

As the War against Indian America closed, the federal government shifted its concentration toward the goal of maneuvering Native peoples toward eventual citizenship. Here, too, its strategy had emerged after expansion, first with the birth of reservations in the 1850s and then with the much more precise blueprints for cultural conversion after the Civil War.

With that came a need to tighten federal authority. One step was an amendment tucked into an appropriations bill passed in 1871. From that point on, it read, no tribe would be recognized as an independent power to be dealt with by treaty. In thirty-five words Congress upended the legal assumption that had guided dealings with Indian peoples since the birth of the republic. All previous treaties were to be followed, but all future arrangements would be through mutual agreements ratified by Congress. As with the Dawes Act, this shift was supported by both reformers and those with crasser motives. Reformers condemned the treaty system as a sham that gave Indians an illusion of independence while committing them to surrendering land and resources under terms that were never fulfilled and that they had no power to force. House members were flexing political muscle, ending an arrangement that had them appropriating funds for treaties they had no voice in making.[28] The change had relatively little practical effect in the short run, though by the 1890s pressure was building to interfere with treaties before 1871, in particular by opening tribal lands. When Kiowa chief Lone Wolf resisted one such effort, the U.S. Supreme Court in 1903 ruled that Congress possessed, and in fact had possessed from the start, a plenary power to abrogate any treaty. With that, Congress could open reservations through the Dawes Act without any pretense of agreements with tribal leaders.[29]

As for control within reservations, the issue was brought dramatically into focus in 1883. On the Brulé Lakota reservation a bitter dispute between two prominent men, Crow Dog and Spotted Tail, ended with the murder of the second by the first. When a Dakota territorial court sentenced Crow Dog to hang, he appealed, arguing that Washington had no authority over crimes committed on tribal land by one Indian on another. In *Ex Parte Crow Dog* the U.S. Supreme Court agreed and ordered the Lakota's release. Congress responded with the Major Crimes Act (1885), which gave states and territories jurisdiction over cases of murder and six other crimes committed wholly by Indians on any reservation inside its borders. A Supreme Court decision upholding this act the next year in effect gave Congress a virtually unchecked authority, in the words of a legal scholar at the time, to "govern the Indians as its own subjects . . . as it sees fit."[30]

By then other mechanisms were taking charge in matters well beyond murder. In 1883 Congress created the Code of Indian Offenses to regulate a widening range of behaviors. Those charged would be arrested by agent-appointed Indian police and brought before agent-appointed tribal presiders of Courts of Indian Offenses. The code first focused on religious and other ceremonies but soon turned to offenses from personal grooming to neglecting "to adopt habits of industry" and passing too much time "in idleness and loafing."[31] By the turn of the century these courts were operating on about two of three reservations.

Telling people how to worship and dress was beyond the most generous views of constitutional limits, but the Constitution applied only to citizens, which Indians weren't. The Fourteenth Amendment declared everyone born or naturalized in the country to be citizens, but it applied only to those under Washington's jurisdiction, and because in 1868 tribes were technically other nations, that left them out. Then, three years later, when Congress declared that tribes in fact were not independent nations, there was no swap for citizenship and its rights. Some argued, as did one reformer, that the government should follow the "stupendous precedent" of emancipation and accept that "the way to fit men for citizenship is to make them citizens," but others, led by Henry

Dawes, opposed immediate citizenship in favor of letting allotment take its course of gradual preparation for full membership in the national family. That side carried the day. As citizenship was opened (with limits) to millions of freedmen, Native peoples were held beyond its embrace until deep into the next century. Until then they were in a legal netherland, with essentially neither power nor rights.[32]

With that, the government was free to proceed with its three-pronged campaign of cultural makeover. In changing Indians' economic foundations, the Dawes Act was called one long step forward by declaring that once tribal members were allotted their own lands, they were, or soon would be, one in practice and values with the hundreds of thousands of white farmers working western lands. A second step was education. Schooling, Interior Secretary Henry Teller wrote in 1883, would turn the Indian "if not [into] a valuable citizen, at least one from whom danger need not be apprehended." A reformer a decade later went farther. If children would spend just five years in the classroom, "savagery would cease and the government support of Indians would be a thing of the past."[33] The majority of schools were ones attended during the day, although by 1877 reservations had forty-eight with students living full-time apart from families, the better to bear down on the work at hand. As warfare ended, the pace and scope of education accelerated and spread. Congressional funding grew more than twenty-five times between 1879 and 1894, and the number of those enrolled by nearly five times.

The strategy changed as well. In 1875 Capt. Richard Henry Pratt took seventy-two Comanche, Kiowa, and Southern Cheyenne men, leaders in the resistance that ended the year before at Palo Duro Canyon, to confinement at Fort Marion near Saint Augustine, Florida. His efforts to school them in English and the fundamentals of mainstream life inspired him to place them at Virginia's Hampton Institute, where they would share classrooms with children of freedpeople. That in turn drew more attention from reformers and won him permission to establish his own institute in abandoned army barracks at Carlisle, Pennsylvania, in 1879.[34] Pratt would say that as an Indian educator he was a Baptist, not in the congregational sense but in his belief that full immersion into white American culture would lead, as in baptism in Christian theology, to death and rebirth, here not symbolic but culturally real. Students had their hair cut and were issued standard uniforms, were forbidden to speak Native languages, and spent half of their time learning the standard curriculum and half toward the goal of economic conversion, practicing the labors and skills of manual and agrarian arts. They were further immersed in a new life by "outing," living with white families during summer recess. Carlisle began with 150 students. By 1890 there were nearly a thousand. The perceived success of Pratt's approach led to nine more off-reservation schools by 1890, all in the West. On reservations emphasis also shifted from day to boarding schools. In 1887 there were 111 boarding schools with an average attendance of more than 8,000, plus 2,500 students in 110 day schools.[35]

Native response was mixed. Some families, recognizing a new reality, sent their children willingly while others refused, sometimes hiding sons and daughters from agents who might resort to finding and seizing them and sending them off. Some problems were quickly apparent. Living closely packed in dormitories was a perfect setting for the spread of disease. There were epidemics of influenza, measles, and mumps, but tuberculosis and trachoma, a highly contagious eye disease with results ranging from painful irritation to full-blown blindness, were the worst. The extent of illness is unclear, though an early report told of nearly one in five of Platt's early students dying in school or soon after being sent home, and a later more systematic study of boarding schools on five reservations found only one in five students wholly clear of tuberculosis symptoms.[36]

Many southeastern and western politicians had little faith in Indian education, a residual of earlier sentiments on Black and Native inferiority. Using education to improve Indians, Sen. John Ingalls of Kansas thought, was as futile as reading to longhorns in order to turn them into Durhams. Financial support slackened after 1884, but the system continued to grow. At the turn of the century there were 307 schools, 24 of them off-reservation boarding schools, with more than 21,500 students attending.[37] By then the curriculum and textbooks were standardized and the system overseen by a superintendent of education. Still, the number of students in classes on any given day seems to have been under a third of those of school age. Even if the formal goal was feasible—that, as an early superintendent put it, the classroom would be the anteroom to usher the "rising generation" into "fraternal and harmonious relationship with their white fellow-citizens"—it is worth wondering whether that goal was practically in reach.[38]

Considering education, the Lake Mohonk Conference in 1884 stressed the third essential of cultural conversion. "[An Indian] must have a Christian education" if he was to meet his civilized duties. The duty in turn of "the Christian people of the country" was to exert through schools "a strong moral and religious influence." Without that, "true civilization of the Indian is impossible."[39] The "Christian" in "Christian education," in fact, was close to redundant. It was assumed that schools, even when not run by persons of the cloth, would include religious instruction and cultivate Christian values, broadly defined.

From the start, in fact, the spiritual was inseparable from every part of the assimilation campaign. John Wesley Powell stressed the need to "shatter the Indian's attachment to his sacred homeland." By moving a tribe to a new home, its "Gods are abandoned and all its religion. . . . That is, everything most sacred to Indian society is yielded up."[40]

As here, the work was not only to inscribe the Christian life. It was also to erase the one before it. The "old heathenish dances" were a "great hindrance" to civilizing Indians, Secretary of the Interior Teller wrote in 1882. They should be outlawed, along with polygamy and the influence of holy men. The Courts of Indian Offenses concentrated there, specifically "the sun dance, scalp dance, or war dance or any other similar feast" as well as any "so-called medicine men" who would use "any arts of a conjurer to prevent Indians from abandoning their barbarous rites" or practicing traditional healing. The list was expanded to include men wearing their hair long, to either sex painting their bodies, and to performing "give-away" ceremonies, all of them associated with "dances that are degrading and so-called religious rites that are immoral."[41]

Barely a decade after the Sioux War, as significant resistance from Apaches was ending, the follow-up to military control might seem to be complete. Virtually all western Indians were consigned to reservations. Their lands were being turned to other uses and the lands' potentials were developed on others' terms. In authority over the reservations were agents who had claim to deciding what Indians would eat, what they would wear, how they formed their families, whether and where and when their children would go to school, how they would talk to God and what they would say, how they should work, and when they were sitting around too much.

As with much of the Native experience, however, what seemed obvious to others was often something else entirely.

Resistance, Adjustment, Persistence

Defeating Natives in the field and taking their lands turned out to be a lot easier than controlling how they lived afterward. Some Indians went along with assimilation programs, but others worked to deflect, subvert, and adapt them to their own needs as they perceived them. They did this with considerable success. Take, for instance, dances. Agents who forbade some dances and discouraged the rest found that they could at best limit them—and thus limit, at best, the values and beliefs behind them. Dances in turn were adapted as expressions of new spiritual practices and, usually performed in a symbolically unifying circle, as a means of redefining and reinforcing a collective identity, both within and among various groups.[42]

Dancing was an enactment of a broader evolving resistance. Often Indians used the very means that had been used to bring them to heel. The irreducible purpose of a reservation, the foundation of the government's programs, was to keep its charges under physical control, starting with keeping them in place. Doing that might seem easy enough, but it was not. Residents were not forbidden to leave, but they did require permission and passes, and while agents denied many requests and tried to restrict the rest, they quickly found their efforts, as with dances, both impractical and ignored. Historian Justin Gage has methodically documented more than 1,200 trips, almost certainly an undercount, among reservations from Minnesota to Arizona to Oregon and Indian Territory between 1880 and 1890 (see map 10). More than a third were apparently without permission. Some went alone or with a few others, some in groups of nearly a hundred.[43] Much of the traveling was via the horses that Indians were allowed to keep, but much was by rail, often over hundreds of miles.

Personal family visits inevitably led to wider conversations among widely separated groups, which led to social gatherings, some quite large. In 1883 six hundred persons converged, mostly by rail, in Winnemucca, Nevada, to visit and dance. Gatherings in turn led to cultural diffusions. As agents were working to suppress the Sun Dance in its heartland on the plains, Utes in the Great Basin were adopting it after visits from their former enemies, the Lakotas. The suppression of intertribal warfare was supposed to unite all tribes on the road to assimilation, but friendly visits brought a dawning sense of former enemies' living in a common fix. There were stunning diplomatic realignments. No peoples had fought more bitterly in the wake of the grass revolution than the Pawnees of the eastern plains with the horseback alliance of Cheyennes, Arapahos, Kiowas, and Comanches to the west. As early as 1871 Pawnees arranged visits with them all to repair relations. Later Lakotas, so recently military lords of the northern plains, visited back and forth with several longstanding foes: Crows, Mandans, Arikaras, Hidatsas, and Pawnees.[44]

Education, another tool of assimilation, had similar effects. In an off-reservation boarding school young students from widely scattered tribes were tossed together in daily and intimate contact as they never would have been otherwise. The psychological effects could be devastating, but the same unmooring could cultivate a kinship based on shared experiences in the classroom and on remembered traumas back home. Essential to the educational effort was the teaching of English. That allowed a bonding that went far beyond off-reservation schools. By 1889 many tribes had a critical mass of persons literate in English.[45] The official intent was to bind dozens of cultures into a common national identity, but it also provided a lingua franca to explore how the various tribes were both a people together and a people apart, distinct in their pasts from the non-Native majority and brought together by their present predicaments.

It added up to Indian education's prime irony. Richard Henry Pratt famously said that he meant "to kill the Indian to save the man." Indians, he was saying, could survive in the emerging America only if their previous identity was eradicated. Before reservations, however, there had been no Indian identity to eradicate. Identities were rooted in tribes, and within them clans and bands, and within them families. Native identity was a dazzling diversity. Education moved it toward a single focus and provided the language to describe and express it. To use Pratt's term, education did not so much kill as create "the Indian."

As literacy spread, Indians used another unifying technology, the postal system, to cultivate their own sense of connection. They wrote letters within tribes and among tribes, to students at boarding schools and to parents back home, from one set of leaders to others and back again. The topics were universal—family welfare, births and deaths and marriages, the dailiness of life everywhere—but also revelations of reservation life: warnings of diseases and epidemics ("the Dr can't help people from dying"), reports of dances, disputes among tribal groups and factions, and strategies for resisting governmental policies. The point is less that Indians were discussing and celebrating and grousing about common concerns. It is more that they were finding that they *had* concerns in common, that some were unique to them as Indians, and that, as Indians, they might find common ways to respond.

One was through yet another tool meant to transform them—religion. Since the late colonial period new religions had arisen among Native peoples, usually at the tipping point of military defeat. They shared a few traits. Usually prophetic figures told of divine visions promising their people's survival and spiritual integrity if new rituals and behaviors were followed. Some predicted an apocalyptic banishing of white invaders, a resurrection of Native dead, and a return of an earlier time. Particulars usually combined traditional customs with elements and teachings of Christianity. They transcended tribal identities and cultivated a sense of unity rooted in a relationship to divine power.

MAP 10. (*opposite*) Trips between selected reservations and other locations, 1880–90. Reservation tribes visited extensively with one another, forming alliances among former enemies, blending traditions, and developing a sense of common identity and responses to common challenges of their new lives, including new religions. Map by Erin Greb. From Justin Gage, *We Do Not Want the Gates Closed between Us: Native Networks and the Spread of the Ghost Dance* (Norman: University of Oklahoma Press, 2020), 80, map 2. © 2020 University of Oklahoma Press. Reprinted by permission of the publisher.

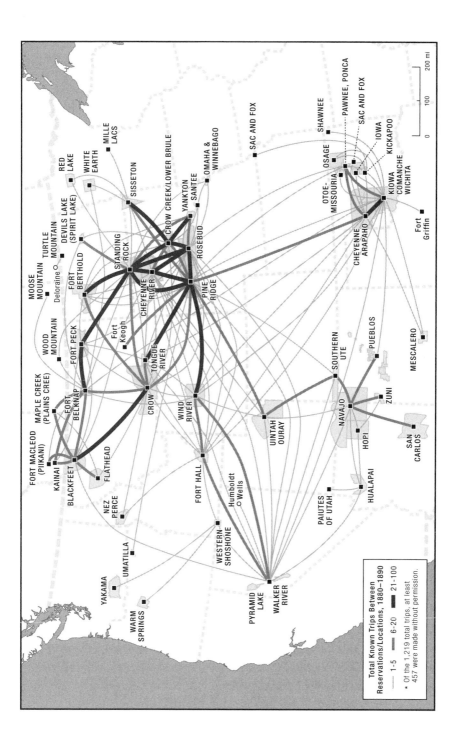

MILLE
LACS

RED
LAKE

WHITE
EARTH

SISSETON

SAC AND FOX

DEVILS LAKE
(SPIRIT LAKE)

CROW CREEK/LOWER BRULE

YANKTON
SANTEE

OMAHA &
WINNEBAGO

SHAWNEE

PAWNEE, PONCA

SAC AND FOX

IOWA

KICKAPOO

MOOSE
MOUNTAIN

TURTLE
MOUNTAIN

STANDING
ROCK

FORT
BERTHOLD

Deloraine

ROSEBUD

OTOE-
MISSOURIA

OSAGE

KIOWA
COMANCHE
WICHITA

CHEYENNE
RIVER

PINE
RIDGE

CHEYENNE
ARAPAHO

Fort
Griffin

WOOD
MOUNTAIN

FORT PECK

Fort
Keogh

TONGUE
RIVER

PUEBLOS

MESCALERO

FORT MACLEOD
(PIIKANI)

MAPLE CREEK
(PLAINS CREE)

FORT
BELKNAP

CROW

WIND
RIVER

SOUTHERN
UTE

ZUNI

KAINAI

FLATHEAD

UINTAH
OURAY

NAVAJO

BLACKFEET

NEZ
PERCE

FORT HALL

Humboldt
Wells

HOPI

SAN
CARLOS

UMATILLA

WESTERN-
SHOSHONE

PAIUTES
OF UTAH

HUALAPAI

YAKAMA

WARM
SPRINGS

PYRAMID
LAKE

WALKER
RIVER

200 mi

100

0

Total Known Trips Between
Reservations/Locations, 1880–1890

1-5   6-20   21-100

* Of the 1,219 total trips, at least
457 were made without permission.

Most notable of the several earlier religions in the East was that centering on the Shawnee brothers Tenskwatawa (or The Prophet or The Open Door) and Tecumseh from around 1809 to 1815. Farther west, in the 1860s Smohalla, a prophet in the Columbia Valley, preached a divine revelation, based on the sanctity of the earth, that promised that white colonization would "fade away into a dim and horrible dream" if sacred rules were kept and a ritual dance (Washat) performed. His followers, called Dreamers, included Chief Joseph of the Nez Perces.[46]

Two such religions arose later in the century. Peyotism, or the peyote religion, took its name from a cactus native to northeastern Mexico.[47] The plant's aboveground portion, its "button," was a hallucinogenic that inspired a rite among Mescalero Apaches after the Civil War that spread to the Comanches and Kiowas by the mid-1870s and then to others on the plains and Great Basin. The all-night rite in a tipi centered on a crescent-shape altar holding a large peyote button. Besides consumption of peyote (chewed or taken as a powder or tea), rituals included songs, prayer, contemplative silence, and the use of a drum, staff, eagle bone whistle, cigarettes, and other paraphernalia. Significantly, the peyote rite took first took focus on the Comanche-Kiowa agency exactly as those tribes made their last, failed try at controlling Comancheria, and it spread to the southern plains groups within ten to fifteen years of their final failures. It preserved some traditions, possibly spirit quests as well as song themes and patterns and long-tailed spiritual practices, yet set them alongside teachings and values hammered home on reservations—self-reliance and hard, steady work, monogamy and marital fidelity, abstinence from alcohol. The religion grafted Christian elements onto traditional belief. Two Comanche peyote songs translate as:

> Coyote, coming down

and

> Jesus have mercy on us, come down![48]

In the wake of outward defeat, the peyote religion was both spiritual persistence and spiritual accommodation. It adapted to new realities in part by being, as one student puts it, "nationalistic," not in the sense meant by assimilationists but by rising beyond tribal boundaries and expressing a common identity born of common difficulties and threats. It declared a Native distinctiveness, cultural endurance, spiritual equality, and pride.

The second religion, that of the Ghost Dance, was far more widespread and, in the short term, of far greater consequence.[49] Its first iteration was in 1869 around Walker River in western Nevada. A Northern Paiute, Wodziwob, introduced a round dance inspired by prophetic visions that assured future curative powers and prosperity through weather control as well as a return of the Native dead and the vanishing of whites.[50] The movement spread to the Pacific Northwest before dying down, then revived much more vigorously in the late 1880s. Much more is known about this second movement. Its prophetic figure, the Paiute Wovoka (Jack Wilson), had known Wodziwob as a teenager. He, too, proclaimed a future of divine protection and, by some accounts, a disappearance of whites if believers accepted new teachings and faithfully performed the new rituals, including a circle dance that gave the two movements their name.

The Ghost Dance has often been portrayed both as reactionary, a reflex to reverse the unstoppable flow of events, and also, as officials would claim at the time, a call for violent resistance against white authority. There is no credible evidence for the second claim. As for the first, the historian Louis Warren argues persuasively that the Ghost Dance is better understood as an adaptation to changes, not a rejection of them. As older systems of status were losing their hold, for instance, the Ghost Dance offered new openings to younger men. It preached the value of literacy and the need to take up agriculture and perform wage labor, and to answer the anxieties of that new material world, it offered an ecstatic release and spiritual affirmation. As with peyotism, it did so through some elements of Christian traditions, including anticipation of a coming messiah at an end time, and in fact it bore striking similarities to new Christian charismatic religions responding in their own ways to the stresses of the modernizing America. Most obviously it was a consolidating force, both within and among tribes, at a time of fragmentation and dislocation.

Just as striking was how the religion spread. News moved via Native connections that had been increasingly grooved across the interior West since the earlier Ghost Dance movement. There were dozens of visits via rail to Wovoka in Nevada, including one of 1,600 persons in 1890, especially from Lakotas, Cheyennes, Arapahos, Kiowas, and Comanches, but also from others as far-flung as Navajos, Utes, Blackfeet, and Crows. There were dozens more visits among the tribes to consider the movement and learn its rituals. The spreading literacy born of schools on and off reservations—several prominent Ghost Dance advocates were Carlisle graduates—was especially put to use. Some wrote to whites to describe and explain the movement. Others explored and debated it among themselves. Of those probably the majority stayed uncommitted, and many, like Comanche chief Quanah Parker, emphatically rejected it. Still others followed the religion's spread through another medium born of a late-century technology, mass-produced newspapers. An agent for the Nez Perces wrote that they were keeping up with events in the same way he was, by reading the press.

The result was something triply remarkable. A new Native religion appeared, responsive to its changing world while expressing a distinctive Indian identity and spiritual kinship. Its followers spread it through the very means that were supposed to suppress such expressions of independence. And its rise and spread led to what would have been unthinkable even a generation before—a vigorous, sometimes contentious conversation among tribes across half the continent, one that presumed a need for collective contact because they all had common options as they coped with the same dilemmas.

Government response to the Ghost Dance varied across the West, a typical blend of puzzlement, misunderstanding, suspicion, and some hostility. The last built into one of the most infamous and tragic moments of Indian-white relations. The movement found special traction among the Cheyennes, Arapahos, Kiowas, and Lakotas. In all but the last the government met it with a wary toleration, but in South Dakota (made a state as the religion arrived there) several factors came together to trigger a crisis. Tensions were already high. In 1889 Gen. George Crook maneuvered to secure a dubious agreement that broke the Sioux reservation into five components and opened half of tribal lands to white settlement. Then an oblivious Congress cut rations by a fifth just as the plains were struck by a severe drought. Amid growing resentment, Short Bull, Kicking Bear, Good Thunder, and other leaders in the summer of 1890 visited Wovoka by rail and returned with the new gospel, which soon gathered a growing attention.

From there events moved along two tracks. Relations among the Lakota bands and factions evolved in kaleidoscopic patterns—conversations, pro and con, about the religion, recriminations over the loss of land, maneuvering over new tribal boundaries, mixed strategies over all of it—while the government found in the Ghost Dance a simplistic focus to the unrest and confusion. They saw all its supporters as resistant traditionalists and its opponents as accepting progressives, which was nothing close to the case, and they warned, virtually without evidence, that it was an inspiration for a violent resistance. That its followers conducted the dances in remote areas far from white observation heightened the agents' suspicions. In November 1890 Gen. Nelson Miles sent six thousand troops to the area, including the Seventh Cavalry, fourteen years after the Custer disaster.

As tensions increased, official attention naturally turned to the most famous Lakota (in white eyes), the Hunkpapa chief and holy man Sitting Bull (Tatanka

Iyotake). He had returned from Canada to surrender in 1881 and now lived in a cabin on the Grand River in the Standing Rock reserve. There was less dancing at Standing Rock than at other agencies, and an apparently skeptical Sitting Bull did not take part, but he allowed the dances in his camp and he challenged agent James McLaughlin's right to suppress religious practice: "You must not say anything about our Pray: because [we] did not say nothing about your Pray," he dictated in a letter. That, with his deep dislike toward the man he found to be a "disaffected intriguer" and "man of low cunning," was enough to cause McLaughlin, as well as the commander at nearby Fort Yates, to order Sitting Bull's arrest by Indian police at dawn on December 15.[51] When his followers tried to stop them, fighting broke out, and the famous chief, his son, and several others, including the leader of the police, died.

Panic (but not the predicted uprising) followed. The chief of the Minneconjou Lakotas, Spotted Elk (Big Foot), and about four hundred of his band fled the Cheyenne River reservation into the Badlands, joined by some Hunkpapas from Standing Rock, but after a couple of weeks, sick with pneumonia, he decided to surrender at Pine Ridge. Troops of the Seventh Cavalry intercepted him on the way and ordered him to camp along nearby Wounded Knee Creek. The next morning the reinforced Seventh under Col. James Forsyth surrounded the camp, with four Hotchkiss guns trained on them. The assembled men were told to surrender all weapons. Accounts of what came next are varied and confused: a rifle discharged during a struggle for it, or a medicine man threw dirt into the air and called on warriors to act, or some Lakota men tried to escape. Whatever the facts, a shot or shots were fired. Most Lakota men died in the fusillade that followed immediately. Warriors used what firearms they had to cover a retreat, but many more, mostly women and children, were killed in a ravine where they sought shelter. At least two hundred Indians died in the massacre. Sixty-five soldiers were killed or wounded.[52]

The Wounded Knee Massacre is usually treated as an end point, something close to a dead stop in the western narrative. That is partly a matter of timing and horror. It came at the end of 1890 with a popular sense that a new America was emerging and an older one passing, and nothing was more associated with the older than the impression of free-roaming Indians, especially the western Sioux who had crushed Custer but now fell before the Hotchkiss guns at Wounded Knee. Particulars of the carnage appeared in the first reports and have been detailed ever since. Boys in school uniforms were mown down while playing leapfrog as the firing began—a deafening barrage "like the sound of tearing canvas." In the ravine the bullets "were like hail coming down," a survivor recalled, "and nothing could be seen for the smoke." A sergeant saw bodies "in big heaps, piled on each other. Women, the children in their arms, young and old."[53] Photographs brought the horror home: Spotted Elk, his body frozen during a storm following the slaughter, appears to be trying to rise from his death pose; men, paid two dollars per corpse, toss bodies into wagons and then into a burial pit. The images match the mood of the time: here was the death of something, a violent corner sharply turned.

Wounded Knee was obviously as clear an exhibit as imaginable of Washington's ultimate physical command over Indian peoples and, with that, its rough control of the lands brought into the nation forty years earlier. But the popular image of the massacre as a stark ending and of its victims, as Louis Warren puts it, as "primitives trapped like wild animals in the cage of modernity," gets it badly wrong.[54] Wounded Knee was an especially bloody twist to Native westerners' evolving response to their new reality. As Washington insisted, Indians across the West were indeed adapting, but they were adapting at least as much on their own terms as on the government's. They would keep at it. The Ghost Dance, as well as the debates around it, persisted in the United States and Canada at least into the 1920s.[55] The peyote religion continued and spread (with peyote buttons broadcast through the mails) and became the Native American Church. Its use of peyote was confirmed in a later amendment to the Indian Religious Freedom Act of 1978.

Religion was a mirror to much else. As from the first contact with Europeans, Native history would continue to be one of adaptation to both opportunities and constrictions and of the persistence of cultures in the face of assaults and denials. Reservations became homelands and new spiritual centers. On some of them residents became expert ranchers.[56] For all its tragedy and loss, the Native story from expansion to Wounded Knee was also one of continuity and survival, of old lives adapting and emerging into new. That story continues.

It mirrors the West's. The close of the century is often seen as the end of an experience, summed up in the term *frontier*, that was distinctive and largely confined in its themes and consequences, while in fact the meanings of the emerging West are both far richer and more lasting than that. Expansion and the great coincidence set in motion developments that, looking back, were revelatory of a changing nation and of where it was headed in the century ahead.

23 ➤ Creating the West

"What is that?" Col. Richard Mason's question to William Sherman in the spring of 1848, as he pointed at the gravel on his desk, is worth asking again three decades later, this time about the country beyond the ninety-eighth meridian. Roughly two million square miles had come into a coherence. Although as diverse in geography and human makeup as anything its size in the hemisphere, it could honestly be called one thing, the West. Its disparate parts were bound physically by networks that had effectively shrunk its distances and blurred its differences to the nation and world. It was bound into an arrangement of power—of governments and authorities—that was set into a larger one that united the expanded nation. An ethnic and racial ordering was in place. Its economic character had taken form. All of this had come into a sharpening focus within well less than a lifetime. Looking forward from 1848, the most remarkable thing about the West in 1880 was that it *was*.

For that, the implications of Sherman's answer to Colonel Mason were in no small part responsible. What I have suggested as the great coincidence—the final expansion to the Pacific simultaneous with John Marshall's moment on the American River—had an impact difficult to overestimate. It set in motion changes as rapid and convulsive as in any comparable time of American history. Those changes in turn were vital to what I have called the Greater Reconstruction. During the thirty or so years after the expansion of the 1840s, America was transformed. All the developments behind that transformation were already under way, but all accelerated sharply with expansion and gold. Some changes were concentrated in the West, some in the East, but they were often in vigorous conversation, and the effects of all were felt from coast to coast.

Together those changes essentially remade the nation. To watch them as they did their work is to see how the American West and the new America were born together. To follow them into the generations ahead is to see the West continue to be a prime actor in the national narrative. The lessons are there in the stories.

Charles Gallagher grew up in a ranching family on Duck Creek, about twenty miles north of Ely, Nevada. With his eight siblings he played and worked in the creek valley and in the desert hills around it. White settlement was barely a sprinkle—there were more than 3,200 acres for each newcomer in the 1880s—and only twenty years earlier an army surveyor wrote that until recently no non-Indians, "not even a Mormon," had dared to cross that part of the territory.[1] That changed when an enterprising Utahn blazed a trail to herd cattle to the gold diggings, then the army plotted a wagon road so troops in California could have quicker access to the troublesome Saints. The road was soon a major trunk of the overland trail used by freighters, thousands of immigrants, jouncing stagecoaches, and, briefly, the Pony Express. In 1861 the link became electrified with the passage of the first telegraph connection to the Pacific, and eight years later the Central Pacific, more than a hundred miles to the north, reduced local traffic but brought far more of the world within practical reach. With a spyglass Charles could follow a thirty-two-mule freight train for three days as it labored between Ely and the rail stop at Wells. By then a local mail coach brought the Gallaghers parcels from home, the *London Illustrated News*, and the occasional astonishment. At thirteen, Charles watched a driver unload something as yet unseen in White Pine County: bananas.[2]

The American West was born connected. It was both a creature of, and a contributor to, a global revolution in movement that had begun early in the century and gathered a terrific momentum in the 1840s.[3] Between 1840 and 1880 railroad trackage in Europe and the United States grew more than thirty times. During the same years the screw propeller accelerated transoceanic travel. Thirty-six years after the Morse-Vail telegraph's first test in 1844, the nation's more than a quarter million miles of wire were connected into systems reaching to Europe, India, and Australia. This greatest compression of distance in human history came precisely as the far West was diplomatically acquired, then politically organized, vigorously explored, militarily subdued, and considerably, if patchily, occupied and worked to new purposes. Passage from the Missouri River to California was reduced from five or six months to five days, and if the telegraph system were clear, information made the trip in seconds.

Paradoxically, the revolution's unifying power at first threatened to tear the nation apart. The new country's accessibility inspired the most passionate hopes among opposing interests in the older America, in particular those in the Southeast and Northeast. Competition for the first rail connection to the

Pacific reconfigured the political order and began the final tumble of events toward Fort Sumter. The nation was nearly destroyed in part because it was suddenly possible to bind it together far more effectively. After the war that connectedness helped consolidate the preserved Union. By 1880 the country whose distances and isolation had daunted easterners had access to everything from mining machinery to cellos, which bound it as well into what Felipe Fernández-Armesto reminds us was the start of "the most active period of intercultural traffic ever."[4] In the 1880s San Francisco's D. Ghirardelli and Company, founded in 1849 by an Italian arriving via Peru, was importing nearly half a million pounds of cocoa beans annually to make the chocolate it shipped to satisfy sweet desires in China and Japan. Fashionable San Francisco women were wearing modified kimonos of the new Japonisme style. In the rainforest nine hundred miles up the Amazon River, audiences in the rubber-rich city of Manaus were applauding operas at Teatro Amazonas, lit by nearly two hundred Italian chandeliers, and on Duck Creek in Nevada, Charles Gallagher was eating his banana.

The connected West was a splashy demonstration of travel's new meanings. Movement across the continent could be a temporary, even fleeting step in a person's life, as suggested by the metaphor for heading west—to "see the elephant." What had recently been a lifetime commitment could be a sojourn to the exotic not much more lasting than a visit to the circus. Westering became part of countless family histories, tales handed down of peach-fuzz ancestors laid low by cholera or by an imagined Indian massacre, stories of going bust on a Dakota farm, being fooled by desert mirages, or following the "dirty plate route" among California ranches as a vagabond.[5] The paradox was that these stories typically dwelled on the new country's strangeness, its distant otherness, and yet the stories' very existence, as a vast body of enduring oral literature, bound the West into the nation's collective memory and identity. The pattern played out in many variations. The West was a favored destination in a new phenomenon birthed by the collapse of distance, the vacation, including to the world's first national park. Travel became increasingly vicarious. Periodicals published scores of articles to feed the public's fascination. Henry Morton Stanley got his first public attention by reporting on wild railroad towns and interviewing Bill Hickok before heading to Africa and presuming to find Dr. David Livingstone.

There is a revealing irony to the binding of the West and America. Then and ever since the emerging West has been pictured as distant both in space and experience, while in fact it was more truly a projection of an emerging new America, from its mines and megafarms to its particulars of everyday life.

Charles Gallagher's family spent evenings around their family pump organ for songs on sheet music sent from Boston. Kansan Elam Bartholomew lived in a two-story sod house with carpets, a large library, and cushiony reading chairs. Because much of the West was born connected, much was also born modern.

That is one key to understanding how the creation of the West fits into the national narrative. It was fundamentally different from earlier stages of national expansion. Only a few generations earlier, travelers going westward from North Carolina or Pennsylvania found themselves increasingly disconnected from what they had left, and by necessity, they reverted to earlier, more rudimentary ways of living. They certainly remained somewhat aware of the world they had left, but taking close part in that world would have to wait on the easing of their isolation. Not so in the far West. From the 1850s on, travelers to Colorado, Montana, Utah, or California found some of the nation's most efficient and productive farms and ranches, most innovative technologies, and most vigorous scientific pursuits, not to mention sod-house libraries and desert ranchers singing the latest popular songs.

The older story, in short, reversed. Before, moving westward in space meant moving backward in time. Now, to move into the connected West was to largely stay in the present and, often enough, to step toward the future. Visiting the West was less a trip to the rim of national life than a schooling in where America was heading. Nowhere was this shown more vividly than in the western economy, its forms and functions, and in its role in propelling the nation into a new era.

Priming a Nation's Pump

Dutch Flat, California, began in 1851 as a placer-mining site and grew as a waystation, first for wagon and mule traffic over the Sierra, then for the Central Pacific on its way to Nevada. It then boomed as a hydraulic mining town that hosted society and cultural accoutrements, including an opera house, that earned it a grand nickname: "the Athens of the Foothills." In 1876 the journalist Albert Webster made a visit. On his first morning, after breakfasting with forty miners, men powerful "both physically and in the use of language," he strolled neighborhoods of shaded cottages and store-lined streets of bantering storekeepers. That changed just beyond the town limits. There he found "heaps of whitish gravel" and cliffs bare of earth or vegetation: a hydraulic operation that he found astonishing in accomplishment and appalling in its devastation. He peered into a pit two hundred feet deep, where day laborers worked with the same drudge as with any quarrymen anywhere ("the same weary lifting of the feet ... the same non-communication"). With considerable relief he returned to his comfortable hotel and a jug of iced claret.[6]

There is at least one incontestable point about expansion of the 1840s. The West that was born connected was also found to be a chest of resources vital to the growth of national power in its rawest sense: industrial and agrarian output, economic influence, and military brawn. The gifts came in spurts. First came gold, which gave a jolt to an expanding and diversifying economy that helped produce the longest period of sustained economic growth in American history (1841–56).[7] Next came copper, the most important non-precious metal of the era. In 1865 three-quarters of the nation's output was from Michigan. Twenty years later the national total had grown nearly nine times over, and two-thirds of it came from Montana and Arizona. Western petroleum would fuel the next stage of the movement revolution, then uranium would set loose yet more power and help make the United States the most formidable military force in human history. In 2013 Wyoming's annual coal output was greater than the next six states combined (and one of those was Montana). Molybdenum is a metal used to harden steel and to make the most durable modern alloys, crucial among many other ways to building spacecrafts. The world's greatest single source today, turning out more than twice as much as the next producer, is at Climax, Colorado, fewer than fifteen miles from Leadville, an early gold-turned-silver camp whose production by 1880 was among the most prodigious on earth. As its benefits unfolded over time, it became impossible to measure even roughly the West's contribution to America's ascent to power and global influence.

Expansion, gold, and the movement revolution also allowed the new country to take vigorous part, and often to take the lead, in the nation's economic reconstruction. Its long-distance connections gave it an edge in moving into new modes of production. At a time of new agricultural methods and technologies, California needed no time to replace older ways because, once Native peoples were dispossessed, there were no older ways to replace. Giant farms with gang plows and steam-driven threshers could appear within months. To choreograph the trade in California grain produced by those new technologies, Isaac Friedlander used the telegraph to juggle the come-and-go of ships from China to England. New enterprises took on even newer forms. Placer mining evolved quickly into the enormous industrial mechanism of hydraulicking, while gold and silver lode mines and processing sites were as advanced an industrial undertaking as any other in the world. In its financing, environmental manipulation, labor force, and legal strategies, California ranching before the Civil War was an early anticipation of the economic order that would epitomize industrial life in the reconstructed nation. In a variation of being born modern, the West did not retool. It just tooled.

Open to innovation and full of resources fit for large-scale development, much of the new West, as in America generally, favored an order with power concentrated toward the top, with its options narrowing toward the bottom and with the disparities in its income and independence widening in between. This is by no means to say that the West had no claim to its image, then and now, as a place of individual opportunity. The Homestead Act was arguably the government's most emphatic embrace of the ideals individual and familial opportunity, and recent work suggests it was much more successful in its avowed goals than critics have claimed.[8] Even in California, which set a high bar in the orgiastic monopolization of land, homesteaders found a surprising leeway for settling.[9] Early cattle drovers might move into big-time ranching, some boomtown prostitutes became propertied madams, and every new town had niches filled by merchants, hostelers, carpenters, liverymen, barbers, tobacconists, saloonkeepers, schoolteachers, tailors, and others.

Still, the overall picture is clear. Aided by friendly legislation and manipulation of federal and state laws, monopolists dominated vast areas of western lands. Mining and ranching were among the most corporatized businesses in the nation. Thirty years after the West was acquired, much of its economy was a model of the corporate market capitalism dominating the East and much of the world.

That made westerners, especially those wed to extractive economies, dramatically vulnerable to a prominent peril in the new nation—cycles of heady booms and calamitous busts. Early California ranching surged and shriveled, victim to erratic rainfall and the bounce of supply and demand. When Friedlander's grain empire collapsed in 1877, the face value of stock in the Comstock mines exceeded the assessed worth of all real property in San Francisco. A few years later, when investors from San Francisco to Berlin lost it all, another supposedly sure bet brought a flood of capital into hundreds of corporate ranches before the combination of western weather and overstocking sent it all into a tumble. Few were immune to these swings. Sixty years before the ranching disaster, their production of bison robes for a global market brought Plains Indians considerable dividends (and mounting problems). Then a new industrial market appeared for leather, and new producers, white hide hunters, stepped in to reap the benefits before that boom, too, came to bust. The hide hunters lost their jobs. The Indians lost their economy and their independence.

America's growth into an economic powerhouse cannot begin to be understood apart from how the opening West fed it. Neither can the West be understood apart from how it took its form from the economic reconstruction it was helping to make. The new country expanded the nation's economy and life in another way. From the start the West increasingly directed the nation's energies in new geographical directions. That in turn bound America into parts of the world it had scarcely known at the time of the great coincidence.

Orienting

In early 1858 the appropriately named *Asia* set sail from San Francisco to Hong Kong. On board were about four hundred Chinese. That was common enough. Every year a sizable portion of Chinese in California made the trip home, sometimes to stay, sometimes to pay family respects and tend to business before heading back. These travelers, however, were different. They were dead.[10]

As paleontologists were digging up fossilized dinosaur skeletons and anthropologists were looting Indian graves for skulls, Chinese in California were gathering the bones and bodies of their fellow sojourners and shipping them home. Cultural tradition placed great stress on one's burial at the home place in ground that was properly sited by a fengshui master and properly respected and maintained by descendants. Burial in alien soil condemned the dead to lonely, ghostly wandering.

In *jianyun*, the business of repatriating human remains, some dead bodies were disinterred and put in coffins, and the bones of others were cleaned and boxed up. The spirits of others, whose remains were lost, were ritually called out and placed in "spirit boxes." All were shipped to Hong Kong where after ritual welcome they were moved to their place of origin for final burial. The total fee was seven to ten dollars each, with perhaps two to five dollars of it for the trip itself. For American merchantmen the trade was modest but, given its source, imminently dependable.

During the second half of the nineteenth century, the United States turned its attention increasingly to the far, far West, into the Pacific Ocean and to the islands within it and the peoples around its rim. The growing place of the Pacific world and Asia in national concerns would be another of the nation's defining features in the century that followed. Even more than the other changes brought by expansion, the emerging West played prominently in this change, America's growing Orientation.

In the years just prior to expansion, the nation's merchants had shown a growing interest in the Pacific world, from its whales to its bird excrement. Gold and the breakneck growth of population gave the impulse a terrific jolt. The forty-eighters, gold hunters from around the rim, created a market quickly fed from Australia, Chile, Peru, China, and Hawaii, and California soon was the commercial focus of the largest ocean on earth. With the promise of connections across the continent, a new crop of visionaries appeared, with more than a few cracked pots. William Gilpin, Colorado's first territorial governor, predicted that a *"Continental Railroad"* to California and eventually across the Bering Straits would spawn a new global civilization centered between Asia and Europe. Its capital would be Gilpin's current address: Denver.[11]

Pacific visions and railroad hopes first fed the growing antagonism between the Northeast and Southeast, but even then Asian dreaming could anticipate the common hopes that would emerge after the war. California senator William Gwin, a Mississippi slaveholder, and New York abolitionist William Seward became fast friends who pushed for the annexation of Hawaii and the purchase of Russian territories in the Pacific Northwest. Gwin strongly endorsed schemes for an American presence on Siberia's Amur River that would give American businessmen "ready and facile access" to Mongolia, Manchuria, and northern China. Ten years after Seward had first urged the Southeast and Northeast to set aside their quarreling for a shared destiny in the Pacific, he repeated his plea to accept their common purpose in "the chief theater in the events of the world's great hereafter." The key to that destiny was trade. "Commerce," he wrote, "is the god of boundaries."[12]

The centerpiece of those hopes was Cmdre. Matthew Perry's opening of Japan to American trade in 1853–54. The "constantly accumulating capital" from California and Australian mines, he wrote in his report, demanded an aggressive expansion of Pacific commerce, and to that end a series of voyages in 1854 and 1855, together called the Northern Pacific Expedition, surveyed an enormous area with an eye to whaling, fisheries, and trade in "vegetable productions, wood, mineral wealth coal or metals."[13] It found a better route from Australia to China and charted a long stretch of China's coast, the Sea of Okhotsk and the area around Japan's largest island, the Sakhalin Islands, and the Aleutian Islands.[14] In scope and accomplishment, the explorations rivaled any others during a golden era of global exploration. As with the railroad surveys of the western interior, forging new connections included a scientific probing that added to yet another new field in which the United States took the lead—oceanography. The key figure here was Lt. Matthew Fontaine Maury, appointed head of the United States Naval Observatory in 1844.[15] Maury compiled and analyzed many thousands of entries in ships' logbooks as well as movements of right and sperm whales to map ocean currents and to show the prevailing water temperatures and wind patterns. With the help of an ingenious sounding device invented by a young midshipman, John Mercer Brooke, Maury also ordered the first attempts at mapping the ocean floor, at first along the thirty-ninth parallel of the Atlantic. The culmination was the publication of

The Physical Geography of the Sea (1855), often considered the first true work of oceanography.[16] The sudden interest in the Pacific opened a far larger vista for Maury, and by 1858 his charts covered the great ocean and added to the decade's scientific advances. Off Russia's Kamchatka Peninsula, Brooke's record sounding, three and a half miles down, brought up tiny mollusk shells refuting the belief that things could sink only so far into the depths.[17]

By the time the Civil War began, the federal government and a variety of civilian interests had traced out thousands of miles of maritime connections and explored the Pacific's commercial potentials and its scientific lessons. Interest revived after the war, as always focusing on commerce and resources.[18] Trade in and out of the Golden Gate nearly doubled in value during the decade after 1870. Exports, large and small, grew prodigiously—iron and steel by nearly three times, fruit two and a half times, lamps and chandeliers more than twice over.[19] With the boom in grain production, most wheat exports went to Europe, but far eastern ports increasingly drew the trade in flour. By 1878–79 barrels of flour shipped around the Pacific were three and a half times that sent to Europe.[20] As for imports, goods landed at San Francisco grew in value five times over between 1860 and 1880, mostly from around the Pacific. The largest jump was in raw silk from China and Japan. France and Italy had long dominated global silk manufacture, but before the war the United States began using lightweight power looms, and after the Pacific rail connection opened a direct, far cheaper route from Asia, the value of raw silk from China into San Francisco grew from about $600,000 in 1875 to more than $10 million five years later, and in another six years that from China, Japan, and Hong Kong grew by half again as much. Silk production in the Northeast, led by New Jersey, roughly doubled in value every decade from 1860 to 1900. By early in the twentieth century the United States was the world's leader in the industry.[21] Other trade developed in parallel. There was Hawaiian sugar, encouraged by a reciprocity treaty, and on the day the final spike was driven on the transcontinental, the first order of Japanese tea was shipped via rail to Saint Louis.[22]

The Pacific turn shaped the nation in other ways, even down to its intoxications, figurative and literal. As the imagined threat of Chinese immigration became a national bugaboo, politicians became positively tipsy in expounding on how "celestials" threatened workers and families from San Francisco to Boston. Chinese men, who competed unfairly because they had no families to support, somehow threatened to overrun the country as they reproduced like gerbils. More particularly, politicians warned of opium smoking's threat to the national character, especially among its youth. Opiate use was in fact increasing across the nation, one more case, especially baleful, of the partnered influence of expansion and the Civil War. As the smoking habit spread eastward, mostly among prostitutes, gamblers, and others of the demimonde, many more became addicted from treatment for illness and battlefield wounds, as Union doctors were issued more than ten million opium pills.[23] Anti-Chinese feeling had effects well beyond the nation. As Mae Ngai writes, the polemics born in California—that the Chinese were a "coolie race" that always would "under-live and undersell" white competitors—were adopted and repeated in gold rushes across the globe, especially in Australia and South Africa. Exclusion became a state policy of Anglophone nations as they expanded their own power and sought to contain China's across the globe.[24]

Over its first thirty years the remade America that was bridging the continent's distances and developing the West's resources by modern techniques was also turning its gaze and interests so far westward that they were in the Far East. Like the other changes, the Pacific turn was a herald of the century ahead, and many looked toward Asia with a new sense of rightful belonging. The vision of some went beyond commerce and knowledge.

At the ceremonial sinking of the transcontinental's final spike, wires had been wound around it and run to a telegraphic key, so when Leland Stanford famously swung the sledge to drive home the spike (possibly missing, but hitting something metallic), he completed a circuit and sent a single impulse to inform the world that the job was done. Meanwhile, in San Francisco, a wire had been run from the receiver at the city hall to the firing mechanism of an artillery piece at Fort Point on the city's bay. The instant that Stanford's blow connected, the fifteen-inch Parrott gun sent a shell through the Golden Gate into the Pacific, toward the next rim of American ambition. Twenty-nine years later, and fifty years after the great coincidence, the United States annexed Hawaii and took the Philippines.[25]

Domesticating the West

Late in his life, Grove Karl Gilbert thought a lot about sludge. In particular he studied with extraordinary care and vigor the debris washed out of the Sierra Nevada by hydraulic mining between 1855 and 1884. To calculate its passage he measured minutely material washed through a "hydraulic laboratory" of flumes, tedious work occasionally relieved by a couple of hours at his other great passion—billiards. Gilbert's report, published in 1918, the year before his death, described how the "debris wave" was still moving like "a great body of storm water," 1.295 billion cubic yards of the stuff. Enough had made its way into San Francisco Bay to reduce the amount of water flowing into it, which allowed the incoming tide to push the tidal bar outside the bay gradually closer in. Were it not for ebb tides, Gilbert calculated, waste from the hydraulics would have shut the Golden Gate.

Gilbert was a celebrated geologist who with Clarence Dutton and John Wesley Powell had used the Henry Mountains to pose an overarching portrait of how every acre on the planet was in a slow-motion quest for equilibrium between the earth's pressures and the erosive power of water, wind, and temperature. His study of hydraulic mining drew on that work, but with one great difference. The forces at work on the Henry Mountains were entirely natural, but the process he now studied was a partnership between timeless laws and a new sort of human creativity. Gilbert concluded that he was measuring something unprecedented. On the slopes of the Sierra Nevada people had become like uplift and erosion themselves, a geomorphic force reshaping the world at its foundations.

Each new opportunity to exploit western resources required expansive changes to the land that offered them. As a result much of the country west of the Missouri River, roughly two-thirds of the continental United States, was made over in part or in whole. The land was worn away and tunneled into, moved from here to there, cleared of much of what was native—floral, faunal, and human— and repopulated with what was alien. It was the most varied and widespread environmental transformation in American history. It was also, in the word's broadest meaning, a massive domestication. Every square mile of the continent had been well used by people for millennia, but never before or after would land be made over for human purpose on such a scale in so many ways in such a brief span of time. This was also domestication as conquest. Intentionally or not, a farmer plowing his acres and a corporation raising cattle were both denying to others what they had long used for their own survival.

The domestication was never close to total—it never can be, anywhere— nor was it, in the word's common sense, benign, as in gentling a horse. A core principle of environmental history is that people are always changing their worlds and that their worlds are always changing them back, often in unpredicted and unhappy ways. The changes in the West were truly profound. So was the clapback.

The examples were especially vivid where they began, on the Pacific coast before the Civil War. The hydraulic mining that Gilbert studied accomplished in a day what would take thousands of years through natural erosion. The water was carried by wooden rivers that by 1860 ran three times the length of the first transcontinental railroad.[26] Lode mining drew millions more trees into the earth—if made into planks a foot wide and an inch thick, Comstock's lumber would have stretched 150,000 miles—as it sent millions of tons of rocks to the surface. Meanwhile the ranching firm of Miller and Lux was reengineering and disrupting much of the ecology of the Central Valley. The new floral species carried from the East and the Old World on the coats of animals or in cargoes of goods displaced native vegetation more rapidly and extensively, writes one authority, than anywhere at any time on earth before.[27]

The postwar spread of cattle ranching eastward from California and northward out of Texas was the most rapid and extensive expansion of pastoralism in human history, which is to say that rarely have ecosystems over such a space been altered so quickly and thoroughly. Most obvious was a massive ungulate swap, with imported cattle replacing the bison, but ranching also reduced drastically a large tribe of animals—elk, deer, pronghorns, and even grizzly bears, native to the Great Plains—which broke apart the webs of complex interrelationships among these and dozens of other animal and plant species. Fencing-off of water sources further disrupted vital routines of wild residents.[28] An area larger than western Europe was faunally repopulated, florally made over, and redirected to uses it had never known, all inside of forty years.

Farming brought its own changes. California's agricultural acreage multiplied more than seven hundred times in the twenty years after 1850. Then the focus shifted from the West's western to eastern edge. Kansas's farm acreage, less than a third of California's in 1870, pulled slightly ahead ten years later, even as California's grew by a third. As the pattern held across much of the plains, much of the wildflowers, grasses, shrubs, and forbs that had charmed early overlanders were grazed away by cattle or replaced by grasses of the plowmen's choosing, especially corn and wheat. This disrupted whole communities of life, from snakes to beetles, butterflies to lizards. Simply by plowing and grazing the swards along a few Montana rivers farmers and ranchers annihilated one of the western hemisphere's most prolific species, the Rocky Mountain locust.

Others followed variations of the same script. Companies used increasingly mechanized (and extraordinarily wasteful) means to steadily increase the harvest of Northern California's gigantic redwoods. In 1874 Humboldt and Mendocino Counties together accounted for 110 million board feet a year. A quarter of a century later more than a third of the redwoods were gone. Because a single tree might be two millennia old, timbermen in effect were destroying millions of years of life. Redwoods make their own weather; coastal fog condenses in their high canopy and drips up to four inches of water a day. Removing the trees literally changed the climate. Wolverines, martens, fishers, and grizzlies declined or vanished as deer and elk invaded to eat the new brushes and grasses.[29]

The unprecedented transformations brought impressive disruptions. As the waste from hydraulics poisoned rivers, raised their beds, flooded their towns, and turned farms into barren mudflats, the huge blowers in lode mines belched out hot, foul air that joined the smoke and fumes from smelters to produce the "villainous vapors" and "cough-compelling odors" a visitor suffered around Central City and Black Hawk, Colorado.[30] Disruption of the tallgrass and midgrass prairie, the largest ecosystem in the United States, invited troublesome invaders, including tumbleweeds that hitchhiked in with German Russian immigrants. Unadapted newcomers were disastrously vulnerable. Indigenous grasses exploited any rainfall with roots up to ten feet long and as dense as an Old Testament beard. The roots of wheat and corn reach only a foot or so into the soil, so when rains slackened corn harvests fell to as little as three bushels per acre. Up to a third of the settlers survived only through charity and outside support. Another ecological unsettling was unseen. Immigration and new settlements introduced new pathogens—cholera, measles, influenza, whooping cough, malaria, smallpox, and others—into the biota of Native bodies with effects ranging from painful to devastating.

The disorderings reached across both hemispheres. When Argentine cattle herds could not supply enough leather for gaskets and belts in factories in the East and Europe, western hide hunters sent plains bison to the lip of extinction, lubricating their .45-caliber rifles with the oil of whales being slaughtered across the Atlantic and Pacific. Bison bones were ground into fertilizer, part of a European agricultural revolution that earlier had drawn on Peruvian bird guano. Eastern tanneries took their name from tannin, a compound needed to convert hides to leather. It was found in the tree bark of slow-growing black oaks and eastern hemlocks in the Catskill and Adirondack Mountains of western Pennsylvania and New York. As factories ate the bison, the tanneries ate the forests, eventually more than a million acres a year. Like the bison carcasses on the plains, the trees, stripped of their bark, were left to rot.[31]

As the East was moving toward crisis in the 1850s, resolving it bloodily by 1865, and then coping with the aftermath, the West was being physically reengineered into a regional engine that would cut the means of living from under tens of thousands of Native peoples, would power the new nation's explosive economic growth and rise to global power, and would set loose environmental troubles that continue to bedevil the land's possessors today. Just as the birth of the West was inseparable from that of the new America, so neither can be understood outside of the environmental changes and consequences that were themselves an introductory course in what it would mean to be modern.

Chasing Understanding

In 1867 Charles Hazelius Sternberg, seventeen, left upstate New York for western Kansas to join his older brother, George, the post surgeon at Fort Harker. George had a ranch, and while working cattle on it Charles found his calling. In eroded sandstones he came across impressions of leaves of trees that had flourished on the edge of a shallow sea more than seventy million years earlier. Caught up in images of magnolias, cinnamon, sassafras, and sweetgum where there was now a treeless plain, he "would make it my business," he wrote forty years later, "to collect facts from the crust of the earth" that would help unveil the story of life.[32] Sternberg soon turned to fossils of creatures from the ancient sea. With three hundred dollars from Edward Drinker Cope he worked the Kansas chalk beds in the summer of 1876, choking on alkali dust, stung by black gnats. He contracted malaria and was in a fit of ague when he discovered a skeleton of *Clidastes tortor*, a twelve-foot predatory aquatic lizard he and Cope presented the next year in Saint George's Hall in Philadelphia. Later that year he and Cope worked the Montana badlands, looking over their shoulders for Lakotas who had recently dispatched George Custer on the Little Bighorn.

Sternberg continued to uncover fossils across western North America for more than fifty years. His finds, such as the magnificent Triceratops in London's Natural History Museum, are in major depositories across the world. Meanwhile, his brother George, devastated by his young wife's death at Fort Harker from cholera, devoted himself to the study of disease. By 1893, when he was appointed surgeon general, he was the nation's leading bacteriologist. It was Geroge Sternberg who tapped Walter Reed (who had begun his career treating western soldiers and Indians, including Geronimo) to go to Cuba to crack the mystery of yellow fever.

The second half of the nineteenth century was one of the most fertile times in the history of science. Advances in the western world touched on the history of the earth, its structural dynamics, and the mechanics of its climate. They probed the processes of life, including its origins and how people sicken and die. Some of the weightiest work was done in the United States. Its scientific contributions were as much a part of its emergence as a global presence as its growing economic flex and commercial spread, and as with the rest of recasting the nation, much of that work was in the West. As with the rest, the scientists' work was also a work of conquest. It imposed one understanding of the world over others that were there before it, and as part of that understanding it set the country's indigenous peoples in the lower ranks of a racial order that scientists certified as natural and proper. Like railroads and the ecological metamorphosis, the West's scientific endeavors were a unifying force that situated the region and nation within a global order of knowledge and, through that, of power.

Science winds through every chapter of the West's creation. It is most obvious in the evolving efforts by the federal government to learn how best to use its new country, starting in the 1850s to understand better what the nation had acquired and to find the best ways across and around it. The surveys that laid out possible rail routes to the Pacific all had their teams of scientists who gathered information and specimens presented in sumptuously illustrated (and fabulously costly) volumes featuring hundreds of new species of plants and animals, geological surveys, descriptions of Native peoples, and glossaries of their languages. John Strong Newberry provided the first strata tracing of the Grand Canyon, the ultimate geological laboratory, while on a foray to find the best military route into the region. As the government reached beyond the coast into the Pacific with hopes of yet more resources and commerce, its voyages returned with yet more new understandings that helped create the new field of oceanography.

The next stage, after the war, focused on grasping the country's potentials, work given to the federal surveys led by John Wesley Powell, Clarence King, Ferdinand Hayden, and George Wheeler. Their eyes, too, were always toward development, but always collection and description were done for their own sake. In the era's most pursued field, geology, the West was arguably its most active site. The "American school," led by Powell, King, Clarence Dutton, Grove Karl Gilbert, and others, made fundamental breakthroughs in both how the earth was formed and, eon by eon, the story of that formation. The surveys, one of the most expansive scientific projects of the century, gathered similarly in fields ranging from zoology to linguistics to archeology.

The second phase overlapped with a third—the study of how resources, once found and catalogued, could best be exploited. Starting in the 1850s the Smithsonian Institution (founded three months after war was declared on Mexico) began gathering data on rainfall across the country and published a landmark survey. With the telegraph's magic, reports from western weather stations, mostly military posts, were coordinated with others to reveal the first detailed weather patterns, coast to coast, and with that the first reliable forecasts. The goal was again pragmatic, to alert Great Lakes shippers and eastern farmers and merchants to coming storms, but in figuring out whether it would be storm or shine in Chicago and Baltimore, scientists put together how the West's landforms, the currents of air above them, streams within oceans, and the turn of the earth all interacted to determine enduring climates and the endless variations of daily weather. John Wesley Powell then applied those breakthroughs to describe the unbridgeable limits of the West's new economies, and in answer to those limits he especially encouraged ranching in the semiarid West. As ranching spread and connected regions, it spread a baffling disease that threatened to cripple this new international business. The federal government responded with its first focused effort to solve a medical mystery. Theobald Smith's and F. L. Kilbourne's discovery that Texas ticks were the culprits was the first description of a vector disease—a key step in unpuzzling malaria, sleeping sickness, bubonic plague, yellow fever, and other maladies, which in turn helped lessen human suffering for millions while saddling millions more with the miseries of colonialism. The U.S. Entomological Commission's effort to fight the plague of the Rocky Mountain locust was a model of deep analysis of a species that anticipated scores of federal programs to assist the nation's farmers.

Science was another fine demonstration of the pervasive influence of the movement revolution. Besides directly inspiring discoveries through the rail surveys, it catalyzed work across the West by bringing people and information into ever closer contact. O. C. Marsh found his first fossilized equid bones at a stop on a spontaneous ride on the Union Pacific, still being built. His two top field men were a meat hunter for the railroad and a theology student who found his way to Colorado by ship and rail from the University of Oxford. Both got Marsh's attention when they sent him telegrams about their finds. Charles Sternberg got his first break when the eminent paleobotanist Leo Lesquereux visited the young man's remote army post in western Kansas. Michigander James Cook worked as a sailor, Texas Ranger, cattle drover, and Indian scout before catching the fossil-hunting bug from Marsh in Nebraska. His exploration of a rich fossil bed on his ranch produced treasures from the early Miocene. *Moropus cooki*, a three-toed ungulate eight feet tall at the shoulder, is named for him.[33] Just as the West's domestication was part of global disruptions of the natural order, so its science was shaking up the world's human relations. The work of Cook, Sternberg, Marsh, Cope, and others, supported by Washington, universities, and corporate kingpins like Andrew Carnegie, brought critical advances in Darwinism and natural selection, an intellectual and cultural revolution that forced a rethinking of people's relation to God.

Science was also rethinking the relation of people to people, in particular how this people or that did or did not fit into different races and, from that, how each race related to the others. Here, too, the West played a crucial role. It was another sort of laboratory, in this case for the study of its peoples and where they supposedly belonged in the reconstructed America and in the human order.

Reconstructing Race

Nathan C. Meeker was a staunch prohibitionist, agricultural reformer, evangelical Christian, and follower of Horace Greeley and Charles Fourier. After founding a reformist colony that became Greeley, Colorado, he was appointed agent to the Ute reservation on the western side of the state. He quickly set about to educate his charges in religion and the proper agrarian life, but just as quickly he was frustrated. After his white employees plowed five acres, he wrote, some Ute men and women dropped in some potato seeds, then took off for weeks on a hunt. The Utes mostly tolerated Meeker until the increasingly angry agent ordered their horse racetrack plowed up and planted in cabbages. That brought enough of a response for him to call in troops, whereupon several men shot and killed him and ten employees.

A bit more than three weeks later an army command regained control, but in the meantime Ute leaders took Meeker's wife, Arvilla, their daughter, Josephine, and a woman employee as hostages. At one point one of the men, Quinkent, threatened Josephine with a rifle to her forehead and mocked her by singing "Swing Low, Sweet Chariot." His ten-year-old son joined in the jeering. The boy had been a favorite of the agent's family—Josephine had taught him English—and as had many on the reservation, he had been given an English name. By one account it was "Frederick Douglass."[34]

The thirty years after 1848 witnessed by far the greatest changes in racial and ethnic relations that the nation would ever know. The greatest change in terms of numbers came with the Civil War and its aftermath, when more than four million African Americans were emancipated and given a halting invitation into citizenship, but the process had begun between 1846 and 1848 when more than a hundred thousand Hispanos were declared citizens and about a third of a million Indian peoples were brought within the nation's borders. The gold rush and what it triggered drew hundreds of thousands of others from Europe and Asia, some of them, notably the Chinese, bearing cultures rarely encountered here before.

The disordering was a key part of the Greater Reconstruction. Out of it emerged a new racial arrangement that, in its way, unified the new nation as much as its continental infrastructure and its expansive West-fed economy. It was not unifying in the sense of setting all its peoples on an equal footing—there were glaring inequalities—but, formally at least, it did unite the new human mix in the national polity under common goals and common presumptions about how to achieve those goals. As it turned out, these led also to common patterns of frustration and failure and to an ongoing conversation over the nature and boundaries of citizenship.

The unsettling began in the West but was always in resonance with the East. Expansion and Marshall's discovery brought efforts to impose a new order of white rule—the "second conquest" of California of 1849–52, the violent marginalization of Hispanos, and elsewhere the determination to keep the new country largely free of Black Americans. Truly establishing Black slavery in the new country became increasingly untenable, and yet the West, as the projecting ground for eastern interests and ideals, steadily drove apart pro- and anti-slavery advocates in the East. In the thick catalogue of ironies of the day, this should be near the front: as the actual West leaned heavily toward white supremacy, the imagined West and the emotions it inspired provoked the war that gave millions of Black slaves their freedom.

Close to that irony should be another: the war that gave freedom to eastern slaves took a long step toward taking it away from western Indians. The immediate impulse was from the near obsession with connectivity, the need to bind the expanded America into one. During the Civil War military efforts to control vital roads to the Pacific broke the power of tribes on the central plains, the Great Basin, and New Mexico, and after the war other connectors, railroads and the telegraph, helped give the army an unbeatable edge. By then retooling the land and tapping its wealth was undoing Native life and consigning Indians to whatever slot the government chose in the new racial order.

Unsettling racial relations from Atlantic to Pacific raised a fundamental question: Who was an American? Who qualified—racially, ethnically, and in cultural nature and potential—to be inside the nation's political and cultural household? The question obviously had been there from the start, but expansion, gold, and civil war pushed it to center stage, and it has stayed there, or close by, ever since. Often enough, its back-and-forth conversation has been between West and East.

That conversation drew especially on what in other ways was connecting the West into a wider world—science. "Race science" (or pseudoscience), claiming to categorize and rank humanity as separate races, arose roughly coincident with expansion, and it was pursued with special vigor in the West. Besides plotting weather fronts and cataloguing insects, those in what Powell called the "Science of Man" were using potsherds, skulls, and language syntax to situate Indians among the world's races. Others aimed to do the same for Africans, including African Americans enslaved in the Southeast. The rankings universally assigned both Africans and Indians (and Hispanos and Chinese) to places near or at the bottom of a global arrangement.

Scientists differed, however, on what the rankings meant, and that difference spoke to nothing less than the future composition of American society. Polygenists argued that each race was a different species. The traits and abilities of each had been there from the start, so races were frozen, unchanging in their potentials, or lack of them. Monogenists held that all races had a common origin and were moving along a common path of progress. Some (namely Caucasians, the race of the theorizers) had advanced farther than the others, but all had the same possibilities and in the grand scheme of things all were on the way to the same goals.

Peel back the scientific gloss, and the basic division was between some who advocated a permanent political and cultural domination by white Americans ("white" defined as they chose) and others willing to open the national family more broadly, albeit on conditions they laid down. Seen that way, the three decades after 1848 saw the introduction of dueling visions of citizenship that has continued for the fourteen decades after that.

At the end of the Civil War the second vision guided federal policy. Its prime focus was on freedpeople and western Indians, the one to fashion the first steps toward citizenship, the other to do the same while setting Indians aside on reservations so the redeemed republic could be fully united. What is striking is how the government's approach toward one was so similar to that toward the other.

For a glimpse at the Indian side, consider the "peace medals" given by nineteenth-century presidents to friendly Native leaders. On one side of each is the current president in profile, on the other are images of the current vision of what Indian relations ought to be. The medals that Lewis and Clark handed out had a simply coiffed Jefferson and on the reverse images of a basic economic exchange—clasped hands, a peace pipe and hatchet, a common trade good, and the words "Peace and Friendship." Scan sixty years ahead. On the verso of Lincoln is a man in full feathered headdress plowing behind a horse. In the background are a church and schoolhouse. In front of the school, children are playing baseball. Change the faces and setting and the scene would describe the vision soon to hatch for emancipated enslaved Blacks. Freedmen were to walk behind their own plows as freeholding farmers. As Indian children were schooled in English and standard curricula as well as in national identity and prevailing values, sons and daughters of former slaves would advance toward citizenship by attending schools under the Freedmen's Bureau (hopes of baseball games were less explicit). Central to the values pressed on Native peoples was the evangelical Christianity that inspired those working with freedpeople through institutions like the American Missionary Association and in individuals like Oliver O. Howard, head of the Freedmen's Bureau.[35]

Both efforts relied on agricultural and manual training, education, and Christianity as avenues of cultural incorporation. And both efforts failed.

Emancipation's reformist impulses weakened, partly through exhaustion and frustration over spotty results, partly through pressures to reunify the older republic under white rule. Unlike freedpeople, Indians were cultural outsiders with their own economies, religions, and ways of teaching their children about both. The snarled changes brought by federal programs resulted in deepening divisions among tribal factions and between generations. Economies meant to be self-supporting more often were self-defeating. The result was sometimes a flash of bloody resistance like that on Nathan Meeker's Ute reservation, but for the most part the reservations meant to become prospering arcadias were what Alfred Terry called "national alms houses, called agencies." The government's goal for freedpeople proved beyond its willingness to pursue. The government's goal for Indians proved beyond its ability to comprehend.

As for other minorities in the new order, federal officials in the Southwest used the Thirteenth Amendment, Civil Rights Act of 1866, and the "Peon Law" the next year to suppress somewhat debt peonage, especially among field workers, but the Hispanic and Anglo elite continued to resist the intrusion, and debt peonage and the economic caste system continued deep into the next century. Meanwhile—the ironies accumulate—a peonage system strikingly similar to the one in the Southwest was saddled on freedpeople in the Southeast as white landholders reasserted control over the economy.[36] In California the Thirteenth Amendment was used *against* the Chinese. Republicans argued that it freed them from their labor contracts, but that was bad news. Once unbound, the toadying Chinese would never be able to truly join in a free labor economy. Judged beyond the powers of assimilation, the Chinese became the only population ever to be excluded from admission on the basis of ethnicity.[37]

As postwar policies for a new racial order waned, the alternative vision from the 1850s reasserted itself, arguing unbridgeable differences among races and an unchanging ranking of superior and inferior. Impoverished Indians were again called retrogrades who should surrender what remained of their land to those who knew how to use it. Black Americans again were infantilized as slow and simple and incapable of civic responsibility. After 1880 they were held under the white boot by a half century of intimidation and lynching startlingly like the suppression of Hispanos during the previous thirty years in California and the Southwest.[38] Hispanos there were pictured as sleepy exotics. These people of color became people of local color, which is another thing altogether. Chinese were deemed culturally infectious and so hopelessly alien that all doors had to be shut against them.

After 1900 the older rhetoric soared, now also targeting the "new" immigrants from eastern and southern Europe. In 1851 the polygenist Josiah Nott had scoffed at the "delusion" that "mankind [is] a *unit*" and that some utopian system could make all peoples "great, good and happy." Sixty-five years later in his best-selling *The Passing of the Great Race* Madison Grant scorned the "fatuous belief" in the "brotherhood of man" and the failed faith that social environment and education could raise up Poles, Italians, Russians, Asians, Blacks, or Indians anywhere close to cultural snuff.[39] As with so many changes begun with expansion, these reverberated globally. An international eugenics movement drew heavily on the American "race science" of the 1850s. In the 1930s, Charles King writes, Germany's National Socialists believed they were "not so much inventing a race-obsessed state as catching up with one."[40] Adolph Hitler spoke admiringly of the nation that had "gunned down the millions of redskins to a few hundred thousands, and now keep[s] the modest remnant under observation in a cage," and the theorist behind the laws forbidding the marriage of Jews to those of German blood (whatever that meant) grounded his ideas in the legal treatment of American Indians, including their confinement to reservations.[41]

After Allied forces crushed the Reich's attempts at a new racial order, national policy swung back toward the vision of expanded citizenship—a widening of the door for immigrants in 1965 and with that a surge in Asian immigration, legislation and social movements to undo restrictions imposed on Black Americans early in the century, the same to address discrimination against Hispanos and Indian peoples, and a withering (but not disappearance) of popular interest and state legislation for eugenics. The vacillations continue. As of this writing there is a resurgence of white supremacist movements, legislation effectively restricting voting by racial minorities, anti-Asian rhetoric and violence, and expanded efforts to restrict nonwhite immigration including, for Hispanos, physical barriers.

Particulars have changed, but the patterns are clear. Among the many ways they helped remake the nation after expansion, developments in the West helped set the terms of an ongoing exchange over who is eligible to be members of the American polity and its social household—of just how *pluribus* should be our *unum*. By one standard the government's initial goal of raising up its newly admitted members remains imperfectly met. Civic equality in the American family implied a rising economic hope, but as the nation followed its extraordinary ascent as an economic superpower, the three populations invited in after 1848 have remained where they were at the start—at the rear. In 2010 seven of the ten poorest counties in the contiguous United States were dominated by Indian peoples, Hispanos, and African Americans. They were in South Dakota, along the Texas border, and in Louisiana and Mississippi. The continental racial order that emerged after the great coincidence continues to bind America, West and East, measured here by the era's failed promises.

The American West was both the child and the midwife of the new United States. The emerging West and modernizing America both have their stories, and each deserves its own telling, yet each story is inextricable from the other. Each at first was a story of unsettling and disruption, and together the two nearly tore the nation apart, but three decades or so after the stories began, the Northeast and Southeast were stitched uneasily back together, and roughly one-half of the expanded nation had coalesced into what was by far its largest and most diverse section. The changes running through the two stories—continental connections, steep economic growth and conversion, the Pacific turn, the land made over, scientific and technological acceleration, and racial reordering—weave into and build on one another.

There can be no untangling the strands of this Greater Reconstruction, and their very knottiness might encourage us to ask what lessons the stories hold. William Sherman did. In 1886 he looked back and found it all good. Although he had his doubts about how we did it, he wrote his brother, taking California was "essential to the world's progress." After all, our seizure and domination of it "at once began that wonderful development" that now promised the nation even grander things ahead.[42]

Any comparable stretch of years, however, especially one with anything like the changes during these, can have no clear balance between gain and cost. The particulars here are obvious: a nation's surge of power and affluence, hundreds of thousands dead or dispossessed, widening opportunities for millions, millions living out promises denied, land turned to homesteads and to Denver and Phoenix and Salt Lake City, land stolen and turned into poisoned grotesqueries. The consequences remain; yesterday makes today. As for tomorrow and how best to use it, the stories and their voices offer up hints and provocations.

In the autumn of 1878 Heinmot Tooyalakekt (Thunder Rising to Loftier Mountain Heights) was living in northeast Indian Territory near the town of Baxter Springs. The white public knew him as Chief Joseph, a tall, broad-faced figure among the Nez Perce (Nimiipu) people of the Pacific Northwest. Washington had consigned him and close to four hundred others to this place they called Eeikish Pah, roughly "The Heat" or "Hell," months after a running fight with the army that had stretched about 1,500 miles from Idaho, across the Rocky Mountains and Montana plains before Joseph surrendered, just shy of the

Canadian border, to Gen. Nelson Miles and Gen. Oliver Howard, former head of the Freedmen's Bureau.

The press had portrayed Joseph as a brilliant war leader but his gift had always been diplomacy, and now he set out to use his celebrity to curry popular support to allow his people to return home. A congressional delegation was in the territory to study whether tribes there should be under military or civilian authority. What did Joseph think? Neither, he answered: "We should have one law to govern [all of] us and we should all live together." "One law for Indians and all citizens of the United States?" asked an incredulous Rep. J. H. Stewart. "All should be citizens," Joseph answered. The Nez Perces had fought because the government had taken "everything that was dear to us . . . our horses, cattle, land, and streams of water." But they had lost. Now they accepted that they were Americans, which after all is what Washington had insisted, and they embraced American values: "Liberty is good and great," including the liberty to go home if they wished.

Then Joseph raised his sights. Washington now commanded the country, and as it felt out the way ahead, it ought to look for answers in the very places it had taken. They were "as large as the people inhabiting" them and not just in the sense of having enough room for them all. He spoke of the sun's generosity and of the earth's gifts and implied that all who lived by them had capacities just as great. As the country opened itself to its people, its people could enlarge its true possibilities through their own generosity of spirit and vision.

Joseph was asking the men he now called his fellow Americans how their story thus far had measured up to that standard. Nearly a century and a half later the question is still worth asking, both about the birth of the West and about all that has followed: In a nation continental in scale and with potentials that still unfold, how might the national character grow and deepen to match the promise of national expansion? Joseph's advice were his last words in any official record: "The way is as big as the land."[43]

Notes

Prelude

1. I have used the dates for when Texas formally joined the Union and when the Treaty of Guadalupe Hidalgo was formally declared in effect.
2. Silbey's particular concern was politics of the 1850s, but his point applies much more broadly. Silbey, "Civil War Synthesis."
3. Recent works have added to the several older surveys of expansion: Howe, *What Hath God Wrought*, chapters 17–20; Clary, *Eagles and Empire*; Woodworth, *Manifest Destinies*; Merry, *Country of Vast Designs*.
4. Merk, "British Party Politics," 653.
5. Cutler, *Correspondence of James K. Polk*, 449.
6. The estimate is from Clary, *Eagles and Empire*, 412.
7. The amount is calculated from 393,093 square miles for the full Texas annexation, 529,017 square miles for the Mexican Cession, and 286,500 square miles for land under the Oregon Treaty. Because its eastern border was not clearly marked at the time, the last is an informed estimate.
8. Farnham, *Travels in the Great Western Prairies*, 246–48.
9. Irving, *Astoria*, 213–14.
10. Graebner, *Empire on the Pacific*, 27–29.
11. *Debates and Proceedings*, 682–83.
12. Farnham, *Travels in the Californias*, 252.
13. Utley, *After Lewis and Clark*.
14. Goetzmann, *Exploration and Empire*, 249.
15. Goetzmann, *Exploration and Empire*, 266–70, 277–79.
16. The essential work remains Horsman, *Race and Manifest Destiny*.
17. Churchill, "Thomas Jefferson Farnham," 536.
18. Whitney, *Project for a Railroad*, iii. On the ideological connection between technology and cultural dominance, see Adas, *Dominance by Design* and Adas, *Machines as the Measure of Men*.
19. Stegner, "Who Are the Westerners?," 36.

Part 1. Unsettling America

1. Bowles, *Our New West*, v.
2. May, *Manifest Destiny's Underworld*, 127.

1. The Great Coincidence

1. Sherman, *Personal Memoirs*, vol. 1, 68–69, 81–82; USCD Serial Set 557, 504–19.
2. USCD Serial Set 537, 10; Sherman, *Personal Memoirs*, 108.
3. On Marshall, see Gay, *James W. Marshall*; Parsons, *Life and Adventures*.
4. Paul, *California Gold Discovery*.
5. Paul, *California Gold Discovery*, 119.
6. Berry, "Gold! but How Much?," 246–55; Ely, "Gold—Its Production in All Countries," 241–50; Chevalier, *Of the Probable Fall*, 41–42; Vilar, *History of Gold and Money*, 351; Ridgeway, *Summarized Data*, 11.
7. Sutter and Marshall, "Discovery of Gold," 202.
8. McGinty, *Haraszthy at the Mint*, 30–31.
9. Roske, "World Impact," 187–232; Phinney, "Gold Production," 647–79; Monaghan, *Australians and the Gold Rush*; Monaghan, *Chile, Peru*.
10. Marx, *Contribution*; Nash, "A Veritable Revolution," 288–89.
11. Seidman, *Fools of '49*, 17.
12. USCD Serial Set 557, 508.
13. Eldredge, *History of California*, 182–85; *Gold Regions of California*, 22.
14. Lyman, *History of Oregon*, vol. 4, 121–24; Bancroft, *Works*, vol. 2, 42–47.
15. Greer, "Wandering Kamaainas," 221–25; Kuykendall, *Hawaiian Kingdom*, 319–20.
16. Wright, "Making of Cosmopolitan California, Part I," 325; Guinn, "Sonoran Migration," 31–36.
17. Wright, "Making of Cosmopolitan California, Part I," 326; Monaghan, *Chile, Peru*; Joy, *Chili Gulch*.
18. Monaghan, *Australians and the Gold Rush*, 38, 99.
19. Paul, *California Gold*, 44–45; Hittel, *Resources of California*, 14–15.
20. William Perkins, "El Campo de los Sonoraenses, or Three Years Residence in California," BaL, 25; Johnson, *Sights in the Gold Region*, 197.
21. Conlin, *Bacon, Beans, and Galantines*, 183–86; Horsman, *Feast or Famine*, 195–221.
22. Churchill, *"Little Sheaves,"* 89–90.
23. Monaghan, *Chile, Peru*, 135.
24. Simpson, *Three Weeks in the Gold Mines*.
25. Stillson, *Spreading the Word*, 28.
26. "Method of Washing Gold Dust," 232.
27. Roberts, *American Alchemy*, 65.
28. Watkins, "Reveloidal Spindle." In 1869 Porter had a prototype built and tested. It didn't work.
29. Stillson, *Spreading the Word*, 61–72; Wyman, "Outfitting Posts."
30. Stillson, *Spreading the Word*, 70.
31. Shumate, *California of George Gordon*, 82.
32. Lewis, "South American Ports of Call," 55–66; Kemble, "Gold Rush by Panama," 45. For firsthand accounts of the first voyage to California around Cape Horn, including those by two men later prominent in California affairs, Mark Hopkins and J. Ross Browne, see Ramirez, *From New York to San Francisco*.

33. Kemble, *Panama Route*, 33–35.

34. Marryat, *Mountains and Molehills*, 18; Johnson, *Sights in the Gold Region*, 32; Joseph W. Revere Album, 9–12, HL.

35. Ferris, "Gold Hunters of California," 930.

36. Pratt, "Gold Hunters of California," 906; Delgado, *To California by Sea*, 54–55.

37. Kemble, *Panama Route*, 254.

38. Unruh, *Plains Across*, 119; Faragher, *Women and Men*, 195.

39. The classic study is Mattes, *Great Platte River Road*.

40. Unruh, *Plains Across*, 414; Bagley, *With Golden Visions*, 248.

41. Unruh, *Plains Across*, 402–3.

42. Watson, "Traveling Traditions," 81.

43. Unruh, *Plains Across*, 397.

44. Addison M. Crane journal, June 22, 1852, HL. One historian writes that, although women were more likely to comment on the aesthetics of the land, both sexes mentioned the beauty of the country more than any other topic. Faragher, *Women and Men*, 14.

45. Thomas D. Sanders reminiscence, 27–28, DPL; John L. Johnson journal, April 2, 1851, BL.

46. Clark, *Gold Rush Diary*, 28.

47. Applegate, *Recollections of My Boyhood*, 14–15; Hafen, *Overland Routes*, 128; Holmes, *Bloomer Girl*, 18–19; Brayer, *Pike's Peak . . . or Busted!*, 8–9.

48. Howard and Riley, "'Thus You See,'" 29.

49. Holmes, *Bloomer Girl*, 18–19; William Tell Parker diary, July 22, 1850, HL.

50. Unruh, *Plains Across*, 185. Unruh recorded 186 deaths at the hands of Indians during the prime rush years of 1849–52, or about a tenth of a percent.

51. "Diary of the Overland Trail," 193; Hafen, *Overland Routes*, 145; Perry Kline reminiscence, 34–35, CSHS.

52. On illness and difficulties generally, see Olch, "Treading the Elephant's Tail."

53. Lorenz, "Scurvy in the Gold Rush," 473–519.

54. Powers and Younger, "Cholera on the Overland Trails."

55. Unruh, *Plains Across*, 124; "Diary of David DeWolf."

56. Eli and Mary Bloyed to W. M. Tigand, November 13, 1852, Eli and Mary Bloyed Letters, UA.

57. West, *Growing up with the Country*, 36–41; Unruh, *Plains Across*, 409–13.

58. Mattes, *Great Platte River Road*, 82; Unruh, *Plains Across*, 408.

59. There is remarkably little certainty about mortality rates in the Unites States before 1900. One estimate sets the crude death rate in 1870–80 at 23.66 per thousand persons, or 2.366 percent, and other work suggests that during the 1840s and 1850s, the years of the great migration over the trails, the rate was higher. See Haines and Steckel, *Population History*, 305–69; Haines, "White Population," 305–69. This would make the mortality rate on the trails seem about double or triple that of the nation. The national rate, however, is for a full year, while that of the trails measures only the four months or so of travel, so in practical terms the overland death rate was well above the nation's. Muddling matters further is

the fact that overland mortality was higher in the earlier years, and much higher in 1849 and 1852, the heaviest years of travel. For those crossing in other years, the rate would have been significantly lower. On the other hand, national rates were far higher among children five years old and younger. If the comparison were between grown males heading west and those staying home, presumably the death rate on the trails would be significantly higher, especially from 1849 to 1852, although more in balance before and after those years. It's complicated.

60. Joseph Fish autobiography, 23, AHS. Of cooking in the wind, one woman wrote that "them that eat the most breakfast eat the most sand." Howard and Riley, "'Thus You See,'" 29.

61. Bagley, *With Golden Dreams*, 272.

62. Unruh, *Plains Across*, 390; Clark, *Gold Rush Diary*, 61–62.

63. Anonymous, "Overland Journey to Colorado, 1863," journal, DPL.

64. Bagley, *With Golden Dreams*, 320–21.

65. Faragher, *Women and Men*, 195.

66. Watson, "Traveling Traditions," 80–81; Spring, *Bloomer Girl*; Porter, *By Ox Team to California*, 27–28.

67. Royce, *Frontier Lady*, 8–9; Watson, "Traveling Traditions," 75, 78–79.

68. Opie and Opie, *Lore and Language*, 2; West, "Child's Play," 2–15.

69. Royce, *Frontier Lady*, 11.

70. Elizabeth Keys's family stopped on Sunday, but, "dreadful to tell," the men went fishing. (That turned out to be no sin, she added dryly, "as they caught nothing to speak of.") Faragher, *Women and Men*, 95–96.

71. Schlissel, *Women's Diaries*, 151; Faragher, *Women and Men*, 190.

72. Schlissel, *Women's Diaries*, 151; Faragher, *Women and Men*, 139.

73. Hafen, *Overland Routes*, 40, 140–41; William F. Denniston, "Journal of Travels in Central America and California, 1849–1850," HL.

2. Division and Multiplication

1. Kennedy, *Texas*, 395–96.

2. Binkley, *Expansionist Movement*, 93.

3. Frazier, *Blood and Treasure*, 9.

4. Clay and Jones, "Migrating to Riches," 1003–1110; Smith, *Freedom's Frontier*, 40.

5. The following is based on Cronon, *Nature's Metropolis*; North, *Economic Growth*; Taylor, *Transportation Revolution*; Egnal, *Clash of Extremes*; Stover, *Iron Road*; Thomas, *Iron Way*.

6. North, *Economic Growth*, 251.

7. USCD Serial Set 1137, 104.

8. Wright, "Making of Cosmopolitan California, Part I," 339.

9. Cotterill, "Southern Railroads"; Cotterill, "Beginnings of Railroads."

10. For a summary of the effects of these changes on sectional conflict, see Binder, "Transportation Revolution."

11. Unruh, *Plains Across*, 227.

12. Unruh, *Plains Across*, 129–32; McChristian, *Fort Laramie*, 47–49.

13. Hafen and Gussow, *Arapaho-Cheyenne Indians*, 49; Hedges, *Pikes Peak*, 13–14.
14. Penniston and Miller day books, December 12, 1866, NSHS. Other entries mention "dope" and "pain killer."
15. On private enterprise along the trails, see Unruh, *Plains Across*, 267–301. Particulars are on 278 and 284.
16. John Eagle to Margaret Eagle, June 28, 1852, John Eagle Letters, HL; Page, *Wagon West*, 123; Holliday, *Rush for Riches*, 131; Perkins, *Three Years in California*, 263.
17. Nelson, "Trip to the Post Office."
18. For a selection of the best work from the voluminous writing on the pony express: Ridge, "Reflections"; Reinfeld, *Pony Express*; Settle and Settle, *Saddles and Spurs*; Corbett, *Orphans Preferred*; Bloss, *Pony Express*.
19. On this important western enterprise: Settle and Settle, *Saddles and Spurs*; Majors, *Seventy Years*.
20. USCD Serial Set 1025, 1408–11, 1484; Hafen, *Overland Mail*, 45–46.
21. Stiles, *First Tycoon*, 170–222.
22. McGuinness, *Path of Empire*, 54–83; Otis, *Isthmus of Panama*; McCullough, "Steam Road."
23. Unruh, *Plains Across*, 120; Kemble, *Panama Route*, 254.
24. Paul, "Beginnings of Agriculture," 18.
25. Hardy, "Agricultural Changes," 219.
26. Paul, "Beginnings of Agriculture," 19; Hardy, "Some Economic Aspects," 146.
27. Adams, "Historical Background," 35–36; Paul, "Wheat Trade"; Paul, "Beginnings of Agriculture," 19–23.
28. Cleland, *Cattle on a Thousand Hills*, 103–9; Jensen, "Cattle Drives"; Atkinson, "Cattle Drives from Arkansas"; Gates, *California Ranchos* 17–21; *Governor's Annual Message*, 25. The astounding price of up to five hundred dollars per head is noted in Bancroft, *History of California*, vol. 7, 54n. For a fascinating diary of an early cattle drive from Texas to California, see Haley, "Log of the Texas-California Cattle Trail."
29. Caughey, *California*, 310–11.
30. Hardy, "Some Economic Aspects," 143.
31. Igler, *Industrial Cowboys*.
32. Paul, "Beginnings of Agriculture," 17–18; Engstrand, *William Wolfskill*; Schoenman, *Father of California Wine*, 13–37.
33. Silver, "Farming Facts," 176–83.
34. Prevost, *California Silk Grower's Manual*, vii. In the late 1860s wealthy San Franciscans, doubtless encouraged by the Pioneer Silk Growers and Manufacturers Association, bankrolled a Sacramento valley plantation. Its six hundred thousand mulberry trees and two large cocooneries produced "some of the finest raw silk ever shown in any country" until a heatwave killed every one of its two million worms. Vaught, *After the Gold Rush*, 205–6; *Memorial of Committee*.
35. Cronise, *Natural Wealth*; Hittel, *Resources of California*. The heroic vegetal claims are in the latter, p. 183.
36. Haraszthy, *Grape Culture*, xx.

37. St. Clair, "Gold Rush." For a detailed description of early industrial development, see Bancroft, *History of California*, vol. 7, 75–101.

38. St. Clair, "Gold Rush," 194.

39. Walker, "Industry Builds the City," 37–38.

40. Pendergrast, *Uncommon Grounds*; Bonsall, *More Than They Promised*.

41. Delgado, *To California by Sea*, 78.

42. On the prelude to this period as a background to increasing American interest and presence in Pacific trade, see Blussé, *Visible Cities*.

43. Igler, *Great Ocean*, 33–35.

44. Igler, *Great Ocean*, 117–28; Davis et al., *In Pursuit of Leviathan*, 19; Bradley, "Hawaii and the American Penetration," 277–86.

45. Cox, *Mills and Markets*, 74–79; Cox, *Lumberman's Frontier*, 266–69.

46. Cox, *Mills and Markets*, 75.

47. Bethel, "Golden Skein," 256; Barker, *Memoirs of Elisha Oscar Crosby*, 19–20; Taylor, *Eldorado*, 162–63; MacMullen, *Paddle-Wheel Days*, 24–33.

48. Winther, *Express and Stagecoach Days*, 14–15.

49. Clappe, *Shirley Letters*, 5–6.

50. Winther, *Express and Stagecoach Days*, 81–95, 150–58; Winther, "Stage-Coach Service."

51. Bethel, "Golden Skein"; Howard, *Sierra Crossing*, 62–64.

52. On development of the express business in California, see Wiltsee, *Pioneer Miner*; Winther, *Express and Stagecoach Days*. For a more general history, see Stimson, *History of the Express Companies*.

53. Wiltsee, *Pioneer Miner*, 37–39; William Brown to "Dear Parents," April 7, 1850, and to "My Dear Mother," February 13, 1851, William A. Brown papers, HL. One company's route was typical. Its partners went first to Marysville from Sacramento by steamboat, then ferried the mail eighty more miles to the headwaters of the Yuba River. Comstock, *Gold Diggers*, 308.

54. Delano, *Pen Knife Sketches*, 27; Holliday, *Rush for Riches*, 131; Schafer, *California Letters*, 59.

55. Wheat, "'California's Bantam Cock,'" 390, 235.

56. McWilliams, *California*, 25.

3. Letting Blood

1. USCD Serial Set 537, 54.

2. Johnson, *Roaring Camp*, 208; John Hovey, "Historical Account of the Troubles between Chilean and American Miners in the Calavaros Mining District," HL.

3. Hittell, *History of California*, 705n.

4. For a summary of these events, see Johnson, *Roaring Camp*, 210–15.

5. Harris, *Gila Trail*, 133.

6. The German literary traveler Friedrich Gerstäcker wrote a slightly comic version of one of these confrontations. Gerstäcker and Cosgrove, "French Revolution."

7. Peterson, *Manifest Destiny*, 43, 66–67; Hittell, *History of California*, 708–9.

8. Nasatir, *French in the California Gold Rush*; Rohrbough, *Rush to Gold*, 143–61, 200; John Hovey, "Account of the Troubles between American Miners and the French-

men of the Garde Mobile at Mokelumne Hill," HL. A French writer urged sending a fleet to California to insure interested parties could protect their interests. Nasatir, *French in California Gold Rush*, 12.

9. The term is most associated with the sociologist Edward E. Telles, who pays special attention to gradations based on color within Latin American cultures. Telles, *Pigmentocracies*.

10. For studies of the rhetoric of expansion and its stereotyping of non-Anglos, see Horsman, *Race and Manifest Destiny*; Almaguer, *Racial Fault Lines*; Brantlinger, *Dark Vanishings*.

11. Clappe, *Shirley Letters*, 131; Monaghan, *Chile, Peru*, 157.

12. Canfield, *Diary of a Forty-Niner*, 39–40.

13. For an excellent recent study of the complex political struggles over issues of bound labor during the gold rush and afterwards, see Smith, *Freedom's Frontier*.

14. Pitt, "Beginnings of Nativism," 26–27.

15. Shaw, *Golden Dreams*, 86–88.

16. Rohrbough, *Rush to Gold*, 196.

17. Pitt, "Beginnings of Nativism," 25–26; Monaghan, *Chile, Peru*, 152–70; Bancroft, *Works*, vol. 33, 402–4.

18. John Hovey, "Account of the Troubles between American Miners and the Frenchmen of the Garde Mobile at Mokelumne Hill," HL; Joy, *Chili Gulch*; Ayers, *Gold and Sunshine*, 46–58; Monaghan, *Chile, Peru*, 243–48.

19. Monaghan, *Chile, Peru*, 152–70.

20. Weber, *New Spain's Northern Frontier*, 302.

21. Peterson, "Foreign Miner's Tax," 267.

22. Kenny, "Nativism," 134.

23. Peterson, "Foreign Miner's Tax," 265, 269.

24. Heckendorn and Wilson, *Miners and Business Men's Directory*, 40–43.

25. Peterson, *Manifest Destiny*, 69–70.

26. Johnson, *Roaring Camp*, 36; Kenny, "Nativism," 136–38.

27. Carrigan and Webb, "Lynching of Persons of Mexican Origin," 422.

28. Faragher, *Eternity Street*, 2.

29. A selection from the large literature on racial violence in the Southeast in the latter nineteenth century: Tolnay and Tolnay, *Festival of Violence*; Brundage, *Lynching in the New South*; Finnegan, *Deed So Accursed*; Wright, *Racial Violence in Kentucky*; *Lynching in America*. Some attention recently has been given to placing lynching in a wider national and international context: Pfeifer, *Roots of Rough Justice*; Pfeifer, "Lynching beyond Dixie"; Seguin and Rigby, "National Crimes."

30. For a fine consideration of the issues and challenges of understanding lynching, East and West, see Carrigan, "Strange Career of Judge Lynch."

31. Carrigan and Webb, "Lynching of Persons of Mexican Origin," 411. See also Carrigan and Webb, *Forgotten Dead*.

32. Vandal, *Rethinking Southern Violence*, 47–48, 167.

33. The figures are calculations by John Mack Faragher based on research for his study of Los Angeles homicides, Faragher, *Eternity Street*. They can be found

through the Criminal Justice Research Center of the Ohio State University: https://cjrc.osu.edu/research/interdisciplinary/hvd/united-states/los-angeles-1830 -1874. My great thanks to Faragher both for access to his work and for advice about its uses. Given the relatively small numbers of homicides in any given year (with the same true of figures for the Red River Valley of Louisiana), rates are more reliable over longer spans of time, such as those used here. Faragher found 302 murders for 1850 to 1865 and estimates that another sixty likely occurred.

34. Other works on lynching in the West during these years are Carrigan, *Making of a Lynching Culture*; Leonard, *Lynching in Colorado*; Day-Gonzales, *Lynching in the West*.

35. John Eagle to Margaret Eagle, February 10, 1853, John H. Eagle Letters, HL.

36. The most thorough study of the ordeal of California Indians after the gold discovery is Madley, *American Genocide*. See also Lindsay, *Murder State*.

37. Rawls, "Gold Diggers," 28; Timothy Osborn journal, October 20, 1850, BaL.

38. Collins, *Sam Ward*, 23–24.

39. Timothy Osborn journal, October 20, 1850, BaL; Johnson, *Roaring Camp*, 220–22; Hurtado, *Indian Survival*, 112–17; Rawls, "Gold Diggers," 28–45. The estimates are from *Gold Regions of California*, 272.

40. Hurtado, *John Sutter*, 76.

41. Heizer and Elsasser, *Natural World*, 97–98; Steward, "Two Paiute Autobiographies," 434, 437–38.

42. Heizer and Elsasser, *Natural World*, 110–11.

43. White, *Yankee Trader*, 107, 110.

44. William Tell Parker diary, July 22, 1850, HL.

45. Elijah Renshaw Potter, "Reminiscences of the Early History of Northern California and of the Indian Troubles," BaL; Clark, *Journals of Alfred Doten*, vol. 1, 67.

46. Madley, *American Genocide*, 185.

47. Elijah Renshaw Potter, "Reminiscences of the Early History of Northern California and of the Indian Troubles," BaL.

48. Madley, *American Genocide*, 354, 533.

49. Madley, *American Genocide*, 174–75, 190–207.

50. Madley, *American Genocide*, 227, 238, 244, 253.

51. Madley, *American Genocide*, 199–200, 237–38, 250, 253, 289.

52. Madley, *American Genocide*, 163–71.

53. USCD Serial Set 974, 650; Madley, "California's Yuki Indians," 323; Phillips, *Indians and Indian Agents*.

54. Madley, *American Genocide*, 170, 260. For Beale's revealing testimony in its entirety, see USCD Serial Set 688, 377–80.

55. William Ralganal Benson, "The Facts of Stone and Kelseyville Massacre," typescript, BaL.

56. Madley, *American Genocide*, 115–38. For a collection of differing accounts of the incident, including both military and Indian sources, see Heizer, *Collected Documents*.

57. Madley, *American Genocide*, 534–50.

58. The laws are reprinted in Heizer, *Destruction of California Indians*, 220–26.

59. Hurtado, *Indian Survival*, 203–4; Hurtado, "'Hardly a Farm House.'"

60. H. C. Bailey, "California in '53: From the Reminiscences of H. C. Bailey," BaL; Rawls, *Indians of California*, 96–97; Carpenter, "Among the Diggers," 391; Madley, "California's Yuki Indians," 313.

61. Heizer, "Indian Servitude," 415.

62. Palmer, *History of Mendocino County*, 459; Carranco and Beard, *Genocide and Vendetta*; Madley, "California's Yuki Indians"; Norton, *Genocide in Northwestern California*.

63. Cook, *Aboriginal Population*, 107.

64. Miller, "Whatever Happened"; Browne, "Coast Rangers," 307.

65. *Majority and Minority Reports*, 3–4; Tassin, "Chronicles of Camp Wright"; Miller, "Whatever Happened"; Madley, *American Genocide*, 280.

66. *Martial Law in Round Valley*.

67. Carranco and Beard, *Genocide and Vendetta*, 115–16; Madley, *American Genocide*, 318–20.

68. Phillips, *"Bringing Them under Subjugation,"* 20–35; Phillips, *Indians and Indian Agents*, 37–56; Madley, *American Genocide*, 202–3, 318–19; Baumgardner, *Killing for Land*, 198–218.

69. The estimates are by Benjamin Madley. Madley, *American Genocide*, 481–522, 351.

70. Stewart, "Bret Harte," 272; USCD Serial Set 1033, 15.

71. Gardner, "March of the 2nd Dragoons," 49–57.

72. Powers and Leiker, "Cholera among the Plains Indians."

73. Mooney, *Calendar History*, 289; West, *Contested Plains*, 88–89.

74. Finley McDiarmid, "Daily Remarks," September 10, Finley McDiarmid letters, BaL.

75. I have suggested the term "confessional conquest" elsewhere: West, *Last Indian War*, 87.

76. USCD Serial Set 688, 402.

77. Madley, *American Genocide*, 212. Revealingly, Weller's proposal for a hundred thousand dollars in "supplies and presents" for Indians was substituted for an unsuccessful request for reimbursement for all losses from "Indian depredations" before June 1852. The thrust of his arguments was to relieve California of the costs of supporting Indians after the Senate had rejected treaties that would have created their nineteen federal reservations—the rejection that Weller himself had helped engineer two months before. *Congressional Globe*, August 11, 1852, Senate, 32nd Cong., 2171–72, 2175.

78. For a summary of population estimates based on twenty-seven sources, see Madley, *American Genocide*, 347.

79. Benjamin Madley convincingly makes the case for genocide: Madley, *American Genocide*, 350–59. For an exchange of views, beginning with an argument by Gary Clayton Anderson that the tragedy is better defined as ethnic cleansing, see Anderson, "The Native Peoples of the American West."

80. Watts, "How Bloody Was Bleeding Kansas."

81. Madley, *American Genocide*, 460.

82. Stansbury, *Expedition*, 43–44.

4. The Horse and the Hammer

1. Hulbert, "Ancestry of the Horse," 32.

2. Flores, *Horizontal Yellow*, 96.

3. Of the many sources on the rise and spread of horse domestication, among the best are Kelekna, *Horse in Human History*; Anthony, "Bridling Horse Power"; Kurst, *Man and Horse*; Chamberlin, *Horse*.

4. Anthropologists debate whether the horse culture was genuinely revolutionary. Some, notably Clark Wissler in an early article on the issue, argue that a horse was simply a more efficient tool that offered advantages in traditional lives. Others, such as Clyde Wilson, argue that horses, more than a tool, represented an expanded access to energy itself. Obviously I favor the latter argument. Wissler, "Influence of the Horse"; Wilson, "Inquiry."

5. Kelekna, *Horse in Human History*, 21–91.

6. For an excellent summary of the movements of tribes that came with the acquisition of horses, see Calloway, *One Vast Winter Count*, chapter 6. For other works on tribal movements, conflicts and alliances, see Hämäläinen, *Comanche Empire*; Kavanagh, *Comanche Political History*; Anderson, *Indian Southwest*; White, "Winning of the West"; Mayhall, *Kiowas*; Hyde, *Indians of the High Plains*; Hoebel, *Cheyennes*; Ewers, *Horse in Blackfoot Culture*; Binnema, *Common and Contested Ground*.

7. Haynes, "Northward Spread"; Jacobsen and Eighmy, "Mathematical Theory."

8. Prince and Steckel, "Nutritional Success."

9. Robert P. Higheagle, "Songs by Sitting Bull," Walter Stanley Campbell Collection, box 104, folder 18, ou.

10. Trennert, *Alternative to Extinction*, 133.

11. Powell, *People of the Sacred Mountain*, 115–16, 162–63.

12. DeLay, *War of a Thousand Deserts*, 138, 318–40; DeLay, "Wider World."

13. DeLay, *War of a Thousand Deserts*; DeLay, "Independent Indians."

14. Fenn, *Pox Americana*, 198–258, 274; Pearcey, "Smallpox Outbreak"; Simmons, "New Mexico's Smallpox Epidemic"; Hämäläinen, "Western Comanche Trade Center."

15. Hämäläinen, "Politics of Grass."

16. Moore, *Cheyenne Nation*, 164–67; Moore, "Dynamics of Scale."

17. Barry, *Beginning of the West*, 781, 787.

18. More than three-quarters of a million were shipped through New Orleans between 1825 and 1830. A reported ninety thousand a year passed through Saint Louis during the decade after 1835. In the late 1840s independent estimates set the number of robes from the upper Missouri through Saint Louis at 110,000 annually. Burlingame, "Buffalo in Trade and Commerce," 266, 268, 277–78; Lippincott, "Century and a Half"; Chittenden, *American Fur Trade*, 807; Isenberg, *Destruction of the Bison*, 105–6. In the mid-1850s an Indian agent reported that tribes along the Arkansas were killing 112,000 bison annually, about ten per person, a number

that included their own consumption as well as trade; among the more commercially active Cheyennes and Arapahos the ratio was thirteen to one. This was roughly twice the number needed for subsistence, with the others obviously taken for the robe trade. J. W. Whitfield to Superintendent of Indian Affairs, January 5, 1856, Office of Indian Affairs, Letters Received, Upper Arkansas Agency; Brown, "*Comancheria* Demography, 1805–1830."

19. Prime hides were of cows (bulls were too big) taken in the fall when their fur was thick, which concentrated the killing on females pregnant from the summer rut, in effect taking two for one. Many hides were never sent because they were not up to par or were botched during processing. By some accounts three bison died for every robe shipped to market. Allen, *History of the American Bison*, 563.

20. *Annual Report of the Commissioner of Indian Affairs*, 128.

21. The Treaty of Fort Laramie, sometimes called the Treaty of Horse Creek, is discussed in the following chapter.

22. Beck, *First Sioux War*; McCann, "Grattan Massacre"; McChristian, *Fort Laramie*, 69–88; Hafen and Young, *Fort Laramie*, 221–30; Hyde, *Spotted Tail's Folk*, 48–58.

23. USCD Serial Set 788, 21.

24. Keyes, *Fifty Years' Observations*, 253.

25. *Congressional Globe*, January 31, 1855, 33rd Cong., 2nd sess., 494–95.

26. Fleming claimed that the Lakotas had been committing desperate depredations on immigrants throughout the summer, that High Forehead had come to the Mormon train to shoot the cow, that the animal's death had left its owner destitute, that Fleming had to respond or "give up entirely all protection of emigrants," that Conquering Bear had agreed to give up High Forehead, and that, as he was writing, the Lakotas were menacing the fort. Evidence is clear that none of this was true. USCD Serial Set 788, 2. Davis's claim took on some credibility when a few warriors attacked a stage, killed the driver, and took ten thousand dollars. A winter count for that year described 1854 as "Much Money." McChristian, *Fort Laramie*, 89.

27. The standard biography is Adams, *General William S. Harney*.

28. Clow, "William S. Harney."

29. On the battle, the campaign that followed, and the events surrounding them, see Paul, *Blue Water Creek*; Beck, *First Sioux War*; Adams, *William S. Harney*, 125–38; Clow, "Mad Bear"; Clow, "General William S. Harney."

30. Taylor, *Gouverneur Kemble Warren*, 27–28.

31. USCD Serial Set 859.

32. USCD Serial Set 859, 4.

33. For an excellent discussion of this council and its implications, including the resumption of warfare with the Crows, see Bray, "Lone Horn's Peace."

34. Hyde, *Red Cloud's Folk*, 82; USCD Serial Set 975, 668–69.

35. Utley, *Frontiersmen in Blue*, 72–75; Anderson, *Conquest of Texas*, 252–58. Anderson credits the double line of forts as effective; Utley does not.

36. Olmsted, *Journey through Texas*, 285–86, 298.

37. USCD Serial Set 659, 6, 23–24.

38. USCD Serial Set 811, 67–69.

39. USCD Serial Set 943, 136–41; Utley, *Frontiersmen in Blue*, 154–57; Hutton, *Apache Wars*, 31–33.

40. Utley, "Bascom Affair"; McChristian, "Eyewitness to the Bascom Affair." One historian argues that relations had worsened prior to the episode. Sweeney, "Cochise"; Hutton, *Apache Wars*, 37–55. Hutton's excellent recent book *Apache Wars* tells Mickey Free's remarkable story.

41. Quoted in Utley, *Frontiersmen in Blue*, 175.

42. USCD Serial Set 611, 207–13.

43. The best accounts of the events that follow are Schwartz, *Rogue River Indian War*; Beckham, *Requiem for a People*.

44. USCD Serial Set 858, 63.

45. Schwartz, *Rogue River Indian War*, 148–49.

46. West, *Last Indian War*, 61–67.

47. USCD Serial Set 858, 45–46; USCD Serial Set 876, 186; USCD Serial Set 955.

48. USCD Serial Set 876, 190; USCD Serial Set 906, 236; USCD Serial Set 975, 341–42. For Stevens's lengthy defense, with accompanying documents, see *Message of the Governor*.

49. USCD Serial Set 975, 344–48, 383–403; Cutler, "Your Nations"; Kip, *Army Life*.

50. Harney added suggestions of how the army might go a bit Native, refitting troops with buffalo coats and lined moccasins and using tipis for lodging. Clow, "William S. Harney," 246.

51. Ball, *Army Regulars*, 24–25; USCD Serial Set 811, 60.

52. Kip, *Army Life*, 71.

53. Anderson, *Conquest of Texas*, 310–11, 316–17; USCD Serial Set 975, 259, 273.

54. USCD Serial Set 975, 396, 403.

5. Conquest in Stutter-Step

1. The total size of the United States in 1848 was 3,090,214 square miles. The size of what would become Kansas, Nebraska, South Dakota, North Dakota, Montana, Idaho, New Mexico, Arizona, California, Colorado, Wyoming, Nevada, Oregon, Washington, and Utah was 1,474,713 square miles, or 47.7 percent of the whole.

2. For the surprisingly revealing story of the creation and evolution of western state boundaries, see Everett, *Creating the American West*.

3. Lamar, *Far Southwest*, 91.

4. Lamar, *Far Southwest*, 88.

5. Lamar, *Far Southwest*, 89.

6. Bender, *March of Empire*, 48; Frazer, *Forts and Supplies*.

7. USCD Serial Set 659, 24.

8. Abel, *Official Correspondence*, 431.

9. Abel, *Official Correspondence*, 425–28; Utley, *Frontiersmen in Blue*, 86–89; Ball, *Army Regulars*, 20–21.

10. Utley, *Frontiersmen in Blue*, 89; Ball, *Army Regulars*, 21–22; Twitchell, *Historical Sketch*, 10; Lamar, *Far Southwest*, 99; "Address to the People of New Mexico," August 28, 1860, HL.

11. Lamar, *Far Southwest*, 108.

12. Richards, *Isaac I. Stevens*, 273–78.

13. USCD Serial Set 881, 40. Later he charged that the six were "the main original cause of the war."

14. Richards, *Isaac I. Stevens*, 280–81.

15. *A Brief Notice of the Recent Outrages*, 12.

16. Galloway, "Private Letters," 546.

17. *ARGLO*, 1851, 5, 46.

18. *ARGLO*, 1855, 3; *ARGLO*, 1861, 7, 20.

19. Besides the largely uncritical Robinson, *Land in California*, the best sources on this complex story are Gates, "Public Land Disposal"; Gates, "Adjudication"; Gates, "California's Embattled Settlers"; Pitt, *Decline of the Californios*; Vaught, "Tale of Three Land Grants"; Pisani, "Squatter Law."

20. Gates, "Adjudication," 216.

21. George, *Our Land and Land Policy*, 15.

22. Gates, "Public Land Disposal," 162.

23. Gates, "Public Land Disposal," 168. The reference specifically was to the federal grant for school lands.

24. For a provocative new look at contests for land in the 1850s and their relation to the anti-monopoly movement, see Shelton, *Squatter's Republic*.

25. Prucha, *Great Father*, 319–23.

26. *Congressional Globe*, 30th Cong., 2nd sess., new series, no 33, 514.

27. Prucha, *Great Father*, 322.

28. The best single treatment is Trennert, *Alternative to Extinction*.

29. *ARCIA*, 1850, 4.

30. *ARCIA*, 1848–49, 8.

31. USCD Serial Set 570, 942–43; Trennert, *Alternative to Extinction*, 32, 50.

32. Kapler, *Indian Affairs*, 1074–75.

33. For accounts of this important council, see McChristian, *Fort Laramie*, 53–61; Hafen and Young, *Fort Laramie*, 177–96; Hoig, *White Man's Paper Trail*, 85–96; Nadeau, *Fort Laramie and the Sioux Indians*, 66–92; Trennert, *Alternative to Extinction*, 186–92; Hill, "Great Indian Treaty Council of 1851."

34. *Missouri Republican*, October 24, 1851.

35. *Missouri Republican*, October 29, 1851.

36. Chittenden and Richardson, *Life, Letters, and Travels*, 682.

37. *Missouri Republican*, October 24, 1851.

38. Hafen and Young, *Fort Laramie*, 185–87.

39. Chittenden and Richardson, *Life, Letters, and Travels*, 683.

40. Hafen and Young, *Fort Laramie*, 195.

41. The point about Indians' finding meaning in daily details of such councils is well made in Fixico, "As Long as the Grass Grows."

42. For an excellent recent history of the Lakotas from their beginnings into the twentieth century, with a particularly good coverage on this period, see Hämäläinen, *Lakota America*.

43. Hämäläinen, *Lakota America*, 216–22; White, "Winning of the West."

44. *Missouri Republican*, November 9, 1851.

45. Bray, "Lone Horn's Peace."

46. *Missouri Republican*, October 26, 1851.

47. *Missouri Republican*, November 23, 1851. On this crucial misunderstanding, see Price, "Lakotas and Euroamericans."

48. Chittenden and Richardson, *Life, Letters, and Travels*, 683.

49. Oliva, "Fort Atkinson," 226.

50. Thian, *Notes Illustrating the Military Geography*. The numbered departments soon were named geographically: Texas, New Mexico, Pacific, and the West. In 1858 a separate Department of Utah was formed from the Department of the West, and Departments of California and Oregon formed from the Department of the Pacific.

51. USCD Serial Set 1079, 208–29.

52. USCD Serial Set 1818, vol. 4, 122.

53. USCD Serial 827, vol. 18, 452. This document provides a fascinating overview of the conditions around health and sickness in the military at midcentury.

54. Utley, *Frontiersmen in Blue*, 36; Coffman, *Old Army*, 59.

55. USCD Serial Set 894, 7; Wooster, *American Military Frontiers*, 123. The average rate of desertion from 1820 to 1860 was 15 percent, according to Wooster, 68–69.

56. Quoted in Wooster, *American Military Frontiers*, 132. The vitriolic correspondence between the two ran to 254 pages when published. See USCD Serial Set 880. The quotes are on 252, 254.

57. USCD Serial Set 690, 362.

58. *Missouri Republican*, November 23, 1851.

59. USCD Serial Set 832.

60. For a recent persuasive argument that the first transcontinentals were at the time unnecessary, except at either end, and their construction and administration wrongheaded and corrupt, see White, *Railroaded*.

61. USCD Serial Set 585, 4.

62. For an excellent summary of the efforts inspired by interest in a transcontinental line, see Goetzmann, *Exploration and Empire*, 265–302.

63. Hafen and Hafen, *Fremont's Fourth Expedition*.

64. Stansbury, *Expedition*.

65. Goetzmann, *Exploration and Empire*, 285–86.

66. USCD Serial Set 760, 132–33.

67. USCD Serial Set 759, 10–11; Goetzmann, *Exploration and Empire*, 290.

68. USCD Serial Set 762.

69. The basic source is Jackson, *Wagon Roads West*.

70. USCD Serial Set 984, 63; USCD Serial Set 959, 2; Thompson, *Edward F. Beale*, 103–23.

71. Winther, *Old Oregon Country*, 202–13; Peterson, *John Mullan*.

72. Goetzmann, *Exploration and Empire*, 292–93.

73. USCD Serial Set 1058, 97–98; Barba, *Balduin Mollhausen*.

74. Wheat, *Mapping the Trans-Mississippi West*, 84–91.

75. Goetzmann, *New Lands, New Men*, 178.

76. USCD Serial Set 763, 71; USCD Serial Set 766, 111–12; USCD Serial Set 761, plate 21; USCD Serial Set 760, 102.

77. USCD Serial Set 763, 49.

6. Carnal Property

1. The classic argument is that of Charles W. Ramsdell, though it should be noted that he was referring only to New Mexico and Utah Territories, where slavery was made an option in the Compromise of 1850. Ramsdell, "Natural Limits of Slavery."

2. William G. Kephart to Salmon Chase, March 27, 1851, reel 9, microfilm collection, Salmon P. Chase papers, Rothemere Library, University of Oxford.

3. The standard work on opposition to slavery in the West, resting on both economic and racial reasons, remains Berwanger, *Frontier against Slavery*.

4. Browne, *Report of the Debates*, 144.

5. Browne, *Report of the Debates*, 137–38.

6. Richards, "Unwelcome Settlers."

7. For a breakdown of the vote by county, see Woodward, *Rise and Early History*, appendix I.

8. Johannsen, *Frontier Politics*, 33–46; Taylor, "Slaves and Free Men."

9. Taylor, *In Search of the Racial Frontier*, 76; Smith, *Freedom's Frontier*, 237–45.

10. Richards, *California Gold Rush*, 67–73; Browne, *Report of the Debates*, 43–44.

11. Goodwin, *Establishment of State Government*, 131.

12. Goodwin, *Establishment of State Government*, 108–10; Richards, *California Gold Rush*, 73–77.

13. Richards, *California Gold Rush*, 73.

14. Clay and Jones, "Migrating to Riches"; Wright, "Making of Cosmopolitan California, Part I."

15. Smith, *Freedom's Frontier*, 113, 69–72.

16. Parish and Gadsden, "Project," 171–75.

17. Ellison, "Movement for State Division"; Richards, *California Gold Rush*, 137–38.

18. Lapp, *Blacks in Gold Rush*, 65; Smith, *Freedom's Frontier*, 40. Lapp estimates 300–400 Black slaves in the early 1850s and 500–600 during the years before the Civil War, including those who had returned to the East but not those missed by enumerators or hidden by their masters.

19. After approving of the *Scott* decision, the legislature resolved that "we believe the people are the proper tribunal to settle all questions which concern themselves." *Acts of the Legislative Assembly*, 72.

20. McConaghy, "Deplorable State," 16–26.

21. Sunseri, *Seeds of Discord*, 117–18; Lamar, *Far Southwest*, 77–78.

22. Stegmaier, "Law That Would Make Caligula Blush." See also Hays, "Curious Case"; Kiser, "'Charming Name.'" The law's sponsor tossed in a bit of the sentiment prevailing elsewhere. Establishing a legal racial hierarchy, he said, would "tend to elevate our own class of free laborers." For the laws on debt peonage and the slave code, see "Laws of the Territory of New Mexico," 24–27, 64–70.

23. Stegmaier, "Law That Would Make Caligula Blush," 210. *Harper's Weekly*, April 6, 1861, 210, in a table purporting to be based on the census, notes twenty-four slaves.

24. Stegmaier, "Law That Would Make Caligula Blush," 225–26.

25. On slavery and the law in Utah, see Lythgoe, "Negro Slavery in Utah"; Lythgoe, "Negro Slavery and Mormon Doctrine"; Beller, "Negro Slaves in Utah," 122–26; Christensen, "Negro Slavery in the Utah Territory."

26. *Journal of Discourses*, vol. 10, 110. Young told Horace Greeley in 1859 that slavery in Utah was "useless and unprofitable" as well as a "curse to the masters." Greeley, *Overland Journey*, 212.

27. *Acts, Resolutions, and Memorials*, 81–82. The connection with support of polygamy is argued in Gordon and Shipps, "Fatal Convergence."

28. Bringhurst, "Mormons and Slavery"; Rich, "True Policy for Utah."

29. Beller, "Negro Slaves in Utah," 126.

30. Johannsen, *Frontier Politics*, 76–77. Republicans also denounced abolitionism and declared themselves the "white man's party." Given attitudes in the West toward slavery, Republicans nationally were moving toward popular sovereignty as the solution to the question of slavery expansion.

31. Johannsen, *Frontier Politics*, 30. Nor were free Blacks more than a tiny fragment of the western population. The 1860 census reported that in the entire span of newly acquired land, African Americans numbered 4,312, well under a single percent of the population, and 95 percent of those were in California. Blacks in Oregon, Washington, Nevada, Utah, and New Mexico totaled 226, less than a tenth of a percent of the population.

32. For some of the more useful sources in the expanding literature on the Southeast's ambitions, see Johnson, *River of Dark Dreams*; May, *Southern Dream*; May, "Epilogue to the Missouri Compromise"; Horne, *Deepest South*; Karp, *Vast Southern Empire*; Hammond, "'High Road to a Slave Empire.'"

33. Keehn, *Knights of the Golden Circle*; Bridges, "Knights of the Golden Circle"; Crenshaw, "Knights of the Golden Circle."

34. May, *Southern Dream*, 144, 159–60; May, "Young American Males," 884–85. While adamantly opposed to any threat to the Union, Houston hoped to stabilize the border and to use victory in Mexico as a step toward the White House. He was willing to use the hot desire for more slave states to his advantage. Friend, *Sam Houston*, 306–9.

35. Johnson, *River of Dark Dreams*, 299; USCD Serial Set 546, 661.

36. *Congressional Globe*, 32nd Cong., 2nd sess., 280–84.

37. Pike, *Address*, 7–8.

38. Karp, *Vast Southern Empire*, 190–93. Buchanan worked throughout his presidency to acquire Cuba, even as domestic events made congressional approval of any expansion of slavery increasingly unlikely and eventually, as one congressman put it, "a great delusion" among its proponents. May, *Southern Dream*, 163–89. The quote is on 171.

39. Miller, *Treaties and Other International Acts*, 361–66; USCD Serial Set 1023, 16–17.

40. Waite, "Jefferson Davis," 548–50; *Congressional Globe*, 35th Cong., 1st Sess., appendix, 28.

41. For an excellent survey of Davis's pro-slavery vision for the West, see Waite, "Jefferson Davis."

42. USCD Serial Set 758, 3–30.

43. Parish and Gadsden, "Project"; Leonard L. Richards, *California Gold Rush*, 125–26.

44. Miller, *Treaties and Other International Acts*, 361–66.

45. Kiser, *Turmoil on the Rio Grande*, 84–87.

46. Waite, "Jefferson Davis," 540. The quotation is from Russell, *Improvement of Communication*, 26.

47. Wright, *Political Economy*, 155; Levy, *Ages of American Capitalism*, 182–84.

48. Levy, *Ages of American Capitalism*, 184.

49. *Congressional Globe*, 31st Cong., 1st sess., 203; Oakes, *Scorpion's Sting*, 182–84.

50. Maizlish, *Strife of Tongues*, 133.

51. Morrison, *Slavery and the American West*, 174, 183, 210.

52. William Kephart to Salmon P. Chase, March 27, 1851, reel 9, microfilm collection, Salmon P. Chase papers, Rothemere Library, University of Oxford; Lowenthal, *Mind and Art of Abraham Lincoln*, 137, 138, 141; Basler, *Collected Works of Abraham Lincoln*, vol. 4, 183.

53. Holt, *Fate of Their Country*, 92–127; Hughes, *Letters and Recollections*, 144, 157; Morrison, *Slavery and the American West*, 167–70, 202, 216.

54. Livingstone, *Livingstone's History*, 40.

55. Freeman, *Field of Blood*, xxiv.

56. *Congressional Globe*, 36th Cong., 2nd sess., December 5, 1860, 10.

57. Freeman, *Field of Blood*, 10.

58. Holt, *Fate of Their Country*, 4, 30.

59. Deverell, "Convalescence and California."

60. Smith, *Freedom's Frontier*, 50; Freeman, *Field of Blood*, 261.

61. Magliari, "Free State Slavery," 159.

62. The best recent treatments of the Southwest are Kiser, *Borderlands of Slavery*; Reséndez, *Other Slavery*, 242–46, 277–94.

63. On *genízaros*, see Magnani, "Plains Indians"; Archibald, "Acculturation and Assimilation"; Brooks, *Captives and Cousins*; Gutierrez, *When Jesus Came*.

64. Kiser, *Borderlands of Slavery*, 88–111.

65. Kiser, *Borderlands of Slavery*, 12.

66. Kiser, *Borderlands of Slavery*, 100–101. For the law, see USCD Serial Set 652, 49–50.

67. Weber, *Mexican Frontier*, 211; Kiser, *Borderlands of Slavery*, 13–14.

68. DeLay, "Blood Talk"; Reséndez, *Other Slavery*, 279–80. In a meticulous survey of Catholic church records, using baptisms to estimate the number and location of Navajo captives, David M. Brugge found that captured Navajos were dispersed among households throughout the century. Of 799 households identified as having Navajo captives, 744 had only 1 or 2. Of the rest, one had 7 and another 8. Brugge, *Navajos*, 122.

69. Reséndez, *Other Slavery*, 280.

70. Frank McNitt, *Navajo Wars*, 441–46.

71. Reséndez, *Other Slavery*, 286; Dunlay, *Kit Carson*, 283.

72. Kiser, *Borderlands of Slavery*, 98.

73. USCD Serial Set 1279, 326.

74. Reséndez, *Other Slavery*, 294.

75. Heizer, "Indian Servitude," 414–16.

76. Cook, *Conflict*, 304; Bagley, *With Golden Visions*, 396–97.

77. Hurtado, *John Sutter*, 152–58.

78. Camp, *James Clyman*, 174.

79. Madley, *American Genocide*, 146–48; Reséndez, *Other Slavery*, 262–64; Hurtado, *Indian Survival*, 92–95; USCD Serial Set 557, 347–48.

80. Reséndez, *Other Slavery*, 264.

81. Bell, *Reminiscences*, 48–49.

82. Magnani, "Plains Indians," 353–58.

83. ARCIA, 1861, 149.

84. ARCIA, 1886, 315.

85. Rawls, *Indians of California*, 90.

86. Heizer, "Indian Servitude," 415.

87. Gerber, "Origin of California's Export," 55. Albert Hurtado questioned the extent of Indian labor in grain production, especially by the late 1850s. Hurtado, *Indian Survival*, 165–66. But Michael Magliari confirms Gerber's point in a close study of one California county, showing the essential role of bound Indian labor in agriculture. Magliari, "Free State Slavery."

88. The best summaries of the Mormon chapter of Indian bondage are Cannon, "'To Buy Up the Lamanite Children'"; Cannon, "Adopted or Indentured"; Reséndez, *Other Slavery*, 266–77. See also Jones, "'Redeeming' the Indian"; Van Hoak, "And Who Shall Have the Children."

89. On Mormons and Indians, see Brooks, "Indian Relations"; Bennion, "Captivity, Adoption"; Farmer, *On Zion's Mount*, 54–104.

90. Reséndez, *Other Slavery*, 268–70.

91. Bennion, "Captivity, Adoption," 259–72.

92. Hastings, *Emigrants' Guide*, 132.

93. Kiser, "Charming Name," 176.

94. USCD Serial Set 688, 35; Reséndez, *Other Slavery*, 250.

95. Hastings, *Emigrants' Guide*, 132.

96. Hastings, *Emigrants' Guide*, 114; Cooke, *Conquest of New Mexico*, 34–35.

97. Cook, *Conflict*, 305; Reséndez, *Other Slavery*, 260.

98. Ayers, "Soldier's Experience," 261; Reid, *Reid's Tramp*, 141–42; Kiser, *Borderlands of Slavery*, 97; Kiser, "Charming Name," 177.

99. Kiser, "Charming Name," 177.

100. Kiser, "Charming Name," 174.

101. Reséndez, *Other Slavery*, 295.

102. USCD Serial Set 474, 46. His concluding comments are reprinted in Gilpin, *Mission*, 124.

103. Reséndez, *Other Slavery*, 277.

7. The Fluid West

1. This doctrine was first espoused by Smith in a sermon in April of 1844. See Cannon and Dahl, *Smith's King Follett Discourse*; Cannon, "King Follett Discourse."
2. Winn, *Exiles*, 62–105; Arrington and Bitton, *Mormon Experience*, 44–64.
3. "A Girl's Letters."
4. On the common passion of Mormons and Methodists to embody their religious visions in the West, see Gordon and Shipps, "Fatal Convergence."
5. Winn, *Exiles*, 79.
6. The standard work on the conflict in Missouri now is Kinney, *Mormon War*.
7. Smith and Smith, *History*, vol. 2, 165.
8. Bennett, *History of the Saints*, 5–6; Winn, *Exiles*, 144.
9. Quinn, "Council of Fifty"; Ehat, "'It Seems like Heaven'"; Hansen, *Quest for Empire*; Andrus, "Joseph Smith." For a recently published volume of the minutes of this important part of the Mormon story, see Grow and Godfrey, *Council of Fifty Minutes*.
10. Andrus, "Joseph Smith," 140.
11. O'Dea, *Mormons*, 82.
12. The standard work is Morgan, *State of Deseret*.
13. Bigler, *Forgotten Kingdom*, 51.
14. Bigler, "'Lion in the Path.'"
15. Bigler and Bagley, *Mormon Rebellion*, 93; Bigler, "'Lion in the Path,'" 9–10.
16. Gunnison was killed in October 1853 in a camp along the Sevier River by Pahvant Indians led by a Mormon convert, Kanosh, apparently in revenge for the murder of Kanosh's father by overlanders. An army command sent the next year to exact punishment found that nothing had been done to arrest to killers. In a trial the army commander called "abortive," three Pahvants were convicted of manslaughter and promptly escaped. Bigler, *Forgotten Kingdom*, 92.
17. USCD Serial Set 956, 115–16, 118–19.
18. USCD Serial Set 920, 7.
19. Bigler and Bagley, *Mormon Rebellion*, 75–76.
20. USCD Serial Set 956, 115–16, 118–19, 224.
21. Bigler, *Forgotten Kingdom*, 125, 127.
22. Hosea Stout diary, April 16, 1857, HL.
23. Reeve, *Religion of a Different Color*, 215–46; Deverell, "Thoughts from the Farther West," 11–13. The quote from the *Daily Tribune* is in Reeve, 230.
24. Bigler and Bagley, *Mormon Rebellion*, 105.
25. USCD Serial Set 956, 34–35; Bigler, *Forgotten Kingdom*, 183–84; Bigler and Bagley, *Mormon Rebellion*, 161–62; Bigler, "Aiken Party Executions," 458.
26. MacKinnon, "125 Years," 233–34.
27. Bigler and Bagley, *Mormon Rebellion*, 140. James Martineau Diary, September 28, October 13, 1857, HL; Henry Ballard Journal, May 24, 1858, HL.
28. USCD Serial Set 956, 46.
29. Bigler, "Crisis at Fort Limhi, 1858."

30. Rogers, *Unpopular Sovereignty*, 165–66.

31. On one such episode, see Bigler, "Aiken Party."

32. In a letter to a San Francisco newspaper, the killer, Hector McLean, had boasted of the murder and added that the people of western Arkansas "agree with me." Published the nearly a month before the arrival of the immigrants, the letter was surely available and probably widely known in Utah. Bigler, *Forgotten Kingdom*, 162n. Two scholars of the church have suggested the opposition of the two denominations as one possible factor in the massacre. Gordon and Shipps, "Fatal Convergence."

33. USCD Serial Set 4377, 14–15.

34. Bigler and Bagley, *Mormon Rebellion*, 145–47.

35. James Martineau diary, May 1, 1857, HL.

36. MacKinnon, "125 Years of Conspiracy Theories."

37. Auchampaugh, *Robert Tyler*, 180–81.

38. Childers, *Failure of Popular Sovereignty*, 225.

39. Rawley, *Race and Politics*, 81.

40. Similarly, Senator Atchison encouraged a cheering crowd to give murderers and horse thieves fair trials but to "hang . . . [an] Abolitionist without judge or jury." Etcheson, *Bleeding Kansas*, 34; Rawley, *Race and Politics*, 85–86.

41. Thayer, *History of the Kansas Crusade*, 2.

42. The Lawrence *Kansas Free State* charged that controlling Kansas was key to the schemes of the "Slave Power" to give a foothold to its "peculiar institution" in the free states, so they next could establish it on a "firmer basis." Quoted in Dailey, "Josiah Miller," 70.

43. Wilder, *Annals of Kansas*, 57–58.

44. *Kansas Question*. The quotations are on 4 and 5.

45. Etcheson, *Bleeding Kansas*, 101–7; Malin, "Judge Lecompte"; "Notes on the Proslavery March"; Goodrich, *War to the Knife*, 114–17. The single fatality was one of the "posse" struck by masonry falling from the hotel.

46. USCD Serial Set 869, 8, 30. From 2,905 eligible voters in a recent census, proslavery candidates in the legislative election managed to garner 5,427 votes. The ratio of illegal to legal votes in one district was 45 to 1.

47. Childers, *Failure of Popular Sovereignty*, 256–58. The quotation is on 178.

48. Etcheson, *Bleeding Kansas*, 201. For the constitution, amended but still in effect, see USCD Serial Set 1060.

49. Johnson, "Emigrant Aid Company," 431. Of the two thousand who came with the company, an estimated third soon headed back East. New Englanders made up scarcely 4 percent of Kansans in 1855 and 1860.

50. Thayer, *History of the Kansas Crusade*, 88.

51. "Will Kansas Be a Free State?" *The Liberator*, June 1, 1855.

52. Shelton, *Squatter's Republic*, 53–59. Free-soil newspapers like the *Kansas Free State* stressed the baneful effects of slavery on whites and kept concerns for slaves well in the background. Cecil-Fronsman, "'Advocate the Freedom.'"

53. Etcheson, *Bleeding Kansas*, 120.

54. Gates, *Fifty Million Acres*, 49.

55. Rawley, *Race and Politics*, 83.

56. Gates, *Fifty Million Acres*, 53.

57. Watts, "How Bloody Was Bleeding Kansas." The quote is on 120–21. Watts found that of all killings 44 percent were over property and personal disputes, 35 percent over slavery.

58. ARCIA, 1854, 10; Ostler, *Surviving Genocide*, 347–56.

59. Miner and Unrau, *End of Indian Kansas*, 11.

60. Ostler, *Surviving Genocide*, 344–47; ARCIA, 1854, 10–11.

61. Miner and Unrau, *End of Indian Kansas*, 16, 20–24; Mullis, *Peacekeeping on the Plains*, 119–52.

62. For a report on this episode, see USCD Serial Set 1122.

63. Gates, *Fifty Million Acres*, 116–21, 140–42.

64. Malin, *John Brown*, 206.

65. Gates, *Fifty Million Acres*, 6–7.

66. Johannsen, *Frontier Politics*, 30.

67. A[braham] Rencher to W. H. Seward, April 14, 1861, New Mexico Territorial Papers, National Archives, RG 59, T17, roll 2.

8. Continental Reckoning

1. One of many examples: Hess, *Civil War in the West*.

2. The standard work remains Josephy, *Civil War*.

3. For a perceptive and immensely readable account of events in the Southwest, see Nelson, *Three-Cornered War*.

4. For his vociferous opposition Henry Hamilton, editor of the *Los Angeles Star*, was briefly imprisoned on Alcatraz Island in 1862. Goldman, "Southern Sympathy"; Robinson, *Los Angeles*; Robinson, "California Copperhead."

5. WR, Series 1, vol. 50, part 1, 472.

6. McKee, *Narrative*, 27; Feather, "Territories of Arizona," 16–19.

7. Waldrip, "New Mexico," 176.

8. WR, Series 1, vol. 4, 73; Isern, "Colorado Territory," 61.

9. For an account of one of Sibley's scouts: Johnson and Clough, *Battles and Leaders*, vol. 2, 700; Noel, *Autobiography*, 56–57.

10. Finch, *Confederate Pathway*; Hall, "Colonel James Reily's Diplomatic Missions"; WR, series 1, vol. 4, 170.

11. For two detailed accounts of the campaign, see Hall, *Sibley's New Mexico Campaign*; Frazier, *Blood and Treasure*.

12. Perrine, "Battle of Valverde"; Colton, *Civil War*, 26–34; Josephy, *Civil War*; Hall, *Sibley's New Mexico Campaign*, 83–103.

13. Hall, *Sibley's New Mexico Campaign*, 110–11, 115. A Confederate veteran later wrote that southern troops had destroyed large amounts of supplies left in Albuquerque and Santa Fe by the retreating Federals. Why they did was a mystery, except that "our men were getting drunk on the whisky and our commander had never been sober." Noel, *Autobiography*, 61.

14. Scott, *Glory, Glory*, 119; Hollister, *Boldly They Rode*, 48.

15. Of the many accounts of this battle, these are most useful. Scott, *Glory, Glory*, 139–80; Hall, *Sibley's New Mexico Campaign*, 141–60; Colton, *Civil War*, 149–80; Whitford, *Colorado Volunteers*, 85–127; Josephy, *Civil War*, 75–85.

16. A survivor hoped that "the day is not far distant when Gen. Sibley will be hung." Colton, *Civil War*, 92–98; Noel, *Autobiography*, 63; Hollister, *Boldly They Rode*, 170; *WR*, Series 1, vol. 9, 511–12.

17. Masich, *Civil War in Arizona*, 10.

18. Hunt, *James Henry Carleton*, 192–98; Masich, *Civil War in Arizona*, 9–13.

19. Hunt, *James Henry Carleton*, 29–32, 325–34.

20. *WR*, Series 1, vol. 50, part 1, 700; Masich, *Civil War in Arizona*, 29.

21. Masich, *Civil War in Arizona*, 46; Finch, *Confederate Pathway*, 128–30, 140–46.

22. On the Confederacy's ephemeral Arizona Territory, see Waite, *West of Slavery*, 190–96; Kiser, *Turmoil on the Rio Grande*, 143–88.

23. *WR*, Series 1, vol. 9, 586–87; *WR*, Series 1, vol. 50, part 1, 127–33; Masich, *Civil War in Arizona*, 236–42; Nelson, "Civil War from Apache Pass."

24. Matthews, *Golden State*, 190–92; Hunt, *Army of the Pacific*, 305–9; Clendenen, "Confederate Spy"; Finch, "Arizona in Exile." The man Davis tapped for the fanciful seizure of the Southwest was Lansford W. Hastings, author of an early emigrant guide to California. For his proposal to Davis, see *WR*, Series 1, vol. 50, part II, 700–701.

25. A survivor of the Texan retreat compared it to Napoleon's from Moscow. Noel, *Autobiography*, 60.

26. Johnson, *Founding the Far West*; Green, "Abraham Lincoln"; Pomeroy, "Lincoln," 362–68.

27. Buchanan, "James A. McDougall," 209. The Senate vote was held in April 1864, prior to Nevada's two senators taking office.

28. Madley, *American Genocide*, 299–303, 316–18, 321–24.

29. Madley, *American Genocide*, 289.

30. *ARCIA*, 1863, 94; Madley, *American Genocide*, 306–7.

31. Tegeder, "Lincoln and the Territorial Patronage," 88.

32. Etulain, *Lincoln Looks West*, 197.

33. Etulain, *Lincoln Looks West*, 135–36.

34. Murphy, *Frontier Crusader*; Murphy, "William F. M. Arny."

35. Tegeder, "Lincoln and Patronage." The quotation is on 90.

36. Etulain, *Lincoln and Oregon Country*, 81–88.

37. Matthews, *Golden State*, 173–87; Ethington, *Public City*, 170–207.

38. Malone and Roeder, *Montana*, 74–80; Hamilton, *From Wilderness to Statehood*, 273–99; Athearn, "Civil War Days"; Davidson and Tash, "Confederate Backwash"; Thane, "Active Acting Governor." The Confederate presence, though real, was exaggerated by Republican partisans: Thane, "Myth of Confederate Sentiment."

39. Lamar, *Dakota Territory*, 83, 88.

40. Twain, *Roughing It*, 192.

41. Lamar, *Dakota Territory*, 85.

42. Hamilton, *From Wilderness to Statehood*, 283–84.

43. Hafen, *Colorado and Its People*, 283–86.

44. Hafen, *Colorado and Its People*, 286.

45. Pomeroy, *Territories and the United States*, 1.

46. Beal and Wells, *History of Idaho*, vol. 1, 348–54.

9. Civil War and the "Indian Problem"

1. For a fine recent work on the war in Indian Territory, see Warde, *When the Wolf Came*. Also Trickett, "Civil War in the Indian Territory"; Fischer, *Western Territories*, 101–13; Rampp and Rampp, *Civil War in Indian Territory*; and Abel, *American Indian*.

2. Foreman, *History of Oklahoma*, 100–105; Morton, "Confederate Government Relations"; Brown, *Life of Albert Pike*, 361–71; Nichols, *Lincoln and the Indians*, 25–41.

3. Meserve, "Chief Opothleyahola," 446–50.

4. USCD Serial Set 1138, 5–6.

5. USCD Serial Set 1157, 301.

6. USCD Serial Set 1157, 280. For a summary account of this appalling episode, see Danziger, "Office of Indian Affairs."

7. USCD Serial Set 1220, 453; USCD Serial Set 1248, 437; ARCIA, 1865, 32.

8. Wardell, *Political History*, 175; Thornton, "History, Structure, and Survival," 92–96.

9. The essential account of these events is Anderson, *Massacre in Minnesota*. See also Heard, *History of the Sioux War*; Anderson, *Little Crow*; Anderson and Woolworth, *Through Dakota Eyes*; Follwell, *History of Minnesota*, vol. 2, 209–64; Oehler, *Great Sioux Uprising*; Berg, *38 Nooses*. For a rare and provocative view that sets the events within the wider context of the evolving nation, its policies, and visions, see Hahn, "Slave Emancipation," 307–30.

10. Heard, *History of Sioux War*, 42; Nichols, *Lincoln and the Indians*, 65–74.

11. Follwell, *History of Minnesota*, 233.

12. Anderson and Woolworth, *Through Dakota Eyes*; USCD Serial Set 1163, 29.

13. Berg, *38 Nooses*, 232–33; Anderson, *Massacre in Minnesota*, 260–62.

14. Anderson, *Massacre in Minnesota*, 283–84.

15. Taylor, *Sioux War*, 12.

16. On the Crow Creek experience, see Danziger, "Crow Creek Experiment"; Hyman, "Survival at Crow Creek."

17. Commissioner of Indian Affairs William Dole wrote privately that the Winnebagoes were "a people who without any fault of their own have been compelled to surrender their homes in deference to popular clamor." William P. Dole to "Dear Sir," May 6, 1863, Letterbook, 1862–1863, 43, HM 47123, William P. Dole Papers, HL.

18. Hyman, "Survival at Crow Creek," 108–9.

19. USCD Serial Set 1279, 401–2, 413.

20. The news was contained in a series of reports from the venerable Jesuit priest Pierre De Smet, who had been sent by the government to ascertain the situation on the upper Missouri. USCD Serial Set 1220, 420–25; Beck, *Columns of Vengeance*.

21. Utley, *Frontiersmen in Blue*, 272–74; WR, vol. 22, part 1, 558–60.

22. Utley, *Frontiersmen in Blue*, 275; Scott and Kempcke, "Journey into the Heart of Darkness"; Pfaller, "Sully's Expedition."

23. Utley, *Frontiersmen in Blue*, 270–71; ARCIA, 1863, 196. The agent, Samuel Latta of the Upper Missouri Agency, stressed that without military protection no immigrants crossing the northern plains or using the Missouri River would be safe.

24. Madsen, *Shoshoni Frontier*, 14.

25. ARCIA, 1862, 198.

26. Madsen, *Shoshoni Frontier*, 135–40.

27. Madsen, *Shoshoni Frontier*, 137.

28. On Connor, see Madsen, *Glory Hunter*.

29. Madsen, *Shoshoni Frontier*, 169, 154; WR, vol. 50, part 2, 144, and part 1, 185. Connor did have a legal pretense for the attack. A federal judge had sworn out warrants for the arrest of Bear Hunter and two other chiefs.

30. WR, vol. 50, part 1, 185.

31. Blackhawk, *Violence over the Land*, 254.

32. For accounts of the battle and massacre, see Madsen, *Glory Hunter*, 65–87; Madsen, *Shoshoni Frontier*, 179–200; Christensen, *Sagwitch*, 41–58; Josephy, *Civil War*, 257–59; Schlinder, "Bear River Massacre."

33. On the distinction, see Madsen, *Encounter*.

34. Madsen, *Shoshoni Frontier*, 189–92.

35. Madsen, *Shoshoni Frontier*, 201–16.

36. WR, vol. 41, part 2, 644, 661. A reporter for the *New York Times* (September 8, 1864) added that a "perfect carnival" of murder and destruction along the Platte road included "rebel Indians" and Confederate bushwhackers.

37. WR, vol. 41, part 3, 903, and part 4, 259.

38. Connor finally arrived in Denver on November 14, his command still back in Wyoming. Chivington told him that he had no troops to spare, which was true enough, since that was the day he had sent them to Fort Lyon for the attack on Black Kettle. A frustrated Connor reported a week later that, denied help by an unnamed officer, he could only advise waiting until early spring for a campaign, "before the savages break their winter encampments." Then he left for Utah. WR, vol. 41, part 1, 908.

39. Hyde, *Life of George Bent*, 151–52.

40. Roberts and Halaas, "Written in Blood," 22–32.

41. Hoig, *Sand Creek Massacre*, 162.

42. "A Brief Chronology."

43. USCD Serial Set 1220, 300, 312.

44. Josephy, *Civil War*, 273.

45. WR, vol. 15, 579.

46. USCD Serial Set 1279, 177–79.

47. Masich, *Civil War in Arizona*, 62, 67.

48. Braatz, *Surviving Conquest*, 92–99; Farish, *History of Arizona*, vol. 4, 103, 107–8.

49. Cremony, *Life among the Apaches*, 201.

50. USCD Serial Set 1279, 108.

51. Utley, *Frontiersmen in Blue*, 247–53.

52. Iverson, *Diné*, 49, 51; USCD Serial Set 1279, 126.

53. USCD Serial Set 1279, 126.

54. Dunlay, *Kit Carson*, 292–93; Kelly, *Navajo Roundup*.

55. WR, Series 1, vol. 34, chapter 46, part 1, 73.

56. On the campaign against the Navajos, see Kelly, *Navajo Roundup*; Trafzer, *Kit Carson Campaign*; Dunlay, *Kit Carson*, 276–301.

57. On the final weeks of the campaign and the exodus to New Mexico, see Kelly, *Navajo Roundup*, 110–58; Bailey, *Long Walk*, 162–68.

58. WR, Series I, vol. 50, part 2, 187.

59. The road, known as the Sawyers Road after its superintendent, James Sawyer, was meant to run more than thirteen hundred miles to Virginia City, Montana, bypassing entirely the main overland route. See USCD Serial Set 1256; Jackson, *Wagon Roads West*, 281–96; Paul, "Galvanized Yankee."

60. Hafen and Hafen, *Powder River Campaigns*, 46–48, 75–76, 80–81, 98; Springer, *Soldiering in Sioux Country*, 53.

61. *ARCIA*, 1857, 15.

62. Kappler, *Indian Affairs*, vol. 2, 852.

63. USCD Serial Set 1220, 149, 150; *ARCIA*, 1861, 29.

64. Between 1861 and 1865, 398,314 square miles were surrendered by treaty. The amount between 1867 and 1872 was 265,382 square miles and between 1874 and 1877, 194,836 square miles. The figures are based on map analysis of treaty boundaries. My thanks to Anne Marie Martin for her help in these calculations. The figures are a bit misleading. Most of the land surrendered was in the intermontane region, a great bleed of land in Utah, Nevada, southern Idaho, and a wide corridor of the overland route, where the density of Indian population was low and well away from the most formidable centers of resistance. The rest was from the bogus Treaty of Fort Wise, land in Colorado and the central plains that remained, to say the least, contested. Still, the sheer size of the loss suggested how rapidly Indian independence was eroding.

65. Kelly, *Navajo Roundup*, 100; USCD Serial Set 1279, 4.

66. Thompson, *Army and the Navajo*, 160.

67. USCD Serial Set 1176, 10–11.

68. *ARCIA*, 1874, 150–51.

69. Public resentment was great enough that Carleton published a lengthy defense of the reservation. Thompson, "'To the People of New Mexico.'"

70. Thompson, *Army and the Navajo*, 61–67.

71. *ARCIA*, 1857, 183–87.

72. For an argument that the flawed experiment was a "successful failure," see Thompson, *Army and the Navajo*, 158–65.

73. Wilson and Davis, *Herndon's Informants*, 357–60; Turner and Turner, *Mary Todd Lincoln*, 284–85.

Part 2. Things Come Together

1. Vevier, "American Continentalism," 323–35.
2. Seward, *Works*, vol. 1, 51–93. The passages referenced are on 74–75 and 84.

10. Iron Bands and Tongues of Fire

1. Reid, *Telegraph in America*, 488.
2. On the telegraph in the United States, see Harlow, *Old Wires and New Waves*; John, *Network Nation*; Starr, *Creation of the Media*; Schwoch, *Wired into Nature*.
3. Highton, *Electric Telegraph*; Prescott, *History, Theory*.
4. Most authorities acknowledge that among the many advances contributing to the Morse-Vail telegraph, Henry's was especially important. Taylor, *Historical Sketch*; Dickerson, *Joseph Henry*.
5. Morse's recollection is in a letter written in September 1837 to Secretary of Treasury Levi Woodbury reprinted in Vail, *American Electro Magnetic Telegraph*, 152.
6. Harlow, *Old Wires and New Waves*, 306.
7. Wolff, *Western Union*.
8. U.S. Statutes at Large, June 16, 1860, 36th Cong., 1st sess., chapter 137, 41–42.
9. Smith, *Rocky Mountain Mining Camps*, 172–73; Irey, "A Social History of Leadville," 278.
10. Shuman, "Report on the Statistics of Telegraphs and Telephones," 784–85.
11. Beatrice Electric Company Records, NSHS.
12. Schwoch, *Wired into Nature*, 107–47; Kennan, *Tent Life in Siberia*.
13. A customer in San Francisco paid six dollars to send ten words to New York and forty-five cents per word beyond the ten, but a six-dollar message was cut from ten to seven words because each telegram had to include its date and place of origin—thus the pricey rate of $0.8743 per word.
14. USCD Serial Set 2177, 4–5.
15. Wolff, *Western Union*.
16. Reid, *Telegraph in America*, 496.
17. Shuman, "Report on the Statistics of the Telegraph," 484–85.
18. Blondheim, *News over the Wires*.
19. For a discussion of the implication of this, see Wenzlheumer, *Connecting the Nineteenth-Century World*, 30–59.
20. Holmes, "Bread and the Newspaper," 348.
21. Morse and Morse, *New System of Geography*, 56.
22. Of the many histories of the Pacific railroad, I found these the most reliable and useful: Klein, *Union Pacific*; White, *Railroaded*; Bain, *Empire Express*; Athearn, *Union Pacific Country*.
23. Thomas Fitzpatrick to A. Cumming, November 19, 1853, in USCD Serial Set 690, 370.
24. Johanssen, *Letters of Stephen A. Douglas*, 270–71.
25. The politician was Rep. George Bliss of Ohio, quoted in Davis, *Union Pacific Railway*, 69.

26. Farnham, "Grenville Dodge"; Lavender, "For Sale."
27. White, *Railroaded*, 38. For a fine and concise account of the intricate maneuvering to construct the first line, including its shenanigans, see 1–38.
28. White, *Railroaded*, 22.
29. White, *Railroaded*, 23.
30. The comment about Train is in Richardson, *Beyond the Mississippi*, 565.
31. Bain, *Empire Express*, 172.
32. Riegel, *Story of Western Railroads*, 89.
33. Lavender, "For Sale," 8; White, *Railroaded*, 19.
34. Triooman, *History of the Union Pacific*, 51 The quote is from the later House report on the investigation of the Crédit Mobilier. USCD Serial Set 1577, 170.
35. White, *Railroaded*, 35; Fogel, *Union Pacific*, 70–73.
36. For a recent work portraying the construction of the line as an early effort of conquest and colonization through a partnership of government, business, and the military, picturing the story from the perspective of Indian peoples and Chinese, see Karuka, *Empire's Tracks*.
37. USCD Serial Set 2507, 3206.
38. Griswold, *Work of Giants*, 145.
39. The topic of Chinese workers on the railroad, and that of Chinese generally, is elusive because of the almost total lack of evidence from the hands of Chinese themselves. For two recent efforts to explore the topic, see Chang, *Ghosts of Gold Mountain*; Dearinger, *Filth of Progress*.
40. Griswold, *Work of Giants*, 112; Kraus, *High Road*, 110–11.
41. Bain, *Empire Express*, 360–62.
42. *Sacramento Reporter* and *Sacramento Union*, respectively, both on July 30, 1870.
43. Saxton, "The Army of Canton," 151.
44. Karuka, *Empire's Tracks*, 90. An impassioned survey of mistreatment of Chinese, especially after 1868, is Pfaelzer, *Driven Out*.
45. Gilliss, "Tunnels of the Pacific Railroad," 162, 167.
46. *Sacramento Union*, April 8, 1867, quoted in Bain, *Empire Express*, 330.
47. Gilliss, "Tunnels of the Pacific Railroad," 158–59.
48. Dodge, *How We Built the Union Pacific*, 142–43; Vance, *North American Railroad*, 179.
49. Vance, *North American Railroad*, 176.
50. Farnham, "Grenville Dodge."
51. Farnham, "Grenville Dodge," 645–47.
52. On this important process, developed shortly before the start of construction of the railway, see *Burnettizing*.
53. Bain, *Empire Express*, 475, 479.

11. Connections Real and Imagined

1. Croffut's *Trans-Continental Tourist's Guide*.
2. Foner, *Reconstruction*, 379.
3. Summers, *Railroads*.

4. Green, "Origins of the Credit Mobilier," 238–51.

5. USCD Serial Set 1038, 48.

6. *Chicago Tribune*, May 11, 1869.

7. For a readable if a bit sensationalized history of these towns, see Kreck, *Hell on Wheels*.

8. Stanley, *My Early Travels*, 166.

9. Stelter, "Birth of a Frontier Boom Town," 22.

10. Homsher, *South Pass*, 17–18; Stanley, *My Early Travels*, 166–67; Bowles, *Our New West*, 56; Monahan, *Julesburg*, 170.

11. *Frontier Index*, March 6, November 13, 1868. Files are at the Western History Collections, Denver Public Library.

12. The chapters are in Bain, *Empire Express*.

13. Williams, *Great and Shining Road*, 150–51.

14. *Frontier Index*, September 15, 1868.

15. Dodge wrote that he and half a dozen others were looking for a suitable pass through the Laramie Mountains when a band of warriors attacked. He and his men held them off "with our Winchesters" until rescued by cavalry, then on the way back to camp he came upon the easy grade the Union Pacific eventually used—the vital break that allowed them across the continental divide. Evans pass, however, was found by its namesake, James Evans, nearly a year later. Dodge's own diary and letters make it clear that the Lakota attack was an invention. Dodge, *How We Built the Union Pacific*, 20–21; Farnham, "Grenville Dodge."

16. Stanley, *My Early Travels*, 202–5. This record of the council is especially interesting because elsewhere in his book Stanley repeats the claim of Indians poised to attack all along the route. That his detailed descriptions of the chiefs' words are likely accurate is suggested by their exact correlation to more limited quotations from the journals of the commissioners. See Deloria and DeMallie, *Proceedings*.

17. Stands In Timber, *Cheyenne Memories*, 387–89; Grinnell, *Fighting Cheyennes*, 263–68.

18. Seymour, *Incidents of a Trip*, 89–90; Stanley, *My Early Travels*, 154–58; Bain, *Empire Express*, 388–89.

19. Ames, *Pioneering the Union Pacific*, 329.

20. Sabin, *Building the Pacific Railway*, 192.

21. Sabin, *Building the Pacific Railway*, 196.

22. Gilliss, "Tunnels of the Pacific Railroad," 170–71.

23. *Chicago Tribune*, May 11, 1869; Todd, *Sunset Land*, 245.

24. Sawyer's first attempt at laying out the road in 1865 had aborted, opposed by the Lakotas and Cheyennes as part of the Powder River campaign led by Gen. Patrick Connor. The following year, however, he succeeded USCD Serial Set 1256. See also Jackson, *Wagon Roads West*, 281–96.

25. Walker, "Freighting from Guaymas to Tucson."

26. Cummins, "Toll Roads."

27. Burke's day books and business records show the extent of his prosperous business. They are in the John Bratt Papers, NSHS. Henry Stanley mentioned his encounter with the ferryman in Stanley, *My Early Travels*, 129–30.

28. Noyes, *Story of Ajax*, 19.

29. Winther, *Old Oregon Country*, 107, 211.

30. Winther, *Old Oregon Country*, 178.

31. Watt, "Experiences of a Packer," 46–47.

32. Talkington, "Mullan Road," 306.

33. Rolfe, "Overland Freighting," 286; Hafen and Gussow, *Arapaho-Cheyenne Indians*, 49; Wyman, "Freighting," 26.

34. Winther, "Place of Transportation," 390–93; Rolfe, "Early Day Los Angeles"; Rice, "Early Freighting," 73–80.

35. Majors, *Seventy Years*; Settle and Settle, *War Drums and Wagon Wheels*.

36. Lowe, *Five Years a Dragoon*, 354–56.

37. Hadley, "Plains War in 1865," 274. Individuals like William Fulton worked under government and private contracts hauling usually for about a penny a pound per hundred miles. It added up. In the summer of 1866, Fulton carried 300,000 pounds from Nebraska City to Salt Lake City at $0.18 a pound, a gross income of $54,000. Fulton, "Freighting and Staging Days in Early Days," 263.

38. Wyman, "Freighting," 26–27.

39. Madsen and Madsen, *North to Montana*, 109–12.

40. Majors, *Seventy Years*, 202–5.

41. McCain, "Trip from Atchison, Kansas," 95–98.

42. Rusling, *Across America*, 237; Porter, *By Ox Team to California*, 38.

43. Chandless, *Visit to Salt Lake*, 13–21; Lass, *From the Missouri to the Great Salt Lake*; Munn, "Reminiscences of My Life—From Boyhood," typescript, nshs; Wood, "Coad Brothers"; Jackson, *Time Exposure*, 101–37; Doyle, *Bound for Montana*, 215, 217–18, 227; Bratt, *Trails of Yesterday*.

44. uscd Serial Set 881, 154.

45. Macintyre, *Man Who Would Be King*; Marsh, *The Camel*, 188; Leonard, *The Camel*.

46. uscd Serial Set 720, 61–68; uscd Serial Set 975, 456–91. The quote is on 491.

47. *Congressional Globe*, 31st Cong., 2nd sess., March 3, 1851, 826–27; Lesley, *Uncle Sam's Camels*; Fowler, *Camels to California*.

48. Fleming, "Jefferson Davis's Camel Experiment," 151; Kramer, "Short, Unhappy Life"; Johnson, *Last Camel Charge*, 3–8; Connelly, "American Camel Experiment."

49. Winther, *Old Oregon Country*, 119; Lewis, "Camel Pack Trains"; DeQuille, "Camels in the Mines."

50. Fleming, "Jefferson Davis's Camel Experiment," 142.

51. uscd Serial Set 1080, 436.

52. On Holladay, his career and the intricate maneuvers around contracts for these stage routes, see Frederick, *Ben Holladay*.

53. Bates, *American Marine*, 467.

54. For a fascinating digital illustration of the spread of post offices in the West, done by Cameron Blevins and Jason Heppler at Stanford University's Spatial History Project, see "Geography of the Post," http://web.stanford.edu/group/spatialhistory /cgi-bin/site/project.php?id=1059. And for the role of the post in opening the West, see Blevins, *Paper Trails*.

55. Burton, *Look of the West*, 27.

56. Hudson, *Scamper through America*, 152–53; McClure, *Three Thousand Miles*, 103; Hutchings, *In the Heart of the Sierras*, 212; West, "Splendid Misery," 86.

57. Barnes, *From the Atlantic to the Pacific*, 70; Earl of Dunraven, *Great Divide*, 37; Bowles, *Our New West*, 70.

58. Pumpelly, *Across America*, 4; Ludlow, *Heart of the Continent*, 127.

59. Murphy, *Rambles in North-Western America*, 173–74.

60. Pumpelly, *Across America*, 2–5; Ludlow, *Heart of the Continent*, 131.

61. The phrase is from a fine recent book: Bryan, *American Elsewhere*.

62. Colden, *Memoir*, 145.

12. Maps

1. Worster, *River Running West*, 159–60.

2. Goetzmann, *Exploration and Empire*, 541.

3. Pyne, *How the Canyon Became Grand*, 18.

4. Goetzmann, *Exploration and Empire*, 306.

5. Worster, *River Running West*, 109–53.

6. Powell, *Exploration of the Colorado River*, 213.

7. Darrah, "Sumner Journal," 121.

8. Darrah, "Sumner Journal," 121.

9. Powell, *Exploration*, iii–iv.

10. Powell, *Exploration*, 214–16.

11. Powell, *Exploration*, 264–67, 274–75.

12. Titiev, "Hopi Salt Expedition," 244–58. For an account of a recent retracing of the pilgrimage, see Engelhard, "Salt Pilgrimage," 211–20.

13. Powell, *Exploration*, 247.

14. Bartlett, *Great Surveys*, and Goetzmann, *Exploration and Empire* remain the two best works on these surveys.

15. Worster, *River Running West*, chapters 6–8 is now the standard source for Powell's work in these years.

16. Goetzmann, *Exploration and Empire*, 559–61.

17. Quoted in Worster, *River Running West*, 320.

18. King understandably has attracted considerable historical attention. See Wilkins, *Clarence King*; Sandweiss, *Passing Strange*; Sachs, *Humboldt Current*, 185–228.

19. King, *Report of the Geological Exploration of the Fortieth Parallel*.

20. On Hayden, see Cassidy, *Ferdinand V. Hayden*; Foster, *Strange Genius*; Bartlett, *Great Surveys*, 489–529.

21. For discussions of the survey work of these two prominent figures, see Kinsey, *Thomas Moran*; Hales, *William Henry Jackson*.

22. Bartlett, *Great Surveys*, 333–72; Dawdy, *George Montague Wheeler*.

23. Wheeler, *Report upon United States Geographical Surveys*, 45.

24. Goetzmann, *Exploration and Empire*, 478.

25. Goetzmann, *Exploration and Empire*, 487.

26. The point is made in Goetzmann, *Exploration and Empire*, 502.

27. Schmeckebier, *Catalogue and Index*, 9–44.

28. On Holmes see Fernlund, *William Henry Holmes*.

29. Historians have given remarkably little attention to Whitney. An early exception is Brewster, *Life and Letters of Josiah Dwight Whitney*.

30. Brewer, *Up and Down California* (1930).

31. On the survey, see Beidleman, *California's Pioneer Naturalists*, 307–56.

32. Goetzmann, *Exploration and Empire*, 442, 447.

33. Macomb, *Report of the Exploring*, 54.

34. Macomb, *Report of the Exploring*, 501, 496–97.

35. Bradley, "Report of Frank H. Bradley," 223.

36. Goetzmann, *Exploration and Empire*, 379–82.

37. Wilkins, *Great Diamond Hoax*; Woodard, *Diamonds in the Salt*; Wilkins, *Clarence King*, 154–72.

38. *First, Second, and Third Annual Reports*, 14–15.

39. Smith, "Rain Follows the Plow."

40. Powell, *Report on the Lands of the Arid Regions*. Powell's work and influence is considered later.

41. Powell, "Lesson of Connemaugh." The quote is on 153.

42. Macomb, *Report of the Exploring*, 54.

43. Ives, *Report upon the Colorado River of the West*, 42.

44. Powell, *Exploration*, 152–53.

45. Gilbert, *Report on the Geology of the Henry Mountains*.

46. Pyne, *Grove Karl Gilbert*, 83–95; Pyne, "Certain Allied Problems in Mechanics."

47. Powell, *Exploration*.

48. Powell, *Exploration*, 162.

49. Pyne, *How the Canyon Became Grand*, 150.

50. *American Journal of Science and Arts*, 2nd ser., 2 (November 1848), 288–89. The discovery was reported by Hiram A. Prout, a Saint Louis physician.

51. Warren, *Joseph Leidy*.

52. Leidy, *Extinct Mammalian Fauna*.

53. Sternberg, *Life of a Fossil Hunter*.

54. Breithaupt, "Railroads, Blizzards, and Dinosaurs," 446–48; Rea, *Bone Wars*, 15.

55. Hay, *Bibliography and Catalogue*.

56. Osborn, *Cope*, 185.

57. Hayden, *Preliminary Report*, 317; Hayden, *Fifth Annual Report*, 317.

58. Marsh, "Polydactyl Horses."

59. Marsh, *Odontornithes*.

60. An earlier bird, *Archaeopteryx*, was later found also to have teeth, but a skull revealing that was not found and described until 1884, four years after Marsh published his study.

61. Marsh, "Introduction and Succession of Vertebrate Life," 352.

62. Schuchert and LeVene, *O. C. Marsh*, 428, 247.

63. Schuchert and LeVene, *O. C. Marsh*, 428–29.

13. The "Science of Man"

1. Hafen and Hafen, *Diaries of William Henry Jackson*, 309–10.
2. Jackson, "First Official Visit," 157.
3. On Grinnell and his association and defense of Indians, see Hagan, *Theodore Roosevelt*.
4. Powell, *People of the Sacred Mountain*, xv.
5. Powell did not use this term until the bureau's fourteenth annual report, although he made clear that the pursuit had guided the bureau from the start. Powell, *Fourteenth Annual Report*, xxix.
6. Wheeler, *Report upon United States Geographical Surveys*.
7. U.S. Geological Survey, *Contributions to North American Ethnography*.
8. Gatschet, *Klamath Indians*; Riggs, *Dakota-English Dictionary*.
9. Gatschet, *Klamath Indians*, 166–67; Powers, *Tribes of California*, 166–67.
10. Powers, *Tribes of California*, 186.
11. Morgan, *Systems of Consanguinity*, 166.
12. Bieder, *Science Encounters the Indian*, 222.
13. Powell, *Fourteenth Annual Report*, xxix.
14. Powell, *Fourteenth Annual Report*, xxvii.
15. Morgan, *Ancient Society*.
16. Murphee, "Evolutionary Anthropologists."
17. Morgan, *Houses and House-Life*, 42–43.
18. Powers, *Tribes of California*, 119, 132–33, 401–18; Gatschet, *Klamath Indians*, 3, xl, xxxix.
19. Fowler, *Anthropology of the Numa*, 38; Hoxie, *Final Promise*, 24.
20. USCD Serial Set 1337, 17; USCD Serial Set 1619, 26.
21. Nott and Gliddon, *Indigenous Races*, 219–21.
22. Lamb, "Army Medical Museum," 625.
23. Bieder, *Brief Historical Survey*, 36–37, 45.
24. Lamb, "Army Medical Museum," 628.
25. Betts, "Yale College Expedition," 665.
26. Quoted in Bieder, *Brief Historical Survey*, 30.
27. Fabian, *Skull Collectors*; Thomas, *Skull Wars*; Bieder, *Brief Historical Survey*.
28. For a sampling of the literature on the evolution of ideas on race, see Stanton, *Leopard's Spots*; Gossett, *Race*; Malcomson, *One Drop of Blood*; Takaki, *Iron Cages*.
29. On Agassiz's ideas on the topic, see Lurie, "Louis Agassiz."
30. Morton, *Crania Americana*, 5–7; Nott and Gliddon, *Types of Mankind*, xxxii–xxxiii; Nott, "Statistics," 280.
31. Nott, "Statistics," 80.
32. Dorsey, *Cegiha Language*, 681–82; Powers, *Tribes of California*, 661–62.
33. Metcalf, "Interest and Importance," 227; Hitchcock, "First Anniversary Address," 271.
34. Harte, *Poems*, 279–80.

35. William Henry Rideing's time with the Wheeler expedition and Ernest Ingersoll's with Hayden, for instance, both inspired and became part of longer works: Rideing, *A-Saddle in the Wild West*; Ingersoll, *Crest of the Continent*.

36. Betts, "Yale College Expedition."

37. Rideing, "Wheeler Expedition," 802.

38. Schuchert and LeVene, *O. C. Marsh*, 116–18.

39. Robinson, "Creation of Yosemite Valley"; Muir, "Studies in the Sierra."

40. King was at least ambivalent on the question. He found much in favor of glacial formation, and in fact had argued as much to Whitney, but as Whitney's protégé he apparently felt obliged to stand by his mentor publicly. King, *Systematic Geology*, 477–78, 792; Wilkins, *Clarence King*, 188–89.

41. King, "Catastrophism and Evolution." Interestingly, while geological catastrophism has been rejected, recent work in evolution has given some credibility to a corresponding approach. Eldredge, "Revisiting."

42. Parkman, *Heroes of To-Day*, 15.

43. Muir, "Explorations," 140–41.

44. Sandweiss, *Passing Strange*, 54.

45. Muir, "In the Heart of the California Alps." Quotes are on 350 and 351.

46. Muir, "Snow-Storm on Mount Shasta." Quote on 529.

47. King, *Mountaineering*, 154–57, 89. The reference to himself as a "pioneer" is in the preface to the fourth edition.

48. There were certainly differences among them. King had disdain for any who regarded mountains with transcendental rapture without attempting to understand them scientifically, and he tried to distinguish between his own emotional response and his appreciation as a scientist, though he could not quite pull it off. For his own thoughts on it, see King, *Mountaineering*, 295–97. For a brief discussion on the differences between King and Muir, see Worster, *Passion for Nature*, 187–90.

49. King, *Mountaineering*, 339, 301–2, 133–34; Dutton, *Tertiary History*, 36–37.

50. Quoted in Michael P. Cohen, *Pathless Way*. Clarence King to Clarence Dutton, October 12, [1880?], Clarence King Letterbook no. 1, United States Geological Survey (Private), Clarence King/James D. Hague Papers, HL.

51. Starr, *Americans and the California Dream*, 180.

52. Emerson, "Progress of Culture," 171.

53. Rieppel, *Assembling the Dinosaur*.

54. Dutton, *Tertiary History*, 86.

55. *Congressional Globe*, 42nd Cong., 2nd sess., 159, 199, 657.

56. The phrase is from Haines, *Yellowstone Story*, xviii.

57. The extent of wildlife at the time the park was created has been a matter of some controversy. Some have argued that the present abundance is the result of animals being pushed into the mountains by settlement of the lower regions they preferred. Historians Paul Schullery and Lee Whittlesey, however, have examined all available early travel accounts and found that virtually all that mention game and all remark on its abundance. Yellowstone's unique conditions, they argue,

attracted game even when animals generally shunned the high country. See Schulery, *Searching for Yellowstone*, 41–50.

58. The account of this group, known as the Folsom-Cook-Peterson party, was published in July 1870 by Chicago's *Western Monthly Magazine*.

59. Hayden, "Wonders of the West."

60. Langford, "Wonders of Yellowstone, I"; Langford, "Wonders of Yellowstone, II."

61. Bonney and Bonney, *Battle Drums and Geysers*, 387; Scott, *Yellowstone*, 172–84.

62. Haines, *Yellowstone Story*, 170–72; Langford, "Wonders of Yellowstone, I," 3. Doane was effusive about the Yellowstone valley only two days' ride from what would be the park boundary: "Excepting the Judith Basin, I have seen no district in the western territories so eligible for settlement."

63. Norton, *Wonder-Land Illustrated*, 82; Strahorn, *Resources of Montana*; Richardson, *Wonders of Yellowstone*.

64. Ludlow, *Report on a Reconnaissance*, 22, 36, 37.

65. Ludlow, *Report on a Reconnaissance*, 14; Strong, *Trip to the Yellowstone*, 99–100.

66. Strahorn, *Fifteen Thousand Miles*, 79, 81.

67. Examples of promotional guides, all with obvious connections to the Northern Pacific: Wylie, *Yellowstone National Park*; McElrath, *Yellowstone Valley*; Haupt, *Yellowstone National Park*; Winser, *Yellowstone National Park*.

68. A contemporary estimate of twenty to thirty thousand visitors is far too high, but there was an undeniable surge in tourism. Topping, *Chronicles of the Yellowstone*; Bartlett, *Yellowstone*, 43–45.

69. Hampton, *How the U.S. Cavalry*, 36.

70. Senator George Vent of Missouri was one of the leaders of the opposition to the lease. During the debate over the original act, one of its backers had warned that unless the place remained public land "some person may go there and plant himself right across the only path that leads to these wonders" and charge all comers to see the wonders that belonged to all, and now, Vent said, that had happened anyway. It was time for Washington to take back the scenery. *Congressional Globe*, 42nd Cong., 2nd sess., 697; *Congressional Record*, 47th Cong., 2nd sess., 3484.

71. An appendix to an early guide estimated expenses: Haupt, *Yellowstone National Park*, 175–77.

72. Ludlow, *Report on a Reconnaissance*, 27; Haines, *Yellowstone Story*, 218.

73. Guie and McWhorter, *Adventures in Geyser Land*, 64; Ludlow, *Report on a Reconnaissance*, 26–29.

74. The committee included such luminaries as Joseph Henry, O. C. Marsh, John Wesley Powell, and George Wheeler. USCD Serial Set 1809, 44.

75. Ludlow, *Report on a Reconnaissance*, 35–36; Strong, *Trip to the Yellowstone*, 92–93.

76. For a summary of proposed legislation during these years, see Crampton, *Early History of Yellowstone*, 37–41.

77. Hampton, *How the U.S. Cavalry*, 66.

78. Crampton, *Early History of Yellowstone*, 78–81.

79. Synge, *Ride through Wonderland*, 60–61.

80. The market for elk tusks on the eastern market rose from fifty cents to up to fifty dollars. In 1916, 257 elk carcasses were found, the animals killed only for their tusks. Jacoby, *Crimes against Nature*, 133–36.

81. On Indians in national parks generally, see Spence, *Dispossessing the Wilderness*; Burnham, *Indian Country*; Catton, *Inhabited Wilderness*; Keller and Turek, *American Indians*.

82. Schullery, *Searching for Yellowstone*, 15.

83. Nabokov and Loendorf, *Restoring a Presence*; Janetski, *Indians of Yellowstone*.

84. West, *Last Indian War*, 214–19.

85. USCD Serial Set 1850, 985; USCD Serial Set 1960, 573.

86. A literary tourist assured his readers that "the traveller in the Park will see or hear no more of [Indians] than if he was in the Adirondacks or White Mountains." Wingate, *Through the Yellowstone Park*, 140; Winser, *Yellowstone National Park*, 22.

87. USCD Serial Set 1960, 605.

88. USCD Serial Set 1960, 597–604. Quote is on p. 600.

89. Niagara Falls is 167 feet tall, Yosemite Falls 2,425 ft.

90. Bowles, *Our New West*, 375–76; Richardson, *Our New States and Territories*, 49.

91. Olmsted's comments, originally delivered in 1865, have been reprinted as Olmstead and Rhode, "Overview of California."

92. Solnit, *Savage Dreams*, 318–20.

93. Jackson, *Bits of Travel*, 20.

94. Spence, *Dispossessing the Wilderness*, 103–8; Burnham, *Indian Country*, 20–21.

95. Some visitors responded pragmatically; one woman sighed that the geysers had enough hot water to launder all America's soiled clothes. Harrison, *Summer's Outing*, 70.

96. Harrison, *Summer's Outing*, 70; Earl of Dunraven, *The Great Divide*, 225.

97. The traveler Dr. Wayland Hoyt quoted in Winser, *Yellowstone National Park*, 73–74.

98. Luke, *Adventures and Travels*, 2.

99. Philetus C. Norris journals, 90, HL.

14. The World's Convention

1. *Ninth Census of the United States*, vol. 1, 340.

2. The classic study is Higham, *Strangers in the Land*. For a survey of the scholarship on nativism, see Gerstle, "Inclusion, Exclusion."

3. White, *Eastern Establishment*, 109.

4. Three basic texts on race and its place in imagining the emerging West are Horsman, *Race and Manifest Destiny*; Pierce, *Making the White Man's West*; Brantlinger, *Dark Vanishings*.

5. Fisher, *Builder of the West*, 202–3.

6. *Ninth Census of the United States*, vol. 1, 336.

7. *Ninth Census of the United States*, vol. 1, 386, 641; West, "Five Idaho Mining Towns," 111, 118.

8. *Tenth Census of the United States*, vol. 1, 3, 492–95.

9. Trimble, *Mining Advance*, 140; Clappe, *Shirley Letters*, 121.

10. William P. Daingerfield to "J," August 18, 1850, William P. Daingerfield letters, BaL. The "golden eggs" comment was from a journalist describing the crowds passing through Kansas City for the Colorado gold fields in 1859: Hafen and Hafen, *Reports from Colorado*, 117. For an overview of the polyglot influx with the gold rush, see Wright, "Making of Cosmopolitan California, Part I"; Wright, "Making of Cosmopolitan California, Part II."

11. Billington, *Land of Savagery*, 65.

12. The Union Pacific sold nearly two million acres in Nebraska between 1869 and 1879 at prices averaging from $3.02 to $5.55 per acre. Combs, "Union Pacific Railroad," 19; Hedges, "Colonization Work," 321.

13. Emmons, *Garden in the Grasslands*, 110.

14. Hedges, "Colonization Work," 321.

15. Hedges, "Colonization Work," 318.

16. Hedges, "Colonization Work," 330–31; Overton, *Burlington West*, 359–60, 369; Combs, "Union Pacific Railroad," 11.

17. Jackson, *Time Exposure*, 102; Goddard, *Where to Emigrate*, 12; Emmons, *Garden in the Grasslands*, 109.

18. Rickey, *Forty Miles a Day*, 18.

19. Hansen, "Official Encouragement of Immigration to Iowa"; Zabel, "To Reclaim the Wilderness"; Henke, "Imagery"; Blodgett, "Colorado Territorial Board of Immigration"; Goddard, *Where to Emigrate*, 12.

20. David M. Emmons, *Garden in the Grasslands*, 35–37.

21. Walther and Taylor, *Resources and Advantages*, 26; Walther, *The State of Nebraska*, 5.

22. Goddard, *Where to Emigrate*, 12.

23. Overton, *Burlington West*, 422. A promotional book from the Chicago, Rock Island and Pacific claimed its lands were home to people "from every corner of the Globe," but when it got down to particulars, it cited the English, the "exiled sons of Erin," "the economic Highlander," and "the hardy Norsemen, the Swede, the Dane, the Bohemian, the ever industrious German." *Great West*, 6. My thanks to Jason Pierce for pointing out this passage.

24. Batchelder, "Sketch of the History," 251; Brown, *State of Nebraska*, 12; Crockett, *Black Towns*.

25. The first ten entries under the letters B, H, and S were examined in Meyer, *Western Jewry*.

26. Rowse, *Cousin Jacks*.

27. Emmons, *Butte Irish*.

28. *Tenth Census of the United States, 1880*, I, 495; Warrin and Gomes, *Land*.

29. A study after the turn of the century showed that about half of the Basque herders in Nevada, Idaho, and Oregon came from six villages in the old country. Douglass and Bilbao, *Amerikanuak*; Rolle, *Westward the Immigrants*, 171–79; Turk, "Selling the Heartland," 150–59; Luebke, "Ethnic Group Settlement," 418–19.

30. Hale, *Danes in North America*, 58–59.
31. Hendricks, "Recollections," 90–204.
32. Hoglund, *Finnish Immigrants*, 35.
33. Sinn, *Pacific Crossing*, 43–91, 314–19. For a summary of estimated Chinese immigration before 1882, see Coolidge, *Chinese Immigration*, 498.
34. Chen, "Internal Origins"; Liu, "Social Origins"; Tong, *Chinese Americans*, 19–29.
35. Hom, *Songs of Gold Mountain*, 185.
36. Timothy Coffin Osborn journal, December 26, 1850, BaL; G. M. Murrell to Eliza Murrell, n.d. [1851–53], letter, HL; White, *Yankee Trader*, 122.
37. Coolidge, *Chinese Immigration*, 22.
38. Estimated gold production in California between 1852 and 1855 declined by more than 30 percent, from $81.3 million to $55.4 million. Paul, *California Gold*, 345.
39. G. D. Phillips to [James Wylie Mandeville], January 4, 1853, letter, HL. For a provocative and extended look at the role of religion in the consideration of assimilating Chinese and Indians, see Paddison, *American Heathens*.
40. The two essential works on the anti-Chinese movement are Saxton, *Indispensable Enemy*; Lew-Williams, *Chinese Must Go*.
41. For an excellent discussion of the early and evolving meanings of "coolie," see *Analysis of the Chinese Question*; Jung, *Coolies and Cane*, 1–38.
42. Jung, *Coolies and Cane*, 6–13.
43. Coolidge, *Chinese Immigration*, 33; Hittell, *History of California*, 4: 187.
44. Quoted in a letter from Chinese leaders to the governor in *Analysis of the Chinese Question*, 13.
45. Hittell, *History of California*, 4: 187.
46. Johnson, *Roaring Camp*, 248; Coolidge, *Chinese Immigration*, 36–37; Chiu, *Chinese Labor in California*, 23, 28–29.
47. Coolidge, *Chinese Immigration*, 70–71.
48. *People v. Hall*, 4 Cal. 399 (California Supreme Court 1854).
49. Nee and Nee, *Longtime Californ'*, 37; Frank and Chappell, *History and Business Directory*, 148–49; Raymond, *Statistics of Mines and Mining*, 243.
50. Dobie, *San Francisco's Chinatown*, 50.
51. Wheat, "'California's Bantam Cock,'" 348–49.
52. *New York Times*, October 27, 1876.
53. *Ninth Census of the United States*, vol. 1, 730; Raymond, *Statistics of Mines and Mining*, 243.
54. Liping Zhu, *Chinaman's Chance*.
55. *Ninth Census of the United States*, vol. 1, 8.
56. Nevada *Journal* quoted in Speer, *Humble Plea*, 36; *Report of Joint Select Committee Relative to the Chinese Population*.
57. Virginia City *Gold Hill News*, March 9, 1864; Virginia City *Territorial Enterprise*, February 8, 1868, September 24, 1868, February 11, 1871, June 24, 1871, all in Russell M. Magnaghi Collection, BaL.
58. Lanctot, *Chinese and English Phrase Book*.
59. Wong, *English-Chinese Phrase Book*.

60. Chiu, *Chinese Labor in California*, 30. Chinese proved to be masters of river mining, adapting coordinated labor and new techniques to exploit streams long after others had given them up. See Rohe, "Chinese River Mining."

61. Booker, *Down by the Bay*, 14–29.

62. USCD Serial Set 1734, 1190.

63. Lew-Williams, *Chinese Must Go*, 34–35.

64. On opium smoking, the debate around it, and its political effects, see Courtwright, "Opiate Addiction in the American West," 23–31; Ahmad, *Opium Debate*; Ahmad, "Opium Smoking"; Sinn, *Pacific Crossing*, 191–218; Lowe, "'Secret Friend.'"

65. Sinn, *Pacific Crossing*, 203; Kane, *Opium-Smoking*, 17.

66. De Quille, *History of the Big Bonanza*, 392.

67. Ahmad, *Opium Debate*, 36–50; Mathews, *Ten Years in Nevada*, 259–60.

68. Ahmad, "Opium Smoking," 57.

69. The point is made in Richard White, *Republic for Which It Stands*, 381.

70. Abrams, "Polygamy," 707; USCD Serial Set 1734.

71. A sampling of these opinions: USCD Serial Set 1734, iv–vii, 13–14, 97, 202, 117, 133, 199–205, 383. For an example of more positive testimony, including support for naturalization, see that of the Methodist minister Otis Gibson, 396–436.

72. Mathews, *Ten Years*, 260–61; Lew-Williams, *Chinese Must Go*.

73. Paddison, *American Heathens*, 139–73.

74. Saxton, *Indispensable Enemy*, 138–39.

75. In Texas Blacks made up 31 percent of its population in 1870, but there were virtually none (and few whites) beyond the ninety-eighth meridian, the line usually used as where the West starts, and in 1890 they made up less than 3 percent of the non-Indian population west of the ninety-eighth meridian, and more than half of those were in Bejar County (San Antonio). My thanks to Marie Ford for helping with these calculations.

76. Saunt, "Paradox of Freedom," 64–65.

77. Abel, *American Indian in the Civil War*; Zellar, *African Creeks*; Littlefield, *Cherokee Freedmen*.

78. *Ninth Census of the United States, 1870*, vol. 1, 12, 23; *Tenth Census of the United States, 1880*, vol. 1, 387.

79. The county is Wilkinson County, Mississippi, where the census recorded 13,144 Blacks in 1860. *Ninth Census of the United States, 1870*, vol. 1, 42–43.

80. Richard, "Unwelcome Settlers," 173–74.

81. For an overview of Blacks in the urban West, see Taylor, *In Search of the Racial Frontier*, 192–221.

82. Taylor, *In Search of the Racial Frontier*, 194–98; Richard, "Unwelcome Settlers," 193–94.

83. On the long history and considerable extent of cattle raising in the South, see Guice, "Cattle Raisers." A well-known close study of the slave economy states that on cotton plantations slaves devoted nearly as much time to raising livestock as to raising cotton (25 vs. 34 percent of labor time). Fogel and Engerman, *Time on the Cross*, 42.

84. Taylor, *In Search of the Racial Frontier*, 160–61; Searles, "Taking Out the Buck."

85. Massey, *Black Cowboys*, 117–30; Haley, *Charles Goodnight*, 242.

86. Leckie, *Buffalo Soldiers*; Schubert, *Voices of the Buffalo Soldier*; Schubert, *Black Valor*; Dobak and Phillips, *Black Regulars*; Billington, *New Mexico's Buffalo Soldiers*.

87. Taylor, *In Search of the Racial Frontier*, 169.

88. Schubert, "Suggs Affray"; Sorenson, *Iron Riders*; Longellier, "Buffalo Soldiers."

89. Schubert, *Black Valor*.

90. *Ninth Census of the United States, 1870*, vol. 1, 30; *Tenth Census of the United States, 1880*, vol. 1, xxxvii. Texas and Indian Territory are excluded.

91. USCD Serial Set 1900, 175–215, 532. Smith's affidavit is on p. 213. At the end of 1876 President Grant sent to Congress a list, nearly a hundred pages long, of about four thousand southern Blacks murdered, maimed, or whipped since 1868. Van Deusen, "Exodus of 1879," 13.

92. Hinger, *Nicodemus*, 31; Painter, "Kansas Fever," 71.

93. Hinger, *Nicodemus*.

94. Schwendemann, "St. Louis and the 'Exodusters,'" 32–33.

95. Athearn, *In Search of Canaan*, 159–63.

96. Painter, *Exodusters*, 198.

97. Campney, *This Is Not Dixie*; Friefield et al., "African American Homesteader 'Colonies.'"

98. Painter, "Kansas Fever," 71.

99. For differing estimates of the number of Black cowboys, see Durham and Jones, *Negro Cowboys*, 44; Porter, *Negro on the American Frontier*, 495; Hunter, *Trail Drivers of Texas*, 453; Taylor, *In Search of the Racial Frontier*, 156–58; Jordan, *North American Cattle-Ranching Frontiers*, 215, 220–21; Massey, *Black Cowboys*, xiii–xiv.

100. Taylor, *In Search of the Racial Frontier*, 344n.

101. Searles, "Taking Out the Buck"; Duke and Frantz, *6,000 Miles of Fence*, 172.

102. Richter, *Army in Texas*, 153.

103. Taylor, *In Search of the Racial Frontier*, 175–76.

104. USCD Serial Set 1900, 105.

105. Kerber, "Abolitionist Perception," 294.

106. USCD Serial Set 1899. The Democratic majority report is iii–viii, quotations from v–viii. The Republican minority report is ix–xxv, quotations on xiii and xxv.

107. Miller, *Unwelcome Immigrant*, 173; Commons, *Documentary History*, 80–83.

108. Jung, *Coolies and Cane*.

109. Athearn, *In Search of Canaan*, 105–7; Painter, *Exodusters*, 237.

110. On three key cases, see Albin, "Perkins Case"; Franklin, "Archy Case"; Hayden, "Biddy Mason's Los Angeles." Lee's departure for the gold fields on Canada's Frazier River was part of a considerable movement of Blacks across the international border during these troubling years. Edwards, "'War of Complexional Distinction.'"

111. Taylor, *In Search of the Racial Frontier*, 215–18.

112. Berwanger, *Frontier against Slavery*, 144–57; Berwanger, "Reconstruction on the Frontier."

15. Crew Cultures and Cribs

1. The new estimate is from Hacker, "Census-Based Count of the Civil War Dead." For an exchange on this reliability of this new estimate, see Marshall, "Great Exaggeration"; Hacker, "Demographic Impact."

2. As a comparison of localities, New York County in 1880 was 51.0 percent female, Providence County in Rhode Island 52.0 percent, and Suffolk County in Massachusetts 52.5 percent, while San Francisco County was 56.6 percent male, Arapaho County (Denver) in Colorado 60.7 percent, and Idaho's Boise County 81.3 percent.

3. In 1870 and 1880, for instance, Kansas was 55.4 percent and 53.8 percent male, Nebraska 57.2 and 55.0 percent.

4. Davis, *Frontier America*, 114–15; Faragher, *Women and Men*, 189–96.

5. The term "crew cultures" is James Belich's. For his discussion, see Belich, *Making Peoples*, 428–36. The quote is on 428.

6. Belich, *Replenishing the Earth*, 323–24.

7. Perkins, "El Campo de los Sonoraenses," 198; Johnson, *Roaring Camp*, 110–11.

8. Paul and West, *Mining Frontiers*, 213–14.

9. Johnson, *Roaring Camp*, 123.

10. Johnson, *Roaring Camp*, 170.

11. Gerstäcker, *Narrative of a Journey*, 236.

12. Helper, *Land of Gold*, 37; Thompson, *Reminiscences*, 59.

13. Edward Austin to sister, September 21, 1849, Edward Austin letters, BaL.

14. Hurtado, "Sex, Gender, Culture," 5.

15. Mountford, "Pacific Gold Rushes," 89; Johnson, *Roaring Camp*, 155.

16. James and Raymond, *Comstock Women*, 30.

17. Barsness, *Gold Camp*, 210; Silver City, Idaho, *Owyhee Avalanche*, September 21, 1866. An early historian of the Comstock Lode estimated the per capita annual consumption there was five gallons of hard liquor and fifteen gallons of beer. Lord, *Comstock Mines*, 377.

18. Goode, *Outposts of Zion*, 438.

19. Mountford, "Pacific Gold Rushes," 89; Johnson, *Roaring Camp*, 155; Clappe, *Shirley Letters*, 79.

20. Courtwright, *Violent Land*, 2–3. For a survey of earlier works that emphasize the lawlessness of the West, see McGrath, *Gunfighters*, 261–66.

21. Belich, *Replenishing the Earth*, 323–24; Wilk, "Extractive Economy."

22. The literature on western violence is considerable. For a selection of overviews, see Brown, "Violence"; Brown, *Strain of Violence*; Hollon, *Frontier Violence*; Bellesiles, "Western Violence"; McGrath, "Violence and Lawlessness."

23. Helper, *Land of Gold*, 29. Helper is clearly not including Indians killed during those years. If the total non-Native population living in California during those six years is estimated roughly at 1,130,000, the homicide rate would be 372 per 100,000 persons, meaning someone who lived through those years had 1 chance in 45 of being murdered. Of the 87,164 Union troops engaged at Antietam, 2,108 died. A soldier thus had 1 chance in 41 of not surviving the day.

24. Dykstra, *Cattle Towns*, 142–48; Perrigo, "Law and Order," 47. Dykstra later added two homicides to the forty-five cited in his book.

25. Dykstra, "Overdosing on Dodge City"; Dykstra, "Body Counts"; Dykstra, "Quantifying the Wild West."

26. To reach such a figure, the number of homicides is divided by the average population multiplied by the number of years over which the murders occurred, with the quotient then expanded per 100,000 adult persons. In San Luis Obispo County, California, for instance, there were 40 murders between 1850 and 1865. If that number is divided by the adult population (17,523, which is the average annual population of 1,095 multiplied by 16, for the years 1850 to 1865), and the result (.00228) is then multiplied by 100,000, the result is the homicide rate: 228. While a bit complicated, the method is a commonsensical way to measure the clip at which people killed each other, adjusting for populations and how they and the number of murders changed over time.

27. McKanna, "Enclaves of Violence," 400; Monkkonen, "Western Homicide," 609–10; Reed, "Homicide on the Nebraska Panhandle," 254.

28. McGrath, "Violence and Lawlessness," 134.

29. McKanna, "Enclaves of Violence," 400.

30. Reed, "Homicide on the Nebraska Panhandle," 149–50; Monkkonen, "Western Homicide," 610–12.

31. Prassel, *Western Peace Officer*.

32. Reed, "Homicide on the Nebraska Panhandle" 154–55; del Mar, *Beaten Down*, 49.

33. For a discussion of the West's high homicide rates in terms of social disorganization theory, see Reed, "Homicide on the Nebraska Panhandle."

34. The argument is developed in Moore, *Cow Boys and Cattle Men*.

35. Perkins, "El Campo de los Sonoraenses," 183; Paul, *Victorian Gentlewoman*, 175–78.

36. Clark, *Journals of Alfred Doten*, 858, 867, 926.

37. For an elaborated argument that California's mining towns were less a departure from American Victorian culture than a crucible for the making of it, see Roberts, *American Alchemy*.

38. Addison Crane diary, May 26, 1852, HL.

39. Solomon Gorgas, "Journal of an Overland Trip to California, 1850–1851," June 30, 1850, HL.

40. Gibbens, *This Is a Strange Country*, 88, 83, 91.

41. Harlow C. Thompson, "Across the Continent on Foot," 21, NL; C. Westover to wife, November 10, 18??, BL; Peavy and Smith, *Women in Waiting*, 33; David DeWolf to Matilda, June 17, 1849, David DeWolf letters, HL. On miners longing for distant families, see Rotter, "'Matilda for God's Sake Write.'"

42. Roberts, *American Alchemy*, 193. Roberts also has an excellent discussion of wives remaining at home, 169–95.

43. Peavy and Smith, *Women in Waiting*, 179–210.

44. Roberts, *American Alchemy*, 171, 174–76, 189–91, 194.

45. Peavy and Smith, *Women in Waiting*, 39.

46. For a rare look at this understudied aspect of the much studied Civil War, see Leonard, *Yankee Women*.
47. Armitage, "Household Work."
48. Anne Jones Davies diary, September 15, 1882, to March 1, 1883, KHS. She provided 60 percent of the family income.
49. Linnaeus B. Rauck interview, 41/158–59, Indian-Pioneer Collection, OHS.
50. O'Kieffe, *Western Story*, 36–37; Blanche McCullough interview, SWC. On the essential roles of women in household production on the agrarian frontier, see Riley, "'Not Gainfully Employed.'"
51. Clappe, *Shirley Letters*, 72.
52. Lydia Walker to mother, October 2, 1872, Walker Family Papers, BL.
53. Hafen, "Diary of Mrs. A. C. Hunt." The quotation is on 169.
54. Bargo, "Women's Occupations."
55. Underwood, "Pace of Their Own Lives"; Riley, *Building and Breaking Families*, 137–38; West, *Growing Up with the Country*, 179–210.
56. The numbers are based on summaries in Bargo, "Women's Occupations."
57. The best survey of western prostitution is Butler, *Daughters of Joy*. For a discussion of the earlier literature, see West, "Scarlet West." For two state and five localized studies, see Nichols, *Prostitution, Polygamy*; MacKell, *Brothels, Bordellos and Bad Girls*; Goldman, *Gold Diggers*; Leonard and Walliman, "Prostitution and Changing Morality"; Petrik, "Capitalists with Rooms"; Barnhart, *Fair but Frail*.
58. James and Raymond, *Comstock Women*, 318.
59. Petrik, "Queens of the Silver Dollar," 113.
60. Nichols, *Prostitution, Polygamy*, 64; Butler, *Daughters of Joy*, 15.
61. Of forty-five prostitutes in the 1880 census for Laramie and Cheyenne, Wyoming Territory, eighteen, or 40 percent, were listed as married. Petrik, "Queens of the Silver Dollar," 119–20.
62. On procurement in San Francisco, including through international networks, see Jonathan Cordero, "White Girls for Red Lights."
63. In Montana's early fluid economy, by one study, as many as one prostitute in three acquired enough wherewithal to move up in society and out of the business, if they chose to. Petrik, "Queens of the Silver Dollar," 117.
64. Nichols, *Prostitution, Polygamy*, 68.
65. Nichols, *Prostitution, Polygamy*, 68; Irey, "Social History," 235; Butler, *Daughters of Joy*, 68; Clark, *Journals of Alfred Doten*, 976.
66. Lillard, "Literate Woman," 88; West, *Growing up with the Country*, 67, 69.
67. De Pew, "William A. Hammill."
68. There is a considerable literature on women homesteaders: Patterson-Black, "Women Homesteaders"; Bauman, "Single Women Homesteaders"; Garceau, "Single Women Homesteaders"; Harris, *Long Vistas*; Hensley, *Staking Her Claim*; Lindgren, *Land in Her Own Name*. On the General Land Office's evolving approach toward homesteading women, see Muhn, "Women and the Homestead Act."
69. Edwards et al., *Homesteading the Plains*, 129–40; Harris, *Long Vistas*, 78; Bauman, "Single Women Homesteaders," 52–53.

70. Garceau, "Single Women Homesteaders," 12–16.
71. Stewart, *Letters of a Woman Homesteader*, 215.
72. For a fascinating tracing and unraveling of Stewart's story, see Smith, "Single Women Homesteaders."
73. Edwards et al., *Homesteading the Plains*, 148–50.
74. Matsuda, "West and the Legal State of Women"; Kahn, *Democratization of Invention.*
75. Browne, *Report of the Debates*, 259, 268, 264, 258–59.
76. August, "Spread of Community-Property Law"; Schuele, "Community Property Law"; McMurray, "Beginnings of the Community Property System."
77. Riley, *Building and Breaking Families*, 116–17; Griswold, *Family and Divorce in California*, 78–79, 28; Griswold, "Apart but Not Adrift."
78. Bennett, *Boom Town Boy*, 25–26. Desertion was common enough in rural areas to force the land office to figure how to fit abandoned wives into homestead law. Muhn, "Women and the Homestead Act," 301–7.
79. Flora Edna Hunter to "Dear Friends," October 17, 1879; fragment, November 1879; to "Dear Friends," April 18, 1880; to "Dear Friends," May 11, 1880; to "Friends at home," September 5, 1880, Henry S. Chrisman Collection, NSHS. My thanks to Steve Schecter for alerting me to this collection.
80. Lewis, *Effects of White Contact*, 38–40.
81. For various views on how the experience of Plains Indian women changed, see Liberty, "Hell Came with Horses"; Albers, "Sioux Women in Transition"; Klein, "Political-Economy of Gender"; Beyreis, "'If You Had Fought Bravely'"; Medicine, "'Warrior Women.'"
82. The term is from Jameson, "Bringing It All Back Home," 191.
83. Hurtado, *Intimate Frontiers*, 87–88.
84. Virginia City *Territorial Enterprise*, June 14, July 30, 1872; Hattori, "'And Some of Them Swear.'"
85. The evolving relations between Natives and newcomers as seen through the lens of family is a pervasive theme in a brilliant reexamination of the history of the West before the Civil War: Hyde, *Empires, Nations, and Families.*
86. Swagerty, "Marriage and Settlement Patterns"; Faragher, "Americans, Mexicans, Metis"; West, *Way to the West*, 119–22; Sarah Hively journal, May 5, 1863, DPL.
87. Hurtado, "Sex, Gender, Culture," 15.
88. Ann Braude, "Baptism of a Cheyenne Girl."
89. Blackwood, "Sexuality and Gender."
90. On Hispanic women in the Southwest, with particular attention to intermarriages, see Myres, "Mexican Americans and Westering Anglos"; Dysart, "Mexican Women in San Antonio"; Miller, "Cross-Cultural Marriages"; Trulio, "Anglo-American Attitudes."
91. González, *Refusing the Favor*, 40, 45.
92. Lecompte, "La Tules and the Americans"; Cook, *Doña Tules.*
93. Montoya, *Translating Property*, 63–68; Riley, *Building and Breaking Families*, 95–99; Johnson, "Sharing Bed and Board"; Jagodinsky, "Territorial Bonds."

94. Sinn, *Pacific Crossing*, 222–23.

95. Sinn, *Pacific Crossing*, 221–26; McKeown, "Transnational Chinese Families."

96. Hom, *Songs of Gold Mountain*, 146.

97. Peffer, *If They Don't*, 6. Three scholars on this topic have set the number of Chinese prostitutes in the city in 1870 at 1,426, 1,452, and 1,565. I have used the average of the three: 1,481. Peffer, *If They Don't*, 124n13. A study of Chinese women in Virginia City, Nevada, estimates that at least one in four listed as prostitutes was in fact a concubine or second wife. Chung, "Their Changing World," 208–9.

98. On Chinese prostitution, see especially Tong, *Unsubmissive Women*; Peffer, *If They Don't*; Hirata, "Free, Indentured, Enslaved."

99. Hirata, "Free, Indentured, Enslaved," 16–18.

100. Tong, *Unsubmissive Women*, 21; Zhu, *Chinaman's Chance*, 119.

101. On the Page Act, see Abrams, "Polygamy, Prostitution"; Peffer, "Forbidden Families"; Chan, "Exclusion of Chinese Women."

102. Abrams, "Polygamy, Prostitution," 700–701.

103. Abrams, "Polygamy, Prostitution," 702. For the decision, see 103 U.S. 581–611.

Part 3. Worked into Being

1. Clarence Mayo to family, April 18, May 2, May 5, May 8, June 2, June 10, July 2, July 13, August 15, September 9, October 3, 1880, C. H. Mayo papers, HL.

2. White, *The Organic Machine*; White, "'Are You an Environmentalist,'" 171–85.

3. Ingersoll, "From the Fraser to the Columbia," 871.

4. *Corbett, Hoye & Co.'s 5th Annual Denver City Directory*; *Corbett, Hoye, & Co.'s Directory of the City of Denver*.

16. Cattle and the New America

1. For a fine recent interpretive history of ranching and the emergence of the beef industry see Specht, *Red Meat Republic*.

2. Isenberg, *Mining California*, 109.

3. Hackel, *Children of Coyote*, 67–74.

4. Cleland, *Cattle on a Thousand Hills*, 103–9; Atkinson, "Cattle Drives"; Jensen, "Cattle Drives from the Ranchos"; Gates, *California Ranchos*, 17–21; *Governor's Annual Message*, 25.

5. Jordan, *North American Cattle-Ranching Frontiers*, 245–47; Burcham, *California Range Land*; Isenberg, *Mining California*, 123.

6. Isenberg, *Mining California*, 122–23; Cleland, *Cattle on a Thousand Hills*, 109–14.

7. Gates, *California Ranchos*, 23.

8. Burcham, *California Range Land*, 123–24; Burcham, "Cattle and Range Forage," 142–43.

9. Westerly fronts coming inland from the Pacific are heavy with moisture and bring considerable precipitation until they are wrung dry as they rise up the Coastal Range. Where they bring it, however, varies usually by season. During the summer a large anticyclonic—a high pressure system—cell typically moves from a thousand or so miles out in the Pacific eastward across northern California, blocking the moist fronts from moving southward and leaving central and

Southern California with little rainfall. Then, in the late fall and winter, the cell turns and moves southwestward, out to sea, effectively opening the door for rain-bearing fronts to come ashore farther south and water the country that had been left dry for several months. Through adaptation the grasses in that region have their growing seasons from roughly November to March and April. Their growth season, that is, ends as that of grasses east of the Rocky Mountains begins. Cattlemen working by eastern standards thus pastured their cattle for fattening just as annual grasses were dying off. California's nutritious perennial grasses were especially vulnerable. To survive over the dry summers, they rely on reserves stored in their roots. Summer grazing taxed those reserves, often fatally. The consequence was replacement of most of those perennials by invasive weedy annuals, part of a wider degeneration of California range forage. Burcham, *California Range Land*, 71–73; Burcham, "Cattle and Range Forage," 147.

10. Burcham, "Cattle and Range Forage," 148.
11. Brewer, *Up and Down California* (2003), 243.
12. Igler, *Industrial Cowboys*, 22–25; Isenberg, *Destruction of the Bison*, 124–25; Cleland, *Cattle on a Thousand Hills*, 127–30.
13. Brewer, *Up and Down California* (2003), 509–10. Isenberg, *Mining California*, 136; Cleland, *Cattle on a Thousand Hills*, 134.
14. Cleland, *Cattle on a Thousand Hills*, 131.
15. Isenberg, *Mining California*, 123.
16. Wickson, *Rural California*, 216–17; Jordan, *North American Cattle-Ranching Frontiers*, 246–47.
17. The essential study of Miller and Lux is Igler, *Industrial Cowboys*.
18. William Miller was born Heinrich Alfred Kreiser. The one story of his name change has it that he was offered a nontransferable steamer ticket to California by a friend, Henry Miller. Anxious to get to the gold country and worried about having the ticket canceled, he assumed Miller's name and never reverted to Heinrich Kreiser. The story may be true. Igler, *Industrial Cowboys*, 15–16.
19. Igler, *Industrial Cowboys*, 16–17; Clay, *My Life on the Range*, 27.
20. Gates, "Public Land Disposal," 172; Igler, *Industrial Cowboys*, 88.
21. Fischer, *Cattle Colonialism*.
22. An essential work is Towne and Wentworth, *Shepherd's Empire*. For an extensive bibliography on the subject, there is Etulain, *Sheep and Sheepmen*.
23. Wentworth, "Eastward Sheep Drives."
24. Saitua, *Basque Immigrants*; Warrin, "Immigrant Path to Social Mobility."
25. Horowitz, *Putting Meat*, 18.
26. USCD Serial Set 1266, 69.
27. Skaggs, *Prime Cut*, 51–52.
28. Cronon, *Nature's Metropolis*, 225–30; Corey, *Meat and Man*, 37–29; Horowitz, *Putting Meat*, 43–48.
29. Cronon, *Nature's Metropolis*, 207–13, 220–23.
30. Dale, *Range Cattle Industry*, 26.
31. Jordan, *North American Cattle-Ranching Frontiers*, 215–17.

32. McCoy, *Historic Sketches*, 94.

33. McCoy, *Historic Sketches*, 44.

34. Webb, *Great Plains*, 222–23.

35. Shannon, *Farmer's Last Frontier*, 199.

36. Gard, *Chisholm Trail*; Worcester, *Chisholm Trail*; Dary, *Cowboy Culture*, 168–97; Dykstra, *Cattle Towns*; Haley, *Charles Goodnight*, 198–216.

37. Osgood, *Day of the Cattleman*, 131.

38. Gordon, "Report on Cattle," 21; Skaggs, *Prime Cut*, 55; Nimmo, *Report in Regard to the Range*, 28.

39. Jordan, *North American Cattle-Ranching Frontiers*, 208.

40. Abbott and Smith, *We Pointed Them North*, 60.

41. Westermeier, *Trailing the Cowboy*, 23.

42. Two early works estimated that up to a third of the drovers were African American or Mexican, but later, more careful work has revised that figure dramatically downward. Quintard Taylor, the leading authority on African Americans in the West, shows that even in Texas Black cowboys made up only about 4 percent of the ranching work force in 1880. The portion on cattle drives was likely below even that. Durham and Jones, *Negro Cowboys*, 44–45; Porter, "Negro Labor"; Taylor, *In Search of the Racial Frontier*, 156–58.

43. Abbott and Smith, *We Pointed Them North*, 63.

44. "Driving Cattle from Texas to Iowa."

45. Lomax, *Cowboy Songs*, 231–32.

46. Dary, *Cowboy Culture*, 193.

47. Skaggs, *Cattle-Trailing Industry*, 27–40.

48. Skaggs, *Cattle-Trailing Industry*, 3.

49. Skaggs, *Cattle-Trailing Industry*, 13–26, 33–39.

50. Skaggs, *Cattle-Trailing Industry*, 13–17, 63, 66–67; Emmett, *Shanghai Pierce*.

51. Jordan, *North American Cattle-Ranching Frontiers*, 220.

52. Murrah, *C. C. Slaughter*, 4–9; Haley, *Charles Goodnight*, 14–32.

53. On the key figure in the birth of cattle ranching in Montana and in Montana development, see Milner and O'Connor, *As Big as the West*.

54. Nimmo, *Report in Regard to the Range*, 170–74; Jackson, *Enterprising Scot*, 74; Frink et al., *When Grass Was King*, 235; Dale, *Cow Country*, 93–94.

55. Gordon, "Report on Cattle," 47–74. The numbers for 1870 included cattle on farms, those for 1880 on both ranches and farms.

56. "Recollections of Joseph E. Ray on Friends and Fillmore," HL; Walker, "Longhorns Come to Utah."

57. Jordan, *North American Cattle-Ranching Frontiers*, 222.

58. Hunter, *Trail Drivers of Texas*, 411–13.

59. Latham, *Trans-Missouri Stock Raising*, 6; Strahorn, *Hand-Book of Wyoming*, 28–31, 35.

60. Jackson, *Enterprising Scot*, 75.

61. Gressley, *Bankers and Cattlemen*, 69–71, 75.

62. Haley, *XIT Ranch*; Duke and Frantz, *6,000 Miles of Fence*.

63. Clay, *My Life on the Range*, 131.
64. Jackson, *Enterprising Scot*, 75–83; Mothershead, *Swan Land and Cattle Company*.
65. All of the many full biographies of Roosevelt treat his time in the Dakotas. See especially Silvestro, *Theodore Roosevelt in the Badlands*; White, *Eastern Establishment*; Jenkinson, *Free and Hardy Life*.
66. Andrews, *Splendid Pauper*; Rico, *Nature's Noblemen*, 45–82.
67. Von Richtofen, *Cattle-Raising on the Plains*, 12–14, 91.
68. Gressley, *Bankers and Cattlemen*, 109. The amount represented money pledged, not truly invested.
69. Brisbin, *Beef Bonanza*, 27.
70. Stuart, *Forty Years on the Frontier*, 327.
71. Wilkeson, "Cattle-Raising on the Plains," 792–93.
72. Jackson, *Enterprising Scot*, 78.
73. The standard work is McCallum and McCallum, *Wire That Fenced the West*.
74. The government had given railroads alternate sections along the right of way to sell, with the other alternate sections retained by the government. A rancher could buy alternating railroad sections and fence along one border, stop when he reached an adjoining government section, leave a gap of a few inches and continue fencing along the border of the next one he owned. The rancher's fence was entirely on land he owned, yet the effect was to enclose twice that, often tens of thousands of acres, and to leave the public land wholly within his private hands. A court challenge in Wyoming confirmed the ranchers' right to the strategy. Osgood, *Day of the Cattleman*, 212–14.
75. Wheeler, "Texas Panhandle Drift Fences," 25–35.
76. Osgood, *Day of the Cattleman*, 218–19.
77. USCD Serial Set 2362, 535.
78. Stuart, *Forty Years on the Frontier*, 227.
79. The best summary of the calamity of 1886 on the southern plains is Wheeler, "Blizzard of 1886."
80. On the devastating winter of 1886–87, see Rackley, "Hard Winter 1886–1887"; Fletcher, "Hard Winter in Montana"; Howard, 157–61.
81. Abbott and Smith, *We Pointed Them North*, 176.
82. Osgood, *Day of the Cattleman*, 219–21; Dale, *Range Cattle Industry*, 108–10.
83. The mix of anecdotal evidence and harder numbers, plus unreliable figures for the cattle population prior to the winter and what was clearly a checkered story of much heavier losses in some places than others, leave estimates all over the place. A study of Wyoming suggests losses at somewhat above 15 percent, while the cost elsewhere, as in Montana, was clearly higher. There the assessed number of cattle declined by 30 percent between 1886 and 1887. Larson, "Winter of 1886–87."
84. Von Richtofen, *Cattle-Raising on the Plains*, 54.
85. Jackson, *Enterprising Scot*, 121.
86. *Cheyenne Daily Sun*, November 3, 1887.
87. Gordon, "Report on Cattle," 74; U.S. Census Bureau, *Statistical Atlas of the United States*, 459.

88. For a description of the midwestern system and its rise to dominance, not just on the plains but across the West, see Jordan, *North American Cattle-Ranching Frontiers*, 267–307.

17. Wind, Fever, and Indians Unhorsed

1. Coffin, *Winds*.
2. Only in 1883 did the maps show coverage coast to coast. The first was in *Monthly Weather Review*, 11, no. 1 (January 1883). The *Review* continues to be published today. Whitnah, *History of the Weather Bureau*.
3. Schott, *Tables and Results*, 120.
4. Powell, *Report on the Lands*, vii.
5. Stegner, *Beyond the Hundredth Meridian*, 212.
6. Ward, *Practical Exercises*, 11–46.
7. Harrington, *History of the Weather Map*, 327.
8. Robinson, "Telegraph and the Weather Service," 146.
9. See the influential essay, originally published in 1856, Ferrel, "Essay on the Winds." On Ferrel, see Abbe, *Memoir of William Ferrel*.
10. Russell, "Prediction of Cold-Waves."
11. Garriott, "Types of Storms."
12. USCD Serial Set 830, 363–70; *Sailing Directions*.
13. Bent, *Bent Family*, 128–29; Johnson, *Dictionary of American Biography*, 206.
14. Bent, "Meteorology."
15. On anxiety in Illinois and other midwestern areas used for fattening Texas cattle, see Hoganson, "Meat in the Middle," 71–74.
16. Mohler, *Texas or Tick Fever*, 124–25; Havins, "Texas Fever."
17. Zissner, *Biographical Memoir*; Hall, "Theobald Smith."
18. On the relative contributions of the several investigators, see *Proceedings of the American Veterinary Medical Association*, 266–69; Hall, "Theobald Smith," 235–39.
19. Smith and Kilbourne, *Investigation*, 105.
20. Mohler, *Texas or Tick Fever*, 21–23.
21. Smith and Kilbourne, *Investigation*, 105.
22. Kruif, *Microbe Hunters*, 250.
23. Zissner, *Biographical Memoir*, 272.
24. Cox, "History of the Discovery"; Ross, *Prevention of Malaria*, 14.
25. On yellow fever, its ravages, and the solving of its origin and transmission, see, among other works, Dickerson, *Yellow Fever*; Crosby, *American Plague*; Pierce and Writer, *Yellow Jack*; Keith, *Fever Season*; Bean, *Walter Reed*.
26. At the end of 1893, the year Smith and Kilbourne's report was published, Reed wrote to Smith to ask, "Would it be asking too much, if I should beg a copy of your paper?" Walter Reed to Theobald Smith, December 5, 1893, Philip S. Henry Walter Reed Yellow Fever Collection, University of Virginia Library.
27. Gorgas, *Sanitation in Panama*.
28. Hedren, *After Custer*, 113.

29. Hämäläinen, *Comanche Empire*, 303; Anderson, *Conquest of Texas*, 342; Schoolcraft, *Information*, 702.

30. Hämäläinen, *Comanche Empire*, 303–23; Anderson, *Conquest of Texas*, 302–26.

31. Hämäläinen, *Comanche Empire*, 315–20.

32. Hämäläinen, *Comanche Empire*, 317–19; Anderson, *Conquest of Texas*, 357.

33. Hämäläinen, *Comanche Empire*, 329.

34. Wallace, "Ranald S. Mackenzie," 144–46.

35. *Papers relating to Talks and Councils*, 60.

36. Grinnell, *Fighting Cheyennes*, 318.

37. West, *Last Indian War*, 170–74, 292–93.

38. USCD Serial Set 1800, 448–49.

39. USCD Serial Set 1899, 4–5; Berthrong, *Cheyenne and Arapaho*, 25; Hoig, *Perilous Pursuit*, 30–32.

40. USCD Serial Set 1680, 775; Pierce, *Most Promising*, 170–71; Hagan, *United States–Comanche Relations*, 128.

41. *ARCIA*, 1878, 35.

42. For an essay on the nutritional effects on Indians of substituting cattle for bison, and also on the substitution's negative effects on the grazing of pastures, see Barsh, "Substitution."

43. USCD Serial Set 2174, 261–62.

44. USCD Serial Set 2174, 59, 63.

45. USCD Serial Set 1899, 39. The Cheyenne and Arapaho agency census of 1883 listed 6,139 persons. Assuming a family numbered between 5 and 7 persons, the number of cattle needed to provide 6 to 8 animals per family would range from 5,262 to 9,822. *ARCIA*, 1883, 60.

46. *ARCIA*, 1882, 66. Taking Whirlwind's estimate that 8 cows would be needed per family to get ranching under way, and assuming 6 persons per family, an agency would need 1.33 cows per person. The report of the commissioner of Indian affairs for 1882 showed 0.52 cattle per person on the Cheyenne and Arapaho reservation, 0.61 per person on the Lakotas' Pine Ridge Reservation, and 0.11 per person on their Rosebud Reservation.

47. USCD Serial Set 1899, 4–5, 29, 34; USCD Serial Set 2174, 159.

48. USCD Serial Set 2018, 138; USCD Serial Set 2174, 58.

49. Dale, *Range Cattle Industry*, 79n.

50. For an egregious example, see Specht, *Red Meat Republic*, 49–50.

51. USCD Serial Set 2165, 59–60.

52. Dale, "Ranching"; Hagan, "Kiowas, Comanches, and Cattlemen"; Hagan, *Quanah Parker*, 91–117.

53. Dale, "Cherokees in the Confederacy," 48.

54. Berthrong, *Cheyenne and Arapaho Ordeal*, 105.

55. USCD Serial Set 2165, 54.

56. Eastman, *From the Deep Woods*, 80.

57. *ARCIA*, 1892, 454.

58. Wickson, *Rural California*, 215.

59. Latham, *Trans-Missouri*, 5.

18. Breaking the Land

1. Farm acreage in Kansas and California grew by 53,408,000 acres between 1870 to 1900. The increase was 45,652,000 acres for the other states (Maine, New Hampshire, Vermont, Massachusetts, Rhode Island, Connecticut, New York, New Jersey, Pennsylvania, Ohio, Indiana, Illinois, Michigan, Wisconsin, Delaware, Maryland, Virginia, West Virginia, North Carolina, South Carolina, Georgia, and Florida). U.S. Census Bureau, *Historical Statistics*, part 1, 460.
2. Powell, *Report on the Lands*, 3–4.
3. *Centennial Edition*, 26.
4. U.S. Census Bureau, *Historical Statistics*, part 1, 459–60.
5. *Manual of the Railroads*, v.
6. A reported 152,000 metric tons of wheat were exported in 1866, and in 1880, 4,170,000 metric tons. Between 1870 and 1880, wheat and flour exports rose from about 50,000,000 to more than 180,000,000 bushels. Mitchell, *International Historical Statistics*, 167, 279; Rothstein, "American West," 298.
7. *Fourth Annual Report*, 27.
8. On state and territorial efforts to promote immigration, see Hansen, "Official Encouragement"; Zabel, "To Reclaim the Wilderness"; Henke, "Imagery"; Blodgett, "Colorado Territorial Board."
9. Walther and Taylor, *Resources and Advantages*, 26; Walther, *State of Nebraska*, 5; *Nebraska: A Sketch of Its History*, 9–10; Batchelder, "Sketch of the History."
10. Overton, *Burlington West*, 159; Emmons, *Garden in the Grasslands*, 35–37; Hedges, "Colonization Work," 315–16.
11. Donaldson, *Public Domain*, 350.
12. Raney, "Timber Culture Acts."
13. The figure is based on the land office being open five days a week for eight hours a day. Fite, *Farmer's Frontier*, 36.
14. Decker, "Great Speculation," 376–77.
15. Gates, "Homestead Act in an Incongruous Land System."
16. *Public Aids to Transportation*, 107–15.
17. Between 1862 and 1871, Washington granted railroads six acres for every one taken to final entry as homesteads. White, *Railroaded*, 24–25; Donaldson, *Public Domain*, 355; Julian, "Railway Influence," 252.
18. A report from the General Land Office in 1888, based on reports from land office across the West and elsewhere, details the various speculative uses of the land laws. My thanks to David Wishart for notice of this source and others used in this section. *Annual Report of the Commissioner of the General Land Office*, 46–91.
19. USCD Serial Set 2378, 205. By further manipulating the law, a timber entryman could hold the land for up to thirteen years. McIntosh, "Use and Abuse," 355, 360.
20. LeDuc, "State Disposal," 399.
21. Gates, *History of Public Land Law*, 443.
22. Donaldson, *Public Domain*, 1220; McIntosh, "Use and Abuse," 353.

23. Decker, "Great Speculation," 375; Edwards et al., *Homesteading the Plains*, 189–93; Ruede, *Sod-House Days*, 212.

24. Estimates were that at least half Kansas farms in the late 1880s were mortgaged and three out of four in the Dakotas. USCD Serial Set 2405, 423; Brewer, "Eastern Money"; Mappin, "Farm Mortgage"; Spearman, "Great American Desert," 239–40.

25. Gleed, "Western Lands," 470; USCD Serial Set 2636, 66; Decker, "Great Speculation," 366–68, 375–78.

26. Spearman, "Great American Desert," 238; Sokolofsky, "Success and Failure," 108.

27. For an argument by a leading historian that land-jobbers have played as valued a role in expansion as "ax-swinging pioneers," and a fine survey of the literature on the role and impact of speculation and speculators, see Billington, "Origin of the Land Speculator," 204–12, and Swierenga, "Land Speculation."

28. USCD Serial Set 2378, 202.

29. Edwards et al., *Homesteading the Plains*, 25–29.

30. *Public Aids to Transportation*, 107–11.

31. Gates, "Homestead Act: Free Land Policy," 38–39. For insights into this process and a classic study showing the sequence from rapid turnover in farm population gradually toward stability, see Malin, "Turnover of Farm Population."

32. Bancroft, *Works*, vol. 33, 65–66.

33. J. D. Hoppe to son, January 28, February 13, 1853, Jacob D. Hoppe Letters, Special Collections, University of North Carolina Library, Chapel Hill, North Carolina.

34. Robert La Motte to mother, December 16, 1850, La Motte Family Papers, BaL; Henry Sheldon Anable journal, September 12, 13, 1852, BaL; John Eagle to Margaret, July 10, 1853, John H. Eagle Letters, HL.

35. Wickson, *California Vegetables*, 11–12; Vaught, *After the Gold Rush*.

36. Nimmo, *Report in Regard to the Range*, 29.

37. Paul, "Beginnings of Agriculture," 17–18; Engstrand, *Wolfskill*; McGinty, *Haraszthy at the Mint*; Haraszthy, *Grape Culture*; Schoenman, *Father of California Wine*, 13–37.

38. *Tenth Census of the United States, 1880*, vol. 3, *Agriculture*, 6, 13, 17.

39. Brock, *Report on the Internal Commerce*, xxxiv, xli, xxxiv, xli, 1108.

40. Brock, *Report on the Internal Commerce*, 350; Bates, *American Marine*, 162.

41. Brewer, "Report on the Cereal Production," 386.

42. Nimmo, *Report in Regard to the Range*, 30–31.

43. "Immense Wheat Farms," *Pacific Rural Press*, September 7, 1872.

44. Walker, *Conquest of Bread*, 164.

45. Walker, *Conquest of Bread*, 133.

46. For a useful summary, see Olmstead and Rhode, "Overview."

47. Wik, "Some Interpretations," 78.

48. Rogin, *Introduction of Farm Machinery*; Schlebecker, "Combine Made in Stockton," 21.

49. Davis, "Wheat in California," 449.

50. On the remarkable Friedlander, see Paul, "Wheat Trade"; Vaught, *After the Gold Rush*.

51. Vaught, *After the Gold Rush*, 150–51.
52. *New York Times*, July 20, 1878; Paul, "Great California Grain War," 164.
53. *New York Times*, April 16, 1877, May 4, 1877, July 20, 1878; Vaught, *After the Gold Rush*, 165.
54. Meinig, "Wheat Sacks Out to Sea," 13–18; Meinig, *Great Columbia Plain*, 224–26, 251, 498–500. The quotation is from "Wheat Sacks," 14.
55. Meinig, *Great Columbia Plain*, 201–61. The quotation is on 248.
56. *Tenth Census of the United States, 1880*, vol. 3, *Agriculture*, 6, 13.
57. The comparisons are between exports from San Francisco as recorded for 1869 and 1877, those for the United States during the same years, and the average annual value of exports from New York City, New Orleans, Boston, Philadelphia, Baltimore, and Galveston, 1871–80. Brock, *Report on the Internal Commerce*, 1120–21; U.S. Census Bureau, *Historical Statistics*, part 1, 885; Smith, *Port of New York*, 114.
58. Brock, *Report on the Internal Commerce*, lxxxviii–lxxxix.
59. U.S. Census Bureau, *Historical Statistics*, part 1, 460–63.
60. USCD Serial Set 1446, 16; Miller, *Soldiers and Settlers*, 61.
61. Miller, *Soldiers and Settlers*, 131–32; Frazer, *Forts and Supplies*, 187; USCD Serial Set 1911, 447.
62. Arrington, *Great Basin Kingdom*, 61.
63. Arrington, *Great Basin Kingdom*, 148–52.
64. Arrington, *History of Idaho*, 276.
65. Bagley, *Frontiersman*, 262; Bigler and Bagley, *Army of Israel*, 445–46; Thomas, *Early Irrigation*, 50–55.
66. Clyde, "History of Irrigation," 29; Brough, *Irrigation in Utah*, 75–76, 81.
67. For a useful overview of the development of Mormon irrigation, see Arrington and May, "'Different Mode of Life.'"
68. Nelson, *Mormon Village*.
69. Abruzzi, "Ecology, Resource Redistribution."
70. Bitton and Wilcox, "Transformation," 65–68.
71. *Gazetteer of Utah*, 43–44.
72. Arrington, *Great Basin Kingdom*, 205–11.
73. For an excellent study of one such colony in Alpine, Utah, in comparison to two other non-Mormon western settlements, see May, *Three Frontiers*.
74. Arrington, *Great Basin Kingdom*, 61.
75. Steinel, *History of Agriculture*, 124–30.
76. West, *Contested Plains*, 253; *Resources of Colorado*, 12; Steinel, *History of Agriculture*, 50–51; Wyckoff, *Creating Colorado*, 127.
77. May, *Three Frontiers*, 97.
78. Schwantes, *In Mountain Shadows*, 96–97.
79. Leeson, *History of Montana*, 851; Coon, "Influence of the Gold Camps," 590–93; Arrington, *Great Basin Kingdom*, 61.
80. Leeson, *History of Montana*, 607–8.
81. May, *Three Frontiers*, 97–101; May, "Middleton's Agriminers."

82. Olmstead and Rhode, "Overview," 94, 102.

83. Drache, *Day of the Bonanza.*

84. U.S. Bureau of the Census, *Ninth Census,* vol. 3, 81, 367. The scores that were the basis of the rankings were found by dividing a county's production in bushels, first, by the county population and, second, by its number of improved acres. The two quotients were multiplied by each other. The score was the square root of the product.

19. Domination and Extinction

1. *ARCIA*, 1872, 9, 11, 14.

2. Morgan, *Ancient Society,* 4–12. The quote is on 4.

3. Although they vary somewhat in themes and opinions, there are several excellent surveys of Indian policy during these years. See Hoxie, *Final Promise*; Fritz, *Movement*; Prucha, *American Indian Policy*; Priest, *Uncle Sam's Stepchildren*; Keller, *American Protestantism.*

4. Vattel, *Law of Nations,* 35–36.

5. Hagan, "Private Property," 126–28.

6. *Proceedings of the Thirteenth Annual Meeting,* 36–37.

7. USCD Serial Set 1337, 4.

8. Prucha, *American Indian Policy,* 14–16; Prucha, *Great Father,* 485–86.

9. USCD Serial Set 1279; USCD Serial Set 1337.

10. USCD Serial Set 1337, 16.

11. USCD Serial Set 1337, 7, 16–17.

12. Kappler, *Indian Affairs,* 984–89, 998–1007, 1012–25.

13. *ARCIA*, 1881, 46.

14. Hebard, *Washakie,* 81–140.

15. *ARCIA*, 1876, 153; Arrowsmith, "Teaching and the Liberal Arts," 3.

16. "Grievances of the Nez Perces: Speeches of Shadow of the Mountain, or Lawyer (Head Chief,) and Gov. Lyon, at Lewiston, Idaho Territory, August 23st, 1864," Broadside, BL.

17. *ARCIA*, 1874, 248; *ARCIA*, 1875, 288, 91, 89, 214, 270.

18. *ARCIA*, 1870, 219–20; *ARCIA*, 1876, 23; *ARCIA*, 1881, 46–47.

19. *Tenth Census of the United States,* vol. 3, 159; *ARCIA*, 1880, iii. Economist Leonard Carlson argues that reservation farming before allotment was more successful than scholars have recognized. His figures, however, confirm the limited amount of land under cultivation by 1880. Carlson, "Learning to Farm"; Carlson, *Indians, Bureaucrats, and Land.*

20. Keller, *American Protestantism,* 47–61.

21. Neill, *Effort and Failure,* 9.

22. U.S.Bureau of Indian Affairs, *Report of Board of Inquiry,* lxiii.

23. *Proceedings of the Third Annual Meeting*; Hoxie, *Final Promise,* 11–12; *ARCIA*, 1880, xvii.

24. On the Dawes Act and its evolution and effects up to the turn of the century, see Otis, *Dawes Act.*

25. C. Joseph Genetin-Pilawa argues that there was considerably more debate over the course toward forced allotment and that there were viable alternatives seriously considered along the "crooked path" to the final law: Genetin-Pilawa, *Crooked Paths*.
26. Prucha, *Great Father*, 629.
27. Hoxie, *Final Promise*, 154.
28. Among the most useful of many works on allotment: Hoxie, *Final Promise*; Greenwald, *Reconfiguring*; Lewis, *Neither Wolf nor Dog*; Prucha, *Great Father*, 659–86; Black, *American Indians*, 103.
29. USCD Serial Set 1938, 10.
30. *ARCIA*, 1856, 97.
31. James, *Account of an Expedition*, 476, 480–81; McHugh, *Time of the Buffalo*, 16–17.
32. Flores, "Bison Ecology," 470–71; Isenberg, *Destruction of the Bison*, 27–29; Hornaday, *Extermination*, 535.
33. Isenberg, *Destruction of the Bison*, 130–31.
34. For three traditional and one more recent and analytical look at the hunt, see Branch, *Hunting of the Buffalo*; Gard, *Great Buffalo Hunt*; Sandoz, *Buffalo Hunters*; Isenberg, *Destruction of the Bison*.
35. Allen, *History of the American Bison*, 67.
36. Collinson, *Life in the Saddle*, 55.
37. Hornaday, *Extermination*, 499.
38. Colpitts, *Pemmican Empire*.
39. Hornaday, *Extermination*, 509; Gard, *Great Buffalo Hunt*, 267.
40. Hornaday, *Extermination*, 498; Barnett, "Historical Geography."
41. For a vigorous exchange on this question, see Smits, "Frontier Army"; Dobak, "Army and the Buffalo"; Smits, "More on the Army."
42. Mayer and Roth, *Buffalo Harvest*, 61–62.
43. Isenberg, *Destruction of the Bison*, 156–60. A chastened Mayer laid out the financial pitfalls of the business and estimated a typical hunter was lucky to make a thousand dollars a year. Mayer and Roth, *Buffalo Harvest*, 61–67.
44. West, "Bison R Us," 221–22.
45. Dawson, "Reconsidered."
46. The estimates are from the best single source on the Rocky Mountain locusts by Jeffrey Lockwood. My numbers here are different because I have used the more reliable estimate of the bison population, twenty-eight million, rather than Lockwood's forty-five million. See Lockwood, *Locust*, 20–21, 163–64.
47. Lockwood, *Locust*, 158.
48. Lockwood, *Locust*, 21–23, 235.
49. Hayden, *Ninth Annual Report*, 614–15.
50. Frances E. Moore, "Memories of a Pioneer in Kansas," reminiscence, KHS; Crofford, "Pioneer Days," 131; Woodin, *Recollections*, 16–17; U.S. Department of the Interior, *First Annual Report of the United States Entomological Commission*, 215.
51. Lockwood, *Locust*, 48–64; U.S. Department of the Interior, *First Annual Report of the United States Entomological Commission*, 350–420.

52. Lockwood, *Locust*, 39–43.

53. Lockwood, *Locust*, 86.

54. Riley also published a report under his own name that summarized much of the first commission report. Riley, *Locust Plague*.

55. John Wesley Powell had found that the years when grasshoppers were abundant were times of "many festivities" as basin Indians gathered and roasted these "very great delicacies," and archeologists later determined that an hour's gathering of drowned grasshoppers along the Great Salt Lake equaled the caloric value of forty-three McDonald's Big Mac hamburgers. Madsen, "Grasshopper in Every Pot," 22–25; Fowler et al., *John Wesley Powell*, 26. A few years later a controversial short book appeared in England in favor of insect-eating, or entomophagy. Holt, *Why Not Eat Insects?*

56. U.S. Department of the Interior, *First Annual Report of the United States Entomological Commission*, 437–43.

57. Leeson, *History of Montana*, 607–8.

58. On this point and on the implications for current policy, see Lockwood, "Fate of the Rocky Mountain Locust." Isenberg, *Destruction of the Bison*, 156–60.

20. When the West Turned Inside Out

1. Kent Curtis makes the point forcefully: "Gold rushes were not caused by gold discoveries, but rather . . . gold 'discoveries' were produced by far-flung ambitions of an expansionist nation." Curtis, "Producing a Gold Rush." The quote is on 278.

2. Bernstein, *Power of Gold*, 219–29; Mountford and Tuffnell, *Global History*.

3. *Scientific American* (September 20, 1879, 177) has a brief article on Edison's platinum hopes. He thought he might get three thousand pounds annually from a single site by using Chinese labor. See also Lingenfelter, *Bonanzas and Borrascas*, 320–22.

4. For descriptions of the basics of placer mining, see Young, *Western Mining*, 108–24; Paul, *California Gold*, 50–66; Rohe, "Origins and Diffusion." The quote is in Carson, *Recollections*, 6.

5. Borthwick, *Three Years*, 122–23.

6. Rohe, "Origins and Diffusion," 141.

7. Paul, *California Gold*, 150–51.

8. J. C. Coates to Jane S. Coates, Letter, August 6, 1852, HL.

9. Rodman W. Paul, *California Gold*, 149. California's state mineralogist examined records to two companies and found the ratio of gravel to mined gold varied from more than 1.6 million to about 12 million to 1. *Second Report of the State Mineralogist*, 115–16.

10. For accounts of the early development of hydraulic mining, see Kelley, "Forgotten Giant" 343–56; Paul, *California Gold*, 152–60; Isenberg, *Mining California*, 23–51; Rohe, "Hydraulicking in the American West," 18–35; Young, *Western Mining*, 125–39.

11. May, *Origins of Hydraulic Mining*.

12. *Second Report of the State Mineralogist*, 73.

13. Browne and Taylor, *Reports upon the Mineral Resources*, 23.

14. Kelley, "Forgotten Giant," 354–55; Evans, "Hydraulic Mining in California," 327–29.

15. Evans, "Hydraulic Mining in California," 335; *Second Report of the State Mineralogist*, 116.

16. Paul, *California Gold*, 160–62; Isenberg, *Mining California*, 29–30; Lingenfelter, *Bonanzas and Borrascas*, 74–77; Holliday, *Rush for Riches*, 204–6; Evans, "Hydraulic Mining in California," 333–34.

17. The standard work now is Johnston, *Mercury and the Making of California*. For a good brief account of mercury production, see Isenberg, *Mining California*, 47–50. See also Splitter, "Quicksilver at New Almaden"; St. Clair, "New Almaden"; *Second Report of the State Mineralogist*, 170–78.

18. For contemporary accounts, see Kuss, *Memoir*; Browne, "Down in the Cinnabar Mines"; Wells, "Quicksilver Mines."

19. Raymond, *Mining Industry*, 10–11.

20. Foote, "California Mining Camp," 480; "Quicksilver Mine of New Almaden," 103.

21. Bowie, *Practical Treatise*, 266.

22. Browne and Taylor, *Reports upon Mineral Resources*, 174–77; St. Clair, "New Almaden," 281; Bowie, *Practical Treatise*, 244.

23. A French company estimated the labor cost of working a sluice to a hydraulic at six to one, a long tom at seventeen to one and a rocker at seventy to one. Browne, *Report of J. Ross Browne*, 125. See a series of charts showing gross value of gold taken compared with labor and other costs in Bowie, *Practical Treatise*, 279.

24. Evans, "Hydraulic Mining in California," 334–35; *Second Report of the State Mineralogist*, 170.

25. *Second Report of the State Mineralogist*, 80; Bowie, *Practical Treatise*, 264; Farley, "Yuba Hydraulic Mines," 221.

26. Lingenfelter, *Bonanzas and Borrascas*, 76.

27. Paul, *California Gold*, 155.

28. Wellington and Behre, *Ore Deposits*, 420, 427.

29. Lingenfelter, *Bonanzas and Borrascas*, 79,83, 79–83, 134–37; Young, *Western Mining*, 142–45; Paul and West, *Mining Frontiers*, 138–49; Rohe, "Origins and Diffusion."

30. Raymond, *Statistics of Mines and Mining*, 258.

31. Raymond, *Statistics of Mines and Mining*, 341.

32. Raymond, *Statistics of Mines and Mining*, 334; Young, *Western Mining*, 144–45.

33. Paul, *Mining Frontiers*, 143–44.

34. Zhu, *Chinaman's Chance*, 161–63.

35. The stories of burros-as-prospectors, clearly apocryphal, have many variations, including at least one bird dog finding gold while retrieving a pheasant. Young, *Western Mining*, 142; Wardner, *Jim Wardner*, 58, 74.

36. Moore, "Silver King"; Ed Schieffelin to Mrs. Mary Throckmorton, January 31, February 1, 1880; Ed Schieffelin to "Dear Friend," May 12, 1881; Ed Schieffelin to "Aunt Mary," November 6, 1881, Edward Schieffelin Papers, HL; Craig, *Portrait of a Prospector*.

37. Beebe and Clegg, *Legends*.

38. James, *Roar and the Silence*, 68; Peterson, "Comstock Couple," 44–49; Paine, *Eilley Orrum*.

39. James, *Roar and the Silence*, 13. On 13–20 James has an excellent explication of popular stories of James Finney and Henry Comstock and how they emerged in early histories of Virginia City and the Comstock Lode.

40. The Comstock Lode has attracted many historians. Far and away the best modern study is James, *Roar and the Silence*. Among the more notable earlier works are Lord, *Comstock*; de Quille, *History of the Big Bonanza*; Smith, *History of the Comstock Lode*; Shinn, *Story of the Mine*; Church, *Comstock Lode*.

41. Lord, *Comstock*, 311.

42. Paul and West, *Mining Frontiers*, 56–80; Becker, *Geology of the Comstock Lode*, 5.

43. King, *Report of the Geological Exploration*, vol. 3, 60.

44. James, *Roar and the Silence*, 54–56.

45. Bailey, *Supplying the Mining World*, 15; de Quille, *History of the Big Bonanza*, 121–22.

46. Young, *Western Mining*, 151–54, 214–15.

47. On the phenomenon of extreme heat in the Comstock, see Church, *Comstock Lode*, 176–220; Becker, *Geology of the Comstock Lode*, 228–66.

48. Church, *Comstock Lode*, 189.

49. Lord, *Comstock*, 394.

50. Young, *Western Mining*, 166–71; Bailey, *Supplying the Mining World*, 15–16; James, *Roar and the Silence*, 58.

51. On the Sutro tunnel, see Young, *Western Mining*, 254–60; James, *Roar and the Silence*, 88–89; Bailey, *Supplying the Mining World*, 16–17; Stewart and Stewart, *Adolph Sutro*, 191–208.

52. *Frank Leslie's Illustrated Newspaper*, March 9, 1878. The journalist in this article reported that the Consolidated Virginia used 4,800 candles daily.

53. Lord, *Comstock*, 389; Watkins, *Gold and Silver*, 209.

54. James, *Roar and the Silence*, 84–88.

55. For a summary of the trials of Comstock mining, see Lord, *Comstock*, 389–406. The table of accidents is on 404. See also de Quille, *History of the Big Bonanza*, 145–54.

56. Vrtis, "Gold Rush Ecology," 24, 26.

57. Becker, *Geology of the Comstock Lode*, 6–7. Becker estimated that in the end the Comstock's bullion was 57 percent silver and 43 percent gold.

58. Almarin Paul's story is in every worthwhile history of the Comstock. Examples: Paul and West, *Mining Frontiers*, 64–66; Smith, *History of the Comstock Lode*, 41–45; James, *Roar and the Silence*, 46–48; Bailey, *Supplying the Mining World*, 11–13; Lord, *Comstock*, 84–88. For an especially detailed description of the process and its chemistry, see Hague, *Mining Industry*, 193–293.

59. Bailey, *Supplying the Mining World*, 26.

60. Bailey, *Supplying the Mining World*, 7.

61. Twain, *Roughing It*, 233–34.

62. Ingersoll, *Crest of the Continent*, 218.

63. Raymond, *Statistics of Mines and Mining*, 348.

64. Paul and West, *Mining Frontiers*, 121–24; Lingenfelter, *Bonanzas and Borrascas*, 187–89; Hague, *Mining Industry*, 577–88; Paul, "Colorado as a Pioneer," 40–45; Fell, "Nathaniel P. Hill."

65. The essential contemporary source on Leadville and an essential early work on the science of mining is Emmons, *Geology and Mining Industry*.

66. Paul and West, *Mining Frontiers*, 127–32; Fell, *Ores to Metals*, 87–89; Fell, "'To the Task, Metallurgists!,'" 54–56.

67. Fell, *Ores to Metals*, 51, 140–41.

68. Fell, *Ores to Metals*, 139.

69. West, *Saloon*, 108–9.

70. Becker, *Geology of the Comstock Lode*, 8–11.

71. Lord, *Comstock*, 124.

21. Legal Wrestling, the Land Convulsed

1. The mean average altitude of major lode mines in seven western states and territories in 1880 (6,554 feet) was only 129 feet below the highest point east of the Mississippi River (Mount Mitchell, 6,684 feet). The mean altitude in Colorado was 9,784 feet; four mines were above 12,000 feet. King, *Statistics and Technology*, 110.

2. Lord, *Comstock*, 125.

3. For accessible summaries of the development of mining law, see Ellison, "Mineral Land Question"; Leshy, *Mining Law*, 9–23; Paul, *California Gold*, 210–39. For two early classic works, see Yale, *Legal Titles*; Lindley, *Treatise on the American Law*.

4. Paul, *California Gold*, 214–16.

5. Lindley, *Treatise on the American Law*, 43.

6. Shinn, *Story of the Mine*, 139–41.

7. King, *History*; Carlson, "History of the San Francisco Mining Exchange"; Lingenfelter, *Bonanzas and Borrascas*, 103.

8. Lingenfelter, *Bonanzas and Borrascas*, 321.

9. Lingenfelter, *Bonanzas and Borrascas*, 88.

10. Shinn, *Story of the Mine*, 136; King, *History*, 78.

11. Shinn, *Story of the Mine*, 144–45.

12. Paul, *California Gold*, 234.

13. Lord, *Comstock*, 177.

14. USCD Serial Set 1938, 2; Smith, *History of the Comstock Lode*, 66–67.

15. Lingenfelter, *Bonanzas and Borrascas*, 91–92.

16. Shinn, *Story of the Mine*, 129; James, *Roar and the Silence*, 62.

17. James, *Roar and the Silence*, 62.

18. Smith, *History of the Comstock Lode*, 67. The story is a bit open to question. The same riposte is often attributed to Alexander Stephens, vice president of the Confederacy. An early instance is in *The Guardian*, 30, no. 6 (June 1879): 167.

19. Smith, *History of the Comstock Lode*, 71–76; Lord, *Comstock*, 167–71.

20. King, *Statistics and Technology*, 156–60.

21. Lord, *Comstock*, 172–77.
22. Shinn, *Story of the Mine*, 135.
23. Lord, *Comstock*, 174–76.
24. King, *Statistics and Technology*, 111.
25. St. Clair, "Gold Rush," 203.
26. On California banking, see Doti and Schweikart, *California Bankers*; Doti and Schweikart, *Banking*; Schweikart and Doti, "From Hard Money"; Willis, *Federal Reserve Bank*.
27. Trusk, "Sources of Capital." See especially 177–81.
28. Lingenfelter, *Bonanzas and Borrascas*, 88; Walker, "California's Golden Road," 183.
29. U.S. Census Bureau, *Historical Statistics*, part 1, 462.
30. Walker, "California's Golden Road," 183; Stevenson, "Old and New Pacific Capitals," 435.
31. Caughey, "Californian and His Environment," 197.
32. Rohe, "Origins and Diffusion," 144.
33. Moerenhout, *Inside Story*, 18–21.
34. Rohe, "Origins and Diffusion," 146–49.
35. Sawyer, *Way Sketches*, 118.
36. (Helena) *Montana Post*, May 20, 1865.
37. Browne, *J. Ross Browne*, 234; Smith, *Mining America*, 61.
38. Rohe, "Man as Geomorphic Agent," 8.
39. Young, *Western Mining*, 122; Brereton, "Mining Techniques," 291; Paul, *California Gold*, 164; Kelley, "Forgotten Giant," 349.
40. Rohe, "Man as Geomorphic Agent," 6, 9; Sherriffs, "Gold Mine Waste," 197; Vischer and Axe, "Trip to the Mining Regions," 332; Brockett, *Our Western Empire*, 107; Lawrence, *Silverland*, 174–75.
41. USCD Serial Set 2028, 12; *Second Report of the State Mineralogist*, 77–81; Holliday, *Rush for Riches*, 270–74.
42. Ziebarth, "California's First Environmental Battle," 276–77.
43. Louis Janin to "My Dear Father," March 29, 1863, box 29, folder 9, Janin Family Papers, HL. My thanks to Warren Dym to alerting me to these papers.
44. Isenberg, *Mining California*, 48–49; Wells, "Quicksilver Mines," 39.
45. Isenberg, *Mining California*, 50; Beesley, "Beyond Gilbert," 77.
46. Brosnan, *Uniting Mountain and Plain*, 157; Rohe, "Man and the Land," 337.
47. King, *Statistics and Technology*, 147–48.
48. Rohe, "Man and the Land," 307; Spence, "Western Mining," 107.
49. Brosnan, *Uniting Mountain and Plain*, 146–54; Isenberg, *Mining California*, 41–42; Vrtis, "Gold Rush Ecology," 26–27; Evans, "Hydraulic Mining in California," 333–34.
50. The standard work is Kelley, *Gold vs. Grain*. See also Ziebarth, "California's First Environmental Battle"; Lowell, "Where Have All the Flowers Gone?" For a lively account, see Holliday, *Rush for Riches*, 282–99.
51. *Report of the State Engineer*, 15, 21; *Cases Argued*, 760.
52. Holliday, *Rush for Riches*, 294, 294.

53. *Cases Argued*, 753–813. The quotations are on 769 and 813.

54. Smith, *Mining America*, 75–79.

55. *Cases Argued*, 812.

56. Paul, *California Gold*, 165; Greenland, *Hydraulic Mining*, 85–86.

57. Nevins, *Selected Writings*, 96.

58. Mathews, *Ten Years in Nevada*, 168.

59. Foote, "California Mining Camp," 480.

60. *Proceedings and Debates*, 754. Clark was speaking before the territorial constitutional convention and arguing that Butte be established as the new state capital. He thought that other Montana cities would be better off with "more smoke and less diphtheria."

61. Smith, *Mining America*, 61.

62. Smith, *Mining America*, 46.

22. The Final Undoing

1. *ARCIA*, 1857, 138; West, *Contested Plains*, 106–7; Holliday, *Rush for Riches*, 60.

2. Washington began to shift its forces decisively away from the South to the West in 1868, and by 1870 the percentage of companies stationed in the West had risen from 39 percent to 58 percent. Downs, *After Appomattox*, 232–33, 264–65.

3. Utley, *Frontier Regulars*, 12–23; Utley, "Chained Dog," 19. Annual pay for enlisted men ranged from a pitiful $156 to $264.

4. *ARCIA*, 1868, 10.

5. Downs and Masur, *World the Civil War Made*, 6–7. Downs and Masur apply their term to both Washington's military and administrative presence in the South and West.

6. In the U.S.-Mexico War the official rolls of the army included 31,034 regular troops and 73,582 volunteers; in the Civil War the Union army at its peak in 1863 included more than 600,000 men. The official tally of battle deaths in the first war was 1,551; the conservative estimate for the Union in the second was 110,000. The effective number of troops in the West probably never exceeded 20,000. The official number of battle deaths between 1850 and 1885 was 1,150. Upton, *Military Policy*, 215–18; Peters, *Indian Battles*.

7. For thoughtful accounts of two instances, see Grinnell, *Two Great Scouts*; Calloway, "'The Only Way Open to Us.'"

8. Utley, "Chained Dog," 24.

9. Hoig, *Peace Chiefs*, 69–73; Grinnell, *Fighting Cheyennes*, 145–46.

10. Gary Clayton Anderson has argued ably that the Lakotas were beginning to adjust to this crippling disadvantage, evolving toward a sense of nationhood and more collected authority. They remained divided, however, and in the end it was too little too late. Anderson, *Sitting Bull*.

11. Scott, *True Copy*, 57, 60.

12. *ARCIA*, 1883, 36; U.S. War Department, *Annual Report of the Chief Signal Officer*, 180. My thanks to Professor James Schwoch for pointing me toward these reports and what they reveal.

13. The engagements are Bear River battle or massacre (January 29, 1863), campaign in Canyon de Chelly (January 12–14, 1864), Sand Creek Massacre (November 24, 1864), and the Washita battle or massacre (November 27, 1868).
14. Chalfant, *Hancock's War*; Jones, *Treaty*.
15. Greene, *Washita*; Brill, *Custer*; Hoig, *Battle of the Washita*.
16. Filipiak, "Battle of Summit Springs"; King, "Republican River Expedition"; King, *War Eagle*, 170–95, 281–92.
17. See chapter 7 herein.
18. Writing on the Sioux War is extensive enough to have inspired a two-volume bibliography: O'Keefe, *Custer*. Here is a selection of older standards and newer takes on it: Stewart, *Custer's Luck*; Gray, *Centennial Campaign*; Connell, *Son of the Morning Star*; Viola, *Little Bighorn*; Hardorff; Philbrick, *Last Stand*; Donovan, *Terrible Glory*; Greene, *Yellowstone Command*; Greene, *Morning Star Dawn*. Excellent accounts can be found as well in biographies of the war's most famous participants: Utley, *Cavalier in Buckskin*; Stiles, *Custer's Trials*; Ambrose, *Crazy Horse and Custer*; Wert, *Custer*; Monaghan, *Custer*; Barnett, *Touched by Fire*; Utley, *Lance and the Shield*; Reilly, *Sitting Bull*; St. George, *To See with the Heart*; Bray, *Crazy Horse*; Powers, *Killing of Crazy Horse*.
19. U.S. Census Bureau, *Historical Statistics*, part 1, 459–60.
20. Jackson, *Custer's Gold*.
21. Cozzens, *Earth Is Weeping*, 218–20.
22. Hutton, *Phil Sheridan*, 301.
23. Utley, *Lance and the Shield*, 176.
24. Greene, *Morning Star Dawn*.
25. Greene, *Morning Star Dawn*, 160.
26. West, *Last Indian War*; Greene, *Beyond Bear's Paw*.
27. Hutton, *Apache Wars*; Haley, *Apaches*.
28. Prucha, *Great Father*, 527–33.
29. Pommersheim, *Broken Landscape*, 125–51; Clark, *Lone Wolf*.
30. Prucha, *Great Father*, 678–79; Haring, *Crow Dog's Case*. Haring describes in some detail earlier erosion of tribal authority on reservations.
31. Prucha, *American Indian Policy*, 208–9; ARCIA, 1892, 29; ARCIA, 1868, 13–14.
32. Prucha, *Great Father*, 681–86.
33. Hoxie, *Final Promise*, 58, 67.
34. Hoxie, *Final Promise*, 53–58.
35. Adams, *Education for Extinction*, 57, 59; ARCIA, 1868, xv–xvi.
36. Adams, *Education for Extinction*, 124–35.
37. Hoxie, *Final Promise*, 61; ARCIA, 1868, 635.
38. The quote is in ARCIA, 1868, 94. The census of 1910 showed 67,934 Indian children between ages 5 and 14. Assuming those attending school in 1900 were of ages 6–7 to 15–17, it seems reasonable that they were fewer than a third of those of that cohort.
39. Prucha, *American Indian Policy*, 265.
40. Talbot, "Spiritual Genocide," 19.

41. Prucha, *American Indian Policy*, 208–9; ARCIA, 1892, 29; ARCIA, 1902, 13–14.

42. Ellis, "'We Don't Want'"; Ellis, "'There Is No Doubt.'"

43. Gage, *We Do Not Want*. A good bit of what follows is from Gage's remarkable study of the development of intertribal contact and exchange during these crucial years.

44. Gage, *We Do Not Want*, 92, 86–87, 123–24.

45. Gage, *We Do Not Want*, 32. Literacy rates in 1889 on twenty-five reservations ranged from 2.2 to 63.7 percent. The average was 18 percent.

46. Ruby and Brown, *Dreamer-Prophets*; Relander, *Drummers and Dreamers*.

47. Among the most useful of the many sources on peyote and the peyote religion are Barre, *Peyote Cult*; Stewart, *Peyote Religion*; Slotkin, *Peyote Religion*; Bee, "Peyotism."

48. McAllester, *Peyote Music*, 29, 31.

49. The most influential work on the Ghost Dance long was Mooney, *Ghost-Dance Religion*. A recent thoroughgoing reinterpretation is Warren, *God's Red Son*. Of the many other works on the topic, these are especially useful: Gage, *We Do Not Want*; Andersson, *Lakota Ghost Dance*; Andersson, *Whirlwind*; Utley, *Last Days*; Kehoe, *Ghost Dance*; Thornton, *We Shall Live Again*.

50. On the movement's beginnings, see Hittman, "1870 Ghost Dance at Walker River" and for its spread, Du Bois, "1870 Ghost Dance."

51. Warren, *God's Red Son*, 280; Gage, *We Do Not Want*, 206.

52. The most complete history of the massacre and events leading up to and following it is Greene, *American Carnage*.

53. Burnham, *Song of Dewey Beard*, 67; Greene, *American Carnage*, 238, 281.

54. Warren, *God's Red Son*, 289.

55. Gage, *We Do Not Want*, 239.

56. Iverson, "Building toward Self-Determination"; Iverson, *When Indians Became Cowboys*; Hoxie, "From Prison"; Harmon, *Reclaiming the Reservation*.

23. Creating the West

1. Simpson, *Report of the Explorations*, 25.

2. Charles D. Gallagher, "Life at Gallagher's Gap," Oral History Collection, UN-R.

3. Howe, *What Hath God Wrought* features a brilliant elaboration on the importance of this revolution in movement prior to expansion.

4. Fernández-Armesto, *Foot in the River*, 226.

5. On the last, see Parker, "Along the Dirty Plate Route," 16–20; Igler, *Industrial Cowboys*, 131–32, 141–44.

6. Webster, "Day at Dutch Flat," 302–4.

7. Davis and Weidenmier, "America's First Moderation."

8. Edwards et al., *Homesteading the Plains*.

9. Sides, *Backcountry Ghosts*.

10. Sinn, *Pacific Crossing*, 267. For a full discussion of the return of remains to China see 265–95.

11. Gilpin, *Central Gold Region*.

12. Kushner, "Visions"; McPherson, "Interest"; Vevier, "Collins Overland Line," 237–53. The quotes are from Kushner, 302, 306.

13. Perry, *Narrative of the Expedition*, 173; "North Pacific Expedition," 314.

14. Goetzmann, *New Lands, New Men*, 349–56; Cole, "Ringgold-Rodgers-Brooke Expedition."

15. For an excellent summary of Maury's remarkable career, see Goetzmann, *New Lands, New Men*, 300–330. See also Williams, *Matthew Fontaine Maury*.

16. Maury, *Physical Geography*.

17. Maury, *Explanations*, 416–17, 420; Goetzmann, *New Lands, New Men*, 351; Habersham, *North Pacific Surveying*, 327, 335–42.

18. Maury, *Explanations*, 263.

19. The figures in this paragraph and the one that follows are from Brock, *Report on the Internal Commerce*, 1098–1124.

20. Meissner, "Bridging the Pacific"; Davis, "California Breadstuffs." The figures are from Davis, 604–7.

21. Ma, "Modern Silk Road," 335–39; Mason, "American Silk Industry," 144; Wyckoff, *American Silk Manufacture*, 75–76. On the American silk industry, see Field et al., *American Silk*.

22. *New York Times*, May 12, 1869.

23. Courtwright, "Opiate Addiction in the American West"; Courtwright, "Opiate Addiction as a Consequence."

24. Ngai, "Chinese Question"; Ngai, *Chinese Question*. My thanks to Professor Ngai for an early look at her fine book.

25. *New York Times*, May 12, 1869. As a crude measure of American involvement in the Pacific world, five of the next six declared and undeclared conflicts were either fought entirely in Asia or begun or ended there: the Spanish-American War, the Filipino conflict, World War II, and the Korean and Vietnamese wars. Only World War I had no significant action in the Pacific. Expansion began what ironically might be called the "Pacification" of American military history.

26. Paul, *California Gold*, 164.

27. Burcham, *California Range Land*, 148.

28. As one of scores of examples, bison and prairie dogs complemented one another in their grazing habits. Krueger, "Feeding Relationships."

29. For an excellent discussion of the redwood timbering and its various effects, see Isenberg, *Mining California*, 75–98.

30. Rohe, "Man and the Land," 336–37.

31. Rutkow, *American Canopy*, 126–27; Isenberg, *Destruction of the Bison*, 132.

32. Sternberg, *Life of a Fossil Hunter*, 17.

33. Cook, *Fifty Years*, 273–82.

34. Dawson, *Ute War*, 108–11.

35. Richardson, *Christian Reconstruction*; Butler, "Union of Church and State."

36. Kiser, "'Charming Name'"; Smith, "Emancipating Peons"; Montoya, "Not-So-Free Labor"; Kiser, "Persistence."

37. Smith, "Emancipating Peons," 60–71; Smith, *Freedom's Frontier*, 217–30; Aarim-Heriot, *Chinese Immigrants*.

38. Violence against Hispanics by no means ended, especially in Texas between 1910 and 1920, where a recent study estimates deaths by mob lynching and by authorities without trial somewhere between several hundred to several thousand. Martinez, *Injustice Never Leaves You*, 6–7.

39. Nott, "Diversity," 114; Grant, *Passing*, 14.

40. King, *Gods of the Upper Air*. On the considerable literature on the influence of the United States on Nazi racial theorizing, see especially Kuhl, *Nazi Connection*; Whitman, *Hitler's American Model*.

41. Whitman, *Hitler's American Model*, 9, 113–20; Krieger, "Principles of the Indian Law."

42. Thorndike, *Sherman Letters*, 370–71.

43. USCD Serial Set 1835, 78–79.

Bibliography

Sources in the bibliography are divided into two categories, government documents and other published sources. Government documents in turn are divided into unpublished and published sources. The first, from the congressional serial set, are listed by serial set numbers, which are used to identify sources in the notes. The second include sources published by the federal and state governments. The other published nongovernment works include both primary and secondary materials.

AHS: Arizona Historical Society, Tucson.
ARCIA: U.S. Bureau of Indian Affairs. *Annual Reports of the Commissioner of Indian Affairs.* Washington DC: U.S. Government Printing Office, 1848–1903.
ARGLO: U.S. Department of the Interior. *Annual Reports of the Commissioner of the General Land Office.* Washington DC: U.S. Government Printing Office, 1851–88.
BaL: Bancroft Library, University of California, Berkeley.
BL: Beinecke Library, Yale University, New Haven CT.
CSHS: Colorado State Historical Society (History Colorado).
DPL: Western History Collections, Denver Public Library, Denver CO.
HL: Henry E. Huntington Library, San Marino CA.
KHS: Kansas Historical Society, Topeka.
MHS: Montana Historical Society, Helena.
NL: Newberry Library, Chicago IL.
NSHS: Nebraska State Historical Society, Lincoln.
OHS: Oklahoma Historical Society, Oklahoma City.
OU: Western History Collections, University of Oklahoma Library, Norman.
SWC: Oral History Collection, Southwest Collection, Texas Tech University, Lubbock.
UA: Special Collections, University of Arkansas Library, Fayetteville.
UN-R: University of Nevada–Reno Library, Reno.
USCD: U.S. Congressional Documents. Unpublished.
WR: *The War of the Rebellion: A Compilation of the Official Records of the Union and Confederate Armies.* Washington DC: U.S. Government Printing Office, 1880–1901.

U.S. Congressional Documents: Unpublished

Serial Set 474: "The Committee on the Post Office and Post Roads." 1846. S.Doc. 306, 29th Cong., 1st sess.

Serial Set 537: "Message from the President of the United States to the Two Houses of Congress." 1848. H.Exec.Doc. 1, 30th Cong., 2nd sess.

Serial Set 546: "Canal or Railroad between the Atlantic and Pacific Oceans." 1849. H.Rpt. 145, 30th Cong., 2nd sess.

Serial Set 557: "Message from the President of the United States, Communicating Information Called for by a Resolution of the Senate of the 17th Instant in Relation to California and New Mexico." 1850. S.Exec.Doc. 18, 31st Cong., 1st sess.

Serial Set 570: "Message from the President of the United States to the Two Houses of Congress." 1849. H.Exec.Doc. 5, pt. 2, 31st. Cong., 1st sess.

Serial Set 585: "Railroad to the Pacific, House Report 439." 1850. 31st Cong., 1st sess.

Serial Set 611: "Message from the President of the United States to the Two Houses of Congress." 1851. Sen.Exec.Doc. 1, pt. 1, 32nd Cong., 1st sess.

Serial Set 652: "New Mexico: Letter from the Secretary of the Territory of New Mexico, Transmitting Copies of the Acts, Resolutions, &c., of That Territory." 1852. H.Misc.D. 4, 32nd Cong., 1st. sess.

Serial Set 659: "Message from the President of the United States to the Two Houses of Congress." 1852. S.Exec.Doc. 1, pt. 2, 32nd Cong., 2nd sess.

Serial Set 688: "Report of the Secretary of the Interior, Communicating . . . a Copy of the Correspondence between the Department of the Interior and the Indian Agents and Commissioners in California." 1853. Exec.Doc. 4, 33rd Cong., Special Senate Session.

Serial Set 690: "Message from the President of the United States to the Two Houses of Congress." 1853. S.Exec.Doc. 1, pt. 1, 33rd Cong., 1st sess.

Serial Set 720: "Report of the Commissioner of Patents for the Year 1853; Agriculture." 1854. H.Exec.Doc 39, pt. 2, 33rd Cong., 1st sess,

Serial Set 758: "Reports of Explorations and Surveys, to Ascertain the Most Practicable and Economical Route for a Railroad from the Mississippi River to the Pacific Ocean Made under the Direction of the Secretary of War, Vol. I." 1855. Sen.Exec. Doc 78, pt. 1, 33rd Cong., 2nd Sess.

Serial Set 760: "Reports of Explorations and Surveys, to Ascertain the Most Practicable and Economical Route for a Railroad from the Mississippi River to the Pacific Ocean, Vol. III." 1855. Sen.Exec.Doc. 78, pt. 3, 33rd Cong., 2nd sess.

Serial Set 761: "Reports of the Explorations and Surveys to Ascertain the Most Practical and Economical Route for a Railroad from the Mississippi River to the Pacific Ocean, Vol. IV." 1855. S.Exec.Doc. 78, pt. 4, 33rd Cong., 2nd sess.

Serial Set 762: "Reports of the Explorations and Surveys to Ascertain the Most Practical and Economical Route for a Railroad from the Mississippi River to the Pacific Ocean, Vol. V." 1855. S.Exec.Doc. 78, pt. 5, 33rd Cong., 2nd sess.

Serial Set 763: "Reports of the Explorations and Surveys to Ascertain the Most Practical and Economical Route for a Railroad from the Mississippi River to the Pacific Ocean, Vol. VI." 1855. S.Exec.Doc. 78, pt. 6, 33rd Cong., 2nd sess.

Serial Set 766: "Reports of the Explorations and Surveys to Ascertain the Most Practical and Economical Route for a Railroad from the Mississippi River to the Pacific Ocean, Vol. IX." 1855. S.Exec.Doc. 78, pt. 9, 33rd Cong., 2nd sess.

Serial Set 788: "Engagement between United States Troops and Sioux Indians." 1855. H.Exec.Doc. 63, 33rd Cong., 2nd sess.

Serial Set 811: "Message from the President of the United States to the Two Houses of Congress." 1855. S.Exec.Doc. 1, pt. 2, 34th Cong., 1st sess.

Serial Set 827: "Statistical Report on the Sickness and Mortality in the Army of the United States." 1856. S.Exec.Doc. 96, 34th Cong., 1st sess.

Serial Set 830: "Narrative of the Expedition of an American Squadron to the China Seas and Japan, Performed in the Years 1852, 1853, and 1854, under the Command of Commodore M.C. Perry, United States Navy." 1856. H.Exec.Doc. 97, pt. 2, 33rd. Cong., 2nd sess.

Serial Set 832: "Report on the United States and Mexican Boundary Survey." 1857. Sen. Exec.Doc 108, pt. 1, 34th Cong., 1st sess.

Serial Set 858: "Indian Hostilities in Oregon and Washington." 1856. H.Exec.Doc. 93, 34th Cong., 1st sess.

Serial Set 859: "Council with the Sioux Indians at Fort Pierre." 1856. H.Exec.Doc. 130, 34th Cong., 1st sess.

Serial Set 869: "Kansas Affairs." 1856. H.Rpt. 200, 34th Cong., 1st sess.

Serial Set 876: "Message from the President of the United States to the Two Houses of Congress." 1856. S. Exec.Doc. 5, no. 2, 34th Cong., 3rd sess.

Serial Set 880: "Message from the President of the United States . . . Certain Information Respecting the Pay and Emoluments Lieutenant General Scott." 1857. Sen.Exec. Doc. 34, 34th Cong., 3rd. sess.

Serial Set 881: "Message from the President of the United States to the Two Houses of Congress, Respecting the Proclamation of Martial Law in the Territory of Washington." 1857. S.Exec.Doc. 41, 34th Cong., 3rd sess.

Serial Set 894: "Message from the President to the Two Houses of Congress." 1856. H.Exec.Doc. 1, pt. 2, 34th Cong., 3rd sess.

Serial Set 906: "Message from the President of the United States to the Two Houses of Congress." 1857. H.Exec.Doc. 76, 34th Cong., 3rd. sess.

Serial Set 920: "Message of the President of the United States to the Two Houses of Congress." 1858. S.Exec.Doc. 11, pt. 2, 35th Cong., 1st sess.

Serial Set 943: "Message from the President of the United States to the Two Houses of Congress." 1857. H.Exec.Doc. 2, pt. 2, 35th Cong., 1st sess.

Serial Set 955: "Expenses of Indian Wars in Washington and Oregon Territories." 1858. H.Exec.Doc. 45, 35th Cong., 1st sess.

Serial Set 956: "The Utah Expedition, Message from the President of the United States." 1858. H.Exec.Doc. 71, 35th Cong., 1st sess.

Serial Set 974: "Message from the President of the United States to the Two Houses of Congress." 1858. Sen.Exec.Doc. 1, pt. 1, 35th Cong., 2nd sess.

Serial Set 975: "Message of the President of the United States to the Houses of Congress." 1858. Sen.Exec.Doc. 1, pt. 2, 35th Cong., 2nd sess.

Serial Set 984: "Report of the Secretary of the Interior, Communicating Reports upon the Pacific Wagon Roads Constructed on the Direction of That Department." 1859. Sen.Exec.Doc. 36, 35th Cong., 2nd sess.

Serial Set 1023: "Message from the President of the United States to the Two Houses of Congress." 1860. S.Exec.Doc. 2, pt. 1, 36th Cong., 1st sess.

Serial Set 1025: "Message from the President of the United States to the Two Houses of Congress." 1859. Sen.Exec.Doc. 2, pt. 3, 36th Cong., 1st sess.

Serial Set 1033: "Report of the Secretary of the Interior . . . the Correspondence between the Indian Office and the Present Superintendents and Agents in California, and J. Ross Browne, Esq." 1860. S.Exec.Doc 46, 36th Cong., 1st sess.

Serial Set 1058: "Report upon the Colorado River of the West, Explored in 1857 and 1858 by Lieutenant Joseph C. Ives." 1861. H.Exec.Doc. 90, 36th Cong., 1st sess.

Serial Set 1060: "Kansas Constitution: Copy of the Constitution Adopted by the Convention at Wyandot, for the State of Kansas." 1860. H.Misc.Doc. 6, 36th Cong., 1st sess.

Serial Set 1079: "Message from the President of the United States to the Two Houses of Congress." 1860. S.Exec.Doc. 1, part 2, 36th Cong., 2nd sess.

Serial Set 1080: "Message from the President of the United States to the Two Houses of Congress." 1860. S.Exec.Doc. 1, pt. 3, 36th Cong., 2nd sess.

Serial Set 1122: "Letter of the Secretary of the Interior . . . In Relation to the 'Half-Breed Kaw Lands' on the Kansas River, in the State of Kansas." 1862. S.Exec.Doc. 58, 37th Cong., 2nd sess.

Serial Set 1137: "Letter from the Secretary of the Interior, Communicating a Preliminary Report on the Eighth Census." 1862. H.Exec.Doc. 116, 32nd Cong., 2nd sess.

Serial Set 1138: "Relief to Indian Refugees in Southern Kansas; Letter from J.P. Usher, Assistant Secretary of the Interior, in Answer to Resolution of the House of 28th Ultimo Relative to Mode and Amount of Relief Extended to Indian Refugees in southern Kansas." 1862. H.Exec.Doc. 132, 32nd Cong., 2nd sess.

Serial Set 1157: "Message of the President of the United States to the Two Houses of Congress." 1862. H.Exec.Doc. 1, pt. 2, 37th Cong., 3rd sess.

Serial Set 1163: "Indian Tribes in the Northwest: Message from the President of the United States, in Answer to Resolution of the House of the 18th December Last, Respecting the Cause of the Recent Outbreaks of the Indian Tribes in the Northwest." 1863. H.Exec.Doc. 68, 37th Cong., 3rd sess.

Serial Set 1176: "Letter of the Secretary of the Interior, Communicating Papers in Relation to Providing the Means of Subsistence for the Navajo Indians of New Mexico, upon a Reservation at the Bosque Redondo, on the Pecos River." 1864. S.Exec.Doc. 36, 38th Cong., 1st sess.

Serial Set 1220: "Message of the President of the United States to the Two Houses of Congress." 1864. H.Exec.Doc. 1, pt. 5, 38th Cong., 2nd sess.

Serial Set 1248: "Message of the President of the United States to the Two Houses of Congress." 1864. H.Exec.Doc. 1, pt. 2, 39th Cong., 1st sess.

Serial Set 1256: "Wagon Road from Niobrara to Virginia City: Letter from the Secretary of the Interior, in Answer to a Resolution of the House of February 16, Relative to a Wagon Road from Niobrara to Virginia City." 1866. H.Exec.Doc. 58, 39th Cong., 1st sess.

Serial Set 1266: "Report of the Commissioner of Agriculture for 1865." 1866. H.Exec. Doc. 136, 39th Cong., 1st. sess.

Serial Set 1279: "Condition of the Indian Tribes: Report of the Joint Special Committee Appointed under Joint Resolution." 1865. S.Rpt. 156, 39th Cong., 2nd sess.

Serial Set 1337: "Report of Indian Peace Commissioners: Message from the President of the United States, Transmitting Report of the Indian Peace Commissioners." 1868. H.Exec.Doc. 97, 40th Cong., 2nd sess.

Serial Set 1440: "Letter from the Secretary of War, Communicating the Report of Lieutenant Gustavus C. Doane upon the So-Called Yellowstone Expedition of 1870." 1871. Ex.Doc. 51, 41st Cong., 3rd sess.

Serial Set 1446: "Report of the Secretary of War." 1870. H.Exec.Doc. 1, pt. 2, vol. 1, 41st Cong., 3rd sess.

Serial Set 1610: "Ute, Pai-Ute, Go-si Ute, and Shoshone Indians." 1874. H.Exec.Doc. 157, 43rd Cong., 1st sess.

Serial Set 1680: "Report of the Secretary of the Interior." 1875. H.Exec.Doc. 1, pt. 5, vol. 1, 44th Cong., 1st sess.

Serial Set 1734: "Report of the Joint Special Committee to Investigate Chinese Immigration." 1877. S.Rpt.689, 44th Cong., 2nd sess.

Serial Set 1800: "Report of the Secretary of the Interior." 1878. vol. 1, H.Exec.Doc. 1, pt. 5, 45th Cong., 2nd sess.

Serial Set 1809: "Yellowstone National Park: Letter from the Secretary of the Interior, in Regard to the Better Protection of the National Park from Injury." 1878. H.Exec. Doc. 75, 45th Cong., 2nd sess.

Serial Set 1818: "The Reorganization of the Army: A Report of the Sub-committee of the Committee on Military Affairs relating to the Reorganization of the Army." 1878. H.Misc.Doc. 56, 45th Cong., 2nd sess.

Serial Set 1835: "Testimony Taken by the Joint Committee Appointed to Take into Consideration the Expediency of Transferring the Indian Bureau to the War Department." 1879. S.Misc.Doc. 53, 45th Cong., 3rd sess.

Serial Set 1850: "Report of the Secretary of the Interior." 1878. H.Exec.Doc. 1, pt. 5, vol. 1, 45th Cong., 3rd sess.

Serial Set 1899: "Select Committee to Examine into the Circumstances Connected to the Removal of the Northern Cheyennes from the Sioux Reservation to the Indian Territory." 1880. S.Rpt.708, 46th Cong., 2nd sess.

Serial Set 1900: "Report and Testimony of the Select Committee of the United States Senate to Investigate the Causes of the Removal of the Negroes from the Southern States to the Northern States." 1880. S.Rpt. 693, pt. 1, 46th Cong., 2nd sess.

Serial Set 1911: "Report of the Secretary of the Interior." 1880. H.Exec.Doc. 1, pt. 5, vol. 2, 46th Cong., 2nd sess.

Serial Set 1938: "Lands in Severalty to Indians." 1880. H.Rpt. 1576, 46th Cong., 2nd sess.

Serial Set 1938: "Survey of Mineral Lands." 1880. H.Rpt. 1747, 49th Cong., 2nd sess.

Serial Set 1960: "Report of the Secretary of the Interior." 1881. H.Exec.Doc. 1, pt. 5, vol. 11, 46th Cong., 3rd sess.

Serial Set 2018: "Report of the Secretary of the Interior." 1882. H.Exec.Doc. 1, pt. 5, vol. 2, 47th Cong., 1st sess.

Serial Set 2028: "Mining Debris in California Rivers." 1882. H.Exec.Doc. 98, 47th Cong., 1st sess.

Serial Set 2165: "Documents and Correspondence relating to Leases of Lands in the Indian Territory to Citizens of the United States for Cattle-Grazing and Other Purposes." 1884. S.Exec.Doc. 54, 48th Cong., 1st sess.

Serial Set 2174: "Select Committee to Examine into the Condition of the Sioux and Crow Indians." 1884. S.Rpt.283, 48th Cong., 1st sess.

Serial Set 2177: "Report of the Committee on Post Offices and Post Roads, United States Senate, on Postal Telegraph." 1884. S.Rpt. 577, 48th Cong., 1st sess.

Serial Set 2362: "Report on the Committee on Indian Affairs, United States Senate, on the Condition of the Indians in Indian Territory, and on Other Reservations." 1886. S.Rpt. 1278, pt. 1, 49th Cong., 1st sess.

Serial Set 2378: "Report of the Secretary of the Interior." 1885. H.Exec.Doc. 1, pt. 5, vol. 1, 49th Cong., 1st sess.

Serial Set 2405: "Report of the Commissioner of Agriculture." 1886. H.Exec.Doc. 378, 49th Cong., 1st sess.

Serial Set 2636: "Report of the Secretary of the Interior." 1888. H.Exec.Doc. 1, vol. 5, pt. 1, 50th Cong., 2nd sess.

Serial Set 4377: "Mountain Meadows Massacre." 1902. H.Exec.Doc. 605, 57th Cong., 1st sess.

U.S. Congressional Documents: Published

Abel, Annie Heloise, ed. *The Official Correspondence of James S. Calhoun While Indian Agent at Santa Fe and Superintendent of Indian Affairs in New Mexico*. Washington DC: U.S. Government Printing Office, 1915.

Allen, Joseph Asaph. *History of the American Bison, Bison Americanus, Extracted from Ninth Annual Report of the United States Geological Survey*. Washington DC: U.S. Government Printing Office, 1877.

Annual Report of the Commissioner of Indian Affairs. Washington DC: U.S. Government Printing Office, 1853.

Annual Report of the Commissioner of the General Land Office for the Year 1888. Washington DC: U.S. Government Printing Office, 1888.

Becker, George F. *Geology of the Comstock Lode and the Washoe District with Atlas*. Washington DC: U.S. Government Printing Office, 1882.

Bradley, Frank H. "Report of Frank H. Bradley, Geologist." In *Sixth Annual Report of the United States Geological Survey of the Territories*. Washington DC: U.S. Government Printing Office, 1873.

Brewer, Wm. H. "Report on the Cereal Production of the United States." *Tenth Census of the United States*, vol. 3. Washington DC: U.S. Government Printing Office, 1883.

Brock, S. G. *Report on the Internal Commerce of the United States for the Year 1890, Part II*. Washington DC: U.S. Government Printing Office, 1891.

Browne, J. Ross, and James W. Taylor. *Reports upon the Mineral Resources of the United States*. Washington DC: U.S. Government Printing Office, 1867.

Coffin, James H. *Winds of the Northern Hemisphere*. Washington DC: Smithsonian Institution, 1853.

Crampton, Louis C. *Early History of Yellowstone National Park and Its Relations to National Park Policies*. Washington DC: U.S. Government Printing Office, 1932.

Dutton, Clarence E. *Tertiary History of the Grand Cañon District*. Washington DC: U.S. Government Printing Office, 1882.

Emmons, Samuel Franklin. *Geology and Mining Industry of Leadville, Colorado*. Washington DC: U.S. Government Printing Office, 1886.

Ewers, John C. *The Horse in Blackfoot Indian Culture, with Comparative Material from Other Western Tribes*. Washington DC: U.S. Government Printing Office, 1955.

Ferrel, William. "An Essay on the Winds and Currents of the Ocean." *Popular Essays on the Movements of the Atmosphere*. Professional Papers of the Signal Service, no. 12. Washington DC: Office of the Chief Signal Officer, 1882.

First, Second, and Third Annual Reports of the United States Geological Survey of the Territories for the Years 1867, 1868, and 1869, under the Department of the Interior. Washington: U.S. Government Printing Office, 1873.

Fowler, Don D., Robert C. Euler, and Catherine S. Fowler. *John Wesley Powell and the Anthropology of the Canyon Country*. Geological Survey Professional Paper 670. Washington DC: U.S. Government Printing Office, 1969.

Gates, Paul W. *History of Public Land Law Development*. Washington DC: U.S. Government Printing Office, 1968.

Gatschet, Albert Samuel. *The Klamath Indians of Southwestern Oregon*. Washington DC: U.S. Government Printing Office, 1890.

Gilbert, G. K. *Report on the Geology of the Henry Mountains*. Washington DC: U.S. Government Printing Office, 1877.

Gordon, Clarence W. "Report on Cattle, Sheep, and Swine, Supplementary to Enumeration of Live Stock on Farms in 1880." Supplement to the *Tenth Census of the United States*, vol. 4.

Hague, James D. *Mining Industry*. Washington DC: U.S. Government Printing Office, 1870.

Harrington, Mark W. "History of the Weather Map." *Report of the International Meteorological Congress*, United States Weather Bureau Bulletin No. 11. Washington DC: Weather Bureau, 1894.

Hayden, F. V. *Ninth Annual Report of the United States Geological and Geographical Survey of the Territories*. Washington DC: U.S. Government Printing Office, 1877.

———. *Preliminary Report of the United States Geological Survey of Montana and Portions of Adjacent Territories*. Washington DC: U.S. Government Printing Office, 1872.

Hornaday, William T. *The Extermination of the American Bison*. Washington DC: U.S. Government Printing Office, 1889.

Ives, Joseph C. *Report upon the Colorado River of the West, Part III*. Washington DC: U.S. Government Printing Office, 1861.

Kappler, Charles J. *Indian Affairs: Laws and Treaties*. Vols. 1–7. Washington DC: U.S. Government Printing Office, 1904.

King, Clarence. *Report of the Geological Exploration of the Fortieth Parallel*. 7 Vols. Washington DC: U.S. Government Printing Office, 1870–80.

———. *Statistics and Technology of the Precious Metals*. Washington DC: U.S. Government Printing Office, 1885.

Ludlow, William. *Report on a Reconnaissance from Carroll, Montana Territory, on the Upper Missouri, to the Yellowstone National Park*. Washington DC: U.S. Government Printing Office, 1876.

Macomb, J. N. *Report of the Exploring Expedition from Santa Fe, New Mexico, to the Junction of the Grand and Green Rivers with Geological Report by Prof. J. S. Newberry*. Washington DC: U.S. Government Printing Office, 1876.

Marsh, O. C. *Odontornithes: A Monograph on the Extinct Toothed Birds of North America*. Washington DC: U.S. Government Printing Office, 1880.

Miller, David Hunter, ed. *Treaties and Other International Acts of the United States of America*. Vol. 6. Washington DC: U.S. Government Printing Office, 1931.

Mohler, John R. *Texas or Tick Fever and Its Prevention*. Washington DC: U.S. Government Printing Office, 1906.

Morgan, Henry Lewis. *Houses and House-Life of the American Aborigines*. Washington DC: U.S. Government Printing Office, 1881.

Neill, Edward D. *Effort and Failure to Civilize the Aborigines: Letter to Hon. N. G. Taylor, Commissioner of Indian Affairs*. Washington DC: U.S. Government Printing Office, 1868.

Nimmo, Joseph. *Report in Regard to the Range and Ranch Cattle Business in the United States*. Washington DC: U.S. Government Printing Office, 1885.

Powell, J. W. *First Annual Report of the Bureau of Ethnology*. Washington DC: U.S. Government Printing Office, 1881.

———. *Fourteenth Annual Report of the Bureau of Ethnology*. Washington DC: U.S. Government Printing Office, 1896.

———. *Report on the Lands of the Arid Regions of the United States*. Washington DC: U.S. Government Printing Office, 1879.

Powers, Stephen. *Tribes of California*. Washington DC: U.S. Government Printing Office, 1877.

Raymond, W. Rossiter. *Statistics of Mines and Mining in the States and Territories West of the Rocky Mountains*. 8 vols. Washington DC: U.S. Government Printing Office, 1869–77.

Ridgeway, Robert H. *Summarized Data of Gold Production*. Department of Commerce, Economic Paper 6. Washington DC: U.S. Government Printing Office, 1929.

Robinson, J. H. "The Telegraph and the Weather Service." *Proceedings of the Second Convention of Weather Bureau Officials.* Washington DC: U.S. Government Printing Office, 1902.

Schmeckebier, L. F. *Catalogue and Index of the Publications of the Hayden, King, Powell, and Wheeler Surveys.* Department of the Interior, United States Geological Survey Bulletin no. 222. Washington DC: U.S. Government Printing Office, 1904.

Schott, Charles A. *Tables and Results of the Precipitation, in Rain and Snow, in the United States.* Washington DC: Smithsonian Institution, 1872.

Simpson, J. H. *Report of the Explorations across the Great Basin of the Territory of Utah.* Washington DC: U.S. Government Printing Office, 1876.

Smith, Theobald, and F. L. Kilbourne. *Investigation into the Nature, Causation, and Prevention of Texas, or Southern Cattle Fever.* Washington DC: U.S. Department of Agriculture, Bureau of Animal Industry, 1893.

Strong, William E. *A Trip to the Yellowstone National Park in July, August, and September, 1875.* Washington DC: U.S. Government Printing Office, 1876.

Tenth Census of the United States. Vol. 4. Washington DC: U.S. Government Printing Office, 1883.

U.S. Bureau of Indian Affairs. *Papers relating to Talks and Councils Held with the Indians in Dakota and Montana Territories in the Years 1866–1869.* Washington DC: U.S. Government Printing Office, 1910.

———. *Report of Board of Inquiry Convened by Authority of Letter of the Secretary of the Interior of June 7, 1877, to Investigate Certain Charges against S. A. Galpin, Chief Clerk of the Indian Bureau, and Concerning Irregularities in Said Bureau.* Washington DC: U.S. Government Printing Office, 1878.

U.S. Census Bureau. *Historical Statistics of the United States: Colonial Times to 1970.* 2 vols. Washington DC: Bureau of the Census, 1975.

———. "Reports on the Agencies of Transportation in the United States, Including the Statistics of Railroads, Steam Navigation, Canals, Telegraphs and Telephones." In *Tenth Census of the United States*, vol. 4. Washington DC: U.S. Government Printing Office, 1880.

———. *Statistical Atlas of the United States.* Washington DC: U.S. Government Printing Office, 1914.

U.S. Department of the Interior. *First Annual Report of the United States Entomological Commission for the Year 1877.* Washington DC: U.S. Government Printing Office, 1877.

U.S. Department of the Interior. *Second Report of the United States Entomological Commission for the Years 1878 and 1879, relating to the Rocky Mountain Locust and the Western Cricket.* Washington DC: U.S. Government Printing Office, 1880.

U.S. Department of Transportation. *Public Aids to Transportation.* Vol. 2. Washington DC: U.S. Government Printing Office, 1938.

U.S. Geological Survey. *Contributions to North American Ethnology.* 8 vols. Washington DC: U.S. Government Printing Office, 1877–93.

U.S. War Department. *Annual Report of the Chief Signal Officer to the Secretary of War for the Year 1878.* Washington DC: U.S. Government Printing Office, 1878.

Upson, Emory. *The Military Policy of the United States.* Washington DC: U.S. Government Printing Office, 1912.

Wheeler, George M. *Report upon the United States Geographical Surveys West of the One Hundredth Meridian.* 7 vols. Washington: U.S. Government Printing Office, 1875–89.

Zissner, Hans. *Biographical Memoir of Theobald Smith, 1859–1934.* Washington DC: National Academy of Sciences, 1936.

State Government Documents

Acts, Resolutions, and Memorials, Passed by the First Annual, and Special Sessions, of the Legislative Assembly, of the Territory of Utah. Great Salt Lake City, Utah Territory: Brigham H. Young, 1852.

Acts of the Legislative Assembly of the Territory of Washington. Olympia: Edward Furste, 1858.

A Brief Notice of the Recent Outrages Committed by Isaac I. Stevens, Governor of Washington Territory. Olympia, Washington, 1856.

Browne, J. Ross. *Report of the Debates in the Convention of California, on the Formation of the State Constitution, in September and October 1849.* Washington DC: John T. Tower, 1850.

DeGroot, Henry. "Hydraulic and Drift Mining." In *Appendix: Papers Supplementary to the Report of the State Mineralogist,* 133–90. Sacramento: State Office, 1882.

Laws of the Territory of New Mexico, Session of 1858–59. Santa Fe: A. De Marle.

Majority and Minority Reports of the Special Joint Committee on the Mendocino War. Sacramento: C. T. Botts, 1860.

Proceedings and Debates of the Constitutional Convention Held in the City of Helena, Montana, July 4th, 1889, August 17th, 1889. Helena: State Publishing, 1921.

Report of the State Engineer to the Legislature of the State of California, Part III. Sacramento: Office of the State Engineer, 1880.

Report of the Committee on Internal Improvements: On the Use of Camels on the Plains. California Senate Document 24. Sacramento: B. B. Redding, State Printer, 1855.

Second Report of the State Mineralogist of California. Sacramento: State Office, 1882, 73.

Published Works

Aarim-Heriot, Najia. *Chinese Immigrants, African Americans, and Racial Anxiety in the United States, 1848–1882.* Urbana: University of Illinois Press, 2003.

Abbe, Cleveland. *Memoir of William Ferrel, 1817–1891.* Washington DC: National Academy of Sciences, 1892.

Abbott, E. C. (Teddy Blue), and Helena Huntington Smith. *We Pointed Them North: Recollections of a Cowpuncher.* Norman: University of Oklahoma Press, 1982.

Abel, Annie Heloise. *The American Indian in the Civil War, 1862–1865.* Lincoln: University of Nebraska Press, 1992.

Abrams, Kerry. "Polygamy, Prostitution, and the Federalization of Immigration Law." *Columbia Law Review* 105, no. 3 (April 2005): 641–716.

Abruzzi, William S. "Ecology, Resource Redistribution, and Mormon Settlement in Northeastern Arizona." *American Anthropologist* 91, no. 3 (September 1989): 642–55.

Adams, David Wallace. *Education for Extinction: American Indians and the Boarding School Experience, 1875–1928.* Lawrence: University Press of Kansas, 1995.

Adams, Frank. "The Historical Background of California Agriculture." In *California Agriculture: By Members of the Faculty of the College of Agriculture University of California*, edited by Claude B. Hutchinson, 1–50. Berkeley: University of California Press, 1946.

Adams, George Rollie. *General William S. Harney: Prince of Dragoons.* Lincoln: University of Nebraska Press, 2001.

Adas, Michael. *Dominance by Design: Technological Imperatives and America's Civilizing Mission.* Cambridge: Harvard University Press, 2006.

———. *Machines as the Measure of Men: Science, Technology, and the Ideologies of Western Dominance.* Ithaca: Cornell University Press, 1989.

Ahmad, Diana L. *The Opium Debate and Chinese Exclusion Laws in the Nineteenth-Century American West.* Reno: University of Nevada Press, 2007.

———. "Opium Smoking, Anti-Chinese Attitudes, and the American Medical Community." *American Nineteenth Century History* 1, no. 2 (Summer 2000): 53–69.

Albers, Patricia C. "Sioux Women in Transition: A Study of Their Changing Status in Domestic and Capitalist Sectors of Production." In *The Hidden Half: Studies of Plains Indian Women*, edited by Patricia C. Albers and Beatrice Medicine, 175–234. Lanham MD: University Press of America, 1983.

Albin, Ray R. "The Perkins Case: The Ordeal of Three Slaves in Gold Rush California." *California History* 67, no. 4 (December 1988): 215–27.

Almaguer, Tomás. *Racial Fault Lines: The Historical Origins of White Supremacy in California.* Berkeley: University of California Press, 1994.

Ambrose, Stephen E. *Crazy Horse and Custer: The Parallel Lives of Two American Warriors.* New York: Anchor, 1996.

Ames, Charles Edgar. *Pioneering the Union Pacific: A Reappraisal of the Builders of the Railroad.* New York: Appleton-Century-Crofts, 1969.

An Analysis of the Chinese Question: Consisting of a Special Message of the Governor, and, in Reply Thereto, Two Letters of the Chinamen, and a Memorial of the Citizens of San Francisco. San Francisco: San Francisco Herald, 1852.

Anderson, Gary Clayton. *The Conquest of Texas: Ethnic Cleansing in the Promised Land, 1820–1875.* Norman: University of Oklahoma Press, 2005.

———. *The Indian Southwest: Ethnogenesis and Reinvention.* Norman: University of Oklahoma Press, 1999.

———. *Little Crow: Spokesman for the Sioux.* Saint Paul: Minnesota Historical Society Press, 1986.

———. *Massacre in Minnesota: The Dakota War of 1862, the Most Violent Ethnic Conflict in American History.* Norman: University of Oklahoma Press, 2019.

———. "The Native Peoples of the American West: Genocide or Ethnic Cleansing?" *Western Historical Quarterly* 47, no. 4 (Winter 2016): 407–34.

———. *Sitting Bull and the Paradox of Lakota Nationhood*. New York: Longman, 1996.

Anderson, Gary Clayton, and Alan R. Woolworth. *Through Dakota Eyes: Narrative Accounts of the Minnesota Indian War of 1862*. Saint Paul: Minnesota Historical Society Press, 1988.

Andersson, Rani Henrik. *A Whirlwind Passed through Our Country: Lakota Voices of the Ghost Dance*. Norman: University of Oklahoma Press, 2019.

———. *The Lakota Ghost Dance of 1890*. Lincoln: University of Nebraska Press, 2008.

Andrews, Allen. *Splendid Pauper*. New York: J. B. Lippincott, 1968.

Andrus, Hyram L. "Joseph Smith and the West." *BYU Studies* 2, no. 2 (Spring/Summer 1960): 129–47.

Anthony, David W. "Bridling Horse Power: The Domestication of the Horse." In *Horses through Time*, edited by Sandra L. Olsen, 57–82. Boulder CO: Roberts Rinehart, 1997.

Applegate, Jesse. *Recollections of My Boyhood*. Roseburg OR: Press of Review Publishing, 1914.

Archibald, Robert. "Acculturation and Assimilation in Colonial New Mexico." *New Mexico Historical Review* 53, no. 3 (July 1978): 205–17.

Armitage, Susan H. "Household Work and Childrearing on the Frontier: The Oral History Record." *Sociology and Social Research* 63, no. 3 (April 1979): 467–74.

Arrington, Leonard J. *Great Basin Kingdom: An Economic History of the Latter-Day Saints, 1830–1900*. Urbana: University of Illinois Press, 2005.

———. *History of Idaho*. Moscow: University of Idaho Press, 1994.

Arrington, Leonard J., and Davis Bitton. *The Mormon Experience: A History of the Latter-Day Saints*. New York: Alfred A. Knopf, 1979.

Arrington, Leonard J., and Dean May. "'A Different Mode of Life': Irrigation and Society in Nineteenth-Century Utah." In *Agriculture in the Development of the Far West*, edited by James H. Shideler, 3–20. Washington DC: Agricultural History Society, 1975.

Arrowsmith, William. "Teaching and the Liberal Arts: Notes toward an Old Frontier." In *The Liberal Arts and Teacher Education: A Confrontation*, edited by Donald N. Bigelow, 3–26. Lincoln: University of Nebraska Press, 1971.

Athearn, Robert G. "Civil War Days in Montana." *Pacific Historical Review* 29, no. 1 (February 1960): 19–34.

———. *In Search of Canaan: Black Migration to Kansas, 1879–1880*. Lawrence: Regents Press of Kansas, 1978.

———. *Union Pacific Country*. Chicago: Rand McNally, 1971.

Atkinson, J. H. "Cattle Drives from Arkansas to California Prior to the Civil War." *Arkansas Historical Quarterly* 28, no. 3 (Autumn 1969): 275–81.

Auchampaugh, Philip Gerald. *Robert Tyler: Southern Rights Champion, 1847–1866; A Documentary Study Chiefly of Antebellum Politics*. Duluth MN: Himan Stein, 1934.

August, Ray. "The Spread of Community-Property Law to the Far West." *Western Legal History* 3, no. 1 (Winter/Spring 1990): 35–66.

Ayers, James J. *Gold and Sunshine: Reminiscences of Early California*. Boston: Gorham Press, 1922.

Ayers, John. "A Soldier's Experience in New Mexico." *New Mexico Historical Review* 24, no. 4 (October 1949): 259–66.

Bagley, Will, ed. *Frontiersman: Abner Blackburn's Narrative.* Salt Lake City: University of Utah Press, 1992.

———. *With Golden Visions Bright before Them: Trails to the Mining West, 1849–1852.* Norman: University of Oklahoma Press, 2012.

Bailey, L. R. *The Long Walk: A History of the Navajo Wars, 1846–68.* Los Angeles: Westernlore Press, 1964.

Bailey, Lynn R. *Supplying the Mining World: The Mining Equipment Manufacturers of San Francisco, 1850–1900.* Tucson: Westernlore Press, 1996.

Bain, David Haward. *Empire Express: Building the First Transcontinental Railroad.* New York: Viking, 1999.

Ball, Durwood. *Army Regulars on the Western Frontier, 1848–1861.* Norman: University of Oklahoma Press, 2001.

Bancroft, Hubert Howe. *The Works of Hubert Howe Bancroft.* Vol. 33, *History of California, 1848–1859.* San Francisco: History Company, 1888.

———. *The Works of Hubert Howe Bancroft.* Vol. 2, *History of Oregon.* San Francisco: History Company, 1888.

Barba, Preston. *Balduin Mollhausen, the German Cooper.* Philadelphia: University of Pennsylvania Press, 1914.

Bargo, Michael. "Women's Occupations in the West in 1870." *Journal of the West* 32 (January 1993): 30–45.

Barker, Charles Albro, ed. *Memoirs of Elisha Oscar Crosby: Reminiscences of California and Guatemala from 1849 to 1864.* San Marino CA: Huntington Library, 1945.

Barnes, Demas. *From the Atlantic to the Pacific, Overland.* New York: D. Van Nostrand, 1866.

Barnett, Le Roy. "An Historical Geography of the Nineteenth Century Buffalo Bone Commerce on the Northern Great Plains." Michigan State University, 1979.

Barnett, Louise. *Touched by Fire: The Life, Death, and Mythic Afterlife of George Armstrong Custer.* New York: Henry Holt, 1996.

Barnhart, Jaqueline Baker. *The Fair but Frail: Prostitution in San Francisco, 1849–1900.* Reno: University of Nevada Press, 1986.

Barre, Weston. *The Peyote Cult.* New York: Schocken, 1969.

Barsh, Russel L. "The Substitution of Cattle for Bison on the Great Plains." In *The Struggle for the Land: Indigenous Insight and Industrial Empire in the Semiarid World,* 103–26. Lincoln: University of Nebraska Press, 1990.

Barsness, Larry. *Gold Camp: Alder Gulch and Virginia City, Montana.* New York: Hastings House, 1962.

Bartlett, Richard A. *Great Surveys of the American West.* Norman: University of Oklahoma Press, 1962.

———. *Yellowstone: A Wilderness Beseiged.* Tucson: University of Arizona Press, 1985.

Basler, Roy P., ed. *The Collected Works of Abraham Lincoln.* Vol. 4. New Brunswick: Rutgers University Press, 1953.

Batchelder, George Alexander. "A Sketch of the History and Resources of Dakota Territory [1870]." In *South Dakota Historical Collections*, vol. 14, comp. State Department of History. Pierre SD: Hipple Printing, 1928.

Bates, William W. *American Marine: The Shipping Question in History and Politics*. Boston: Houghton Mifflin, 1892.

Bauman, Paula M. "Single Women Homesteaders in Wyoming, 1880–1930." *Annals of Wyoming* 58, no. 1 (Spring 1986): 39–53.

Baumgardner, Frank H., III. *Killing for Land in Early California: Indian Blood at Round Valley*. New York: Algora, 2005.

Beal, Merrill D., and Merle W. Wells. *History of Idaho*. Vol. 1. New York: Lewis Historical Publishing, 1959.

Bean, William B. *Walter Reed: A Biography*. Charlottesville: University of Virginia Press, 1982.

Beck, Paul N. *Columns of Vengeance: Soldiers, Sioux, and the Punitive Expeditions, 1863–1864*. Norman: University of Oklahoma Press, 2013.

———. *The First Sioux War: The Grattan Fight and Blue Water Creek, 1854–1856*. Lanham MD: University Press of America, 2004.

Beckham, Stephen Dow. *Requiem for a People: The Rogue Indians and the Frontiersmen*. Corvalis: Oregon State University Press, 1971.

Bee, Robert L. "Peyotism in North American Indian Groups." *Transactions of the Kansas Academy of Science* 68, no. 1 (Spring 1965): 13–61

Beebe, Lucius, and Charles Clegg. *Legends of the Comstock Lode*. Stanford: Stanford University Press, 1950.

Beesley, David. "Beyond Gilbert: Environmental History and Hydraulic Mining in the Sierra Nevada." *Mining History Journal* 7 (2000): 71–80.

Beidleman, Richard G. *California's Pioneer Naturalists*. Berkeley: University of California Press, 2006.

Belich, James. *Making Peoples: A History of the New Zealanders from Polynesian Settlement to the End of the Nineteenth Century*. Honolulu: University of Hawaii Press, 1996.

———. *Replenishing the Earth: The Settler Revolution and the Rise of the Anglo-World, 1783–1939*. New York: Oxford University Press, 2009.

Bell, Major Horace. *Reminiscences of a Ranger or, Early Times in Southern California*. Los Angeles: Yarnell, Caystile and Mathes, 1881.

Beller, Jack. "Negro Slaves in Utah." *Utah Historical Quarterly* 2, no. 4 (October 1929): 122–26.

Bellesiles, Michael A. "Western Violence." In *A Companion to the American West*, edited by William Deverell, 162–78. Malden MA: Blackwell, 2004.

Bender, Averam B. *The March of Empire: Frontier Defense in the Southwest, 1848–1860*. Lawrence: University Press of Kansas, 1952.

Bennett, Edwin Lewis. *Boom Town Boy*. Chicago: Sage, 1966.

Bennett, John C. *The History of the Saints; or, and Exposé of Joe Smith and Mormonism*. Boston: Leland and Whiting, 1842.

Bennion, Michael Kay. "Captivity, Adoption, Marriage and Identity: Native American Children in Mormon Homes, 1847–1900." M.A. thesis, University of Nevada, Las Vegas, 2012.

Bent, Allen H. *The Bent Family in America: Being Mainly a Genealogy of the Descendants of John Bent*. Boston: David Clapp and Son, 1900.

Bent, Silas. "Meteorology of the Mountains and Plains of North America, as Affecting the Cattle-Growing Industries of the United States." In *Proceedings of the First National Convention of Cattle Growers of the United States*, 92–97. Saint Louis: B. P. Studley, 1884.

Berg, Scott W. *38 Nooses: Lincoln, Little Crow, and the Beginning of the Frontier's End*. New York: Pantheon, 2014.

Bernstein, Peter L. *The Power of Gold: The History of an Obsession*. New York: John Wiley and Sons, 2000.

Berry, Thomas Senior. "Gold! But How Much?" *California Historical Quarterly* 55, no. 3 (Fall 1976): 246–55.

Berthrong, Donald J. *The Cheyenne and Arapaho Ordeal: Reservation and Agency Life in the Indian Territory, 1875–1907*. Norman: University of Oklahoma Press, 1976.

Berwanger, Eugene H. *The Frontier against Slavery: Western Anti-Negro Prejudice and the Slavery Extension Controversy*. Urbana: University of Illinois Press, 1967.

———. "Reconstruction on the Frontier: The Equal Rights Struggle in Colorado, 1865–1867." *Pacific Historical Review* 46, no. 3 (August 1975): 313–30.

Bethel, A. C. W. "The Golden Skein: California's Gold-Rush Transportation Network." *California History* 72, no. 4 (Winter 1998/1999): 250–75.

Betts, C. W. "The Yale College Expedition of 1870." *Harper's New Monthly Magazine* 43, no. 257 (October 1871): 663–72.

Beyreis, David. "'If You Had Fought Bravely I Would Have Sung for You': The Changing Roles of Cheyenne Women during Nineteenth-Century Plains Warfare." *Montana: The Magazine of Western History* 69, no. 1 (Spring 2019): 3–20.

Bieder, Robert E. *A Brief Historical Survey of the Exploration of American Indian Remains*. Boulder: Native American Rights Funds, 1990.

———. *Science Encounters the Indian, 1820–1880: The Early Years of American Ethnology*. Norman: University of Oklahoma Press, 1986.

Bigler, David L. "The Aiken Party Executions and the Utah War, 1857–1858." *Western Historical Quarterly* 38, no. 4 (Winter 2007): 457–76.

———. "'A Lion in the Path': Genesis of the Utah War, 1857–1858." *Utah Historical Quarterly* 76, no. 1 (Winter 2008): 4–21.

———. "The Crisis at Fort Limhi, 1858." *Utah Historical Quarterly* 35, no. 2 (Spring 1967): 121–36.

———. *Forgotten Kingdom: The Mormon Theocracy in the American West*. Spokane WA: Arthur H. Clark, 1998.

Bigler, David L., and Will Bagley, eds. *Army of Israel: Mormon Battalion Narratives*. The Mormons and the American Frontier. Spokane WA: Arthur H. Clark, 2000.

———. *The Mormon Rebellion: America's First Civil War, 1857–1858*. Norman: University of Oklahoma Press, 2011.

Billington, Monroe. *New Mexico's Buffalo Soldiers, 1866–1900*. Niwot: University Press of Colorado, 1991.

Billington, Ray Allen. *Land of Savagery, Land of Promise: The European Image of the American Frontier in the Nineteenth Century*. New York: W. W. Norton, 1981.

———. "The Origin of the Land Speculator as a Frontier Type." *Agricultural History* 19, no. 4 (October 1945): 204–12.

Binder, John J. "The Transportation Revolution and Antebellum Sectional Disagreement." *Social Science History* 35, no. 1 (Spring 2011): 19–57.

Binkley, William Campbell. *The Expansionist Movement in Texas, 1836–1850*. University of California Publications in History, vol. 13. Berkeley: University of California Press, 1925.

Binnema, Theodore. *Common and Contested Ground: A Human and Environmental History of the Northwestern Plains*. Norman: University of Oklahoma Press, 2001.

Bitton, Davis, and Linda Wilcox. "The Transformation of Utah's Agriculture." In *The Twentieth-Century American West: Contributions to an Understanding*, edited by Thomas G. Alexander and John F. Bluth, 57–84. Midvale UT: Charles Redd Center for Western Studies, 1983.

Black, Jason Edward. *American Indians and the Rhetoric of Removal and Allotment*. Jackson: University Press of Mississippi, 2015.

Blackhawk, Ned. *Violence over the Land: Indians and Empires in the Early American West*. Cambridge: Harvard University Press, 2006.

Blackwood, Evelyn. "Sexuality and Gender in Certain Native American Tribes: The Case of Cross-Gender Females." *Signs* 10, no. 1 (Autumn 1984): 27–42.

Blevins, Cameron. *Paper Trails: The US Post and the Making of the American West*. New York: Oxford University Press, 2021.

Blodgett, Ralph E. "The Colorado Territorial Board of Immigration." *Colorado Magazine* 46, no. 3 (Summer 1969).

Blondheim, Manahem. *News over the Wires: The Telegraph and the Flow of Public Information*. Cambridge: Harvard University Press, 1994.

Bloss, Roy S. *Pony Express: The Great Gamble*. Berkeley: Howell-North, 1959.

Blussé, Leonard. *Visible Cities: Canton, Nagasaki, and Batavia and the Coming of the Americans*. Cambridge: Harvard University Press, 2008.

Bonney, Orrin H., and Lorraine Bonney. *Battle Drums and Geysers: The Life and Journals of Lt. Gustavus Cheyney Doane, Soldier and Explorer of the Yellowstone and Snake River Regions*. Chicago: Sage, 1970.

Bonsall, Thomas E. *More Than They Promised: The Studebaker Story*. Palo Alto: Stanford University Press, 2000.

Booker, Matthew Morse. *Down by the Bay: San Francisco's History between the Tides*. Berkeley: University of California Press, 2013.

Borthwick, J. D. *Three Years in California*. Edinburgh and London: William Blackwood and Sons, 1857.

Bowie, Aug. J. *A Practical Treatise on Hydraulic Mining in California*. New York: D. Van Nostrand, 1885.

Bowles, Samuel. *Our New West*. Hartford: Hartford, 1869.

Braatz, Timothy. *Surviving Conquest: A History of the Yavapai Peoples*. Lincoln: University of Nebraska Press, 2003.

Bradley, Harold Whitman. "Hawaii and the American Penetration of the Northeastern Pacific, 1800–1845." *Pacific Historical Review* 12, no. 3 (September 1943): 277–86.

Branch, E. Douglas. *The Hunting of the Buffalo*. New York: D. Appleton, 1929.

Brantlinger, Patrick. *Dark Vanishings: Discourse on the Extinction of Primitive Races, 1800–1930*. Ithaca: Cornell University Press, 2003.

Bratt, John. *Trails of Yesterday*. Lincoln: University Publishing, 1921.

Braude, Ann. "The Baptism of a Cheyenne Girl." In *The Study of Children in Religions: A Methods Handbook*, edited by Susan B. Ridgley, 236–51. New York: New York University Press, 2011.

Bray, Kingsley M. *Crazy Horse: A Lakota Life*. Norman: University of Oklahoma Press, 2006.

———. "Lone Horn's Peace: A New View of Sioux-Crow Relations, 1851–1858." *Nebraska History* 66, no. 1 (Spring 1985): 28–47.

Brayer, Herbert O., ed. *Pike's Peak . . . or Busted! Frontier Reminiscences of William Hawkins Hedges*. Evanston IL: Branding Iron, 1954.

Breithaupt, Brent H. "Railroads, Blizzards, and Dinosaurs: A History of Collecting in the Morrison Formation of Wyoming during the 19th Century." *Modern Geology* 23, no. 1–4 (July 1998): 441–64.

Brereton, Roslyn. "Mining Techniques in the California Goldfields in the 1850s." *Pacific Historian* 20, no. 3 (Fall 1976): 286–302.

Brewer, H. Peers. "Eastern Money and Western Mortgages in the 1870s." *Business History Review* 50, no. 3 (Autumn 1976): 356–80.

Brewer, William H. *Up and Down California in 1860–1864: The Diary of William H. Brewer*. Berkeley: University of California Press, 2003.

———. *Up and Down California in 1860–1864: The Journal of William H. Brewer*. Edited by Francis P. Farquar. New Haven: Yale University Press, 1930.

Brewster, Edwin Tenney. *Life and Letters of Josiah Dwight Whitney*. Boston: Houghton Mifflin, 1909.

Bridges, C. A. "The Knights of the Golden Circle: A Filibustering Fantasy." *Southwestern Historical Quarterly* 44, no. 3 (January 1941): 287–302.

"A Brief Chronology of Battles and Skirmishes, 1864–65." *Colorado Heritage*, Autumn 1996.

Brill, Charles J. *Custer, Black Kettle, and the Fight on the Washita*. Norman: Red River Books, 2002.

Bringhurst, Newell G. "The Mormons and Slavery: A Closer Look." *Pacific Historical Review* 50, no. 3 (August 1981): 329–38.

Brisbin, James S. *The Beef Bonanza: or, How to Get Rich on the Plains*. Philadelphia: J. B. Lippincott, 1881.

Brockett, L. P. *Our Western Empire: or, the New West beyond the Mississippi*. Philadelphia: Bradley, 1881.

Brooks, James. *Captives and Cousins: Slavery, Kinship, and Community in the Southwest Borderlands*. Chapel Hill: University of North Carolina Press, 2002.

Brooks, Juanita. "Indian Relations on the Mormon Frontier." *Utah State Historical Society* 12, no. 1–2 (January–April 1944).

Brosnan, Kathleen A. *Uniting Mountain and Plain: Cities, Law, and Environmental Change Along the Front Range*. Albuquerque: University of New Mexico Press, 2002.

Brough, Charles Hillman. *Irrigation in Utah*. Baltimore: Johns Hopkins Press, 1898.

Brown, George L. *The State of Nebraska as a Home for Emigrants*. Omaha NE: Republican Printing, 1875.

Brown, Richard Maxwell. *Strain of Violence: Historical Studies of American Violence and Vigilantism*. New York: Oxford University Press, 1975.

———. "Violence." In *The Oxford History of the American West*, edited by Clyde A. Milner II, Carol A. O'Connor, and Martha A. Sandweiss, 393–425. New York: Oxford University Press, 1994.

Brown, Walter Lee. *A Life of Albert Pike*. Fayetteville: University of Arkansas Press, 1997.

Browne, J. Ross. "Coast Rangers of California." *Harper's New Monthly Magazine* 23, no. 135 (August 1861): 306–16.

———. "Down in the Cinnabar Mines." *Harper's New Monthly Magazine* 31, no. 185 (October 1865): 545–61.

———. *J. Ross Browne: His Letters, Journals, and Writings*. Albuquerque: University of New Mexico Press, 1969.

Brugge, David M. *Navajos in the Catholic Church Records of New Mexico*. Santa Fe: School for Advanced Research Press, 2010.

Brundage, W. Fitzhugh. *Lynching in the New South: Georgia and Virginia, 1880–1930*. Urbana: University of Illinois Press, 1993.

Bryan, Jimmy L., Jr. *The American Elsewhere: Adventure and Manliness in the Age of Expansion*. Lawrence: University Press of Kansas, 2017.

Buchanan, Russell. "James A. McDougall: A Forgotten Senator." *California Historical Society Quarterly* 15, no. 3 (September 1936): 199–212.

Burcham, L. T. *California Range Land: An Historico-Ecological Study of the Range Resource of California*. Sacramento: Department of Natural Resources, 1957.

———. "Cattle and Range Forage in California: 1770–1880." *Agricultural History* 35, no. 3 (July 1961): 140–49.

Burnettizing: Or the Process of Preventing the Rapid Decay of Timber by the Use of Chloride of Zinc. Lowell: Proprietors of the Locks and Canals of the Merrimack River, 1859.

Burnham, Philip. *Indian Country, God's Country: Native Americans and the National Parks*. Washington DC: Island Press, 2000.

———. *Song of Dewey Beard: Last Survivor of the Little Big Horn*. Lincoln: Bison, 2014.

Burton, Richard Francis. *The Look of the West, 1860: Across the Plains to California*. Lincoln: University of Nebraska Press, 1963.

Butler, Aaron Jason. "A Union of Church and State: The Freedmen's Bureau and the Education of African Americans in Virginia from 1865–1871." PhD dissertation, College of William and Mary, 2013.

Butler, Anne M. *Daughters of Joy, Sisters of Misery: Prostitutes in the American West, 1865–90.* Urbana: University of Illinois Press, 1985.

Calloway, Colin G. *One Vast Winter Count: The Native American West before Lewis and Clark.* Lincoln: University of Nebraska Press, 2003.

———. "'The Only Way Open to Us': The Crow Struggle for Survival in the Nineteenth Century." *North Dakota History* 53, no. 1 (1986): 25–34.

Camp, Charles L., ed. *James Clyman, Frontiersman.* Portland OR: Champoeg, 1960.

Campney, Brent M. S. *This Is Not Dixie: Racist Violence in Kansas, 1861–1927.* Norman: University of Illinois Press, 2015.

Canfield, Chauncey L. *The Diary of a Forty-Niner.* San Francisco: M. Shepard, 1906.

Cannon, Brian Q. "Adopted or Indentured, 1850–1870: Native Children in Mormon Households." In *Nearly Everything Imaginable: The Everyday Life of Utah's Mormon Pioneers,* edited by Ronald W. Walker and Doris R. Dant, 341–57. Provo: Brigham Young University Press, 1999.

———. "'To Buy Up the Lamanite Children as Fast as They Could': Indentured Servitude and Its Legacy in Mormon Society." *Journal of Mormon History* 44, no. 2 (April 2018): 1–35.

Cannon, Donald Q. "The King Follett Discourse: Joseph Smith's Greatest Sermon in Historical Perspective." *BYU Studies* 18, no. 2 (Winter 1978): 179–92.

Cannon, Donald Q., and Larry E. Dahl. *The Prophet Joseph Smith's King Follett Discourse.* Provo: Religious Studies Center, Brigham Young University, 1983.

Carlson, Leonard A. *Indians, Bureaucrats, and Land: The Dawes Act and the Decline of Indian Farming.* Westport: Greenwood, 1981.

———. "Learning to Farm: Indian Land Tenure and Farming before the Dawes Act." In *Property Rights and Indian Economies: The Political Economic Forum,* edited by Terry L. Anderson, 67–84. Lanham MD: Rowan and Littlefield, 1992.

Carlson, Wallin John. "A History of the San Francisco Mining Exchange." M.A. thesis, University of California, Berkeley, 1928.

Carpenter, Helen M. "Among the Diggers of Thirty Years Ago." *Overland Monthly* 21, no. 122 (February 1893): 146–55.

Carranco, Lynwood, and Estle Beard. *Genocide and Vendetta: The Round Valley Wars of Northern California.* Norman: University of Oklahoma Press, 1981.

Carrigan, William D. *The Making of a Lynching Culture: Violence and Vigilantism in Central Texas.* Urbana: University of Illinois Press, 2006.

———. "The Strange Career of Judge Lynch: Why the Study of Lynching Needs to Be Refocused on the Mid-Nineteenth Century." *Journal of the Civil War Era* 7, no. 2 (June 2017): 293–312.

Carrigan, William D., and Clive Webb. *Forgotten Dead: Mob Violence against Mexicans in the United States, 1848–1928.* New York: Oxford University Press, 2013.

———. "The Lynching of Persons of Mexican Origin or Descent in the United States, 1848 to 1928." *Journal of Social History* 37, no. 2 (2003): 411–38.

Carson, James H. *Recollections of the California Mines; an Account of the Early Discoveries of Gold, with Anecdotes and Sketches of California and Miner's Life, and a Description of the Great Tulare Valley.* Oakland CA: Biobooks, 1950.

Cases Argued and Determined in the Circuit and District Courts of the United States. Saint Paul: West, 1884.

Cassidy, James G. *Ferdinand V. Hayden: Entrepreneur of Science.* Lincoln: University of Nebraska Press, 2000.

Catton, Theodore. *Inhabited Wilderness: Indians, Eskimos, and National Parks in Alaska.* Albuquerque: University of New Mexico Press, 1997.

Caughey, John W. *California.* New York: Prentice-Hall, 1940.

———. "The Californian and His Environment." *California Historical Society Quarterly* 51, no. 3 (Fall 1972): 1972.

Cecil-Fronsman, Bill. "'Advocate the Freedom of White Men, as Well as That of Negroes': The *Kansas Free State* and Antislavery Westerners in Territorial Kansas." *Kansas History: A Journal of the Central Plains* 20, no. 2 (Summer 1997): 102–15.

Centennial Edition of the Fourth Annual Report of the State Board of Agriculture. Topeka: George W. Martin, 1876.

Chalfant, William Y. *Hancock's War: Conflict on the Southern Plains.* Norman: Arthur H. Clak, 2010.

Chamberlin, J. Edward. *Horse: How the Horse Has Shaped Civilizations.* New York: BlueBridge, 2006.

Chan, Sucheng. "The Exclusion of Chinese Women." In *Entry Denied: Exclusion and the Chinese Community in America,* edited by Sucheng Chan, 94–146. Philadelphia: Temple University Press, 1991.

Chandless, William. *A Visit to Salt Lake: Being a Journey across the Plains and a Residence in the Mormon Settlements of Utah.* London: Smith, Elder, 1857.

Chang, Gordon H. *Ghosts of Gold Mountain: The Epic Story of the Chinese Who Built the Transcontinental Railroad.* Boston: Houghton Mifflin Harcourt, 2019.

Chen, Yong. "The Internal Origins of Chinese Emigration to California Reconsidered." *Western Historical Quarterly* 28, no. 4 (Winter 1997): 520–46.

Chevalier, Michel. *Of the Probable Fall of the Value of Gold: The Commercial and Social Consequences Which May Ensue, and the Measures Which It Invites.* Manchester: Alexr. Ireland, 1859.

Childers, Christopher. *The Failure of Popular Sovereignty: Slavery, Manifest Destiny, and the Radicalization of Southern Politics.* Lawrence: University Press of Kansas, 2012.

Chittenden, Hiram Martin, and Alfred Talbot Richardson, eds. *Life, Letters, and Travels of Father Pierre-Jean DeSmet, S.J., 1801–1873.* Vol. 2. New York: Francis F. Harper, 1905.

Chiu, Ping. *Chinese Labor in California: An Economic Study.* Madison: State Historical Society of Wisconsin, 1963.

Christensen, James B. "Negro Slavery in the Utah Territory." *Phylon Quarterly* 18, no. 3 (3rd Quarter 1957): 398–405.

Christensen, Scott R. *Sagwitch: Shoshone Chieftain, Mormon Elder, 1822–1887.* Logan: Utah State University Press, 1999.

Chung, Sue Fawn. "Their Changing World: Chinese Women on the Comstock, 1860–1910." In *Comstock Women: The Making of a Mining Community,* edited by Ronald M. James and Elizabeth Raymond, 203–28. Reno: University of Nevada Press, 1998.

Church, John A. *The Comstock Lode: Its Formation and History*. New York: John Wiley & Sons, 1879.

Churchill, Charles B. "Thomas Jefferson Farnham: An Exponent of American Empire in Mexican California." *Pacific Historical Review* 60, no. 4 (November 1991): 517–37.

Churchill, Mrs. C. M. *"Little Sheaves" Gathered while Gleaning after Reapers: Being Letters of Travel Commencing in 1870, and Ending in 1873*. San Francisco, 1874.

Clappe, Louise Amelia Knapp. *The Shirley Letters from California Mines in 1851–52*. San Francisco: T. C. Russell, 1922.

Clark, Blue. *Lone Wolf v. Hitchcock: Treaty Rights and Indian Law at the End of the Nineteenth Century*. Lincoln: University of Nebraska Press, 1994.

Clark, Thomas D., ed. *Gold Rush Diary: Being the Journal of Elisha Douglass Perkins on the Overland Trail in the Spring and Summer of 1849*. Lexington: University of Kentucky Press, 1967.

Clark, Walter Van Tilburg, ed. *The Journals of Alfred Doten, 1849–1903*. Vol. 1. Reno: University of Nevada Press, 1973.

Clary, David A. *Eagles and Empire: The United States, Mexico, and the Struggle for a Continent*. New York: Bantam, 2009.

Clay, John. *My Life on the Range*. Chicago: Privately Printed, 1924.

Clay, Karen, and Randall Jones. "Migrating to Riches? Evidence from the California Gold Rush." *Journal of Economic History* 68, no. 4 (December 2008): 997–1027.

Cleland, Robert Glass. *The Cattle on a Thousand Hills*. San Marino CA: Huntington Library, 1951.

Clendenen, Clarence C. "A Confederate Spy in California: A Curious Incident of the Civil War." *Southern California Quarterly* 45, no. 3 (September 1963): 219–34.

Clow, Richmond L. "General William S. Harney on the Northern Plains." *South Dakota History* 16, no. 3 (Fall 1986): 229–48.

———. "Mad Bear: William S. Harney and the Sioux Expedition of 1855–1856." *Nebraska History* 61, no. 2 (Summer 1980): 133–51.

———. "William S. Harney." In *Soldiers West: Biographies from the Military Frontier*, 42–58. Lincoln: University of Nebraska Press, 1987.

Clyde, George D. "History of Irrigation in Utah." *Utah Historical Quarterly* 27, no. 1 (January 1959): 27–36.

Coffin, James H. *Winds of the Northern Hemisphere*. Washington DC: Smithsonian Institution, 1853.

Coffman, Edward M. *The Old Army: A Portrait of the American Army in Peacetime, 1784–1898*. New York: Oxford University Press, 1986.

Cohen, Michael P. *The Pathless Way: John Muir and the American Wilderness*. Madison: University of Wisconsin Press, 1984.

Colden, Cadwallader D. *Memoir, Prepared at the Request of a Committee of the Common Council of the City of New York.. at the Celebration of the Completion of the New York Canals*. New York: W. A. Davis, 1825.

Cole, Allan B. "The Ringgold-Rodgers-Brooke Expedition to Japan and the Northern Pacific, 1853–1859." *Pacific Historical Review* 16, no. 2 (May 1947): 152–62.

Collins, Carvel, ed. *Sam Ward in the Gold Rush.* Stanford CA: Stanford University Press, 1949.

Collinson, Frank. *Life in the Saddle.* Norman: University of Oklahoma Press, 1972.

Colpitts, George. *Pemmican Empire: Food, Trade, and the Last Bison Hunts in the North American Plains.* Cambridge: Cambridge University Press, 2015.

Colton, Ray C. *The Civil War in the Western Territories: Arizona, Colorado, New Mexico, and Utah.* Norman: University of Oklahoma Press, 1959.

Combs, Barry B. "The Union Pacific Railroad and the Early Settlement of Nebraska, 1868–1880." *Nebraska History* 50, no. 1 (Spring 1969): 1–21.

Commons, John R., ed. *A Documentary History of American Industrial Society.* Cleveland OH: Arthur H. Clark, 1910.

Comstock, David Allan. *Gold Diggers and Camp Followers.* Grass Valley CA: Comstock Bonanza Press, 1982.

Conlin, Joseph R. *Bacon, Beans, and Galantines: Food and Foodways on the Western Mining Frontier.* Reno: University of Nevada Press, 1986.

Connell, Evan S. *Son of the Morning Star.* New York: Harper and Row, 1985.

Connelly, Thomas L. "The American Camel Experiment: A Reappraisal." *Southwestern Historical Quarterly* 69, no. 4 (April 1966): 442–62.

Cook, James H. *Fifty Years on the Old Frontier, as Cowboy, Hunter, Guide, Scout, and Ranchman.* New Haven: Yale University Press, 1923.

Cook, Mary J. Straw. *Doña Tules: Santa Fe's Courtesan and Gambler.* Albuquerque: University of New Mexico Press, 2007.

Cook, Sherburne F. *The Aboriginal Population of the North Coast of California.* University of California Anthropological Records, 79–129. Berkeley: University of California Press, 1956.

———. *The Conflict between the California Indian and White Civilization.* Berkeley: University of California Press, 1960.

Cooke, Philip St. George. *The Conquest of New Mexico and California: An Historical and Personal Narrative.* New York: G. P. Putnam's Sons, 1878.

Coolidge, Mary Roberts. *Chinese Immigration.* New York: Henry Holt, 1909.

Coon, S. J. "Influence of the Gold Camps on the Economic Development of Western Montana." *Journal of Political Economy* 38, no. 5 (October 1930): 580–99.

Corbett, Christopher. *Orphans Preferred: The Twisted Truth and Lasting Legend of the Pony Express.* New York: Broadway, 2003.

Corbett, Hoye & Co.'s 5th Annual Denver City Directory. Denver: Corbett, Hoye, 1877.

Corbett, Hoye, & Co.'s Directory of the City of Denver. Denver: Corbett, Hoye, 1880.

Cordero, Jonathan. "White Girls for Red Lights: The Procurement of American and European Girls for the Purpose of Prostitution in San Francisco, 1860–1900." *Journal of the West* 51, no. 1 (Winter 2012): 20–29.

Corey, Lewis. *Meat and Man: A Study of Monopoly, Unionism, and Food Policy.* New York: Viking Press, 1950.

Cotterill, R. S. "The Beginnings of Railroads in the Southwest." *Mississippi Valley Historical Review* 8, no. 4 (March 1924): 318–26.

———. "Southern Railroads, 1850–1860." *Mississippi Valley Historical Review* 10, no. 4 (March 9924): 396–405.

Courtwright, David T. "Opiate Addiction as a Consequence of the Civil War." *Civil War History* 24, no. 2 (June 1978): 101–11.

———. "Opiate Addiction in the American West." *Journal of the West* 21, no. 3 (July 1982): 23–31.

———. *Violent Land: Single Men and Social Disorder from the Frontier to the Inner City.* Cambridge: Harvard University Press, 1996.

Cox, Thomas R. *The Lumberman's Frontier: Three Centuries of Land Use, Society, and Change in America's Forests.* Corvallis: Oregon State University Press, 2010.

———. *Mills and Markets: A History of the Pacific Coast Lumber Industry to 1900.* Seattle: University of Washington Press, 1974.

Cozzens, Peter. *The Earth Is Weeping: The Epic Story of the Indian Wars for the American West.* New York: Alfred Knopf, 2016.

Craig, R. Bruce, ed. *Portrait of a Prospector: Edward Schieffelin's Own Story.* Norman: University of Oklahoma Press, 2017.

Cremony, John. C. *Life among the Apaches.* San Francisco and New York: A. Roman, 1868.

Crenshaw, Ollinger. "The Knights of the Golden Circle: The Career of George Bickley." *American Historical Review* 47, no. 1 (October 1941): 23–50.

Crockett, Norman L. *The Black Towns.* Lawrence: University Press of Kansas, 1979.

Crofford, Mrs. H. E. "Pioneer Days in North Dakota." *North Dakota Historical Quarterly* 2, no. 2 (Summer 1928): 129–37.

Croffut's Trans-Continental Tourist's Guide. New York: George A. Croffut, 1873.

Cronise, Titus Fey. *The Natural Wealth of California.* San Francisco: H. H. Bancroft, 1868.

Cronon, William. *Nature's Metropolis: Chicago and the Great West.* New York: W. W. Norton, 1991.

Crosby, Molly Caldwell. *The American Plague: The Untold Story of Yellow Fever, the Epidemic That Shaped Our History.* New York: Berkeley, 2006.

Cummins, D. H. "Toll Roads in Southwestern Colorado." *Colorado Magazine* 29, no. 2 (April 1952): 98–104.

Curtis, Kent. "Producing a Gold Rush: Ambitions and the Northern Rocky Mountains, 1853–1863." *Western Historical Quarterly* 40, no. 3 (Autumn 2009): 275–97.

Cutler, Don. "Your Nations Shall Be EXTERMINATED." *MHQ: The Quarterly Journal of Military History* 22, no. 3 (Spring 2010): 46–53.

Cutler, Wayne, ed. *Correspondence of James K. Polk.* Vol. 10. Nashville: Vanderbilt University Press, 2004.

Dailey, Dennis M. "Josiah Miller, an Antislavery Southerner: Letters to Father and Mother." *Kansas: A Journal of the Central Plains* 36, no. 2 (Summer 2013): 66–89.

Dale, Edward E. "The Cherokees in the Confederacy." *Journal of Southern History* 13, no. 2 (May 1947): 160–85.

———. *Cow Country.* Norman: University of Oklahoma Press, 1965.

———. "Ranching on the Cheyenne-Arapaho Reservation, 1880–1885." *Chronicles of Oklahoma* 6, no. 1 (March 1928): 35–51.

———. *The Range Cattle Industry*. Norman: University of Oklahoma Press, 1930.

Danziger, Edmund J., Jr. "The Crow Creek Experiment: An Aftermath of the Sioux War of 1862." *North Dakota History* 37, no. 2 (Spring 1970): 105–23.

———. "The Office of Indian Affairs and the Problem of Civil War Indian Refugees in Kansas." *Kansas Historical Quarterly* 35, no. 3 (Autumn 1969): 257–75.

Darrah, William Culp, ed. "J. C. Sumner's Journal." *Utah Historical Quarterly* 15, no. 1–4 (January–October 1947).

Dary, David. *Cowboy Culture: A Saga of Five Centuries*. Lawrence: University Press of Kansas, 1981.

Davidson, Stanley R., and Dale Tash. "Confederate Backwash in Montana Territory." *Montana: The Magazine of Western History* 17, no. 4 (October 1967): 50–58.

Davis, Horace. "California Breadstuffs." *Journal of Political Economy* 2, no. 4 (September 1894): 517–35.

———. "Wheat in California." *Overland Monthly and Out West Magazine* 1, no. 5 (November 1868): 442–52.

Davis, James E. *Frontier America, 1800–1840: A Comparative Demographic Analysis of the Settlement Process*. Glendale CA: Arthur H. Clark, 1977.

Davis, John Patterson. *The Union Pacific Railway: A Study in Railway Politics, History, and Economics*. Chicago: S. C. Griggs, 1894.

Davis, Joseph, and Marc D. Weidenmier. "America's First Moderation." *Journal of Economic History* 77, no. 4 (December 2017): 1116–43.

Davis, Lance E., Robert E. Gallman, and Karin Gleiter. *In Pursuit of Leviathan: Technology, Institutions, Productivity, and Profits in American Whaling, 1816–1906*. Chicago: University of Chicago Press, 1997.

Dawdy, Doris O. *George Montague Wheeler: The Man and the Myth*. Athens OH: Swallow Press, 1993.

Dawson, David D. "Reconsidered: The Buffalo Hunters on the Southern Plains." MA thesis, University of Arkansas, 1990.

Dawson, Thomas F. *The Ute War: A History of the White River Massacre*. Denver: Tribune, 1879.

Day-Gonzales, Ken. *Lynching in the West: 1850–1935*. Durham: Duke University Press, 2006.

Dearinger, Ryan. *The Filth of Progress: Immigrants, Americans, and the Building of Canals and Railroads in the West*. Oakland: University of California Press, 2016.

The Debates and Proceedings in the Congress of the United States. Washington DC: Gales and Seaton, 1855.

Decker, Leslie E. "The Great Speculation: An Interpretation of Mid-continent Pioneering." In *The Frontier in American Development: Essays in Honor of Paul Wallace Gates*, edited by David M. Ellis. Ithaca: Cornell University Press, 1969.

De Kruif, Paul. *Microbe Hunters*. New York: Harcourt, Brace, 1926.

Delano, Alonzo. *Pen Knife Sketches; or, Sketches of the Old Block*. Sacramento: Union Office, 1853.

DeLay, Brian. "Blood Talk: Violence and Belonging in the Navajo-New Mexico Bor- derland." In *Contested Spaces of Early America*, edited by Juliana Barr and Edward Countryman, 229–56. Philadelphia: University of Pennsylvania Press, 2014.

———. "Independent Indians and the U.S.-Mexican War." *American Historical Review* 112 (2007): 35–68.

———. *War of a Thousand Deserts: Indian Raids and the U.S.-Mexican War*. New Haven: Yale University Press, 2008.

———. "The Wider World of the Handsome Man: Southern Plains Indians Invade Mexico, 1830–1846." *Journal of the Early Republic* 27 (2007): 83–113.

Delgado, James P. *To California by Sea: A Maritime History of the California Gold Rush*. Columbia: University of South Carolina Press, 1990.

del Mar, David Peterson. *Beaten Down: A History of Interpersonal Violence in the West*. Seattle: University of Washington Press, 2002.

Deloria, Vine, Jr., and Raymond DeMallie, eds. *Proceedings of the Great Peace Commis- sion of 1867–1868*. Washington DC: Institute for the Development of Indian Law, 1975.

De Pew, Kathryn. "William A. Hammill, Early Colorado Pioneer of Georgetown." *Colo- rado History* 32, no. 4 (October 1955): 266–79.

de Quille, Dan. "Camels in the Mines." *New Mexico Historical Review* 24, no. 1 (January 1949): 54–61.

———. *History of the Big Bonanza*. Hartford CT: American Publishing, 1877.

Deverell, William. "Convalescence and California: The Civil War Comes West." *South- ern California Quarterly* 90, no. 1 (Spring 2008): 1–26.

———. "Thoughts from the Farther West: Mormons, California, and the Civil War." *Journal of Mormon History* 34, no. 2 (Spring 2008): 1–19.

"Diary of the Overland Trail 1849 and Letters 1849–50 of Captain David DeWolf." *Transactions of the Illinois State Historical Society for the Year 1925*, vol. 32, 183–222.

Dickerson, Edward N. *Joseph Henry and the Magnetic Telegraph*. New York: Charles Scribner's Sons, 1885.

Dickerson, James L. *Yellow Fever: A Deadly Disease Poised to Kill Again*. Amherst NY: Prometheus, 2006.

Di Silvestro, Roger. *Theodore Roosevelt in the Badlands: A Young Politician's Quest for Recovery in the American West*. New York: Walker, 2010.

Dobak, William A. "The Army and the Buffalo: A Demur, A Response to David D. Smits's 'The Frontier Army and the Destruction of the Buffalo: 1865–1883.'" *Western Historical Quarterly* 26, no. 2 (Summer 1995): 197–202.

Dobak, William A., and Thomas D. Phillips. *The Black Regulars, 1866–1898*. Norman: University of Oklahoma Press, 2001.

Dobie, Charles Caldwell. *San Francisco's Chinatown*. New York: D. Appleton-Century, 1936.

Dodge, Grenville M. *How We Built the Union Pacific Railway*. Council Bluffs IA: Mon- arch, 1910.

Donovan, James. *A Terrible Glory: Custer and the Little Bighorn, the Last Great Battle of the American West*. New York: Little, Brown, 2008.

Doti, Lynne Pierson, and Larry Schweikart. *Banking in the American West: From the Gold Rush to Deregulation*. Norman: University of Oklahoma Press, 1991.

——. *California Bankers, 1848–1993*. Needham Heights MA: Ginn, 1994.

Douglass, William A., and Jon Bilbao. *Amerikanuak: Basques in the New World*. Reno: University of Nevada Press, 1975.

Downs, Gregory P. *After Appomattox: Military Occupation and the Ends of War*. Cambridge: Harvard University Press, 2015.

Downs, Gregory P., and Kate Masur, eds. *The World the Civil War Made*. Chapel Hill: University of North Carolina Press, 2015.

Doyle, Susan Badger, ed. *Bound for Montana: Diaries from the Bozeman Trail*. Helena: Montana Historical Society, 2004.

Drache, Hiram M. *The Day of the Bonanza: A History of Bonanza Farming in the Red River Valley of the North*. Fargo: North Dakota Institute for Regional Studies, 1964.

"Driving Cattle from Texas to Iowa, 1866." *Annals of Iowa* 14, no. 4 (April 1924): 243–62.

Du Bois, Cora. *1870 Ghost Dance*. Lincoln: Bison, 2007.

Duke, C. S., and Joe B. Frantz. *6,000 Miles of Fence: Life on the XIT Ranch of Texas*. Austin: University of Texas Press, 1961.

Dunlay, Tom. *Kit Carson and the Indians*. Lincoln: University of Nebraska Press, 2000.

Dunraven, Earl of. *The Great Divide: Travels in the Upper Yellowstone in the Summer of 1874*. London: Chatto and Windus, 1876.

Durham, Philip, and Everett L. Jones. *The Negro Cowboys*. New York: Dodd, Mead, 1965.

Dutton, Clarence E. *Tertiary History of the Grand Cañon District*. Washington DC: U.S. Government Printing Office, 1882.

Dykstra, Robert R. "Body Counts and Murder Rates: The Contested Statistics of Western Violence." *Reviews in American History* 31, no. 4 (December 2003): 554–63.

——. *The Cattle Towns*. New York: Atheneum, 1972.

——. "Overdosing on Dodge City." *Western Historical Quarterly* 27, no. 4 (Winter 1996): 505–14.

——. "Quantifying the Wild West: The Problematic Statistics of Frontier Violence." *Western Historical Quarterly* 40, no. 3 (Autumn 2009): 321–47.

Dysart, Jane. "Mexican Women in San Antonio, 1830–1860." *Western Historical Quarterly* 7, no. 4 (October 1976): 365–75.

Eastman, Charles A. (Ohiyesa). *From the Deep Woods to Civilization: Chapters in the Autobiography of an Indian*. Boston: Little, Brown, 1916.

Edwards, Malcolm. "'The War of Complexional Distinction': Blacks in Gold Rush California and British Columbia." *California Historical Quarterly* 56, no. 1 (March 1977): 34–45.

Edwards, Richard, Jacob K. Friefeld, and Rebecca S. Wingo, eds. *Homesteading the Plains: Toward a New History*. Lincoln: University of Nebraska Press, 2017.

Egnal, Marc. *Clash of Extremes: The Economic Origins of the Civil War*. New York: Hill and Wang, 2009.

Ehat, Andrew F. "'It Seems like Heaven Began on Earth': Joseph Smith and the Constitution of the Kingdom of God." *BYU Studies* 20, no. 3 (Spring 1980): 1–26.

Eldredge, Niles. "Revisiting Clarence King's 'Catastrophism and Evolution' (1877)." *Biological Theory* 14 (2019): 247–53.

Eldredge, Zoeth Skinner, ed. *History of California*. Vol. 3. New York: Century History, 1915.

Ellis, Clyde. "'There Is No Doubt . . . the Dances Should Be Curtailed': Indian Dances and Federal Policy on the Southern Plains, 1880–1930." *Pacific Historical Review* 70, no. 4 (November 2001): 543–69.

———. "'We Don't Want Your Rations, We Want This Dance': The Changing Use of Song and Dance on the Southern Plains." *Western Historical Quarterly* 30, no. 2 (Summer 1999): 133–54.

Ellison, Joseph. "The Mineral Land Question in California, 1848–1866." In *The Public Lands: Studies in the History of the Public Domain*, edited by Vernon Carstensen, 71–92. Madison: University of Wisconsin Press, 1968.

Ellison, William Henry. "The Movement for State Division in California, 1849–1860." *Southwestern Historical Quarterly* 17, no. 2 (October 1913): 101–39.

Ely, Dr. "Gold—Its Production in All Countries and in All Times, with Full Statistics." *Debow's Review* 18, no. 2 (February 1855): 241–50.

Emerson, Ralph Waldo. "Progress of Culture." In *Letters and Social Aims*, by Ralph Waldo Emerson. Boston: Houghton, Mifflin, 1898.

Emmett, Chris. *Shanghai Pierce: A Fair Likeness*. Norman: University of Oklahoma Press, 1974.

Emmons, David M. *The Butte Irish: Class and Ethnicity in an American Mining Town, 1875–1925*. Urbana: University of Illinois Press, 1990.

———. *Garden in the Grasslands: Boomer Literature of the Central Great Plains*. Lincoln: University of Nebraska Press, 1971.

Emmons, Samuel Franklin. *Geology and Mining Industry of Leadville, Colorado*. Washington DC: U.S. Government Printing Office, 1886.

Engelhard, Michael. "A Salt Pilgrimage." *Interdisciplinary Studies in Literature and Environment* 11, no. 2 (Summer 2004): 211–20.

Engstrand, Iris Higbie. *William Wolfskill, 1789–1866: Frontier Trapper to California Ranchero*. Glendale CA: Arthur H. Clark, 1965.

Etcheson, Nicole. *Bleeding Kansas: Contested Liberty in the Civil War Era*. Lawrence: University Press of Kansas, 2004.

Ethington, Philip J. *The Public City: The Political Construction of Urban Life in San Francisco, 1850–1900*. Cambridge: Cambridge University Press, 1994.

Etulain, Richard W. *Lincoln and Oregon Country Politics in the Civil War Era*. Corvallis: Oregon State University Press, 2013.

———. *Lincoln Looks West: From the Mississippi to the Pacific*. Carbondale: Southern Illinois University Press, 2010.

———. *Sheep and Sheepmen of the American West*. Albuquerque: Center for the American West, 2001.

Evans, Taliesin. "Hydraulic Mining in California." *The Century* 25, no. 3 (January 1883): 323–38.

Everett, Derek R. *Creating the American West: Boundaries and Borderlands*. Norman: University of Oklahoma Press, 2014.

Fabian, Ann. *The Skull Collectors: Race, Science, and America's Unburied Dead.* Chicago: University of Chicago Press, 2010.

Faragher, John Mack. "Americans, Mexicans, Metis: A Community Approach to the Comparative Study of North American Frontiers." In *Under an Open Sky: Rethinking America's Western Past,* edited by William Cronon, George Miles, and Jay Gitlin, 90–109. New York: W. W. Norton, 1992.

———. *Eternity Street: Violence and Justice in Frontier Los Angeles.* New York: W. W. Norton, 2016.

———. *Women and Men on the Overland Trail.* New Haven: Yale University Press, 1979.

Farish, Thomas Edwin. *History of Arizona.* Vol. 4. Phoenix AZ: Filmer Bros., 1916.

Farley, Judson. "The Yuba Hydraulic Mines." *Overland Monthly* 5, no. 3 (September 1870): 213–21.

Farmer, Jared. *On Zion's Mount: Mormons, Indians, and the American Landscape.* Cambridge: Harvard University Press, 2008.

Farnham, Thomas Jefferson. *Travels in the Californias and Scenes in the Pacific Ocean.* New York: Saxton and Miles, 1844.

———. *Travels in the Great Western Prairies: The Anahuac and Rocky Mountains and in the Oregon Territory.* London: Bentley, 1843.

Farnham, Wallace D. "Grenville Dodge and the Union Pacific: A Study of Historical Legends." *Journal of American History* 51, no. 4 (March 1965): 632–50.

Feather, Alali. "The Territories of Arizona." *New Mexico Historical Review* 39, no. 1 (January 1964): 16–31.

Fell, James E., Jr. "Nathaniel P. Hill: A Scientist-Entrepreneur in Colorado." *Arizona and the West* 15, no. 4 (Winter 1973): 315–32.

———. *Ores to Metals: The Rocky Mountain Smelting Industry.* Lincoln: University of Nebraska Press, 1979.

———. "'To the Task, Metallurgists!': Technological Advances in Ore Processing in Colorado, 1858–1914." *Journal of the West* 49, no. 2 (Spring 2010): 50–60.

Fenn, Elizabeth A. *Pox Americana: The Great Smallpox Epidemic of 1775–82.* New York: Hill and Wang, 2001.

Fernández-Armesto, Felipe. *A Foot in the River: Why Our Lives Change—and the Limits of Evolution.* Oxford: Oxford University Press, 2015.

Fernlund, Kevin J. *William Henry Holmes and the Rediscovery of the American West.* Albuquerque: University of New Mexico Press, 2000.

Ferris, A. C. "Gold Hunters of California: Hardships of the Isthmus in '49." *The Century* 41, no. 6 (April 1891): 929–31.

Field, Jacqueline, Marjorie Senechal, and Madelyn Shaw. *American Silk, 1830–1930: Entrepreneurs and Artifacts.* Lubbock: Texas Tech University Press, 2007.

Filipiak, Jack D. "The Battle of Summit Springs." *Colorado Magazine* 41, no. 4 (Fall 1964): 343–54.

Finch, L. Boyd. "Arizona in Exile: Confederate Schemes to Capture the Far Southwest." *Journal of Arizona History* 33, no. 3 (Spring 1992): 27–56.

———. *Confederate Pathway to the Pacific: Major Sherod Hunter and Arizona Territory, C.S.A.* Tucson: Arizona Historical Society, 1996.

Finnegan, Terence. *A Deed So Accursed: Lynching in Mississippi and South Carolina, 1881–1940*. Charlottesville: University of Virginia Press, 2013.

Fischer, John Ryan. *Cattle Colonialism: An Environmental History of the Conquest of California and Hawai'i*. Chapel Hill: University of North Carolina Press, 2015.

Fischer, LeRoy H., ed. *The Western Territories in the Civil War*. Manhattan KS: Sunflower University Press, 1977.

Fisher, John S. *A Builder of the West: The Life of General William Jackson Palmer*. Caldwell ID: Caxton Printers, 1939.

Fite, Gilbert C. *The Farmer's Frontier: 1865–1900*. New York: Holt, Rinehart and Winston, 1966.

Fixico, Donald L. "As Long as the Grass Grows . . . The Cultural Conflicts and Political Strategies of United States—Indian Treaties." In *Ethnicity and War*, edited by Winston A. Van Horne and Thomas V. Tonnesen, 128–49. Madison: University of Wisconsin System American Ethnic Studies Coordinating Committee/Urban Corridor Consortium, 1984.

Fleming, Walter L. "Jefferson Davis's Camel Experiment." *Popular Science Monthly* 174 (February 1909).

Fletcher, Robert S. "The Hard Winter in Montana, 1886–1887." *Agricultural History* 4, no. 4 (October 1930): 123–30.

Flores, Dan. "Bison Ecology and Bison Diplomacy: The Southern Plains from 1800 to 1850." *Journal of American History* 78, no. 2 (September 1991): 465–85.

———. *Horizontal Yellow: Nature and History in the Near Southwest*. Albuquerque: University of New Mexico Press, 1999.

Fogel, Robert William. *The Union Pacific: A Case in Premature Enterprise*. Baltimore: Johns Hopkins Press, 1960.

Fogel, Robert William, and Stanley L. Engerman. *Time on the Cross*. Boston: Little, Brown, 1974.

Follwell, William Watts. *A History of Minnesota*. Vol. 2. Saint Paul: Minnesota Historical Society, 1924.

Foner, Eric. *Reconstruction: America's Unfinished Revolution*. New York: Perennial Classics, 2002.

Foote, Mary Hallock. "A California Mining Camp." *Scribner's Monthly* 15, no. 4 (February 1878): 480–93.

Foreman, Grant. *A History of Oklahoma*. Norman: University of Oklahoma Press, 1942.

Foster, Mike. *Strange Genius: The Life of Ferdinand Vandeveer Hayden*. Niwot CO: Roberts Rinehart, 1994.

Fowler, Harlan D. *Camels to California: A Chapter in Western Transportation*. Stanford: Stanford University Press, 1950.

Frank, B. F., and H. W. Chappell. *The History and Business Directory of Shasta County: Comprising an Accurate Historical Sketch of the County from Its Earliest Settlement to the Present Time*. Redding CA: Redding Independent Book and Job Printing House, 1881.

Franklin, William E. "The Archy Case: The California Supreme Court Refuses to Free a Slave." *Pacific Historical Review* 32, no. 2 (May 1963): 137–54.

Frazer, Robert W. *Forts and Supplies: The Role of the Army in the Economy of the Southwest, 1846–1861.* Albuquerque: University of New Mexico Press, 1983.

Frazier, Donald S. *Blood and Treasure: Confederate Empire in the Southwest.* College Station: Texas A&M University Press, 1995.

Frederick, J. V. *Ben Holladay, the Stagecoach King.* Glendale CA: Arthur H. Clark, 1940.

Freeman, Joanne B. *The Field of Blood: Violence in Congress and the Road to the Civil War.* New York: Farrar, Straus and Giroux, 2018.

Friefield, Jacob K., Mikal Brotnov Eckstrom, and Richard Edwards. "African American Homesteader 'Colonies' in the Settling of the Great Plains." *Great Plains Quarterly* 39, no. 1 (Winter 2019): 11–37.

Friend, Llerena. *Sam Houston, the Great Designer.* Austin: University of Texas Press, 1954.

Frink, Maurice, W. Turrentine Jackson, and Agnes Wright Spring. *When Grass Was King: Contributions to the Western Range Cattle Industry Study.* Boulder: University of Colorado Press, 1956.

Fritz, Henry E. *The Movement for Indian Assimilation, 1860–1890.* Philadelphia: University of Pennsylvania Press, 1963.

Gage, Justin. *We Do Not Want the Gates Closed between Us: Native Networks and the Spread of the Ghost Dance.* Norman: University of Oklahoma Press, 2020.

Galloway, Tod B. "Private Letters of a Government Official in the Southwest." *Journal of American History* 3, no. 4 (October 1909): 541–54.

Garceau, Dee. "Single Women Homesteaders and the Meanings of Independence." *Frontiers* 15, no. 3 (1995): 1–26.

Gard, Wayne. *The Chisholm Trail.* Norman: University of Oklahoma Press, 1954.

———. *The Great Buffalo Hunt.* Lincoln: University of Nebraska Press, 1959.

Gardner, Hamilton, ed. "March of the 2nd Dragoons: Report of Lieutenant Colonel Philip St. George Cooke on the March of the 2nd Dragoons from Fort Leavenworth to Fort Bridger in 1857." *Annals of Wyoming* 27, no. 1 (April 1955): 43–60.

Garriott, E. B. "Types of Storms in January." *Monthly Weather Review,* January 1895, 9–13.

Gates, Paul W. "Adjudication of Spanish-Mexican Land Claims in California." *Huntington Library Quarterly* 21, no. 3 (May 1958): 213–36.

———. *California Ranchos and Farms, 1846–1862: Including the Letters of John Quincy Adams Warren of 1861, Being Largely Devoted to Livestock, Wheat Farming, Fruit Raising, and the Wine Industry.* Madison: State Historical Society of Wisconsin, 1967.

———. "California's Embattled Settlers." *California Historical Society Quarterly* 41, no. 2 (June 1962): 99–130.

———. *Fifty Million Acres: Conflicts over Kansas Land Policy, 1854–1890.* Norman: University of Oklahoma Press, 1997.

———. "The Homestead Act: Free Land Policy in Operation, 1862–1935." In *Land Use Policy and Problems in the United States,* edited by Howard W. Ottoson, 28–46. Lincoln: University of Nebraska Press, 1963.

———. "The Homestead Act in an Incongruous Land System." *American Historical Review* 41, no. 4 (July 1936): 652–81.

———. "Public Land Disposal in California." *Agricultural History* 49, no. 1 (January 1975): 158–78.

Gay, Theressa. *James W. Marshall, the Discoverer of California Gold: A Biography.* Georgetown CA: Talisman, 1967.

Gazetteer of Utah and Salt Lake City Directory. Salt Lake City: Salt Lake Herald, 1869–74.

Genetin-Pilawa, C. Joseph. *Crooked Paths to Allotment: The Fight over Federal Indian Policy after the Civil War.* Chapel Hill: University of North Carolina Press, 2012.

George, Henry. *Our Land and Land Policy, National and State.* San Francisco: White and Bauer, 1871.

Gerber, Jim. "The Origin of California's Export Surplus in Cereals." *Agricultural History* 67, no. 4 (Autumn 1993): 40–57.

Gerstäcker, Friedrich. *Narrative of a Journey round the World: Comprising a Winter-Passage across the Andes to Chili; with a Visit to the Gold Regions of California and Australia, the South Sea Islands, Java, &c.* New York: Harper & Bros., 1853.

Gerstäcker, Friedrich, and George Cosgrove. "The French Revolution." *California Historical Society Quarterly* 17, no. 1 (March 1938): 2–17.

Gerstle, Gary. "Inclusion, Exclusion, and the Making of American Identity." In *Oxford Handbook of American Immigration and Ethnicity*, edited by Ronald H. Bayor, 144–65. New York: Oxford University Press, 2016.

Gibbens, Byrd, ed. *This Is a Strange Country: Letters of a Westering Family, 1880–1906.* Albuquerque: University of New Mexico Press, 1988.

Gilliss, John R. "Tunnels of the Pacific Railroad." In *Transactions: American Society of Civil Engineers*, vol. 1, 155–72. New York: By the Society, 1872.

Gilpin, William. *The Central Gold Region: The Grain, Pastoral, and Gold Regions of North America. with Some New Views of Its Physical Geography; and Observations on the Pacific Railroad.* Philadelphia: Sower, Barnes, 1860.

———. *Mission of the North American People.* Philadelphia: J. B. Lippincott, 1873.

"A Girl's Letters from Nauvoo." *Overland Monthly* 16, no. 96 (December 1890): 616–38.

Gleed, J. Willis. "Western Lands and Mortgages." *The Forum* 11 (1891): 468–71.

Goddard, Frederick. *Where to Emigrate and Why: Homes and Fortunes in the Boundless West and the Sunny South.* Philadelphia: Peoples Pub., 1869.

Goetzmann, William H. *Exploration and Empire: The Explorer and the Scientist in the Winning of the American West.* New York: Alfred A. Knopf, 1966.

———. *New Lands, New Men: America and the Second Great Age of Discovery.* New York: Penguin, 1987.

Goldman, Henry H. "Southern Sympathy in Southern California, 1860–1865." *Journal of the West* 4, no. 4 (October 1965): 577–86.

Goldman, Marion S. *Gold Diggers and Silver Miners: Prostitution and Social Life on the Comstock Lode.* Ann Arbor: University of Michigan Press, 1981.

The Gold Regions of California; Describing the Geography, Topography, History, and General Features of That Country, from the Official Report Transmitted to the American Government by Colonel Mason, Lieutenant-Colonel Fremont, Brigadier-General Jones, Lieutenant Emory, J.S. Folson, Esq. Together with Exclusive Authentic Particulars, and a Coloured Map of the Country. London: Baily Brothers, 1849.

González, Deena J. *Refusing the Favor: The Spanish-Mexican Women of Santa Fe, 1820–1880*. New York: Oxford University Press, 1999.

Goode, William H. *Outposts of Zion with Limnings of Mission Life*. Cincinnati: Poe and Hitchcock, 1864.

Goodrich, Thomas. *War to the Knife: Bleeding Kansas, 1854–1861*. Mechanicsburg PA: Stackpole, 1998.

Goodwin, Cardinal. *The Establishment of State Government in California, 1846–1850*. New York: Macmillan, 1914.

Gordon, Sarah Barringer, and Jan Shipps. "Fatal Convergence in the Kingdom of God: The Mountain Meadows Massacre in American History." *Journal of the Early Republic* 37, no. 2 (Summer 2017): 307–47.

Gorgas, William Crawford. *Sanitation in Panama*. New York: D. Appleton, 1915.

Gossett, Thomas F. *Race: The History of an Idea in America*. Dallas: Southern Methodist University Press, 1963.

Governor's Annual Message to the Legislature of the State of California. Sacramento: B. B. Redding, 1855.

Graebner, Norman A. *Empire on the Pacific: A Story in American Continental Expansion*. New York: Ronald Press, 1955.

Grant, Madison. *The Passing of the Great Race, or the Racial Basis of European History*. New York: Charles Scribner's Sons, 1916.

Gray, John S. *Centennial Campaign: The Sioux War of 1876*. Fort Collins: Old Army Press, 1976.

The Great West. Chicago: Rollings, 1880.

Greeley, Horace. *An Overland Journey, from New York to San Francisco, in the Summer of 1859*. New York: C. M. Saxton, Barker, 1860.

Green, Fletcher. "Georgia's Forgotten Industry: Gold Mining, Part I." *Georgia Historical Quarterly* 19, no. 2 (June 1935): 93–111.

Green, Fletcher M. "Origins of the Credit Mobilier of America." *Journal of American History* 46, no. 2 (September 1959): 238–51.

Green, Michael. "Abraham Lincoln, Nevada, and the Law of Unintended Consequences." *Nevada Historical Society Quarterly* 52, no. 2 (Summer 2009): 85–108.

Greene, Jerome A. *American Carnage: Wounded Knee, 1890*. Norman: University of Oklahoma Press, 2014.

———. *Beyond Bear's Paw: The Nez Perce Indians in Canada*. Norman: University of Oklahoma Press, 2010.

———. *Morning Star Dawn: The Powder River Expedition and the Northern Cheyennes, 1876*. Norman: University of Oklahoma Press, 2003.

———. *Washita: The U.S. Army and the Southern Cheyennes, 1867–1869*. Norman: University of Oklahoma Press, 2004.

———. *Yellowstone Command: Colonel Nelson A. Miles and the Great Sioux War, 1876–1877*. Lincoln: University of Nebraska Press, 1991.

Greenland, Powell. *Hydraulic Mining in California: A Tarnished Legacy*. Western Lands and Waters Series. Spokane WA: Arthur H. Clark, 2001.

Greenwald, Emily. *Reconfiguring the Reservation: The Nez Perces, Jicarilla Apaches, and the Dawes Act.* Albuquerque: University of New Mexico Press, 2002.

Greer, Richard A. "Wandering Kamaainas: Notes on Hawaiian Emigration before 1848." *Journal of the West* 6, no. 2 (April 1967): 221–25.

Gressley, Gene M. *Bankers and Cattlemen.* Lincoln: University of Nebraska Press, 1966.

Grinnell, George Bird. *The Fighting Cheyennes.* Norman: University of Oklahoma Press, 1955.

———. *Two Great Scouts and Their Pawnee Battalion: The Experiences of Frank J. and Luther H. North.* Lincoln: University of Nebraska Press, 1973.

Griswold, Robert L. "Apart but Not Adrift: Wives, Divorce, and Independence in California, 1850–1890." *Pacific Historical Review* 49, no. 2 (May 1980): 265–83.

———. *Family and Divorce in California, 1850–1890.* Albany: State University of New York Press, 1982.

Griswold, Wesley S. *A Work of Giants: Building the First Transcontinental Railroad.* New York: McGraw-Hill, 1962.

Grow, Matthew J., and Matthew C. Godfrey, eds. *The Joseph Smith Papers: Council of Fifty Minutes.* Salt Lake City: Church Historian's Press, 2016.

Guice, John D. W. "Cattle Raisers of the Old Southwest: A Reinterpretation." *Western Historical Quarterly* 8, no. 2 (April 1977): 167–87.

Guie, Heister Dean, and Lucullus Virgil McWhorter. *Adventures in Geyser Land.* Caldwell ID: Caxton Printers, 1935.

Guinn, J. M. "The Sonoran Migration." *Annual Publications of the Historical Society of Southern California* 8, no. 1 (1909–10): 31–36.

Gutierrez, Ramon. *When Jesus Came, the Corn Mothers Went Away.* Stanford: Stanford University Press, 1991.

Habersham, A. W. *The North Pacific Surveying and Exploring Expedition; or, My Last Cruise.* Philadelphia: J. B. Lippincott, 1857.

Hackel, Steven W. *Children of Coyote, Missionaries of St. Francis: Indian-Spanish Relations in Colonial California, 1769–1850.* Chapel Hill: University of North Carolina Press, 2005.

Hacker, J. David. "A Census-Based Count of the Civil War Dead." *Civil War History* 57, no. 4 (December 2011): 307–48.

———. "Has the Demographic Impact of Civil War Deaths Been Exaggerated?" *Civil War History* 60, no. 4 (December 2014): 453–58.

Hafen, LeRoy R. *Colorado and Its People: A Narrative and Topical History of the Centennial State.* Vol. 1. New York: Lewis Historical Publishing, 1948.

———, ed. "Diary of Mrs. A. C. Hunt." *Colorado Magazine* 21, no. 5 (September 1944): 161–70.

———. *The Overland Mail, 1849–1869: Promoter of Settlement, Precursor of Railroads.* Cleveland: Arthur H. Clark, 1926.

———, ed. *Overland Routes to the Gold Fields, 1859, from Contemporary Diaries.* Glendale CA: Arthur H. Clark, 1942.

Hafen, Leroy R., and Zachary Gussow. *Arapaho-Cheyenne Indians*. New York: Garland, 1974.

Hafen, LeRoy R., and Ann W. Hafen, eds. *The Diaries of William Henry Jackson, Frontier Photographer*. Glendale CA: Arthur H. Clark, 1959.

———. *Fremont's Fourth Expedition: A Documentary Account of the Disaster of 1848–1849*. Glendale CA: Arthur H. Clark, 1960.

———. *Powder River Campaigns and Sawyers Expedition of 1865: A Documentary Account Comprising Official Reports, Diaries, Contemporary Newspaper Accounts, and Personal Narratives*. Glendale CA: Arthur H. Clark, 1961.

———. *Reports from Colorado: The Wildman Letters, 1859–1865*. Glendale CA: Arthur H. Clark, 1961.

Hafen, LeRoy R., and Francis Marion Young. *Fort Laramie and the Pageant of the West, 1834–1890*. Glendale CA: Arthur H. Clark, 1938.

Hagan, William T. "Kiowas, Comanches, and Cattlemen, 1867–1906: A Case Study of the Failure of U.S. Reservation Policy." *Pacific Historical Review* 40, no. 3 (1971): 333–55.

———. "Private Property, the Indian's Door to Civilization." *Ethnohistory* 3, no. 2 (Spring 1956): 126–37.

———. *Quanah Parker, Comanche Chief*. Norman: University of Oklahoma Press, 1993.

———. *Theodore Roosevelt and Six Friends of the Indian*. Norman: University of Oklahoma Press, 1997.

———. *United States–Comanche Relations: The Reservation Years*. New Haven: Yale University Press, 1976.

Hague, James D. *Mining Industry*. Washington DC: U.S. Government Printing Office, 1870.

Hahn, Steven. "Slave Emancipation, Indian Peoples, and the Projects of the New American Nation-State." *Journal of the Civil War Era* 3, no. 3 (September 2013): 307–30.

Haines, Aubrey L. *The Yellowstone Story: A History of Our First National Park*. Vol. 1. Gardiner MT: Yellowstone Library Museum Association, 1977.

Haines, Michael R., and Richard H. Steckel. *A Population History of North America*. Cambridge: Cambridge University Press, 2000.

Hale, Frederick, ed. *Danes in North America*. Seattle: University of Washington Press, 1984.

Hales, Peter B. *William Henry Jackson and the Transformation of the American Landscape*. Philadelphia: Temple University Press, 1988.

Haley, James L. *Apaches: A History and Cultural Portrait*. Norman: University of Oklahoma Press, 1997.

Haley, J. Evetts, ed. "A Log of the Texas-California Cattle Trail, 1854, I." *Southwestern Historical Quarterly* 35, no. 3 (January 1932): 208–37.

———. *Charles Goodnight, Cowman and Plainsman*. Boston and New York: Houghton Mifflin, 1936.

———. *The XIT Ranch of Texas and the Early Days of the Llano Estacado*. Norman: University of Oklahoma Press, 1953.

Hall, Martin Hardwick. "Colonel James Reily's Diplomatic Missions to Chihuahua and Sonora." *New Mexico Historical Review* 31, no. 3 (July 1956): 232–53.

———. *Sibley's New Mexico Campaign*. Austin: University of Texas Press, 1960.

Hall, M. C. "Theobald Smith as a Parasitologist." *Journal of Parasitology* 21, no. 4 (August 1935): 231–43.

Hamilton, James McClellan. *From Wilderness to Statehood: A History of Montana, 1805–1900*. Portland OR: Binfords & Mort, 1957.

Hammond, John Craig. "The 'High Road to a Slave Empire': Conflict and the Growth and Expansion of Slavery on the North American Continent." In *The World of the Revolutionary American Republic: Land, Labor, and the Conflict for a Continent*, edited by Andrew Shankman, 346–69. New York: Routledge, 2014.

Hampton, H. Duane. *How the U.S. Cavalry Saved Our National Parks*. Bloomington: Indiana University Press, 1971.

Hansen, Klaus J. *Quest for Empire*. East Lansing: Michigan State University Press, 1967.

Hansen, Marcus Lee. "Official Encouragement of Immigration to Iowa." *Iowa Journal of History and Politics* 19, no. 2 (April 1921).

Haraszthy, A. *Grape Culture, Wines, and Wine-Making: With Notes upon Agriculture and Horticulture*. New York: Harper and Brothers, 1862.

Hardorff, Richard G., ed. *Lakota Recollections of the Custer Fight: New Sources of Indian-Military History*. Spokane WA: Arthur H. Clark, 1991.

Hardy, Osgood. "Agricultural Changes in California, 1860–1900." In *Proceedings of the Pacific Coast Branch of the American Historical Association*, 216–30, 1929.

———. "Some Economic Aspects of the Gold Age in California." In *Proceedings of the Pacific Coast Branch of the American Historical Association*, 141–50, 1927.

Haring, Sidney L. *Crow Dog's Case: American Indian Sovereignty, Tribal Law, and United States Law in the Nineteenth Century*. Cambridge: Cambridge University Press, 1994.

Harlow, Alvin F. *Old Wires and New Waves: The History of the Telegraph, Telephone, and Wireless*. New York: D. Appleton-Century, 1936.

Harmon, Alexandra. *Reclaiming the Reservation*. Seattle: University of Washington Press, 2019.

Harrington, Mark W. *History of the Weather Map*. Washington DC: Weather Bureau, 1894.

Harris, Benjamin Butler. *The Gila Trail: The Texas Argonauts and the California Gold Rush*. Norman: University of Oklahoma Press, 1960.

Harris, Katherine. *Long Vistas: Women and Families on Colorado Homesteads*. Niwot: University Press of Colorado, 1993.

Harrison, Carter H. *A Summer's Outing and the Old Man's Story*. Chicago: Dibble, 1891.

Harte, Bret. *Poems and Two Men of Sandy Bar: A Drama*. New York: Houghton Mifflin, 1896.

Hastings, Lansford W. *The Emigrants' Guide to Oregon and California*. Cincinnati: G. Conclin, 1845.

Hattori, Eugene M. "'And Some of Them Swear like Pirates': American Indian Women in Nineteenth-Century Virginia City." In *Comstock Women: The Making of a Mining Community*, edited by Ronald M. James and Elizabeth Raymond, 229–45. Reno: University of Nevada Press, 1998.

Haupt, Herman. *The Yellowstone National Park.* New York: J. M. Stoddart, 1883.

Havins, T. R. "Texas Fever." *Southwestern Historical Quarterly* 52, no. 2 (October 1948): 147–62.

Hayden, Delores. "Biddy Mason's Los Angeles, 1851–1891." *California History* 68, no. 3 (Fall 1989): 86–99.

Hayden, F. V. "The Wonders of the West—II: More about the Yellowstone." *Scribner's Monthly* 3, no. 4 (February 1872): 388–96.

Haynes, Francis. "The Northward Spread of Horses among the Plains Indians." *American Anthropologist* 40 (1938): 429–37.

Hays, John P. "The Curious Case of New Mexico's Pre–Civil War Slave Code." *New Mexico Historical Review* 92, no. 3 (Summer 2017): 251–83.

Hämäläinen, Pekka. *The Comanche Empire.* New Haven: Yale University Press, 2008.

———. *Lakota America: A New History of Indigenous Power.* New Haven: Yale University Press, 2019.

———. "The Politics of Grass: European Expansion, Ecological Change, and Indigenous Power in the Southwest Borderlands." *William and Mary Quarterly* 67, no. 2 (April 2010): 173–208.

———. "The Western Comanche Trade Center: Rethinking the Plains Indian Trade System." *Western Historical Quarterly* 29, no. 4: 485–514.

Heard, Isaac V. D. *History of the Sioux War, and Massacres of 1862 and 1863.* New York: Harper & Bros., 1863.

Hebard, Grace Raymond. *Washakie: An Account of Indian Resistance of the Covered Wagon and Union Pacific Railroad Invasions of Their Territory.* Cleveland: Arthur H. Clark, 1930.

Heckendorn, J., and W. A. Wilson. *Miners and Business Men's Directory for the Year Commencing January 1st, 1856: Embracing a General Directory of the Citizens of Tuolumne, and Portions of Calaveras, Stanislaus, and San Joaquin Counties.* Columbia CA: Clipper Office, 1856.

Hedges, James B. "The Colonization Work of the Northern Pacific Railroad." *Mississippi Valley Historical Review* 13, no. 3 (December 1926).

Hedges, William Hawkins. *Pikes Peak . . . or Busted! Frontier Reminiscences of William Hawkins Hedges.* Evanston IL: Branding Iron Press, 1954.

Hedren, Paul L. *After Custer: Loss and Transformation in Sioux Country.* Norman: University of Oklahoma Press, 2011.

Heizer, Robert F., ed. *Collected Documents on the Causes and Events in the Bloody Island Massacre of 1850.* Berkeley: Archeological Research Facility, 1973.

———. *The Destruction of California Indians: A Collection of Documents from the Period 1847 to 1865 in which Are Described Some of the Things That Happened to Some of the Indians of California.* Santa Barbara: Peregrine Smith, 1974.

———. "Indian Servitude in California." In *History of Indian-White Relations: Handbook of North American Indians,* vol. 4, edited by Wilcomb E. Washburn, 414–16. Washington DC: Smithsonian Institution, 1988.

Heizer, Robert F., and Albert B. Elsasser. *The Natural World of the California Indians.* Berkeley: University of California Press, 1980.

Helper, Hinton R. *The Land of Gold: Reality versus Fiction.* Baltimore: Henry Taylor, 1855.

Hendricks, Carl Luvig. "Recollections of a Swedish Buffalo Hunter." *Swedish Pioneer Historical Quarterly* 32, no. 3 (July 1981): 190–204.

Henke, Warren A. "Imagery, Immigration and the Myth of North Dakota, 1890–1933." *North Dakota History* 38, no. 4 (Fall 1971).

Hensley, Marcia Meredith. *Staking Her Claim: Women Homesteading in the West.* Glendo WY: High Plains Press, 2008.

Hess, Earl J. *The Civil War in the West: Victory and Defeat from the Appalachians to the Mississippi.* Chapel Hill: University of North Carolina Press, 2012.

Higham, John. *Strangers in the Land: Patterns of American Nativism, 1860–1925.* New York: Atheneum, 1963.

Highton, Edward. *The Electric Telegraph: Its History and Progress.* London: John Weale, 1852.

Hill, Burton S. "The Great Indian Treaty Council of 1851." *Nebraska History* 47 (1966): 85–110.

Hinger, Charlotte. *Nicodemus: Post-Reconstruction Politics and Racial Justice in Western Kansas.* Norman: University of Oklahoma Press, 2016.

Hirata, Lucie Cheng. "Free, Indentured, Enslaved: Chinese Prostitutes in Nineteenth-Century America." *Signs* 5, no. 1 (Autumn 1979): 2–30.

Hitchcock, Edward. "First Anniversary Address before the Association of American Geologists." *American Journal of Science and Arts* 40 (April 1841): 232–75.

Hittel, John S. *The Resources of California, Comprising Agriculture, Mining, Geography, Climate, Commerce, Etc. Etc.* San Francisco: A. Roman, 1863.

Hittell, Theodore H. *History of California.* Vols. 3 and 4. San Francisco: N. J. Stone, 1897.

Hittman, Michael. "1870 Ghost Dance at the Walker River Reservation: A Reconstruction." *Ethnohistory* 20, no. 3 (Summer 1973): 247–78.

Hoebel, E. Adamson. *The Cheyennes: Indians of the Great Plains.* Fort Worth: Harcourt Brace Javonovich College Publishers, 1978.

Hoganson, Kristin L. *The Heartland: An American History.* New York: Penguin, 2019.

———. "Meat in the Middle: Converging Borderlands in the U.S Midwest, 1865–1900." *Journal of American History* 98, no. 4 (March 2012): 1025–51.

Hoglund, A. William. *Finnish Immigrants in America, 1880–1920.* Madison: University of Wisconsin Press, 1960.

Hoig, Stan. *The Battle of the Washita: The Sheridan-Custer Indian Campaign of 1867–69.* Garden City NY: Doubleday, 1976.

———. *The Peace Chiefs of the Cheyennes.* Norman: University of Oklahoma Press, 1980.

———. *Perilous Pursuit: The U.S. Cavalry and the Northern Cheyennes.* Boulder: University Press of Colorado, 2002.

———. *The Sand Creek Massacre.* Norman: University of Oklahoma Press, 1961.

———. *White Man's Paper Trail: Grand Councils and Treaty-Making on the Central Plains.* Boulder: University Press of Colorado, 2006.

Holliday, J. S. *Rush for Riches: Gold Fever and the Making of California.* Berkeley: University of California Press, 1999.

Hollister, Ovando. *Boldly They Rode: A History of the First Colorado Regiment of Volunteers.* Lakewood CO: Golden Press, 1949.

Hollon, W. Eugene. *Frontier Violence: Another Look.* New York: Oxford University Press, 1974.

Holmes, Julia Archibald. *A Bloomer Girl on Pike's Peak, 1858.* Denver: Denver Public Library, 1949.

Holt, Michael F. *The Fate of Their Country: Politicians, Slavery Extension, and the Coming of the Civil War.* New York: Hill and Wang, 2004.

Holt, Vincent M. *Why Not Eat Insects?* London: Field and Tuer, 1885.

Hom, Marlon K. *Songs of Gold Mountain: Cantonese Rhymes from San Francisco Chinatown.* Berkeley: University of California Press, 1987.

Homsher, Lola M. *South Pass, 1868: James Chisholm's Journal of the Wyoming Gold Rush.* Lincoln: University of Nebraska Press, 1960.

Horne, Gerald. *The Deepest South: The United States, Brazil, and the African Slave Trade.* New York: New York University Press, 2007.

Horowitz, Roger. *Putting Meat on the American Table: Taste, Technology, Transformation.* Baltimore: Johns Hopkins University Press, 2006.

Horsman, Reginald. *Feast or Famine: Food and Drink in American Westward Expansion.* Columbia: University of Missouri Press, 2008.

———. *Race and Manifest Destiny: The Origins of American Racial Anglo-Saxonism.* Cambridge: Harvard University Press, 1981.

Howard, Joseph Kinsey. *Montana: High, Wide, and Handsome.* Lincoln: University of Nebraska Press, 2003.

Howard, N. Jill, and Glenda Riley. "'Thus You See I Have Not Much Rest.'" *Idaho Yesterdays* 37, no. 3 (Fall 1993): 27–35.

Howard, Thomas Frederick. *Sierra Crossing: First Roads to California.* Berkeley: University of California Press, 1998.

Howe, Daniel Walker. *What Hath God Wrought: The Transformation of America, 1815–1848.* New York: Oxford University Press, 2007.

Hoxie, Frederick E. *A Final Promise: The Campaign to Assimilate the Indians, 1880–1920.* Cambridge: Cambridge University Press, 1989.

———. "From Prison to Homeland: The Cheyenne River Indian Reservation before WWI." *South Dakota History* 10, no. 1 (January 1979): `1–24.

Hudson, T. S. *A Scamper through America; or, Fifteen Thousand Miles of Ocean and Continent in Sixty Days.* London: Griffith & Farran, 1882.

Hughes, Sarah Forbes, ed. *Letters and Recollections of John Murray Forbes.* Vol. 1. Boston: Houghton Mifflin, 1899.

Hulbert, Richard, Jr. "The Ancestry of the Horse." In *Horses through Time*, edited by Sandra Olsen, 13–34. Boulder: Roberts Rinehart, 1997.

Hunt, Aurora. *The Army of the Pacific: Its Operations in California, Texas, Arizona, New Mexico, Utah, Nevada, Oregon, Washington, Plains Region, Mexico, Etc. 1860–1866.* Glendale CA: Arthur H. Clark, 1951.

———. *Major General James Henry Carleton, 1814–1873: Western Frontier Dragoon.* Glendale CA: Arthur H. Clark, 1958.

Hunter, J. Marvin, ed. *The Trail Drivers of Texas: Interesting Sketches of Early Cowboys and Their Experiences on the Range and on the Trail during the Days That Tried Men's Souls—True Narratives Related by Real Cow-Punchers and Men Who Fathered the Cattle Industry in Texas*. Nashville TN: Cokesbury Press, 1925.

Hurtado, Albert L. "'Hardly a Farm House—a Kitchen without Them': Indian and White Households on the California Borderland Frontier in 1860." *Western Historical Quarterly* 13, no. 3 (July 1982): 245–70.

———. *Indian Survival on the California Frontier*. New Haven: Yale University Press, 1988.

———. *Intimate Frontiers: Sex, Gender and Culture in Old California*. Albuquerque: University of New Mexico Press, 1999.

———. *John Sutter: A Life on the North American Frontier*. Norman: University of Oklahoma Press, 2006.

———. "Sex, Gender, Culture, and a Great Event." *Pacific Historical Review* 68, no. 1 (February 1999): 1–19.

Hutchings, J. M. *In the Heart of the Sierras: The Yo Semite Valley*. Oakland: Pacific Press, 1888.

Hutton, Paul Andrew. *The Apache Wars: The Hunt for Geronimo, the Apache Kid, and the Captive Boy Who Started the Longest War in American History*. New York: Crown, 2016.

———. *Phil Sheridan and His Army*. Lincoln: University of Nebraska Press, 1985.

Hyde, Anne F. *Empires, Nations, and Families: A New History of the North American West, 1800–1860*. Lincoln: University of Nebraska Press, 2011.

Hyde, George E. *Indians of the High Plains: From the Prehistorical Period to the Coming of Europeans*. Norman: University of Oklahoma Press, 1959.

———. *Life of George Bent: Written from His Letters*. Norman: University of Oklahoma Press, 1968.

———. *Red Cloud's Folk: A History of the Oglala Sioux Indians*. Norman: University of Oklahoma Press, 1937.

———. *Spotted Tail's Folk: A History of Brulé Sioux*. Norman: University of Oklahoma Press, 1961.

Hyman, Collete A. "Survival at Crow Creek, 1863–1866." *Minnesota History* 61, no. 4 (Winter 2008–9): 148–61.

Igler, David. *The Great Ocean: Pacific Worlds from Captain Cook to the Gold Rush*. New York: Oxford University Press, 2013.

———. *Industrial Cowboys: Miller & Lux and the Transformation of the Far West, 1850–1920*. Berkeley: University of California Press, 2001.

Ingersoll, Ernest. *The Crest of the Continent: A Summer's Railroad Ramble through the Rocky Mountains*. New York: R. R. Donnelly & Sons, 1885.

———. "From the Fraser to the Columbia." *Harper's New Monthly Magazine* 68, no. 408 (July 1884): 869–82.

Irey, Eugene Floyd. "A Social History of Leadville, Colorado during the Boom Days, 1877–1881." PhD dissertation, University of Minnesota, 1951.

Irving, Washington. *Astoria, or Anecdotes of an Enterprise beyond the Rocky Mountains*. Philadelphia: Carey, Lea, & Blanchard.

Isenberg, Andrew C. *The Destruction of the Bison: An Environmental History, 1750–1920.* Cambridge: Cambridge University Press, 2000.

———. *Mining California: An Ecological History.* New York: Hill and Wang, 2005.

Isern, Thomas D. "Colorado Territory." *Journal of the West* 16, no. 2 (April 1977).

Iverson, Peter. "Building toward Self-Determination: Plains and Southwestern Indians in the 1940s and 1950s." *Western Historical Quarterly* 16, no. 2 (April 1985): 163–73.

———. *Diné: A History of the Navajos.* Albuquerque: University of New Mexico Press, 2002.

———. *When Indians Became Cowboys: Native Peoples and Cattle Ranching in the American West.* Norman: University of Oklahoma Press, 1994.

Jackson, Donald. *Custer's Gold: The United States Cavalry Expedition of 1874.* Lincoln: University of Nebraska Press, 1966.

Jackson, Helen Hunt. *Bits of Travel at Home.* Boston: Little, Brown, 1909.

Jackson, W. H. "First Official Visit to the Cliff Dwellings." *Colorado Magazine* 1, no. 4 (May 1924).

Jackson, William Henry. *Time Exposure: The Autobiography of William Henry Jackson.* New York: G. P. Putnam's Sons, 1940.

Jackson, W. Turrentine. *The Enterprising Scot: Investors in the American West after 1873.* Edinburgh: Edinburgh University Press, 1968.

———. *Wagon Roads West: A Study of Federal Road Surveys and Construction in the Trans-Mississippi West, 1846–1869.* Berkeley: University of California Press, 1952.

Jacobsen, R. Brooke and Eighmy, Jeffrey L. "A Mathematical Theory of Horse Adoption on the North American Plains." *Plains Anthropologist* 25, no. 90 (November 1980): 333–41.

Jacoby, Karl. *Crimes against Nature: Squatters, Poachers, Thieves, and the Hidden History of American Conservation,* 2001.

Jagodinsky, Katrina. "Territorial Bonds: Indenture and Affection in Intercultural Arizona." In *On the Borders of Love and Power: Families and Kinship in the Intercultural American Southwest,* edited by David Wallace Adams and Crista DuLuzio, 255–77. Berkeley: University of California Press, 2012.

James, Edwin. *Account of an Expedition from Pittsburgh to the Rocky Mountains.* Vol. 1. Philadelphia: H. C. Carey and I. Lea, 1823.

James, Ronald. *The Roar and the Silence: A History of Virginia City and the Comstock Lode.* Reno: University of Nevada Press, 1998.

James, Ronald M., and C. Elizabeth Raymond, eds. *Comstock Women: The Making of a Mining Community.* Reno: University of Nevada Press, 1998.

Jameson, Elizabeth. "Bringing It All Back Home: Rethinking the History of Women and the Nineteenth-Century West." In *A Companion to the American West,* edited by William Deverell, 179–99. Malden MA: Blackwell, 2004.

Janetski, Joel C. *Indians of Yellowstone Park.* Salt Lake City: University of Utah Press, 1987.

Jenkinson, Clay S. *A Free and Hardy Life: Theodore Roosevelt's Sojourn in the American West.* Bismarck: Dakota Institute, 2011.

Jensen, James M. "Cattle Drives from the Ranchos to the Gold Fields of California." *Arizona and the West* 2, no. 4 (Winter 1960): 341–52.

Johannsen, Robert W. *Frontier Politics on the Eve of the Civil War*. Seattle: Washington University Press, 1955.

———. *The Letters of Stephen A. Douglas*. Urbana: University of Illinois Press, 1961.

John, Richard R. *Network Nation: Inventing American Telecommunications*. Cambridge: Belknap Press, 2010.

Johnson, Allen, ed. *Dictionary of American Biography*. Vol. 1. New York: Charles Scribner's Sons, 1927.

Johnson, David Alan. *Founding the Far West: California, Oregon, and Nevada, 1840–1890*. Berkeley: University of California Press, 1992.

Johnson, Forrest Bryant. *The Last Camel Charge: The Untold Story of America's Desert Military Experiment*. New York: Berkley Caliber, 2012.

Johnson, R. U., and C. C. Clough Buel, eds. *Battles and Leaders of the Civil War, Being for the Most Part Contributions by Union and Confederate Officers*. Vol. 2. New York: The Century, 1887–88.

Johnson, Samuel A. "The Emigrant Aid Company in Kansas." *Kansas Historical Quarterly* 1, no. 5 (November 1932): 429–41.

Johnson, Susan L. *Roaring Camp: The Social World of the California Gold Rush*. New York: W. W. Norton, 2002.

———. "Sharing Bed and Board: Cohabitation and Cultural Difference in Central Arizona Mining Towns, 1863–1873." In *The Women's West*, edited by Susan Armitage and Elizabeth Jameson, 77–91. Norman: University of Oklahoma Press, 1987.

Johnson, Theodore T. *Sights in the Gold Region, and Scenes by the Way*. New York: Baker and Scribner, 1849.

Johnson, Walter. *River of Dark Dreams: Slavery and Empire in the Cotton Kingdom*. Cambridge: Harvard University Press, 2013.

Johnston, Andrew Scott. *Mercury and the Making of California: Mining, Landscape, and Race, 1840–1890*. Boulder: University Press of Colorado, 2013.

Johnston, William G. *Experiences of a Forty-Niner*. Pittsburgh, 1892.

Jones, Douglas. *The Treaty of Medicine Lodge Creek: The Story of the Great Treaty Council as Told by Eyewitnesses*. Norman: University of Oklahoma Press, 1966.

Jones, Sondra. "'Redeeming' the Indian: The Enslavement of Indian Children in New Mexico and Utah." *Utah Historical Quarterly* 67, no. 3 (Summer 1999): 220–41.

Jordan, Terry G. *North American Cattle-Ranching Frontiers: Origins, Diffusion, and Differentiation*. Albuquerque: University of New Mexico Press, 1993.

Josephy, Alvin M., Jr. *The Civil War in the American West*. New York: Alfred A. Knopf, 1991.

Joy, Emmett P. *Chili Gulch*. Berkeley: Bancroft Library, 1964.

Julian, George W. "Railway Influence in the Land Office." *North American Review* 136, no. 316 (March 1883): 237–57.

Jung, Moon-Ho. *Coolies and Cane: Race, Labor, and Sugar in the Age of Emancipation*. Baltimore: Johns Hopkins University Press, 2006.

Kahn, B. Zorina. *The Democratization of Invention: Patents and Copyrights in American Economic Development, 1790–1920*. Cambridge: Cambridge University Press, 2005.

Kane, H. H. *Opium-Smoking in America and China*. New York: G. P. Putnam's Sons, 1882.

The Kansas Question: Senator Sumner's Speech, Reviewing the Action of the Federal Administration upon the Subject of Slavery in Kansas. Cincinnati: George S. Blanchard, 1856.

Karp, Matthew. *This Vast Southern Empire: Slaveholders at the Helm of American Foreign Policy*. Cambridge: Harvard University Press, 2016.

Karuka, Manu. *Empire's Tracks: Indigenous Nations, Chinese Workers, and the Transcontinental Railroad*. Berkeley: University of California Press, 2019.

Kavanagh, Thomas W. *Comanche Political History: An Ethnohistorical Perspective, 1706–1875*. Lincoln: University of Nebraska Press, 1996.

Keehn, David C. *Knights of the Golden Circle: Secret Empire, Southern Secession, Civil War*. Baton Rouge: Louisiana State University Press, 2013.

Kehoe, Alice Beck. *The Ghost Dance: Ethnohistory and Revitalization*. New York: Holt, Rinehart, and Winston, 1989.

Keith, Jeanette. *Fever Season: The Story of a Terrifying Epidemic and the People Who Saved a City*. New York: Bloomsbury, 2012.

Kelekna, Pita. *The Horse in Human History*. Cambridge: Cambridge University Press, 2009.

Keller, Robert H., Jr. *American Protestantism and United States Indian Policy, 1869–82*. Lincoln: University of Nebraska Press, 1983.

Keller, Robert H., and Michael F. Turek. *American Indians and National Parks*. Tucson: University of Arizona Press, 1998.

Kelley, Robert L. "Forgotten Giant: The Hydraulic Gold Mining Industry in California." *Pacific Historical Review* 23, no. 4 (November 1954): 343–56.

——. *Gold vs. Grain: The Hydraulic Mining Controversy in California's Sacramento Valley*. Glendale CA: Arthur H. Clark, 1959.

Kelly, Lawrence C. *Navajo Roundup: Selected Correspondence of Kit Carson's Expedition against the Navajo, 1863–1865*. Boulder CO: Pruett, 1970.

Kemble, John Haskell. "The Gold Rush by Panama, 1848–1851." *Pacific Historical Review* 18, no. 1 (February 1949): 44–56.

——. *The Panama Route, 1848–1869*. Berkeley: University of California Press, 1943.

Kennan, George. *Tent Life in Siberia: A New Account of an Old Undertaking*. New York: G. P. Putnam's Sons, 1910.

Kennedy, William. *Texas: The Rise, Progress, and Prospects of the Republic of Texas*. Vol. 2. London: R. Hastings, 1841.

Kenny, William, R. "Nativism in the Southern Mining Region of California." *Journal of the West* 12, no. 1 (January 1973): 126–38.

Kerber, Linda. "The Abolitionist Perception of the Indian." *Journal of American History* 62, no. 2 (September 1975): 271–95.

Keyes, Erasmus D. *Fifty Years' Observations of Men and Events: Civil and Military*. New York: Charles Scribner's Sons, 1884.

King, Charles. *Gods of the Upper Air: How a Circle of Renegade Anthropologists Reinvented Race, Sex, and Gender in the Twentieth Century.* New York: Doubleday, 2019.

King, Clarence. "Catastrophism and Evolution." *American Naturalist* 11, no. 8 (August 1877): 449–70.

———. *Mountaineering in the Sierra Nevada.* Boston: James R. Osgood, 1874.

King, James T. "The Republican River Expedition, June–July, 1869, II: The Battle of Summit Springs." *Nebraska History* 41, no. 4 (December 1960): 281–98.

———. *War Eagle: A Life of General Eugene A. Carr.* Lincoln: University of Nebraska Press, 1963.

King, Joseph L. *History of the San Francisco Stock Exchange Board.* New York: Arno Press, 1975.

Kinney, Brandon G. *The Mormon War: Zion and the Missouri Extermination Order of 1838.* Yardley PA: Westholme, 2011.

Kinsey, Joni Louise. *Thomas Moran and the Surveying of the American West.* Washington DC: Smithsonian Institution Press, 1992.

Kip, Lawrence. *Army Life on the Pacific: A Journal of the Expedition against the Northern Indians, the Tribes of the Coeur d'Alenes, Spokans, and Pelouzes, in the Summer of 1858.* New York: Redfield, 1859.

Kiser, William S. *Borderlands of Slavery: The Struggle over Captivity and Peonage in the American Southwest.* Philadelphia: University of Pennsylvania Press, 2017.

———. "A 'Charming Name for a Species of Slavery': Political Debate on Debt Peonage in the Southwest, 1840s–1860s." *Western Historical Quarterly* 45, no. 2 (Summer 2014): 169–89.

———. "The Persistence of Unfree Labor in the American Southwest." *Western Historical Quarterly* 52, no. 3 (Autumn 2021): 259–80.

———. *Turmoil on the Rio Grande: History of the Mesilla Valley, 1846–1865.* College Station: Texas A&M University Press, 2011.

Klein, Alan M. "The Political-Economy of Gender: A 19th-Century Plains Indian Case Study." In *The Hidden Half: Studies of Plains Indian Women,* by Patricia Albers and Beatrice Medicine, 143–73. Lanham MD: University Press of America, 1983.

Klein, Maury. *Union Pacific.* Garden City NY: Doubleday, 1987.

Kramer, Stanley. "The Short, Unhappy Life of the U.S. Camel Cavalry." *American History Illustrated* 22, no. 1 (March 1987): 52–57.

Kraus, George. *High Road to Promontory: Building the Central Pacific (Now the Southern Pacific) across the High Sierra.* Palo Alto CA: American West, 1969.

Krieger, Henrich. "Principles of the Indian Law and the Act of June 18, 1934." *George Washington Law Review* 3, no. 3 (March 1935): 279–308.

Krueger, Kirsten. "Feeding Relationships among Bison, Pronghorn, and Prairie Dogs: An Experimental Analysis." *Ecology* 67, no. 3 (June 1986): 760–70.

Kuhl, Stefan. *The Nazi Connection: Eugenics, American Racism, and German National Socialism.* New York: Oxford University Press, 2002.

Kurst, Matthew J. *Man and Horse in History.* Alexandria VA: Plutarch, 1983.

Kushner, Howard I. "Visions of the Northwest Coast: Gwin and Seward in the 1850s." *Western Historical Quarterly* 4, no. 3 (July 1973): 295–306.

Kuss, M. H. *Memoir of the Mines and Works of Almaden*. San Francisco: Dewey, 1879.

Kuykendall, Ralph S. *The Hawaiian Kingdom, 1778–1854: Foundation and Transformation*. Honolulu: University of Hawaii, 1938.

Lamar, Howard Roberts. *Dakota Territory, 1861–1889: A Study of Frontier Politics*. New Haven: Yale University Press, 1956.

———. *The Far Southwest, 1846–1912: A Territorial History*. New Haven: Yale University Press, 1966.

Lamb, D. S. "The Army Medical Museum in American Anthropology." In *Proceedings of the Nineteenth International Congress of Americanists*, 625–32. Washington DC: By the Secretary, 1917.

Lanctot, Benoni. *Chinese and English Phrase Book: With the Chinese Pronunciation Indicated in English Specially Adapted for the Use of Merchants, Travelers and Families*. San Francisco: A. Roman, 1867.

Langford, N. P. "The Wonders of Yellowstone." *Scribner's Monthly* 1, no. 2 (May 1871): 1–17.

———. "The Wonders of Yellowstone." *Scribner's Monthly* 2, no. 2 (June 1871): 113–28.

Lapp, Rudolph M. *Blacks in Gold Rush California*. New Haven: Yale University Press, 1977.

Larson, Alfred. "The Winter of 1886–87 in Wyoming." *Annals of Wyoming* 14, no. 1 (January 1942): 5–17.

Latham, Hiram. *Trans-Missouri Stock Raising: The Pasture Lands of North America: Winter Grazing*. Denver: Old West, 1962.

Lavender, David. "For Sale: An Empire, $1,500 Down." *American West* 6, no. 3 (May 1969): 6–12, 29–32, 62–63.

Lawrence, George A. *Silverland*. London: Chapman and Hall, 1873.

Leckie, William H. *The Buffalo Soldiers: A Narrative of the Negro Cavalry in the West*. Norman: University of Oklahoma Press, 1967.

Lecompte, Janet. "La Tules and the Americans." *Arizona and the West* 20, no. 3 (Autumn 1978): 215–30.

LeDuc, Thomas. "State Disposal of the Agricultural College Land Scrip." In *The Public Lands: Studies in the History of the Public Domain*, edited by Vernon Carstensen, 395–410. Madison: University of Wisconsin Press, 1968.

Leeson, Michael A. *History of Montana. 1739–1885*. Chicago: Warner, Beers, 1885.

Leidy, Joseph. *The Extinct Mammalian Fauna of Dakota and Nebraska*. Philadelphia: J. B. Lippincott, 1869.

Leonard, Arthur Glyn. *The Camel: Its Uses and Management*. New York: Longmans, 1894.

Leonard, Carol, and Isador Walliman. "Prostitution and Changing Morality in the Frontier Cattle Towns of Kansas." *Kansas History* 2, no. 1 (Spring 1973): 34–53.

Leonard, Elizabeth D. *Yankee Women: Gender Battles in the Civil War*. New York: W. W. Norton, 1994.

Leonard, Stephen J. *Lynching in Colorado, 1859–1919*. Niwot: University Press of Colorado, 2002.

Leshy, John D. *The Mining Law: A Study in Perpetual Motion*. Washington DC: Resources for the Future, 1987.

Lesley, Lewis Burt, ed. *Uncle Sam's Camels: The Journal of May Humphreys Stacey Supplemented by the Report of Edward Fitzgerald Beale (1857–1858)*. Cambridge: Harvard University Press, 1929.

Levy, Jonathan. *Ages of American Capitalism: A History of the United States*. New York: Random House, 2021.

Lewis, David Rich. *Neither Wolf nor Dog: American Indians, Environment, and Agrarian Change*. New York: Oxford University Press, 1994.

Lewis, Oscar. *The Effects of White Contact upon Blackfoot Culture, with Special Reference to the Role of the Fur Trade*. New York: J. J. Augustin, 1942.

——. "South American Ports of Call." *Pacific Historical Review* 18, no. 1 (February 1949): 56–66.

Lewis, William S. "The Camel Pack Trains in the Mining Camps of the West." *Washington Historical Quarterly* 19, no. 4 (October 1928): 271–84.

Lew-Williams, Beth. *The Chinese Must Go: Violence, Exclusion, and the Making of the Alien in America*. Cambridge: Harvard University Press, 2018.

Liberty, Margot. "Hell Came with Horses: Plains Indian Women in the Equestrian Era." *Montana: The Magazine of Western History* 32, no. 3 (Summer 1982): 10–19.

Lillard, Richard G., ed. "A Literate Woman in the Mines." *Mississippi Valley Historical Review* 31, no. 1 (June 1944): 81–98.

Limerick, Patricia Nelson. *The Legacy of Conquest: The Unbroken Past of the American West*. New York: Norton, 1987.

Lindgren, H. Elaine. *Land in Her Own Name: Women as Homesteaders in North Dakota*. Norman: University of Oklahoma Press, 1991.

Lindley, Curtis H. *A Treatise on the American Law relating to Mines and Mineral Lands: Within the Public Land States and Territories and Government the Acquisition and Enjoyment of Mining Rights in Lands of the Public Domain*. San Francisco: Bancroft-Whitney, 1897.

Lindsay, Brendan C. *Murder State: California's Native American Genocide, 1846–1873*. Lincoln: University of Nebraska Press, 2012.

Lingenfelter, Richard E. *Bonanzas and Borrascas: Gold Lust and Silver Sharks, 1848–1884*. Norman: University of Oklahoma Press, 2012.

Littlefield, Daniel F. *The Cherokee Freedmen: From Emancipation to American Citizenship*. Westport: Greenwood, 1978.

Liu, Haiming. "The Social Origins of Early Chinese Immigrants: A Revisionist Perspective." In *The Chinese in America: A History from Gold Mountain to the New Millennium*, edited by Susie Lan Cassel, 21–36. Walnut Creek CA: Rowman & Littlefield, 2002.

Livingstone, William. *Livingstone's History of the Republican Party*. Detroit: William Livingstone, 1900.

Lockwood, Jeffrey A. "The Fate of the Rocky Mountain Locust, *Melanoplus Spretus* Walsh: Implications for Conservation Biology." *Terrestrial Arthropod Reviews* 3, no. 2 (2010): 129–60.

——. *Locust: The Devastating Rise and Mysterious Disappearance of the Insect That Shaped the American Frontier*. New York: Basic, 2004.

Lomax, John A., comp. *Cowboy Songs and Other Frontier Ballads*. New York: Sturgis and Walton, 1916.

Longellier, John P. "Buffalo Soldiers in Big Sky Country." *Montana: The Magazine of Western History* 68, no. 1 (Autumn 2018): 41–56.

Lorenz, Antony J. "Scurvy in the Gold Rush." *Journal of the History of Medicine and Allied Sciences* 12, no. 4 (October 1957): 473–519.

Lowe, Percival G. *Five Years a Dragoon ('49 to '54) and Other Adventures on the Great Plains*. Kansas City MO: Franklin Hudson, 1906.

Lowe, Sharon. "The 'Secret Friend': Opium in Comstock Society, 1860–1887." In *Comstock Women: The Making of a Mining Community*, edited by Ronald M. James and C. Elizabeth Raymond, 95–112. Reno: University of Nevada Press, 1998.

Lowell, Waverly B. "Where Have All the Flowers Gone? Early Environmental Litigation." *Prologue* 21, no. 3 (Fall 1989): 247–55.

Lowenthal, David. *The Mind and Art of Abraham Lincoln, Philosopher Statesman: Texts and Interpretations of Twenty Great Speeches*. Lanham: Lexington, 2012.

Ludlow, Fitz Hugh. *The Heart of the Continent: A Record of Travel across the Plains and in Oregon with an Examination of the Mormon Principal*. New York: Hurd and Houghton, 1870.

Luebke, Frederick C. "Ethnic Group Settlement on the Great Plains." *Western Historical Quarterly* 8, no. 4 (October 1977): 405–30.

Luke, L. D. *Adventures and Travels in the New Wonder Land of Yellowstone Park, Big Trees, and Yosemite Valley*. Utica NY: Press of Curtiss & Childs, 1886.

Lurie, Edward. "Louis Agassiz and the Races of Man." *Isis* 45, no. 3 (September 1954): 227–42.

Lyman, Horace S. *History of Oregon: The Growth of an American State*. Vol. 4. New York: North Pacific Publishing Society, 1903.

Lynching in America: Confronting the Legacy of Racial Terror. Montgomery: Equal Justice Initiative, 2017.

Lythgoe, Dennis L. "Negro Slavery and Mormon Doctrine." *Western Humanities Review* 21, no. 4 (Autumn 1967): 327–38.

———. "Negro Slavery in Utah." *Utah Historical Quarterly* 39, no. 1 (Winter 1971): 40–54.

Ma, Debin. "The Modern Silk Road: The Global Raw-Silk Market, 1850–1930." *Journal of Economic History* 56, no. 2 (June 1996): 330–55.

Macintyre, Ben. *The Man Who Would Be King: The First American in Afghanistan*. New York: Farrar, Straus and Giroux, 2004.

MacKell, Jan. *Brothels, Bordellos and Bad Girls: Prostitution in Colorado, 1860–1930*. Albuquerque: University of New Mexico Press, 2004.

MacKinnon, William P. "125 Years of Conspiracy Theories: Origins of the Utah Expedition of 1857–58." *Utah Historical Quarterly* 52, no. 3 (Summer 1984): 212–30.

MacMullen, Jerry. *Paddle-Wheel Days in California*. Stanford CA: Stanford University Press, 1944.

Madley, Benjamin. *An American Genocide: The United States and the California Indian Catastrophe*. New Haven: Yale University Press, 2016.

———. "California's Yuki Indians: Defining Genocide in Native American History." *Western Historical Quarterly* 39, no. 3 (Autumn 2008): 303–32.

Madsen, Betty M., and Brigham D. Madsen. *North to Montana! Jehus, Bullwhackers, and Muleskinners on the Montana Trail.* Salt Lake City: University of Utah Press, 1980.

Madsen, Brigham D. *Encounter with the Northwestern Shoshoni at Bear River in 1863: Battle or Massacre?* Dello G. Dayton Memorial Lecture. Ogden UT: Weber State College Press, 1984.

———. *Glory Hunter: A Biography of Patrick Edward Conner.* Salt Lake City: University of Utah Press, 1990.

———. *The Shoshoni Frontier and the Bear River Massacre.* Salt Lake City: University of Utah Press, 1985.

Madsen, David B. "A Grasshopper in Every Pot." *Natural History* 98, no. 7 (July 1989): 22–25.

Magliari, Michael F. "Free State Slavery: Bound Indian Labor and Slave Trafficking in California's Sacramento Valley, 1850–1864." *Pacific Historical Review* 81, no. 2 (May 2012): 155–92.

Magnani, Russell M. "Plains Indians in New Mexico: The *Genizaro* Experience." *Great Plains Quarterly* 10, no. 2 (Spring 1990): 86–95.

Maizlish, Stephen E. *A Strife of Tongues: The Compromise of 1850 and the Ideological Foundations of the American Civil War,* 2018.

Majors, Alexander. *Seventy Years on the Frontier: Memoirs of a Lifetime on the Border.* Chicago: Rand, McNally, 1893.

Malcomson, Scott. *One Drop of Blood: The American Misadventure of Race.* New York: Farrar, Straus and Giroux, 2001.

Malin, James C. *John Brown and the Legend of Fifty-Six.* Philadelphia: American Philosophical Society, 1942.

———. "Judge Lecompte and the Sack of Lawrence, Part 1." *Kansas Historical Quarterly* 20, no. 7 (August 1953): 465–94.

———. "The Turnover of Farm Population in Kansas." In *History and Ecology: Studies of the Grassland,* ed. Robert P. Swierenga, 269–99. Lincoln: University of Nebraska Press, 1984.

Malone, Michael P., and Richard B. Roeder. *Montana: A History of Two Centuries.* Seattle: University of Washington Press, 1976.

Manual of the Railroads of the United States for 1878–79. New York: H. V. and H. W. Poor, 1878.

Mappin, W. F. "Farm Mortgages and the Small Farmer." *Political Science Quarterly* 4, no. 3 (September 1889): 433–51.

Marryat, Frank. *Mountains and Molehills, or Recollections of a Burnt Journal.* London: Longman, Brown, Green and Longmans, 1855.

Marsh, George Perkins. *The Camel: His Organization, Habits, and Uses Considered with Reference to His Introduction into the United States.* Boston: Gould and Lincoln, 1856.

Marsh, O. C. "Introduction and Succession of Vertebrate Life in America." *American Journal of Science and Art* 14, no. 83 (November 1877): 337–78.

———. "Polydactyl Horses, Recent and Extinct." *American Journal of Science* 102 (June 1879): 499–505.

Marshall, Nicholas. "The Great Exaggeration: Death and the Civil War." *Journal of the Civil War Era* 4, no. 1 (March 2014): 3–27.

Martial Law in Round Valley, Mendocino Co., California. Ukiah City CA: Herald Office, 1863.

Martinez, Monica Munoz. *The Injustice Never Leaves You: Anti-Mexican Violence in Texas.* Cambridge: Harvard University Press, 2020.

Marx, Karl. *A Contribution to the Critique of Political Economy.* Chicago: Charles H. Kerr, 1911.

Masich, Andrew E. *The Civil War in Arizona: The Story of the California Volunteers, 1861–1865.* Norman: University of Oklahoma Press, 2006.

Mason, Frank R. "The American Silk Industry and the Tariff." *American Economic Association Quarterly* 11, no. 4 (December 1910): 1–182.

Massey, Sara R., ed. *Black Cowboys of Texas.* College Station: Texas A&M University Press, 2000.

Mathews, Mrs. M. M. *Ten Years in Nevada; or Life on the Pacific Coast.* Buffalo: Baker, Jones, 1880.

Matsuda, Mari J. "The West and the Legal State of Women: Explanations of Frontier Feminism." *Journal of the West* 24 (January 1985): 47–56.

Mattes, Merrill J. *The Great Platte River Road: The Covered Wagon Mainline via Fort Kearny to Fort Laramie.* Lincoln: Nebraska State Historical Society, 1969.

Matthews, Glenna. *The Golden State in the Civil War: Thomas Starr King, the Republican Party, and the Birth of Modern California.* Cambridge: Cambridge University Press, 2012.

Maury, M. F. *Explanations and Sailing Directions to Accompany the Wind and Current Charts.* Philadelphia: E. C. and J. Biddle, 1855.

———. *The Physical Geography of the Sea.* New York: Harper and Brothers, 1855.

May, Dean L. "Middleton's Agriminers: The Beginnings of an Agricultural Town." *Idaho Yesterdays* 28 (Winter 1985): 2–11.

———. *Three Frontiers: Family, Land, and Society in the American West, 1850–1900.* Cambridge: Cambridge University Press, 1994.

May, Philip Ross. *Origins of Hydraulic Mining in California.* Oakland: Holmes, 1970.

May, Robert E. "Epilogue to the Missouri Compromise: The South, the Balance of Power, and the Tropics in the 1850s." *Plantation Society* 1, no. 2 (June 1979): 201–25.

———. *Manifest Destiny's Underworld: Filibustering in Antebellum America.* Chapel Hill: University of North Carolina Press, 2002.

———. *The Southern Dream of a Caribbean Empire, 1854–1861.* Baton Rouge: Louisiana State University Press, 1973.

———. "Young American Males and Filibustering in the Age of Manifest Destiny: The United States Army as a Cultural Mirror." *Journal of American History* 78, no. 3 (December 1991): 857–86.

Mayer, Frank H., and Charles B. Roth. *The Buffalo Harvest.* Denver: Sage, 1958.

Mayhall, Mildred P. *The Kiowas.* Norman: University of Oklahoma Press, 1952.

McAllester, David P. *Peyote Music*. Viking Fund Publications in Anthropology, no. 13. New York: Viking Fund, 1949.

McCain, G. S. "A Trip from Atchison, Kansas to Laurette, Colorado: Diary of G. S. McCain." *Colorado Magazine* 27, no. 2 (April 1950): 95–98.

McCallum, Henry D, and Frances T. McCallum. *The Wire That Fenced the West*. Norman: University of Oklahoma Press, 1965.

McCann, Lloyd E. "The Grattan Massacre." *Nebraska History* 37, no. 1 (March 1956): 1–25.

McChristian, Douglas C. *Fort Laramie: Military Bastion of the High Plains*. Norman OK: Arthur H. Clark, 2008.

McClure, A. K. *Three Thousand Miles through the Rocky Mountains*. Philadelphia: J. B. Lippincott, 1869.

McConaghy, Lorraine. "The Deplorable State of Our National Affairs: The Civil War in Washington Territory." *Journal of the West* 51, no. 3 (Summer 2012): 16–26.

McCoy, Joseph G. *Historic Sketches of the Cattle Trade of the West and Southwest*. Glendale CA: Arthur H. Clark, 1940.

McCullough, David. "Steam Road to El Dorado." *American Heritage* 27, no. 4 (June 1976): 54–59.

McElrath, Thomas P. *The Yellowstone Valley. What It Is, Where It Is, and How to Get to It*. Saint Paul: Pioneer, 1880.

McGinty, Brian. *Haraszthy at the Mint*. Los Angeles: Dawson's Book Shop, 1975.

McGrath, Roger D. *Gunfighters, Highwaymen and Vigilantes*. Berkeley: University of California Press, 1984.

———. "Violence and Lawlessness on the Western Frontier." In *Violence in America*, vol. 1, *The History of Crime*, edited by Ted Robert Gurr, 122–45. Newbury Park: Sage, 1989.

McGuinness, Aims. *Path of Empire: Panama and the California Gold Rush*. Cornell: Ithaca University Press, 2008.

McHugh, Tom. *The Time of the Buffalo*. Lincoln: University of Nebraska Press, 1972.

McIntosh, C. Barron. "Use and Abuse of the Timber Culture Act." *Annals of the Association of American Geographers* 63, no. 3 (September 1975): 347–62.

McKanna, C. V. "Enclaves of Violence in Nineteenth-Century California." *Pacific Historical Review* 73, no. 3 (August 2004): 391–424.

McKee, James Cooper. *Narrative of the Surrender of a Command of U.S. Forces at Fort Fillmore, N.M., in July, 1861, at the Breaking Out of the Civil War*. New York, 1881.

McKeown, Adam. "Transnational Chinese Families and Chinese Exclusion, 1875–1943." *Journal of American Ethnic History* 18, no. 2 (Winter 1999): 73–110.

McMurray, Orrin K. "The Beginnings of the Community Property System in California and the Adoption of the Common Law." *California Law Review* 3, no. 5 (July 1915): 359–80.

McNitt, Frank. *Navajo Wars: Military Campaigns, Slave Raids, and Reprisals*. Albuquerque: University of New Mexico Press, 1972.

McPherson, Hallie M. "The Interest of William McKendree Gwin in the Purchase of Alaska, 1854–1861." *Pacific Historical Review* 3, no. 1 (March 1934): 28–38.

McWilliams, Carey. *California: The Great Exception*. New York: Current, 1949.

Medicine, Beatrice. "'Warrior Women': Sex Role Alternatives for Plains Indian Women." In *The Hidden Half: Studies of Plains Indian Women*, edited by Patricia C. Albers and Beatrice Medicine, 267–80. Lanham MD: University Press of America, 1983.

Meinig, Donald W. *The Great Columbia Plain: A Historical Geography, 1805–1910*. Seattle: University of Washington Press, 1968.

——. "Wheat Sacks out to Sea: The Early Export Trade from the Walla Walla Country." *Pacific Northwest Quarterly* 45, no. 1 (January 1954): 13–18.

Meissner, Daniel. "Bridging the Pacific: California and the China Flour Trade." *California History* 76, no. 4 (December 1997).

Memorial of Committee of Pioneer Silk Growers of California to the Legislature. Sacramento: D. W. Gelwicks, 1867.

Merk, Frederick. "British Party Politics and the Oregon Treaty." *American Historical Review* 37, no. 4 (July 1932): 653–77.

Merry, Robert W. *A Country of Vast Designs: James K. Polk, the Mexican War, and the Conquest of the American Continent*. New York: Simon and Schuster, 2009.

Meserve, John B. "Chief Opothleyahola." *Chronicles of Oklahoma* 9, no. 4 (December 1931): 439–54.

Metcalf, Samuel L. "The Interest and Importance of Scientific Geology as a Subject for Study." *The Knickerbocker* 3, no. 4 (April 1834): 225–34.

"Method of Washing Gold Dust in California." *Hunt's Merchants' Magazine and Commercial Review* 20, no. 2 (February 1849): 232.

Meyer, Martin A. *Western Jewry: An Account of the Achievements of the Jews and Judaism in California, Including Eulogies and Biographies*. San Francisco: Emanu-el, 1916.

Miller, Darlis A. "Cross-Cultural Marriages in the Southwest: The New Mexico Experience, 1846–1900." *New Mexico Historical Review* 57, no. 4 (October 1982): 335–59.

——. *Soldiers and Settlers: Military Supply in the Southwest, 1861–1885*. Albuquerque: University of New Mexico Press, 1989.

Miller, David Hunter, ed. *Treaties and Other International Acts of the United States of America*. Vol. 6. Washington DC: U.S. Government Printing Office, 1931.

Miller, Stuart Creighton. *The Unwelcome Immigrant: The American Image of the Chinese, 1785–1882*. Berkeley: University of California Press, 1969.

Miller, Virginia P. "Whatever Happened to the Yuki?" *Indian Historian* 8, no. 2 (Fall 1975): 6–12.

Milner, Clyde A., and Carol A. O'Connor. *As Big as the West: The Pioneer Life of Granville Stuart*. New York: Oxford University Press, 2009.

Miner, Craig, and William E. Unrau. *The End of Indian Kansas: A Study of Cultural Revolution, 1854–1871*. Lawrence: University Press of Kansas, 1978.

Mitchell, B. R. *International Historical Statistics: The Americas, 1750–1993*. New York: Stockton Press, 1998.

Moerenhout, Jacques Antoine. *The Inside Story of the Gold Rush*. San Francisco: California Historical Society, 1935.

Mohler, John R. *Texas or Tick Fever and Its Prevention*. Washington DC: U.S. Government Printing Office, 1906.

Monaghan, Jay. *Australians and the Gold Rush: California and Down Under*. Berkeley: University of California Press, 1966.

——. *Chile, Peru, and the California Gold Rush of 1849*. Berkeley: University of California Press, 1973.

——. *Custer: The Life of General George Armstrong Custer*. Lincoln: University of Nebraska Press, 1971.

Monahan, Doris. *Julesburg and Fort Sedgwick: Wicked City—Scandalous Fort*. Sterling CO: By the author, 2009.

Monkkonen, Eric. "Western Homicide: The Case of Los Angeles, 1830–1870." *Pacific Historical Review* 74, no. 4 (November 2005): 603–18.

Montoya, Maria E. "The Not-So-Free Labor in the American Southwest." In *Empire and Liberty: The Civil War and the West*, edited by Virginia Scharff, 159–74. Berkeley: University of California Press, 2015.

——. *Translating Property: The Maxwell Land Grant and the Conflict over Land in the American West, 1840–1900*. Berkeley: University of California Press, 2002.

Mooney, James. *Calendar History of the Kiowa Indians*. Washington DC: Smithsonian Institution Press, 1979.

——. *The Ghost-Dance Religion and the Sioux Outbreak of 1890*. Chicago: University of Chicago Press, 1965.

Moore, Jacqueline M. *Cow Boys and Cattle Men: Class and Masculinities on the Texas Frontier, 1865–1900*. New York: New York University Press, 2010.

Moore, John H. *The Cheyenne Nation: A Social and Demographic History*. Lincoln: University of Nebraska Press, 1987.

——. "The Dynamics of Scale in Plains Indian Ethnohistory." *Papers in Anthropology* 23, no. 2 (1982): 225–46.

Moore, Richard E. "The Silver King: Ed Schieffelin, Prospector." *Oregon Historical Quarterly* 87, no. 4 (Winter 1986): 367–87.

Morgan, Dale L. *The State of Deseret*. Logan: Utah State University Press, 1987.

Morgan, Lewis Henry. *Ancient Society, or Researches in the Lines of Human Progress from Savagery through Barbarism to Civilization*. Chicago: Charles H. Kerr, 1877.

——. *Systems of Consanguinity and Affinity of the Human Family*. Washington DC: Smithsonian Institution, 1870.

Morrison, Michael A. *Slavery and the American West: The Eclipse of Manifest Destiny and the Coming of the Civil War*. Chapel Hill: University of North Carolina Press, 1997.

Morse, Jedidiah, and Sidney Edwards Morse. *A New System of Geography, or a View of the Present State of the World*. Boston: Richardson and Lord, 1822.

Morton, Ohland. "Confederate Government Relations with the Five Civilized Tribes." *Chronicles of Oklahoma* 31, no. 2 (Summer 1953): 189–204.

Morton, Samuel George. *Crania Americana; or, a Comparative View of the Skulls of Various Aboriginal Nations of North and South America*. Philadelphia: J. Dobson, 1839.

Mothershead, Harmon Ross. *The Swan Land and Cattle Company, Ltd*. Norman: University of Oklahoma Press, 1971.

Mountford, Benjamin. "The Pacific Gold Rushes and the Struggle for Order." In *A Global History of Gold Rushes*, 88–108. Berkeley: University of California Press, 2018.

Mountford, Benjamin, and Stephen Tuffnell, eds. *A Global History of Gold Rushes*. Berkeley: University of California Press, 2018.

Muhn, James. "Women and the Homestead Act: Land Department Administration of a Legal Imbroglio, 1863–1934." *Western Legal History* 7, no. 1 (Winter/Spring 1994): 283–307.

Muir, John. "Explorations in the Great Tuolumne Cañon." *Overland Monthly* 11 (1873): 139–47.

———. "In the Heart of the California Alps." *Scribner's Monthly* 20, no. 3 (July 1880): 345–53.

———. "Snow-Storm on Mount Shasta." *Harper's New Monthly Magazine* 55, no. 328 (September 1877): 521–30.

———. "Studies in the Sierra, I: Mountain Sculpture." *Overland Monthly* 12, no. 5 (May 1874): 393–403.

Mullis, Tony R. *Peacekeeping on the Plains: Army Operations in Bleeding Kansas*. Columbia: University of Missouri Press, 2004.

Murphee, Idus L. "The Evolutionary Anthropologists: The Progress of Mankind; The Concepts of Progress and Culture in the Thought of John Lubbock, Edward B. Tylor, and Lewis H. Morgan." *Proceedings of the American Philosophical Society* 105, no. 5 (June 1961): 265–300.

Murphy, John Mortimer. *Rambles in North-Western America from the Pacific Ocean to the Rocky Mountains*. London: Chapman and Hall, 1879.

Murphy, Lawrence R. *Frontier Crusader: William F. M. Arny*. Tucson: University of Arizona Press, 1972.

———. "William F. M. Arny: Secretary of New Mexico Territory." *Arizona and the West* 8, no. 4 (Winter 1966): 323–38.

Murrah, David J. *C. C. Slaughter: Rancher, Banker, Baptist*. Austin: University of Texas Press, 1981.

Myres, Sandra L. "Mexican Americans and Westering Anglos: A Feminine Perspective." *New Mexico Historical Review* 57, no. 4 (October 1982): 317–33.

Nabokov, Peter, and Lawrence Loendorf. *Restoring a Presence: American Indians and Yellowstone National Park*. Norman: University of Oklahoma Press, 2004.

Nadeau, Remi. *Fort Laramie and the Sioux Indians*. Englewood Cliffs NJ: Prentice-Hall, 1967.

Nasatir, A. P. *The French in the California Gold Rush*. New York: American Society of the French Legion of Honor, 1934.

Nash, Gerald D. "A Veritable Revolution: The Global Economic Significance of the California Gold Rush." *California History* 77, no. 4 (Winter 1998–99): 276–92.

Nebraska: A Sketch of Its History, Resources and Advantages It Offers to Settlers. Nebraska City: Morning Chronicle, 1870.

Nee, Victor G., and Brett de Bary Nee. *Longtime Californ': A Documentary Study of an American Chinatown*. Stanford: Stanford University Press, 1986.

Nelson, Eric A. "A Trip to the Post Office in 1848: The Story of the First Overland Mail to California." *Overland Journal* 27, no. 1 (Spring 2009): 18–25.

Nelson, Lowry. *The Mormon Village: A Pattern and Technique of Land Settlement.* Salt Lake City: University of Utah Press, 1952.

Nelson, Megan Kate. "The Civil War from Apache Pass." *Journal of the Civil War Era* 6, no. 4 (December 2016): 510–35.

——. *The Three-Cornered War: The Union, the Confederacy, and Native Peoples in the Fight for the West.* New York: Scribner, 2020.

Nevins, Allan, ed. *Selected Writings of Abram S. Hewitt.* New York: Columbia University Press, 1937.

Ngai, Mae M. "The Chinese Question: The Gold Rushes and Global Politics, 1849–1910." In *A Global History of Gold Rushes*, edited by Benjamin Mountford and Stephen Tuffnell, 109–36. Berkeley: University of California Press, 2018.

——. *The Chinese Question: The Gold Rushes and Global Politics.* New York: W. W. Norton, 2021.

Nichols, David A. *Lincoln and the Indians: Civil War Policy and Politics.* Columbia: University of Missouri Press, 1978.

Nichols, Jeff. *Prostitution, Polygamy, and Power: Salt Lake City, 1847–1918.* Urbana: University of Illinois Press, 2002.

Noel, Theophilus. *Autobiography and Reminiscences of Theophilus Noel.* Chicago: Tho. Noel, 1904.

North, Douglass C. *The Economic Growth of the United States, 1790–1860.* New York: W. W. Norton, 1966.

"The North Pacific Expedition." *Scientific American* 8, no. 40 (June 1853): 314.

Norton, Harry J. *Wonder-Land Illustrated; or, Horseback Rides through Yellowstone National Park.* Virginia City MT: By the Author, 1873.

Norton, Jack. *Genocide in Northwestern California: When Our Worlds Cried.* San Francisco: Indian Historian Press, 1979.

"Notes on the Proslavery March against Lawrence." *Kansas Historical Quarterly* 11, no. 1 (February 1942): 45–64.

Nott, J. C., and Geo. R. Gliddon. *Indigenous Races of the Earth: New Chapters of Ethnological Inquiry.* Philadelphia: J. B. Lippincott, 1857.

——. *Types of Mankind; or, Ethnological Researches Based upon the Ancient Monuments, Paintings, Sculptures, and Crania of Races.* Philadelphia: Lippincott, Grambo, 1855.

Nott, Josiah C. "Diversity of the Human Race." *DeBow's Review* 10, no. 2 (February 1851): 113–32.

——. "Statistics of Southern Slave Population." *DeBow's Review* 4, no. 3 (November 1847): 275–89.

Noyes, Alva J. *The Story of Ajax: Life in the Big Hole Basin.* Helena: State Publishing, 1914.

O'Dea, Thomas F. *The Mormons.* Chicago: University of Chicago Press, 1957.

Oehler, C. M. *The Great Sioux Uprising.* New York: Oxford University Press, 1959.

O'Keefe, Michael, ed. *Custer, the Seventh Cavalry, and the Little Big Horn: A Bibliography*. Norman: Arthur H. Clark, 2012.

O'Kieffe, Charles. *Western Story: The Recollections of Charley O'Kieffe, 1884–1898*. Lincoln: University of Nebraska Press, 1960.

Olch, Peter D. "Treading the Elephant's Tail: Medical Problems on the Overland Trails." *Overland Journal* 6, no. 1 (1988): 25–33.

Oliva, Leo E. "Fort Atkinson on the Santa Fe Trail, 1850–1854." *Kansas Historical Quarterly* 40, no. 2 (Summer 1974): 212–33.

Olmstead, Alan L., and Paul Rhode. "An Overview of California Agricultural Mechanization, 1870–1930." *Agricultural History* 62, no. 3 (Summer 1988): 86–112.

Olmsted, Frederick Law. *A Journey through Texas, or, a Saddle-Trip on the South-Western Frontier*. New York: Dix, Edwards, 1857.

Opie, Iona, and Peter Opie. *The Lore and Language of Schoolchildren*. Oxford: Clarendon Press, 1960.

Osborn, Henry Fairchild. *Cope: Master Naturalist; The Life and Letters of Edward Drinker Cope with a Bibliography of His Writings Classified by Subject*. Princeton: Princeton University Press, 1931.

Osgood, Ernest Staples. *The Day of the Cattleman*. Minneapolis: University of Minnesota Press, 1929.

Ostler, Jeffrey. *Surviving Genocide: Native Nations and the United States from the American Revolution to Bleeding Kansas*. New Haven: Yale University Press, 2019.

Otis, D. S. *The Dawes Act and the Allotment of Indian Lands*. Norman: University of Oklahoma Press, 1973.

Otis, F. N. *Isthmus of Panama: History of the Panama Railroad; and of the Pacific Mail Steamship Company*. New York: Harper and Brothers, 1867.

Overton, Richard C. *Burlington West: A Colonization History of the Burlington Railroad*. Cambridge: Harvard University Press, 1941.

Paddison, Joshua. *American Heathens: Religion, Race, and Reconstruction in California*. Berkeley: University of California Press, 2012.

Page, Elizabeth. *Wagon West: A Story of the Oregon Trail*. New York: Farrar & Rinehart, 1930.

Paine, Swift. *Eilley Orrum, Queen of the Comstock*. Indianapolis: Bobbs-Merrill, 1929.

Painter, Nell Irwin. *Exodusters: Black Migration to Kansas after Reconstruction*. New York: Alfred A. Knopf, 1977.

———. "The Kansas Fever Exodus of 1879." In *Strangers and Neighbors: Relations between Blacks and Jews in the United States*, edited by Maurianne Adams and John Bracey, 66–83. Amherst: University of Massachusetts Press, 1977.

Palmer, Myron L. *History of Mendocino County, California: Comprising Its Geography, Geology, Topography, Climatography, Springs and Timber*. San Francisco: Aley, Bowen, 1880.

Parish, John C., and James Gadsden. "A Project for a California Slave Colony in 1851." *Huntington Library Bulletin* 8 (October 1935): 171–75.

Parker, Paul P. "Along the Dirty Plate Route." *California Folklore Quarterly* 3, no. 1 (January 1944): 16–20.

Parkman, Mary R. *Heroes of To-Day*. New York: Century, 1918.

Parsons, George Frederic. *The Life and Adventures of James W. Marshall, the Discoverer of Gold in California*. Sacramento: James W. Marshall and W. Burke, 1870.

Patterson-Black, Sheryll. "Women Homesteaders on the Great Plains Frontier." *Frontiers* 1, no. 2 (Spring 1976): 67–88.

Paul, R. Eli, ed. "A Galvanized Yankee along the Niobrara River." *Nebraska History* 70, no. 2 (Summer 1989): 146–57.

Paul, R. Eli. *Blue Water Creek and the First Sioux War, 1854–1856*. Norman: University of Oklahoma Press, 2004.

Paul, Rodman W. "The Beginnings of Agriculture in California: Innovation vs. Continuity." *California Historical Quarterly* 52, no. 1 (Spring 1973): 16–27.

——. *California Gold: The Beginning of Mining in the Far West*. Lincoln: University of Nebraska Press, 1964.

——. *The California Gold Discovery: Sources, Documents, Accounts and Memoirs relating to the Discovery of Gold at Sutter's Mill*. Georgetown CA: Talisman Press, 1966.

——. "Colorado as a Pioneer of Science in the Mining West." *Mississippi Valley Historical Review* 47, no. 1 (June 1969): 34–50.

——. "The Great California Grain War: The Grangers Challenge the Wheat King." *Pacific Historical Review* 27, no. 4 (November 1958): 331–49.

——. *A Victorian Gentlewoman in the Far West: The Remembrances of Mary Hallock Foote*. San Marino: Huntington Library, 1972.

——. "The Wheat Trade between California and the United Kingdom." *Mississippi Valley Historical Review* 45, no. 3 (December 1958): 391–412.

Paul, Rodman, and Elliott West. *Mining Frontiers of the Far West, 1848–1880*. Albuquerque: University of New Mexico Press, 2001.

Pearcey, Thomas L. "The Smallpox Outbreak of 1779–1782: A Brief Comparative Look at Twelve Borderland Communities." *Journal of the West* 34, no. 1 (January 1997): 26–37.

Peavy, Linda, and Ursula Smith. *Women in Waiting in the Westward Movement: Life on the Home Frontier*. Norman: University of Oklahoma Press, 1994.

Peffer, George Anthony. "Forbidden Families: Emigration Experiences of Chinese Women under the Page Law, 1875–1882." *Journal of American Ethnic History* 6, no. 1 (Fall 1986): 28–46.

——. *If They Don't Bring Their Women Here: Chinese Female Immigration before Exclusion*. Urbana: University of Illinois Press, 1999.

Pendergrast, Mark. *Uncommon Grounds: The History of Coffee and How It Transformed Our World*. New York: Basic, 2010.

Perkins, William. *Three Years in California: William Perkins' Journal of Life at Sonora, 1849–1852*. Berkeley: University of California Press, 1964.

Perrigo, Lynn I. "Law and Order in Early Colorado Mining Camps." *Mississippi Valley Historical Review* 28, no. 1 (June 1941): 41–62.

Perrine, David P. "The Battle of Valverde, New Mexico Territory, February 21, 1862." In *Civil War Battles in the West*, ed. LeRoy H. Fischer, 26–38. Manhattan KS: Sunflower University Press, 1981.

Perry, Matthew C. *Narrative of the Expedition of an American Squadron to the China Seas and Japan*. Washington DC: Beverly Tucker, 1856.

Peters, Joseph P., comp. *Indian Battles and Skirmishes on the American Frontier, 1790–1898*. New York: Argonaut Press, 1966.

Peterson, Keith C. *John Mullan: The Tumultuous Life of a Western Road Builder*. Pullman: Washington State University Press, 2014.

Peterson, Richard H. "Comstock Couple: The Triumphs and Tragedy of Sandy and Eilley Bowers." *The Californians* 7, no. 3 (September–October 1989): 44–49.

——. "The Foreign Miner's Tax of 1850 and Mexicans in California: Exploitation or Expulsion?" *Pacific Historian* 20, no. 3 (Fall 1976): 265–72.

——. *Manifest Destiny in the Mines: A Cultural Interpretation of Anti-Mexican Nativism in California, 1848–1853*. Saratoga CA: R. and E. Research Associates, 1975.

Petrik, Paula. "Capitalists with Rooms: Prostitution in Helena, Montana, 1865–1900." *Montana: The Magazine of Western History* 31, no. 2 (April 1981): 28–41.

——. "Queens of the Silver Dollar: The Social and Economic Structure of Prostitution in the Far West, 1865–1900." *European Contributions to American Studies* 16, no. 3 (1989): 109–27.

Pfaelzer, Jean. *Driven Out: The Forgotten War against Chinese Americans*. Berkeley: University of California Press, 2007.

Pfaller, Louis O. S. B. "Sully's Expedition of 1864 Featuring the Killdeer Mountain and Badlands Battles." *North Dakota History* 31, no. 1 (January 1964): 25–77.

Pfeifer, Michael J., ed. "Lynching beyond Dixie: American Mob Violence outside the South," 2013.

——. *Roots of Rough Justice: Origins of American Lynching*. Urbana: University of Illinois Press, 2011.

Philbrick, Nathaniel. *The Last Stand: Custer, Sitting Bull, and the Battle of the Little Bighorn*. New York: Viking, 2010.

Phillips, George Harwood. *"Bringing Them under Subjugation": California's Tejon Indian Reservation and Beyond, 1852–1864*. Lincoln: University of Nebraska Press, 2004.

——. *Indians and Indian Agents: The Origins of the Reservation System in California, 1849–1852*. Norman: University of Oklahoma Press, 1997.

Phinney, J. T. "Gold Production and the Price Level: The Cassell Three Percent Estimate." *Quarterly Journal of Economics* 47, no. 4 (August 1933): 647–79.

Pierce, Jason. *Making the White Man's West: Whiteness and the Creation of the American West*. Boulder: University Press of Colorado, 2016.

Pierce, John R., and Jim Writer. *Yellow Jack: How Yellow Fever Ravaged America and Walter Reed Discovered Its Deadly Secrets*. New York: John Wiley and Sons, 2005.

Pierce, Michael D. *The Most Promising Young Officer: A Life of Ranald Slidell Mackenzie*. Norman: University of Oklahoma Press, 1993.

Pike, Albert. *Address on the Southern Pacific Railroad*. New Orleans: Emile La Sere, 1855.

Pisani, Donald J. "Squatter Law in California, 1850–1858." *Western Historical Quarterly* 25, no. 3 (Autumn 1994): 277–310.

Pitt, Leonard. "The Beginnings of Nativism in California." *Pacific Historical Review* 30, no. 1 (February 1961): 22–38.

————. *The Decline of the Californios: A Social History of the Spanish-Speaking Californians*. Berkeley: University of California Press, 1966.

Pomeroy, Earl S. "Lincoln, the Thirteenth Amendment, and the Admission of Nevada." *Pacific Historical Review* 12, no. 4 (December 1943): 362–68.

————. *The Territories and the United States, 1861–1890: Studies in Colonial Administration*. Philadelphia: University of Pennsylvania Press, 1947.

Pommersheim, Frank. *Broken Landscape: Indians, Indian Tribes and the Constitution*. New York: Oxford University Press, 2009.

Porter, Kenneth W. "Negro Labor in the Western Cattle Industry, 1866–1900." *Labor History* 10, no. 3 (1966): 346–74.

Porter, Kenneth Wiggins. *The Negro on the American Frontier*. New York: Arno Press, 1971.

Porter, Lavinia Honeyman. *By Ox Team to California: A Narrative of Crossing the Plains in 1860*. Oakland: Oakland Enquirer, 1910.

Powell, John Peter. *People of the Sacred Mountain: A History of the Northern Cheyenne Chiefs and Warrior Societies*. Vol. 1. San Francisco: Harper and Row, 1981.

Powell, J. W. *The Exploration of the Colorado River and Its Canyons*. New York: Dover Publications, 1961.

————. "The Lesson of Connemaugh." *North American Review* 149 (1889): 150–56.

Powers, Ramon, and James N. Leiker. "Cholera among the Plains Indians: Perceptions, Causes, Consequences." *Western Historical Quarterly* 29, no. 3 (August 1998): 317–40.

Powers, Ramon, and Gene Younger. "Cholera on the Overland Trails, 1832–1869." *Kansas Quarterly* 5, no. 2 (Spring 1973): 32–49.

Powers, Thomas. *The Killing of Crazy Horse*. New York: Alfred A. Knopf, 2010.

Prassel, Frank R. *The Western Peace Officer: A Legacy of Law and Order*. Norman: University of Oklahoma Press, 1972.

Pratt, Julius H. "Gold Hunters of California. To California, by Panama, in 1849." *The Century* 41, no. 6 (April 1891): 901–17.

Prescott, George B. *History, Theory, and Practice of the Electric Telegraph*. Boston: Tichnor and Fields, 1860.

Prevost, Louis. *California Silk Grower's Manual*. San Francisco: H. H. Bancroft, 1867.

Price, Catherine. "Lakotas and Euroamericans: Contrasted Concepts of 'Chieftanship' and Decision-Making Authority." *Ethnohistory* 41, no. 3 (Summer 1994): 447–64.

Priest, Loring Benson. *Uncle Sam's Stepchildren: The Reformation of United States Indian Policy*. New Brunswick: Rutgers University Press, 1942.

Prince, Joseph M., and Richard H. Steckel. "Nutritional Success on the Great Plains: Nineteenth-Century Equestrian Nomads." *Journal of Interdisciplinary History* 33, no. 3 (Winter 2003): 353–84.

Proceedings of the Third Annual Meeting of the Lake Mohonk Conference of Friends of the Indian. Philadelphia: Sherman, 1886.

Proceedings of the Thirteenth Annual Meeting of the Lake Mohonk Conference of Friends of the Indian, 1895. Lake Mohonk NY: Lake Mohonk Conference, 1896.

Prucha, Francis Paul. *American Indian Policy in Crisis: Christian Reformers and the Indian, 1865–1900*. Norman: University of Oklahoma Press, 1976.

———. *The Great Father: The United States Government and the American Indians.* Lincoln: University of Nebraska Press, 1984.

Pumpelly, Raphael. *Across America and Asia: Notes of a Five Years' Journey around the World.* New York: Leypoldt & Holt, 1870.

Pyne, Stephen J. "Certain Allied Problems in Mechanics: Grove Karl Gilbert at the Henry Mountains." In *Two Hundred Years of Geology in America: Proceedings of the New Hampshire Bicentennial Conference on the History of Geology,* 225–38. Hanover NH: University Press of New England, 1979.

———. *Grove Karl Gilbert: A Great Engine of Research.* Austin: University of Texas Press, 1980.

Pyne, Stephen. *How the Canyon Became Grand: A Short History.* New York: Viking, 1998.

"The Quicksilver Mine of New Almaden." *Hutchings' California Magazine* 1, no. 3 (September 1856): 97–105.

Quinn, D. Michael. "The Council of Fifty and Its Members, 1844 to 1945." *BYU Studies* 20, no. 2 (Winter 1980): 1–34.

Rackley, Barbara Fifer. "The Hard Winter 1886–1887." *Montana: The Magazine of Western History* 21, no. 1 (Winter 1971): 50–59.

Ramirez, Salvador A. *From New York to San Francisco Via Cape Horn in 1849: The Gold Rush Voyage of the Ship "Pacific": An Eyewitness Account.* Carlsbad CA: Tentacled Press, 1985.

Rampp, Lary C., and Donald L. Rampp. *The Civil War in Indian Territory.* Austin: Presidial Press, 1975.

Ramsdell, Charles W. "The Natural Limits of Slavery." *Mississippi Valley Historical Review* 16, no. 2 (September 1929): 151–71.

Raney, William F. "The Timber Culture Acts." *Proceedings of the Mississippi Valley Historical Association* X, no. II (1919–20 1921): 219–29.

Rawley, James A. *Race and Politics: "Bleeding Kansas" and the Coming of the Civil War.* Philadelphia: J. B. Lippincott, 1969.

Rawls, James J. "Gold Diggers: Indian Miners in the California Gold Rush." *California Historical Quarterly* 55, no. 1 (Spring 1976): 28–45.

———. *Indians of California: The Changing Image.* Norman: University of Oklahoma Press, 1984.

Raymond, Rossiter W. *Mining Industry of the States and Territories of the Rocky Mountains.* New York: J. B. Ford, 1874.

Rea, Tom. *Bone Wars: The Excavation of Andrew Carnegie's Dinosaur.* Pittsburgh: Pittsburgh University Press, 2004.

Reed, Eric Melvin. "Homicide on the Nebraska Panhandle Frontier, 1867–1901." *Western Historical Quarterly* 50, no. 2 (Summer 2019): 137–60.

Reeve, W. Paul. *Religion of a Different Color: Race and the Mormon Struggle for Whiteness.* New York: Oxford University Press, 2015.

Reid, James D. *The Telegraph in America: Its Founders, Promoters, and Noted Men.* New York: Derby Brothers, 1879.

Reid, John C. *Reid's Tramp; or, a Journal of Incidents of Ten Months Travel through Texas, New Mexico, Arizona, Sonora, and California.* Selma AL: John Hardy, 1858.

Reilly, Edward J. *Sitting Bull: A Biography*. Westport CT: Greenwood, 2007.

Reinfeld, Fred. *Pony Express*. Lincoln: University of Nebraska Press, 1966.

Relander, Click. *Drummers and Dreamers*. Seattle: Northwest Interpretive Center, 1986.

Reséndez, Andrés. *The Other Slavery: The Uncovered Story of Indian Enslavement in America*. Boston: Houghton Mifflin Harcourt, 2016.

Resources of Colorado, by the Board of Trade of Denver City, Colorado. Brooklyn: Union Steam Presses, 1868.

Rice, William B. "Early Freighting on the Salt Lake-San Bernadino Trail." *Pacific Historical Review* 11, no. 1 (March 1942): 73–80.

Rich, Christopher B., Jr. "The True Policy for Utah: Servitude, Slavery, and 'an Act in Relation to Service.'" *Utah Historical Quarterly* 80, no. 1 (Winter 2012): 54–74.

Richard, K. Keith. "Unwelcome Settlers: Black and Mulatto Oregon Pioneers, Part II." *Oregon Historical Quarterly* 84, no. 2 (Summer 1983): 173–205.

Richards, Kent D. *Isaac I. Stevens: Young Man in a Hurry*. Provo: Brigham Young University Press, 1979.

Richards, Leonard L. *The California Gold Rush and the Coming of the Civil War*. New York: Alfred A. Knopf, 2007.

Richardson, Albert D. *Beyond the Mississippi: From the Great River to the Great Ocean*. Hartford CT: American Publishing, 1867.

Richardson, Albert Deane. *Our New States and Territories; Being Notes of a Recent Tour of Observation through Colorado, Utah, Idaho, Nevada, Oregon, Montana, Washington Territory and California*. New York: Beadle, 1866.

Richardson, James, ed. *Wonders of Yellowstone*. New York: Scribner, Armstrong, 1873.

Richardson, Joe M. *Christian Reconstruction: The American Missionary Association and Southern Blacks, 1861–1890*. Athens: University of Georgia Press, 1986.

Richter, William L. *The Army in Texas During Reconstruction, 1865–1870*. College Station: Texas A&M University Press, 1987.

Rickey, Don. *Forty Miles a Day on Beans and Hay*. Norman: University of Oklahoma Press, 1963.

Rico, Monica. *Nature's Noblemen: Transatlantic Masculinities and the Nineteenth-Century American West*. New Haven: Yale University Press, 2013.

Rideing, William Henry. *A-Saddle in the Wild West*. London: J. C. Nimmo and Bain, 1879.

———. "Wheeler Expedition in Southern Colorado." *Harper's New Monthly Magazine* 52, no. 312 (May 1876): 793–807.

Ridge, Martin. "Reflections on the Pony Express." *Montana: The Magazine of Western History* 46, no. 3 (Autumn 1996): 2–13.

Riegel, Robert Edgar. *The Story of Western Railroads*. New York: Macmillan, 1926.

Rieppel, Lukas. *Assembling the Dinosaur: Fossil Hunters, Tycoons, and the Making of a Spectacle*. Cambridge: Harvard University Press, 2019.

Riley, Charles V. *The Locust Plague in the United States: Being More Particularly a Treatise on the Rocky Mountain Locust or So Called Grasshopper, As It Occurs East of the Rocky Mountains*. Chicago: Rand, McNally, 1877.

Riley, Glenda. *Building and Breaking Families in the American West*. Albuquerque: University of New Mexico Press, 1996.

———. "'Not Gainfully Employed': Women on the Iowa Frontier, 1833–1870." *Pacific Historical Review* 49, no. 2 (May 1980): 237–64.

Roberts, Brian. *American Alchemy: The California Gold Rush and Middle Class Culture.* Chapel Hill: University of North Carolina Press, 2000.

Roberts, Gary L., and David Fridtjof Halaas. "Written in Blood: The Soule-Cramer Sand Creek Massacre Letters." *Colorado Heritage,* Winter 2001, 22–32.

Robinson, J. H. "The Telegraph and the Weather Service." In *Proceedings of the International Convention of Weather Bureau Officials.* Washington DC: U.S. Government Printing Office, 1902.

Robinson, John W. "A California Copperhead: Henry Hamilton and the Los Angeles Star." *Arizona and the West* 23, no. 3 (Autumn 1981): 213–30.

———. "The Creation of Yosemite Valley: A Scientific Controversy from the Nineteenth Century." *Pacific Historian* 24, no. 4 (Winter 1980): 376–85.

———. *Los Angeles in Civil War Days, 1860–65.* Los Angeles: Dawson's Book Shop, 1977.

Robinson, W. W. *Land in California: The Story of Mission Lands, Ranchos, Squatters, Mining Claims, Railroad Grants, Land Scrip, Homesteads.* Berkeley: University of California Press, 1948.

Rodriguez, Sarah. "'The Greatest Nation on Earth': The Politics and Patriotism of the First Anglo American Immigrants to Mexican Texas, 1820–1824." *Pacific Historical Review* 86, no. 1 (February 2017): 50–83.

Rogers, Brent M. *Unpopular Sovereignty: Mormons and the Federal Management of Early Utah Territory.* Lincoln: University of Nebraska Press, 2017.

Rogin, Leo. *The Introduction of Farm Machinery in Its Relation to the Productivity of Labor in the Agriculture of the United States during the Nineteenth Century.* University of California Publications in Economics, vol. 9. Berkeley: University of California Press, 1931.

Rohe, Randall E. "Chinese River Mining in the West." *Montana: The Magazine of Western History* 46, no. 3 (Autumn 1996): 14–29.

———. "Hydraulicking in the American West." *Montana: The Magazine of Western History* 35, no. 2 (Spring 1985): 18–35.

———. "Man and the Land: Mining's Impact in the Far West." *Arizona and the West* 28, no. 4 (Winter 1986): 299–338.

———. "Man as Geomorphic Agent: Hydraulic Mining in the American West." *Pacific Historian* 27, no. 1 (1983): 1–20.

———. "Origins and Diffusion of Traditional Placer Mining in the West." *Material Culture* 18, no. 3 (Fall 1986): 127–66.

Rohrbough, Malcolm J. *Rush to Gold: The French and the California Gold Rush, 1848–1854.* New Haven: Yale University Press, 2013.

Rolfe, Frank. "Early Day Los Angeles: A Great Wagon Train Center." *Historical Society of Southern California Quarterly* 35, no. 4 (December 1953): 305–18.

Rolle, Andrew. *Westward the Immigrants: Italian Adventurers and Colonists in an Expanding America.* Niwot: University Press of Colorado, 1999.

Roske, Ralph J. "The World Impact of the California Gold Rush, 1848–1857." *Arizona and the West* 5, no. 3 (Autumn 1963): 187–232.

Ross, Ronald. *Prevention of Malaria*. New York: E. P. Dutton, 1910.

Rothstein, Morton. "The American West and Foreign Markets, 1850–1900." In *The Frontier in American Development: Essays in Honor of Paul Wallace Gates*, edited by David M. Ellis, 381–406. Ithaca: Cornell University Press, 1969.

Rotter, Andrew J. "'Matilda for God's Sake Write': Women and Families on the Argonaut Mind." *California History* 58, no. 2 (Summer 1979): 128–41.

Rowse, A. L. *The Cousin Jacks: The Cornish in America*. New York: Scribner, 1969.

Royce, Sarah. *A Frontier Lady: Recollections of the Gold Rush and Early California*. New Haven: Yale University Press, 1933.

Ruby, Robert H., and John A. Brown. *Dreamer-Prophets of the Columbia Plateau: Smohalla and Skolaskin*. Norman: University of Oklahoma Press, 1989.

Ruede, Howard. *Sod-House Days: Letters from a Kansas Homesteader, 1877–78*. New York: Columbia University Press, 1937.

Rusling, James F. *Across America: Or, the Great West and the Pacific Coast*. New York: Sheldon, 1874.

Russell, Robert R. *Improvement of Communication with the Pacific Coast as an Issue in American Politics, 1783–1864*. Cedar Rapids: Torch Press, 1948.

Russell, T. "Prediction of Cold-Waves from Signal Service Weather Maps." *American Journal of Science* 40, no. 240 (December 1890): 463–75.

Rutkow, Eric. *American Canopy: Trees, Forests, and the Making of a Nation*. New York: Scribner, 2012.

Sabin, Edwin L. *Building the Pacific Railway*. Philadelphia: J. B. Lippincott, 1919.

Sachs, Aaron. *The Humboldt Current: Nineteenth-Century Exploration and the Roots of American Environmentalism*. New York: Viking, 2006.

Sailing Directions and Nautical Remarks, by Officers of the Late U.S. Naval Expedition to Japan, Under the Command of Commodore M. C. Perry. Washington DC: A. O. P. Nicholson.

Saitua, Iker. *Basque Immigrants and Nevada's Sheep Industry: Geopolitics and the Making of an Agricultural Workplace*. Reno: University of Nevada Press, 2019.

Sandoz, Mari. *The Buffalo Hunters: The Story of the Hide Men*. New York: Hastings House, 1954.

Sandweiss, Martha A. *Passing Strange: A Gilded Age Tale of Love and Deception across the Color Line*. New York: Penguin, 2009.

Saunt, Claudio. "The Paradox of Freedom: Tribal Sovereignty and Emancipation During Reconstruction." *Journal of Southern History* 70, no. 1 (February 2004): 63–94.

Sawyer, Lorenzo. *Way Sketches: Containing Incidents of Travel across the Plains from St. Joseph to California in 1850*. New York: E. Eberstadt, 1926.

Saxton, Alexander. "The Army of Canton in the High Sierra." *Pacific Historical Review* 35, no. 2 (May 1966): 141–52.

———. *The Indispensable Enemy: Labor and the Anti-Chinese Movement in California*. Berkeley: University of California Press, 1971.

Schafer, Joseph, ed. *California Letters of Lucius Fairchild*. Madison: State Historical Society of Wisconsin, 1931.

Schlebecker, John T. "The Combine Made in Stockton." *Pacific Historian* 10, no. 1 (Autumn 1966): 15–22.

Schlinder, Harold. "The Bear River Massacre: New Historical Evidence." *Utah Historical Quarterly* 67, no. 4 (Fall 1999).

Schlissel, Lillian. *Women's Diaries of the Westward Journey.* New York: Schocken, 1982.

Schoenman, Theodore, ed. *Father of California Wine: Agoston Haraszthy.* Santa Barbara: Capra Press, 1979.

Schoolcraft, Henry R. *Information Respecting the History, Condition and Prospects of the Indian Tribes of the United States, Part V.* Philadelphia: J. B. Lippincott, 1855.

Schubert, Frank N. *Black Valor: Buffalo Soldiers and the Medal of Honor, 1870–1898.* Wilmington: Scholarly Resources, 1997.

———. "The Suggs Affray: The Black Cavalry in the Johnson County War." *Western Historical Quarterly* 4, no. 1 (January 1973): 57–68.

———. *Voices of the Buffalo Soldier: Records, Reports, and Recollections of Military Life and Service in the West.* Albuquerque: University of New Mexico Press, 2003.

Schuchert, Charles, and Clara Mae LeVene. *O. C. Marsh: Pioneer in Paleontology.* New Haven: Yale University Press, 1940.

Schuele, Donna C. "Community Property Law and the Politics of Married Women's Rights in Nineteenth-Century California." *Western Legal History* 7, no. 1 (Winter/Spring 1994): 245–81.

Schullery, Paul. *Searching for Yellowstone: Ecology and Wonder in the Last Wilderness.* Boston: Houghton Mifflin, 1997.

Schwantes, Carlos A. *In Mountain Shadows: A History of Idaho.* Lincoln: University of Nebraska Press, 1991.

Schwartz, E. A. *The Rogue River Indian War and Its Aftermath, 1850–1980.* Norman: University of Oklahoma Press, 1997.

Schweikart, Larry, and Lynne Pierson Doti. "From Hard Money to Branch Banking: California Banking in the Gold-Rush Economy." *California History* 77, no. 4 (Winter 1998): 209–32.

Schwendemann, Glen. "St. Louis and the 'Exodusters' of 1879." *Journal of Negro History* 46, no. 1 (January 1961): 32–46.

Schwoch, James. *Wired into Nature: The Telegraph and the North American Frontier.* Urbana: University of Illinois Press, 2018.

Scott, Darrell, ed. *A True Copy of the Record of the Official Proceedings at the Council in the Walla Walla Valley, 1855.* Fairfield WA: Ye Galleon Press, 1985.

Scott, Kim Allen. *Yellowstone Denied: The Life of Gustavus Cheyney Doane.* Norman: University of Oklahoma Press, 2007.

Scott, Kim Allen, and Ken Kempcke. "A Journey into the Heart of Darkness." *Montana: The Magazine of Western History* 50, no. 4 (Winter 2000): 2–17.

Scott, Robert. *Glory, Glory, Glorieta: The Gettysburg of the West*: Boulder: Johnson, 1992.

Searles, Michael N. "Taking Out the Buck and Putting In a Trick: The Black Working Cowboy's Art of Breaking and Keeping a Good Cow Horse." *Journal of the West* 44, no. 2 (Spring 2005): 53–60.

Seguin, Charles, and David Rigby. "National Crimes: A New National Data Set of Lynchings in the United States, 1883–1941." *Socius* 5 (2019): 1–9.

Seidman, Laurence I. *The Fools of '49: The California Gold Rush, 1848–1856.* New York: Alfred A. Knopf, 1976.

Settle, Raymond W., and Mary Lund Settle. *Saddles and Spurs: The Pony Express Saga.* Harrisburg PA: Stackpole, 1955.

———. *War Drums and Wagon Wheels: The Story of Russell, Majors, and Waddell.* Lincoln: University of Nebraska Press, 1966.

Seward, William H. *Works of William H. Seward,* vol. 1. New York: Redfield, 1853.

Seymour, Silas. *Incidents of a Trip from the Great Platte Valley to the Rocky Mountains and the Laramie Plains.* New York: D. Van Nostrand.

Shannon, Fred A. *The Farmer's Last Frontier: Agriculture, 1860–1897.* New York: Harper and Row, 1945.

Shaw, William. *Golden Dreams and Waking Realities: Being the Adventures of a Gold-Seeker in California and the Pacific Islands.* London: Smith, Elder, 1851.

Shelton, Tamara Venit. *A Squatter's Republic: Land and the Politics of Monopoly in California, 1850–1900.* Berkeley: University of California Press, 2013.

Sherman, William T. *Personal Memoirs of Gen. W. T. Sherman.* Vol. 1. New York: Charles L. Webster, 1890.

Sherriffs, Alex, Jr. "Gold Mine Waste—A Mineral Commodity." *California Geology* 24, no. 10 (October 1971): 196–97.

Shinn, Charles Howard. *The Story of the Mine, as Illustrated by the Great Comstock Lode of Nevada.* New York: Appleton, 1896.

Shumate, Albert. *The California of George Gordon and the 1849 Sea Voyages of His California Association.* Glendale CA: Arthur H. Clark, 1976.

Sides, Josh. *Backcountry Ghosts: California Homesteaders and the Making of a Dubious Dream.* Lincoln: University of Nebraska Press, 2021.

Silbey, Joel H. "The Civil War Synthesis in American Political History." *Civil War History* 10, no. 2 (June 1964): 130–40.

Silver, J. S. "Farming Facts for California Immigrants." *Overland Monthly,* July 1868, 176–83.

Simmons, Marc. "New Mexico's Smallpox Epidemic of 1780–1781." *New Mexico Historical Review* 41, no. 4: 319–26.

Simpson, Henry I. *Three Weeks in the Gold Mines, or Adventures with the Gold Diggers in California in August, 1848.* New York: Joyce, 1848.

Sinn, Elizabeth. *Pacific Crossing: California Gold, Chinese Migration, and the Making of Hong Kong.* Hong Kong: Hong Kong University Press, 2013.

Skaggs, Jimmy M. *The Cattle-Trailing Industry: Between Supply and Demand, 1866–1890.* Lawrence: University Press of Kansas, 1973.

———. *Prime Cut: Livestock Raising and Meatpacking in the United States, 1607–1983.* College Station: Texas A&M University Press, 1986.

Slotkin, James Sydney. *The Peyote Religion: A Study in Indian-White Relations.* New York: Octagon, 1975.

Smith, Alexander. *Port of New York Annual.* New York: Smith's Port, 1919.

Smith, Duane A. *Mining America: The Industry and the Environment, 1800–1980.* Lawrence: University Press of Kansas, 1987.

———. *Rocky Mountain Mining Camps: The Urban Frontier.* Lincoln: University of Nebraska Press, 1967.

Smith, Grant. *The History of the Comstock Lode, 1850–1897.* Reno: University of Nevada Press, 1943.

Smith, Henry Nash. "Rain Follows the Plow: The Notion of Increased Rainfall for the Great Plains, 1845–1880." *Huntington Library Quarterly* 10, no. 2 (February 1947): 169–93.

Smith, Joseph, and Heman C. Smith, comps. *History of the Church of Jesus Christ of the Latter Day Saints.* Vol. 2. Lamoni IA: Board of Publication of the Reorganized Church of Jesus Christ of the Latter Day Saints, 1897.

Smith, Sherry L. "Single Women Homesteaders: The Perplexing Case of Elinore Pruitt Stewart." *Western Historical Quarterly* 22, no. 2 (May 1991): 163–83.

Smith, Stacey L. "Emancipating Peons, Excluding Coolies." In *The World the Civil War Made,* edited by Gregory P. Downs and Kate Masur, 46–74. Chapel Hill: University of North Carolina Press, 2015.

———. *Freedom's Frontier: California and the Struggle over Unfree Labor, Emancipation, and Reconstruction.* Chapel Hill: University of North Carolina Press, 2013.

Smith, Theobald, and F. L. Kilbourne. *Investigation into the Nature, Causation, and Prevention of Texas, or Southern Cattle Fever.* Washington DC: U.S. Department of Agriculture, Bureau of Animal Industry, 1893.

Smits, David D. "The Frontier Army and the Destruction of the Buffalo: 1865–1883." *Western Historical Quarterly* 25, no. 3 (Autumn 1994): 312–38.

———. "More on the Army and the Buffalo: The Author's Reply." *Western Historical Quarterly* 26, no. 2 (Summer 1995): 203–8.

Sokolofsky, Homer E. "Success and Failure in Nebraska Homesteading." *Agricultural History* 42, no. 2 (April 1968): 102–8.

Solnit, Rebecca. *Savage Dreams: A Journey into the Landscape Wars of the American West.* Berkeley: University of California Press, 2014.

Sorenson, George. *Iron Riders: Story of the 1890s Fort Missoula Buffalo Soldier Bicycle Corps.* Missoula: Pictorial Histories, 2012.

Spearman, Frank H. "The Great American Desert." *Harper's New Monthly Magazine* 77, no. 458 (July 1888): 232–46.

Specht, Joshua. *Red Meat Republic: A Hoof-to-Table History of How Beef Changed America.* Princeton: Princeton University Press, 2019.

Speer, William. *An Humble Plea: Addressed to the Legislature of California, in Behalf of the Immigrants from the Empire of China to This State.* San Francisco: Office of the Oriental, 1856.

Spence, Clark C. "Western Mining." In *Historians and the American West,* edited by Michael P. Malone, 96–120. Lincoln: University of Nebraska Press, 1983.

Spence, Mark David. *Dispossessing the Wilderness: Indian Removal and the Making of the National Parks.* New York: Oxford University Press, 2000.

Splitter, Henry Winfred. "Quicksilver at New Almaden." *Pacific Historical Review* 26, no. 1 (February 1957): 33–50.

Spring, Agnes Wright. *A Bloomer Girl on Pike's Peak, 1858: Julia Archibald Holmes, First White Woman to Climb Pike's Peak.* Denver: Denver Public Library, 1949.

Springer, Charles H. *Soldiering in Sioux Country: 1865.* San Diego CA: Frontier Heritage Press, 1971.

Stands In Timber, John. *Cheyenne Memories.* New Haven: Yale University Press, 1967.

Stanley, Henry M. *My Early Travels and Adventures in America and Asia.* Vol. 1. New York: Charles Scribner's Sons, 1895.

Stansbury, Howard. *An Expedition to the Valley of the Great Salt Lake of Utah.* Philadelphia: Lippincott, Grambo, 1855.

Stanton, William. *The Leopard's Spots: Scientific Attitudes toward Race in America.* Chicago: University of Chicago Press, 1960.

Starr, Kevin. *Americans and the California Dream, 1850–1915.* New York: Oxford University Press, 1973.

Starr, Paul. *The Creation of the Media: Political Origins of Modern Communications.* New York: Basic, 2004.

St. Clair, David J. "The Gold Rush and the Beginnings of California Industry." *California History* 77, no. 4 (Winter 1998–99): 185–208.

———. "New Almaden and California Quicksilver in the Pacific Rim Economy." *California History* 78, no. 4 (Winter 1994–95): 278–94.

Stegmaier, Mark J. "A Law That Would Make Caligula Blush? New Mexico Territory's Unique Slave Code, 1859–1861." *New Mexico Historical Review* 87, no. 2 (Spring 2012): 209–42.

Stegner, Wallace. *Beyond the Hundredth Meridian: John Wesley Powell and the Second Opening of the West.* New York: Penguin, 1992.

———. "Who Are the Westerners?" *American Heritage* 38, no 8 (December 1987): 34–41.

Steinel, Alvin. *History of Agriculture in Colorado.* Fort Collins: State Agricultural College, 1926.

Stelter, Gilbert A. "The Birth of a Frontier Boom Town: Cheyenne in 1867." *Annals of Wyoming* 39, no. 1 (April 1967): 5–36.

Sternberg, Charles H. *The Life of a Fossil Hunter.* Bloomington: Indiana University Press, 1990.

Stevenson, Robert Louis. "Old and New Pacific Capitals." In *The Works of Robert Louis Stevenson.* Vol. 2. New York: Charles Scribner's Sons, 1892.

Steward, Julian. "Two Paiute Autobiographies." *University of California Publications in American Archaeology and Ethnology* 33, no. 5 (1934): 423–38.

Stewart, Edgar Irving. *Custer's Luck.* Norman: University of Oklahoma Press, 1955.

Stewart, Elinore Pruitt. *Letters of a Woman Homesteader.* New York: Houghton Mifflin, 1914.

Stewart, George R., Jr. "Bret Harte on the Frontier: A New Chapter of Biography." *Southwest Review* 11, no. 3 (April 1926): 265–73.

Stewart, Omer C. *The Peyote Religion: A History*. Norman: University of Oklahoma Press, 1987.

Stewart, Robert E., Jr., and Mary Frances Stewart. *Adolph Sutro: A Biography*. Berkeley: Howell-North, 1962.

St. George, Judith. *To See with the Heart: The Life of Sitting Bull*. New York: G. P. Putnam's Sons, 1996.

Stiles, T.J. *Custer's Trials: A Life on the Frontier of a New America*. New York: Knopf, 2016.

———. *The First Tycoon: The Epic Life of Cornelius Vanderbilt*. New York: Alfred A. Knopf, 2009.

Stillson, Richard T. *Spreading the Word: A History of Information in the California Gold Rush*. Lincoln: University of Nebraska Press, 2006.

Stimson, A. L. *History of the Express Companies: And the Origin of American Railroads*. New York, 1858.

Stover, John F. *Iron Road to the West: American Railroads in the 1850s*. New York: Columbia University Press, 1978.

Strahorn, Carrie Adell. *Fifteen Thousand Miles by Stage*. New York: G. P. Putnam's Sons, 1911.

Strahorn, Robert E. *The Hand-Book of Wyoming and Guide to the Black Hills and Big Horn Regions for Citizen, Emigrant, and Tourist*. Cheyenne WY: By the author, 1877.

———. *The Resources of Montana Territory and Attractions of Yellowstone National Park*. Helena: Montana Legislature, 1879.

Strong, William E. *A Trip to the Yellowstone National Park in July, August, and September, 1875*. Washington DC: U.S. Government Printing Office, 1876.

Stuart, Granville. *Forty Years on the Frontier as Seen in the Journals and Reminiscences of Granville Stuart, Gold-Miner, Trader, Merchant, Rancher and Politicians*. Cleveland: Arthur H. Clark, 1925.

Summers, Mark W. *Railroads, Reconstruction, and the Gospel of Prosperity: Aid under the Radical Republicans, 1865–1877*. Princeton: Princeton University Press, 1984.

Sunseri, Alvin R. *Seeds of Discord: New Mexico in the Aftermath of the American Conquest, 1846–1861*. Chicago: Nelson-Hall, 1979.

Sutter, John A., and James W. Marshall. "The Discovery of Gold in California." *Hutchings' Illustrated California Magazine* 2, no. 17 (November 1857): 194–202.

Swagerty, William R. "Marriage and Settlement Patterns of Rocky Mountain Trappers and Traders." *Western Historical Quarterly* 11, no. 2 (April 1980): 159–80.

Sweeney, Edwin R. "Cochise and the Prelude to the Bascom Affair." *New Mexico Historical Review* 64, no. 4 (Fall 1989): 427–46.

Swierenga, Robert P. "Land Speculation and Its Impact on American Economic Growth and Welfare: A Historiographical Overview." *Western Historical Quarterly* 8, no. 3 (July 1977): 283–302.

Synge, Georgiana. *A Ride through Wonderland*. London: Sampson Low, Marston, 1892.

Takaki, Ronald. *Iron Cages: Race and Culture in 19th Century America*. New York: Oxford University Press, 2000.

Talbot, Steve. "Spiritual Genocide: The Denial of American Indian Religious Freedom, from Conquest to 1934." *Wičazo Ša Review* 21, no. 2 (Autumn 2006): 19.

Talkington, Henry. "Mullan Road." *Washington Historical Quarterly* 7, no. 4 (October 1916): 301–6.

Tassin, A. G. "Chronicles of Camp Wright." *Overland Monthly* 10, no. 55 (July 1887): 24–32.

Taylor, Bayard. *Eldorado; or, Adventures in the Path of Empire*. Vol. 1. New York: George P. Putnam, 1850.

Taylor, Emerson Gifford. *Gouverneur Kemble Warren: The Life and Letters of an American Soldier, 1830–1882*. Boston: Houghton Mifflin, 1932.

Taylor, George Rogers. *The Transportation Revolution, 1815–1860*. New York: Rinehart, 1951.

Taylor, James W. *The Sioux War, What Shall We Do with It? The Sioux Indians, What Shall We Do with Them? A Reprint of Papers Communicated to the St. Paul Daily Press, in October, 1862*. Saint Paul: Press Printing, 1862.

Taylor, Quintard. *In Search of the Racial Frontier: African Americans in the American West, 1528–1990*. New York: W. W. Norton, 1998.

———. "Slaves and Free Men: Blacks in the Oregon Country, 1840–1860." *Oregon Historical Quarterly* 83, no. 2 (Summer 1982): 153–70.

Tegeder, Vincent G. "Lincoln and the Territorial Patronage: The Ascendency of the Radicals in the West." *Mississippi Valley Historical Review* 35, no. 1 (June 1948): 77–90.

Telles, Edward E. *Pigmentocracies: Ethnicity, Race, and Color in Latin America*. Chapel Hill: University of North Carolina Press, 2014.

Thane, James L., Jr. "An Active Acting Governor: Thomas Francis Meagher's Administration in Montana Territory." *Journal of the West* 9, no. 4 (October 1970): 537–51.

———. "The Myth of Confederate Sentiment in Montana." *Montana: The Magazine of Western History* 17, no. 2 (April 1967): 14–19.

Thayer, Eli. *A History of the Kansas Crusade, Its Friends and Its Foes*. New York: Harper & Brothers, 1889.

Thian, Raphael P., comp. *Notes Illustrating the Military Geography of the United States, 1813–1880*. Austin: University of Texas Press, 1979.

Thomas, David Hurst. *Skull Wars: Kennewick Man, Archaeology, and the Battle for Native Identity*. New York: Basic, 2000.

Thomas, George. *Early Irrigation in the Western States*. Salt Lake City: University of Utah Press, 1948.

Thomas, William G. *The Iron Way: Railroads, the Civil War, and the Making of Modern America*. New Haven: Yale University Press, 2011.

Thompson, William. *Reminiscences of a Pioneer*. San Francisco, 1912.

Thompson, Gerald. *The Army and the Navajo*. Tucson: University of Arizona Press, 1976.

———. *Edward F. Beale and the American West*. Albuquerque: University of New Mexico Press, 1983.

———, ed. "'To the People of New Mexico': Gen. Carleton Defends the Bosque Redondo." *Arizona and the West* 14, no. 4 (Winter 1972): 347–66.

Thorndike, Rachel Sherman. *The Sherman Letters: Correspondence between General Sherman and Senator Sherman from 1837 to 1891.* New York: Da Capo Press, 1969.

Thornton, Russell. "History, Structure, and Survival: A Comparison of the Yuki (*Ukomno'm*) and Tolowa (*Hush*) Indians of Northern California." *Ethnology* 25, no. 2 (April 1986): 119–30.

———. *We Shall Live Again: The 1870 and 1890 Ghost Dance Movements as Demographic Revitalization,* 1986.

Titiev, Mischa. "A Hopi Salt Expedition." *American Anthropologist* 39, no. 2 (April–June 1937): 244–58.

Todd, John. *The Sunset Land; or, the Great Pacific Slope.* Boston: Lee and Shepard, 1870.

Tolnay, Stewart E., and E. M. Beck. *A Festival of Violence: An Analysis of Southern Lynchings, 1882–1930.* Urbana: University of Illinois Press, 1995.

Tong, Benson. *The Chinese Americans.* Boulder: University Press of Colorado, 2003.

———. *Unsubmissive Women: Chinese Prostitutes in Nineteenth-Century San Francisco.* Norman: University of Oklahoma Press, 1994.

Topping, E. S. *The Chronicles of the Yellowstone.* Saint Paul: Pioneer Press, 1883.

Towne, Charles Wayland, and Edward N. Wentworth. *Shepherd's Empire.* Norman: University of Oklahoma Press, 1946.

Trafzer, Clifford E. *The Kit Carson Campaign: The Last Great Navajo War.* Norman: University of Oklahoma Press, 1982.

Trennert, Robert A., Jr. *Alternative to Extinction: Federal Indian Policy and the Beginnings of the Reservation System, 1846–51.* Philadelphia: Temple University Press, 1975.

Trickett, Dean. "The Civil War in the Indian Territory." *Chronicles of Oklahoma* 17, no. 3 (September 1939): 315–27.

Trimble, William J. *The Mining Advance into the Inland Empire.* New York: Johnson Reprint Corp., 1972.

Trottman, Nelson. *History of the Union Pacific: A Financial and Economic Survey.* New York: Ronald Press, 1923.

Trulio, Beverly. "Anglo-American Attitudes toward New Mexican Women." *Journal of the West* 12 (April 1973): 229–39.

Trusk, Robert Joseph. "Sources of Capital of Early California Manufactures, 1850 to 1880." PhD dissertation, University of Illinois, 1960.

Turk, Eleanor L. "Selling the Heartland: Agents, Agencies, Press, and Policies Promoting German Emigration to Kansas in the Nineteenth Century." *Kansas History* 12, no. 3 (Autumn 1989): 150–59.

Turner, Justin G., and Linda Levitt Turner. *Mary Todd Lincoln: Her Life and Letters.* New York: Alfred A. Knopf, 1972.

Twain, Mark. *Roughing It.* Berkeley: University of California Press, 1993.

Twitchell, Ralph E. *Historical Sketch of Governor William Carr Lane.* Albuquerque: Historical Society of New Mexico, 1917.

Underwood, Kathleen. "The Pace of Their Own Lives: Teacher Training and the Life Course of Western Women." *Pacific Historical Review* 55, no. 4 (November 1986): 513–30.

Unruh, John D., Jr. *The Plains Across: The Overland Emigrants and the Trans-Mississippi West, 1840–60.* Urbana: University of Illinois Press, 1979.

Upton, Emory. *The Military Policy of the United States.* Washington DC: U.S. Government Printing Office, 1912.

Utley, Robert M. *After Lewis and Clark: Mountain Men and the Paths to the Pacific.* Lincoln: University of Nebraska Press, 2004.

———. *Cavalier in Buckskin: George Armstrong Custer and the Western Military Frontier.* Norman: University of Oklahoma Press, 2001.

———. "A Chained Dog: The Indian-Fighting Army." *American West* 10, no. 4 (July 1973): 18–24.

———. *Frontier Regulars: The United States Army and the Indian, 1866–1891.* Lincoln: University of Nebraska Press, 1973.

———. *Frontiersmen in Blue: The United States Army and the Indian, 1848–1865.* Lincoln: University of Nebraska Press, 1967.

———. *The Lance and the Shield: The Life and Times of Sitting Bull.* New York: Ballantine, 1993.

———. *Last Days of the Sioux Nation.* New Haven: Yale University Press, 1963.

Vail, Alfred. *The American Electro Magnetic Telegraph: With the Reports of Congress, and a Description of All Telegraphs Known, Employing Electricity or Galvanism.* Philadelphia: Lea & Blanchard, 1847.

Vance, James E. *The North American Railroad: Its Origins, Evolution, and Geography.* Baltimore: Johns Hopkins University Press, 1995.

Vandal, Gilles. *Rethinking Southern Violence: Homicides in Post–Civil War Louisiana, 1866–1884.* Columbus: Ohio State University Press, 2000.

Van Deusen, John G. "The Exodus of 1879." *Journal of Negro History* 21, no. 3 (April 1936): 111–29.

Van Hoak, Stephen P. "And Who Shall Have the Children? The Indian Slave Trade in the Southern Great Basin." *Nevada Historical Society Quarterly* 41, no. 1 (Spring 1998): 3–25.

Vattel, Emer de. *The Law of Nations, or, Principles of the Law of Nature, Applied to the Conduct and Affairs of Nations and Sovereigns.* Philadelphia: T. and J. W. Johnson, 1849.

Vaught, David. *After the Gold Rush: Tarnished Dreams in the Sacramento Valley.* Baltimore: Johns Hopkins University Press, 2007.

———. "A Tale of Three Land Grants on the Northern California Borderlands." *Agricultural History* 78, no. 2 (Spring 2004): 140–54.

Vevier, Charles. "American Continentalism: An Idea of Expansion, 1845–1910." *American Historical Review* 65, no. 2 (January 1960): 323–35.

———. "The Collins Overland Line and American Continentalism." *Pacific Historical Review* 28, no. 3 (August 1959): 237–53.

Vilar, Pierre. *A History of Gold and Money.* London: NLB, 1969.

Viola, Herman J. *Little Bighorn Remembered: The Untold Story of Custer's Last Stand.* Times, 1999.

Vischer, Eduard, and Ruth Frey Axe. "A Trip to the Mining Regions in the Spring of 1859." *California Historical Society Quarterly* 11, no. 4 (December 1932): 321–38.

Von Richtofen, Walter Baron. *Cattle-Raising on the Plains of North America.* New York: D. Appleton, 1885.

Vrtis, George. "Gold Rush Ecology: The Colorado Experience." *Journal of the West* 49, no. 2 (Spring 2010): 23–31.

Waite, Kevin. "Jefferson Davis and Proslavery Visions of Empire in the Far West." *Journal of the Civil War Era* 6, no. 4 (December 2016): 536–65.

———. *West of Slavery: The Southern Dream of a Transcontinental Empire.* Chapel Hill: University of North Carolina Press, 2021.

Waldrip, William I. "New Mexico during the Civil War." *New Mexico Historical Review* 28, no. 3 (July 1953): 163–82.

Walker, Don D. "Longhorns Come to Utah." *Utah Historical Quarterly* 30, no. 2 (Spring 1962): 135–47.

Walker, Henry Pickering. "Freighting from Guaymas to Tucson, 1850–1880." *Western Historical Quarterly* 1, no. 3 (July 1970): 291–304.

Walker, Richard A. "California's Golden Road to Riches: Natural Resources and Regional Capitalism, 1848–1940." *Annals of the Association of American Geographers* 91, no. 1 (March 2001): 167–99.

———. *The Conquest of Bread: 150 Years of Agribusiness in California.* New York: New Press, 2004.

———. "Industry Builds the City: The Suburbanization of Manufacturing in the San Francisco Bay Area, 1850–1940." *Journal of Historical Geography* 27, no. 1 (2001).

Wallace, Ernest. "Ranald S. Mackenzie on the Texas Frontier." *Museum Journal* 7–8 (1963–64): xi–214.

Walther, C. F. *The State of Nebraska, Its Resources and Advantages: Where to Emigrate and Why?* Nebraska City: Morning Chronicle Book and Job Office, 1871.

Walther, C. F., and I. N. Taylor. *The Resources and Advantages of the State of Nebraska: Where to Emigrate and Why.* Lincoln NE: State Board of Commissioners of Immigration, 1871.

Ward, Robert DeCourcy. *Practical Exercises in Elementary Meteorology.* Boston: Ginn, 1899.

Warde, Mary Jane. *When the Wolf Came: The Civil War and the Indian Territory.* Fayetteville: University of Arkansas Press, 2013.

Wardell, Morris L. *A Political History of the Cherokee Nation.* Norman: University of Oklahoma Press, 1938.

Wardner, James. *Jim Wardner, by Himself.* New York: Anglo-American Publishing, 1900.

Warren, Leonard. *Joseph Leidy: The Last Man Who Knew Everything.* New Haven: Yale University Press, 1998.

Warren, Louis. *God's Red Son: The Ghost Dance Religion and the Making of Modern America.* New York: Basic, 2017.

Warrin, Donald. "An Immigrant Path to Social Mobility." *California History* 76, no. 4 (Winter 1997): 94–107.

Warrin, Donald, and Geoffrey L. Gomes. *Land, as Far as the Eye Can See: Portuguese in the Far West.* Western Lands and Water Series. Spokane WA: Arthur H. Clark, 2001.

Watkins, T. H. *Gold and Silver in the West: The Illustrated History of an American Dream.* Palo Alto: Bonanza, 1971.

———. "The Reveloidal Spindle and the Wondrous Avitor." *American West* 4, no. 1 (February 1967): 24–27, 69–70.

Watson, Jeanne H. "Traveling Traditions: Victorians on the Overland Trails." *Journal of the West* 33, no. 1 (January 1994): 74–83.

Watt, James W. "Experiences of a Packer in Washington Territory Mining Camps during the Sixties." *Washington Historical Quarterly* 19, no. 4 (October 1928): 285–93.

Watts, Dale E. "How Bloody Was Bleeding Kansas? Political Killings in Kansas Territory, 1854–1861." *Kansas History* 18, no. 2 (Summer 1995): 116–29.

Webb, Walter Prescott. *The Great Plains.* New York: Grosset and Dunlap, 1931.

Weber, David J. *The Mexican Frontier, 1821–1846: The American Southwest under Mexico.* Albuquerque: University of New Mexico Press, 1982.

———, ed. *New Spain's Northern Frontier: Essays on Spain in the American West.* Albuquerque: University of New Mexico Press, 1979.

Weber, Gustavus A. *The Weather Bureau: Its History, Activities, and Organization.* New York: D. Appleton, 1922.

Webster, Albert F. "A Day at Dutch Flat." *Appletons' Journal* 1, no. 4 (October 1876): 302–4.

Wellington, John Finch, and C. H. Behre, eds. *Ore Deposits of the Western States.* New York: American Institute of Mining and Metallurgical Engineers, 1933.

Wells, William V. "The Quicksilver Mines of New Almaden." *Harper's New Monthly Magazine* 27, no. 157 (June 1863): 25–41.

Wentworth, Edward N. "Eastward Sheep Drives from California and Oregon." *Mississippi Valley Historical Review* 28, no. 4 (March 1942): 507–38.

Wenzlheumer, Roland. *Connecting the Nineteenth-Century World: The Telegraph and Globalization.* Cambridge: Cambridge University Press, 2012.

Wert, Jeffry D. *Custer: The Controversial Life of George Armstrong Custer.* New York: Simon and Schuster, 1996.

West, Elliott. "Bison R Us: The Buffalo as Cultural Icon." In *The Essential West: Collected Essays,* by Elliott West, 213–29. Norman: University of Oklahoma Press, 2012.

———. "Child's Play: Tradition and Adaptation on the Frontier." *Montana: The Magazine of Western History* 38, no. 1 (Winter 1988): 2–15.

———. *The Contested Plains: Indians, Goldseekers and the Rush to Colorado.* Lawrence: University Press of Kansas, 1998.

———. "Five Idaho Mining Towns: A Computer Profile." *Pacific Northwest Quarterly* 73, no. 3 (July 1982): 108–20.

———. *Growing Up with the Country: Childhood on the Far Western Frontier.* Albuquerque: University of New Mexico Press, 1989.

———. *The Last Indian War: The Nez Perce Story.* New York: Oxford University Press, 2009.

———. *The Saloon on the Rocky Mountain Mining Frontier.* Lincoln: University of Nebraska Press, 1979.

———. "Scarlet West: The Oldest Profession in the Trans-Mississippi West." *Montana: The Magazine of Western History* 31, no. 2 (April 1981): 16–27.

———. "Splendid Misery: Stagecoach Travel in the Far West." *American West* 18, no. 6 (November/December 1981): 61–65, 83–86.

———. *The Way to the West: Essays on the Central Plains.* Albuquerque: University of New Mexico Press, 1995.

Westermeier, Clifford P., comp. and ed. *Trailing the Cowboy: His Life and Lore as Told by Frontier Journalists.* Caldwell ID: Caxton Printers, 1955.

Wheat, Carl I., ed. "'California's Bantam Cock': The Journals of Charles E. De Long, 1854–1863, Part II." *California Historical Society Quarterly* 9, no. 4 (December 1930): 345–97.

———. *Mapping the Trans-Mississippi West, 1540–1861.* San Francisco: Institute of Historical Cartography, 1960.

Wheeler, David L. "The Blizzard of 1886 and Its Effect on the Range Cattle Industry in the Southern Plains." *Southwestern Historical Quarterly* 94, no. 3 (January 1991): 415–34.

———. "The Texas Panhandle Drift Fences." *Panhandle-Plains Historical Review* 55 (January 1982): 25–35.

White, G. Edward. *The Eastern Establishment and the Western Experience: The West of Theodore Roosevelt, Frederick Remington, and Owen Wister.* Austin: University of Texas Press, 1989.

White, Katherine A., comp. *A Yankee Trader in the Gold Rush: The Letters of Franklin A. Buck.* Boston: Houghton Mifflin, 1930.

White, Richard. "'Are You an Environmentalist or Do You Work for a Living?': Work and Nature." In *Uncommon Ground: Rethinking the Human Place in Nature*, edited by William Cronon, 171–85. New York: Norton, 1996.

———. *The Organic Machine.* New York: Hill and Wang, 1995.

———. *Railroaded: The Transcontinentals and the Making of Modern America.* New York: W. W. Norton, 2011.

———. *The Republic for Which It Stands: The United States during Reconstruction and the Gilded Age, 1865–1896.* New York: Oxford University Press, 2017.

———. "The Winning of the West: The Expansion of the Western Sioux in the Eighteenth and Nineteenth Centuries." *Journal of American History* 65, no. 2 (September 1978): 319–43.

White, William Allen. *A Certain Rich Man.* New York: Macmillan, 1909.

Whitford, William Clarke. *Colorado Volunteers in the Civil War: The New Mexico Campaign in 1862.* Denver: State Historical and Natural History Society, 1906.

Whitman, James Q. *Hitler's American Model: The United States and the Making of Nazi Race Law.* Princeton: Princeton University Press, 2017.

Whitnah, Donald R. *A History of the United States Weather Bureau.* Urbana: University of Illinois Press, 1961.

Wickson, Edward J. *The California Vegetables in Garden and Field: A Manual of Practice, with and without Irrigation, for Semi-Tropical Countries.* San Francisco: Pacific Rural Press, 1913.

———. *Rural California.* New York: Macmillan, 1923.

Wik, Reynold M. "Some Interpretations of the Mechanization of Agriculture in the Far West." In *Agriculture in the Development of the Far West,* edited by James H. Shideler, 73–83. Washington DC: Agricultural History Society, 1975.

Wilder, Daniel W. *Annals of Kansas.* Topeka: George W. Martin, 1875.

Wilk, Richard. "The Extractive Economy: An Early Phase of Globalization of Diet, and Its Environmental Consequences." In *Rethinking Environmental History: World-System History and Global Environmental Change,* edited by Alf Hornborg, J. R. McNeill, and Joan Martinez-Alier, 179–98. Lanham: AltaMira Press, 2007.

Wilkeson, Frank. "Cattle-Raising on the Plains." *Harper's New Monthly Magazine* 72, no. 431 (April 1886): 788–95.

Wilkins, James H., ed. *The Great Diamond Hoax and Other Stirring Incidents in the Life of Asbury Harpending.* San Francisco: James H. Barry, 1913.

Wilkins, Thurman. *Clarence King: A Biography.* New York: Macmillan, 1958.

Williams, Frances Leigh. *Matthew Fontaine Maury, Scientist of the Sea.* New Brunswick: Rutgers University Press, 1963.

Williams, John Hoyt. *A Great and Shining Road: The Epic Story of the Transcontinental Railroad.* New York: Times.

Willis, Parker B. *The Federal Reserve Bank of San Francisco: A Story in American Central Banking.* New York: Columbia University Press, 1937.

Wilson, Douglas L., and Rodney O. Davis, eds. *Herndon's Informants: Letters, Interviews, and Statements about Abraham Lincoln.* Urbana: University of Illinois Press, 1998.

Wilson, H. Clyde. "An Inquiry into the Nature of Plains Indian Cultural Development." *American Anthropologist* 65, no. 2 (April 1963): 355–69.

Wiltsee, Ernest A. *The Pioneer Miner and the Pack Mule Express.* San Francisco: California Historical Society, 1931.

Wingate, George W. *Through the Yellowstone Park on Horseback.* New York: O. Judd, 1886.

Winn, Kenneth H. *Exiles in a Land of Liberty: Mormons in America, 1830–1846.* Chapel Hill: University of North Carolina Press, 1989.

Winser, Henry J. *The Yellowstone National Park. A Manual for Tourists.* New York: G. P. Putnam's Sons, 1883.

Winther, Oscar Osburn. *Express and Stagecoach Days in California: From the Gold Rush to the Civil War.* Stanford: Stanford University Press, 1936.

———. *The Old Oregon Country: A History of Frontier Trade, Transportation and Travel.* Stanford: Stanford University Press, 1950.

———. "The Place of Transportation in the History of the Early Pacific Northwest." *Pacific Historical Review* 11, no. 4 (December 1942): 17–27.

———. "Stage-Coach Service in Northern California." *Pacific Historical Review* 3, no. 4 (December 1934): 386–99.

Wissler, Clark. "The Influence of the Horse in the Development of Plains Culture." *American Anthropologist* 16 (1914): 1–25.

Wolff, Joshua D. *Western Union and the Creation of the American Corporate Order.* Cambridge: Cambridge University Press, 2013.

Wong, Sam. *An English-Chinese Phrase Book Together with the Vocabulary of Trade, Law, Etc.* San Francisco: Cubery, 1875.

Wood, A. B. "The Coad Brothers: Panhandle Cattle Kings." *Nebraska History* 19, no. 1 (January–March 1938): 28–43.

Woodard, Bruce A. *Diamonds in the Salt.* Boulder CO: Pruett, 1967.

Woodin, Katherine Williams Filley. *Recollections of My Childhood on the Nebraska Pioneer Prairie.* Youngtown AZ: Privately printed, 1975.

Woodward, Walter Carleton. *The Rise and Early History of Political Parties in Oregon.* Portland: J. K. Gill, 1913.

Woodworth, Steven E. *Manifest Destinies: America's Westward Expansion and the Road to the Civil War.* New York: Vintage, 2010.

Wooster, Robert. *The American Military Frontiers: The United States Army in the West, 1783–1900.* Albuquerque: University of New Mexico Press, 2009.

Worcester, Donald E. *The Chisholm Trail: High Road of the Cattle Kingdom.* Lincoln: University of Nebraska Press, 1980.

Worster, Donald. *A Passion for Nature: The Life of John Muir.* New York: Oxford University Press, 2008.

———. *A River Running West: The Life of John Wesley Powell.* New York: Oxford University Press, 2001.

Wright, Doris Marion. "The Making of Cosmopolitan California: An Analysis of Immigration, 1848–1870, Part I." *California Historical Society Quarterly* 19, no. 4 (December 1940): 323–43.

———. "The Making of Cosmopolitan California: An Analysis of Immigration, 1848–1870, Part II." *California Historical Society Quarterly* 20, no. 1 (March 1941): 65–71.

Wright, Gavin. *The Political Economy of the Cotton South: Households, Markets, and Wealth in the Nineteenth Century.* New York: W. W. Norton, 1978.

Wright, George C. *Racial Violence in Kentucky.* Baton Rouge: Louisiana State University Press, 1990.

Wyckoff, William. *Creating Colorado: The Making of a Western American Landscape, 1860–1940.* New Haven: Yale University Press, 1999.

Wyckoff, William C. *American Silk Manufacture.* New York, 1887.

Wylie, W. W. *Yellowstone National Park; or the Great American Wonderland.* Kansas City MO: Ramsey, Millett & Hudson, 1882.

Wyman, Walker. "Freighting: A Big Business on the Santa Fe Trail." *Kansas Historical Quarterly* 1, no. 1 (November 1931): 17–27.

———. "The Outfitting Posts." *Pacific Historical Review* 18, no. 1 (February 1949): 14–23.

Yale, Gregory. *Legal Titles to Mining Claims and Water Rights in California: Under the Mining Law of Congress, of July, 1866.* San Francisco: A. Roman, 1867.

Young, Otis E., Jr. *Western Mining: An Informal Account of Precious-Metals Prospecting, Placering, Lode Mining, and Milling on the American Frontier from Spanish Times to 1893*. Norman: University Oklahoma Press, 1970.

Zabel, Orville H. "To Reclaim the Wilderness: The Immigrant's Image of Territorial Nebraska." *Nebraska History* 46, no. 4 (Winter 1965).

Zellar, Gary. *African Creeks: Estelvste and the Creek Nation*. Norman: University of Oklahoma Press, 2007.

Zhu, Liping. *A Chinaman's Chance*. Boulder: University of Colorado Press, 1997.

Ziebarth, Marilyn. "California's First Environmental Battle." *California History* 63, no. 4 (Fall 1984): 294–304.

Index

Duck Creek, Nevada, 434, 435
Dull Knife, 340, 419
Dunraven, Earl of, 213, 254
Durant, Thomas C., 185, 187, 197
Dutch Flat CA, 188, 436
Dutton, Clarence, 222, 225, 229–30, 246, 247, 254, 336, 443, 447
Dykstra, Robert, 282, 497n24
Dym, Warren, 515n43

Eagle, John, 42
Earl, A. B., 285
Eastman, Charles, 343
East North Central region, 347
Echo Canyon, 121, 202
ecology, 84, 444, 445, 447
economic activity, 206, 242, 331, 402
economic growth, 19, 30, 422, 437, 438–39, 445; gold and, 26–27, 34
economic order, 37, 148, 166, 296, 380, 437
economy, 90, 206, 336, 339, 348, 404, 436, 448; expanding, 437; extractive, 438; hunting-gathering-fishing, 44; indus- trializing, 278; ranching/farming, 308
Edison, Thomas, 382
education, 95, 145, 309, 367, 449, 451, 453; Americanization and, 69; assimi- lation and, 425; Christian, 423–24; Indian, 76, 422–23, 423–24, 426; women and, 288–89
Eeikish Pah, 454
Eel River Rangers, 47, 49
Egyptians, horses and, 56
Ein Gut, 259
El Dorado, 9, 39, 77, 126, 417
Elkhorn Ranch, 320
Elko NV: ranches near, 320
elk tusks, market for, 491n80
Elliott, Richard Smith, 227
Ellsworth KS, 314, 316
El Paso TX, 86, 137, 141
emancipation, 134, 170, 241, 272, 275, 421, 452
Emancipation Proclamation, 147
Emerson, Ralph Waldo, 246
emigration, xxvi–xxvii, 37, 124, 142, 226
Emmons, Samuel F., 223, 229

Emory, William H., 84
enslaved persons, 38, 50, 54, 91, 92, 94, 95, 115, 270, 271; former, 165; freedom for, 111, 113, 450; Indian, 107, 108; number of, 97, 471n18; runaway, 131
environment, xx, 155, 416; changes in, xxix, 325
environmental issues, 44, 48, 49, 51, 52, 63, 65, 66, 152, 179, 255, 372–73, 379, 403–10, 443, 445; mining and, 407–8, 409; overland trails and, 15; smelting and, 409
Eocene, 232
epidemics, 54, 55, 286, 334, 423, 426
Episcopalians, 369; Sioux and, 367
Equidae, 52
equipment, mining, 206, 356, 392–93, 394
Equus ferus caballus, 52, 343
Erie Canal, 20, 214
erosion, 4, 44, 88, 159, 188, 219, 230, 382, 404, 405, 443
Escalante River, 222
ethnic relations, 35, 41–42, 261, 433, 449
ethnology, 216, 235, 237, 239
eugenics movement, 453
Eureka Lake and Yuba Canal Co., 386
Evans, James, 192, 484n15
Evans, John, 159–60
evolution, 209–10, 230, 232, 233, 320
Ewell, Richard, 65
exodusters, migration of, 273
expansion, xxvii, xxviii, xxix, 1, 2, 3, 34, 35, 41, 55, 66, 67, 72, 74, 75, 89, 99, 105, 113, 124, 130, 167, 172, 175, 234, 262–63, 279, 294, 336, 432, 444, 450, 453; agricultural, xxvi, 345, 349, 374; deaths attributed to, 51; economic, 438–39; national, 436; rhetoric of, 463n10; southern, 19, 20, 21–22; white, 346
Ex Parte Crow Dog, 421
exploration, 84, 217; global, 440; map of, 85
The Exploration of the Colorado River of the West (Powell), 220
expulsion decrees, 38–39
extinction, 265, 279, 372, 380, 411, 445

Gillespie County TX, 319
Gilpin, William, 112–13, 138, 440
Glidden, J. F., 321
Gliddon, George, 241, 242
Glorieta Pass, 138, 141, 159
Godfrey, Harriet, 286
Goetzmann, William, xxvii, 87, 217–18
gold, 25, 32, 43, 66, 157, 275, 299, 354, 357, 385, 398, 401, 439, 450; camps, 207, 282; discovery of, 28, 33, 41, 84, 102, 169, 212, 264, 302, 361, 381, 382, 406, 411, 417, 464n36; extraction of, 393–94; impact of, 6–7, 30, 34; mining, F45, F46, 6, 9, 65, 382, 386–87, 397, 405, 406, 407, 409, 437, 511n9, 512n23; placer, 382, 383–84, 387, 388; production of, 5–6, 210, 381, 402, 493n38; strikes, 5–6, 7, 44, 48, 63, 68, 145, 155, 175, 262–63, 318, 361, 381, 382, 386, 387, 415
Golden Gate, 31, 262, 355, 357, 441, 442, 443
gold fields, 11, 14, 21, 35, 37, 43, 91, 130, 154, 164, 165, 309, 347, 353; traveling to, 16; wealth from, 26
gold rush, xiv, 9, 10, 30, 39, 63, 68, 205, 258, 294, 305, 347, 355, 383 (map), 492n10, 511n1; agriculture and, 27; bound labor during, 463n13; impact of, 26, 27, 33; Native peoples and, 43–44, 410; road scene from, F31
goldseekers, F4, 6, 7, 8, 9–10, 23, 39, 388; French, 37; migration of, 24–25
Goldwasser, Michael, 261
Goldwater, Barry, 261
Goode, William, 282
Goodnight, Charles, 272, 317, 318, 338
Goodnight-Loving trail, 314
Good Thunder, 430
Gorgas, William, 336
Goshutes, 157
Gould and Curry Mill, F48, 395
grading crews, 188–89
Graham, Nancy, 14
grain, 27, 65, 163, 164, 356, 357, 361, 368, 437; production of, 108, 110, 354, 355, 441, 474n87

Grand Army of the Republic, 281
Grand Canyon, 88, 179, 221, 223, 228, 229, 230, 252, 447; exploration of, 217–18, 220, 222, 246
Grand River, 29, 218, 431
Grant, Madison, 453
Grant, Ulysses S., 161, 204, 370, 495n91; Black Hills and, 418; Peace Policy and, 367; Yellowstone Act and, 247–48
grass energy, 56, 338, 343
grasses, 307, 322, 415; bluestem, 371; domestic, 380; grama, 371; indigenous, 306, 445
grasshoppers, 359, 368, 511n55; drought and, 376; irruptions of, 379. See also Rocky Mountain locusts
grasslands, 90, 307, 313, 365
grass revolution, 51–57, 59, 65, 77, 152, 293, 336–43, 371–72, 425
Grass Valley Silver Mining Co., 400
Grattan, John L., 58, 59, 60, 83, 158; Harney and, 61
grazing, 15, 44, 193–94, 306, 307, 311, 323, 379, 395, 505n42, 519n28
Great Basin, xxvii, 12, 48, 59, 61, 84, 86, 91, 117, 122, 134, 145, 156, 164, 192, 201, 222, 223, 224, 229, 240, 310, 318, 337, 425, 450
great coincidence, 19, 34, 35, 48, 117, 203, 256, 286, 302, 381, 383, 402, 420, 432, 433, 439, 442, 454
Greater Reconstruction, xiv, xx, 433, 449, 454
Great Geyser Basin, 249
"Great Greaser Extermination Meeting," text of, 39–40
Great Lakes, xxv, 20, 21, 99, 326, 447
Great Plains, 49, 52, 54, 59, 75, 76, 125, 179, 209, 229, 237, 262, 310, 313, 328, 330, 346, 376; described, 259; horses and, 53; interrelationships on, 444; migration across, 34; military action on, 416; public land and, 319
The Great Plains (Webb), 313
Great Salt Lake, xxvii, 68, 86, 117, 119, 195, 202, 223, 229, 511n55; farmland near, 364; Mormon exodus to, 11

608 | Index

Honey Lake, 87
Honey Springs OK, 151
Hong Kong, xxvii, 30, 263, 268, 298, 439, 441
Honolulu HI, 7, 30, 281
Hopis, 163, 221, 242
Hopkins, Mark, 183, 186, 188, 458n32; Chinese and, 189, 190
Horse Creek, 78, 81
horse culture, 52, 53, 54, 57, 66, 156–57, 338, 340; rise of, 65, 105
horsemen, F10, 53, 56
horses, F7, F37, 54, 55, 158, 164, 199, 206, 213, 233, 316, 324, 338, 340, 341, 343, 363, 368, 372, 373; domestication of, 466n3; eating, 52–53; evolution of, 209–10; genealogy of, F21; introduction of, 51, 52, 345, 466n6; Native peoples and, 337
Hotel de Starvation, 250
Houston, Sam, 59, 99, 472n34
Howard, Oliver O., 451
Hoyt, Wayland, 491n97
Hualapai Indians, 88
Hudson's Bay Co., xxii, 64
Humboldt County CA: redwoods in, 444
Humboldt River, 12, 49, 156, 157, 223
Humbug Creek, 406
Hunt, Alexander Cameron, 288
Hunt, Ellen: death of, 288
Hunter, Berna, 292–93
Hunter, Flora, 292–93
Hunter, Lyle, 292–93
Hunter, Sherod, 140
hunter-gatherers, 59
hunting, 152, 251, 252, 324, 337, 338, 368, 414; Indian, 45, 372, 374; professional, 373; timing/methods of, 56
Huntington, Collis, 183, 186, 187, 188, 195; Chinese and, 189, 190
Hunt's Merchants' Magazine and Commercial Review, 9
Hurtado, Albert, 474n87
Hutton, Paul Andrew, 468n40
Hydraulic Miners Association, 408
hydraulic mining, F45, F46, 40, 387, 393, 405, 407, 408, 409, 436, 437, 511n10;

advantage of, 406; described, 385–86; equipment for, 29; impact of, 442, 443, 445

Idaho City ID, 361, 388
Idaho County ID: Chinese in, 271
identity, 172, 238, 413; American, 234, 236, 242, 249; collective, 80, 284, 424, 435; national, 451; Native, 426, 430
Ikard, Bose, 272
Iliff, John W., 318
Illinois Central Railroad, 142, 176
Illinois River, 20
immigrants, 3, 10, 15–16, 17–18, 49, 86–87, 134, 261, 310, 331, 332, 360, 434; Black, 273–74; death of, 14–15; German, 153; German-Russian, 445; Mormon, 57; native-born, 21; targeting, 452–53; Welsh, 217
immigration, 23, 130, 131, 156, 360, 445; Asian, 453; Chinese, 262–63, 264, 265, 268, 269, 270, 441
indentures, 109, 110, 145, 296
independence, 9, 23, 172; expressions of, 430; Indian, 411, 419
Independent Order of Odd Fellows, 281
Indian America: defeat of, 73, 419; limitations for, 413, 414–15; threat from, 413
Indian Bureau, 59, 132
Indian Office. *See* Bureau of Indian Affairs
Indian policy, 74, 239–40, 365–66; challenging, 366; Christianity and, 367; surveys of, 509n3
Indian Religious Freedom Act (1978), 432
Indian Rights Association, 369
Indians. *See* Native peoples
Indian Territory, 65, 75, 94, 138, 152, 155, 166, 270, 271, 313, 314, 337, 338, 339, 366, 369, 370, 417, 425, 454; fencing and, 321; relocation to, 150
individualism, 291, 366
industrialization, xxv, 20, 317, 373, 382, 396, 404, 462n37
industry, 39, 44, 91, 305, 357, 362, 437
infrastructure, xxviii, 27, 33, 67, 69, 171, 397, 401, 418, 449

Ingalls, John, 423
Ingersoll, Ernest, 234, 302, 489n35
Ingram, William, 14
integration, 155, 212, 310, 330, 345; western, 203, 243
Inuits, 238
Irish, 242, 353
iron, 29, 400, 441
irrigation, F40, 358, 359, 362, 379, 415, 508n67
Irving, Washington, xxvi
Isatai (Wolf Vagina), 339
Italians, 258, 262, 309, 453
Ives, Joseph Christmas, 88, 218

Jackson, Andrew, 75
Jackson, Helen Hunt: on mining, 410
Jackson, William Henry, 208, 224, 225, 234, 248, 260
Jackson County MO, 116
James, Edwin, 372, 513n39
Japanese, 190
Jefferson, Thomas, 75, 217, 247, 451; Lewis and Clark and, 87
Jefferson River, 379
Jews, 258, 261, 453
Jinshan, attraction to, 262–70
Johnson, Andrew, 276
Johnston, Albert Sidney, 98, 121, 122, 123, 202
Jordan, Terry: ranching and, 314
Jordan River, 360
Joseph, Chief (Heinmot Tooyalakekt), 340, 428, 454, 455
Journal of Commerce, 411
Judah, Theodore, 183, 188
Judith Basin, 324
Julesburg CO, 161, 198
Jurassic period, 232

Kaibab Plateau, 222
Kanab Plateau, 222
Kanakas, 7, 36, 37, 42, 43. *See also* Hawaiians
Kane, Thomas, 122
Kansa Indians, 123
Kansas Academy of Science, 375

Kansas City KS/MO, 174, 199, 273, 312, 316, 319, 411, 492n10
Kansas Free State, 476n42, 476n52
Kansas-Nebraska Act (1854), 96, 127, 128
Kansas Pacific Railroad, 199, 227, 258, 312, 314
Kansas Territory, creation of, 68
Kapurats (He Who Has One Arm). *See* Powell, John Wesley
Kearney, Dennis, 269
Kearny, Stephen Watts, xxiii, xxiv, 60
Kellogg, Noah, 389
Kelly, William Darrah, 249
Kelsey, Andrew, 46
Keogh, Miles, 260
Keys, Elizabeth, 460n70
Kickapoos, 132
Kicking Bear, 430
kidnapping, 47, 109, 148
Kilbourne, F. L., 332, 333, 334, 335, 336, 504n26; Texas ticks and, 378, 448
Killdeer Mountain, 155
King, Charles, 453
King, Clarence, 222, 223, 224, 225, 227, 229, 233, 244, 245, 390–91, 486n18, 489n40, 489n48; mountaineering by, 246; survey by, 447; work of, 226
King, Thomas Starr, 253
kinship, 88, 119, 302, 413; Asian, 120; cultivating, 425; political, 21; spiritual, 430; tribal, 237–38
Kiowas, 53, 57, 80, 81, 159, 272, 337, 338, 339, 340, 341, 342, 343, 367, 421, 422, 425, 428, 430; buffalo war and, 374, 411; concerns about, 61; fighting, 413, 417; horses and, 54; Wovoka and, 429
Kipling, Rudyard, 209
Klamaths, 89, 236, 237, 239
The Knickerbocker, 243
Knights of the Golden Circle, 98, 99
knowledge, xx, 442; folk, 329; global order of, 447; roads and, 83–84, 86–89
Koch, Robert, 332
Konkow Maidu Indians, 47, 48
Korak trappers, 177
Kountze, Augustus, 206

Medicine Lodge Creek, 338, 367
medicine men, 424
medicines, 44, 49, 139, 208, 268
Meek, Fielding B., 225
Meeker, Arvilla, 449
Meeker, Josephine, 449
Meeker, Nathan C., 361, 449, 452
Memphis TN, 99, 334; murders in, 283
Mendocino County CA, 47; redwoods
   in, 444
Menominees, 154
Merced River, 253, 263
mercury, 8, 386, 394, 406407, 512n17
Merk, Frederick, xxii
Mesa Verde, 234
Mesilla NM, 136, 137
Mesilla Valley, 358
Mesozoic, 247
meteorology, 216, 326, 328, 329, 376
Methodists, 71, 115, 218, 369, 415, 475n4
Mexican Cession, 457n7
Mexicans, 43, 48, 62, 162, 165, 205, 258,
   262, 269, 309, 359, 386; expulsion of,
   38; gambling and, 8; goldseeking by,
   39; horses and, 54; labor from, 27;
   portrayal of, 38
Mexican War, 35, 39, 59, 116, 140, 157; His-
   panos and, 37–38
Miamis, 132
Middle Yuba River, 36, 37
Midland Pacific Railroad Co., 208
migration, 18, 34, 65, 273, 376, 459n59;
   animal, 44; described, 15–17; horses
   and, 53; maritime, 25; overland, 9–10,
   20–21, 25, 373
Miles, Nelson, 340, 419, 430
Miles City MT: cattle in, 320, 374
military, 74; assaults by, 46, 59, 337; limits
   of, 411–15. See also Union Army; U.S.
   Army
militia men, F6
militias, 45, 59, 69–70
Miller, Henry (Heinrich Alfred Kreiser),
   28, 309, 310, 313, 321, 444, 501n18; cattle and, 308; haying and, 323
Millett, Eugene, 317

mills, F48, 395, 396, 407; flour, 358; gravity, 393; quartz, 393, 394; stamp, 337,
   393–94
mine owners, 392, 406
mineral rights, 36, 184, 191, 397
miners, F30, 42, 279, 282, 387, 391, 396,
   398, 403; Chinese, 265, 439; energy of,
   410; farmers and, 362; labor from, 27;
   placer gold and, 382, 383; tunnels by,
   384–85
mining, xxix, 8, 43, 91, 226, 281, 289, 302,
   346, 362, 381, 390, 397–404, 406, 435;
   agriculture and, 408; booms in, 205,
   206; changes in, 391; concerns with,
   397, 399; corporatization of, 438;
   drift, 384–85; environmental issues
   and, 407–8, 409; illegal, 400; impact
   of, 388, 403, 409; methods for, 40,
   382; prospects for, 351; railroads and,
   395; river, 383; surface, 393. See also
   hydraulic mining; lode mining; placer
   mining
Mining and Scientific Press, 395
mining camps, 205, 277, 281
mining districts, 36, 401
mining towns, 210, 282, 284, 497n37
Minnesota River, 152
miscegenation, 268, 296
missionaries, xxii, 71, 264, 295
Mississippi River, 20, 181, 312, 514n1; control west of, 412; crossing, 347
Mississippi Valley, xxvi, 363
Missouri Compromise, 67, 125–26, 127, 135
Missouri River, 20–21, 35, 54, 55, 59, 60,
   79, 82, 84, 87, 90, 117, 147, 152, 154, 180,
   204, 206, 293, 326, 327, 330, 374, 379,
   434, 443; crossing, 9, 12, 347; West
   and, 345
Missouri Valley, 21, 55, 176, 237, 312, 360;
   railroad for, 183; trade in, xxii
Mitchell, David D., 77, 78, 79–80, 83, 414;
   Horse Creek and, 81
Mitchell, George, 94
Miwoks, 42, 45, 50
Modocs, 237
Mohave Desert, 237

Mohaves, F10, 89, 161; gender ambivalence and, 295
Mokelumne River, 38
Möllhausen, Heinrich Balduin, 88
molybdenum, 437
Moneypenny, George Washington, 132
Mongolians, 241, 269
monogenesis, 242, 451
Montague, Samuel, 203
Monterey CA, xxiii, xxvi, 4, 7, 23, 30
Montgomery, John, 108
Monthly Weather Review, 326, 504n2
Monument Lake, 202, 204
Moran, Thomas, 224, 225, 248, 249
Morgan, Lewis Henry, 238, 239–40, 242, 365
Mormon Battalion, 359
Mormon Reformation, 119
Mormons, F11, F41, 86, 110–12, 115–16, 118–19, 124, 125, 140, 157, 219, 302, 318, 345, 359, 411, 434, 475n4; accomplishments of, 115, 360–61; civil war and, 116–17; confrontation with, 121–23; exodus of, 118; Indians and, 141; railroad and, 201, 203; recruitment by, 261; settlement by, 119, 361, 362; telegraphs and, 176; Utah Territory and, 114
Morning Star, 340
Moropus cooki, 448
Morrill Act, 350, 351
Morse, Jedidiah, 179–80
Morse, Samuel Finley Breese, xxvii, 174, 179, 180
mortality rate, overland, 15, 459–60n59
Morton, Samuel George, 240, 241
Mosquito Pass, 177
mosquitos (*Aedis aegypti*), 335
Mother Lode, 5, 35, 42
Mountaineering in the Sierra Nevada (Wheeler), 245
Mountain Meadows Massacre, F11, 123–24, 140
Mount Davidson, 409
Mount Shasta, 245
Mount Tyndall, 245

Mount Washburn, 250
movement, 21; advances in, 173; systems of, 21; technology of, 278
movement revolution, 173, 243, 259, 279, 437, 448
Muir, John, 244, 245, 246, 253
mulattoes, 147, 271
mules, 54, 204–10
muleskinners, 210
muleteers, 206
Mullan, John, 87, 205
Mullan Road, 205, 206
Munn, Eugene, 208
murders, 464n26, 497n33; handguns and, 283; number of, 496n23; rate of, 40, 41, 282, 283, 284, 464n33, 496n23, 497n24
Murphy, John Mortimer, 213
Murray, Hugh, 265
Myers, J. J., 318

Nakotas, 152
Napa Valley, 112
National Banking Act, 147
National Indian Defense Association, 370
National Observatory, 175
Native American Church, 432
Native peoples, F31, 1, 12, 36, 39, 42, 51, 76, 110, 111, 118, 165, 166–67, 180, 241, 242, 251–52, 253, 258, 264, 265, 269, 290, 294, 299, 336, 357; cattle and, 341; citizenship and, 421–22; Civil War and, 164, 450; Confederacy and, 150, 151; cultural conversion of, 49, 77; decline of, 49, 111, 145, 411, 412, 415, 445; displaced, 75, 133, 134; engagements with, 70, 136, 187, 412, 413; federal government and, 420–24; gender ambivalence and, 295; genocide of, xxix, 35; gold rush and, 43–44, 410; integration of, 155; killing, xxix, 35, 46–47, 55, 496n23; knowledge of, 242–43; place of, 370–71; policies toward, 134; population of, 43, 47, 415; railroads and, 198–99, 217; relations with, 2, 73, 366, 371; removal of, 166, 302; resistance by,

ranching (*cont.*)
and, 325; expansion of, 309–10; grass
revolution and, 336; Indian, 341;
plains, 330, 337; sheep, 309–10, 323
ranchos, 28, 72, 306, 307, 309
Ratification Jubilee, 271
Rawlins, John A., 193
real estate, 5, 53, 159, 182, 271, 296, 399, 403
reconstruction, 142, 146, 171, 196, 197, 235,
313; economic, 437, 438; national, 302.
See also Greater Reconstruction
Red Cloud, 236, 417
Red River, 41, 339, 464n33
Redwood Agency, 153
redwoods, 33, 444, 519n29
Reed, Samuel, 192
Reed, Walter, 335, 336, 446, 504n26
Reed, W. H. "Bill," 231
Reeder, Andrew, 132
religion, 449; Christian charismatic, 429;
Native, 426, 428, 430, 431; peyote, 428,
432, 518n47
Remington, Frederic, 258
Rencher, Abraham, 135
Reno, Marcus, 418
*Report of the Lands of the Arid Regions of
the United States* (Powell), 327, 328,
330
Republican Party, 104, 122, 128, 142, 146,
159, 275, 348; popular sovereignty
and, 472n30; slavery and, 96; Unionist Democrats and, 147
Republic of Texas, xxi, 19
Republic of the Pacific, 137
Reséndez, Andrés, 107, 112
reservations, 48, 220, 294, 318, 343, 369,
370, 449, 451, 452, 453; boundaries of,
79; internal removal and, 76; purpose
of, 425; as spiritual centers, 432; treaties and, 166–67; trips between, 427
(map)
revolution: communication, 173, 175;
ecological, 325, 336; industrial, 373;
knowledge, xx; technological, 99,
279–80, 345. *See also* grass revolution;
movement revolution
Reynold, Joseph, 418

Richardson, Albert, 253
Richmond Enquirer, 104
Richtofen, Walter Baron von, 320, 323
Rideing, William Henry, 489n35
Riley, Charles Valentine, 378, 379, 380,
511n54
Rio Grande, xxii, xxiii, 19, 55, 62, 68, 137,
138, 140, 141, 156, 161, 169, 358
Rio Grande Valley, 61, 68, 161, 163, 322
roads, 171; building, 156, 175, 196, 204;
knowledge and, 83–84, 86–89
Roberts, Brian, 497n42
Robinson, Charles, 131, 134
Rock Island Railroad, 347
Rock Springs WY, 192, 301, 302
Rocky Mountain locusts (*Melanoplus
spretus*), F44, 379, 510n46; aggressions
of, 380; anatomy of, 378; biomass of,
376; extinction of, 376, 379, 380, 444;
fighting, 377–78, 379, 448; fried, 379.
See also grasshoppers
Rocky Mountains, xxvii, 12, 24, 59, 61, 76,
86, 87, 89, 102, 117, 125, 126, 133, 145,
149, 169, 177, 224, 225, 227, 269, 302,
327, 329, 330; crossing, 191, 193, 214,
223; geology of, 218; gold strikes in,
387
Roe, Joseph, 318
Rogue River Indians, 63
Roller Pass, 12
Rollins, James, 183
Roman Catholics, 69, 166, 168; Flatheads
(Salish) and, 367
Roosevelt, Theodore, 320, 323, 503n65
Rosebud Reservation, 505n46
Ross, John, 150, 151
Ross, Ronald, 334, 335
Round Valley, 47, 48, 50, 143
Royce, Josiah, 39
Royce, Sarah, 16
Ruef, Abraham, 261
Rush, Jacob, 14
Rusling, James E., 208
Russell, Andrew, 203
Russell, Charles Marion, 324, 330–31
Russell, Majors and Waddell (freighting
firm), 23, 24, 206–7

Wheeler, George M., 226, 227, 236, 244, 489n35; survey by, 224–25, 447
"When the Big Cramps Take Place" (1849), 4849
Whigs, xxiii
Whilkut, 143
Whipple, Amiel W., 86, 87
Whirlwind, 341–42, 505n46
White, Francis, 208
White, Richard, 183, 302, 350
white Americans: political/cultural domination by, 451; population of, 411, 415
White Mountain Apache Reservation, 369
White Mountains, 491n86
White Pine County NV, 434
white supremacy, 96, 242, 450
White Thunder, 342
Whitfield, J. W., 467n18
Whitney, Asa, xxvii, xxviii
Whitney, Josiah Dwight, 225, 226, 245, 487n29, 489n40
Whittlesey, Lee, 489n57
Wichita KS, 314, 375
Wichitas, 105, 368
Willamette River, xxii, xxvi
Willamette Valley, 68, 301, 357, 364
Williamson, J. H., 274
Wilmot Proviso, 104
Wilson, Clyde, 466n4
Wilson, Jack. See Wovoka
Wind River Mountains, 218
Winds of the Northern Hemisphere (Coffin), 326
Winnebagoes, 154, 479n17
Winnemucca NV, 319, 425
winter storms, 55–56, 343
Wirt County VA, 255
Wishart, David, 506n18
Wissler, Clark: horse culture and, 466n4
Wodziwob, 429
Wohaw, F50
Wolfskill, William, 28, 354
Wolverine Rangers, 15
women: economic opportunities for, 287–88; education and, 288–89; family

roles and, 287; of the fringe, 293–99; frontier effect and, 292; migration of, 286–93; property rights and, 291–92; social opportunities for, 287; traditional roles for, 288–89. See also Chinese women; Native women
women's rights, marriage and, 296
Woodbury, Levi, 482n5
Wooden, Katherine, 377
Wood Lake, 153
Wood River, gold strike at, 382
Woodruff, Edward, 408
Woodruff v. North Bloomfield (1882), 409
Woods, Daniel, 281
Wool, John E., 63, 64, 70
Workingmen's Party, 269
World War I, 291, 519n25
World War II, 411, 519n25
Wounded Knee Massacre, 272, 431–32
Wovoka (Jack Wilson), 429
Wright, Gavin, 101
Wright, George, 64, 65–66, 140, 340, 368
Wyandotte KS, 130, 273
Wyandotte constitution, 130

XIT Ranch, 274, 319–20

Yahi, 265
Yakimas, 64
Yanas, 42, 143
Yavapais, 161, 162, 413
Yellow Jacket mine, 393
Yellowstone Act (1872), 247–48
Yellowstone National Park, 68, 248–49, 254, 489–90n57; Indians and, 252; lease to, 250; mysteries of, 249
Yellowstone National Park Improvement Co., 250
Yellowstone River, 154, 223, 248, 379, 418; lower falls of, F24
Yellowstone Valley, 224, 254, 364, 490n62
Yerba Buena, 33
Yokuts, 43
Yolo County CA, 354
Yosemite Falls, 253
Yosemite National Park, 272, 2563
Yosemite Valley, 246, 249, 253

In the History of the American West Series

One Vast Winter Count: The American
West before Lewis and Clark
by Colin G. Calloway

Empires, Nations, and Families: A History of
the North American West, 1800–1860
by Anne F. Hyde

Making a Modern U.S. West: The Contested
Terrain of a Region and Its Borders, 1898–1940
by Sarah Deutsch

Continental Reckoning: The American
West in the Age of Expansion
by Elliott West

To order or obtain more information on
these or other University of Nebraska Press
titles, visit nebraskapress.unl.edu.